The Chief Justice

This volume brings together leading scholars of the courts who employ social science theory and research to explain the role of the Chief Justice of the U.S. Supreme Court. They consider his appointment, office, powers, and influence both within the Court and in the American system of government more generally. The chief justice is the one who presides over oral arguments and the justices' private conferences. He speaks first in those conferences, presents cases and other matters to the other justices, and assigns the Court's opinions in all cases in which he votes with the majority. In addition, he presides over the Judicial Conference of the United States, a policymaking body composed of lower court federal judges. As Chief Justice Charles Evans Hughes wrote, the Chief Justice of the U.S. Supreme Court is "the most important judicial officer in the world."

David J. Danelski is the Mary Lou and George Boone Centennial Professor Emeritus at Stanford University.

Artemus Ward is Professor of Political Science at Northern Illinois University.

The Chief Justice

APPOINTMENT *and* INFLUENCE

Edited by
DAVID J. DANELSKI
and
ARTEMUS WARD

UNIVERSITY OF MICHIGAN PRESS
ANN ARBOR

Published in the United States of America by the
University of Michigan Press
Manufactured in the United States of America
♾ Printed on acid-free paper

2019 2018 2017 2016 4 3 2 1

A CIP catalog record for this book is available from the British Library.

Library of Congress Cataloging-in-Publication Data

Names: Danelski, David Joseph, 1930– editor. | Ward, Artemus, 1971– editor.
Title: The Chief Justice : appointment and influence / edited by David J. Danelski and Artemus Ward.
Description: Ann Arbor : University of Michigan Press, 2016. | Includes bibliographical references and index.
Identifiers: LCCN 2016006531 | ISBN 9780472119912 (hardcover : alk. paper) | ISBN 9780472121953 (e-book)
Subjects: LCSH: United States. Supreme Court.
Classification: LCC KF8748 .C385 2016 | DDC 347.73/2634—dc23
LC record available at http://lccn.loc.gov/2016006531

To our mentors, C. Herman Pritchett and Doris Marie Provine

Chief Justices of the United States are rarer than Presidents. A Chief Justice cannot escape history.
–Felix Frankfurter

The experiences of a Chief Justice are like those of an impresario with his company of artists.
–William Howard Taft

[To be an effective Chief Justice requires] a conviction that you have to be fair in the assignment of opinions—this ensures good feelings all around—and an extraordinary capacity for persuading others to a point of view.
–William J. Brennan Jr.

Contents

~ Tables

Figures

Introduction

SHELDON GOLDMAN

The position of Chief Justice of the United States is widely recognized by scholars and observers of American law and politics as an immensely important one in the fashioning of law and by extension public policy. Thus it is surprising that relatively little scholarly attention from the perspective of social science, particularly in recent years, has been devoted to the Chief Justice qua Chief Justice.[1] This wonderful collection of never-before-published studies of the chiefs helps to fill the research gap. In the introductory remarks that follow, I will offer first an overview of the office of chief justice, then a review of how the chief justice and judicial behavior on the Court have been studied, and then a brief overview of the studies that make up this book.

I. The Office of Chief Justice

The chief justice has both formal and informal powers that enable him (thus far only men have served as chief) to place his stamp on the Court. Indeed, there is a long tradition of writing about and conceptualizing different historical periods of the Supreme Court in terms of the chief justice who served during those times. Most famous historically is the Court under the leadership of Chief Justice John Marshall, known as "the Marshall Court." More contemporaneously, we use the terms "the Warren Court," "the Burger Court," "the Rehnquist Court," and since 2005, "the Roberts Court." These terms define not only a historical time period but also connote the thrust of judicial policymaking during each period.

The Warren Court (1953–1969), for example, is characterized by a major expansion of civil liberties including First Amendment freedoms, the rights of those accused of crime, and equal protection of the law, particularly concerning racial equality and political equality. The Burger Court (1969–1986), on the other hand, has been characterized as being unsympathetic to the rights of the accused and unwilling to expand civil liberties in general, with the important exception, however, of gender equality.

The successor Rehnquist Court (1986–2005) saw a retrenchment in many areas of civil liberties but not gender equality and, in fact, in the realm of protection of gays from discrimination, the Court broke new ground. But the Rehnquist Court has also been seen as a Court that reopened what were thought to have been long-settled questions of the scope of federal government power in the realm of economic regulation and social welfare, laying the foundation for the potential undoing of much of constitutional law since 1937. Chief Justice Rehnquist undoubtedly furthered his conservative economic agenda during his chief justiceship.

Now the Roberts Court (2005–), under John Roberts's leadership, appears to have continued the conservative economic agenda of Rehnquist's and additionally has prodded the Court in a more conservative direction on racial but not gay rights equality. It should be clear, and the chapters in this volume make it abundantly clear, that the individual occupying the office of chief justice has the potential to use his powers to influence the course of judicial policy. And that is why the selection of a chief justice may be perhaps the single most consequential personnel decision a president can make (part II of this volume focuses on the selection of the chief).

While it is not my purpose to offer a complete catalogue of the powers of the chief justice, it is useful to recount the highlights. On the Court itself, the chief justice:

- presides over oral argument in public sessions of the Court;
- presides over the closed conferences where the justices discuss the disposition of cases, petitions, and other matters brought to the Court;
- in the conference, speaks first and is able to orient and frame the issues for discussion;
- assigns the writing of the Opinion of the Court when voting with the majority;
- has major responsibility for screening all cases that come to the Court and making recommendations to his colleagues as to which cases the Court should hear;
- is chief administrator for the Court and thus is at the center of activity and information as to the status and scheduling of cases and the status of opinion writing.

As the head of the U.S. court system, the chief justice has numerous duties and powers. Recently, attention has been given to the chief justice's power to unilaterally appoint members of the secret surveillance court that is tasked with granting or denying the federal government's request of search warrants to gather intelligence data from telephone and other electronic forms of communication both domestically and internationally. Chief Justice John Roberts has appointed primarily conservative Republicans with a background in criminal prosecution, and this has caused popular concern as to whether these judges are sufficiently alert to possible abuses of the surveillance program.[2]

The chief justice presides over the Judicial Conference of the United States, a body consisting of the chief judges of the appeals courts and one district court from each circuit. The conference is the administrative policymaking organization for the federal judicial system. The chief justice appoints committees that formulate legislative proposals concerning the federal courts, recommendations for additional judgeships and other judicial system personnel, salary recommendations, budgets, and revisions to the rules of criminal and civil procedure. The conference accepts, modifies, or rejects these recommendations. Recommendations are then transmitted to the appropriate congressional committees.

The chief justice selects the director of the Administrative Office of the U.S. Courts and oversees the work of that office in preparing the federal court system budget, the supervision of clerical and secretarial personnel as well as probation officers, undertaking the necessary staff work for the Judicial Conference, and also congressional liaison. The Administrative Office assembles detailed statistics on the work of the federal courts and the workings of the justice system and issues annual reports that in recent years have been available online.

Still another administrative task of the chief justice is serving as chair of the Board of the Federal Judicial Center, which coordinates and plans educational and training programs, for example, seminars for newly sworn in federal district judges, U.S. magistrates, and bankruptcy judges. The Federal Judicial Center undertakes research into the workings of the judicial system, maintains an ongoing database of biographical information on every federal judge, past and present, and develops new technology to assist the courts.

Not only does the chief justice have unique leadership and administrative responsibilities on the Supreme Court and as head of the federal judicial system, the chief justice historically has been the guardian if not promoter of the Court's institutional power and prestige. The career of

Chief Justice John Marshall offers countless examples of articulating this role, including the momentous decision in *Marbury v. Madison* that laid the claim of the power of judicial review (and extricated the Court from a sticky political confrontation with the president) and dozens of landmark decisions of American constitutional law that saw the Court develop and exercise judicial power.[3] Fast forward some two hundred years and we see Chief Justice John Roberts acting in an analogous way with his decisive vote and opinion that preserved the constitutionality of "Obamacare" in the 2012 presidential election year (and also extricated the Court from a sticky political confrontation with a president running for re-election).

II. How the Chief Justice and Judicial Behavior Have Been Studied

The chief justice has traditionally been studied in judicial biographies that have focused on the man and not necessarily the office. Such studies, while bringing insights into understanding the individuals studied and insights into how the Supreme Court has functioned, nevertheless were approached by the methods of history and not the systematic application of the methods of social science.[4] Neither theories of judicial decisional behavior nor theories of small-group dynamics were used in these judicial biographies. No systematic analyses of voting data were undertaken.

In the nineteenth century and into the twentieth, the study of law and courts was based on a mechanical conceptualization of law as legal science. Law was seen as something that could be found and applied mechanically to the case at hand in an exact, logical, and completely detached and value-free manner. In the twentieth century, study of the Supreme Court, including the chief justice, began to be informed first by the legal realists (primarily housed in a handful of law schools) and then by the political behavioralists (primarily housed in political science departments).

Legal realism, developed by some judges and law professors, particularly as applied to decisions of the Supreme Court, emphasized the human aspect of judging. Realists saw judges, particularly at the higher court levels, as having wide discretion in how they interpreted or applied the facts, statutes, the U.S. Constitution, rules of procedure, and court precedent. Legal realists sought to understand how courts and the justice system really work.

At about the same time that legal realism was being developed and used as a mode of analysis and a basis for critiques of the Court's conservative decisions, in the 1920s and 1930s the political science discipline underwent a transformation of its own in its approach to the study of politics. Political scientists sought to focus on how political institutions really work, how decisions are really made, and who benefits and how from those decisions. This new emphasis on political realism led to the development of quantitative and statistical methods and the adoption of a distinctive social science approach. Much later in the twentieth century and into the twenty-first, statistical modeling became commonplace for the study of behavior (which is demonstrated by many of the studies in this volume).

The breakthrough that began the development of the behavioral approach to the study of courts and judges was made by University of Chicago political science professor C. Herman Pritchett, who began where the legal realists left off. Pritchett focused on the Supreme Court and was concerned with the voting alignments and policy preferences of the justices in decisions that were decided nonunanimously (an objective indicator that the justices had discretion in how to decide the cases). Pritchett viewed the justices as political actors whose attitudes regarding the substantive issues before them helped shape the use of their discretion and thus helped to shape their votes and opinions. He discovered voting blocs among the justices in nonunanimous decisions the existence of which strongly suggested that the justices' "value systems are differently constructed and weighted, that their political, economic, and social views contrast in important respects."[5] David J. Danelski was a student of Pritchett's.

In the late 1950s and into the 1960s, Danelski, along with Walter Murphy (another student of Pritchett's), Glendon Schubert, Joseph Tanenhaus, Sidney Ulmer, Harold Spaeth, and others began to build on Pritchett's work and also to develop new methods for the study of judicial behavior. (The first section of chapter 2 offers Danelski's firsthand account of what he calls "writing on a blank slate" during this period.) The social science approach to judicial decision making was used to map the attitudes and values of judges, test the linkages of background variables to decisional proclivities, analyze the small-group dynamics of the Supreme Court and other collegial courts, examine the saliency of fact patterns to judicial voting, and to explore decision making from the standpoint of judicial role theory, among other scholarly pursuits. Toward the end of the twentieth century and into the next, social science approaches have been used to examine strategic voting, the saliency of law and precedent, and the relationship of attitudes to judicial reasoning.

Danelski, using the social-psychological concepts of leadership, was the first political scientist to study how chief justices do or do not do their job of marshalling the Court. The fruits of Danelski's work formed the basis of his doctoral dissertation supervised by Professor Pritchett from which was drawn the classic convention paper that is printed in its entirety for the first time in this book (chapter 1).

III. The Studies in This Book

This volume, the first of its kind, explores various facets of the chief justice and his work in the 15 chapters prepared for this book by leading young and established scholars of judicial politics.

Part I sets the stage for this focus on the chief justice with the three chapters by Danelski. Chapter 1 is the complete conference paper Danelski delivered in 1960 at the annual meeting of the American Political Science Association. This path-breaking paper applied the social-psychological concepts of task and social leadership in the small-group setting to understand the behavior and effectiveness of chief justices and their courts. Drawing upon the private papers of several justices, Danelski demonstrated the utility of these social science concepts and opened the eyes of judicial politics scholars to the rich mine of data to be found in the papers. Danelski used these data to explore the small-group dynamics of the Supreme Court under the leadership of Chief Justices Taft, Hughes, and Stone. The paper was subsequently published in abridged form on a number of occasions, cementing its stature as a classic in the literature and dramatically changing the way political scientists viewed individual chief justices as well as the office of chief justice. He also reviews the literature that ensued from the paper.

In chapter 2, Danelski focuses on the chief justice's exercise of his opinion-assignment power when voting with the majority. Taking as his point of departure a convention paper he delivered in 1960 that formed the basis for a chapter in his doctoral dissertation, he revisits the data that were the basis for that chapter and ties his findings to more recent quantitative work, which he reviews. The empirical work originated by Danelski on the opinion-assignment behavior of the chief justice thus continues through the present using more advanced methods than were known and used by judicial politics scholars more than a half century ago. Chapters 7 and 8, as well as subsequent chapters in part III, are prime examples of the advances in methodology.

Chapter 3, by Danelski, was conceived as a sequel to and considers the same territory as chapter 1 but with the use of Jungian personality theory as interpreted and developed by Isabel Briggs Myers. Danelski posits the linkage between personality and the chief justice's exercise of leadership.

In discussing the chief justices' personalities, he considers their ambitions, their rise to the chief justiceship, their relationships with their colleagues, and such incidental matters as persuading colleagues to retire when old age or illness prevents them from doing their work and deciding when they themselves should retire.

Part II consists of two chapters that focus on the appointment of the chief justice. Christine Nemacheck in chapter 4 provides a qualitative analysis of the nine appointments and one failed nomination (that of Abe Fortas) to the chief justice position from early in the twentieth century through the present. Drawing on archival materials in presidential libraries, Nemacheck builds on the work of Henry Abraham[6] and David Yalof,[7] one of Danelski's students, on presidential appointments to the Supreme Court. Potential leadership ability is certainly a variable that presidents have considered when choosing a chief justice.

Kevin McMahon, in his contribution (chapter 5), focuses on the confirmation of Supreme Court justices and chief justices in particular and uses, in part, Stephen Skowronek's typology of American presidents in political time to explain easy as opposed to difficult confirmations.[8] Like the Nemacheck chapter, McMahon focuses on the past ten nominations to chief justice.

Part III offers eight chapters analyzing various facets of the chief justice's influence on the bench. Chapter 6, by Timothy Johnson and Charles Gregory, explores the question of the chief justice's influence on his colleagues during oral argument. They examine how the associate justices interacted with the chief justice and the extent of deference they showed. Their focus is on Chief Justices Burger, Rehnquist, and Roberts (his first four terms). Johnson and Gregory found that during oral argument, chief justices talked more and sought to shape the debate. In other words, the chiefs sought to exercise task leadership. The finding that associate justices do not cut off the chief in midsentence as often as they interrupt other associates suggests that associate justices recognize the special leadership role of the chief justice. In a separate analysis of the language used by Chief Justice Roberts directed toward the attorneys during oral argument, Johnson and Gregory found evidence of the exercise of social leadership.

In chapter 7, Paul Wahlbeck, Alyx Mark, Ryan Krog, and Phillip Winginger focus on forecasting opinion assignment during the Roberts Court. They develop a statistical model drawing on data from the 2004 through 2009 Supreme Court terms, and they test that model with the 2010 term. They find that Chief Justice Roberts used his opinion-assignment power much like his predecessors in that a mix of variables were involved: ideological positions of the associates, strategic considerations, need for an equitable distribution of the workload, and the Court's organizational needs.

Charles Cameron and Tom Clark in chapter 8 were concerned with ideological voting behavior on the Supreme Court and in particular the influence of the chief justice on the most important cases. Their finding that the ideology of the chief justice dramatically affects the extent of liberal outcomes is tied to the chief justice's power of assigning the writing of the Opinion of the Court (when voting with the majority). Cameron and Clark, in effect, demonstrate that the chief justice's task leadership impacts ideological outcomes on the Court.

Amy Steigerwalt, Pamela Corley, and Artemus Ward in chapter 9 explore the role of the chief justice in encouraging unanimous decision making and, in particular, whether a new chief justice has a "honeymoon period" whereby conflict is muted and unanimity is enhanced. They examined appeals from lower federal courts that were decided by the Supreme Court between the 1946 and 2011 terms. They looked for opinion consensus and not just outcome consensus. Their findings that not all chiefs have a "honeymoon," and that there is a variation among those that do, tie in part into the leadership and personality variables discussed in particular in chapter 3.

In chapter 10, Brandon Bartels and Phillip Wininger look at still another facet of chief justice leadership: whether chiefs more than associate justices pursue institutional maintenance. For the chiefs this means building larger coalitions when the chief is the author of the majority opinion. They also explore whether the chiefs, more than the associates, emphasize authoritative precedent in their opinions, thus underscoring institutional legitimacy and the image of the Court as a court of law. They analyze data from 1946 to 2010, encompassing five chief justices. That the findings are mixed only underscores the difficulty of empirically demonstrating certain aspects of leadership—and again we can speculate that the results are somehow linked to personality variables.

Social leadership is the focus of chapter 11. Ryan Black, Ryan Owens, and Justin Wedeking looked at every written opinion between 1946 and 2012 using textual analysis software programs that differentiated "agreeable" from "disagreeable" language in majority opinions. They tested whether chief justices in their opinions used more "agreeable" and less "disagreeable" language than associate justices did in their majority opinions. Also they examined the language of majority decisions not written by the chief in which the chief did not join. This measure of social leadership, admittedly only one facet or indicator, failed to yield evidence of social leadership by the chief justices studied. But the study is reflective of the new generation of empirically oriented scholars who imaginatively search for measures of leadership and do not flinch when they come up empty-handed.

Chapter 12 has an ambitious agenda. Drawing on all the majority, concurring, and dissenting opinions of the justices from 1789 through 2000, the authors, Douglas Rice and Christopher Zorn, examine the extent to which a new chief justice affects the exercise of task and social leadership. They do this indirectly by way of a computerized analysis of the linguistic content of all opinions. The authors posit that task leadership is tied to the amount of emotional language in opinions while social leadership is linked to the tone of that language varying from positive (indicative of social leadership) to negative (indicative of weak or no social leadership). Their suggestive findings are many, but of greatest import is their support of Danelski's findings of task and social leadership in the Taft, Hughes, and Stone Courts.

The final chapter in part III, chapter 13, by Kirk Randazzo and Rebecca Reid, aims to focus on the chief justice's leadership in statutory construction cases. Their data set is from the Warren, Burger, and Rehnquist Courts and is limited to cases concerning congressional statutes that are clearly liberal or conservative. They posit that statutory language inhibits the role of ideology in judicial voting behavior. Their findings are numerous and provide some support for their hypotheses, although evidence concerning chief justice leadership is more suggestive than demonstrated.

Part IV consists of two chapters concerned with the chief justice's efforts, in addition to judicial decision making, to enhance institutional legitimacy and to promote administrative reform. Chapter 14, by Richard Vining and Teena Wilhelm, address the chief justice's administrative leadership by analyzing the chief justice's annual Year-End Report on the Federal Judiciary and his calls for legislation to meet the needs of the judicial branch. Chief Justice Warren Burger was the innovator of the annual report. Interestingly, Burger and Rehnquist used the annual reports to promote agenda items much more than did Roberts. But also, Vining and Wilhelm found that there is a relationship between the number of years in office as chief justice and the number of agenda items in the report.

Shawn Fettig and Sara Benesh, in chapter 15, examine chief justices and their concern for protecting the Court's reputation and image. They draw on examples of chief justices including Chief Justice Hughes's opinion assignments, his meetings with Justice Owen Roberts during the summer of 1936 that eventually resulted in "the switch in time that saved nine," Chief

Justice Earl Warren's quest for unanimity in *Brown v. Board of Education*,[9] Chief Justice Rehnquist's opinion in *Dickerson v. United States*[10] reaffirming *Miranda v. Arizona*,[11] and Chief Justice John Roberts's opinion in *National Federation of Independent Business v. Sebelius*[12] upholding the Affordable Care Act ("Obamacare"), among other examples.

IV. Epilogue

This exciting and imaginative collection of empirical research on various facets of the chief justice has a common denominator. Each chapter is concerned with leadership and as such they of necessity have their intellectual roots in the remarkable and path-breaking scholarship of Danelski. Although this volume was neither intended nor designed as a festschrift, it is clear that Danelski's influence continues through the current generation of scholars. His contributions are immense, and he is unquestionably a key founder of the field of judicial politics and the study of chief justices. This volume not only advances the field in the study of chief justices and their impact, it also serves as a tribute to David J. Danelski's life work.

NOTES

1. But see Elliot Slotnick, "Who Speaks for the Court? Majority Opinion Assignment from Taft to Burger," *American Journal of Political Science* 23 (1979): 60–77; and Robert J. Steamer, *Chief Justice: Leadership and the Supreme Court* (Columbia: University of South Carolina Press, 1986).

2. See Charlie Savage, "Newest Spy Court Pick Is a Democrat But Not a Liberal," *New York Times*, August 20, 2013. But see Charlie Savage and Scott Shane, "Top Secret Court Castigates N.S.A. on Surveillance: E-Mail from Americans: Judge Found Violations of the Constitution in a 2011 Ruling," *New York Times*, August 22, 2013, p. 1.

3. 5 U.S. 137 (1803).

4. Some notable biographies include Alpheus T. Mason, *Harlan Fiske Stone: Pillar of the Law* (New York: Viking, 1956) and Merlo J. Pusey, *Charles Evans Hughes*, 2 vols. (New York: Macmillan, 1951). Other publications containing data on the chief justice's role in the Court's decision-making process are Charles Evans Hughes, *The Supreme Court of the United States, Its Foundations, Methods and Achievements: An Interpretation* (New York: Columbia University Press, 1928); Edwin McElwain, "The Business of the Supreme Court as Conducted by Charles Evans Hughes," *Harvard Law Review* 63 (1949): 5–26; Felix Frankfurter, "Chief Justices I Have Known," in *Of Law and Men*, ed. Philip Elman (New York: Harcourt, Brace, 1956), 111–36; and David J. Danelski and Joseph S. Tulchin, eds., *The Autobiographical Notes of Charles Evans Hughes* (Cambridge, MA: Harvard University Press, 1973).

5. C. Herman Pritchett, *The Roosevelt Court: A Study in Judicial Politics and Values 1937–1947* (New York: Macmillan, 1948), xii.

6. Henry J. Abraham, *Justices, Presidents, and Senators: A History of U.S. Supreme Court Appointments from Washington to Bush II* (Lanham, MD: Rowman & Littlefield, 2008).

7. David A. Yalof, *Pursuit of Justices: Presidential Politics and the Selection of Supreme Court Nominees* (Chicago: University of Chicago Press, 1999).

8. Stephen Skowronek, *The Politics Presidents Make: Leadership from John Adams to George Bush* (Cambridge, MA: Harvard University Press, 1993).

9. 347 U.S. 483 (1954).

10. 530 U.S. 428 (2000).

11. 384 U.S. 436 (1966).

12. 567 U.S. ___ (2012).

PART I

The Earliest Social Science Studies of the Chief Justice Revisited

DAVID J. DANELSKI

In 1960, I delivered two related papers at professional meetings—one at the Midwest Conference of Political Scientists and the other at the American Political Science Association meeting. The first paper was an empirical study of opinion assignment by the chief justice;[1] the second paper was a theoretical study of the chief justice's influence in the Supreme Court's decisional process.[2] In 1961, Walter F. Murphy and C. Herman Pritchett published an abridged version of the APSA paper in *Courts, Judges, and Politics*.[3] In 1968, Thomas P. Jahnige and Sheldon Goldman published another abridged version of the same paper in *The Federal Judicial System: Readings in Process and Behavior*.[4] Both versions were widely reprinted in other anthologies on judicial behavior and American politics.[5] One version is still in print.[6]

Chapter 1 is the unabridged version of the 1960 APSA paper, which is more comprehensive, more theoretical, and hence more useful for research purposes than its abridged versions. It presents a social-psychological theory of leadership in the Supreme Court and applies it to data drawn from the papers of William Howard Taft, Charles Evans Hughes, and Harlan Fiske Stone at the Library of Congress. The paper focuses particularly on the five phases of the Court's decisional process: case selection, oral argument, conference decision making, opinion assignment, and opinion writing. The gist of the theory is that two types of leadership—task and social leadership—are necessary for cohesion, productivity, and satisfaction in the Court, which are the basis of efficient decision making.

In the past fifty-five years, more than 150 books, articles, and dissertations have discussed, relied on, or cited one version or another of the 1960 APSA paper. Viewed by scholars as an "important,"[7] "significant,"[8] "seminal,"[9] and "classic"[10] work, it has been cited in studies of chief judges of lower federal courts,[11] state courts of last resort,[12] foreign courts,[13] and the British House of Lords.[14] It has also been cited in studies assessing the leadership of Chief Justices John Marshall,[15] Morrison Remick Waite,[16] Edward Douglass White,[17] William Howard Taft,[18] Charles Evans Hughes,[19] Harlan Fiske Stone,[20] Fred M. Vinson,[21] Earl Warren,[22] Warren Burger,[23] William H. Rehnquist,[24] and John Roberts.[25]

Thomas G. Walker's analysis of the 1960 APSA paper is the most perceptive in the literature.[26] After discussing the paper at length, he concluded that it "provided a bridge between competing schools of thought and frequently opened the door to research questions that younger generations of judicial politics scholars could pursue armed with their new their new theoretical insights and methodological skills."[27]

Chapter 2 revisits the 1960 Midwest Conference paper, which, except for a two-and-a-half-page excerpt on the strategic aspects of opinion assignment by the chief justice, has never been published.[28] The chapter summarizes the paper's major findings and compares them to the findings of recent studies of opinion assignment that used multivariate analysis and sophisticated modeling.

The 1960 Midwest Conference paper marked the beginning of the opinion-assignment literature. Among the scholars who relied on or cited the paper or its summary were S. Sidney Ulmer,[29] David W. Rohde,[30] William P. McLauchlan,[31] Gregory J. Rathjen,[32] Dennis Haynes,[33] Elliot Slotnick,[34] Saul Brenner,[35] Jan Palmer,[36] Harold Spaeth,[37] Robert J. Steamer,[38] Sue Davis,[39] Beverly Blair Cook,[40] Sandra L. Wood,[41] Forrest Maltzman and Paul J. Wahlbeck,[42] Drew Noble Lanier,[43] and Linda Greenhouse.[44]

Chapter 3 revisits the 1960 APSA paper for the purpose of exploring the relationship between personality and leadership in the Supreme Court, a subject that had been mentioned in the paper but not pursued. The chapter is, in effect, a sequel to the 1960 APSA paper. Both studies deal with leadership and both explore uncharted territory, using social science theory and archival data to explain judicial behavior. The former draws on social psychology. The latter draws on the personality theory of C. G. Jung, as interpreted and developed by Isabel Briggs Myers.

The two leadership studies are bookends of a scholar's career that spanned more than half a century, yet they constitute a single work and should be read together, for each informs the other.

NOTES

1. David J. Danelski, "Opinion Assignment by the Chief Justice," a paper delivered at the Midwestern Conference of Political Scientists in Bloomington, Indiana, April 28, 1960. A revised version of the paper is a chapter in David J. Danelski, "The Chief Justice and the Supreme Court" (PhD diss., University of Chicago, 1961).

2. David J. Danelski, "The Influence of the Chief Justice in the Decisional Process of the Supreme Court," a paper delivered at the American Political Science Association meeting in New York City, September 9, 1960.

3. Walter F. Murphy and C. Herman Pritchett, eds., *Courts, Judges, and Politics* (New York: Random House, 1961), 497–508.

4. Thomas P. Jahnige and Sheldon Goldman, eds., *The Federal Judicial System* (New York: Holt, Rinehart, & Winston, 1968), 147–60.

5. See Thomas G. Walker, "David J. Danelski: Social Psychology and Group Choice," in *The Pioneers of Judicial Behavior*, ed. Nancy Maveety (Ann Arbor: University of Michigan Press, 2003), 254.

6. Walter F. Murphy, C. Herman Pritchett, Lee Epstein, and Jack Knight, *Courts, Judges, and Politics* (New York: McGraw-Hill, 2005).

7. Joel K. Goldstein, "Leading the Court: Studies in Influence as Chief Justice," *Stetson Law Review* 40 (2011): 721.

8. Theodore L. Becker, *Political Behavioralism and Modern Jurisprudence* (Chicago: Rand McNally, 1965), 37.

9. Frank B. Cross and Stefanie A. Lindquist, "The Decisional Significance of the Chief Justice," *University of Pennsylvania Law Review* 154 (2006): 1665.

10. Jeffery Morris, "'What Heaven Must Be Like': William Howard Taft as Chief Justice," *Supreme Court History Yearbook* (1983): 92.

11. Virginia Hettinger, Stefanie A. Lindquist, and Wendy L. Martinek, "The Role and Impact of Chief Judges on the United States Courts of Appeals," *Justice Systems Journal* 24 (2003): 91–117.

12. Craig R. Ducat and Victor E. Flango, *Leadership in State Supreme Courts: Roles of the Chief Justice* (Beverly Hills, CA: Sage, 1976), 6–8.

13. Russell Smyth and Paresh Kumar Narayan, "Hail to the Chief! Leadership and Change in the Level of Consensus in the High Court of Australia," *Journal of Empirical Studies* 1 (2004): 399–421.

14. Alan Paterson, *The Law Lords* (Toronto: University of Toronto Press, 1982), 105.

15. Robert G. Seddig, "John Marshall and the Origins of Supreme Court Leadership," *University of Pittsburgh Law Review* 36 (1974–75): 765.

16. D. Grier Stephenson, "The Chief Justice as Leader: The Case of Morrison Remick Waite," *William and Mary Law Review* 14 (1973): 899.

17. Walter F. Pratt Jr., *The Supreme Court under Edward Douglass White* (Columbia: University of South Carolina Press, 1999), 60–61.

18. Goldstein, "Leading the Court," 732–33.

19. Ibid., 723–27.

20. Ibid., 734–35; William Wiecek, *The Birth of the Modern Constitution: The United States Supreme Court, 1941–53* (New York: Cambridge University Press, 2006), 58–62.

21. James E. St. Claire and Linda C. Gugin, *Chief Justice Fred M. Vinson of Kentucky* (Lexington: University Press of Kentucky, 2002), 171–74.

22. Leo Katcher, *Earl Warren: A Political Biography* (New York: McGraw-Hill, 1967), 350.

23. Goldstein, "Leading the Court," 736–37.

24. Ibid., 737–40.

25. Mark Tushnet, "The First (and Last?) Term of the Roberts Court," *Tulsa Law Review* 42 (2006–07): 502.

26. Walker, "David J. Danelski: Social Psychology and Group Choice," 251–57.

27. Ibid., 265.

28. See Murphy and Pritchett, *Courts, Judges, and Politics*, 503–5.

29. S. Sidney Ulmer, "The Use of Power in the Supreme Court: The Opinion Assignments of Earl Warren, 1953–1960," *Journal of Public Law* 30 (1970): 49, 51, 53, 55, 64.

30. David W. Rohde, "Strategy and Ideology: The Assignment of Majority Opinions in the United States Supreme Court" (PhD diss., University of Rochester, 1971), 13–14, 16, 31, 87. Rohde published most of his dissertation in two articles in the *Midwest Journal of Political Science* in 1972.

31. William P. McLauchlan, "Research Note: Ideology and Conflict in Supreme Court Opinions, 1946–1962," *Western Political Quarterly* 25 (1972): 16, 27.

32. Gregory J. Rathjen, "Policy Goals, Strategic Choice, and Majority Opinion Assignments in the Supreme Court: A Replication," *American Journal of Political Science* 18 (1974): 714.

33. Dennis Haynes, "Rolling Back the Top on Chief Justice Burger's Desk," *University of Pittsburgh Law Review* 39 (1977): 631, 631, 637, 642, 646.

34. Elliot E. Slotnick, "Who Speaks for the Court: The Chief Justice and the Assignment of Majority Opinions" (PhD diss., University of Minnesota, 1976), passim. Slotnick published most of his dissertation in political science journals in 1978 and 1979.

35. Saul Brenner, "Strategic Choice and Opinion Assignment on the Supreme Court: A Reexamination," *Western Political Quarterly* 35 (1982): 205, 206. Between 1984 and 1992, Brenner cited one version or another of the Midwest Conference paper in at least seven other journal articles and book chapters.

36. Saul Brenner and Jan Palmer, "The Time Taken to Write Majority Opinions as a Determinant Opinion Assignment on the Vinson Court," *Judicature* 72 (1988): 179.

37. Harold Spaeth, "Distributive Justice: Majority Opinions in the Burger Court," *Judicature* 67 (1984): 300, 301.

38. Robert J. Steamer, *Chief Justice, Leadership, and the Supreme Court* (Columbia: University of South Carolina Press, 1986), 214.

39. Sue Davis, "Power on the Court: Chief Justice Rehnquist's Assignments," *Judicature* 74 (1990): 67.

40. Beverly Blair Cook, "Testing a Model of Opinion Assignment: The Burger Court" (paper presented at the 1992 meeting for the American Political Science Association): 22, Beverly Blair Cook Papers, Newcomb Archives, Tulane University.

41. Sandra L. Wood, Linda Camp Keith, Drew Noble Lanier, and Ayo Ogun-

dele, "Opinion Assignment and the Chief Justice, 1888–1940," *Social Science Quarterly* 81 (2000): 798, 800.

42. Forrest Maltzman and Paul J. Wahlbeck, "A Conditional Model of Opinion Assignment on the Supreme Court," *Political Research Quarterly* 57 (2004): 551, 553, one of a series of assignment studies done by the authors between 1996 and 2006 that used multivariate analysis.

43. Drew Noble Lanier and Sandra Wood, "Moving on Up: Institutional Position and the Chief Justice," *American Review of Politics* 22 (2001): 93, 95, 97, 104.

44. Linda Greenhouse, "Chief Justice Roberts in His Own Voice," *Judicature* 97 (2013): 90, 91.

1 ~ The Influence of the Chief Justice in the Decisional Process of the Supreme Court*

DAVID J. DANELSKI

In theory, the relationship among the justices of the Supreme Court of the United States is one of equality, and frequently the chief justice is referred to as first among equals. Rarely, however, is there equality in practice. Some justices are more able, more persuasive, or more personable than others; thus, they are more influential that others in decisional process. The chief justice by virtue of his office has a unique opportunity for leadership. He is in the key figure in the Court's certiorari practice. He presides in open court and over the secret conferences where he usually presents each case to his associates, giving his opinion first and voting last. He assigns the opinion of the Court in virtually all cases when he votes with the majority, and, as a practical matter, he decides when the opinion will be announced. But the chief justiceship does not guarantee leadership. It only offers its incumbent an opportunity to lead. Optimum leadership inheres in the combination of the office and an able, persuasive, personable judge.

The chief justiceship has lived and grown in the shadow of judicial secrecy. Data cannot be obtained about it for purposes of analysis by direct observation of the chief justice's participation in the decisional process of the Court. Manuscripts, memoirs, interviews, and the Court's official reports are the chief available sources of data. Although one must be wary of coming too close to the present, lest disclosures embarrass Court members still on the bench, a study of the chief justiceship, to be worthwhile, must be close enough to the present to yield generalizations useful in understanding the office today. In an effort to avoid both difficulties, the period

*This chapter is the original, unabridged version of a paper delivered at the American Political Science Association meeting in New York, on Sept. 8, 1960.

from 1921 to 1946—the era of Chief Justices Taft, Hughes, and Stone—was selected for analysis.

The first section of this paper sets out basic definitions and hypotheses drawn principally from social psychology. Sections II through VI develop these hypotheses and apply them to data concerning the chief justice's participation in the decisional process of the Court. A caveat is in order: this is a tentative and exploratory study. The data are fragmentary and do not measure up to the standards of modern social science for rigorous analysis. In such a situation, one can only analyze the data with the rigor they admit. That is what is attempted here.

I. Some Theoretical Considerations

Leadership in the Supreme Court is best understood in terms of influence: CJ influences J to do x to the extent that CJ performs some activity y as a result of which J chooses to do x.[1] Explicit in this definition are the two concepts, activity and interaction. Activity simply refers to things Court members do, for example, voting and writing opinions. Interaction refers to activity by one member of the Court to which another member responds, for example, conference discussion and opinion assignment. Interaction is indispensable to influence, for if J does not respond to CJ's activity, J cannot choose to do x as the result of y. Influence, however, implies more than surface activity and interaction, for frequently underlying those phenomena are expectations, thoughts, and feelings of CJ and J.[2]

Expectations are evaluative standards applied to an incumbent of a position, such as the chief justice, and a set of those expectations defines his role.[3] The term "expectation" is used in the normative sense (CJ *should* do y) rather than in the predictive sense (CJ *will* do y).[4] Role is an important concept in the analysis of judicial behavior because the expectations the chief justice and justices hold for themselves and each other affect their activity. Conversely, activity affects expectations. The chief justice, by his activity, can create new expectations and to some extent thereby redefine his roles and even the role of the justices. Chief Justice Hughes, for example, did this when he established the "special list" for disposing of unmeritorious certiorari cases without conference discussion. Thereafter, the chief justice was expected to determine initially which certioraris should be considered in conference, and if a justice wanted a case transferred from the "special list" so that it might be discussed and voted upon, the chief justice was expected to do so upon request.[5]

Likeability is an important dimension of influence. Like other persons,

Court members tend to like some of their associates more than others, to be indifferent to some, and perhaps even to dislike others. Chief Justice Taft, for example, regarded Justice Van Devanter as "the closest friend [he had] on the Court," and when he was fatally ill in January 1930, Van Devanter was the only member of the Court who was allowed to see him.[6] Applying sociometry to the personal documents of justices, the social structure of the Court can be diagrammed, and the various relationships described by Moreno emerge: the "isolated individual" (McReynolds, ca. 1921–1926), the "star" or greatly preferred member (Taft, 1921–1930), etc.[7] As this paper will show, the social structure of the Court is significant in decisional process, and likeability is an important variable in influence, for it affects the interactions among Court members.

Esteem is another important dimension of influence. It is the value of a Court member as perceived by his associates primarily in terms of ability. The member who is regarded as having the best ideas in conference and being best able to handle the tough cases assigned him for opinion is ordinarily highly esteemed by his associates. Of course, there may be differences of opinion as to who is the most able member of the Court, the next most able, etc., but there is no doubt that such ranking occurs.[8] A factor that may affect the perceived value of a Court member is the esteem he carries over from previous high-status positions, such as president, presidential candidate, secretary of state, etc. The position of chief justice in itself, however, probably adds only a little to the esteem of its incumbent in the eyes of his associates. In the Court his esteem depends more upon his overall ability and how well he fulfills his role as chief justice. The highly esteemed chief justice has near maximal influence potential, for his associates will tend to act on the premise: "I value you and your opinions CJ, so I shall do as you wish."

In terms of influence, then, the ideal chief justice is a persuasive, esteemed, able, and well-liked judge who perceives, fulfills, and even expands his role as head of the Court. One might ask: influence for what? The more important objects of influence are the attainment of: (1) a majority vote for the chief justice's position, (2) written opinions satisfactory to him, (3) social cohesion in the Court, and (4) unanimous decisions. In the close case, where a justice is wavering in his vote, influence may be the difference between a decision one way or another. Since the chief justice assigns virtually all cases when he votes with the majority, the content of an opinion is to some degree determined by his selection of the Court's spokesman. Unless there is cohesion among the justices, the Court cannot be a true collegial decision-making body. And where there is high cohesion, unanimous decisions will be frequent, for unanimity arises from the give and take of compromise. Thus the main objects of influence go to the heart of the Court's decisional process.

II. The Decision to Make a Decision

Today, the appellate jurisdiction of the Court is almost entirely discretionary.[9] Therefore, the threshold decision to take or not to take a case for review is crucial; six out of seven cases go no further in the Court's decisional process. Standing at the threshold of the Court's discretionary jurisdiction is the chief justice. All the justices examine the petitions for certiorari and jurisdictional statements, but the chief justice's examination must be particularly careful, for it is his duty to present them in conference. Chief Justice Taft's preparation of certioraris was like Holmes' preparation: not done so thoroughly as to decide the cases but thoroughly enough to decide whether or not they should be brought before the Court.[10] Chief Justice Hughes, however, made very complete and thorough preparation, usually going into the merits of each case and often deciding it "then and there in his own mind."[11] Apparently Chief Justice Stone, who was prone to defer judgment for days and even weeks after cases were argued, usually prepared the certioraris and jurisdictional statements only to determine whether the Court should exercise its jurisdiction.[12]

Until the middle 1930s, every petition for certiorari was presented in conference by the chief justice and voted upon by the Court. At the beginning of a term, some 250 to 300 certioraris would be awaiting disposition. Taft scheduled daily conferences to dispose of them, taking up fifty to sixty cases a day.[13] At first Hughes followed Taft's procedure, presenting and disposing of as many as a hundred petitions for certiorari in a single afternoon.[14] Then he established a unanimous consent procedure in which the chief justice was the key figure. If the chief justice decided that a petition for certiorari was frivolous or otherwise did not merit conference discussion, he placed it on a "special list" that was circulated to the associates. Upon request, any case on the special list would be transferred to the regular take-up list,[15] but cases remaining on the special list were automatically denied certiorari without discussion. Hughes disposed of about 60 percent of the petitions for certiorari via the special list, and rarely did a justice challenge his list.[16] Challenges were also relatively rare during Stone's chief justiceship.[17]

The innovation of the special list increases the influence potential of the chief justice. Petitions he wants discussed in conference are taken up automatically, but petitions are not so easily transferred from the special to the regular list. The associate justice who challenges the special list must be well prepared and willing to disagree openly with the chief justice. To the extent, therefore, that a justice does not prepare thoroughly or is hesitant to disagree with the chief justice, because he likes or esteems him or for some other reason, the chief justice's influence increases proportionately.[18]

The chief justice's second opportunity for influence during this phase of the decisional process arises when he presents the petitions for certiorari and jurisdictional statements to the conference, for he gives his views first and usually speaks longer than any of his associates. The influence of the chief justice in conference is considered later, but a word as to the time spent on petitions for certiorari and jurisdictional statements is in order here. Frequently when Hughes finished his presentation of those cases, his associates had nothing to add,[19] and when there was a discussion, he limited it, bearing in mind his rule that the average certiorari petition could not be allowed more than three and a half minutes.[20] During Taft's chief justiceship, the average certiorari case received about ten minutes, but Taft felt that too much time was devoted to certiorari cases, thus limiting discussion of argued and submitted cases.[21] During Stone's chief justiceship, "petitions for certiorari and jurisdictional statements," said Justice Douglas, "were never more fully or carefully discussed."[22]

Taft admitted that his conference activity in regard to certioraris was not very influential: when the Court votes on certioraris, he said, "I'm usually in the minority . . ."[23] Hughes was more influential partly because of his rigorous control of discussion. In the three and one-half minutes he allowed each certiorari petition, there could be little discussion, for usually it would take that long to present the case and vote. Thus, by virtually monopolizing the time available, he greatly influenced the certiorari and probable jurisdiction decisions. Conversely, Stone's influence was probably less than Hughes's because of the expanded discussion of certioraris and jurisdictional statements during his chief justiceship.

III. Oral Argument

When the Court hears oral argument, the chief justice is only in a little better position than his associates to influence the decisional process. As presiding officer, he has some discretion in extending counsel's time for argument, but beyond that, his influence depends primarily upon his esteem and interaction.[24] For oral argument is a period of deliberation in which Court members frequently arrive at tentative decisions that usually accord with their final votes.[25]

Court members participate in open court deliberation by questioning counsel and making comments from the bench. Formally, the chief justice cannot restrict his associates in such interaction, but if he is highly esteemed, his wishes as to excessive questioning of counsel probably will be respected.[26] Nonetheless, it is pretty much every judge for himself, and a judge who has made up his mind, is well prepared, and initiates interactions may wittingly or unwittingly influence his associates' tentative decisions.

Apparently Hughes did. One of his reasons for going to the merits of a case and often deciding it when it was before him at the certiorari stage was "always to be ahead of the Court and at least abreast of counsel" when the case was argued.[27] He realized that arguments of counsel in four out of five cases, as one justice confided in 1948, were "not good,"[28] and thus he guided the "frightened," the "timid," and the "incompetent" with helpful questions.[29] "Is your argument so and so," he would say, stating the argument for counsel. When counsel agreed, he would say, "Now the Court would like to hear from you on these other points," indicating what he thought should be argued.[30] In a series of genial questions, it was not uncommon for Hughes to indicate subtly what he thought the Court's decision should be,[31] something his associates could not help but notice. Both Taft and Stone questioned counsel, Stone more actively as chief justice than as associate justice,[32] but neither of them did so in the grand and influential manner of Hughes.

IV. In Conference

In conference, the chief justice is in a favorable position to influence his associates. In order to explain the nature of his influence at this stage of the decisional process a theory of conference leadership is necessary. Relying principally upon the empirical studies of decision-making groups by Bales,[33] Slater,[34] and Berkowitz,[35] the following theory has been constructed: The primary task of the conference is the decision of cases through interaction. In making decisions, some Court members initiate and receive more interaction than others. Usually one member makes more suggestions, gives more opinions, orients the discussion more frequently, and successfully defends his ideas more often than the others. Generally, he is regarded as having the best ideas for the decision of cases and is highly esteemed by his associates. Thus he emerges as task leader of the conference. He is apt to be an intense man, and, in concentrating on the Court's decisions, his response to the emotional needs of his associates is apt to be secondary. The interaction involved in deciding cases tends to cause conflict, tension, and antagonism, which if allowed to get out of hand would make the intelligent decision of cases virtually impossible. Negative aspects of interaction are counterbalanced by interactions relieving tension and showing solidarity and agreement. One member usually performs more such activity than the others. He invites orientation, opinions, and suggestions and in general attends to the emotional needs of his associates by affirming their value as individuals and Court members. Generally, he is the best-liked member of the conference and emerges as its social leader. Not only is he well-liked; usually he wants to be well-liked. He is apt to dislike conflict, and its avoidance may be a felt necessity for him. Thus it would be difficult for him to assume task leadership.

Yet the chief justice can be both task and social leader.[36] While his task leadership is not primarily derived from his office, the fact that he speaks first in conference tends to maintain such leadership if he has an independent claim to it. Also his control of the conference process puts him in a favorable position to exercise social leadership, for he can minimize exchanges that contribute toward negative feelings among Court members and perform other activity that favorably disposes his associates toward him. Assuming he performs both aspects of leadership well and fulfills the important expectations of his role, his influence in conference is great. Other important consequences are: (1) Conflict in conference tends to be minimal. (2) Court members tend to be socially cohesive. (3) Court members tend to be satisfied with the conference. (4) The conference tends to be productive in terms of the number of decisions made for the time spent. Rarely, however, are both aspects of leadership combined in a single individual. Typically, leadership is shared in conference. If it is positively shared, that is, if a chief justice who is social leader forms a coalition with a justice who is task leader and they work together, a situation prevails that is similar to the one in which both aspects of leadership are combined in the chief justice. Such coalitions ordinarily occur where the personal relations between the chief justice and the task leader are fairly close. But if leadership is negatively shared, that is, if the chief justice and the task leader do not work together and even compete against each other, then not only does the chief justice's influence in conference tends to decrease, but conflict tends to increase, and cohesion, satisfaction, and production tend to decrease.

There was positive sharing of leadership during Taft's chief justiceship: Taft was social leader and his good friend and appointee, Van Devanter, was task leader. Evidence of Van Devanter's esteem and task leadership is abundant.[37] Taft, time and time again, asserted that Van Devanter was the most able justice on the Court.[38] If the Court were to vote, he said, that would be its judgment too.[39] Chief Justice Taft admitted that he did not know how he could get along without Van Devanter in conference, for Van Devanter kept the Court consistent with itself, and "his power of statement and his immense memory make him an antagonist in conference who generally wins against all opposition."[40] Van Devanter's contemporaries saw him as "a man with great physical vigor, a powerful intellect and a driving and dominant personality,"[41] a man who was "absorbed by his work" and yet had a sense of humor but "not of the frivolous or merry sort," but "always dignified."[42] At times, Van Devanter's ability actually embarrassed Taft, and he wondered if it might not be better to have Van Devanter run the conference himself.[43] "Still," mused the former president, "I must worry along until the end of my ten years, content to aid in the deliberation when there is a difference of opinion."[44] In other words, Taft was content to perform the functions of social leadership. Clearly he was the best-liked member of his Court, and he wanted to be liked.[45] His friendship with Van Devanter was especially close,[46] but he valued the friendship of each of his colleagues, including McReynolds, whom he characterized as a "grouch."[47]

Discussion in the Taft-Van Devanter conference was described in 1928 as being of "the freest character,"[48] and naturally this led to some conflict. But when the justices disagreed, it was usually, as Brandeis said, "without any ill feeling"; it was "all very friendly."[49] Taft, however, disliked conflict of any kind. The "clash of minds" at the conference table made him tense.[50] When tensions rose in conferences he frequently sought to relieve them with his humor,[51] and when the justices could not agree, he tried to mediate their differences.[52] During his chief justiceship, the justices were satisfied with the conferences. "Things go happily in the conference room," Brandeis remarked. "The judges go home less tired emotionally and less weary physically than in White's day."[53] Holmes said the 1922 term was the most pleasant year he had spent on the Court, which he credited to Taft.[54] The Court was fairly cohesive. Personal relations among the justices were amiable.[55] There even appeared to be a tacit *rapprochement* between McReynolds and Brandeis.[56] Despite differences of opinions, there was compromise and teamwork among the liberal and conservative justices alike.[57] And there was production. The Court under Taft for the first time in more than fifty years came close to clearing its docket. Taft's influence in conference was probably as great as it could have been, for his coalition with Van Devanter gave him power he would not have had otherwise.

Task and social leadership were combined in Hughes. Overall, he was the most esteemed member of his Court.[58] His prior high positions undoubtedly contributed to his esteem, but primarily it was due to his performance in conference. His associates could always be sure that he was well prepared. Blessed with a photographic memory,[59] he would summarize comprehensively and accurately the facts of each case. When he finished, he would look up and say with a smile: "Now I will state where I come out."[60] Then he would outline his views as to how the case should be decided. Sometimes that was all the discussion a case received, and the justices proceeded to vote for the disposition suggested by the chief. Where there was a discussion, the justices gave their views in order of seniority without interruption, stating why they concurred or dissented from the chief's views. After the justices had their say, Hughes would review the discussion, pointing out his agreement and disagreement with the views expressed.[61] Then he usually called for a vote. In terms of interaction, Hughes was the key figure of the conference. He made more suggestions, gave more opinions, and oriented the conference more than any other member. He not only did most of the talking; his associates' remarks were usually addressed to him, and they discussed the views he initially presented. Clearly, Hughes was conference task leader. His personality was in some respects similar to Van Devanter's. "The Chief Justice was an intense man," said Justice Roberts. "When he had serious business to transact he allowed no consideration to interfere with his operations. He was so engrossed in the vital issue that he had not time for lightness and pleasantry."[62]

Yet Hughes's relationship with his associates was genial and cordial, and he was regarded as being "considerate, sympathetic, and responsive."[63] Never in the eleven years that Roberts sat with Hughes in conference did he see him lose his temper. Never did he hear him pass a personal remark or even raise his voice. Never did he witness him interrupting or engaging in controversy with an associate.[64] Despite his popular stereotype, Hughes had a "keen sense of humor," which aided in keeping differences in conference from becoming discord.[65] On the whole, he was well liked. Roberts, who felt toward Hughes "much as a son or younger brother might feel," said, "Men whose views were as sharply opposed as those of Van Devanter and Brandeis, or those of Sutherland and Cardozo, were at one in their admiration and affectionate regard for their presiding officer."[66] Roberts could well have added Holmes, Black, Reed, Frankfurter, Douglas, and McReynolds.[67]

However, Justice Stone's feelings were ambivalent. From the beginning of Hughes's chief justiceship, he thought Hughes did not allow adequate time for discussion in conference. He told McReynolds that he was dissenting in a certain case because he had not been given an opportunity to state his views in conference.[68] Stone was also critical of Hughes's presentation of cases. Hughes, he said, would greatly overelaborate "unimportant details" and then dispose of the vital questions "in a sentence or two."[69] Stone referred to a portion of Hughes's presentation of the AAA case as "painful elaboration."[70] Oddly, Hughes was not aware of Stone's attitude, for Stone never openly challenged Hughes's methods, even when he had strong feelings about them. Why did not Stone speak out? If he had pressed his views in conference, Hughes could not have stopped him. Perhaps Hughes' esteem among his associates tended to inhibit discussion generally; for, as Frankfurter said, the "moral authority" exerted by the chief "inhibited irrelevance, repetition, and fruitless discussion."[71] It might have inhibited relevant and fruitful discussion as well. Stone's ambivalence toward Hughes might also be traced to his conception of the chief justice's role in conference that he learned during Taft's chief justiceship. Since leadership had been shared in the Taft Court, Taft had been a more permissive presiding officer, and Stone apparently felt that Hughes should have presided in a similar manner.[72]

Although there was some conflict in the Hughes conference, Hughes used his position as presiding officer to cut off discussion that showed signs of deteriorating into wrangling.[73] Socially, the Hughes Court was fairly cohesive. Justice Roberts said that though the Court was divided on constitutional policy, there was a feeling of "personal cordiality and comradeship" among the "justices."[74] Stone, as we have seen, was not satisfied with the conference, and there is some evidence that Cardozo shared Stone's feelings.[75] On the other hand, Roberts and Frankfurter, just to mention two justices, were highly satisfied with the Hughes conferences.[76] Conference production reached the highest point in the Court's history under Hughes and has never been equaled. Unquestionably, Hughes's influence in conference was great.

During Stone's chief justiceship, conference leadership was negatively shared. U.S. Court of Appeal Judge Augustus Hand apparently foresaw this when Stone was promoted to the center chair. Hand wanted Hughes to remain on the bench, and, from what he had heard, "the rest of the Court sincerely had the same desire, for they knew the peril of a lack of firm leadership." He hoped that Stone would fill the bill, but he had qualms. Stone, he said, "never seemed . . . a sure bet as a leader because of a certain inability to express himself orally and to maintain a position in a discussion."[77]

Stone departed from the conference role cut out for him by Hughes. When he presented cases, he lacked the apparent certitude of his predecessor, and, at times, his statement indicated that he was still groping for a solution.[78] In that posture the case would be passed down to his associates. Justices would speak out of turn,[79] and Stone did little to control their debate.[80] Instead, like his younger associates, he would join in the debate with alacrity, "delighted to take on all comers around the conference table."[81] "Jackson," he would say, "that's damned nonsense." "Douglas, *you* know better than that."[82] In other words, Stone was still acting like an associate justice, and in the free and easy interaction of the conference, his presumptive task leadership began to slip from his grasp.

Eventually, Black emerged as leading contender for task leadership of the conference.[83] Although Stone thought that Black was able, he distrusted his unorthodox approach, and no coalition developed as in the Taft Court.[84] Most of the justices, having served under Hughes, probably expected that Stone should lead in conference much in the same manner as his predecessor.[85] When he did not, a problem arose that is similar to the one studied by Heyns, who suggested that if a designated leader of a conference group does not perform the task functions expected of him, the group will tend to accept leadership from one of its other members. But if the designated leader performs his task functions, members who act like leaders will tend to be rejected by the group.[86] Stone's case is ambiguous, for Stone performed some task functions. Thus some justices accepted Black's assertion of task leadership and others did not. Douglas, Murphy, and Rutledge esteemed and liked Black and went along with his leadership, which, as senior associate justice, he was able to reinforce by usually speaking before them in conference and by assigning opinions when Stone dissented.[87] Roberts, Frankfurter, and Jackson, however, rejected Black's leadership, regarding him as a usurper of functions that were properly Stone's.[88] Reed, who was inclined toward Black, stood in the middle. Since Black asserted task leadership, a word might be said about his personality. His former law clerk, John P. Frank, described him in the following terms: "Black is a very, very tough man. When he is convinced, he is cool hard steel. . . . His temper is usually in close control, but he fights, and his words may occasionally have a terrible edge. He can be a rough man in an argument."[89]

Debates in conference were heated in the Stone Court, and a social leader was needed to sooth ruffled tempers, relieve tensions created by interaction, and maintain solidarity. Stone might have performed this function, but he did not. He did not use his control over the conference's process, as Hughes did, to cut off debate leading to irreconcilable conflict. He did not remain neutral when controversies arose so that he could be in a position to mediate them. As Professor Mason said, "He was totally unprepared to cope with the petty bickering and personal conflict in which his

Court became engulfed."[90] In sum, he did not provide the conference with adequate social leadership.

The combination of negative sharing of leadership and the failure of social leadership increased conflict in conference during Stone's chief justiceship. The conflict was not friendly as in Taft's day; rather, it was acrimonious and at times descended to the level of personalities. Even Stone's integrity was challenged.[91] Cohesion in the Court decreased.[92] Satisfaction with the conference also decreased. Frankfurter warned Stone about the dangers of justices speaking out of turn after the first conference,[93] and a year later he was appalled at the "easy-going, almost heedless way in which views on Constitutional issues touching the whole future direction of this country were floated."[94] Extended discussion meant conferences that frequently lasted until after six in the evening and sometimes were continued on into the following week.[95] "On more than one Saturday," Frankfurter noted, "the discussion after four-thirty gave evidence of fatigued minds and occasionally of frayed nerves." He longed for the taut four-hour conference of the Hughes Court, for he felt that the justices of the Stone Court were not always well prepared and conference discussion was often unfocused.[96] Production decreased. The Court under Stone decided as many cases as the Hughes Court did, but the time spent in conference to do so was just about double. It is probably safe to say that Stone's influence in conference was no greater than that of some of his associates.

Hughes was probably the most influential conference leader in modern times because he was able to perform both the task and social functions of leadership. Those functions are to some degree incompatible, and ordinarily a chief justice will be predisposed to perform either the task or social function, but not both. Quite likely Taft's strong dislike of conflict and his desire to be liked would have prevented him from becoming task leader even if he had the ability and esteem of Van Devanter. This, too, may have been the reason for Stone's failure as task leader. For Justice Jackson said, "Stone dreaded conflict,"[97] and the description of Black as "a very, very tough man" could not be applied to Stone. Stone, it would seem, was made of the intellectual, but not of the emotional, stuff that task leaders are made of. By comparison, it would seem that Hughes possessed those elements. But there was more than that to Hughes's success as conference leader. He had all the advantages of Taft and Stone and few of their disadvantages. He apparently had more esteem than Taft when he had come to the Court as chief justice, and on the Court he had more esteem than either Taft or Stone. Like Hughes, he had the advantage of having been a Court member, but unlike Hughes, Stone had the disadvantage of having difficulty in disassociating himself from his former role as an associate justice. The principal thing Hughes had learned during his service with Chief Justice White was how not to preside in conference. He thought White had failed as a leader because he did not focus and control conference discussions. As chief justice, Hughes intended to act otherwise. He had a clear conception of his role in conference and acted accordingly.[98] One might well conclude that Hughes understood the task and social functions of leadership and rationally sought to perform them to maintain his leadership in the Court.

V. Assignment of the Court's Opinion

In all cases in which the chief justice votes with the majority, he may write the Court's opinion or assign it to one of his associates who voted with him.[99] Opinion assignment is a significant exercise of influence because the selection of the Court's spokesman may be instrumental in:

(1) Determining the value of a decision as a precedent, that is, depending upon the writer, an opinion may be placed on one ground rather than another or two grounds instead of one, or deal narrowly or broadly with the issues.
(2) Making a decision as acceptable to the public.
(3) Holding the chief justice's majority together in close cases.
(4) Persuading dissenting associates to join in the Court's opinion.

Taft and Hughes assigned 95 percent of the cases decided during their tenures. Stone's assignment average was slightly more than 85 percent. Usually justices accept their assignments without question.[100]

The chief justice has maximal control over an opinion if he assigns it to himself, and undoubtedly chief justices have retained many important cases for that reason. The chief justice's self-assignment in "big cases" is generally accepted by his colleagues. In fact, they expect him to write in those cases to lend the prestige of his office to the Court's pronouncements.[101] In varying degrees, chief justices have fulfilled this expectation. Taft wrote opinions in 34 percent of the "important constitutional cases"[102] decided while he was chief justice. Hughes's and Stone's percentages were 29 and 18 respectively.

When the chief justice does not speak for the Court, his influence lies primarily in his assignment of important cases to justices who generally agree with him. From 1925 to 1930, Taft designated his fellow conservatives, Sutherland and Butler, to speak for the Court in 50 percent of the important constitutional cases assigned to associate justices. From 1932 to 1937, Hughes, who agreed more with Roberts, Van Devanter, and Sutherland than with the rest of his associates, assigned 44.2 percent of the important constitutional cases to Roberts and Sutherland. From 1943 to 1945, Stone assigned 55.5 percent of those cases to Douglas and Frankfurter. During that period, only Reed agreed more with Stone than with Frankfurter, but Douglas agreed with Stone less than any other justice except Black. Stone had high regard for Douglas's ability, and this may have been Stone's overriding consideration in his assignments to Douglas.[103]

The chief justice might seek to influence dissenting justices to join in the Court's opinion by adhering to one or both of the following assignment rules:

Rule 1: Assign the case to the justice whose views are the closest to the dissenters on the assumption that his opinion would take a middle approach upon which both majority and minority could agree.

Rule 2: Where there are blocs on the Court and a bloc splits, assign the case to a majority member of the dissenters' bloc on the assumption that he would take a middle approach upon which both majority and minority could agree and that the minority justices would be more likely to agree with him because of general mutuality of agreement.

There is some evidence that early in Taft's chief justiceship he followed Rule 1 occasionally and assigned himself cases in an effort to win over dissenters. An analysis of his assignments from 1925 to 1930, however, indicates that he apparently did not adhere to either of the above rules with any consistency. Stone's assignments from 1943 to 1945 show the same thing. In other words, Taft and Stone did not generally use their assignment power to influence their associates for the purpose of achieving unanimity. An analysis of Hughes's assignments from 1932 to 1937, however, indicates that he probably did. He appears to have followed Rule 1 when either the liberal or conservative bloc dissented intact. When the liberal bloc dissented, Roberts, who was then a center judge, was assigned 46.5 percent of the opinions. The remaining 53.5 percent were divided among the conservatives, apparently according to their degree of conservatism: Sutherland, 25 percent; Butler, 17.8 percent; McReynolds, 10.7 percent.[104] When the conservative bloc dissented, Hughes divided 63 percent of the opinions between himself and Roberts.

Hughes probably also followed Rule 2 to some extent. When the left bloc split, Brandeis was assigned 22.2 percent of the cases he could have received compared with his 10.2 percent assignment average for unanimous cases. When the right bloc split, Sutherland was assigned 16.1 percent of the decisions he could have received compared with his 10.2 percent assignment average for unanimous cases. He received five of the six cases assigned the conservatives when their bloc was split. One of those cases was *Powell v. Alabama*,[105] which Hughes had assigned to Sutherland "probably in the hope that he could bring over Justices Butler and McReynolds while some of the more 'liberal' Justices could not."[106]

If the chief justice is to be well liked, he must appear to be generous, considerate, and impartial in assigning cases, particularly important cases. Taft was considered generous in his assignments,[107] and that undoubtedly contributed to his likeability. Hughes said he tried to assign each justice the same proportion of important cases and especially took into account the feelings of the senior justices.[108] Justice Roberts thought Hughes's assignments were generous and considerate,[109] and Justice Frankfurter wrote that no chief justice had equaled Hughes in the "skill, wisdom, and disinterestedness" with which he assigned opinions.[110] Justice Stone, however, thought otherwise. During the early and middle 1930s, he felt that Hughes was not assigning him as many important cases as he should have received.[111] Just as Stone felt slighted by Hughes in the matter of assignments, so did Justices Murphy and Rutledge during Stone's chief justiceship. Stone was aware of this, but he did little about it.[112]

How often the chief justice uses his assignment power to influence his colleagues cannot be determined with certainty. Besides influence, there are other reasons underlying opinion assignment, such as equality of case distribution, ability, and expertise.[113] Nonetheless, every assignment presents the chief justice with an opportunity for influence.

VI. The Final Phase: Persuasion and Unanimity

In the last stage of the decisional process, opinions are written, circulated, discussed, and approved or disapproved. Final decision near, Court members have their last chance to persuade each other. The results of interaction during this period can be highly significant: opinion modification, increase or decrease in the size of a majority, and even the reversal of a conference decision. Again the chief justice is in a favorable position for purposes of influence. Standing at the center of intra-Court communication, he ordinarily knows better than any of his associates the status of each case—who is having trouble writing an opinion, who is overworked, who is wavering in his vote, etc.—and if he is so inclined, he can play an active role in reconciling differences, seeking compromises, and attaining unanimity. Since, as a practical matter, he decides when an opinion will be announced, he can delay the announcement in hope of augmenting the Court's majority. What the chief justice actually does greatly depends upon how he views his role in this final phase of the decisional process.

Seldom has a chief justice had a more definite conception of his role as Court unifier than Taft. The chief justice, he said, "is expected to promote teamwork by the Court so as to give weight and solidarity to its opinions."[114] He believed his predecessor, White, earnestly sought to avoid divisions by skillfully reconciling differences among the justices, and he intended to do the same.[115] His aim was unanimity, but he was willing to admit that at times dissents were justifiable and perhaps even a duty. Dissent was proper, he thought, in cases where a Court member strongly believed the majority erred in a matter involving important principle or where a dissent might serve some useful purpose, such as convincing Congress to pass certain legislation.[116] But in other cases, a justice should be a good member of the team, silently acquiesce in the views of the majority, and not try to make a record for himself by dissenting.[117]

Taft's conception of the function of the dissent was shared by most of his colleagues, and when he sought to unite them, his efforts were accepted as proper and consistent with his role as chief justice. New justices joining the Taft Court were indoctrinated in the no-dissent-unless-absolutely-necessary tradition, and most of them learned it well. Justice Butler gave it classic expression on the back of one of Stone's slip opinions:

> I voted to reverse. While this sustains your conclusion to affirm, I still think reversal would be better. But I shall in silence acquiesce. Dissents seldom aid in the right development or statement of the law. They often do harm. For myself I say: "lead us not into temptation."[118]

Even Stone, who was not so sure about the no-dissent tradition, usually went along with it, acquiescing in the appropriate cases.[119]

Taft enjoyed moderate success in his efforts to attain unanimity. During his first year as chief justice, he united the Court in a number of cases in which the White Court had been "grievously divided."[120] Usually he would assign himself such cases and try to write an opinion that would bring in the dissenters. That meant he had to make concessions to justices like Brandeis, but he was willing to exchange concessions for votes. When there were divisions in cases he assigned to others that could be reconciled, Taft would try to mediate between majority and minority (at times with the help of Van Devanter) in an effort to attain unanimity.[121] If there was any chance of winning over a dissenter, Taft would frequently let the case go over a few conferences with hope that time would work in his favor.[122]

Hughes easily assumed the role of Court unifier that Taft had cut out for him, for he believed that unanimity should be sought where it could be attained without sacrificing strongly held convictions.[123] Like Taft, he distinguished two types of cases, those involving matters of important principle and those of lesser importance. The former were dissent-worthy; the latter were not. As to the cases of lesser importance, Hughes felt it was better to have the law settled one way or the other regardless of his own ideas as to the correct disposition of the case, and if the majority voted contrary to his view, he would change his vote.[124] For example, in a case involving statutory construction, Hughes wrote to Stone: "I choke a little at swallowing your analysis, still I do not think it would serve any useful purpose to expose my views."[125]

Like Taft, Hughes mediated differences of opinion between contending blocs, and in order to get a unanimous decision, he would try to find common ground upon which all could stand. He was willing to modify his own opinions to hold or increase his majority, and if this meant he had to put in some disconnected thoughts or sentences, in they went. In cases assigned to others, he would suggest the addition or subtraction of a paragraph if by doing so he could save a dissent or concurring opinion.[126] According to Justice Roberts, dissents were thus avoided in some cases in which agreement seemed impossible.[127] But unlike Taft, Hughes apparently seldom held up the delivery of an opinion in an effort to secure another vote or two. He made his attempt to secure unanimity, and if it failed, the case was usually handed down as soon as the opinions were ready.[128]

Hughes's efforts to attain unanimity were fairly successful. Even in the cases which invalidated New Deal legislation, the Court was fairly intact. Of the eleven such cases, five were unanimous, and two were decided 8 to 1.[129] The tradition of "no dissent unless absolutely necessary" continued, and in a host of lesser cases Court members acquiesced in silence. The Roosevelt appointees, particularly, showed remarkable restraint in the matter of dissents while serving under Hughes.[130] Frankfurter, who had the best record, registered only seven dissents in his three years with Hughes. The New Deal justices were baptized in the old tradition concerning dissent, but whether they would retain the faith after Hughes left the Court was another matter.

As an associate justice, Stone prized the right to dissent and occasionally rankled under the no-dissent-unless-absolutely-necessary tradition of the Taft and Hughes Courts.[131] As chief justice, he did not believe it appropriate for him to dissuade Court members from dissenting in individual cases by persuasion or otherwise. A chief justice, he thought, might admonish his associates generally to exercise restraint in the matter of dissents and seek to find common ground for decision, but beyond that he should not go.[132] Stone usually went no further. His activity or lack of it in this matter gave rise to new expectations on the part of his associates as to their role and the role of the chief justice regarding unanimity and dissent. A new tradition of great freedom of individual expression displaced the tradition of Taft and Hughes Courts. This explains in part the unprecedented number of dissents and separate opinions during Stone's chief justiceship.

Chief Justice Stone, nonetheless, exercised some influence in the final phase of the decisional process. In *Edwards v. California*,[133] one of the first cases heard by the Court after he became chief justice, he persuaded Justice Byrnes to change his conference vote, and the switch resulted in a decision based on the commerce clause rather than on the privileges and immunities clause of the Constitution.[134] He also influenced the content of many opinions, especially those of Justice Murphy, by suggesting additions and deletions.[135] Although justices who voted against Stone in conference would occasionally go along with his opinions,[136] he usually made no concerted effort to attain unanimity. He recognized, however, that unanimity in certain cases was desirable, and in a few cases he sought it. One of those cases was the Nazi Saboteur Case;[137] another was the case of General Yamashita.[138] Although the Saboteurs' Case "bristled with difficulties and possibilities of disagreement," Stone was able to get a unanimous decision after "patient negotiation."[139] That, however, was relatively early in his chief justiceship. As the new tradition of freedom in the matter of dissents became more established, unanimity became difficult to attain. That was the situation when the Yamashita case arose toward the end of Stone's chief justiceship. Stone assigned himself the case and sought to hold his majority of six and win over, if possible, the two dissenters, Murphy and Rutledge. Not only was he unsuccessful, Murphy and Rutledge were apparently antagonized by the attempt, for when they read their dissents, Yamashita's lawyer, A. Frank Reel, said their tones were bitter and their language sharp. Justice Rutledge said, "Not with ease does one find his views at odds with the Court's in a matter of this character and gravity. Only the most deeply felt convictions could force one to differ. That reason alone leads me to do so now, *against strong consideration for withholding dissent*." "As he uttered the last clause," said Reel, "Rutledge carefully turned and nodded in the chief justice's direction."[140] After departing from the tradition of Taft and Hughes in regard to dissent, it seems odd that Stone should seek unanimity in a type of case the old tradition did not embrace.

The unprecedented number of dissents and concurrences during Stone's chief justiceship can be only partly attributed to the displacing of the old tradition of loyalty to the Court's opinion. A major source of difficulty appears to have been the free and easy expression of views in conference. Whether the justices were "dead sure" of their grounds or not,[141] they spoke up and many times took positions from which they could not easily back down, and given the heated debate that sometimes occurred in the Stone conference, the commitment was not simply intellectual. What began in conference frequently ended with elaborate justification as concurring or dissenting opinions in the United States Reports. This, plus Stone's passiveness in seeking to attain unanimity, is probably the best explanation for what Professor Pritchett characterized as "the multiplication of division" in the Stone Court.[142]

VII. Conclusions

The task of the political writer, said John Morley, is not simply to describe governmental institutions, but to "penetrate to the secret of their functions."[143] To attempt to do this with the chief justiceship is difficult, for involved are complex relationships among the chief justice and justices and their influence upon each other. The office provides the chief justice with an opportunity for influence, but it does not guarantee it. To exercise influence, he must perform activity that to some extent results in his associates choosing to do what he wants them to do. His success depends largely upon his likeability and esteem in the Court and upon his perception and fulfillment of his role.

For a chief justice to be maximally effective, he must be simultaneously task and social leader, as Hughes was, or he must work in coalition with the justice who is task leader, as Taft worked with Van Devanter. For the social structure of the Court and the attainment of its goals depend upon how ably the task and social functions of leadership are performed. If they are performed in a Hughes or Taft-Van Devanter configuration of leadership, conflict will tend to remain with the bounds of calm, rational, orderly deliberation. Court members will tend to be socially cohesive and satisfied with their work, which makes for a spirit of compromise and teamwork essential to true collegial decision. Finally, the Court will tend to do its work with greater dispatch, and in a time when the Court decides more than a thousand cases a year, that is of some significance.

This study has implications that go beyond the chief justiceship. It indicates that concepts and hypotheses from social psychology can be used in political and historical analysis. In a sense, this study has dealt with the hardest case, for good data concerning the decisional process of the Supreme Court are fragmentary and difficult to obtain. The concepts and hypotheses suggested here, however, might be applied more rigorously to other governmental decision-making bodies whose processes are not so cloaked in secrecy. Perhaps we are approaching an era in which Morley's hope for the study of politics will be realized.

NOTES

1. See Felix E. Oppenheim, "An Analysis of Political Controls: Actual and Potential," *Journal of Politics* 20 (1958): 516.

2. Cf. George C. Homans, *The Human Group* (New York: Harcourt, Brace, 1950), 37–40. For purposes of this study, expectations, thoughts, and feelings are postulated. The postulation arises out of the observation of activity and is used to observe and analyze other similar activity.

3. See Neal Gross, Ward S. Mason, and Alexander McEachern, *Explorations in Role Analysis* (New York: Wiley, 1958).

4. Cf. Chief Justice Vinson's statement about Charles Evans Hughes: "He was precise and decisive in playing the role he believed the Chief Justice *ought* to play." 338 U.S. xxviii (1950).

5. See infra, discussion at note 15.

6. Taft to Charles Taft, June 8, 1927; Taft to Horace D. Taft, June 29, 1927; Taft to Van Devanter, Jan. 7, 1930, Library of Congress, Manuscript Division, William Howard Taft Papers.

7. See J. L. Moreno, *Who Shall Survive?* (Washington: Nervous and Mental Disease Press, 1934), passim; Gordon W. Allport, *The Use of Personal Documents in Psychological Science* (New York: Social Science Research Council, 1942), 46–47, 50, 108–10.

8. See Henry F. Pringle, *The Life and Times of William Howard Taft*, 2 vols. (New York: Farrar & Rinehart, 1939), 2:968–72; Alpheus Thomas Mason, *Harlan Fiske Stone: Pillar of the Law* (New York: Viking, 1956), 793; Steven T. Early, Jr., "James Clark McReynolds and the Judicial Process," (PhD diss., University of Virginia, 1954), 90; Fred Rodell to Editor, *New York Time Book Review* July 24, 1960, 24; Charles Evans Hughes, Biographical Notes, 12, Library of Congress, Manuscript Division, Charles Evans Hughes Papers. [Hughes's "Biographical Notes" were subsequently edited by David J. Danelski and Joseph S. Tulchin and published as *The Autobiographical Notes of Charles Evans Hughes* by Harvard University Press in 1973.]

9. Chief Justice Warren said in an address at the annual American Law Insti-

tute meeting in 1954 that "it is only accurate to a degree to say that our jurisdiction in cases on appeal is obligatory as distinguished from discretionary on certiorari." Quoted by Frederick Bernays Wiener, "The Supreme Court's New Rules," *Harvard Law Review* 68 (1954): 51.

10. Holmes to Lewis Einstein, May 19, 1927, Library of Congress, Manuscript Division, Oliver Wendell Holmes Jr., Papers.

11. Edwin McElwain, "The Business of the Supreme Court as Conducted by Chief Justice Hughes," *Harvard Law Review* 63 (1949), 13. McElwain was a former law clerk of Chief Justice Hughes.

12. Alpheus Thomas Mason, *Harlan Fiske Stone: Pillar of the Law* (New York: Viking Press, 1956), 792; William O. Douglas, "Chief Justice Stone," *Columbia Law Review* 46 (1946), 693; Alfred McCormack, "A Law Clerk's Recollections," ibid., 716; Bennett Boskey, "Mr. Chief Justice Stone," *Harvard Law Review* 59 (1946): 1200.

13. Taft to Brethren, Sept. 27, 1928; Taft to Horace D. Taft, Sept. 22, 1929, Taft Papers.

14. Hughes to Stone, Oct. 1, 1931, Library of Congress, Manuscript Division, Harlan F. Stone Papers; Hughes to Brandeis, Oct. 1, 1931, University of Louisville Law School, Louis D. Brandeis Papers; McElwain, "The Business of the Supreme Court," 15.

15. Hughes to Stone, Sept. 30, 1935, Feb. 25, 1938, Sept. 30, 1940, Stone Papers; Merlo J. Pusey, *Charles Evans Hughes*, 2 vols. (New York: Macmillan, 1951), 2:672.

16. Ibid.

17. Stone's papers indicate that his special lists were challenged fewer than ten times in five years.

18. Few of the justices of the pre-1937 Court under Hughes, said an anonymous writer (probably a former law clerk), "made a careful study of the records or briefs of cited authorities before they went to conference." Quoted by John P. Frank, "Harlan Fiske Stone: An Estimate," *Stanford Law Review* 9 (1957): 629 n. 31. During Stone's chief justiceship, too, Court members were not always fully prepared for the conferences. Frankfurter to Stone, ca. Oct. 22, 1942; Rutledge to Stone, Feb. 1, 1946, Stone Papers.

19. Owen J. Roberts, "Address to the Association of the Bar of the City of New York and the New York County Lawyers' Association," December 12, 1948, *Proceedings of the Bar and Officers of the Supreme Court of the United States in Memory of Charles Evans Hughes* (Washington: privately published, 1950), 122–23.

20. McElwain, "The Business of the Supreme Court," 14.

21. Taft to Charles P. Taft II, Oct. 23, 1927, Taft Papers.

22. Douglas, "Chief Justice Stone," 695.

23. Taft to McKenna, April 20, 1923, Taft Papers.

24. Chief Justices Taft and Stone were lenient in this regard, but Hughes was not. When the hour ordinarily given counsel for argument was over, Hughes invariably required counsel to stop. See McElwain, "The Business of the Supreme Court,"17.

25. Charles Evans Hughes, *The Supreme Court of the United States: Its Foundations, Methods and Achievements: An Interpretation* (New York: Columbia University

Press, 1928), 61–62; Frederick Bernays Wiener, "Oral Advocacy," *Harvard Law Review* 62 (1948): 58 n. 7; Robert H. Jackson, "Advocacy Before the United States Supreme Court," *Cornell Law Review* 37 (1951): 2.

26. Felix Frankfurter, "Chief Justices I Have Known," in *Of Law and Men: Papers and Addresses of Felix Frankfurter, 1939–1956*, ed. Philip Elman (New York: Harcourt, Brace, 1956), 134, 141. Disturbed by incessant questioning of counsel, Chief Justice White was once heard to moan in audible stage whisper: "I want to hear the argument." "So do I damn him," growled his neighbor, Justice Holmes. Quoted in John W. Davis, "The Argument on Appeal," *American Bar Journal*, 26 (1940): 898.

27. McElwain, "The Business of the Supreme Court," 13.

28. Wiener, "Oral Advocacy," 56.

29. Robert H. Jackson, Autobiographical Notes, quoted in Eugene C. Gerhart, *America's Advocate: Robert H. Jackson* (Indianapolis: Bobbs-Merrill, 1958), 146.

30. Merlo J. Pusey, "Mr. Chief Justice Hughes," in *Mr. Justice*, ed. Allison Dunham and Philip B. Kurland (Chicago: University of Chicago Press, 1956), 153.

31. McElwain, "The Business of the Supreme Court," 16.

32. Charles Fahy, "Mr. Chief Justice Stone," *Harvard Law Review* 59 (1946): 1198.

33. Robert F. Bales, *Interaction Process Analysis: A Method for the Study of Small Groups* (Chicago: University of Chicago Press, 1950); "The Equilibrium Problem in Small Groups," chap. iv in Talcott Parsons, Robert F. Bales, and Edward A. Shils, eds. *Working Papers in the Theory of Actions* (Glencoe, IL: Free Press, 1953); "Task Status and Likeability as a Function of Talking and Listening in Decision-Making Groups," in Leonard D. White, ed., *The State of the Social Sciences* (Chicago: University of Chicago Press, 1956), 148–61; "Task Roles and Social Roles in Problem-Solving Groups," in Eleanor E. Maccoby, Theodore M. Newcomb, and Eugene L. Harley, *Readings in Social Psychology* (New York: Holt, 1958), 437–47.

34. Philip E. Slater, "Role Differentiation in Small Groups," *American Sociological Review* 20 (1955): 300–310.

35. Leonard Berkowitz, "Some Effects of Leadership Sharing in Small, Decision-Making Conference Group," (unpublished PhD diss., University of Michigan, 1951); "Sharing Leadership in Small, Decision-Making Groups," *Journal of Abnormal and Social Psychology* 48 (1953): 231–38.

36. Though rare, there are such individuals. See Edgar F. Borgatta, Robert F. Bales, and Arthur S. Couch, "Some Findings Relevant to the Great Man Theory of Leadership," *American Sociological Review* 19 (1954): 755–59.

37. Hughes said that Van Devanter's perspicacity and common sense made him a trusted advisor in all sorts of matters. Chief Justice White relied heavily upon him, and before Hughes accepted the presidential nomination in 1916, Van Devanter was the only member of the Court with whom he discussed the matter. Hughes, Biographical Notes, 220–21, 231. In conference, said Hughes, Van Devanter's "careful and elaborate statements . . . were of the greatest value," ibid., p. 220. Stone said Van Devanter had "great legal ability" and "an accurate and precise mind," and referred to Van Devanter's service in conferences as "invaluable." Stone to Children, Feb. 13, 1941; Stone to Van Devanter, June 2, 1937, Stone Papers. When Taft wrote to Holmes that "209 was affirmed on Van Devanter's suggestion," it was but an instance of what was typical in the Taft Court. March 12, 1928, Taft

Papers. See also Holmes to Laski, May 13, 1919, in Mark DeWolfe Howe, *Holmes-Laski Letters*, 2 vols. (Cambridge, MA: Harvard University Press, 1953), I, 202; Alexander M. Bickel, *The Unpublished Opinions of Mr. Justice Brandeis* (Cambridge, MA: Harvard University Press, 1957), 248; 316 U.S. xix, xxxii, xlii (1941).

38. Taft to Helen Taft Manning, June 11, 1923; Taft to Robert A. Taft, May 3, 1925, Jan. 22, 1927; Taft to Charles P. Taft, June 8, 1927, Taft Papers.

39. Taft to George D. Seymour, June 17, 1926, ibid.

40. Taft to William Lyon Phelps, May 30, 1927, ibid.

41. Remarks of former attorney general William D. Mitchell, 316 U.S. xvii (1941).

42. Ibid., xvii–xviii.

43. Taft to Robert A. Taft, Oct. 23, 1927, ibid. Cf. Slater, who wrote, "[The social leader] will in fact retire into the conventional safety of the 'average Joe.' He may even avoid the performance of task functions altogether, because of the personal threats which task activity might hold for him." "Role Differentiation," 309.

44. Taft to Robert A. Taft, Oct. 23, 1927, Taft Papers.

45. Each summer Taft made it a point to write his colleagues friendly letters that were answered in the same spirit. Apparently he was the only member of his Court who corresponded with all of his associates regularly.

46. "Van Devanter is really the closest friend I have on the Court," wrote Taft, "and we ordinarily work together." Taft to Charles Taft, June 8, 1927; Taft to Horace D. Taft, June 29, 1927. Cf. Slater, "Role Differentiation," 306–7.

47. Taft to Helen Taft Manning, June 11, 1923, Taft Papers.

48. Harlan F. Stone, "Fifty Years' Work of the United States Supreme Court," *American Bar Association Journal* 14 (1928): 436.

49. Quoted in Bickel, *The Unpublished Opinions of Mr. Justice Brandeis*, 203.

50. Taft to Charles P. Taft, Oct. 16, 1921, Taft Papers.

51. "[Y]our humor . . . smoothed the rough places," said the Court's letter to Taft upon his retirement. Feb. 10, 1930. And Holmes wrote earlier that "the Chief Justice makes good humor easier" in conference. Holmes to Taft, April 2, 1922, Taft Papers.

52. Taft to Robert A. Taft, Oct. 23, 1927, ibid.

53. Bickel, *The Unpublished Opinions of Mr. Justice Brandeis*, 203.

54. Taft to Helen Taft Manning, June 11, 1923, Taft Papers.

55. See Joel Francis Paschal, *Mr. Justice Sutherland* (Princeton: Princeton University Press, 1951), 115–17.

56. Holmes to Laski, March 26, 1922, Howe, *Holmes-Laski Letters*, I, 413.

57. See Bickel, *The Unpublished Opinions of Mr. Justice Brandeis*, especially chaps. 1, 5, and 9.

58. Frankfurter has said that if Hughes "made others feel his moral superiority, they merely felt a fact . . . all who served with him recognized the extraordinary qualities possessed by the chief justice." "The Impact of Charles Evans Hughes," in Elman, ed., *Of Law and Men*, 148. Hughes was the only member of the Court to whom McReynolds would defer. Early, "James Clark McReynolds and the Judicial Process," 90. Black said he had "more than impersonal and detached admiration" for Hughes' "extraordinary intellectual gifts." Black to Hughes, June 3, 1941, Hughes Papers. The following contain statements of similar reports: Frankfurter

to Hughes, June 2, 1941; Douglas to Hughes, June 30, 1941; Reed to Hughes, Feb. 24, 1940; Holmes to Hughes, Feb. 10, 1930; ibid.; Learned Hand to Stone, May 29, 1930, Stone Papers; Roberts, "Address," 118–28; Ambrose Doscow (Cardozo's law clerk for the 1933 term), interview by George S. Hellman, June, 1939, Benjamin N. Cardozo Papers, Columbia University. In 1938, Solicitor General Robert H. Jackson told President Roosevelt: "What is urgently needed in the Supreme Court at this time is someone who can interpret the Constitution with scholarship and with sufficient assurance to face Chief Justice Hughes in conference and hold his own in the discussion. Any man you would be likely to name from the west would be possessed of an inferiority complex in the presence of the Chief Justice, who looks like God and talks like God. He would be completely unable to help give direction to the action of the Court." "I think," answered the President, "Felix [Frankfurter] is the only man who could do that job, Bob." Quoted in Gerhart, *America's Advocate*, 165–66.

59. Hughes, Memorandum on Speeches, 5, Hughes Papers.

60. Roberts, "Address," 123.

61. Ibid.

62. Ibid., 127. Cf. Frankfurter, "The Impact of Charles Evans Hughes," in Elman, ed., *Of Law and Men*, 147–48.

63. Roberts, "Address," 123.

64. Ibid., 126.

65. Frankfurter, "'The Administrative Side' of Charles Evans Hughes," in Elman, ed., *Of Law and Men*, 142; "The Impact of Charles Evans Hughes," in ibid., 148–49. "Hughes is an old friend of mine and a very hard worker. He can tell a story and say a funny thing on occasion as well as do his job." Holmes to Lewis Einstein, Feb. 26, 1930, Holmes Papers.

66. Roberts, "Address," 118, 126.

67. The sources mentioned in note 58 contain evidence of affection as well as esteem. Roberts said that when the Court would adjourn for lunch "the Chief Justice relaxed and became the center of a delightful half hour of talk which ranged from the merest local happening to world events. The current business of the Court was completely forgotten in the sociability of the group." Ibid., 121.

68. Stone to McReynolds, April 3, 1930, Stone Papers.

69. Stone Memorandum re *Colgate v. Henry*, ibid.

70. Stone Memorandum re *U.S. v. Butler*, ibid.

71. Frankfurter, "Chief Justices I Have Known," in Elman, ed., *Law and Men*, 135; "'The Administrative Side' of Chief Justice Hughes," ibid., 141.

72. Stone to John Bassett Moore, May 17, 1932, Stone Papers.

73. Pusey, *Charles Evans Hughes*, 2:676, citing an interview with Hughes, Dec. 3, 1946.

74. Roberts, "Address,"126. Cardozo, for example, was fond of Roberts, considered Van Devanter and Sutherland pleasant, and liked the Irish wit of Butler. Doscow, interview by Hellman. See also interview of C. S. Sargent (Cardozo's law clerk from 1936 to 1938) by Hellman, Cardozo Papers.

75. See Howard C. Westwood, Book Review, *Virginia Law Review* 8 (1957), 302. Doscow, however, said that Cardozo considered Hughes a fine chief justice. Doscow, interview by Hellman.

76. Roberts, "Address," 122–28; Frankfurter, "Chief Justices I Known," in Elman, ed., *Of Law and Men*, 133; "'The Administrative Side' of Charles Evans Hughes," ibid., 141–42. "Brandeis thought Hughes the best Chief Justice he had ever known." Alfred Lief, *Brandeis* (New York: Stackpole Sons, 1936), 463.

77. Augustus Hand to Hughes, Oct. 2, 1941, Hughes Papers.

78. Mason, *Harlan Fiske Stone*, 790–91.

79. Frankfurter to Stone, ca. Oct. 12, 1941, Stone Papers.

80. Chief Justice White, who was also promoted from associate justice to chief justice, acted in the same manner. When he encountered a difficult case, frequently he would say in conference: "Here's a baffling case. I don't know what to do with it. God help us!" Rambling debate would usually follow. Hughes, quoted in Pusey, "Mr. Chief Justice Hughes," 154.

81. Remarks of Justice Reed at unveiling of Chesterfield Memorial Tablet for Stone, Aug. 25, 1948. Quoted in Mason, *Harlan Fiske Stone*, 792.

82. Ibid., 795.

83. See John P. Frank, *Mr. Justice Black: The Man and His Opinions* (New York: Knopf, 1949), 134–35, 137; Mason, *Harlan Fiske Stone*, 768, 797; Fred Rodell, "Justice Hugo Black," *American Mercury* 59 (1944): 136–37, 142–43.

84. Mason, *Harlan Fiske Stone*, 793.

85. Roberts wrote to Hughes: "To work under you was the greatest experience and the greatest satisfaction of my life. When you left the Court, the whole picture changed. For me it could never be the same." July 16, 1945. Quoted in Pusey, *Charles Evans Hughes*, 2:802.

86. R. W. Heyns, *Effects of Variation in Leadership on Participant Behavior in Discussion Groups* (PhD diss., University of Michigan, Ann Arbor, 1948).

87. Frank, *Mr. Justice Black*, 137.

88. This is only a partial explanation for Black's rejection by Roberts, Frankfurter, and Jackson. Some further insights into this problem can be obtained by studying the Roberts letter incident, the Jewell Ridge Case controversy, and Jackson's Nuremberg cable. See Gerhart, *America's Advocate*, chap. 15; Mason, *Harlan Fiske Stone*, 641–46, 765–69.

89. Frank, *Mr. Justice Black*, 134–45.

90. Mason, *Harlan Fiske Stone*, 790.

91. See Mason, *Harlan Fiske Stone*, 641; Marquis Childs, *Washington Post*, May 2, 1946, p. 11, cl. 3.

92. See Mason, *Harlan Fiske Stone*, 641–46, 765–69.

93. Frankfurter to Stone, ca. Oct. 12, 1941, Stone Papers.

94. Frankfurter to Stone, Oct. 21, 1942, ibid.

95. Stone to W. Warren Barbour, Jan. 16, 1942, ibid.; Douglas, "Chief Justice Stone," 693.

96. Frankfurter to Stone, ca. Oct. 22, 1942, Stone Papers.

97. Quoted in Mason, *Harlan Fiske Stone*, 769.

98. Pusey, "Mr. Chief Justice Hughes," in *Mr. Justice*, 153.

99. One minor exception to this rule is that a newcomer to the Court is entitled to select his first case for opinion. This is a tradition of long standing. Matthews to Waite, Oct. 5, 1881, Library of Congress, Manuscript Division, Morrison R. Waite Papers.

100. Hughes, *The Supreme Court of the United States*, 59.

101. Frankfurter, "'The Administrative Side' of Chief Justice Hughes," in Elman, ed., *Of Law and Men*, 142. Justice John H. Clarke recalled some years after he retired: "[T]he great cases are written, as they should be, by the Chief Justice." Quoted in Joseph E. McLean, *William Rufus Day* (Baltimore: Johns Hopkins University Press, 1947), 6. Justice Stone, however, apparently felt that Chief Justice Hughes retained too many of the "big cases" during the early and middle 1930s. One of his law clerks during that period commented that Hughes was notorious for keeping the "plums" to himself. Memorandum of Howard C. Westwood, Oct. 30, 1947, Stone Papers.

102. The "important constitutional cases" decided by the Court from 1921 to 1946 were determined by examination of four leading works on the Constitution: Paul A. Freund, Arthur E. Sutherland, Mark De Wolfe Howe, and Ernest J. Brown, *Constitutional Law* (Boston: Little, Brown, 1954); Alfred H. Kelly and Winfred A. Harbison, *The American Constitution: Its Origins and Development* (New York: Norton, 1948); Alpheus T. Mason and William M. Beaney, *American Constitutional Law* (Englewood Cliffs, NJ: Prentice-Hall, 1959); and C. Herman Pritchett, *The American Constitution* (New York: McGraw-Hill, 1959). If a case was discussed in any two of these works, it was considered an "important constitutional case."

103. See Mason, *Harlan Fiske Stone*, 793.

104. For an interesting explanation of Hughes's failure to assign himself any of these cases, see Irving Brant, "How Liberal Is Justice Hughes?" *New Republic* 91 (1937): 295–98, 329–32.

105. 287 U.S. 45 (1932) (7–2).

106. McElwain, "The Business of the Supreme Court," 18.

107. Stone to Thomas Reed Powell, Jan. 30, 1940; Stone to Children, Nov. 23, 1939, Stone Papers.

108. Hughes, Biographical Notes, 1930–1941, 16, Hughes Papers.

109. Roberts, "Address," 124.

110. Frankfurter, "Chief Justices I Have Known," in Elman, ed., *Of Law and Men*, 137.

111. Memorandum of Walter F. Gellhorn. Stone's law clerk during the 1931 term, Jan. 21, 1947; memorandum of Howard C. Westwood, Stone Papers.

112. Mason, *Harlan Fiske Stone*, 602–3, 793.

113. David J. Danelski, "The Assignment of the Court's Opinion by the Chief Justice," an unpublished paper presented at the Midwest Conference of Political Scientists, Indiana University, April 28, 1960.

114. Draft of a tribute to Edward Douglass White, ca. May 1921, Taft Papers.

115. Ibid.

116. Taft to Clarke, Feb. 10, 1922, ibid. An example of the former situation is Taft's dissenting opinion in *Adkins v. Children's Hospital*, 261 U.S. 525 (1923) (5-3). An example of the latter is Taft's dissent in *Gooch v. Oregon Shortline R.R.*, 258 U.S. 22 (1922) (5-3), which was an effort to get "Congress to extend the Cummins Amendment to persons." Ibid.

117. Taft to Charles D. Hilles, Dec. 3, 1922, ibid.

118. Slip opinion, *The Malcolm Baxter, Jr.*, 277 U.S. 323 (1928) (9-0), Stone Papers. Butler, apparently thinking this was a good statement or at least one the chief

justice would like to see, had a copy of it made and sent to Taft on May 19, 1928, Taft Papers.

119. Mason, *Harlan Fiske Stone*, 263.

120. White to McReynolds, May 13, 1921, James C. McReynolds Papers, Alderman Library, University of Virginia. Three of the most important of these cases were *American Steel Foundries v. Tri-City Trades Council*, 257 U.S. 184 (1921) (8-1), in which Taft won over Holmes and Brandeis; *Bailey v. Drexel Furniture Co.*, 259 U.S. 20 (1922) (8-1), in which Taft again won over Holmes and Brandeis; and *Coronado Co. v. United Mine Workers*, 259 U.S. 344 (1922) (9-0), in which Taft won over Holmes, Day, Brandeis, and Clarke. In the first and last cases, Taft made important concessions to the would-be dissenters. Other important cases in which Taft achieved unanimity or won over crucial votes are *Hill v. Wallace*, 259 U.S. 44 (1922) (9-0); *Carroll v. U.S.*, 267 U.S. 132 (1925) (7–2); *Pierce v. Society of Sisters*, 268 U.S. 510 (9-0). These cases are cited as illustrative. If all cases during Taft's chief justiceship were considered, two hundred unexpressed dissenting votes would be a conservative estimate.

121. Taft to Helen H. Taft, April 3, 1924; Brandeis to Taft, Nov. 12, 1926, Taft Papers; Pringle, *The Life and Times of William Howard Taft*, 2:1024–43; Bickel, *The Unpublished Opinions of Mr. Justice Brandeis*, pp. 209–10; Mason, *Harlan Fiske Stone*, 251–60.

122. On January 25, 1927, Taft wrote to Sutherland: "I am inclined to think that it is better not to have the case [*Bedford Co. v. Stone-Cutters Ass'n*, 274 U.S. 37 (1927) (7–2)] rushed through but to give time enough to let us discuss . . . what the issues are—in other words, to let the matter grow cold and take it up again." Taft Papers.

123. Hughes, *Supreme Court of the United States*, 67.

124. Confidential source.

125. Nov. 4, 1939, Stone Papers. The case was *Sanford v. Comm'r*, 308 U.S. 39 (1939) (8–0). Roberts and McReynolds also acquiesced in silence. The case is cited to illustrate what was commonplace in the Hughes Court.

126. McElwain, "The Business of the Supreme Court," 19.

127. Pusey, *Charles Evans Hughes*, 2:677.

128. See Mason, *Harlan Fiske Stone*, 468,789.

129. Hughes made a point of it to mention this in his Biographical Notes, 1930–1941, 24–25, Hughes Papers.

130. See C. Herman Pritchett, *The Roosevelt Court: A Study in Judicial Politics and Values 1937–1947* (New York: Macmillan, 1948), 35–38.

131. Stone to John Bassett Moore, Oct. 21, 1930, April 21, 1932; Stone to Children, Nov. 16, 1939, Stone Papers.

132. Stone to Charles C. Burlingham, Jan. 15, 1944, Jan. 20, 1944; Stone, Memorandum to Court, Jan. 13, 1944, ibid. Stone actually admonished his Court about dissents and concurring opinions in the cited memorandum, which is quoted in Mason, *Harlan Fiske Stone*, 608–9.

133. 314 U.S. 482 (1941) (9-0).

134. See Mason, *Harlan Fiske Stone*, 578–80.

135. Stone to Murphy, Dec. 20, 1941, Jan. 30, 1942, Nov. 4, 1943, June 1, 1944, March 14, 1946; Murphy to Stone, Nov. 4, 1943, Stone Papers.

136. Jackson in *U.S. v. Dick Johnson*, 319 U.S. 302 (1943) (9-0) (Per Curiam);

Rutledge in *Matton Steamboat Co., v. Murphy*, 319 U.S. 412 (9-0) (Per Curiam); Frankfurter in *Corn Products Co. v. FTC*, 324 U.S. 726 (1945) (8-0), ibid.

137. *Ex parte Quirin*, 317 U.S. 1 (1942) (9-0).

138. *In re Yamashita*, 327 U.S. 1 (1946) (6-2).

139. Stone to Hughes, Sept. 25, 1942; Stone to Roger Nelson, Nov. 30, 1942, Stone Papers.

140. A. Frank Reel, *The Case of General Yamashita* (Chicago: University of Chicago Press, 1949), 216.

141. Cf. Frankfurter, "Chief Justices I Have Known," in Elman, ed., *Of Law and Men*, 135.

142. Pritchett, *The Roosevelt Court*, 24.

143. Quoted in Woodrow Wilson, *Congressional Government* (New York: Meridian, 1956), 25.

2 ⁓ An Exploratory Study of Opinion Assignment by the Chief Justice Revisited

DAVID J. DANELSKI

We shall not cease from exploration
And the end of our exploring
Will be to arrive where we started
And know the place for the first time.
—T. S. Eliot

This chapter revisits "The Assignment of the Court's Opinion by the Chief Justice," a fifty-seven-page paper I delivered at the Midwest Conference of Political Scientists in Bloomington, Indiana, on April 28, 1960. At the time, I was a doctoral candidate in political science at the University of Chicago and a first-year instructor at the University of Illinois. It was my first professional paper. Despite its limited publication—a brief excerpt as part of another paper published in an anthology—it is special in the assignment literature.[1] Beverly Blair Cook called it a "seminal" study,[2] and Elliot Slotnick called it a "path-breaking study."[3]

I. Writing on a Blank Slate

I was fortunate to have been present at the creation of judicial behavior as a subfield of political science in the late 1950s. C. Herman Pritchett was my mentor, Walter F. Murphy was a friend and fellow graduate student, and Glendon A. Schubert was an early collaborator. The subfield's pioneers, having virtually no political science literature to draw upon, wrote on a blank slate. They borrowed theories and methods from other disciplines, fashioned their own theories and methods, and conducted exploratory research. I did all three in my study of opinion assignment by the chief justice.

I began my research by reading the biographies of William Howard Taft, Charles Evans Hughes, and Harlan Fiske Stone and examining their papers at the Library of Congress, which revealed their explanations of opinion assignment. I then tested empirically those explanations as well as other explanations, using data from the U.S. Supreme Court Reports.[4] Because Court members viewed "important cases" as special, I analyzed them separately, operationally defining them as cases covered in at least two of four works on the Constitution by law professors, political scientists, and constitutional historians—Freund, Sutherland, Howe, and Brown, *Constitutional Law* (1954); Mason and Beaney, *American Constitutional Law* (1959); Pritchett, *The American Constitution* (1959); and Kelly and Harbison, *The American Constitution: Its Origins and Development* (1948). Since I viewed the Supreme Court as a small group, I selected, for purposes of analysis, periods of Court personnel stability, that is, natural courts. I focused particularly on Courts of greatest duration—Taft (1925–30), Hughes (1932–37), and Stone (1943–45)—and I analyzed opinion assignments in those periods using absolute percentages of assignments and percentages that reflected the justices' availability for assignments.

Much of what I did in my analysis had not been done before, for example separating important cases from other cases for purposes of analysis, defining operationally "important cases," controlling for availability for assignments, focusing on natural courts, and trying to explain opinion assignment empirically.

A. An Assignment Analysis Combining Important and Routine Cases

In an analysis that combined important and routine cases, I found that Taft, Hughes, and Stone took into account the following variables in assigning cases:

1. *Equity.* According to Taft, the chief justice assigns cases to his colleagues "as equally as may be."[5] Hughes described opinion assignment as an "effort of the Chief Justice to distribute the work so that each judge would have about the same amount of work as the others and the same proportion of important cases."[6] Table 2.1, which shows assignment percentages in important and routine cases, indicates the extent to which Taft, Hughes, and Stone equalized work in their Courts.[7]

The main reason for disparity of the above percentages is that some Court members were able to complete their assignments more promptly than others, which, as a term progressed, required the chief justice to assign fewer cases to members who had fallen behind and to reassign some of their cases to others. Among the reasons for justices writing less than the average number of Court opinions were illness (Sutherland, 1925–30),[8] age (Brandeis, 1932–37),[9] procrastination (Sanford, 1925–30),[10] "pen paralysis" (Van Devanter, 1925–30 and 1932–37),[11] and overconscientiousness (Rutledge, 1943–45).[12]

2. *Efficiency.* Efficiency was an important consideration for the chief justices in assigning cases because there was an expectation that the Court would try to clear its docket each term. That is why Taft wanted new appointees to learn to dispose of cases quickly. "Sutherland," Taft wrote to his wife in 1924, "is a very hard worker and gets through his cases promptly. Sanford and Butler have yet to get used to quick disposition of them, but I think they will soon learn."[13] Despite Taft's high hopes, he struggled to get his "team" to clear the Court's docket each term.[14] His experience during the 1926 term is illustrative.

By mid-January 1927, it was clear to Taft that Van Devanter could not write even half of his assigned opinions before the end of the term. A perfectionist who suffered from "pen paralysis," Van Devanter was the Court's least productive opinion writer. Among his assignments during the 1926 term were five cases he had carried over from the previous term, including *Fiske v. Kansas*, which involved the constitutionality of Kansas's syndicalism act.[15] Taft asked Sanford whether he would take *Fiske*. "[A]fter you have written the opinions in the other syndicalism cases that you have, I don't think it will be difficult for you to include this [case]."[16] He asked Stone to

Table 2.1. Assignments of Routine and Important Cases (percentages)

Taft Court (1925–30)		Hughes Court (1932–37)		Stone Court (1943–45)	
Taft	15.0 (15.0)	Hughes	18.1 (18.1)	Stone	19.1 (19.1)
Stone	12.9 (13.3)	Cardozo	13.5 (14.3)	Douglas	11.4 (13.3)
Holmes	12.3 (12.5)	Roberts	12.8 (13.5)	Black	7.9 (12.3)
Butler	11.8 (12.3)	Stone	12.5 (12.5)	Murphy	9.3 (11.8)
Brandeis	11.7 (12.1)	Butler	10.5 (10.5)	Roberts	8.7 (10.1)
McReynolds	11.0 (11.6)	Sutherland	9.8 (10.4)	Reed	7.6 (9.8)
Sanford	8.9 (9.3)	McReynolds	8.9 (9.4)	Jackson	8.2 (9.8)
Sutherland	8.7 (8.7)	Brandeis	8.4 (8.4)	Frankfurter	6.8 (8.2)
Van Devanter	5.1 (5.1)	Van Devanter	2.5 (2.5)	Rutledge	3.8 (5.7)
N = 838		*N* = 806		*N* = 293	

Note: The first number listed for each Court indicates the percentage of assignments by the chief justice; the second number (in parentheses) indicates the percentage of total assignments for each Court member. The percentages for chief justices include per curiam opinions: 1.0 percent for Taft, 5.2 percent for Hughes, and 6.0 percent for Stone.

take another case "to help our dear friend Van, because of his near breakdown."[17] Stone answered, "I shall cheerfully take over No. 48 and try to get you an opinion in it soon."[18] Taft then wrote Sutherland, also asking him to take one of Van Devanter's cases. "You have a pretty heavy load already," acknowledged Taft, "but I don't think this will involve on your part very heavy work."[19]

Before May 1, Taft knew that Van Devanter and Sanford could not finish their assignments before the term's end. On May 3, he commiserated with Sanford: "You are jaded and you are making too much of difficulties that grow in your imagination."[20] He then relieved Sanford of three of his cases, which Brandeis agreed to take. The next day, Sanford came to Taft's chambers to express his gratitude.[21] On May 3, Taft also acted to relieve Van Devanter of many of his cases. "My Dear Van," he wrote. "You have too many cases and are not expected to clean up." He told Van Devanter that he wanted him to keep four of his important cases, but he proposed to distribute the rest of his cases "to others not so loaded. Tactfully, he assured Van Devanter that he was not at fault in falling behind. "I really assigned you too many."[22] Taft then contacted Brandeis, Holmes, and Stone and asked them to take most of Van Devanter's cases.[23] To Stone he wrote, "Will you take Van's case by way of reassignment, No. 492, the Fox River case? I don't think it is necessary for you to speak to him about it. He is very sensitive on all matters of this kind. I have written to him that I am going to take the case away from him and assign it to another."[24] Stone answered, "I shall be very glad to take over No. 492, the Fox River case, especially as I think it will be an interesting case to write."[25] Van Devanter graciously accepted Taft's proposal to reassign most of his cases. "I must assent to the change in assignments proposed in the very considerate note of yesterday," he wrote Taft. "It gives me little pain and embarrassment to have to say this, but I recognize the full propriety of what you propose. The cases must be disposed of. I believe I can take care of those you intend to leave with me."[26] But Taft's assignment problems were not over. Brandeis, he reported, was reluctant about taking two of Van Devanter's cases because he believed Van Devanter "would cherish resentment against him." Perplexed, but only for a moment, Taft took Van Devanter's cases himself and gave Brandeis two of his own. Then, presumably with a chuckle, he wrote to his wife, "The experiences of a Chief Justice are like those of an impresario with his company of artists."[27]

From 1921 to 1946, the most efficient associate justices were Holmes, Stone, Cardozo, and Douglas.

In May 1925, Taft wrote, "I think that [Holmes] will probably have written more opinions than anybody in the Court. He is thirsting for more cases and is willing to take them from other Judges to help them out. His quickness is remarkable."[28] Seven months later, Holmes explained his enthusiasm for writing opinions in a letter to Harold Laski: "I have real intellectual pleasure with my cases this term. They have been sufficiently interesting and to write them shortly and compactly with a hint at general theory when possible is good sport. The Chief called me by telephone to know if a case that he proposed to assign me would be too troublesome. I told him that if he spared me in that way I would have to leave [the Court]. He gave me the case and I polished it off in short metre. I always say, and have probably said to you, there is no such thing as a hard case."[29]

Stone had the same enthusiasm for writing opinions. "[He] was happy in his work, and happy when he was working hard," recalled Harold Leventhal, his law clerk during the 1936 term. "[H]e always moved along with his tasks, even if they were not going well. When he finished an opinion at 4:00 p.m., he started right in on the next case, to get an hour in before his walk. Most of us operate at modest efficiency, only 10% according to William James. Justice Stone operated at 90% efficiency 90% of the time."[30]

Cardozo, who had few interests other than the law, devoted almost all of his time to his judicial work. "He did his work and was never idle," recalled Stone. "There was always the urge to give him new work as soon as the old was disposed of. In view of that fact, he often began work on an assigned case on Saturday night (or as soon as the assignment was made)."[31] To make sure that Cardozo, who had a weak heart, did not work on his opinions on Sundays, Hughes deliberately postponed delivery of his assignments from Saturday evening to Monday morning.[32]

Douglas, like Holmes, was decisive and wrote his opinions quickly. Once he started an opinion, he stayed with it until he finished it. Stone relied heavily on Douglas's efficiency.[33]

3. *Expertise.* Taft sometimes assigned a line of related cases to a single justice. In the mid-1920s, for example, he assigned Sanford three state syndicalism cases—*Gitlow v. New York* (1925), *Fiske v. Kansas* (1927), and *Whitney v. California* (1927). In 1928, he wrote Butler, "In looking over the persons to whom to assign this case of *Black & White Taxi and Transfer Co.* . . . it seems to me that with your having written the New Jersey case it would be easier for you to write the opinion in this case than for others. I shall make it up to you in leaving you out in making other assignments."[34] Taft also took advantage of his colleagues' subject expertise in assigning opinions. "Van Devanter has land law and Indians at his fingers' end," wrote

Holmes to Laski. "McReynolds is the boss of Admiralty."[35] Taft, Holmes, and Stone made up the Court's patent section.[36] From 1925 to 1930, the trio wrote almost 80 percent of the Court's patent opinions. Brandeis, who was the Court's expert in Interstate Commerce Commission cases, wrote the Court's opinions in approximately 60 percent of them from 1921 through 1930.[37]

Hughes and Stone relied less on expertise in assigning opinions than Taft. Under Hughes, McReynolds was no longer "the boss of Admiralty." From 1932 to 1937, Hughes assigned McReynolds only 5 percent of those cases, while assigning himself 40 percent and Butler 15 percent. During the same period, he assigned Brandeis only 23 percent of the ICC cases. Stone and Roberts, however, thrived as patent experts under Hughes. From 1932 to 1937, they wrote 63 percent of the patent opinions. From 1943 to 1945, Douglas joined Stone as a patent expert, writing 27 percent of the patent opinions, while Stone wrote 18 percent.[38]

4. *Holding and Increasing Majorities.* Edwin McElwain, who was Hughes's law clerk during 1938 term, believed that Hughes used his assignment power to hold or increase majorities. According to McElwain, when a bloc split, Hughes would often assign the case to a defecting member of the losing bloc, citing as an example Sutherland in the first Scottsboro case, *Powell v. Alabama* (1932). Hughes probably assigned Sutherland the Court's opinion in that case, wrote McElwain, "with the hope that he could bring over Justices Butler and McReynolds while the more 'liberal' justices could not."[39] McElwain's statement illustrates the marginal hypothesis, which appears to explain much of Hughes's assignment behavior in closely divided cases in the 1932–37 period, for he often assigned the Court opinion to justices who were ideologically closest to the dissenters. From 1932 to 1937, Court members lined up ideologically from left (liberal) to right (conservative) as follows: Stone, Cardozo, Brandeis, Hughes, Roberts, Van Devanter, Sutherland, Butler, and McReynolds.[40] When the right bloc (Van Devanter, Sutherland, Butler, and McReynolds) dissented intact in twenty-two cases, Hughes assigned those 5-4 cases as follows: Hughes, eight; Roberts, six; Cardozo, five; Stone, two; and Brandeis, one. Thus Hughes and Roberts, the marginal justices, wrote for the Court in 63 percent of those cases. When the left bloc (Brandeis, Stone and Cardozo) dissented intact in twenty-eight cases, Hughes assigned those 6-3 cases as follows: Roberts, thirteen; Sutherland, seven; Butler, five; and McReynolds, three. He did not assign any of those cases to himself or Van Devanter. Thus Roberts, the marginal justice, wrote for the Court in 46 percent of those cases. When

the left bloc split in nineteen cases, Hughes assigned those cases as follows: Butler, five; Brandeis, four; Roberts, three; Sutherland, two; and Hughes, one, and when the right bloc split in thirty-five cases, Hughes assigned those cases as follows: Hughes, eight; Cardozo, eight; Roberts, five; Stone, six; Sutherland, five; Brandeis, four; Butler, one. Eliminating Van Devanter from the analysis because he received no assignments in closely divided cases, the marginal justices were Brandeis, Hughes, Roberts, and Sutherland. From 1932 to 1937, Hughes assigned the Court's opinions to those justices in 65 percent of 104 divided cases.[41]

B. *An Assignment Analysis of Important Cases*

In his *Autobiographical Notes*, Hughes wrote that in assigning the Court's opinions, he took into account the feelings of the Court's senior members and "endeavored . . . to give to each Justice the same proportion of important cases, while at the same time equalizing so far as possible the burden of work."[42] Table 2.2 shows that while Taft, Hughes, and Stone may have "endeavored" to give "each Justice the same proportion of important cases," they did so only marginally.

In order to explain the disparity in the percentages, in table 2.2 it is necessary to take into account variables other than those discussed above. Among those variables are ideology, ability, and opinion legitimacy.[43]

1. *Ideology*. Ideology probably explains Taft's assignments of important cases during the 1925–30 period because he assigned himself and his fellow conservatives—Sutherland and Butler—almost 60 percent of those cases, and he assigned Brandeis—the Court's arch liberal—none. Hughes appears to have taken ideology into account in assigning important cases for stra-

Table 2.2. Assignments of Important Cases (percentages)

Taft Court (1925–30)		Hughes Court (1932–37)		Stone Court (1943–45)	
Sutherland	22.7	Hughes	34.0	Douglas	27.3
Taft	18.2	Sutherland	14.9	Frankfurter	18.2
Butler	18.2	Roberts	14.9	Stone	18.2
Holmes	9.1	Brandeis	8.5	Black	13.6
Stone	9.1	Cardozo	8.4	Reed	9.1
Sanford	9.1	McReynolds	6.4	Roberts	4.5
Van Devanter	9.1	Stone	6.4	Jackson	4.5
McReynolds	4.5	Butler	6.4	Murphy	4.5
Brandeis	0.0	Van Devanter	0.0	Rutledge	0.0
N = 22		*N* = 48		*N* = 22	

tegic reasons. "If the court were sharply divided," wrote Merlo J. Pusey, who had interviewed Hughes for his biography, "he tried to avoid extremes by assigning the opinion to the Justice nearest the center, as he did when he assigned Roberts the Agricultural Adjustment Administration Case."[44] From 1932 to 1937, Roberts was ideologically in middle of the Court. He was on Hughes's right and on Van Devanter's and Sutherland's left.[45] Ideology does not, however, explain Stone's assignment of important cases to Douglas, who had been assigned the largest number of important cases. Although Stone voted more frequently with Frankfurter (74 percent) during the 1944 term than any other colleague, he voted least with Douglas (52 percent) and Black (41 percent).[46] Ideology may explain, at least in part, Stone's assignment of important cases to Frankfurter, for Stone assigned Frankfurter more such cases than he assigned any other associate justice, except Douglas. See table 2.2.

2. *Ability.* In his Columbia University lectures in 1927, Hughes said that it "is safe to say that no member of the Supreme Court is under any illusion as to the mental equipment of his brethren. Constant and close association discloses the strength of character and exposes the weakness of each."[47]

Taft often wrote of his colleagues' abilities in his correspondence. "Van Devanter," he wrote in 1927, "is our strongest man. He is of the utmost value to the Court, even if he writes no opinions. Indeed, it would be better if he did not write any opinions because then the others could keep up the work."[48] Two years earlier, Taft had written, "Sutherland is one of the most valuable men on the Court because his constitutional views had been tempered by long political experience—a process which make him a much more useful judge than one who, like Holmes, has had no political experience and proceeds as if the American Constitution were as malleable as the British Constitution."[49] Taft valued Butler because he was a conservative, a team player, and because he was "strong, able and willing."[50] Yet Taft readily acknowledged the ability of the liberals Holmes and Stone. Holmes, he said, was "brilliant," "a well of pure common law undefiled," and Stone was "a learned lawyer," but Taft thought both were often wrong on constitutional questions.[51] He thought that the converse was true of the conservative Sanford. Though he was usually "right" on constitutional questions, Taft thought that Sanford lacked the overall ability of Holmes and Stone. At the bottom of Taft's rank order were Brandeis and McReynolds. Taft acknowledged Brandeis' intellectual capacity and extraordinary grasp in certain areas of the law, but he felt that Brandeis's constitutional views were extreme.[52] He viewed McReynolds as a man of ability who was "spoiled for usefulness" as a judge because he was prejudiced, lazy, and irresponsible.[53]

Hughes undoubtedly believed that some of his colleagues were more able than others, but tactfully he did not say so in his *Autobiographical Notes.* He did say, however, that Van Devanter "was most painstaking and exact," Stone was "able, scholarly, and experienced," Roberts was "a strong judge," and Cardozo was "one of the outstanding jurists of his time." As for his other colleagues, he said that they, too, were "all able men of high character."[54]

According to Mason, Stone took his colleagues' abilities into account in assigning opinions. "An especially tough or interesting opinion," he wrote, "usually went to Douglas, Frankfurter, or Roberts, as the Chief rated their ability highly. Stone also esteemed Black but distrusted his unorthodox approach. Therefore, the New Deal Justice did not get his share of the 'good' cases. The Chief Justice was well aware that he slighted Murphy; he often agreed to give him a 'break,' but in the end Murphy would be nosed out partly because Stone disliked leaving a fine case to the rumination of a law clerk."[55]

Table 2.2 confirms that Taft and Stone rewarded colleagues they considered able with assignments of important cases. Van Devanter was no exception. He received as many assignments of important cases as Sutherland and Butler, but he did not write opinions in those cases because he had to relinquish them for reassignment to other justices. Table 2.2 also partly supports Hughes's claim that he had "endeavored" to give each justice the same proportion of important cases. Except for Van Devanter, who for reasons already mentioned was unavailable for assignments, Hughes distributed important cases more or less evenly to Cardozo, Brandeis, Stone, Butler, and McReynolds, but he clearly favored himself, Sutherland, and Roberts.

In an effort to determine the extent to which Taft, Hughes, and Stone favored certain Court members in the assignment process because of their ability, I did an analysis of opinion assignment that controlled for availability. That analysis, which is presented in table 2.3, shows the percentages obtained by dividing the number of assignments a justice received by the number of times that justice voted with the majority and hence was available for assignments.

The percentages in table 2.3 do not greatly advance explanation of assignments of important cases, but the raw numbers for their calculation do. The numerators in the fractions in the table suggest that equal distribution rather than ability explains more than half of the assignments of important cases to associate justices in the three Courts. Taft and Stone each assigned five justices one or two such cases, and Hughes assigned five justices three or four such cases. Explanations for the justices at the bottom of their rank orders have already been suggested. For Brandeis it was ideology, for Van Devanter it was "pen paralysis," and for Rutledge it was overconscientiousness. Ideology coupled with ability probably explain Taft's assignments to Sutherland and Butler, and ability coupled with efficiency probably explains Hughes's assignments to Sutherland, for Sutherland was the ablest Court conservative who could produce opinions promptly, but his defections from the right bloc and his center-right ideological position in the Court also provide an explanation. Hughes undoubtedly appreciated Roberts's ability, but Roberts's position as a marginal justice is a better explanation for his relatively high percentage of assignments in important cases. Since Stone and Frankfurter mostly voted together in divided cases, ability coupled with ideology appears to be the best explanation for Frankfurter's assignments of important cases, and since Stone voted less frequently with Douglas in divided cases, the best explanation for his assignment of important cases to Douglas is ability coupled with efficiency.

3. *Opinion Legitimacy.* A concern for opinion legitimacy explains assignments in some important cases. "The fact is," wrote former Justice John Hessin Clarke, "the great cases are written, as they should be, by the Chief Justice, and a very large percentage of the cases written by the other Justices are of little general importance."[56] William O. Douglas agreed. "Earl Warren," he wrote, "naturally kept to himself the landmark decisions. The prestige of the office of Chief Justice behind a controversial decision gives it strength and weight. . . . Every Chief Justice when assigning opinions has an eye to public relations and to history—and naturally so."[57]

In assigning cases, wrote Frankfurter, Hughes understood "the impor-

Table 2.3. Assignments of Important Cases to Associate Justices (percentages controlled for availability)

Taft Court (1925–30)		Hughes Court (1932–37)		Stone Court (1943–45)	
Sutherland	27.8 (5/18)	Sutherland	26.9 (7/26)	Frankfurter	50.0 (4/8)
Butler	25.0 (4/16)	Roberts	24.1 (7/29)	Douglas	46.1 (6/13)
Holmes	22.2 (2/9)	Cardozo	16.7 (4/24)	Black	23.1 (3/13)
Stone	18.2 (2/11)	Brandeis	16.7 (4/24)	Roberts	16.6 (1/6)
Sanford	13.3 (2/15)	McReynolds	15.8 (3/19)	Reed	15.4 (2/13)
Van Devanter	11.8 (2/17)	Stone	13.6 (3/22)	Murphy	12.5 (1/8)
McReynolds	6.7 (1/15)	Butler	13.0 (3/23)	Jackson	11.1 (1/9)
Brandeis	0.0 (0/7)	Van Devanter	0.0 (0/25)	Rutledge	0.0 (0/10)

tance of the chief justiceship as a symbol. For there are occasions when an opinion should carry the extra weight which pronouncement by the chief justice gives."[58] According to Pusey, "Hughes assigned himself those cases which he believed to be of such importance that the country would expect the pronouncement of the Court to come from the Chief Justice. . . . When a justice with a reputation as a liberal voted with the majority on the conservative side of a question, he usually got the opinion to write. The same was true in the case of a conservative voting on the liberal side. Hughes constant effort was to enhance public confidence in the entire court as a independent body."[59]

Stone assigned himself fewer important cases than did Taft or Hughes, but Stone did speak for the Court in the "big" war cases—*Ex parte Quirin* (1942), *Hirabayashi v. United States* (1943), and *In re Yamashita* (1946)—which relieved Frankfurter, who told Stone that he was confident that the chief's opinion in *Yamashita* would "measure up to what is worthy of the Chief Justice of the United States."[60]

II. The Tests of Time and Multivariate Analysis

More than fifty years have passed since I delivered the 1960 Midwest Conference paper. During that period, the Supreme Court has become more political, has heard fewer cases, and has tripled the number of its law clerks. Those changes may have affected opinion assignment by the chief justice to an extent that the paper's findings are no longer valid. Whether they do or not can be determined by comparing its findings with findings of subsequent studies of opinion assignments by Chief Justices Warren, Burger, and Rehnquist using multivariate analysis.

In 2003, Thomas G. Walker wrote that the 1960 Midwest Conference paper

> set the stage for future examinations of the opinion assignment power. Such studies have held the attention of judicial behavior scholars over the past several decades. Ulmer's research (1970), for example, extended Danelski's analysis by examining Earl Warren's exercise of the opinion assignment power. Similarly, Slotnick (1978, 1979) published a series of articles evaluating opinion assignment patterns from Taft through Burger. Brenner (1982) and subsequently Maltzman and Wahlbeck (1996) explicitly applied strategic analysis to the opinion assignment process. Those studies, and others of a similar vein, cite [a version of the Midwest Conference paper]

> as the initial attempt to understand the use of opinion assignments as a means of political influence. In fact, subsequent studies employing increasingly sophisticated statistical and theoretical tools have continued to confront the same questions and evaluate the same hypotheses that Danelski laid down during the early period of pioneering studies of judicial behavior.[61]

In 2004, Forrest Maltzman and Paul J. Wahlbeck published "A Conditional Model of Opinion Assignment on the Supreme Court," a multivariate analysis of 3,494 opinion assignments by Chief Justices Warren, Burger, and Rehnquist that tested the relationship between two hypothesized assignment goals: the advancement of the chief justice's policy preferences (ideology) and the attainment of the Court's organizational needs (e.g., equity, efficiency, and expertise).[62] "According to a neo-institutional view of the opinion assignment process," Maltzman and Wahlbeck wrote, "policy motivations are paramount but are constrained by norms compelling the chief to tend to the Court's organizational needs. Organizational factors are little more than a constraint on the chief's ability to advance his policy goals. In contrast, the significant influence attributed to organizational factors might indicate the chief justice pursues goals beyond his policy preferences. Although judicial scholars have recently ascribed primacy to policy goals, they do not always view that as the only goal."[63] To illustrate their point, Maltzman and Wahlbeck chose a study written more than four decades earlier. "For example," they wrote, "when writing about leadership in the Supreme Court, Danelski argued that chief justices regularly strive to lead the institution in such a way that they minimize conflict among the justices and ensure the viability of the Court as a system."[64]

To test the relationship between the chief justice's policy preference goal and the Court's organizational goals, Maltzman and Wahlbeck's conditional model included some of the variables identified in the 1960 Midwest Conference paper. They found that four variables were significantly related to opinion assignments—ideology at the .001 level, equity at .001 level, efficiency at the .001 level, and expertise at the .01 level, which suggested that both policy concerns and organizational needs drive opinion selection. "[E]fficiency and equity," they wrote, "are goals in their own right that are impervious to changes in ideological distance."[65] They also found that two variables condition ideology. The first variable was the size of the conference vote. "When the coalition contains at least two justices more than necessary for a majority," they wrote, "the advantage goes to the chief's ideological allies and grows with the size of the conference majority.

Ideological distance does not affect the assignment choice as the majority coalition approaches minimum winning,"[66] which suggests that marginal justices are more likely to be assigned such cases. Further, "the chief is more likely to assign himself the opinion when the conference coalition is at least three more than necessary to form a majority. When the coalition is smaller, the chief is significantly less likely to assign himself the opinion."[67] The second variable conditioning ideology was case importance. They found that "the Chief Justice is more likely to assign cases that are politically salient or legally important to his ideological allies or himself."[68] Finally, they found that the dynamics of the Court calendar affects the chief justice's assignments. "The chief justice," they wrote, "weighs expertise at the beginning of the term, but not at the end. The 'bonus' applied to a justice for expertise is most pronounced at the beginning of the term, but it diminishes in magnitude as the term advances. Indeed, it is indistinguishable from zero a little more than five months from the end of the term (about January). The same pattern emerges for equity and ideology. . . . At the beginning of a term, the chief's ideological allies and those with fewer cases are significantly more likely to win assignments, but this advantage disappears after about four months. In contrast, the growing impact of efficiency is seen in the positive and significant coefficient for the interaction of efficiency and days remaining in the term. Thus, the chief justice places greater weight on the justices' ability to complete opinions as the term comes to an end."[69]

Although Maltzman and Wahlbeck did not include "opinion legitimacy" in their model, they recognized its importance. In an article on Rehnquist's opinion assignments published in 2005, they wrote that the chief justice uses his opinion assignment "to enhance the legitimacy of the Court's opinions, promote harmony on the bench, and ensure that the Court completes its work," as well as to advance his policy preferences.[70]

The only assignment variable in the 1960 Midwest Conference paper that Maltzman and Walhbeck did not mention in their assignment studies was "ability," which is understandable, for it is a difficult variable to operationalize. Cook recognized that difficulty in her unpublished multivariate analysis of opinion assignment in the Burger Court, yet she included in her model an equivalent variable, "competence," which she reported as statistically significant at the .01 level for "all cases" and at the .001 level for "hard cases." Among other variables in her model were assignment to the "marginal justice," which was significant at the .01 level, and "equity," which was significant at the .001 level.[71]

Despite changes in the Supreme Court and advances in sophisticated analysis of judicial behavior over the past half-century, the findings in 1960 Midwest Conference paper appear to have stood the test of time, for they are consistent with the findings of later assignment studies that employed multivariate analysis. The latter findings are, of course, more reliable, but the former findings have more texture. Viewing both types of findings together tells more about assignment of opinions by the chief justice than either do separately. Thus, as T. S. Eliot wrote, often in our explorations "we arrive where we started" and "know the place for the first time."

NOTES

I am indebted to Thomas G. Walker, whose comments on an early draft helped me improve it.

1. Walter F. Murphy and C. Herman Pritchett, *Courts, Judges, and Politics* (New York: Random House, 1961), 503–6. There are three unpublished versions of the paper—the original paper, Part V of the unabridged 1960 APSA paper, which is chapter 1 of this volume, and David J. Danelski, "The Chief Justice and the Supreme Court" (PhD diss., University of Chicago, 1961), chap. 7, hereafter cited as CJ&SC.

2. Beverly Blair Cook, "Measuring the Significance of U.S. Supreme Court Decisions," *Journal of Politics* 55 (1993): 1128.

3. Elliot E. Slotnick, "Who Speaks for the Court: The Chief Justice and the Assignment of Majority Opinions" (PhD diss., University of Minnesota, 1976), 92.

4. The principal biographies were Henry F. Pringle, *The Life and Times of William Howard Taft: A Biography*, 2 vols. (New York: Farrar & Rinehart, 1939); Merlo J. Pusey, *Charles Evans Hughes*, 2 vols. (New York: Macmillan, 1951); Alpheus Thomas Mason, *Harlan Fiske Stone: Pillar of the Law* (New York: Viking Press, 1956).

5. Taft to Henry Holzer, Feb. 21, 1928, Library of Congress, William Howard Taft Papers.

6. Charles Evans Hughes, *The Supreme Court of the United States: Its Foundations, Methods and Achievements, An Interpretation* (New York: Columbia University Press, 1928), 59.

7. The source of data for tables 2.1–2.3 was the United States Reports.

8. Taft to Sutherland, Aug. 11, 1925; Oct. 3, 1927; Nov. 3, 1927; April 29, 1929; Nov. 25, 1929; Sutherland to Taft, Jan. 25, 1926; Oct. 4, 1927; April 29, 1929, Taft Papers.

9. Brandeis to Bernard Flexner, Feb. 13, 1939, University of Louisville, Louis D. Brandeis Papers; Stone to Children, Feb. 15, 1939, Library of Congress, Harlan Fiske Stone Papers.

10. Taft to Robert A. Taft, May 3, 1925, Taft Papers.

11. David J. Danelski and Joseph S. Tulchin, eds., *The Autobiographical Notes of Charles Evans Hughes* (Cambridge, MA: Harvard University Press, 1973), 171.

12. "Rutledge," recalled Douglas, "was a man . . . whose mill ground very, very

slowly. He was very, very, very conscientious, down to the finest last detail and he would write heavily footnoted opinions that sometimes seemed to be useless expenditures of time and energy on a problem that didn't need that detailed treatment." Transcriptions of interviews of William O. Douglas by Walter F. Murphy (1961), 186, Princeton University, Seely G. Mudd Manuscript Library.

13. Taft to Helen H. Taft, undated, postmarked April 28, 1924, Taft Papers.

14. Danelski, "CJ&SC," 138–39.

15. Taft to Butler, Jan. 14, 1927, Taft Papers.

16. Taft to Sanford, Jan. 26, 1927, ibid.

17. Taft to Stone, Jan. 26, 1927, ibid.

18. Stone to Taft, Jan. 26, 1927, ibid.

19. Taft to Sutherland, Jan. 28, 1927, ibid.

20. Taft to Sanford, May 3, 1927, ibid.

21. Taft to Helen H. Taft, May 4, 1927, ibid.

22. Taft to Van Devanter, May 3, 1927, ibid.

23. Taft to Brandeis, May 3, 1927; Taft to Holmes, May 3, 1927; Taft to Stone, May 3, 1927, ibid.

24. Taft to Stone, May 3, 1927, ibid.

25. Stone to Taft, May 4, 1927, ibid.

26. Van Devanter to Taft, May 4, 1927, ibid.

27. Taft to Helen H. Taft, May 3, 1927, ibid. Hughes also found it necessary to take back cases from Van Devanter. "You are overworked," he would say to Van Devanter. "Let me relieve you of your burden." Quoted in Pusey, *Charles Evans Hughes*, 2:668.

28. Taft to Robert A. Taft, May 17, 1925, Taft Papers.

29. Holmes to Harold Laski, Dec. 17, 1925, in Mark DeWolfe Howe, ed., *Holmes-Laski Letters: The Correspondence of Mr. Justice Holmes and Harold J. Laski, 1916–1935*, 2 vols. (Cambridge, MA: Harvard University Press, 1953), I, 806.

30. Harold Leventhal, "Harlan Fiske Stone," *New York State Bar Journal* 24 (1977): 54.

31. Stone to Benjamin Shein, April 26. 1942, Stone Papers.

32. Stone to Frankfurter, Oct. 18, 1935, ibid.

33. Stone to Jackson, Jan. 2, 1946, ibid.

34. Taft to Butler, Feb. 18, 1928, Taft Papers.

35. Holmes to Harold Laski, Feb. 27, 1929, *Holmes-Laski Letters*, 2:1135.

36. On the reverse side of one of Stone's early patent opinions, Brandeis wrote, "You seem to have qualified the patent section of the Court." The case was *Holland Furniture v. Perkins Glue Co.* (1928). Stone Papers.

37. Danelski, "CJ&SC," 152–56.

38. Ibid., 156–57.

39. Edwin McElwain, "The Business of the Supreme Court as Conducted by Chief Justice Hughes," *Harvard Law Review* 63 (1949): 18.

40. C. Herman Pritchett, *The Roosevelt Court: A Study in Judicial Politics and Values, 1937–1947* (New York: Macmillan, 1948), 242.

41. Danelski, "CJ&SC," 168.

42. Danelski and Tulchin, *Autobiographical Notes*, 302.

43. Taft's percentage of important cases is only 18.2 percent because he was ill during the 1925–30 period. During his entire chief justiceship, he assigned himself 34 percent of the important cases.

44. Pusey, *Charles Evans Hughes*, 2:678.

45. Pritchett, *Roosevelt Court*, 242.

46. Ibid., 246.

47. Hughes, *Supreme Court*, 57.

48. Taft to Horace D. Taft, Jan. 17, 1927, Taft Papers.

49. Taft to Robert A. Taft, May 24, 1925, Taft Papers.

50. Taft to Van Devanter, July 9, 1926, Taft Papers.

51. Taft to Helen H. Taft, May 6, 1928; Taft to Robert A. Taft, April 10, 1927; Taft to Learned Hand, March 3, 1923, ibid.; Pringle, *Life and Times of William Howard Taft*, 2:969–70.

52. Taft to Horace A. Taft, Dec. 26, 1924, Dec. 8, 1929; Taft to Robert A. Taft, Nov. 14, 1926; Dec. 8, 1929; Taft to Charles P. Taft, II, Oct. 31, 1926, Taft Papers.

53. Pringle, *Life and Times of William Howard Taft*, 2:971; Taft to Mrs. Frederick Manning, June 11, 1923; Taft to Robert A. Taft, April 20, 1924, Feb. 1, 1935; Taft to Charles P. Taft, Oct. 31, 1926, Taft Papers.

54. Danelski and Tulchin, *Autobiographical Notes*, 298–300.

55. Mason, *Harlan Fiske Stone*, 793.

56. John Hessin Clarke to Joseph E. McLean, April 23, 1941, quoted in Joseph E. McLean, *William Rufus Day* (Baltimore: Johns Hopkins Press, 1947), 6.

57. Douglas, Draft of autobiography, vol. II, chap. 1, 53–54, Library of Congress, William O. Douglas Papers.

58. Felix Frankfurter, "'Administrative Side' of Chief Justice Hughes," in *Of Law and Men*, ed. Philip Elman (New York: Harcourt, Brace, 1956), 142.

59. Pusey, *Charles Evans Hughes*, 2:678–79.

60. Frankfurter to Stone, Jan. 15, 1946, Stone Papers.

61. Thomas G. Walker, "David J. Danelski: Social Psychology and Group Choice," in *The Pioneers of Judicial Behavior*, ed. Nancy Maveety (Ann Arbor: University of Michigan Press, 2003), 255–56, citing S. Sidney Ulmer, "The Use of Power in the Supreme Court: The Opinion Assignments of Earl Warren, 1953–1960," *Journal of Public Law* 19 (1970); Elliot E. Slotnick, "The Chief Justice and Self-Assignment of Majority Opinions: A Research Note," *Western Political Quarterly* 31 (1978); Elliot E. Slotnick, "Who Speaks for the Court? Majority Opinion Assignment from Taft to Burger," *American Journal of Political Science* 23 (1979); Forrest Maltzman and Paul J. Wahlbeck, "May It Please the Chief: Opinion Assignments in the Rehnquist Court," *American Journal of Political Science* 40 (1996); and Forrest Maltzman, James F. Spriggs II, and Paul J. Wahlbeck, *Crafting Law on the Supreme Court: The Collegial Game* (New York: Cambridge University Press, 2000).

62. Forrest Maltzman and Paul J. Wahlbeck, "A Conditional Model of Opinion Assignment on the Supreme Court," *Political Research Quarterly* 57 (2004): 551–63.

63. Ibid., 551.

64. Ibid., citing Danelski, in *The Federal Judicial System: Readings in Process and Behavior*, ed. Thomas P. Jahnige and Sheldon Goldman (New York: Holt, Rinehart & Winston, 1968), 147–60.

65. Maltzman and Wahlbeck, "A Conditional Model," 559.

66. Ibid., 559–60.
67. Ibid., 561.
68. Ibid.
69. Ibid.
70. Forrest Maltzman and Paul J. Wahlbeck, "Opinion Assignment on the Rehnquist Court," *Judicature* 89 (2005): 122. Wahlbeck made the same statement in his article "Strategy and Constraints on Supreme Court Opinion Assignment," *University of Pennsylvania Law Review* 154 (2006): 1729, 1742, in which he cited a version of the Midwest Conference paper.
71. Beverly Blair Cook, "Testing a Model of Opinion Assignment: The Burger Court," paper presented at the annual meeting for the American Political Science Association, 1992, 5 and table 2, Tulane University, Newcomb Archives, Beverly Blair Cook Papers. In explaining the significance of the equity variable, Cook wrote, "Chief Justice Burger showed little concern for the social harmony of his Court. His purpose in equalizing the total number of assigned cases among justices was to process the workload rather than to satisfy his brethren. His method was to make assignments in the significant cases to the justices with attitudes similar to his own; he then distributed the less significant cases to the available justice at the liberal end of the spectrum. It is not surprising that the chief's behavior caused disaffection among those justices who had few opportunities to fashion the law and policy made by the Court." Ibid., 12. Opinion legitimacy was not a variable in Cook's model, but she did report that Burger assigned himself twelve of twenty-eight "landmark cases" during the seventeen years he was chief justice, which was three times the number of landmark cases he assigned any other justice. Ibid., table 2.1.

3 ~ The Influence of the Chief Justice in the Decisional Process of the Supreme Court Revisited

Personality and Leadership*

DAVID J. DANELSKI

This chapter revisits "The Influence of the Chief Justice in the Decisional Process of the Supreme Court" for the purpose of exploring the relationship between personality and leadership in the Court. Although I was aware of the relationship when I wrote the paper in 1960, I did not explore it because I had no adequate personality theory. Today, there are many personality theories from which to choose. After reviewing the psychological literature, I chose for the present study C. G. Jung's personality theory in *Psychological Types*, as interpreted and developed by Isabel Briggs Myers in *Gifts Differing*.[1]

I. The Jung-Myers Theory

According to the Jung-Myers theory, four preferences structure personality. The first three preferences were in Jung's original theory. Myers added the fourth preference. The four preferences are:

1. Extroversion (E) or Introversion (I), each of which is an attitude that focuses one's attention. Extroverts focus their attention out-

*This chapter is a revision of "The Influence of the Chief Justice Revisited: Personality and Strategy," a paper I prepared for delivery at the 2012 American Political Science Association meeting in New Orleans. I should like to thank Jill Parmer Danelski, David E. Cote, and David A. Yalof for reading and commenting on the paper.

wardly to people and things; introverts focus their attention inwardly toward themselves.[2]

2. Sensation (S) or Intuition (N), each of which is a nonevaluative function for acquiring information or ideas. Sensation involves the five senses and imparts practicality and concreteness. Intuition involves "meanings, relationships, and possibilities that go beyond the information from one's senses; it looks at the bigger picture and tries to grasp the essential patterns."[3]
3. Thinking (T) or Feeling (F), each of which is an evaluative function for assessing information or ideas. Thinking is a process that leads to decisions based on cause-and-effect analysis. Feeling considers what is important to an individual or other people (without requiring that it be logical) and is based on personal values.[4]
4. Perceiving (P) or Judging (J) are lifestyle preferences. The former relies essentially on Sensation or Intuition; the latter relies essentially on Thinking or Feeling. Perception is essentially information gathering about persons, things, and ideas. Judging is essentially is evaluation of matters perceived. Those who prefer Perceiving as a lifestyle are more curious than decisive; those who prefer Judging as a lifestyle are more decisive than curious.[5]

The combination and relative dominance of the four preferences determines an individual's personality type.[6] The first two preferences yield eight general types: extroverted and introverted thinking, feeling, intuitive, and sensing types. All four preferences yield sixteen types. Only three of those sixteen types are relevant in this study: ENFJ (Taft, a feeling extrovert), INTP (Van Devanter and Hughes, thinking introverts), and ENTP (Stone, an intuitive extrovert).

The Jung-Myers theory suggests the following hypotheses concerning task and social leadership: (1) Social leaders are apt to be feeling types. (2) Task leaders are apt to be thinking types. (3) A social leader who is a feeling type can be a successful chief justice if he or she shares task leadership with a thinking type. (4) A task leader who is a thinking type can be a successful chief just if he or she shares leadership with a feeling type. (5) A thinking type can be a successful chief justice if he or she provides both task and social leadership.

With those hypotheses in mind, I re-examined the biographical literature and archival data I collected over many years concerning Taft, Van Devanter, Hughes, and Stone. I then classified their personalities using

Jung-Myers typology as used by Loren E. Pedersen in *Sixteen Men: Understanding Masculine Personality Types.* Those classifications raised the following questions that focused my analysis: Does a judge's personality type affect his or her choice of law as a career or his or her ambition to rise in the judiciary? Why are social leaders apt to be feeling types? Why are task leaders apt to be thinking types? What drew Taft and Van Devanter to each other to become coleaders? Why was Hughes able to provide social leadership when he was known to be an austere and aloof introvert? Why was Stone successful as an associate justice but unsuccessful as a chief justice?

II. William Howard Taft and Willis Van Devanter

Taft's was a feeling extrovert—an ENFJ—whose personality functions were feeling (dominant), intuition (auxiliary), sensation (tertiary), and thinking (inferior) and whose lifestyle preference was judging. The main indicators of the type are a desire for harmonious human contacts, warmth, friendliness, sensitivity to praise and criticism, loyalty, compassion, devotion to a loved person or institution, and attention to the needs of others.[7]

Referring to male ENFJs, Pedersen observed that there are not a lot of them "in the entire population, and among men, they account for only 2.8 percent. (There are twice as many among women, about 4.5 percent.) . . . [It] is a rare type for a man to be, and a difficult one unless he finds suitable channels for expressing his warmth, compassion, and attention to the needs of others."[8] Less than 5 percent of ENFJs find law an attractive profession. They are more likely to become ministers, priests, monks, or actors.[9]

Taft epitomized the feeling extrovert. Above all, he sought harmony among his fellow human beings. Alice Roosevelt Longworth recalled that she had never known "anyone with the equanimity, amiability, and kindliness of Mr. Taft."[10] Others shared Longworth's perception.[11] And probably no one loved the Supreme Court more than Taft. In 1923, he wrote, "[T]he Court . . . , next to my wife and children, is the nearest thing to my heart in life."[12]

Taft and his father, Alphonso, had almost identical personalities. Taft's wife described her father-in-law as "'gentle' beyond anything I ever knew. . . . [H]e was one of the most lovable men that ever lived because he had a wide tolerance and a strange understanding sympathy for everybody."[13] Taft's brother, Horace, described their father as "a combination of strength, sweetness, gentleness, simplicity, and broadmindedness," and he described Will in similar terms. "It was very hard," he wrote, "for anyone to be near him without loving him."[14]

Alphonso Taft had been an Ohio lawyer, trial judge, U.S. attorney general, secretary of war, and diplomatic minister to Vienna and St. Petersburg. Will Taft, like his father, attended Yale College, where by dint of hard work he graduated second in his class. But unlike his father, he did not remain at Yale for his legal education. His biographer, Henry F. Pringle, suggests that Taft reluctantly chose law as a career and attended the Cincinnati Law School because its program required only two hours a day for two years, which left him with ample time to work as a reporter for the local newspaper, enjoy the pleasures of Cincinnati society, and taste "the sweetness of universal popularity."[15] Though he tied for top honors at graduation from law school, he apparently had learned little law. "What I really knew of the law," he later declared, "I learned at the expense of Hamilton County, Ohio, as assistant prosecutor and as judge of the Superior Court."[16]

As a young lawyer and judge, Taft identified with his father's ambition to become a U.S. Supreme Court justice.[17] He also he shared his father's view that it was more important to be chief justice than president. In 1874, the elder Taft wrote Chief Justice Waite, "I have sometimes hoped that if Judge Swayne should retire, there might be a possibility of my being thought of for that place."[18] Swayne did not retire, and when he died in 1881, his place on the Court went to another Ohioan, Stanley Matthews. In 1889, when Matthews died, Will Taft's friends pushed his candidacy for the "Ohio vacancy."[19] At the time, Taft was in his early thirties. Perhaps for that reason, he referred to his friends' efforts as "innocent amusement." Though he knew his chance of success was "one in a million," he thought that the appointment was worth pursuing because it was "so great a prize."[20] When he heard that Justice Harlan had inquired about him, he regarded his friends' efforts as more than "innocent amusement," and he solicited a letter from Governor Joseph B. Foraker to President Harrison.[21] Foraker complied, and Taft thanked him, saying that the letter would bring pleasure to his father, "whose weakness is a too high appreciation of his boys."[22] The appointment went to David J. Brewer, but the efforts of Taft's friends had not been in vain. Ohio congressman Benjamin Butterworth recommended Taft for appointment as U.S. solicitor general, and a few days later Harrison offered Taft the post. Foraker suggested that Taft accept the appointment as a steppingstone to the Supreme Court.[23] Taft, however, feared that the duties of the office would be overwhelming for a young and relatively inexperienced lawyer and sought his father's advice. His father admitted that the job was indeed "Herculean," but he told his son what he wanted to hear: "Go ahead and fear not."[24] So Taft became U.S. solicitor general at the age of thirty-two. In 1864, when Lincoln appointed Salmon Portland

Chase chief justice, Alphonso Taft congratulated him and observed, "To be Chief Justice of the United States is more important than to be President in my estimation."[25] More than sixty years later, Taft would write to Jacob Dickinson, his former secretary of war, "I don't hesitate to say that I would rather have been chief justice than president."[26] That was not only Taft's preference; it was also the preference of his mother, who insisted in 1912: "I do not want my son to be president; he is not my candidate. A place for him on the Supreme Court Bench, where my boy would administer justice, is my ambition for him."[27]

In 1891, as his father lay dying, Taft, then thirty-eight, was waiting to hear whether he would be appointed to the federal circuit bench. Both men knew the appointment was an important step to the Supreme Court, but they did not talk about it in their final conversations. Five days before he died, Alphonso Taft told his son what he had known all of his life. "Will," he said, "I love you beyond expression."[28] That evening, Taft wrote to his wife: "I am not superstitious as you know my darling, but I have a kind of presentment that Father has been a kind of guardian angel to me in that his wishes for my success have been so strong and intense to bring it, and that as his life ebbs away I shall cease to have the luck which has followed me thus far. I have a feeling that I shall not be appointed circuit judge and I shall settle down to a humdrum, commonplace practice in Cincinnati, managing to eke out only enough to support us."[29]

The circuit judgeship came through, and Taft settled into his beloved judicial life, hoping for promotion to the Supreme Court. Writing to his wife after a trip to Washington in 1896, he noted with optimism, "Almost every person I met spoke of my coming here to sit on the Supreme Court as a certainty. . . . Perhaps you think that this is very weak on my part, but when the thing is chimed into one's ears every day, it is hard not to think of the possibilities."[30] Promotion came in 1900, but it was not to the Supreme Court, though it was sold in those terms. President McKinley assured Taft that if he resigned his judgeship to head a commission to the Philippine Islands, he would not suffer. Referring to the Supreme Court, McKinley said, "If I last and the opportunity comes, I shall appoint you."[31] Though McKinley did not last, Theodore Roosevelt honored his predecessor's promise. In 1902, and again in 1906, TR offered Taft the judicial post to which he had aspired. In 1902, Taft felt he could not honorably accept the offer because he felt he was he being kicked upstairs for his policies in the Philippines. In 1906, he wanted to accept, but pressures from his wife and friends to seek the 1908 presidential nomination were so great that he again declined. "Had he been offered the Chief Justiceship," recalled his friend Jack Hammond, "we would have raised no objection. That would indeed have been the achievement of a life ambition."[32] A year and a half later, Taft was elected president. It seemed unbelievable, for his ambition had been judicial, not political. He said he felt "a bit like a fish out of water." Then he revealingly added, "If I were now presiding in the Supreme Court of the United States as chief justice, I should feel entirely at home."[33]

When Chief Justice Fuller died in 1910, Taft had to choose a man for the position that had been the object of his own ambition. He narrowed his consideration to two associate justices, Charles Evans Hughes, whom he had just appointed, and Edward Douglass White, a judge with sixteen years of experience on the Court. One of Taft's considerations was the ages of the two judges. In choosing the sixty-five-year-old White instead of the forty-eight-year-old Hughes, Taft might yet achieve his life's ambition, for he was twelve years younger than White and five years older than Hughes. When he signed White's commission, he said, "There is nothing I would have loved more than being chief justice of the United States. . . . I cannot help seeing the irony in the fact that I, who desired that office so much, should now be signing the commission of another man."[34]

After Taft left the presidency, he continued to long for the chief justiceship, which he believed might still be his, for he told friends and others that White was holding the office for him and that when the Republicans returned to power, White would relinquish it for him.[35] In 1920, Taft supported Warren G. Harding for the presidency and was delighted when the president-elect invited him to Marion, Ohio, for a talk. To Taft's surprise, Harding began talking about cabinet appointments. Hughes, said Harding, had been offered the State Department. "I thought," Taft responded, "Hughes would like to be Chief Justice." Harding said he thought not. "By the way," he added, "I want to ask you whether you would accept a position on the Supreme Court. Because if you would, I'll put you on that Court." Taft told Harding that had been life's ambition, but, he explained, "I am obliged that under the circumstances of having been President, and having appointed three of the present Bench and three others, and having protested against Brandeis, I could not accept any place but the Chief Justiceship."[36] Harding made no response, and Taft left Marion not knowing where he stood. Months passed while Harding remained silent and White made no move to retire. Discouraged, Taft wrote his wife on March 1, 1921: "[W]e may as well possess our souls with humility and suppress our ambitions."[37] Exactly a month later, Taft's friend Gus Karger wrote him from Washington that the matter that so concerned him, the chief justiceship, "rested in the lap of the gods or in the lap of Mr. White."[38] On May

19, White died, leaving the matter entirely "in the lap of the gods." Taft waited impatiently to hear from Harding, but no word came. Then, on June 22, Taft received a letter from Karger, who reported a meeting with Harding. "As I was about to leave, [Harding] stopped me," Karger wrote, "'Tell the Big Chief,' he said, 'that I'm going to put that over about the first of July.'"[39] Taft was elated; his life's ambition was now within his grasp. "Thank you, my dear Gus," he answered, "and God bless you."[40]

Contemporary perceptions of Taft in the legal community confirm that he was a feeling extrovert. "Taft," Felix Frankfurter recalled, "was instinctively genial, with great warmth, and a capacity to inspire camaraderie about him."[41] Others who knew Taft at the Supreme Court wrote that he had an unusually "genial personality . . . which to a large extent contributed to the harmonious working of the Court. Always cheerful in disposition, always beloved by those who came in contact with him, despite differences on questions of law and policy, he [was] able to achieve unison among members of the Court."[42]

Taft's colleagues agreed. When illness forced him retire from the Court in 1930, they sent him the following letter, which Oliver Wendell Holmes had drafted:

> DEAR CHIEF JUSTICE:
>
> We call you Chief Justice still, for we can not quickly give up the title by which we have known you for all these later years and which you have made so dear to us. We cannot let you leave us without trying to tell you how dear you made it. You came to us from achievements in other fields, and with the prestige of the illustrious place that you had lately held, and you showed in a new form your voluminous capacity for work and for getting work done, your humor that smoothed the rough places, your golden heart that has brought you love from every side, and, most of all, from your brethren whose tasks you have made happy and light. We grieve at your illness but your spirit has given life an impulse that will abide whether you are with us or are away.

Every associate justice signed the letter.[43]

Taft's correspondence also confirms that he was a feeling extrovert. Soon after his appointment to the Court, he wrote to his colleague John Hessin Clarke: "In my rusty shortcomings, I shall have to lean much on my colleagues in doing my share of the work. I hope you will be patient and forbearing."[44] James Clark McReynolds's inconsiderate behavior on the Court and his laziness irked Taft, but he restrained his feelings in order to remain on good terms with his crusty colleague. "I am old enough to know," he wrote one of his sons, "that the best way to get along with people with whom you have to live is always to restrain your impatience and consider that doubtless you have peculiarities that try other people."[45] He was also solicitous for the health of his colleagues, and when they were ill, he wrote them encouraging letters. When Sutherland was recovering from an illness at Johns Hopkins Hospital, Taft wrote, "My dear George: . . . Sanford has kept us advised of the messages which you have sent him, so we have followed you with loving interest. Now be a good boy and don't think that you are through until you are really beyond the probability of a retrograde movement."[46] Taft also attended to other personal needs of his colleagues. When Holmes's wife died, he made all arrangements for her funeral. When Taft and his colleagues concluded that Joseph McKenna, who was eighty-two, had to leave the Court because of senility, Taft tactfully and considerately persuaded him to do so. On McKenna's last day on the bench, Taft read a touching letter of farewell from the Court, which he had composed. In response, McKenna reminded his colleagues that he had served under three chief justices, Fuller, White, "and you, my dear Chief Justice." As McKenna finished his statement, the marshal put a basket of red roses in front of him. Such heartfelt gestures were natural for Taft.[47]

Taft had a special relationship with Willis Van Devanter, whom he had appointed to the Court. Less than a week after his nomination as chief justice, Taft wrote Van Devanter, "I am glad to come into close personal and official relations with you."[48] Taft confided to a friend that he did not know how he could get along without Van Devanter, for Van Devanter kept the Court consistent with itself and "his power of statement and his immense memory make him an antagonist who generally wins against all opposition."[49] In recommending Van Devanter for an honorary degree at Yale in 1926, Taft wrote, "The value of a judge in conference, especially in such a court as ours, never becomes known except to the members of the court. Now I don't hesitate to say that Mr. Justice Van Devanter is far and away the most valuable man in our court in all these qualities. We have other learned and valuable members, with special knowledge in particular subjects, but Van Devanter has knowledge in every subject that comes before us. . . . Van Devanter exercises more influence, a good deal, than any other member of the court, just because the members of the court know his qualities."[50] In other words, Van Devanter was the task leader of the Taft Court. Taft told his son Robert that Van Devanter's ability embarrassed him, and he wondered whether it would be better if Van Devanter ran the conference. But Taft was aware that he still had an important role to play in the conference, which was "to aid in deliberation when there is a difference of opinion," that is, to exercise social leadership.[51]

Van Devanter was a thinking introvert—an INTP—whose personality functions were thinking (dominant), intuition (auxiliary), sensation (tertiary), and feeling (inferior) and whose lifestyle preference was perceiving.[52] The main indicators of that type are reserve, detachment, aloofness (except with intimates), analytical orientation, self-containment, creativity, austerity, severity, an inclination to seek perfection, and a disinclination to praise others.[53]

According to Pedersen, INTPs make up 5 percent of the male population and 2 percent of the female population.[54] About 8 percent of INTPs are attracted to law as a career.[55]

INTPs are apt to be strategists because their dominant personality function is thinking, which, as Myers pointed out, involves predicting "the logical consequences of any choice or action. When you use thinking, you decide objectively, based on cause and effect."[56] Referring to INTPs, Pedersen added, "Theirs is a search for causal explanation, for why something is so. Their decisive natures are literally 'ruled' by logic, rationality and objectivity."[57]

One of Van Devanter's former professors at the Cincinnati Law School said that he had "a most excellent legal mind, which had the quality of being able to get to the nubbin of a question, to discover quickly the underlying principle of law, and to state his conclusions in clear, terse English."[58] Van Devanter graduated second in his class in 1881 at the age of twenty-two, a year after Taft had graduated from the same law school. By dint of his intelligence and ambition, Van Devanter rose quickly in the world of law and politics—Cheyenne city attorney at twenty-eight, member of the Wyoming territorial legislature and chairman of its judiciary committee at twenty-nine, chief justice of the Wyoming Territorial Supreme Court at thirty, assistant U.S. attorney general at forty, U.S Court of Appeals judge at forty-six, and U.S. Supreme Court associate justice at fifty-three. When Chief Justice White died on May 19, 1921, Justices McKenna, Day, Clarke, and McReynolds told Van Devanter that they "would be glad to see [him] appointed [chief justice]," and Senator Frank B. Kellogg told Van Devanter that he intended to recommend him for the position, but Van Devanter thought that he could not ethically use those statements to advance his candidacy and thus took no action in his own behalf.[59]

Van Devanter was a typical thinking introvert. His grandson, Willis II, said, "I remember that he was strict, very strict. Kids were to be seen and not heard. He didn't joke [or] take me up in his arms the way I do with my grandchildren." Van Devanter's granddaughter, Ethel Harris, added, "He did care, but he didn't show it. He didn't know how."[60] Herbert Wechsler, Harlan Fiske Stone's law clerk in the 1932 term, remembered Van Devanter as "a very reserved, almost remote, tightly disciplined, person."[61] Former U.S. attorney general William D. Mitchell, who had been Van Devanter's friend for thirty-eight years, said, "Anyone meeting him would have thought, 'Here is man with great physical vigor, a powerful intellect, and a driving power.' . . . Many thought him unusually austere, but he was not so with his friends. He was dignified and reserved, even in his family life. . . . On the bench, he exhibited on some occasions what might be described as withering severity towards lawyers appearing before him. But I learned . . . that in these instances the unfortunate object of his attentions invariably had been guilty of some impropriety or of misstatement,"[62] John W. Davis, who had argued many cases before Van Devanter, recalled that there was "a certain bluntness, almost gruffness" in his questions from the bench.[63] Charles Evans Hughes, who had been Van Devanter's friend for thirty-one years, recalled that he was "painstaking and exact" and "[h]is perspicacity and common sense made him a trusted advisor. . . . Chief Justice White leaned heavily on him and so did Chief Justice Taft."[64] U.S. attorney general Francis Biddle said, "Van Devanter was distinguished for two great judicial qualities. He had, in the first place, a remarkable sense of proportion and never pressed a principle to the extreme. . . . In the second place, he had a most orderly and analytical mind."[65]

Felix Frankfurter said that Van Devanter played "an important role in the history of the Court, though you cannot find it adequately reflected in the opinions written by him because he wrote so few. But Van Devanter was a man of great experience. . . . He had a very clear, lucid mind, the mind . . . of a great architect. He was a beautiful draftsman and an inventor of legal techniques who did much to bring about the reforms which were effectively accomplished by Taft as chief justice," which Taft generously acknowledged. "[W]hatever [Taft] did as chief justice," recalled Frankfurter, "was made possible by his great reliance on him whom he called his 'lord chancellor,' Mr. Justice Van Devanter."[66]

Van Devanter was also a perfectionist, which was one reason for his slowness in writing opinions. Struggling to write perfect opinions, he suffered "pen paralysis."[67] "[B]ut," as Alexander M. Bickel wrote, "he spoke authoritatively and lucidly in conference" and "wielded a decisive influence."[68]

He would sometimes rewrite his colleagues' opinions. Milton F. Handler, Stone's law clerk during the 1926 term, recalled that Van Devanter "would take a Stone opinion and virtually rewrite it from beginning to end."[69] Stone did not object, for he believed that Van Devanter's opinions "were models of judicial exposition, never discursive, redundant, nor sprinkled with irrelevant citations. Simple and direct in statement, orderly, lucid, complete, they gave a hint, but only a hint, of the painstaking care which in fact he gave to their preparation."[70] Taft expected Van Devanter to rewrite his opinions. In sending his opinions to Van Devanter, he would say, "[C]ut and slash as you think wise."[71]

It was almost inevitable that Taft and Van Devanter would share the Court's leadership—Taft as social leader and Van Devanter as task leader—for each needed what the other had. As Myers wrote, feeling types need thinking types to analyze, organize, find flaws, reform what needs reforming, hold consistently to a policy, weigh the law and evidence, fire people when necessary, and stand firm against opposition, while thinking types need feeling types to persuade, conciliate, forecast how others will feel, arouse enthusiasm, teach, sell, advertise, and appreciate the thinking types.[72]

Taft and Van Devanter were intimate friends. According to Nellie Taft's biographer, Carl Anthony, Taft's appointment as chief justice in 1921 "altered the relationship that he and Nellie had created in their immediate post–White House years. . . . Will's new job, in fact, permanently ended the active partnership of the Tafts. Nellie had not learned to appreciate or find in any way interesting the judicial process or the world of law. That her spouse was chief justice made no difference."[73] Perhaps that was a reason for Taft's intimate relationship with Van Devanter. When Taft was indisposed, Van Devanter was his alter ego in the Court, and during Taft's last illness, Van Devanter was the only member of the Court who was permitted to see him. Two months before Taft died, he wrote to Van Devanter: "Nobody will be permitted to call on me except you and Misch [Wendell Mischler, Taft's secretary] and Nellie. . . . Love to Mrs. Van Devanter and yourself. You are a thing of joy forever!"[74] Thus, Taft and Van Devanter's friendship was probably as important as their compatible personalities in explaining their joint leadership of the Court.[75]

Taft, knowing his death was imminent and assured that Hughes, whom he wanted to succeed him, would take his place, resigned from the Court on February 3, 1930. He died a month later at the age of seventy-one. Van Devanter retired from the Court on June 2, 1937, and died on February 8, 1941, at the age of eighty-one.

III. Charles Evans Hughes

Like Van Devanter, Hughes was a thinking introvert—an INTP—whose personality functions were thinking (dominant) intuition (auxiliary), sensation (tertiary), feeling (inferior) and whose lifestyle preference was perceiving. He was highly analytical, detached, self-contained, creative, perfectionistic, austere, aloof, and, at times, severe. According to Jeffery B. Morris, Hughes's reputation for austerity was a factor in Taft's choice of White as chief justice in 1910. "While Taft knew and liked both men," wrote Morris, "Hughes had a reputation for austerity, and White was an especially lovable personality."[76]

Hughes's personality was much like his mother's. "Mother," he recalled, "was . . . delicate, reserved, reflective, and cautious but of strong will. My father's impulses were subject to my mother's wise restraint. . . . My mother in her quiet way was as intellectually ambitious as my father. In her studies, she also found escape from the limitations of her environment. Taking full advantage of every educational opportunity that was open to her, she decided to become a teacher."[77] She put her pedagogical training to use in teaching Hughes while he was still a toddler. He learned to read at three and a half. Before he was six, he was reading and reciting verses from the New Testament, doing mental addition, and studying French and German. When he began the first grade, his education was so advanced that he insisted that formal schooling was for him a waste of time, and, at his request, he was home-schooled, mostly by his mother. Prior to his graduation from high school as salutatorian at the age of thirteen, he had only two and half years of formal education.[78] His mother influenced his character and personality as well as his mind. She instilled in him that he must always do what he believed was right, and whatever he undertook, he had to do thoroughly. When he was a fifteen-year-old college student, she wrote him, "How thankful we are for God's loving care over you & how pleased that you are attentive to your studies and doing well. *Be thorough*, BE THOROUGH, BE THOROUGH in all you undertake."[79] His study of law at Columbia Law School illustrates his thoroughness. During the day, he listened to regular law school lectures. At night, he attended private law "quizzes" and participated in moot court. As a senior, he attended lectures in courses he had taken the year before for purposes of review. His thoroughness paid off. He graduated at the top of his class and passed the New York bar examination with a grade of 99½ percent.[80] Thereafter, thorough preparation characterized his work as a lawyer, investigator, governor, associate justice, presidential candidate, secretary of state, and chief justice. At times, he drove himself to the edge of his endurance and would say to his wife, "It is too much. I simply cannot go on."[81] But after a night's rest, he would go on.[82]

Hughes was ambitious but not for any specific office. "I inherited a continuing ambition to excel in hard work," he told his biographer, Merlo J. Pusey, in 1945, "and to do my job as well as it could be done. I couldn't bear the thought of leaving undone anything which could be done or of not doing my particular work as well as it could be done within my limitations."[83] What explains his phenomenal rise in public life was his strong sense of duty. When nominated for the governorship of New York, he said he did not desire the office and would not be a candidate, but he did not refuse the nomination because that might put him "forever beyond the possibility of rendering public service." Upon his nomination, he wired party leaders: "I shall accept the nomination without pledge other than to do my duty according to my conscience. If elected, it will be my ambition to give the State a sane, efficient and honorable administration, free from the taint of bossism or of servitude to any private interest."[84] Hughes also accepted the Republican presidential nomination in 1916 out of a sense of duty.[85] His strong claims of duty did not, however, deprive him of the satisfaction of a job well done or the thrill of undertaking a challenging assignment.[86]

When White died in 1921, Hughes said that he did not want to be appointed chief justice because it was his duty to continue as secretary of state, and besides he thought that Harding had promised the place to Taft. In 1930, when Hoover offered to appoint him as chief justice to replace Taft, Hughes demurred on the ground that at the age of sixty-seven he was too old. Rejecting Hughes's demurrer, Hoover strongly urged him to accept.[87] "The main thrust of [Hoover's] argument," wrote Pusey, "was that the country would expect the position to go to Hughes and that it was Hughes's duty to accept it."[88] Finally, Hughes acquiesced after Hoover assured him that he believed (wrongly as it turned out) that there would be no fight in the Senate.[89]

When I asked Hughes's daughter Elizabeth Hughes Gossett in 1969 to describe her father's personality, she said that he was "a loving father." Outside of the family, however, he was "aloof, very reserved. But he was intellectual. He didn't mind being by himself. He loved to read. He was aloof in that he didn't make friends easily, [but] he did have some close friends. . . . He was a humble man. He never talked about himself. . . . He was very objective. He just didn't get involved in personal antagonisms or anything like that. . . . He saw both sides. . . . But Father could make up his mind.

He was very leonine. He was a very strong character—very forceful. . . . I don't think it is right to call him a cold pillar of strength. He was very warm. His blue eyes lit up. And he was funny. He told the most wonderful stories—in dialect. And he'd laugh until he'd cry. The tears would just roll down his cheeks. . . . [Some people] were scared of him, I imagine. He was so reserved, so overpowering—his looks, you know, a Jacobean. He was so handsome with that beard and all. He had an overpowering presence."[90]

Hughes's childhood experiences reinforced his introverted personality. "As I had no brother or sister," he recalled, "I learned to play alone."[91] Without playmates, he lived mostly in the adult world of his parents. Concerned about his lack of companions, they discussed the possibly of adopting a child. Having overheard their conversation, he objected. His education, he said, was more important than companionship.[92] He also lived in the world of his imagination. One of his favorite boyhood pastimes was imaginary travel. He would mount his hobbyhorse and set forth on extensive journeys. "I loved to get hold of a travel book," he recalled, "and pretend, with the book before me, to go with my stout steed from place to place. Especially helpful in these excursions were Thomson's *Land and the Book*, descriptive of Palestine with inset pictures, and I traveled up and down the land, reading the descriptions to aid my imagination, as they seemed very familiar in view of my Bible lessons."[93] As a youth, he wandered the streets of New York City, a solitary onlooker, walking from Great Jones Street to the Battery and on to Central Park, Broadway, the Bowery, Chatham Street, Cherry Hill, and Stuyvesant Square. When he became tired, he would "jump on the tail-end of an empty truck and ride joyously with dangling legs."[94]

Scholars agree that self-sufficiency and detachment were important elements of Hughes's personality. "Hughes," wrote the editors of his *Autobiographical Notes*, "was unusually self-sufficient, and his relations with others, with only a few exceptions, were characterized by detachment."[95] Hughes's biographer, Pusey, explained Hughes's detachment as follows: "Personal friendships were less important to him than his work, which absorbed most of the time that other men gave to casual friendly intercourse. And he felt no need to seek personal understanding, sympathy, or solace outside his home."[96] In her psychobiography of Hughes as secretary of state, Betty Glad emphasized his detachment. "Hughes's tight control, his perfectionism, his emotional detachment—all these indicate," wrote Glad, "that he did not wish to explore the darker sides of either his self or his world."[97]

There is less agreement as to Hughes's intellectual ingenuity and creativity. John Lord O'Brien said that Hughes was a "creative genius."[98] Glad believed that Hughes "was simply a hero of the times, an exemplar of the virtues of his age—not a creative genius."[99] Zechariah Chafee, Jr., thought Hughes had a powerful mind that was not exploratory like the minds of Holmes and Cardozo.[100] Hughes, however, demonstrated ingenuity, creativity, and even genius in running the Court. One of his innovations was the special list to expedite the disposition of certiorari petitions and jurisdictional statements. Further, few if any of the chief justices presided in open court with greater grandeur than Hughes. "You know, he stood only about five feet ten," said one of his former law clerks, "but when he presided over the Court, he was ten feet tall."[101] To see Hughes preside, said Frankfurter, "was like witnessing Toscanini lead an orchestra."[102] In conference, wrote John P. Frank, Hughes's skill "reached the point of genius."[103] "Hughes," Alex Bickel observed, "led the Court, as not all Chief Justices have done. He invested with the authority of his own person the uncertain perquisites of the office of primus inter pares, and he did it in a time of crisis, when even the center of the storm could not remain quiet."[104]

Social psychologists would have called Hughes "a great-man leader" because he exercised both the task and social leadership.[105] Such leaders are rare. In the entire history of the Court, there have been only two or three. Hughes had a personality that suited him well for both task leadership and permitted him to exercise social leadership. As Edward F. Pritchard, Jr., Frankfurter's law clerk during the 1939 term, aptly put it, "He ran the Court with a steel fist in a velvet glove."[106] In the conference, his colleagues saw a cool, aloof, detached, severe chief justice. William O. Douglas recalled that Hughes "was a very formidable man. He looked like Jehovah with his beard. He had a very cold eye if he wanted to make it such. He could be very, very severe or very, very warm, but in conference he was always very, very severe."[107] Owen J. Roberts recalled that Hughes "was an intense man. When he had serious business to transact, he allowed no consideration to interfere with his operations. He was so engrossed in the vital issue that he had no time for lightness or pleasantry."[108] Roberts's statement described Hughes's responses to his colleagues' draft opinions, which he seldom praised, as well as his conference behavior.[109] But Roberts acknowledged that outside of the conference, Hughes was warm, friendly, genial, considerate, and sympathetic.[110] Felix Frankfurter said that Hughes "was genial though not promiscuous, full of fun and whimsy, a delightful tease and sparkling storyteller."[111] Holmes wrote a friend in 1930: "Hughes is an old friend of mine and very hard worker. He can tell a story and say a funny thing on occasion as well as do his job."[112] Douglas said that Hughes had "a very keen sense of humor" and a "very bright twinkle in his eye that very seldom appeared during the conference." The Hughes conference, Douglas added, was "a very quick, alert, hard-working process rather than a relaxed conversation."[113]

Did Hughes consciously simulate warmth to ingratiate himself with his colleagues? Harold D. Lasswell has written that persons with detached characters often simulate warmth. What such behavior signifies, he explained, "is simply that intelligent persons can recognize the signs of affective expectation in others and play up, much as a deaf person learns to read lips and to mingle smoothly with those who are not hard of hearing." From detached characters, he added, "useful judges, arbitrators, conciliators, diplomatic negotiators and scientists can be recruited."[114] The simulation hypothesis is plausible, but more plausible is the hypothesis that Hughes's warmth was genuine but situational, that is, it depended on closeness of his relationships and the kind of activities in which he was involved.

Hughes's daughter Elizabeth said that when he was with his family he was "very warm," "funny," and "told the most wonderful stories," but outside his family circle he was "aloof [and] reserved."[115] In other words, he behaved like an extrovert in one situation and like an introvert in another.[116] That is not unusual for thinking introverts, explained Myers, for they are "outwardly quiet, reserved, detached, perhaps even aloof *except with intimates*"[117] (my emphasis). That would explain Hughes's warmth and sociability with his personal family and his judicial family in situations other than the conference and assessment of his colleagues' opinions. Hughes did not make friends easily, but, as his daughter noted, "he did have some close friends."[118] Three of them—Holmes, Van Devanter, and Brandeis—were on the Supreme Court when he rejoined it in 1930.[119] He was especially close to Holmes (there were tears in his eyes when he told Holmes that he had to retire),[120] and it was no accident that he chose Van Devanter and Brandeis to cosign his letter to the Senate Judiciary Committee in the Court packing fight in 1937. Further, he developed close friendships with two young colleagues: Roberts and Douglas. Roberts said that Hughes was like a father or older brother to him, and Douglas said that he had "warm friendship" with Hughes that developed into "almost a father-son relationship."[121] Except for Stone, Hughes had positive relations with all his colleagues, and he was unaware of Stone's negative feelings.[122] In his *Autobiographical Notes*, Hughes wrote, "My relations with all the Justices—both with the seniors and those who came to the Court in the later years—were most happy, and whatever disagreements there were from time to time did not affect our friendship."[123] Jung would have understood why Hughes's friends on the Court were drawn to him. The introverted thinking type, wrote Jung, is "taciturn," but "the better one knows him, the more favorable one's judgment becomes, and his closest friends value his intimacy very highly."[124] Thus Hughes's personality contributed to his social leadership.

Hughes's skill in presiding over the conference also contributed to his social leadership. In conferences, Frankfurter recalled, Hughes "struck the pitch, as it were, for the orchestra. He guided discussion by opening up lines for it to travel, focusing on essentials, evoking candid exchange on subtle and complex issues, and avoiding redundant talk. He never checked free debate, but the atmosphere which he created, and the moral authority which he exerted, inhibited irrelevance, repetition, and fruitless discussion. He was a master of timing: he knew when discussion should be deferred and when brought to issue. He also showed uncommon resourcefulness in drawing elements of agreement out of differences and thereby narrowing, if not always escaping, conflicts."[125]

Hughes's detachment also contributed to his social leadership. As Frankfurter wrote, "He knew when a case was over; he had no lingering afterthoughts born of a feeling of defeat, and thereby avoided the festering of cleavages. Intellectual issues were dealt with by him as such. As a result, differences in opinion did not arouse personal sensitiveness. Partly a disciplined mind, partly long experience at the bar, made him treat a case that was over as over whether victory or defeat fell to his views. This capacity for detachment also reflected his keen sense of humor, which it often pleased him to conceal; partly such detachment must be ascribed to great conservation of energy that saved him from crying over spilt milk."[126] Illustrating Frankfurter's statement, Pusey wrote, "One day the court rejected a decision proposed by Hughes just before the judges went to lunch. Without once adverting to the case, the Chief Justice sat by the junior member who had taken the lead in opposing his view and chatted in the most fascinating manner throughout the lunch period. Grousing over a defeat was as foreign to his nature as gloating over a victory."[127]

Hughes retired from the Court on July 1, 1941, at the age of seventy-nine, because, he said, he could no longer keep up the pace he had set for himself as chief justice.[128] He was the first chief justice in the Court's history to retire. John Jay and Oliver Ellsworth resigned; John Rutledge, who had a recess appointment, failed Senate confirmation; John Marshall, Roger Brooke Taney, Salmon Portland Chase, Morrison Remick Waite, Melville Weston Fuller, and Edward Douglass White all died in office; and Taft resigned a month before his death. Hughes enjoyed seven years of retirement and died on August 27, 1948, at the age of eighty-six.

IV. Harlan Fiske Stone

Harlan Fiske Stone was an intuitive extrovert—an ENTP—whose personality functions were intuition (dominant), thinking (auxiliary), feeling (tertiary), and sensation (inferior) and whose lifestyle preference was perception.[129] The main indicators for this type are inspiration, independence, ingenuity, originality, imagination, ambition, gregariousness, versatility, enthusiasm, loquaciousness, impersonal relations with people, and a penchant for a series of careers or projects.[130]

According to Pedersen, ENTPs make up 6 percent of the male population and 3 percent of the female population.[131] About 8 percent of ENTPs are attracted to law as a career.[132]

Stone resembled his mother physically, temperamentally, and intellectually. Mason described her as "large of frame and feature," "a little on the fleshy side," and "forceful and energetic."[133] A former schoolteacher, she insisted on "intellectual discipline" in her children, which she instilled with mental drills before they were old enough for school.[134] Stone's father, a farmer, had attended public schools and a private academy, but "he was not of a scholarly turn of mind."[135] Stone's parents were strict disciplinarians. "If the boy's offense was serious," wrote Mason, "the culprit was led off to the barn and punished with a horse whip. . . . In later years, [Stone] insisted that his father's harshness had been wholly salutary; it made 'a man' of him. The new generation lacks courtesy, he said, because they were not 'licked enough.' 'When I was a boy I received some mighty valuable whalings, especially when the Governor thought I was not sufficiently polite. That's one thing that makes me so humble nowadays."[136] Stone probably uttered the last sentence tongue-in-cheek, for some of his colleagues thought he was vain.[137] Stone's unruliness continued into his college years at the Massachusetts Agricultural College, which expelled him for brawling. Contrite, he applied to Amherst, which accepted him and gave him an opportunity to prove his mettle.[138] After teaching science in a high school for a year, he went on to Columbia Law School and was a success in a series of careers—lawyer, adjunct law professor, law professor, law school dean, Wall Street lawyer, U.S. attorney general, and Supreme Court associate justice.

A typical intuitive extrovert, Stone was gregarious. According to Alfred McCormack, Stone's law clerk during the 1925 term, Stone was "exceptionally gregarious."[139] But there was an impersonal quality in his relationships with his colleagues and law clerks. Herbert Wechsler, Stone's law clerk during the 1932 term, wrote that Stone "was far from [being] compassionate or warm, but neither intellectually nor socially was he a snob."[140] Douglas recalled that Stone was inclined to be "garrulous" and "gossipy." "[He] relished saying something snide about someone. He was not malicious . . . but he just talked too much," which is to say that, like other intuitive extroverts, he was loquacious.[141]

In January 1929, Stone asked John Bassett Moore, his former Columbia colleague, for "friendly advice" whether he should consider leaving the Court to take the post of secretary of state, a move he believed could lead to the presidency. Moore advised his friend against it, saying, "I hope to see you Chief Justice rather than President."[142] Stone agreed and focused his ambition on becoming chief justice. He had good reason to believe that he would be nominated chief justice, for he had been prominently mentioned in the press in 1929 as Taft's successor, and President Hoover was a close friend. About ten days before Taft resigned, Hoover invited Stone to the White House to discuss candidates for the chief justiceship. At the time, Stone believed he was a candidate, for Hoover wanted to know what he thought of Calvin Coolidge for appointment as an associate justice, which suggested Hoover was considering promoting Stone to the center chair and appointing Coolidge in his place. When Hoover asked him what he thought of Hughes as chief justice, Stone said that he was against his appointment because Hughes was too old, had represented corporations, and had left the Court to run for the presidency. Stone urged Hoover to appoint Benjamin N. Cardozo.[143] According to Stone's secretary, Gertrude Jenkins, Hoover's appointment of Hughes as chief justice was a "terrific disappointment" for Stone, because he felt that he "was entitled to the post and expected it."[144] Howard C. Westwood, Stone's law clerk during the 1933 term, shared Miss Jenkins' view. "I am sure that from a few things that he told me," wrote Westwood in 1947, "that he was deeply disappointed."[145]

Stone disliked Hughes.[146] He privately criticized Hughes's presentation of cases in conference (particularly his failure to allow more time for discussion), his opinion assignments (he claimed that Hughes kept the "plums" for himself), and his failure in the Court-packing fight to consult all the justices before sending his letter in behalf of the Court to the Senate Judiciary Committee.[147] Stone once told a colleague he had dissented in a case because he had not been allowed to present his views in conference.[148] Feeling isolated and unhappy in the early 1930s, he considered returning to the practice of law.[149] As for succeeding Hughes as chief justice, he believed his chances were at best slight. In 1941, when Hughes retired, Stone discounted talk that he might become chief justice, for he believed that Attorney General Robert H. Jackson, whose ambition for the post was as strong as Taft's, would be nominated. But FDR, following the advice of Hughes and Frankfurter, chose Stone over Jackson.[150]

Unlike Taft, Stone did not aspire to the chief justiceship because of any interest in judicial administration. In a letter to a former law school colleague who had commiserated with him when he failed to receive Hoover's nomination as chief justice in 1930, Stone wrote, "After all, being Chief Justice of the Supreme Court is a good deal like being Dean of the Law School—he has to do things the janitor will not do. The post never enlarges the occupant's individual capacity for judicial work, and it may diminish it."[151] Stone expressed a similar view in 1941. "I am much more interested," he wrote, "in studying the cases and writing opinions than I am in doing administrative work of any kind."[152]

Given his personality, it is not surprising that Stone, as an associate justice, enjoyed drawing on his vast knowledge of the law and solving intuitively tough legal and constitutional problems. Holmes had recognized intuition as a source of judicial decision making when he wrote in *Lochner v. New York*, 198 U.S. at 78 (1903): "The decision will depend on judgment or intuition more subtle than any articulate major premise."

Alfred McCormack described Stone's intuitive approach to decision making in a 1926 letter to William O. Douglas, who was then teaching part-time at Columbia Law School. McCormack wrote, "Well, I hope you continue to have success in your teaching. It's great stuff, and the judge [Stone] thinks it's a good foundation for practice. From what I see of him, the way he thinks, and the excellent legal background he has, I should say that it is. He's a great man for hunches. He doesn't carry much loose information in his head. He has anything but an encyclopedic mind, but, by golly, when he sees a legal proposition he can *feel* (McCormack's emphasis) whether it is right or wrong, good or bad, accurate or inaccurate."[153]

"Stone would dictate his opinions," Douglas recalled, "and when he stated a principle of law he would write in parentheses 'cite cases.' The draft would go to the clerk, who would then look for the cases supporting Stone's position."[154] Stone did that in *Ex parte Quirin*, 317 U.S. 1 (1942). While working on the Court's opinion in that case, he wrote to his law clerks: "I am troubled some by the statement from Hall [author of an international law treatise] as to the use of the uniform. . . . I have written the opinion on the assumption that the law is the other way as I think it ought to be."[155]

Stone's great intuitive contributions to constitutional law were his theory of judicial review and his preferred-freedoms doctrine.[156] According to Samuel J. Konefsky, who wrote a book about Stone, his theory of judicial review requires judges to exercise self-restraint in cases involving economic legislation, provided there is a rational basis for such legislation, but the theory allows, indeed encourages, searching judicial scrutiny of legislation "growing out of attempts to curtail fundamental civil rights, particularly the four freedoms of the First Amendment."[157] How did Stone arrive at his theory? Konefsky did not directly answer that question, but Charles Beard, in a prefatory note to Konefsky's book, wrote that the answer lay in Stone's "character," that is, his personality. "It has been said," Beard explained, "that a great man is someone who first does something in the nature of greatness. If this maxim is true, there are few great men in history. On my part, I am inclined to the opinion that a great person is one who discovers [that is, intuits] something that should have long have been obvious and states it with such force and clarity, in favorable circumstances, that they who run and read are astounded and cry out 'of course.'"[158] "Nothing delighted Stone more," wrote Mason, "than to take a morass of conflicting decisions, sort them out, and then restate the rule with reasons having solid substance. His skillful trimming, elaborating, and blending of the Brandeis and Holmes approach makes him one of the creative judges of our time."[159]

Some believed that Stone was a great associate justice because his opinions passed muster not only with his judicial brethren but also with his former academic colleagues, whose approval and praise he cherished.[160] As an associate justice, he was a scholar on the bench, an astute judicial craftsman who was able to justify his intuitive decisions.

Stone's performance as chief justice was another matter. His conference behavior was the antithesis of Hughes's. Stone conducted the conference like an academic seminar or a faculty meeting. All sides of issues were explored, every justice had an opportunity to express his views fully, and there were no time limits. Things soon got out of hand. Justices spoke out of turn, debate became heated, tensions rose, tempers were ruffled, talk went on and on, and Stone failed to calm things down or cut off debate. Instead, he joined in it with alacrity, answering each justice's arguments and counterarguments.[161] "Stone," recalled Douglas, "was one of most argumentative justices in my time."[162] The Stone conferences went on interminably. The Saturday session often continued over into Monday, Tuesday, and even Wednesday. "We were in continual conference," recalled Douglas, "battling every single point, big ones, little ones. It became . . . a great ordeal."[163] Other justices also criticized Stone, including Black and Roberts.[164] Frankfurter said that Stone was "a terrible chief justice . . . inept and lumbering."[165] Exasperated, Frank Murphy blurted out after one conference, "What we need is a new chief justice!"[166]

Stone failed as a social leader largely because he lacked Taft's likeability and restraint, and he failed as a task leader largely because he lacked Hughes's detachment and control of the conference.

Like some intuitive extroverts, Stone's need for affirmation and praise was great.[167] Frankfurter said that Stone was a man of "egregious vanity [who] needed constant petting and who was greatly influenced by praise."[168] John P. Frank, Black's law clerk during the 1942 term, made a similar observation. "Stone," he wrote, "was a man of great ability but also of great vanity, a man of great charm, but also of considerable testiness."[169] Douglas said that it was a joke in the Court that if Stone's law clerk missed citing one of Stone's opinions, he committed a "capital offense," and, as a result, the "proclivity to cite one's own opinions came to be known as 'Stone's disease.'"[170] Mason acknowledged Stone's vanity. "The human streak of vanity," he wrote, "was marked in him. 'A man's got to live with himself,' [Stone] would often say. But he cherished the discerning acclaim of others and loved admiration, attention, and praise. The flattery of classmates . . . showered on him for nearly half a century gave him genuine pleasure. But it rarely trapped him into a false estimate of his own powers or moved him to make a rash decision or take a false hope."[171] That may be, but Stone's vanity nonetheless contributed to his failure as a social leader.

So did his lack of restraint. According to John P. Frank's reading of Mason's biography of Stone, "at one time or another, Stone condemned almost every colleague he had between 1926 and 1946, except Holmes, Sanford (whose presence he did not seem to have noticed), Brandeis, and Douglas—and he got off on the wrong foot with Brandeis."[172] Stone not only criticized his colleagues; he sometimes criticized them indiscreetly to journalists, who published his remarks without attribution.[173] Douglas thought that Stone's published statement casting aspersions on Black's judicial ability might not have been "exactly libelous, [but] it was a very distorted, cruel caricature of a very brilliant, able man. But, again, whether that was the reason that Stone and Black were not close, I don't know. I think it was."[174] As chief justice, Stone got along superficially with his colleagues, but he had no friends in the Court, except perhaps Douglas, who had been his student at Columbia.

Stone's lack of detachment also stemmed from his personality. In acrimonious conference debates, he usually did not remain above the fray so that he could later reconcile differences.[175] Further, for Stone, unlike Hughes, a case was not over after the Court voted on it. At times, defeat in conference festered in his mind, and on at least one occasion he made sarcastic remarks to a colleague who had not voted with him.[176] On another occasion when the Court voted 5 to 4 in a case, Stone looked down the conference table at Douglas and said: "Douglas, I know why some of my brethren went astray. But, for the life of me, I can't understand your vote in this case." "Chief," answered Douglas, "all the law I ever knew, I learned from you." "By God," Stone replied without missing a beat, "You never learned that from me!"[177]

Stone's personality not only explains his failure as chief justice; it also explains his success as an associate justice. Even his critics acknowledged his insightful contributions, though they were unaware that those contributions stemmed largely from his intuitive personality. "If vanity, garrulity, and weaknesses were Stone's personal deficiencies as a judge," wrote Philip B. Kurland, Frankfurter's law clerk during the 1945 term, "they were more than compensated for by other great judicial capacities."[178] And the Harvard constitutional-law quadrumvirate—Paul A. Freund, Arthur E. Sutherland, Mark DeWolfe Howe, and Ernest J. Brown—wrote, "Throughout [Stone's] judicial career he endeavored to look beyond those formulas which offer indecisive comforts of familiarity to considerations of a more conclusive sort."[179]

Recently, Justice John Paul Stevens gave this estimate of Stone: "Stone was unquestionably a great jurist and a great American. There were, however, two imperfections in his career that must be acknowledged. Though a thorough and brilliant scholar, he was an exceptionally poor presiding officer during the Court's deliberations in conference, which sometimes consumed more than two days. And his two most significant wartime opinions—*Ex parte Quirin*, rejecting challenges to their death sentences by putative German saboteurs who had voluntarily surrendered to the FBI, and in *In re Yamashita*, upholding a military tribunal's death sentence imposed on a Japanese general because of atrocities committed by soldiers under his command—may have bent the rule of law in response to perceived military necessity. As Justice Antonin Scalia observed in his dissenting opinion in *Hamdi v. Rumsfeld* (2004), 'The [*Quirin*] case was not this Court's finest hour.'"[180]

On April 22, 1946, three months after the Court decided *Yamashita*, Stone suffered a cerebral hemorrhage in open Court and died the same day at the age of seventy-three.

V. Conclusions

The personalities of chief justices largely explain their successes or failures as social and task leaders. Taft was a great social leader mostly because he was an able feeling extrovert, and he succeeded as a chief justice because he shared leadership with Van Devanter, a task leader who was a thinking introvert. Hughes was a great task leader mostly because he was an able thinking introvert, and he succeeded as a chief justice because he was also an adequate social leader. Stone was a successful associate justice largely because he was an able intuitive extrovert who used his intuition to make important contributions to constitutional law, but, as chief justice, he failed mostly because his personality did not suit him well for either social leadership or task leadership.

This study also illustrates the significance of friendship in the Supreme Court. Taft was a successful social leader largely because of his friendships in the Court, and he was a successful chief justice largely because of his close friendship with Van Devanter, who was his coleader. Hughes's success as a social leader was due largely to his close friendships with Holmes, Van Devanter, Brandeis, Roberts, and Douglas. It is telling that Stone as chief justice had no friends on the Court, except perhaps Douglas.

More than fifty years ago, I concluded the paper this chapter revisits with John Morley's statement that the task of the political writer is not simply to describe governmental institutions but to "penetrate to the secret of their functions."[181] That is a difficult task, but I hope this study and its predecessor have contributed toward that end.

NOTES

1. C. G. Jung, "Psychological Types," in *Collected Works of C.G. Jung*, trans. R.F.C. Hull, vol. 6: 1970–1979 (Princeton: Princeton University Press, 1979); Isabel Briggs Myers with Peter B. Myers, *Gifts Differing* (Palo Alto, CA: Consulting Psychologists Press, 1980). I considered using the Five-Factor Trait model, which is presently dominant in psychological studies of personality, but I chose instead the Jung-Myers theory for three reasons. First, the Five-Factor Trait model is a taxonomy, not a coherent theory. Second, four of the factors in the Five-Factor Trait model—Extroversion, Agreeableness, Conscientiousness, and Openness—are clusters of traits that are similar to four major elements of the Jung-Myers theory. See Oliver P. John, Laura P. Naumann, and Christopher J. Soto, "Paradigm Shift to the Integrative Five Trait Taxonomy," in *Handbook of Personality: Theory and Research*, ed. Oliver P. John, Richard W. Robins, and Lawrence A. Pervin (New York: Guilford Press, 2008), 115, table 4-1. Third, the Jung-Myers theory is compatible with the social-psychological theory of leadership I used in my 1960 APSA paper.

2. Myers, *Gifts Differing*, 7.

3. Myers, quoted in Loren E. Pedersen, *Sixteen Men: Understanding Masculine Personality Types* (Boston: Shambhala, 1993), 20.

4. Ibid., 21.

5. Myers, *Gifts Differing*, 9, 75. For an explanation of Jung's model without Myers's adaptations, see Daryl Sharp, *Personality Types: Jung's Model of Typology* (Toronto: Inner City Books, 1987).

6. Myers, *Gifts Differing*, chap. 9.

7. Ibid., 93; Pedersen, *Sixteen Men*, 154.

8. Pedersen, *Sixteen Men*, 156; Isabel Briggs Myers and Mary H. McCaulley, *Manual: A Guide to Development and Use of the Myers-Briggs Type Indicator* (Palo Alto, CA: Consulting Psychologists Press, 1989), 282.

9. Ibid., 283.

10. Alice Roosevelt Longworth, *Crowded Hours* (New York: Scribners, 1933), 69.

11. Judith Icke Anderson, *William Howard Taft: An Intimate History* (New York: W. W. Norton, 1981), 21–22; Carl Sferrazza Anthony, *Nellie Taft: The Unconventional First Lady* (New York: William Morrow, 2005), 61; James David Barber, *Politics by Humans: Research on American Leadership* (Durham, NC: Duke University Press, 1988), 98.

12. Taft to H. S. Pritchett, April 23, 1923, Library of Congress, Manuscript Division, William Howard Taft Papers.

13. Helen Herron Taft, *Recollections of the Full Years* (New York: Dodd, Meade, 1915), 18.

14. Horace Dutton Taft, *Memories and Opinions* (New York: Macmillan, 1942), 10, 115.

15. See Henry F. Pringle, *The Life and Times of William Howard Taft: A Biography*, 2 vols. (New York: Farrar & Rinehart, 1939), 1:47–53, which are the opening pages of a chapter titled "Reluctant Feet."

16. Ibid., 2:47.

17. Anderson, *William Howard Taft*, 41.

18. Alphonso Taft to Morrison R. Waite, Dec. 7, 1874, Library of Congress, Manuscript Division, Morrison R. Waite Papers.

19. Taft to Alphonso Taft, July 20, 1889, Taft Papers.

20. Taft to Alphonso Taft, Aug. 10, 1889, Sept. 14, 1889, ibid.

21. Taft to Joseph B. Foraker, Sept. 17, 1889, Library of Congress, Manuscript Division, Joseph B. Foraker Papers.

22. Taft to Joseph B. Foraker, Sept. 25, 1889, ibid.

23. Joseph B. Foraker to Taft, Jan. 31, 1891, Taft Papers.

24. Alphonso Taft to Taft, Feb. 1, 1891, ibid.

25. Alphonso Taft to Salmon P. Chase, Dec, 6, 1864, Library of Congress, Manuscript Division, Salmon P. Chase Papers.

26. Anderson, *William Howard Taft*, 260.

27. Ibid., 95–96.

28. Taft to Helen H. Taft, May 16, 1891, Taft Papers.

29. Ibid.

30. Taft to Helen H. Taft, March 25, 1896, ibid.

31. Pringle, *The Life and Times of William Howard Taft*, 1:161.

32. John Hays Hammond, *The Autobiography of John Hays Hammond*, 2 vols. (New York: Farrar & Rinehart, 1935), 2:532. See also Pringle, *Life and Times of William Howard Taft*, 1:313.

33. Taft to W. W. Merrill, Dec. 2, 1908, Taft Papers.

34. Daniel S. McHargue, "President Taft's Appointments to the Supreme Court," *Journal of Politics* 12 (1950): 478–79.

35. Taft to Helen H. Taft, Dec. 26, 1920; Taft to J. M. Dickinson, April 25, 1921, Taft Papers.

36. Taft to Helen H. Taft, Dec. 26, 1920, ibid.

37. Taft to Helen H. Taft, March 1, 1921, ibid.

38. Gus Karger to Taft, April 1, 1920, ibid.

39. Gus Karger to Taft, June 21, 1921, ibid.

40. Taft to Gus Karger, June 22, 1921, ibid.

41. Felix Frankfurter, "Chief Justices I Have Known," in *Of Law and Men: Papers and Addresses of Felix Frankfurter*, ed. Philip Elman (New York: Harcourt, Brace, 1956), 130.

42. Gregory and Charlotte A. Hankin, *Progress of the Law in the Supreme Court, 1929–1930* (Washington: Legal Research Service, 1939), 6.

43. 280 U.S. at v (1930).

44. Taft to Clarke, July 8, 1921, John Hessin Clarke Papers, Case Western Reserve University Library.

45. Taft to Robert A. Taft, Jan. 10, 1926, Taft Papers.

46. Taft to Sutherland, Nov. 3, 1927, Library of Congress, Manuscript Division, George Sutherland Papers.

47. David J. Danelski, "A Supreme Court Justice Steps Down," *Yale Review* 54 (1965): 411–25.

48. Taft to Van Devanter, July 6, 1921, Library of Congress, Manuscript Division, Willis Van Devanter Papers.

49. Taft to William Lyon Phelps, May 30, 1927, Taft Papers.

50. Pringle, *Life and Times of William Howard Taft*, 2:971. Brandeis had a similar view of Van Devanter. Though the two judges were poles apart ideologically, "Brandeis respected Van Devanter for his learning and experience, particularly in the area of federal jurisdiction and procedure. . . . "[O]n Van Devanter's birthday in one of the mid-thirty years, Brandeis wrote him a congratulatory note saying: 'Take the best care of yourself. The Court never needed you more.'" Paul A. Freund, interview with Katie Louchheim, in Katie Louchheim, ed., *The Making of the New Deal: The Insiders Speak* (Cambridge, MA: Harvard University Press, 1983), 99. Freund was Brandeis's law clerk during the 1932 term.

51. Taft to Robert A. Taft, Oct. 23, 1927, Taft Papers.

52. Myers and McCaulley, *Manual*, 18.

53. Myers, *Gifts Differing*, 89–90, 92–93; Pedersen, *Sixteen Men*, 106–7.

54. Ibid., 208.

55. Myers and McCaulley, *Manual*, 286. Of those choosing law as a career, approximately 42 percent have N and T as two of their four personality functions. Myers, *Gifts Differing*, 49.

56. Pedersen, *Sixteen Men*, 20.

57. Ibid., 58.

58. Quoted in the *Saturday Evening Post*, March 18, 1911, 25, Scrapbook, Van Devanter Papers.

59. Van Devanter to John C. Pollock, May 26, 1921, Van Devanter Papers.

60. Quoted in Dana Bieber, "Don't Mess with Willis," http://www.madeinwyoming.net/profiles/van.php.

61. Herbert Weschler, interview with Katie Louchheim, in *Making of the New Deal*, 53.

62. 316 U.S. at xvii–xviii (1942).

63. Ibid. at xxvi.

64. David J. Danelski and Joseph S. Tulchin, eds., *The Autobiographical Notes of Charles Evans Hughes* (Cambridge, MA: Harvard University Press, 1973), 171.

65. 316 U.S. at xxxi–xxxii (1942).

66. Frankfurter, "Chief Justices I Have Known," 119.

67. Danelski and Tulchin, *Autobiographical Notes of Charles Evans Hughes*, 171.

68. Alexander M. Bickel, *The Unpublished Opinions of Mr. Justice Brandeis: The Supreme Court at Work* (Cambridge, MA: Harvard University Press, 1957), 248.

69. Milton F. Handler, "Clerking for Harlan Fiske Stone," *Journal of Supreme Court History Yearbook* (1995): 119. Van Devanter acknowledged that he took "responsibility for the opinions of [colleagues] and worked on them." Van Devanter to John C. Pollock, June 7, 1921, Van Devanter Papers.

70. 86 L. Ed. 1791 (1942).

71. Taft to Van Devanter, Dec. 7, 1921, Van Devanter Papers.

72. Myers, *Gifts Differing*, 121.

73. Anthony, *Nellie Taft*, 375.

74. Taft to Van Devanter, Jan. 7, 1930, Taft Papers. Taft's half-brother Harry wrote Van Devanter soon after Taft's death: "I appreciate your devotion to my brother, particularly during the early stages of his sickness." Harry W. Taft to Van Devanter, March 20, 1930, Van Devanter Papers.

75. It also partly explains their effectiveness in securing the nomination of Pierce Butler to the Supreme Court in 1922. See David J. Danelski, *A Supreme Court Justice Is Appointed* (New York: Random House, 1964), 49–55.

76. Jeffrey B. Morris, "Chief Justice Edward Douglass White and President Taft's Court," *Supreme Court Historical Yearbook* (1982): 36.

77. Danelski and Tulchin, *Autobiographical Notes of Charles Evans Hughes*, 3, 7.

78. Ibid., xiii–xiiv, 14–16, 18–19.

79. Merlo J. Pusey, *Charles Evans Hughes*, 2 vols. (New York: Macmillan, 1951), 1:39.

80. Ibid., 1:69–73; Edwin McElwain, "The Business of the Supreme Court as Conducted by Chief Justice Hughes," *Harvard Law Review* 63 (1949): 6.

81. Danelski and Tulchin, *Autobiographical Notes of Charles Evans Hughes*, 127.

82. Ibid., xix, 127.

83. Pusey, *Charles Evans Hughes*, 1:95.

84. Ibid., 1:149, 172–73.

85. Danelski and Tulchin, *Autobiographical Notes of Charles Evans Hughes*, xvii.

86. Ibid., xvii–xviii.

87. Ibid., 291.

88. Merlo J. Pusey, "The Nomination of Charles Evans Hughes as Chief Justice," *Supreme Court Historical Yearbook* (1982): 96.

89. Danelski and Tulchin, *Autobiographical Notes of Charles Evans Hughes*, 291.

90. Elizabeth Hughes Gossett, interview with the author, Sept. 15, 1969.

91. Danelski and Tulchin, *Autobiographical Notes of Charles Evans Hughes*, 15.
92. Pusey, *Charles Evans Hughes*, 1:12. Presumably Hughes was Pusey's source.
93. Danelski and Tulchin, *Autobiographical Notes of Charles Evans Hughes*, 15.
94. Ibid., 21.
95. Ibid., xix.
96. Pusey, *Charles Evans Hughes*, 1:220.
97. Betty Glad, *Charles Evans Hughes and the Illusions of Innocence* (Urbana: University of Illinois Press, 1966), 111.
98. John Lord O'Brien, *Proceedings of the Bar and Officers of the Supreme Court of the United States in Memory of Charles Evans Hughes* (Washington: privately printed, 1950), 39–40.
99. Glad, *Charles Evans Hughes and the Illusions of Innocence*, 3.
100. Zechariah Chafee Jr., "Charles Evans Hughes," *Proceedings of the American Philosophical Society*, 93 (1949): 279.
101. Author's confidential interview, Sept. 11, 1959.
102. Frankfurter, "Chief Justices I Have Known," 133.
103. John P. Frank, *The Marble Palace: The Supreme Court in Modern Life* (New York: Alfred A. Knopf, 1968), 75–76.
104. Bickel, *Unpublished Opinions of Mr. Justice Brandeis*, 244.
105. See Edgar F. Borgatta, Robert F. Bales, and Arthur S. Couch, "Some Findings Relevant to the Great Man Theory of Leadership," *American Sociological Review* 19 (1954): 755–59.
106. Edward F. Pritchard, Jr., interview with the author, Nov. 4, 1982.
107. William O. Douglas, transcriptions of interviews with Walter F. Murphy, 25, Seeley G. Mudd Manuscript Library, Princeton University. On April 2, 1940, Douglas, referring to remarks Hughes made from the bench in an oral argument by Robert H. Jackson, wrote in his diary, "The C.J. has a wonderful sense of humor." Douglas Diary, Library of Congress, Manuscript Division, William O. Douglas Papers.
108. Owen J. Roberts, Address to the Association of the Bar of the City of New York and the New York County Lawyers' Association, Dec. 12, 1948, in *Proceedings of the Bar and Officers of the Supreme Court of the United States in Memory of Charles Evans Hughes* (Washington, 1950), 127.
109. Myers wrote that thinking introverts "are apt not to know, unless told, what matters emotionally to another person, but they can and should act on the principle that people like to have their merits appreciated and their views respectfully considered. Both the working life and the personal life of introverted thinkers will go better if they take trouble to do two things: say an appreciative word when praise is honestly due, and mention the points on which they agree with another person *before* (Myers's emphasis) bringing up points on which they disagree." *Gifts Differing*, 90. In responding to colleagues' draft opinions, Hughes seldom mentioned the points with which he agreed before giving his criticisms. An example is his response to Stone's opinion in *United States v. Carolene Products Co.*, 304 U.S. 144 (1938), in which Stone wrote his famous footnote 4. Hughes agreed with much in the opinion and footnote, but he did not mention it. Instead, he began his response with this sentence: "I am somewhat disturbed by your Note 4 on page 6." Hughes to Stone, April 18, 1938, Stone Papers.

110. Roberts, Address, 123.

111. Felix Frankfurter, "The Impact of Charles Evans Hughes," in Elman, ed., *Of Law and Men*, 147–48.

112. Holmes to Lewis Einstein, Feb. 10, 1930, Library of Congress, Manuscript Division, Oliver Wendell Holmes, Jr., Papers.

113. Douglas, transcriptions of interviews with Walter F. Murphy, 102.

114. Harold D. Lasswell, *Power and Personality* (New York: W. W. Norton, 1948), 92–93.

115. Elizabeth Hughes Gossett, interview with the author, Sept. 15, 1969.

116. Susan Caine, relying on Brian Little's Free Trait Theory, wrote that "introverts are capable of acting like extroverts for the sake of work they consider important, people they love, or anything they value highly." *Quiet: The Power of Introverts in a World That Can't Stop Talking* (New York: Crown Publishers, 2012), 209. "According to Free Trait Theory," Caine added, "we are born and culturally endowed with certain personality traits—introversion, for example—but we can act out of character in the service of 'core' personal projects." Ibid.

117. Myers, *Gifts Differing*, 89.

118. Elizabeth Hughes Gossett, interview with the author, Sept. 15. 1969.

119. Holmes to Lewis Einstein, Feb. 10, 1930, Holmes Papers; Danelski and Tulchin, *Autobiographical Notes of Charles Evans Hughes*, 298–99; Frankfurter, "Chief Justices I Have Known," 134; Pusey, *Charles Evans Hughes*, 2:667–69; Elizabeth Hughes Gossett, interview with the author, Sept. 15, 1969.

120. Paul Freund, "Charles Evans Hughes as Chief Justice," *Harvard Law Review* 81 (1967): 29.

121. Roberts, Address, 118; William O. Douglas, *An Almanac of Liberty* (Garden City, NY: Doubleday, 1954), 43.

122. Wechsler's interview in Louchheim, *Making of the New Deal*, 54.

123. Danelski and Tulchin, *Autobiographical Notes of Charles Evans Hughes*, 302.

124. Jung, *Psychological Types*, 6:385.

125. Felix Frankfurter, "'The Administrative Side' of Chief Justice Hughes," in Elman, ed., *Of Law and Men*, 141–42.

126. Ibid., 142. Douglas confirmed Frankfurter's views. On January 5, 1940, Douglas wrote in his diary, "The C.J. is a good loser." Douglas Papers.

127. Pusey, *Charles Evans Hughes*, 2:677.

128. Danelski and Tulchin, *Autobiographical Notes of Charles Evans Hughes*, 324.

129. Myers and McCaulley, *Manual*, 18.

130. Myers, *Gifts Differing*, 108–9, 111–12; Pedersen, *Sixteen Men*, 111–12.

131. Pedersen, 208.

132. Myers and McCaulley, *Manual*, 288.

133. Alpheus Thomas Mason, *Harlan Fiske Stone: Pillar of the Law* (New York: Viking Press, 1956), 22.

134. Ibid., 24, 26.

135. Ibid., 17.

136. Ibid., 28–29.

137. Philip B. Kurland, Review of *Harlan Fiske Stone: Pillar of the Law*, by Alpheus Thomas Mason, *Harvard Law Review* 80 (1957): 1321–22.

138. Mason, *Harlan Fiske Stone*, chaps. 3–4.

139. Alfred McCormack, "A Law Clerk's Recollections," *Columbia Law Review* 46 (1946): 718.

140. Herbert Wechsler, undated memorandum [ca. 1947], 4, Stone Papers.

141. Douglas, transcriptions of interviews with Walter F. Murphy, 139–40.

142. Mason, *Harlan Fiske Stone*, 268.

143. John Bassett Moore, handwritten memorandum, Feb. 20, 1930, Library of Congress, Manuscript Division, John Bassett Moore Papers. Alpheus Thomas Mason published the memorandum in *William Howard Taft: Chief Justice* (New York: Simon & Schuster, 1965), 297–98.

144. Gertrude Jenkins to Luther Ely Smith, Oct. 22, 1947, Stone Papers.

145. Howard C. Westwood, memorandum, Oct. 30, 1947, Stone Papers.

146. On Jan. 12, 1940, Douglas recorded in his diary: "Stone harbors deep resentment at Hughes." Douglas Papers. In his interview with Louchheim, Wechsler said, "At the time I was as a law clerk, Stone did not have a happy relationship with Chief Justice Hughes. He resented what he felt was discrimination by Hughes in the assignment of opinions. He felt that he was getting the junky cases whereas Hughes was courting Roberts by giving him more important material. There was quite a genuine hostility, at least on Stone's part." Louchheim, *Making of the New Deal*, 54.

147. Stone to John Bassett Moore, May 17, 1932; Westwood memorandum, Oct. 30, 1947, Stone Papers; Mason, *Harlan Fiske Stone*, 346, 401–2, 416, 451–52. Stone, however, passed his views on the 1937 Court bill to FDR through Irving Brant. Irving Brant to Alpheus Thomas Mason, July 22, 1951, Library of Congress, Manuscript Division, Irving Brant Papers.

148. Stone to McReynolds, April 3, 1930, Stone Papers.

149. Mason, *Harlan Fiske Stone*, 346–47.

150. Ibid., 567–68.

151. Quoted in ibid., 281.

152. Ibid., 7, 568.

153. Alfred McCormack to Douglas, Feb. 18, 1926, Douglas Papers.

154. Draft of Volume II of Douglas's autobiography, Chap. 12, 5, ibid.

155. Stone to Boskey and Morrison, Aug. 14, 1942, Stone Papers. See David J. Danelski, "The Saboteurs' Case," *Journal of Supreme Court History* 1 (1996): 73.

156. See Louis Lusky, "Footnote Redux: A 'Carolene Products' Reminiscence," *Columbia Law Review* 82 (1982): 1100–3.

157. Samuel J. Konefsky, *Chief Justice Stone and the Supreme Court* (New York: Macmillan, 1945), 268–70.

158. Ibid., xxii.

159. Alpheus Thomas Mason, *Harlan Fiske Stone*, vol. 3 of *The Justices of the United States Supreme Court, 1789–1969; Their Lives and Major Opinions*, ed. Leon Friedman and Fred L. Israel (New York: R. R. Bowker, 1969), 2227.

160. See, e.g., Noel T. Dowling to Stone, Dec. 2, 1925, Jan. 26, 1926, March 14, 1927, Jan. 16, 1931, Feb. 10, 1932, Nov. 11, 1933; Stone to Dowling, April 19, 1927, Feb. 8, 1930, Jan. 17, 1931; Thomas Reed Powell to Stone, Jan. 30, 1926, April 23, 1932, Jan. 28, 1935, Jan. 15, 1940; Stone to Powell, Jan. 20, 1931, Jan. 30, 1935, Jan. 22, 1936; John Bassett Moore to Stone, Jan. 29, 1929, May 28, 1931, June 4, 1943; Stone to Moore, May 10, 1927, June 5, 1926, May 6, 1927, May 27, 1931, Stone Papers.

161. Mason, *Harlan Fiske Stone*, 793–94.
162. William O. Douglas, Remarks to the Multnomah County Bar Association, Portland, OR, Sept. 25, 1971, 7, Douglas Papers.
163. William O. Douglas, transcriptions of interviews with Walter F. Murphy, 26.
164. Joe Lash, ed., *From the Diaries of Felix Frankfurter* (New York: W. W. Norton, 1980), 160.
165. Quoted in Edward F. Prichard, Jr., interview with the author.
166. Quoted in Sidney Fine, *Frank Murphy: The Washington Years* (Ann Arbor: University of Michigan Press, 1984), 243.
167. Pedersen, *Sixteen Men*, 162.
168. Quoted in Fine, *Murphy: The Washington Years*, 250. See also Harlan B. Phillips, ed., *Felix Frankfurter Reminisces* (New York: Reynal, 1960), 221.
169. John P. Frank, Review of *Harlan Fiske Stone: Pillar of the Law*, by Alpheus T. Mason, *Stanford Law Review* 11 (1957): 628.
170. Douglas, Remarks to the Multnomah County Bar Association, 7, Douglas Papers.
171. Mason, *Harlan Fiske Stone*, 4. On the same page Mason wrote, "In demeanor Stone was markedly modest and self-effacing. But . . . one was impressed with his commanding presence."
172. Frank, Review of *Harlan Fiske Stone*, 627.
173. Mason, *Harlan Fiske Stone*, 472–76.
174. Douglas, transcriptions of interviews with Walter F. Murphy, 21–22.
175. Mason, *Harlan Fiske Stone*, 790–91, 795.
176. Ibid., 614.
177. Douglas, Remarks to the Multnomah County Bar Association, 7.
178. Kurland, review of *Harlan Fiske Stone*, 1323.
179. Ibid.
180. John Paul Stevens, *Five Chiefs: A Supreme Court Memoir* (New York: Little, Brown, 2011), 36. Cf. Danelski, "The Saboteurs' Case," 61–82.
181. Quoted in Woodrow Wilson, *Congressional Government* (New York: Meridian, 1956), 25.

PART II

Becoming the Chief

DAVID J. DANELSKI

Why does a president nominate one candidate as chief justice and rather than another? To what extent is a nominee's ambition relevant to his or her nomination? Why does the Senate confirm some of the president's nominees and reject others? Do the considerations for nominating a chief justice differ from the considerations for nominating an associate justice? If so, what are those considerations? Why are some candidates willing to accept the chief justiceship but not an associate justiceship? Why are some nominations for the chief justiceship contentious but others are not? Why are some contentious nominations confirmed but not others?

Chapter 3 touched on some of those questions in reporting the ascent of Taft, Hughes, and Stone to the chief justiceship. For Taft, the chief justiceship was his life's ambition. For White, Stone, and Rehnquist, ambitions arose after their appointments as associate justices. Burger's ambition for an appointment either as associate justice or chief justice was as strong as Taft's. Burger, recalled John Ehrlichman, "wanted a seat on the Supreme Court so passionately that he would have agreed to anything to get it."[1] John Mitchell said, "Burger's the first guy to run for the chief justiceship—and get it."[2] Taft insisted that Harding nominate him as chief justice rather than as associate justice because he had been president and had opposed Brandeis's appointment to the Court, but he also wanted the chief justiceship, as did White, Stone, Warren, and Rehnquist, because of the office's historical significance, prestige, and leadership potential.

In chapter 4, Christine L. Nemacheck connects my findings concerning task and social leadership to William H. Rehnquist's nomination as chief justice, which indicates that leadership ability is an important consideration in choosing a chief justice. For Nemacheck, explanation of a presidential nomination of a chief justice is a two-step process. The first step is retrieval of the short lists of candidates from the nominating presidents' papers. The second step is a determination of the reasons for the presidents' final choices from the short list, which Nemacheck makes by examining archival and biographical data.

In chapter 5, Kevin J. McMahon explores the relationship between types of political regimes and contentiousness in the Senate concerning chief justices' nominations. Of the ten nominations McMahon considers, six were not contentious. The Senate approved the nominations of White, Stone, Vinson, and Warren by voice votes, and there were only four votes against Taft's confirmation and three votes against Burger's confirmation. Such strong approval contributes to the chief justiceship's prestige as an institution. Of the four contentious nominations—those of Hughes, Fortas, Rehnquist, and Roberts—the Senate, which the president's party controlled in each instance, failed to confirm only Fortas's nomination. The four nominations had two things in common—strong ideological opposition and nominees with obvious task-leadership potential. Hughes and Rehnquist in fact became task leaders of their Courts. Roberts, wrote Joel K. Goldstein recently, "is perhaps the ablest lawyer to serve as Chief Justice since Hughes. . . . [His] formidable talent and success as an appellate advocate makes him well suited to lead the Court in its tasks."[3] As for Fortas, one of his biographers wrote, "In terms of task leadership, Fortas might have become the best chief justice in the Court's history. He was nothing if not efficient."[4]

NOTES

1. John Ehrlichman, *Witness to Power: The Nixon Years* (New York: Simon & Schuster, 1982), 114. According to Ehrlichman, Burger "was even willing to create another vacancy when Nixon wanted one. . . . The President said he had Burger's promise that Burger would retire before Nixon did so that Nixon could appoint another, younger Chief Justice to carry the Nixon mandate far beyond the Burger and Nixon years." Ibid., 114–15.

2. Quoted in John Dean, *The Rehnquist Choice: The Untold Story of the Nixon Appointment that Redefined the Supreme Court* (New York: Free Press, 2001), 14. According to Dean, Mitchell made the quoted statement in his presence.

3. Joel K. Goldstein, "Leading the Court: Studies in Influence as Chief Justice," *Stetson Law Review* 40 (2011): 753.

4. Laura Kalman, *Abe Fortas: A Biography* (New Haven: Yale University Press, 1990), 334.

4 ~ Selecting the Chief

Presidential Calculation in Appointing Chief Justices

CHRISTINE L. NEMACHECK

> I think that the practice which each of us appears to follow at the close of a day of oral argument—plodding back to his own individual salt mine—is bad for morale. While I know there is work to be done, I am wondering if there would be any substantial sentiment in the Conference in favor of opening either the Justices' Dining Room, or one of the Conference Rooms, to all Justices and law clerks who desire it, for a half hour of coffee or tea at 3:00 PM on at least some afternoons following oral argument.[1]
>
> —Justice William Rehnquist to Chief Justice Warren Burger, September 24, 1973

Many years prior to his own service as Chief Justice of the United States, Associate Justice William Rehnquist sent the above suggestion to Chief Justice Warren Burger. At the time, Rehnquist had served a scant nine months on the Supreme Court, but even as a new associate justice, he sought opportunities to bring his fellow justices together to form relationships that would provide not only social benefits but would improve the work environment at the Court. At the same time, Rehnquist was an ideological outlier on the Court, writing solo dissents so frequently that his law clerks gave him a "Lone Ranger" doll.[2] These characteristics, providing social and administrative leadership on the Court while staking out a consistent legal philosophy that was, particularly in his early years on the Court, in the minority, typified Rehnquist's thirty-plus years of service on the bench. Indeed, upon his death in 2005, Justice Ruth Bader Ginsburg, hardly his ideological ally, called Rehnquist "the fairest, most efficient boss I have ever had."[3]

The importance of Rehnquist's skill in both social and task leadership harks back to David Danelski's early and important contributions to our understanding of the chief justice's role in the Court's process and decisional outcomes. According to Danelski, the most successful chief justices are likely to either possess both of these qualities himself, or benefit from at least one other colleague on the Court who possesses whichever of these qualities the chief personally lacks. But those chiefs who possess neither quality, and are not as fortunate in terms of their colleagues' skills, are likely to experience significant conflict on a Court lacking in cohesion during their tenures as chief.[4]

As chief justice, Rehnquist was known to run a tight ship. Postargument conferences were said to run smoothly and efficiently, and opinions were assigned fairly. Although there is evidence, as would be expected, that Rehnquist acted strategically to assign opinions to ideologically proximate colleagues in close and important cases,[5] he also provided each of the associate justices with opportunities to craft majority opinions. He encouraged timely completion of those opinions by considering in future assignments whether uncirculated majority opinions lingered in the justices' chambers. It was his concern for the smooth functioning of the institution that factored prominently in his decision making.

In addition to his organizational prowess, Rehnquist was widely liked by colleagues across the Court's ideological spectrum. He is said to have gambled on everything from the amount of snow that accumulated on the Court's grounds to election outcomes and the Kentucky Derby.[6] During his time as chief, he went significantly beyond the afternoon coffees he suggested to Chief Justice Burger and enjoyed hosting holiday and end-of-term parties for which he drafted *Jeopardy*-style quiz questions on Court history and other obscure facts.[7] And, perhaps most importantly as the Court's leader, "he never held a grudge."[8]

Chief Justice Rehnquist is widely regarded as a "great" chief.[9] Justice William Brennan asserted that Rehnquist was "the most all-around successful" chief justice of the three (Warren, Burger, and Rehnquist) under whom he served.[10] In his evaluation of the five chief justices with whom he served, Justice John Paul Stevens reported that Rehnquist's colleagues on the Court "all regarded him as a friend who we knew would handle his new responsibilities competently and impartially. He more than fulfilled that expectation throughout his career as chief justice."[11] These accolades are even more impressive than they might otherwise be when considering they come from two of the associate justices with whom Rehnquist was often in disagreement on the substance of the cases before the Court.

Rehnquist, who was appointed as an associate justice by Richard Nixon in 1971 and by Ronald Reagan as the chief justice in 1986, certainly had the qualifications and legal acumen to make a fine Supreme Court justice, and the great majority of his decisions are ones with which his appointing presidents (Richard Nixon and Ronald Reagan respectively) would be pleased. He is one of only three chief justices of the seventeen to have been confirmed by the Senate and served on the Court who rose to that position from the ranks of a sitting associate justice.

Not all chief justices have enjoyed Rehnquist's success. Another one of the few chiefs who was elevated from the rank of associate justice, Chief Justice Harlan Stone, is regarded to have been a largely ineffectual leader. In his description of Stone as a chief justice, Henry Abraham referred more to the characteristics Stone lacked than those he possessed: "Not a first-rate administrator like Taft, not a skillful and disciplinary Court-master like Hughes, not a ruthless craftsman like Marshall, not so persuasive as Taney, not so innovative cum activist as Warren."[12] Conferences led by Stone were often unpleasant meetings where "Court members spoke out of turn, and Stone did little to control their debate," even joining in to tell colleagues that their points were "damned nonsense."[13] Under Stone's leadership, the Court was divisive and fractious.

The role and import of the Chief Justice of the United States has long been recognized and has been subject to substantial analysis.[14] The chief's significance has been recognized both in terms of social leadership as well as the functional and administrative leadership he provides as the head of the nine "little law firms." Evidence shows that who the chief is matters, so how do presidents approach the process of choosing chief justices? Are certain characteristics emphasized in that selection process that differ from the choice of an associate justice? Put simply, how do presidents choose their chiefs?

In this chapter, I analyze the appointment of ten chief justices of the United States, including each chief nominated during the twentieth century and John Roberts's nomination to that position in 2005. In the first section, I examine the constitutional and statutory requirements for the position of Chief Justice of the United States. Then I provide a brief overview of the general literature on Supreme Court appointments and the few studies that address appointments of chief justices more explicitly. In the third section, I apply the literature on Supreme Court appointments to the president's choice of a chief and examine those factors that are unique to the process of selecting a chief justice. In the fourth section, I analyze the nominations of chief justices since 1900, relying on, among other sources, archival research from the papers of the presidents making those decisions. In the final section, I conclude with a brief discussion and suggestions for future research.

I find evidence that although factors traditionally thought important in Supreme Court appointments more generally are also important in choosing chiefs, presidents do approach the process of choosing a chief differently than choosing his associates in several key aspects. First, presidents frequently consider whether chief justice candidates have the leadership and administrative skills Danelski long ago asserted to be crucial to the smooth functioning of the Court as an institution. Additionally, when choosing a chief, presidents see a particularly important role for the advice of current and former justices in deciding on a nominee; the justices' desire to participate in the process also highlights the importance that members of the Court themselves place on the selection of the chief. Finally, presidents face a unique problem in choosing a chief. Unlike the process when choosing an associate justice, there is a readily identifiable pool of prominent candidates for the chief's position, namely the sitting associate justices. While it will come as no surprise to ideologically distant associate justices that they are not considered for the elevation to chief, when there is more than one ideologically proximate candidate for chief, presidents must also consider the divisiveness on the Court that might result from choosing to elevate one of those candidates. In those circumstances, presidents might well decide to choose an outside candidate.

I. The Chief Justice of (the Supreme Court of) the United States: Constitutional and Statutory Requirements

The position of chief justice is the only position in the federal judiciary specifically referred to in the Constitution. Rather than appearing in Article III, where we might expect to see some criteria relevant for service in that leadership position, the sole mention of the role is in Article I as it pertains to the chief's role in the presidential impeachment process. According to Article I, §3, "When the President of the United States is tried, the Chief Justice shall preside." Article II, §2 provides for presidential nomination of "Judges of the supreme Court . . . by and with the Advice and Consent of the Senate." But it makes no distinction between "judges" generally and the "Chief Justice" referred to in the previous article.

It is clear from debate at the Constitutional Convention that the framers intended that there be a chief justice who would lead the Supreme Court. There was debate, for example, over the exact title of the position, which was originally the "Chief Justice of the U.S. Supreme Court" and only later came to be known as the "Chief Justice of the United States." It was Chief Justice Salmon Chase who initially used the title; Congress then embraced it for the first time in July 1866. It was not until Chief Justice Melville Fuller's appointment in 1888 that an actual commission to the position of chief was given the title "Chief Justice of the United States."[15] The change in the title reflects the fact that the chief justice's responsibilities lay not only with the Supreme Court, though that is arguably his most important work, but also as a leader of the judicial branch, and in governing more generally.

As is the case for most of the judiciary, the framework for the chief justice position was provided through statute rather than through the Constitution. Chapter 20, §1 of the Judiciary Act of 1789 actually defined the position, providing that the Supreme Court of the United States would "consist of a chief justice and five associate justices."[16] Other responsibilities accrued through additional statutory language and custom. In his account of the five chief justices under whom he served, Justice John Paul Stevens describes many of the chief's statutorily assigned responsibilities, including choosing district court judges to serve on the Federal Intelligence Surveillance Court, presiding over the Judicial Conference of the United States, approving the work of retired U.S. Supreme Court justices on other federal courts, and serving on a number of boards and commissions, including the Board of the Smithsonian Institution.[17] Of course, many would argue that the chief's most important responsibilities concern the day-to-day running of the Supreme Court, presiding over oral arguments, leading the justices in their confidential conferences and, arguably most important, assigning opinions when he is in the majority.

II. The Appointment Process

The Constitution gives very little guidance on the nomination of justices to the U.S. Supreme Court. The only constitutional requirements come from the language in Article II, §2 requiring that the president nominate judges by and with the consent of the Senate. And there is *no* language to indicate the manner in which the office of chief justice should be filled. The first time the chief justice's seat was filled, the assumption was that President Washington would determine which among the six justices he nominated to the Court would serve as chief, and candidates lobbied him for that honor.[18] On September 24, 1789, Washington sent nominations to the Senate, designating John Jay as the first chief justice.

Although some have argued for alternative methods of choosing the chief justice, including such options as a vote among the sitting members of the Court or using a seniority system,[19] the current selection process, through which the president either nominates a chief from among the sitting associate justices or from candidates outside the Court, has generated little controversy. It is telling, in fact, that apart from a few largely theoretical examinations of alternative processes through which the chief justice might be appointed, there is little to no research focused solely on the appointment of chief justices over time. Instead, the knowledge we have on the appointment of chief justices comes either from historical approaches focused on the life and work of a particular chief justice, or from the literature on Supreme Court nominations more generally, which include discussions of chief justices' appointments as one aspect of their coverage.

Thus, in thinking about the determinants of presidents' choices of candidates to lead the Supreme Court, the literature on appointments to the high court more generally is a reasonable starting point. Much of the work on appointments to the Supreme Court has focused on the confirmation stage of the process.[20] But to a lesser degree, the selection stage of the process (the point in time from which the president has knowledge of a vacancy in that office to the point when a nomination is officially made) has also received scholarly attention.

Henry Abraham provides a meticulous examination of each Supreme Court nomination from Washington's original six to George W. Bush's appointment of Samuel Alito. In this seminal work on Supreme Court appointments, Abraham lays out four criteria that have guided the choice of nominees for the nation's highest bench: (1) objective merit, (2) personal friendship, (3) balancing "representation" or "representativeness" on the Court, and (4) political and ideological compatibility.[21] According to Abraham, political and ideological compatibility encompass such concerns as whether the nominee favors the president's programs and policies, whether he or she will gain the president favor with influential groups and individuals, and whether he or she agrees with the president's understanding of constitutional construction.[22] Merit, on the other hand, involves criteria such as demonstrated judicial temperament, appropriate educational background and training, leadership ability, and collegial sensitivity.[23]

Abraham's work has been the jumping-off point for much of the literature on Supreme Court nominations. By examining the nomination environment and the nominees presidents send to the Senate for confirmation, Abraham's work has expanded our knowledge and understanding of the criteria important in the selection process. But in its discussion of the particulars of each appointment and the candidate actually chosen for nomination, it fails to explain the determinants of presidents' choices more broadly.

Research building on Abraham's work has had a more theoretical focus, particularly in making the connection between the selection and confirmation phases explicit.[24] In his work on Supreme Court nominations, David Yalof considers institutional changes, such as divided government, increased interest group participation, and media attention, and how those changes have affected the nomination process. Yalof finds significant patterns in the selection process, such as the increasing focus on federal appeals court judges as candidates for Supreme Court nomination and the increasing role played by White House and Justice Department staff.[25] These findings are largely consistent with Abraham's criteria, but they move toward a more theoretical understanding of the nomination process.

More recent work on the Supreme Court nomination process uses a theoretical lens to systematically analyze the determinants of presidents' choices of Supreme Court nominees. Specifically, it utilizes theories of strategic behavior and uncertainty to identify factors shaping Supreme Court nominations throughout most of the twentieth century and into the twenty-first.[26] That research further examines the connection between the selection and confirmation stages of the nomination process and finds that presidents act strategically to make their choices with an eye toward lessening uncertainty about their nominees' prospects in the confirmation process as well as their future behavior on the Court. This work concludes that when presidents experience relatively greater institutional constraints, they pursue a political strategy to lessen their uncertainty surrounding the confirmation environment. But when they experience relatively fewer constraints, they strategically pursue an informational strategy to maximize their certainty over a nominee's future, ideologically compatible, behavior on the Court.[27]

Although some have argued that this theoretical approach is too "formulaic" to understand the Supreme Court nomination process,[28] that critique misunderstands the argument. Employing the theoretical framework of strategic behavior and uncertainty, the theory-driven approach does not dismiss the idiosyncrasies of any single nomination. But rather than focusing on those idiosyncrasies or trying to ferret out the differences that make each choice unique, it focuses on explaining the institutional and political constraints that all presidents face in making what many of them argue to be one of their most "serious responsibilities as President."[29] In doing so, it advances our understanding of political conditions that affect all presidents in their efforts to staff the highest level of the third branch of government.

While there are several different approaches aimed at explaining nominations to the high bench, none focus solely on choosing chief justices. Instead, the extant literature on Supreme Court nominations largely treats the appointment to chief justice as one of a number of federal judicial appointments presidents have the opportunity to make. In some cases, a nomination to chief justice has been considered in terms of the attributes of a particular vacancy that might make the process of successfully appointing a candidate more politically difficult.[30] And there are a couple of instances in which authors have considered the chief justice nomination process not from an empirical perspective of seeking to understand why presidents choose the chiefs they do, but by discussing alternative methods that might be used for choosing the chief.[31] Aside from the historical approaches that examine each individual nomination, including those of the chief justices, studies have not been aimed at explaining the nominations of chief justices as a group distinct from their associates.

III. Deliberation Amid Uncertainty

As discussed above, presidents relish the opportunity to appoint justices to the U.S. Supreme Court. While it is not an opportunity that occurs frequently, presidents have, on average, the opportunity to appoint two justices during their time in office. Doing so, of course, allows presidents to affect important public policies long after their own terms in office end. It is an even more rare opportunity, however, for a president to appoint a chief justice. While 112 justices have served on the Supreme Court throughout the history of the United States, only seventeen chief justices have sat in the center chair of the U.S. Supreme Court.[32] That fact gives rise to the question of why presidents choose the chief justice nominees they do.

To answer this question, we can evaluate the historical record to tease out factors particularly important to presidents when choosing a chief justice nominee from a short list of seriously considered candidates.[33] The literature on Supreme Court nominations suggests that presidents ought to act strategically to minimize their uncertainty in choosing chief justices. As mentioned previously, there are two types of uncertainty presidents face in the selection process: uncertainty over their nominees' future behavior on the Court and uncertainty over the confirmation environment.[34] But the uncertainty presidents confront in choosing a chief justice is more complex than what they encounter in choosing an associate. When choosing the chief justice, the behavior on the Court over which presidents are uncertain is not only the positions the justice will take or the opinions he will write, but also the candidate's administrative capabilities, the manner in which he will assign opinions, and the potential repercussions of choosing to elevate one associate justice or making the appointment from outside the Court, to name just a few.

Unlike other presidential appointments, to cabinet departments for example, presidents lack the ability to check the power of their Supreme Court nominees once they are confirmed to life-tenured positions. But by appointing ideologically compatible nominees, presidents can be more certain that once the nominee is on the Court, acting with relatively few institutional constraints, he or she will reach decisions with which their appointing president would agree. Of course, candidates under consideration for such a post would have an incentive to misrepresent their ideological preferences if they were not consistent with the president's ideology. Presidents can lessen their uncertainty over their candidates' preferences in a number of ways; one way is to choose candidates with whom they have been colleagues or friends or with whom they have at least some first-hand experience.

There are many examples of presidents choosing chief justices with whom they have some personal relationship. President Truman, of course, is widely recognized for appointing members of his close "kitchen cabinet" to the Supreme Court. His nomination of Fred Vinson to the position of chief justice fits that mold. Truman and Vinson had long been friends; they served in Congress together, traveled together, and of course prior to nominating him as chief justice, the president had appointed him secretary of the treasury.

Another way presidents can lessen their uncertainty about a nominee's future behavior is to choose nominees who have experience in the public sector; this type of experience might come in the way of state or federal government service. Examples of presidents nominating chief justices with experience in the public sector are numerous. In fact, each of the ten chief justice nominees included in the analysis had served in either the state or federal government, or both.

Another type of experience that can be valuable in lessening uncertainty about a nominee's behavior once confirmed is service on the federal courts. Federal appeals court experience has become particularly prominent among those considered for the Supreme Court over the last twenty to thirty years.

Writing or signing on to opinions concerning many of the very issues that could reach the Supreme Court provides a great deal of information to presidents considering candidates for appointment to the Court.

For a president deliberating on a choice for chief justice, an even more telling type of judicial experience is actual experience on the U.S. Supreme Court. Interestingly, it has historically been unusual for presidents to elevate sitting justices to the center chair. Since the earliest nominations to the Court, only three of the seventeen candidates for chief justice confirmed by the Senate were elevated from the position of associate justice.[35] This practice, however, has become more common in recent years. Since 1900, four of the ten nominees for chief justice vacancies (including Justice Fortas's failed nomination in 1968) were, when nominated, a sitting associate justice of the Supreme Court. In fact, the first successful elevation of an associate justice was President Taft's choice to elevate Edward D. White to become chief justice in 1910.

Candidates' involvement in political activity can also be a valuable indicator of future behavior on the Court. For example, not only would Charles Evans Hughes's experience as an associate justice have elucidated his behavior as chief, his service as the Republican nominee for president in 1916 also helped to clarify his views on issues that might come before the Court. In combination with Hughes's service as the governor of New York, President Hoover had to have felt certain of his chief justice nominee's future behavior on the Court.

In addition to lessening uncertainty over future behavior, presidents also make nominations with an eye toward the constitutionally required confirmation process. Presidents' uncertainty over their nominees' likelihood of confirmation is much greater when the opposite party controls the Senate. In an effort to lessen their uncertainty in facing an opposition Senate, presidents often pursue a political strategy in which they are willing to accept relatively greater uncertainty about a nominee's future behavior on the Court in exchange for greater certainty about their nominee's confirmation prospects. In contrast, when the president's party controls the Senate, they are more likely to pursue an informational strategy aimed at choosing a candidate for the bench about whose future behavior they have more certainty.

Interestingly, in each of the chief justice appointments considered here, with one exception, the president's party controlled the Senate. The one exception was when President Richard Nixon faced an opposition Senate when he nominated Warren E. Burger to become chief justice in 1969. In choosing chief justices to the Supreme Court, presidents since

1900 have thus experienced generally fewer constraints than when nominating associate justices and judges to the lower federal courts. These presidents had greater certainty that their nominees would pass the confirmation hurdle than they would have had the Senate been under opposition control.

As I suggest above, presidents deciding on a candidate for chief justice might well consider other factors beyond those suggested in the Supreme Court nomination literature more generally. The chief is not only a single voice out of nine. He or she has important leadership tasks on the Court, in particular presiding over oral arguments and running the Court's conferences. In recalling the earlier discussion of Chief Justice Rehnquist's success in this position, presidents might consider some of the characteristics he possessed when choosing a chief justice nominee.

According to the evaluations of scholars, close observers of the Court, and his own colleagues, it was Rehnquist's adept organizational and administrative skills, fairness in dealing with his colleagues, efficiency in running the business of the Court, and his ability to create a welcoming social atmosphere that led to his success as chief. As discussed above, Rehnquist possessed what Danelski, in one of the earliest studies of the chief justice, referred to as "task" and "social" leadership;[36] the ability to facilitate the smooth operation of the Court and to provide a functional and collegial workplace. Of course, Rehnquist is not alone among past chief justices in possessing these characteristics. According to Danelski, Charles Evans Hughes was an extremely adept leader of the Court's conferences, running them with authority and confidence, as well as amiability.[37] Thus when deliberating on a choice for chief justice, presidents might do well to consider their candidates' task and social leadership skills.

Finally, presidents would do well to consider the likely effects of their choice for chief on existing relationships among members of the Court. One way to lessen the president's uncertainty in this area is to consult with sitting or former justices. By gathering information from these actors, the president can make a decision that continues, or even enhances, the smooth functioning of the institution.

IV. Choosing the Chief

I examine the president's choice of a chief justice nominee from the pool of candidates seriously considered for that position. By examining the pool of candidates, we can better understand not just the qualities present in the candidates formally nominated for chief justice, but we can gain valuable insight into the calculations made in choosing a particular nominee above other highly qualified and seriously considered candidates.

I restrict my analysis to the period from 1900 to the present. During this time, presidents nominated ten chief justices to the Supreme Court. One of those nominations, President Johnson's advancement of Associate Justice Abe Fortas, was unsuccessful. Another nomination was initially made as a recess appointment. Chief Justice Earl Warren first gained his seat on the Court by a recess appointment in October 1953. Within two months of that appointment, however, his nomination was sent to the Senate and he was confirmed on March 1, 1954.

Much of the information I will discuss on these appointments comes from the papers of the appointing presidents.[38] For most of these nominations, I have been able to develop a short list of candidates presidents considered for appointment as chief justice (see table 4.1). In order to answer the question of why presidents choose the nominees they do, we can compare the chosen candidate to the list of other candidates considered for the position.[39]

There are two chief justice appointments for which I present only the name of the actual nominee on the "short list." The first of these is Warren Burger's. There is simply little information in the Nixon papers on this appointment. The most substantive references to the appointment are in the Haldeman papers and diaries, but that reference is to President Nixon catching his closest advisors by surprise in telling them that he had decided on a nominee, Warren Burger, just days before he made the formal announcement. There is no discussion of other candidates.[40]

The second appointment for which there is only a single name on the "short list" is President Bush's nomination of John Roberts as chief justice. Bush writes in his memoir, *Decision Points*, that three days prior to Roberts's scheduled confirmation hearings for the associate justice position vacated by retiring Justice Sandra Day O'Connor, he learned that Chief Justice Rehnquist had died. Based on Bush's own account, he simply decided to withdraw Roberts's nomination for associate justice and nominate him for the position of chief; he did not consider other candidates.[41] Thus, for the Burger and Roberts nominations, we can assess the factors considered in the appointment, but we cannot compare the actual nominee to those who were considered but not chosen.

In examining presidents' choices of chief justice nominees, it is clear that they do value candidates about whom they have first-hand information. But it is not clear that this personal relationship distinguishes the actual nominee from the other candidates the president considers for the post. For example, President Roosevelt was well-acquainted with both Harlan Stone and Robert Jackson. Indeed, Roosevelt was quite close to Jackson, who had been a long-time supporter of New Deal programs and had served the administration for a short time, first at the Internal Revenue Service and then in the Justice Department, where he eventually served as both solicitor and attorney general. But, in consultation with retiring Chief Justice Hughes and then Associate Justice and frequent advisor Felix Frankfurter, Roosevelt decided to go with Harlan Stone as his nominee for chief. Since Stone had been serving as an associate justice, Roosevelt was then able to nominate Robert Jackson to fill that vacancy.

In Jackson's case, being close to Roosevelt may actually have hurt his

TABLE 4.1. Appointments to Chief Justice of the United States, 1900–Present

President	Vacating Chief Justice	Short List	Actual Nominee
William H. Taft	Melvin Fuller	Charles E. Hughes Edward D. White	Edward D. White
Warren G. Harding	Edward D. White	George Sutherland William H. Taft	William H. Taft
Herbert Hoover	William H. Taft	Charles E. Hughes Harlan F. Stone	Charles E. Hughes
Franklin D. Roosevelt	Charles E. Hughes	Robert H. Jackson Harlan F. Stone	Harlan F. Stone
Harry S. Truman	Harlan F. Stone	Sam G. Bratton Harrie Brigham Chase Robert H. Jackson Robert P. Patterson Orie L. Phillips Fred M. Vinson Peter Woodbury	Fred M. Vinson
Dwight D. Eisenhower	Fred M. Vinson	Harold H. Burton John W. Davis John Foster Dulles Robert H. Jackson John J. Parker Orie L. Phillips Arthur T. Vanderbilt Earl Warren	Earl Warren
Lyndon B. Johnson	Earl Warren	Abe Fortas Henry H. Fowler Cyrus Vance	Abe Fortas[a]
Richard M. Nixon	Earl Warren	Warren E. Burger	Warren E. Burger
Ronald W. Reagan	Warren E. Burger	Robert H. Bork William H. Rehnquist Antonin Scalia	William H. Rehnquist
George W. Bush	William H. Rehnquist	John G. Roberts	John G. Roberts

[a]Not confirmed.

candidacy for chief. In Frankfurter's discussion with Roosevelt, he suggested that the "most decisive consideration, considering the fact that Stone is qualified, is that Bob [Robert Jackson] is of your personal and political family, as it were, while Stone is a Republican."[42] In Frankfurter's opinion, Roosevelt's bipartisanship in the chief justice appointment might increase confidence in him as the country moved toward war.

As discussed previously, President Truman is known more for choosing his cronies to the Supreme Court than any other president, except perhaps President Johnson. Nonetheless, when considering candidates to assume the role of chief justice in the wake of Stone's death in 1946, Fred Vinson was not the only person with close ties to Truman to be considered for the chief justice position. Truman also seriously considered elevating Justice Jackson to the chief's position, but "feuds in the Court" prevented elevating any of the associate justices.[43] In particular, Justice Jackson made public allegations that Justice Black was trying to block his elevation to the center chair.[44]

In other chief justice nominations, none of the candidates who were seriously considered had a close relationship to the president. For example, when President Reagan elevated Justice Rehnquist, he did not have close ties with Rehnquist or the two other candidates, Robert Bork or Antonin Scalia. Thus, in general, it seems that some personal association between a president and candidates seriously considered for the court is common, but that relationship does not necessarily distinguish the actual nominee from the pack of frontrunners.

Another factor that presidents might consider to lessen their uncertainty about a chief justice's future behavior is public service experience. Through a long record of service in the state or federal government, particularly as a member of Congress, candidates would have substantial opportunity to develop their views on important policy issues and to go on the record as to those views. Indeed, chief justice nominees, on average, had spent more than twice as many years in the public sector as had their colleagues on the presidents' short lists.

Fred Vinson, for example, far outpaced any of the runners-up in terms of years of public-sector experience, having served in Congress and then in the executive branch for a total of twenty years. The candidate with the most years after Vinson was Sam Bratton, who had served for nine years in the U.S. Senate. In the case of Herbert Hoover's choice of Charles Evans Hughes in 1930, his nine years of combined government service, including his work as an associate justice of the U.S. Supreme Court and as governor of New York, dwarfed his partner on Hoover's short list for chief justice, Harlan F. Stone, who had only a single year of service as the attorney general.

Thus it seems that as it provides presidents with information on the candidate's future behavior, public-sector experience can improve a candidate's prospects for winning the chief justice nomination. Such public-sector experience is perhaps particularly helpful in providing insight on a candidate's administrative and leadership capacities. As Danelski reminds us, a candidate's abilities both in terms of "task" and "social" leadership are important characteristics for successful chiefs.[45] Certainly one of the factors that recommended him for chief justice was Fred Vinson's twenty years of service through which he had "demonstrated administrative and legislative leadership."[46]

Although substantial attention had been paid to the deal between President Eisenhower and Earl Warren leading to his appointment as chief, Eisenhower did consider waiting to appoint Warren to a vacancy other than the chief justice's seat, or to elevating a sitting associate to the chief's seat and then appointing Warren to fill the vacancy in the associate justice's seat.[47] But Eisenhower also thought Warren's extensive experience in the public sector had much to recommend him as a chief justice. Eisenhower emphasized to his advisors that a candidate for chief justice should have a national reputation. Rather than simply the "legal training, training on the bench" that he thought important for an associate justice, he sought a chief justice with a broader array of experiences akin to those of Chief Justice Marshall.[48] And while Eisenhower considered elevating Justices Jackson or Burton, he abandoned the idea, particularly of Burton, "because he was afraid he [Burton] was not enough of an administrator."[49]

Considering candidates with federal court experience can go a long way toward lessening presidents' uncertainty over future behavior on the Court. Through such service, candidates are on record considering some of the very same kind of issues likely to come before the U.S. Supreme Court. Although lower court judges are constrained by Supreme Court precedent, and thus their decisions may not perfectly reflect those they would reach if they were to serve on the Supreme Court, there are few better indicators of a candidate's legal views.

Not surprisingly, most candidates nominated for chief justice have experience on the federal courts. But so do most of their colleagues who make the presidents' short lists but are not nominated. Thus such service does not necessarily distinguish nominees from the other candidates.

What is particularly interesting in the case of chief justice nominations is that presidents have available an even better indicator of future behavior than lower federal court experience: they can choose to elevate an associate justice to the position of chief. In doing so, they also create another vacancy in an associate justice's seat.

Early in the Court's history, a norm developed against appointing a chief from among the ranks of current or former associate justices. After President Washington's failed attempt to appoint former associate justice John Rutledge, and current associate justice William Cushing's refusal to accept the chief justice nomination, preferring to remain an associate, no president attempted to elevate a sitting justice until President Taft did so in 1910. Although Taft was reportedly at least partially motivated by his own desire to become chief justice one day, he is said to have chosen Justice Edward White for the position for three reasons: because his "'real' politics [were] eminently compatible" with Taft's, because he was "the ablest administrator on the high bench," and he was popular among his colleagues.[50]

More recently, the practice of elevating a sitting associate justice for the chief's position has become commonplace. Including Justice Fortas's failed nomination for chief in 1968, fully one-half of the candidates nominated for chief justice since Taft's choice of Justice White in 1910 have been associate justices.[51] Given presidents' desire to appoint like-minded chief justices about whose future behavior they are relatively more certain, this should not be surprising. In fact, in several of the recent instances where presidents have chosen *not* to elevate a sitting associate justice, the reason for doing so has been rooted in their fear of creating tension on the Court. As discussed previously, when President Truman chose Vinson for chief justice, one of the primary reasons he did not choose to elevate Justice Jackson, whom he seriously considered for the position, was because of the public feud between Jackson and Justice Black. And the echoes of that feud reverberated at the Court even when President Eisenhower considered Justice Jackson for appointment in 1953. Attorney General Herbert Brownell cautioned Eisenhower against elevating Jackson due to difficulties in leading a Court divided in their loyalties.[52]

As mentioned above, presidents have also seized on another source of information to lessen their uncertainty in choosing their chief justices: former chief justices and sitting associates. In at least one case, a retiring chief (Warren Burger) made unsolicited suggestions to the appointing president (Ronald Reagan). When he arrived at the meeting with President Reagan, where he would notify the president of his decision to retire, Warren Burger came with a memorandum containing his own recommendations for his replacement. The memo included six names, among them then Associate Justice William Rehnquist, Judge Robert Bork, and Judge Antonin Scalia,[53] the three serious contenders who also appeared on lists developed by the Justice Department and White House Counsel's Office.

In most cases, however, presidents sought out the advice of current or former members of the Court in deciding on a new chief justice. Other scholars have discussed that appointing presidents sometimes seek the advice of current members of the Court in choosing their Supreme Court nominees more generally,[54] but this seems to be particularly prevalent for presidents deliberating on a nominee for the center seat on the Court. Shortly after Chief Justice Hughes told President Roosevelt he would retire, Roosevelt called Hughes to discuss a successor. Hughes immediately went to the White House to discuss, in person, who would make the best candidate to replace him. He advised Roosevelt that Harlan Stone's record "gave him first claim as chief."[55] And even though President Truman was known for appointing his cronies, he did ask Tom Clark, then attorney general, to speak with former chief justice, Charles Evans Hughes, as well as other current members of the Court to solicit suggestions on the nomination. Truman's friend Fred Vinson was one of the candidates suggested.[56] Although there is some dispute regarding President Hoover's consultations or lack thereof when he appointed Chief Justice Hughes to the Court in 1930,[57] by his own account, Attorney General William Mitchell sent sitting members of the Court to speak with Hughes regarding his availability and interest prior to Hoover's decision to make the appointment.[58]

In the case of President Bush's nomination of John Roberts, Bush has not given any indication that he sought the counsel of current or former justices in his deliberations.[59] However, Roberts's appointment began as an associate justice appointment to Justice Sandra Day O'Connor's seat. As mentioned above, it was only after Chief Justice Rehnquist's death that Bush decided to withdraw the associate justice nomination and appoint him chief, "decid[ing] that John Roberts's leadership ability made him a perfect fit for chief justice."[60] One might even conjecture that President Bush was encouraged to go outside the Court so as to avoid tension between sitting associate justices, particularly Justices Scalia and Thomas, on whom the president said he would model his appointments to the federal judiciary. Indeed, as Chief Justice Rehnquist's health deteriorated, commentators suggested that a kinder, gentler Justice Scalia was mounting a "charm offensive" to position himself for elevation to the center seat.[61]

When they have had the freedom to do so, presidents have minimized their uncertainty over a nominee's future behavior and have chosen the most ideologically proximate candidate for appointment as chief. Examining the short lists of chief justice candidates considered by presidents, it is evident that ideology plays an important role in choosing a chief. On average, presidents' nominees were more than twice as close to the presidents' own ideological positions as were those candidates considered but not chosen.[62]

There are, however, a couple of prominent exceptions to this finding. When President Taft chose Justice White as his nominee for chief over Justice Hughes, ideological compatibility was not the driving force in his decision. Instead, it is widely understood that Taft was at least in part motivated by his desire to appoint a chief who would step down in a more timely manner so as to create a vacancy for Taft himself to assume the role of chief justice. And, indeed, Taft mounted a strong campaign for that nomination even before his fellow Ohioan Warren Harding was inaugurated. Taft made it clear that he "could not accept any place but the Chief Justiceship."[63] Upon White's death, Harding succumbed to the pressure to nominate Taft as chief justice despite his desire to appoint his friend and ideological ally, George Sutherland, to the position.

The importance of ideological compatibility in the process for selecting the chief justice should not be surprising. While it seems clear that presidents consider the characteristics necessary to succeed as the Court's social leader (to use Danelski's term) as well as the administrative aspect of task leadership, presidents also want to ensure their chief justices will provide the kind of ideological leadership the president would if he were setting the agenda and framing the legal questions at conference and, most importantly, in writing or assigning opinions. By choosing a nominee who shares his legal philosophy and understanding of key constitutional issues, presidents can be more certain the Court will reach decisions with which they will agree.

V. Conclusion

In choosing chief justices, presidents take into account many of the factors they consider when choosing associate justices. The process, however, is unique in terms of the kind of uncertainty presidents face. The president seeks a nominee who is an able administrator, who facilitates the smooth and effective operation of the Court, and who does so in a way that leads to the kind of decisions and policy outcomes the president prefers. Of course there are cases where presidents made "mistakes" in the process, President Eisenhower's reported dissatisfaction with Chief Justice Earl Warren being the most widely cited example, but presidents have generally chosen chief justices who behaved in line with their preferences. As chief justice, William Rehnquist was finally able to turn the lone dissents he wrote as an associate justice into majority opinions, particularly in economic and federalism cases, with which Ronald Reagan would have been pleased. And despite the outcome of *National Federation of Independent Business v. Sebelius*,[64] President Bush must be largely pleased with his appointment of Chief Justice John Roberts. Roberts has consistently led the conservative wing of the Court to majorities on cases involving the Second Amendment, campaign finance reform, corporate speech, and affirmative action.

One reason for presidents' relative success in nominating chief justices may stem from the increasing likelihood that their nominees come from the ranks of sitting or former U.S. Supreme Court justices. One could hardly ask for a better predictor of a chief's future behavior on the Court than his or her behavior on that very Court as an associate justice. In terms of the kind of cases a justice hears and the relative freedom a justice enjoys, performance as an associate justice is the best indicator a president could have about future performance. One could imagine, for example, that in nominating John Roberts to fill the vacancy created by Sandra Day O'Connor's retirement, President Bush was planning to evaluate Roberts's performance on the Court during the October 2005 term in anticipation of appointing him chief when Chief Justice Rehnquist retired at the end of that term, as was Rehnquist's plan. Indeed, the many recent Supreme Court nominations of candidates with experience on the federal courts and the federal circuit courts of appeal more specifically indicate that presidents value the insight provided by that particular kind of experience. Although Chief Justice Roberts is almost sure to serve for many years to come, it seems likely that as his tenure draws to a close, appointing presidents might well nominate candidates to the federal courts of appeals, or even to the position of associate justice, with an eye toward evaluating their performance for a year or two in anticipation of an opening in the chief's seat.

Presidents also clearly see the value in consulting with current members of the Court, as well as the departing chief, in choosing their chief justice nominees. These actors can provide unique and valuable information about an internal (i.e., sitting associate justice) candidate's relationship with the other members of the Court and will also alert the president if there is likely to be tension created on the bench by choosing one associate justice over another. Each of these pieces of information helps lessen presidents' uncertainty concerning appointments of chief justices with whom they will forever be connected and whose leadership on the Supreme Court will have lasting political import.

NOTES

1. Letter from Justice William Rehnquist to Chief Justice Warren Burger (Sept. 24, 1973), Library of Congress, Manuscript Division, Papers of Harry A. Blackmun, container 352, folders 7–9, as cited in Linda Greenhouse, "How Not to Be Chief Justice: The Apprenticeship of William H. Rehnquist," *University of Pennsylvania Law Review* 154 (2006).

2. Adam Cohen, "The Justice Dissents," *New York Times*, November 16, 2012, http://www.nytimes.com/2012/11/18/books/review/the-partisan-the-life-of-william-rehnquist-by-john-a-jenkins.html?pagewanted=all&_r=0, accessed May 30, 2013.

3. Linda Greenhouse, "News Was Surprising to Colleagues on the Court," *New York Times*, September 5, 2005, http://www.nytimes.com/2005/09/05/politics/politicsspecial1/05court.html?pagewanted=all, accessed May 30, 2013.

4. David J. Danelski, "The Influence of the Chief Justice in the Decisional Process of the Supreme Court," in *The Federal Judicial System*, ed. Thomas P. Jahnige and Sheldon Goldman (New York: Holt, Rinehart, and Winston, 1968).

5. Forrest Maltzman and Paul J. Wahlbeck, "Opinion Assignment on the Rehnquist Court," *Judicature* 89 (2005).

6. Artemus Ward, "Making Work for Idle Hands: William H. Rehnquist and His Clerks," in *In Chambers: Stories of Supreme Court Law Clerks and Their Justices*, ed. Todd C. Peppers and Artemus Ward (Charlottesville: University of Virginia Press, 2012).

7. John Paul Stevens, *Five Chiefs: A Supreme Court Memoir* (New York: Little, Brown, 2011).

8. Greenhouse, "News Was Surprising to Colleagues."

9. Henry J. Abraham, *Justices, Presidents, and Senators: A History of U.S. Supreme Court Appointments from Washington to Bush II*, 5th ed. (Lanham, MD: Rowman & Littlefield, 2008).

10. Ibid., 277.

11. Stevens, *Five Chiefs*, 170.

12. Abraham, *Justices, Presidents, and Senators*, 183.

13. Danelski, "Influence of the Chief Justice."

14. See, for example, Danelski, "Influence of the Chief Justice"; Joel K. Goldstein, "Leading the Court: Studies in Influence as Chief Justice," *Stetson Law Review* 40 (2011); Forrest Maltzman and Paul J. Wahlbeck, "May It Please the Chief? Opinion Assignments in the Rehnquist Court," *American Journal of Political Science* 40 (1996); Theodore W. Ruger, "The Chief Justice's Special Authority and the Norms of Judicial Power," *University of Pennsylvania Law Review* 154 (2006).

15. Peter G. Fish, "The Office of Chief Justice of the United States: Into the Federal Judiciary's Bicentennial Decade," in *The Office of Chief Justice* (Charlottesville: White Burkett Miller Center of Public Affairs, University of Virginia Press, 1984).

16. The Judiciary Act of 1789, Chapter 20, §1, September 24, 1789. 1 Stat. 73.

17. Stevens, *Five Chiefs*, 42–44.

18. Todd E. Pettys, "Choosing a Chief Justice: Presidential Prerogative or a Job for the Court?" *Journal of Law & Politics* 22 (2006).

19. Ibid.; Edward T. Swaine, "Hail, No: Changing the Chief Justice," *University of Pennsylvania Law Review* 154 (2006).

20. Jeffrey A. Segal, "Senate Confirmations of Supreme Court Justices," *Journal of Politics* 49 (1987); Charles M. Cameron, Albert D. Cover, and Jeffrey A. Segal, "Senate Voting on Supreme Court Nominees: A Neoinstitutional Model," *American Political Science Review* 84 (1990); L. Marvin Overby et al., "Courting Constituents? An Analysis of the Senate Confirmation Vote on Justice Clarence Thomas," *American Political Science Review* 86 (1992); Jeffrey A. Segal, Charles M. Cameron, and Albert D. Cover, "A Spatial Model of Roll Call Voting: Senators, Constituents, Presidents, and Interest Groups in Supreme Court Confirmations," *American Journal of Political Science* 36 (1992); P. S. Ruckman, Jr., "The Supreme Court, Critical Nominations, and the Senate Confirmation Process," *Journal of Politics* 55 (1993); Bryon J. Moraski and Charles R. Shipan, "The Politics of Supreme Court Nominations: A Theory of Institutional Constraints and Choices," *American Journal of Political Science* 43 (1999); Charles R. Shipan and Megan L. Shannon, "Delaying Justice(s): A Duration Analysis of Supreme Court Confirmations," *American Journal of Political Science* 47 (2003); Timothy R. Johnson and Jason Roberts, "Presidential Capital and the Supreme Court Confirmation Process," *Journal of Politics* 66 (2004); Timothy R. Johnson and Jason Roberts, "Pivotal Politics, Presidential Capital, and Supreme Court Nominations," *Congress & the Presidency* 32 (2005); Lee Epstein et al., "The Changing Dynamics of Senate Voting on Supreme Court Nominees," *Journal of Politics* 68 (2006); Jonathan P. Kastellec, Jeffrey R. Lax, and Justin H. Phillips, "Public Opinion and Senate Confirmation of Supreme Court Nominees," *Journal of Politics* 72 (2010); among others.

21. Abraham, *Justices, Presidents, and Senators*, 2.

22. Ibid., 52.

23. Ibid., 326.

24. David A. Yalof, *Pursuit of Justices: Presidential Politics and the Selection of Supreme Court Nominees* (Chicago: University of Chicago Press, 1999); Christine L. Nemacheck, *Strategic Selection: Presidential Nomination of Supreme Court Justices from Herbert Hoover through George W. Bush* (Charlottesville: University of Virginia Press, 2007).

25. Yalof, *Pursuit of Justices*, 6.

26. Nemacheck, *Strategic Selection*.

27. Ibid.

28. Joel K. Goldstein, "Choosing Justices: How Presidents Decide," *Journal of Law and Politics* 26 (2011).

29. Robert Gibbs, White House Press Briefing, May 1, 2009, http://www.whitehouse.gov/the_press_office/Press-Briefing-By-Press-Secretary-Robert-Gibbs-5-1-09, accessed April 1, 2013.

30. George Watson and John A. Stookey, *Shaping America: The Politics of Supreme Court Appointments* (New York: Harper Collins College Publications, 1995).

31. Pettys, "Choosing a Chief"; Swaine, "Hail, No."

32. There is some disagreement as to who should be included on the list of Chief Justices of the United States. I rely on the U.S. Supreme Court's list of chiefs, which includes John Rutledge as the second chief justice (http://www.supremecourt.gov/about/members_text.aspx). Rutledge served as chief justice by virtue of

a recess appointment, though his nomination was rejected when it was sent to the Senate for confirmation. Others (see Ross Davies, "William Cushing: Chief Justice of the United States," *University of Toledo Law Review* 37 (2006)) contend that William Cushing should also be included among the ranks of chief justices as he was nominated and confirmed by the Senate before he declined the position due to ill health. For the purposes of the present examination, it is sufficient to treat the Court's own lists of chief justices as definitive.

33. Although it would be appealing to employ a statistical model to examine this question, the small number of nominations for which we have relevant data (only ten cases, including Justice Fortas's failed nomination in 1968) make this question more appropriate for a qualitative analysis.

34. For a fuller discussion of this theoretical context, see Nemacheck, *Strategic Selection*, chap. 2.

35. This number includes Chief Justice John Jay's appointment, who as the first chief justice could not have been elevated from a sitting position. Chief Justice Charles Evans Hughes, nominated by President Herbert Hoover in 1930, had previously served as an associate justice, but he had resigned from that post in 1916 to run for president. Chief Justice John Rutledge was nominated while an associate justice and served for a few months as a recess appointee, but the Senate refused to confirm him in December 1795.

36. Danelski, "Influence of the Chief Justice."

37. Ibid.

38. These papers are contained in the presidential libraries that are a part of the National Archives and Records Administration. I thank the fine archival staff at each of the following presidential libraries for their assistance in my research on these appointments: the Herbert Hoover Library, the Franklin D. Roosevelt Library, the Harry S. Truman Library, the Dwight D. Eisenhower Library, the Lyndon Baines Johnson Library, the Nixon Presidential Materials Project at the National Archives, and the Ronald Reagan Library. For financial support to conduct this research, I thank the Hoover Presidential Library Association, the Harry S. Truman Library Institute, the Lyndon Baines Johnson Foundation, the Cosmos Club Foundation and the College of William & Mary. The nominations of Edward White and William Taft are exceptions. The lists for those nominations are derived from secondary sources: Abraham, *Justices, Presidents, and Senators*; Daniel S. McHargue, "President Taft's Appointments to the Supreme Court," *Journal of Politics* 12 (1950); Robert C. Post, "Mr. Taft Becomes Chief Justice," *University of Cincinnati Law Review* 76 (2007–2008).

39. For a complete discussion on the development of these short lists, see Nemacheck, *Strategic Selection*, chap. 3.

40. Henry Abraham's discussion of Warren Burger's appointment is consistent with this finding. Abraham refers to Nixon's choice of Burger as "a bona fide lone, personal choice of the chief executive." *Justices, Presidents, and Senators*, 236.

41. It is possible that once President Bush's papers concerning his nomination of Chief Justice Roberts are open, information on other considerations will come to light.

42. Alpheus Thomas Mason, *Harlan Fisk Stone: Pillar of the Law* (New York: Viking, 1956), n. 39, 191, as cited in Abraham, *Justices, Presidents, and Senators*, 183.

43. Papers of Harry S. Truman, President's secretary's files, box 322.
44. Abraham, *Justices, Presidents, and Senators*, 190.
45. Danelski, "Influence of the Chief Justice," 1968.
46. Abraham, *Justices, Presidents, and Senators*, 190.
47. Papers of Dwight D. Eisenhower, Elbert Tuttle Oral History, 1970.
48. Papers of Dwight D. Eisenhower, Bernard M. Shanley Oral History Interview, 1975.
49. Papers of Dwight D. Eisenhower, Ann C. Whitman Diaries.
50. Abraham, *Justices, Presidents, and Senators*, 134.
51. In the case of Hoover's nomination of Hughes for the chief's seat in 1930, Hughes had experience as an associate justice of the Supreme Court, though he had left his seat in 1916 to run as the Republican candidate for president.
52. Yalof, *Pursuit of Justices*, 130.
53. Papers of Ronald Reagan, Peter Wallison memo, 1986. The other three names Chief Justice Burger submitted for consideration included Justice Byron White, Judge J. Clifford Wallace of the U.S. Court of Appeals for the Ninth Circuit, and Judge Edward Re, Chief Judge of the U.S. Court of International Trade.
54. Lawrence Baum, *Supreme Court*, 11th ed. (Washington, DC: CQ Press, 2012).
55. Abraham, *Justices, Presidents, and Senators*, 182.
56. Papers of Harry S. Truman, Papers of Eben Ayers, diaries, 1944–1948.
57. See David Danelski and Joseph S. Tulchin, *The Autobiographical Notes of Charles Evans Hughes* (Cambridge, MA: Harvard University Press, 1973), 292–93.
58. William Mitchell to Merlo Pusey, November 7, 1949, Herbert Hoover Library.
59. As of this writing, President George W. Bush's papers concerning judicial appointments have not yet been made available to researchers. Much of the material will be subject to Freedom of Information Act requests in January 2014.
60. George W. Bush, *Decision Points* (New York: Crown Publishers, 2010), 99.
61. Dana Milbank, "Scalia Showing His Softer Side: Justice Moves into Public Eye with Possible Sights Set on Chief Job," *Washington Post*, March 15, 2005, http://www.washingtonpost.com/wp-dyn/articles/A35096-2005Mar14.html, accessed August 8, 2013.
62. For detail on how ideological measures for nominees and those considered for nomination were developed, see Nemacheck, *Strategic Selection*, 119–21.
63. Post, "Mr. Taft Becomes Chief Justice," 772–73.
64. *National Federation of Independent Business v. Sebelius*, 567 U.S. _____ (2012).

5 ~ Confirming Chiefs

Ideology, Opportunity, and the Court's Center Chair

KEVIN J. MCMAHON

It was an extraordinary day. Indeed, in the history of the Supreme Court, few could compare with what happened on June 12, 1941. For on this day, President Franklin D. Roosevelt made three appointments to the high bench, a historical rarity.[1] First, he named South Carolina's junior senator, James "Jimmy" Byrnes, to a seat left open by the retirement of Justice James McReynolds of Tennessee, the last of the Four Horsemen who together led the charge against the constitutionality of FDR's New Deal legislation in the mid-1930s. Byrnes was one of the leaders of the southern Democrats, and his selection was understood as a reward for his hard work in helping to pass Lend-Lease legislation a few months earlier and to the fact that FDR had ignored earlier requests from southerners to choose "one of their own" for a seat on the nation's highest tribunal.[2] Next, the president chose to elevate Associate Justice Harlan Fiske Stone to the Court's center chair, which was being vacated by the retiring Charles Evans Hughes. With war underway in Europe and on the horizon for the United States, FDR decided to select a jurist for chief who could help unify the nation. The Republican-appointed Stone had served as Calvin Coolidge's attorney general before his appointment to the Court, but he had also written vigorous dissents supporting the constitutionality of the New Deal during the Court's campaign to dismantle it. Finally, the president selected his attorney general, Robert H. Jackson, to fill the Stone seat. Jackson, who had risen through the ranks of the Roosevelt administration, was considered a bright legal mind who would advance a liberal constitutional vision once on the Court. The Senate reacted to FDR's choices with speed. After receiving word of the Byrnes nomination, his colleagues took just eight minutes to confirm him. Stone and Jackson would have to wait a bit longer, but not that much. In fact, a Senate judiciary subcommittee unanimously approved Stone's elevation after a mere two minutes in session. And once their nominations reached the Senate floor, all three were confirmed by a voice vote.[3]

It had not been this easy for the nominee the last time the Court's center chair had been filled, and it would not be so for future chief justice nominees either. In this chapter, I consider the confirmations of last ten of these nominees: Edward D. White (1910), William Howard Taft (1921), Charles Evans Hughes (1930), Harlan Fiske Stone (1941), Fred Vinson (1946), Earl Warren (1954), Abe Fortas (1968), Warren Burger (1969), William Rehnquist (1986), and John Roberts (2005). Notably, the Senate only rejected one of these selections: Lyndon B. Johnson's attempted elevation of Associate Justice Abe Fortas. In addition to Fortas, three others faced significant opposition: Hughes (twenty-six senators opposed), Rehnquist (thirty-three senators opposed), and Roberts (twenty-two senators opposed). While chief justice nominees faced contentious confirmations more often than their counterparts for associate justice slots in the twentieth century, only on rare occasions did their appointment to chief appear to matter to the voting senators.[4] In other words, in reviewing these nominations, the evidence suggests that senators did not behave in a systematically distinctive way when considering a nominee for chief compared to a nominee for an associate seat. To some extent, this is a bit of a surprise. After all, as political scientist David Danelski has detailed in his scholarship on the position, the chief justice plays an instrumental role in the workings of the Court.[5] Given this, it might be expected that senators would view their responsibility in examining the worthiness of a chief justice nominee with a different—more exacting—lens during the confirmation process. But on the other hand, this nondiscriminating positioning should not be surprising at all. In my analysis and in the conclusion, I elaborate on why.

Another factor, however, does seem to have made a difference in whether a particular nomination for chief was contested. In six of the ten nominations under review, there were at least two vacancies on the Court when the Senate voted on the confirmation of a chief justice nominee, primarily because four of the ten were appointed from within. This multivacancy situation created the possibility for strategic action on the part of Senate opponents of the president, and the evidence suggests that on several occasions it altered the calculations—both in terms of the treatment of the nominee and the vote—inherent in the confirmation process.

Put simply, "to those senators itching for conflict, such a scenario provides a perfect opportunity to display both their willingness to compromise and their readiness to fight for their principles."[6] Indeed, on the four occasions when both the chief's seat and one associate slot were vacant, at least one of the two nominees were either rejected or closely contested in the Senate.[7]

In analyzing these chief justice nominations, I build on earlier work where I developed a presidency-focused political regimes approach to understanding shifts in the Supreme Court at certain historical moments.[8] In a 2007 article, I expounded upon that framework by constructing a historical institutional model for understanding presidential success in the Senate for Supreme Court nominees in the twentieth and early twenty-first centuries.[9] There I suggest that such a model "offers more promise" than attitudinal-inspired models "in explaining Senate challenges to presidential attempts to shape the Court through the appointment process. Part of the value of this model stems from its ability to predict party disunity, a prime source . . . of confirmation catastrophes." In focusing on the Senate's treatment of the past ten choices for chief, I rely on this model, and in turn divide the nominees into two groups: the six who faced comparably comfortable confirmations and the four who confronted conflict.[10] While the examination of the second group offers more intriguing insights about the role of the Senate in the confirmation of Supreme Court chiefs, I argue that these nominations generally show that more than ideology, opportunity mattered in how senators treated a nominee for chief. As I explain below, opportunity took different forms and was shaped by several factors, including disunity within the president's party, the timing of the appointment, and the "political time" of the appointing president. Ideology was certainly part of the equation, but it typically was not the sole explanatory factor in Senate votes, in part because the appointing president would more than likely have the opportunity to select a similarly minded nominee if a Senate majority rejected his first choice.[11] Divided government was also a factor for nominations during this period, but on the four occasions when a chief justice nominee was either rejected or contested, the same party controlled both the presidency and the Senate.[12]

Comfortable Confirmations

As I suggested in my 2007 article, the level of the president's political authority—as defined through political scientist Stephen Skowronek's concept of "political time"—was a useful predictor of conflictual confirmations during the twentieth century (see table 5.1 for a summary of his four periods of political time). The concept sheds light on how and why presidents with different levels of authority succeed and fail in the Senate with their selections for the Court, including those chosen for the center chair.[13] More specifically, three factors were particularly important during the twentieth century with regard to the likelihood of a confirmation fight for all high bench nominees: the level of the president's authority, the nominee's perceived ideology, and the timing of the appointment in the president's term. The evidence suggests that reconstructive presidents generally and articulation presidents in the earlier part of their terms had a much easier time in securing confirmation for their High Court nominees. Presidents leading at the end of a politics of articulation (i.e., immediately before the election of a preemptive president) or in the midst of a politics of disjunction faced the greatest difficulty. Preemptive presidents who sought to use a nominee to transform the preexisting legal order also provoked conflict in the confirmation process, no matter the timing of the appointment.

Table 5.2 shows the specific Senate contentiousness rates for each type of president in the twentieth century (for nominees for chief and associate justice), and table 5.3 lists the ten chief justice nominees—also by presidential type—under consideration.[14] In the following sections, I detail the six nominees for chief who faced little or no opposition in the Senate since the beginning of the twentieth century, and I elaborate on the usefulness of this model for explaining their confirmation experiences.

TABLE 5.1. Skowronek's Four Types of Political Regimes

Previously Established Commitments	President's Political Identity—Opposed	President's Political Identity—Affiliated
Vulnerable	Politics of Reconstruction	Politics of Disjunction
Resilient	Politics of Preemption	Politics of Articulation

Note: This table appears under the heading "Recurrent Structures of Presidential Authority," in Skowronek, *The Politics Presidents Make*, 36.

TABLE 5.2. Senate Contentiousness Rates for Twentieth-Century Supreme Court Nominees by Political Regime

Type of Political Regime	Rejection Percentage Rate	Closely Contested Percentage Rate	Overall Contentious Percentage Rate
Reconstruction	7.1	14.3	21.4
Articulation	4.0	12.0	16.0
Disjunction	25.0	25.0	50.0
Preemption	11.8	11.6	23.5

Note: Reprinted from McMahon 2007, 934. In that original table, I offered two figures for articulation presidents based on the difficulty of assessing the confirmation vote of Truman's final nominee, Sherman Minton. Here I include Minton. For a discussion on the vote, see McMahon, "Presidents, Political Regimes, and Contentious Supreme Court Nominations," 940. Given the small sample size, I have not separated out these rates for the chief justice nominees for inclusion in this table. See note 14 for those specific figures.

TABLE 5.3. The Last Ten Chief Justice Nominees by Period of Political Time

Political Time	Nominee	Year	President	Senate Vote
Reconstruction	Stone	1941	F. Roosevelt	Voice
	Rehnquist	*1986*	*Reagan*	*65–33*
Articulation	White	1910	Taft	Voice
	Taft	1921	Harding	Voice
	Vinson	1946	Truman	Voice
	Fortas	**1968**	**Johnson**	**45–43**
	Roberts	*2005*	*G. W. Bush*	*78–22*
Preemption	Warren	1954	Eisenhower	Voice
	Burger	1969	Nixon	74–3
Disjunction	*Hughes*	*1930*	*Hoover*	*52–26*

Note: Rejected nominees in **bold**; closely contested nominees in *italics*.

Stone: A Republican to Lead FDR's Court

According to the model, reconstructive presidents should have an easy time securing the confirmation for their nominees to the Court since they are challenging a severely weakened pre-existing order. And in fact, in the twentieth century, the Senate rejected only one Supreme Court nominee appointed by a reconstructive president (Robert Bork in 1987).[15] Two others endured contentious but ultimately successful confirmations (Hugo Black in 1937 and William Rehnquist's elevation to chief in 1986). Timing and ideology seemingly played a role in these two confirmation battles as both FDR (with Black) and Ronald Reagan (with Rehnquist) saw their first transformative appointment contested in the Senate.[16]

From the standpoint of constitutional decision making of the mid-1930s, the selection of Harlan Fiske Stone could have easily been defined as a transformative appointment as well. But by June 12, 1941, the Court had already made its "switch in time" and FDR had already appointed five men to the Court, thereby establishing a Roosevelt majority. Put another way, by the time of his elevation to chief, Stone's constitutional vision was consistent with the majority of the sitting justices, not in conflict with it. With two vacancies to fill in the first part of 1941, Roosevelt had several options available to him. In choosing to name a well-liked southern senator in Byrnes, a respected Republican justice in Stone (via elevation), and an advocate for liberalism in Jackson, he was able to appeal to a wide swath of constituencies. In turn, there was little opportunity for his opponents in the Senate to mount much of an opposition. And they didn't even try. In writing of the Stone nomination specifically, political scientist Henry

Abraham notes that it was greeted by "a nationwide chorus of praise and acclaim. . . . The press was ecstatic, the judiciary delighted, the intellectual community reassured, Congress happy."[17] The president expressed joy as well, triumphantly telling a private group, "It may not be proper to announce it, but today the Supreme Court is full."[18]

If attitudinalist Jeffrey Segal's ideological ratings—which range from 0 (most conservative) to 1 (most liberal)—are to be believed, liberals in the Senate might have had something to complain about since Stone (with a .300 rating) and Byrnes (.330) were perceived to be far more conservative than Jackson (1.000).[19] But with Charles Evans Hughes and James McReynolds departing, the Court would still be decidedly more liberal with these new justices on the high bench. Moreover, given his authorship of footnote 4 in *Carolene Products* and more importantly his dissents in defense of the constitutionality of the New Deal, not all viewed Stone in such conservative terms. Viewed either way, Stone's elevation was uncontested in the Senate. No senator dissented from the voice vote. So, as the model suggests, the reconstructive Roosevelt was able to appoint his chosen chief without being contested. But in truth, his choice of the appealing Stone—in conjunction with Byrnes and Jackson—made that expectation easy to realize.

White, Taft, and Vinson: Easy Articulation Appointments

As table 5.2 shows, in the twentieth century, articulation presidents had the highest success rate for their appointments to the Court.[20] The Senate rejected only one of their twenty-five nominees, namely, Abe Fortas's elevation to chief, which I discuss below. Three others secured a seat on the Court after a contested confirmation. This is in line with what the model suggests for articulation presidents, who generally seek to appoint jurists to the Court whose thinking is representative of the constitutional principles of a robust regime. In turn, when President William Howard Taft sought to fill the Court's center chair following the death of Melville Fuller in 1910, he had little difficulty in doing so. In fact, the Senate confirmed Edward D. White of Louisiana about an hour after it received his nomination from the president. Like FDR thirty-one years later, Taft likely benefited from being able to make three appointments on the very same day, December 12, 1910.

Despite this easy confirmation victory, Taft was initially concerned about Republican reaction to his choice for chief. He apparently thought that many in the GOP expected him to elevate fellow Republican and recently confirmed associate justice Charles Evans Hughes to that vacancy. Instead, the president chose to cross party—along with religious and battle—lines to select White, who was a leading Democrat, was a Catholic, and had been a soldier in the Confederate army. In contrast to Taft's expectations, the selection of White "was very popular, though [Republican Speaker of the House] Uncle Joe Cannon said: 'If Taft were pope, he'd want to appoint some Protestants to the College of Cardinals.'"[21]

To be sure, if Taft had only had a single vacancy to fill, his party's reaction might have been different. But on the same day, he was also able to name Willis Van Devanter of Wyoming and Joseph Lamar of Georgia to the two associate vacancies. Van Devanter had a long history in Republican Party politics and had served as a judge on the U.S. Eight Circuit Court since 1903. And as a westerner, he certainly pleased that contingent of the party. In choosing a second southerner with Lamar, Taft added evidence to suggestions that he had chosen White based on political calculations, hoping to break the Democrats' stranglehold on the South. While this was clearly part of his decision-making process in his choice for chief, Taft seemingly had other reasons to select White, who was the first sitting justice in history to be elevated to the center chair. Perhaps most importantly, Taft shared White's conservative constitutional outlook. And in this sense, as one instant analysis put it in discussing the choices of White and Lamar, "the South . . . [was] reaping the benefit of her conservatism."[22] Moreover, a poll of the Court's members found that White was the most popular choice to take over as chief, suggesting that he would be most able to lead the Court as Taft desired. Taft's selection of White over Hughes was likely also influenced by the fact that Teddy Roosevelt—Taft's predecessor in the presidency and future challenger—both supported White and disliked the "upstart" Hughes.[23] A final reason centered on the president's own ambitions. He wanted the position for himself one day. Choosing the middle-aged Hughes would likely mean that would never happen. At sixty-six, White's age was more in line with the president's own wants and desires.[24] And given the strong Republican majority in the Senate, confirmation came quickly.[25]

Taft would need to wait just over a decade to get his wish. Ousted from the White House in the 1912 election by Democrat Woodrow Wilson (aided by the GOP-bolting Progressive Roosevelt), Republicans regained the presidency with Warren Harding's election in 1920. Almost as soon as the votes had been counted, Taft started his campaign to secure the Court's center seat, aware that White had agreed to step down once a Republican was elected to the presidency again. Before he had a chance, White died on May 19, 1921. While many reportedly expected Harding to immediately announce Taft as White's replacement, as Abraham writes, "the president procrastinated, hoping for the rumored impending resignation of Associate Justice [John] Clarke to reward his intimate political adviser, ex-Senator George Sutherland. Almost beside himself with anxiety, the now 63-year-old Taft pulled out all the stops and through intermediaries succeeded in convincing the president that no additional vacancy would occur—short of another death."[26] While the overwhelmingly Republican Senate quickly confirmed Taft on the same day of his nomination, four senators did choose to dissent, three progressive Republicans and a populist southern Democrat.[27]

In similar articulation terms, when President Truman made his selection following Harlan Fiske Stone's death in 1946, he chose a nominee unlikely to upset the decidedly Democratic Senate. Fred Vinson of Kentucky was a well-known and popular man in the political circles of Washington and, like Truman's other choices, was a friend of the president. Indeed, according to one report, he was the president's "favorite poker companion."[28] Before FDR appointed him to the U.S. Circuit Court of Appeals for the District of Columbia in 1937, Vinson had served twelve years in the House of Representatives. After six years on the United States Court of Appeals for the District of Columbia, he left to join the executive branch. At the time Truman selected him for the Supreme Court, he was serving as the treasury secretary. And by all accounts, he had been an important advisor to the president during his first year in office.[29]

While Vinson was rated as a liberal on Segal's scale (.750), others viewed him in more conservative terms. Indeed, there was a fair degree of uncertainty about his ideology at the time of his appointment. As Lewis Wood of the *New York Times* wrote, "Vinson's appearance on the court horizon" produced "a great deal of speculation as to his coming position in court philosophy." While some described him as "just a bit to the left of center," general consensus held that he would not join "the 'liberal' wing of the court," which was made up of Hugo L. Black, William O. Douglas, Frank Murphy, and Wiley Rutledge. In fact, after a public spat between Jackson and Black and numerous stories about dissension on the Court, Truman reportedly selected Vinson because he thought he could unify the high bench. Vinson had a reputation as a "skilled conciliator," and after brief consultations with the Court's last two Republican-appointed members, Charles Evans Hughes and Owen Roberts, the president decided that his old friend would be the right fit for the Court's center chair.[30] As the model suggests, the articulation-appointed Vinson faced little resistance in the

Senate, which confirmed him by a voice vote just two weeks after receiving his nomination.

Warren: The Symbol of Liberalism

As Stephen Skowronek has noted, preemptive presidents who seek to challenge the established principles of a resilient pre-existing governing order face great challenges, even the possibility of impeachment.[31] But with his selection of Earl Warren, former Republican vice presidential candidate and current California governor, President Dwight D. Eisenhower did not seek to challenge the Court's emerging liberalism. In fact, Warren's name would come to define the period of the Court's history in which a majority of the justices were most committed to the advancement of a liberal creed. Of course, President Eisenhower did not necessarily intend for the Court to develop in such an ideologically liberal fashion, and he famously complained that two of his appointments who advanced that cause—Warren and William Brennan—had been among the mistakes of his presidency.[32]

But when Eisenhower chose Warren for the Court's center chair, he was not thinking in those ideological terms. Instead, the president was paying off a political debt. During the Republican convention to select the party's presidential nominee, Eisenhower's team reportedly promised Warren a key post in the administration if he supported the general over Senator Robert Taft of Ohio. Warren delivered, helping to secure the nomination for Eisenhower. When Eisenhower filled out his cabinet, though, there was no position that interested Warren, who was then nearing the end of his third term as California governor. So instead, the president told Warren that he would appoint him to the "first vacancy" on the Court.[33] Eight months into his presidency, Chief Justice Vinson died of heart failure, leaving Eisenhower an opportunity to deliver on his second promise to Warren. He did so, making a recess appointment on September 30, 1953.

The choice of Warren was a popular one, and most expected the Senate to easily confirm him once the president formally submitted his name in early 1954. But Republican William Langer of North Dakota and a small band of conservative southern Democrats objected to the nomination, delaying confirmation. As chairman of the Senate Judiciary Committee, Langer was said to be delaying consideration of Warren's nomination because of the dearth of North Dakotans in important positions in the federal government. Another report pointed to other reasons: "the spasm of suspicion now sweeping the country . . . [is] that [Warren's] enemies in California are after him for opposing the loyalty oath at the University of

California; and that one or two southern Senators oppose him because they think he will vote to end racial segregation in the nation's schools."[34] Despite these concerns about Warren's well-known liberalism—with a Segal rating of .750—after six weeks, his critics could delay the committee vote no more. In fact, when the Senate Judiciary Committee finally voted on his nomination, even Langer supported it. Two southerners and a border state senator did not.[35] Nevertheless, five days later the full Senate confirmed him by a voice vote. No dissents were heard, but there were reportedly only about forty senators in the chamber at the time.[36]

Burger: Waiting for Haynsworth?

Richard Nixon was a different type of preemptive president than Eisenhower. While Eisenhower had chosen jurists for the Court unlikely to upset the Senate's apple cart, Nixon used his appointments to the high bench as a means to help him build a Republican electoral majority.[37] During the 1968 presidential race, Nixon—along with third-party candidate George Wallace—had consistently blamed the Warren-led Court's criminal law decisions for the rapid rise in street crime and for the unrest on college campuses and in the nation's riot-ridden inner cities. Moreover, when Nixon captured the presidency after narrowly defeating Vice President Hubert Humphrey, he knew he would have the chance to name the next chief justice due to Warren's retirement and the successful filibuster of Fortas (discussed below). What he couldn't know was by the time he announced that Warren Earl Burger—an ironic name for Nixon's choice to be the next chief—he would have a second vacancy to fill. For on May 15, 1969, under pressure from Nixon's attorney general John Mitchell, Abe Fortas decided to step down from the Court in the face of revelations about financial wrongdoing. The president announced Burger's nomination six days later. With regard to the confirmation process, the timing was significant.

Hailing from Minnesota, Burger reportedly had a record of moderation on civil rights and toughness on "law-and-order" issues. Given this combination, it would have been a difficult for liberals in the Senate—both Democrats and Republicans—to oppose him. Two recent public opinions surveys told the story why it was unwise to challenge a "law-and-order" judge who even the editorial writers at the *New York Times* described as "moderately liberal" on civil rights and other non–criminal justice matters. The first was a January 1969 Gallup poll that showed that 74.4 percent of respondents thought courts did not treat criminals "harshly enough." A paltry 1.9 percent thought courts were "too harsh" in dealing with criminals.

In another poll, begun the day after Burger's nomination, Gallup showed that 52 percent of respondents thought "conservatives" should fill vacancies on the Supreme Court. Only 25 percent thought "liberals" should be selected. So from the perspective of Senate liberals, there was little reason to oppose Burger. As Democrat Lee Metcalf of Montana, a liberal with a reputation as one of the Senate's "constitutional scholars," noted, "He's a better appointee than I had any right to expect. . . . Who knows, he might event be another Warren."[38] Given this reaction, Burger's confirmation was a fairly comfortable one. After six weeks of consideration, the Senate confirmed him by a vote of 74 to 3.

From the perspective of a president's opponents in the Senate, opportunity may come in a variety of forms. So instead of challenging Burger, Senate liberals waited for Nixon's choice to fill the Fortas seat to unleash their distaste for the president's perceived plans for the Court. While the announcement would not be made until near the end of summer, inside the White House Nixon made it clear soon after Fortas's departure that he wanted "a white southern conservative federal judge under age sixty."[39] On August 18, the American public learned his choice was Clement Haynsworth of South Carolina. While Segal rates Burger as more conservative than Haynsworth at the time of their appointments (.115 to .160), Nixon's opponents in the Senate didn't see it that way. To be sure, in their drive to undermine the Haynsworth nomination, opposing senators focused on his ethics more than his ideology. But as political scientist John Massaro has shown, the vote was largely an ideological one.[40] It was also one that divided the GOP, as nearly 40 percent of Republican senators—mostly from Democratic-leaning states—abandoned their recently elected president to oppose the Haynsworth nomination. After his defeat, Nixon countered with another southerner, G. Harrold Carswell (with a Segal rating of .040), who was destined for a Senate defeat as well. And again ideology, not Carswell's questionable qualifications, was the underlying motivation for the opposition.[41]

In the end, it would take the president nearly a year to find a jurist the Senate was willing to confirm. On his third try, he chose Harry Blackmun of Minnesota. Senate liberals viewed Blackmun in similar terms to Burger: a moderately conservative jurist who was unlikely to challenge the Warren Court's path-breaking civil rights decisions. And it is easy to understand why. As one newspaper account noted, like Burger, Blackmun's opinions "stamp him as a moderate on civil rights and civil liberties issues . . . [and] more conservative on criminal suspects' constitutional claims."[42] (Segal's rating of Blackmun is also the same as that of Burger's: .115). In fact, the two had known each other since kindergarten, and Blackmun had even served as Burger's best man at his wedding. So with the Senate denying him his southern justice, Nixon settled on Burger's Minnesota Twin. In turn, Blackmun faced little opposition in the Senate, earning confirmation without a single dissenting vote. As Nixon's experience shows (and as the model suggests), preemptive presidents need to tread carefully to secure confirmation for their nominees for the High Court. Nixon easily succeeded with his choice for chief. But with the Fortas vacancy, he allowed his opponents to define the debate as one about protecting civil rights. As result, he witnessed the Senate reject his two southern selections. Notably, however, the nominee's overall ideology—at least as scored on Segal's attitudinal scale—didn't matter much in these votes. Haynsworth had a more liberal rating than both Burger and Blackmun. Carswell had a more conservative rating. What mattered to those senators in opposition was the individual nominee's views on certain issues, specifically civil rights.

Contentious Confirmations

During the twentieth century, presidents leading during all four types of political time saw their nominees for the Court face contentious confirmations. While candidates nominated by reconstructive and articulation presidents were less likely to face contentiousness in the Senate, as noted above, timing and ideology were additional factors in the confirmation equation. More specifically, both of the century's reconstructive presidents saw their first transformative thinker contested but not rejected.[43] And four of the century's articulation presidents witnessed their last nominee either closely contested or rejected. Notably, on all four occasions—and only on those occasions—the articulation presidency was followed by the election of a preemptive president, suggesting a decline in the pre-existing regime's authority.[44] Two of these appointments were for chief justice: the first by the articulation president Lyndon Johnson (Abe Fortas) and the second by the reconstructive Ronald Reagan (William Rehnquist). I explore both selections below.

The model suggests that disjunctive presidents, who rule over a governing regime whose legitimacy is in free fall, are bound to face hostility in the Senate no matter the timing of the appointment and especially if they select a jurist identified with the principles of the crumbling regime. Herbert Hoover's appointment of Charles Evans Hughes to the Court's center chair fits into that category. Of the ten chief justice nominees I examine in these pages, the two chosen by preemptive presidents—Warren and Burger—did not have a conflictual confirmation. As noted above, however, no matter the timing of the appointment, a preemptive president who selects a jurist who poses too great a challenge to the pre-existing order's constitutional principles is likely to face a conflictual confirmation. The final chief justice nominee under review is the most recent, John Roberts. I separate the Roberts appointment from those of the previous century due the altered confirmation environment that has developed in recent years.

Hughes: The Short Battle Over a Corporate Chief

In replacing the retiring William Howard Taft, the only man to serve both as president and a Supreme Court justice (as chief), President Herbert Hoover chose another man well-known to the American public. On the same day Taft announced his retirement, February 3, 1930, Hoover named Charles Evans Hughes as the next chief. Hughes was familiar with the Court, having left the high bench after six years of service to run for the presidency in 1916. With Republicans firmly in control of the Senate, few expected much of a fight. In fact, the day after the nomination the *New York Times* titled its editorial in support of Hughes "The New Chief Justice."[45] But unbeknownst to the editorial writers at the *Times*, there was discontent brewing in the Senate. Indeed, writing in 1951, Hughes's biographer Samuel Hendel exclaimed that with the possible exception Roger B. Taney, the debate over the confirmation of Hughes was "the most bitter" for a chief justice nominee "in the history of the United States." Hendel continues, "Every known aspect of the life of Charles Evans Hughes commanding the slightest public interest or importance was canvassed in the course of this historic debate."[46]

To be sure, senators who were displeased with the president viewed this high-profile appointment as a means to express their feelings. But more than that, in a nation in economic turmoil following the stock market crash the previous October, Hughes's résumé represented a life lived according to a set of principles whose legitimacy was in sharp decline. In the words of constitutional scholar Paul Freund, Hughes's critics viewed him as a "menacing reactionary." In particular, Senate liberals and southern Democrats combined forces to express their concern about the long list of corporate clients Hughes had served after losing the presidential bid to Woodrow Wilson in 1916. In doing so, they "identified the arguments advanced on behalf of private clients as the judicial philosophy of the counsel."[47] In his their minds, Hughes had served the very interests responsible for the nation's economic ill health and widespread unemployment. As progressive

Republican George Norris of Nebraska noted in opposing his confirmation, "No man in public life so exemplifies the influence of power combinations in the political and financial world as does Mr. Hughes." Norris was also unnerved by the fact that Hughes had left his seat on the Court to run for the presidency and now sought to return to that tribunal. To him, this maneuvering threatened to reduce the Court "to the level of a political machine . . . [which would] inevitably encourage and stimulate political activity on the part of judges of the Supreme Court."[48] When the vote was taken, eleven Republicans joined fifteen Democrats to make up the opposition. But a sufficient number of senators, fifty-two, supported Hughes. Fourteen abstained from the vote. Hughes, who "had long been one of the most prominent members of the Republican party," would now lead the Court as the nation spun more deeply into economic depression.[49]

Senate liberals may have been unsuccessful in blocking Hughes's appointment to chief justice, but before long they would taste victory. On the heels of Hughes's narrow confirmation victory, President Hoover, in a bid to build support in the South, nominated forty-five-year-old John J. Parker to the Court following the death of Justice Edward Sanford on March 8, 1930. As they had done just weeks earlier with Hughes, liberals sought to use the Parker nomination as a means to attack the president. This time they succeeded in denying Hoover his choice. By a vote of 39–41, the Senate rejected a nominee for the Court for the first time in thirty-six years. As suggested above, disjunctive presidents are bound to face difficulty in shaping the Court in their own image, even when they select a jurist of Hughes's stature.

Fortas: "Law-and-Order" and a Confirmation Battle in Campaign Season

As an articulation president with the end of his term in sight, Lyndon Johnson sought to install another strong liberal on a Court under sharp challenge from conservatives in 1968.[50] In doing so, he chose to elevate his close friend Associate Justice Abe Fortas (Segal rating of .845) to replace the retiring Chief Justice Earl Warren and to fill the Fortas vacancy with a fellow Texan, Homer Thornberry.[51] It was not a wise decision. Republicans and conservative southern Democrats in the Senate took delight in grilling Fortas about the Court's decisions on criminal law, including some that were reached before he was even a justice. Fortas felt that because he might decide similar cases in the future—after all he would still remain as an associate justice if the Senate denied his elevation—he could not fully respond to the senators' questions. But Fortas's refusal simply allowed the senators to grill him more, knowing he would be unable to simultaneously unleash a counterattack and maintain his pledge not to answer questions on issues the Court might hear at a later date.

Perhaps more importantly, the Senate's consideration of Fortas took place in the midst of a presidential campaign in which both the Republican nominee, Richard Nixon, and third-party candidate, George Wallace, were stressing crime as a major concern. Significantly, both placed a great deal of blame on the Supreme Court for the lawlessness and unrest across the land. As Nixon repeated throughout the campaign, in his eyes, the Court's decisions "had the effect of seriously hamstringing the peace forces in our society and strengthening the criminal forces." And the American public appeared to agree. According to one survey taken a year after the Fortas filibuster, 82 percent of American men agreed—50 percent "a great deal" and 32 percent "somewhat"—that "recent Supreme Court decisions have made it more difficult to punish criminals."[52]

Some had warned LBJ that he should not attempt to fill the Warren vacancy, that as a lame duck nearing the end of his presidency he should allow the victor of the November vote to choose the next chief. But to LBJ, deferring was not a reasonable option. He viewed the appointment as a way to further infuse his brand of liberalism on the Court for years to come. Unfortunately for him, it was that very brand of liberalism that was attracting the attacks from Nixon and Wallace and putting the Democrats on the defensive. Stated simply, the move backfired. There would not be a Chief Justice Fortas. After a summer of attacks on Capitol Hill, the full Senate finally took up the Fortas nomination in early autumn. With conservative Republicans aligning with southern Democrats, both of whom were upset over many of the Warren Court's decisions, Fortas was unable to overcome a filibuster. With nineteen Democrats breaking with their president, the vote to invoke cloture failed, 45 to 43. The following day, LBJ withdrew the nomination. A month later Richard Nixon captured the presidency.

As noted above, articulation presidents making their last appointment to the Court, particularly one designed to instill new life to their regime's principles, are likely to confront conflict in the Senate. LBJ understood the risks, but he was unwilling to back down and watch the principles he had advocated for during his presidency undermined by the second coming of Richard Nixon. To him, Fortas was worth the fight, even if it ended in failure. To his ideological opponents in the Senate, rejecting Fortas would improve their chances of getting a more like-minded nominee as chief. After all, they had seen the public opinion polls and understood that Nixon was the odds-on favorite to win the vote in November.

Rehnquist: Elevating an Ideological Leader for a Conservative Court

In 1981, Ronald Reagan disappointed social conservatives in his coalition with his first selection for the Court, Sandra Day O'Connor (with a Segal rating of .415). But with his next appointments in 1986, Reagan sought to make amends to that constituency and to advance his own constitutional vision. He did so by elevating the Court's lone "movement" conservative, William H. Rehnquist (Segal rating of .045) to replace the retiring Chief Justice Burger and to fill the associate vacancy with Antonin Scalia (Segal rating of .000). According to political scientist David Yalof, Rehnquist was chosen for the Court's center chair because key players in the Reagan administration held the "view that sitting judges or justices who had a clearly articulated philosophy were the most likely to remain steadfast to their views." Reagan apparently selected Scalia over runner-up Robert Bork because of concerns about the difficulty in confirming both Bork and Rehnquist and because of Scalia's age (he was nine years younger than Bork) and his ethnicity (he would be the first Italian American nominee to the Court).[53]

With the Senate in Republican hands, liberal Democrats understood the difficulty of denying both nominees a seat on the Court, so they focused their energies on undermining Rehnquist's candidacy. Scalia received comparatively lenient treatment and eventually won confirmation without a dissenting vote. Moreover, while Scalia might have been perceived as slightly more conservative according to Segal, Senate liberals had fifteen years' worth of conservative opinions and a collection of "character questions" on which to attack Rehnquist. In particular, Rehnquist's Senate doubters—led by Ted Kennedy of Massachusetts—thought the future chief justice was too far to the right to lead the Court. As Kennedy declared, Rehnquist's "own record of massive isolated dissent" demonstrated that "he is too extreme on race, too extreme on women's rights, too extreme on freedom of speech, too extreme on separation of church and state—too extreme to be Chief Justice." Indeed, the campaign against Rehnquist was geared more at denying him opportunity to lead the Court since he would no doubt retain his seat on the high bench even if he didn't occupy the center chair. But it also allowed liberals like Kennedy an opportunity to publicly challenge the president's plans for the Court in hopes of undermining their appeal, and to perhaps weaken a jurist widely viewed as deeply committed to the conservative cause (as they would successfully accomplish a year later with Robert Bork).[54] To do that, Rehnquist's opponents focused in part on the fact that Reagan was seeking to elevate this "Lone Ranger" of conservatism to the Court's center chair. As constitutional scholar and incoming Yale University president Benno C. Schmidt, Jr., wrote at the time, "The question is whether [Rehnquist's] reactionary constitutional vision is so out of touch with that of his colleagues and the temper of the times that all his powers of intellect and personality cannot overcome the essential isolation that has been the overriding characteristic of his service on the Court to date."[55] Notably, however, Rehnquist and the team assembled by the Reagan White House "did not prepare any defense nor anticipate any issues arising over the significance of being the Chief as opposed to an Associate." Rather, they believed Senate liberals would oppose him based on his ideology.[56]

And indeed, while liberals might have preferred that Rehnquist not lead the Court, their main objections were defined by his ideology, not his location on the bench.[57] At the time, however, it was not sufficient to undermine a nominee's candidacy simply on ideology. So in addition to expressing concerns about how his conservatism would undermine his ability to lead the Court, Rehnquist's critics highlighted the fact that he owned property with constitutionally invalid restricted covenants, had as a clerk to Justice Robert Jackson written a memo of dissent in the historic 1954 *Brown* decision, and as a young man participated in vote suppression (a charge he denied).[58] In the end, Rehnquist was able to sufficiently deflect these criticisms to win confirmation, 65-33. Significantly, Republicans largely held together with only two of the fifty-one in their ranks voting in opposition. Still, given the closeness of the vote, Rehnquist earned the distinction of becoming the chief justice with the highest number of senators opposing his confirmation. As noted above, even reconstructive presidents like Reagan may face difficulty in the Senate when they appoint their first transformative thinker. And in the case of the Senate's objections to Rehnquist's elevation, that resistance was clear. His opponents were profoundly concerned—it turns out rightly—that his elevation to chief marked the turning point to a more conservative brand of constitutional law. As Schmidt wrote days after Reagan selected Rehnquist and Scalia: "These appointments constitute a greater challenge to the received tradition of constitutional law than any we have seen in a half century."[59]

Roberts: The Meaning of Success in a New Confirmation Environment

Antonin Scalia was the second-to-last Supreme Court nominee to earn confirmation without a dissenting vote. The following year, 1987, Reagan's selection of Robert Bork would create an unprecedented confirmation battle that would effectively change the nature of the process. While Clarence

Thomas was able to survive a brutal confirmation process four years later, the other post-Bork nominees of the twentieth century are best described as compromise selections, chosen because they were considered confirmable by the appointing president. Ideology certainly mattered, but on each occasion the appointing president was willing to select a more ideologically moderate nominee to secure a relatively smooth Senate confirmation. More specifically, according to Segal's perceived ideological scores, three of Reagan and George H. W. Bush's choices—O'Connor before Bork and Anthony Kennedy and David Souter after him—were the most moderate Republican-appointed justices since Eisenhower's selection of Potter Stewart in 1959. In addition, Bill Clinton's nominees—Ruth Bader Ginsburg and Stephen Breyer—were the two most moderate nominees appointed by a Democratic president since two of Truman's choices in the 1940s.[60] And he made them even though the Democrats controlled the Senate at the time of both nominations.

By 2005, when President George W. Bush appointed John Roberts to the Court, that formula had changed. By this time, it had become more acceptable in a highly polarized Congress for senators to publicly declare their opposition to a nominee for purely ideological reasons. As Senator Charles Schumer, Democrat of New York, wrote in a 2001 op-ed, "If the president uses ideology in deciding whom to nominate to the bench, the Senate, as part of its responsibility to advise and consent, should do the same in deciding whom to confirm."[61] In fact, by 2005, nominees faced an entirely different form of the Senate's confirmation gauntlet. With the GOP in control, a Republican-appointed nominee who was considered a compromise choice could no longer win confirmation like O'Connor, Kennedy, and Souter had in the 1980s and early 1990s. Instead, Senate Republicans were more interested in engaging in a confirmation battle to ensure an identifiable "movement" conservative a seat on the Court than they were in a compromise choice who would confront little Senate resistance. In other words, they were not interested in a nominee like Harriet Miers (Segal rating of .270), who was selected by George W. Bush in part because she was unlikely to generate much protest from Senate Democrats.[62] Senate Republicans wanted a more reliable conservative. And for this reason, several weeks after announcing the Miers nomination, President Bush yielded to conservative objections and withdrew her name from consideration. In her place, he chose Samuel Alito, a federal judge who had a reputation as a "movement" conservative (Segal rating of .100) who was unlikely to succumb to the "Greenhouse Effect," a term named after longtime *New York Times* Supreme Court reporter Linda Greenhouse and defined as "the pattern in which some Supreme Court Justices have drifted away from the conservatism of their early votes and opinions towards the stated preferences of cultural elites, including left-leaning journalists and the 'liberal legal establishment that dominates at elite law schools,'"[63] To be sure, Alito faced a tougher confirmation than John Roberts had months earlier, but with Republicans in control, conservatives were confident of confirmation. In the end, the Senate approved his nomination by a vote of 58-42. Only one Republican—Lincoln Chafee of Rhode Island—joined the opposition.[64]

As the first nominee of the twenty-first century, John Roberts received high marks for his stellar qualifications. With a Segal rating of .120, he was also pleasing to the Senate Republicans who would later oppose Harriet Miers. While in the past, senators of the opposing (and minority) party might have fully supported a nominee like John Roberts—if only to save their fire for the nominee for the second vacancy—in the highly polarized atmosphere of the 2005 confirmation process the calculation was different. Even though Roberts was the first selection of the newly re-elected George W. Bush—who unlike in 2000 won both the popular and Electoral College vote four years later—twenty-two senators opposed Roberts's nomination to be chief. By historical standards, this was a highly unusual figure, especially since Bush was an articulation president making his first appointment and Roberts was replacing the conservative Rehnquist. Moreover, the level of party polarization in the Senate was stark. In the previous century, any nominee who confronted conflict in the Senate faced bipartisan opposition, even if the number of senators who abandoned their president was small. But in 2005, only Democrats opposed Roberts.

This new trend of more ideological choices and greater partisan opposition has continued during Barack Obama's presidency. His selections of Sonia Sotomayor and Elena Kagan were both sufficiently satisfying to Senate Democrats (Segal ideological ratings of .780 and .730, respectively), and provoked a high level of Republican opposition.[65] With such a small sample size, it is difficult to draw too many conclusions about the developments in this century. In the current environment, however, it seems unlikely that the model that was so useful in predicting contentious confirmations in the twentieth century still holds great value. Of course, when it comes to confirming a chief, we will not likely know for some time. Indeed, since John Roberts is expected to serve on the Court for many years to come, the choice to be the next chief will likely face an entirely different set of confirmation hurdles in the Senate.

Conclusion

During the twentieth century, when the opportunity presented itself—as suggested by the presidency-focused political regimes model outlined above—senators typically voted in ideological and/or political terms on divisive confirmation battles. So, for example, while senators opposing the nominations of Fortas (for chief), Haynsworth, Carswell, and Bork cited specific concerns about those particular jurists, as Massaro has shown, the Senate votes were largely on ideological grounds. Moreover, in my own work, I show how Republican concerns about Nixon's plans for the Court, particularly from GOP senators from the most Democratic states, divided the party and doomed the Haynsworth and Carswell nominations.[66] With their votes then, senators as a group appear to have been far less concerned about the inners workings of the Court and more interested in how a new justice might alter its doctrinal product. For this reason, they tend not to view nominees for chief in starkly distinct terms than those for associate justice. In today's more polarized Senate, the ideological and political motivations are even clearer as even the highest quality of nominees are almost certain to garner negative votes from senators of the opposite party of the president's own. For their part, presidents—at least at certain times—have been more concerned with how a particular individual might perform the duties of chief justice. For example, the elevations of White and Stone and the selection of Vinson were driven in part by how these men would help lead the Court. But there is not much evidence to suggest that senators think in similar terms when voting to confirm or deny a nominee for a seat on the high bench, either in the current or the most recent century.

NOTES

1. This not to say the three had as great an impact on the Court as might have been expected. After all, Byrnes served only a year, and Stone died five years after his elevation. Jackson's service was the most noteworthy, but it was also shorter than expected. He died in 1954 after thirteen years on the high bench.

2. Considered "the most radical man in the Senate" at the time of his appointment, Hugo L. Black of Alabama was not viewed by fellow southerners as one of their own. Joseph Alsop and Turner Catledge, *The 168 Days* (Garden City, NY: Doran, 1938), 301.

3. The Senate confirmed Stone and Jackson on June 27 and July 7, respectively. Only one senator dissented. Democrat Millard Tydings of Maryland opposed Jackson's confirmation.

4. In the twentieth century, of the nine nominees for chief, one was rejected and two were closely contested (for an overall contentiousness rate of 33.3 percent). Of the fifty-one nominees for an associate slot, four were rejected and five were closely contested (for an overall contentiousness rate 17.6 percent). I define a contentious but successful confirmation as one in which at least 20 percent of voting senators opposed the nomination.

5. David Danelski, "The Influence of the Chief Justice in the Decisional Process of the Supreme Court," paper presented at the annual meeting for the American Political Science Association, New York, 1960.

6. Kevin J. McMahon, "Presidents, Political Regimes, and Contentious Supreme Court Nominations: A Historical Institutional Model," *Law & Social Inquiry* 32 (2007): 938.

7. The four were as follows: Fortas (rejected) and Thornberry in 1968; Burger and Haynsworth (rejected) in 1969; Rehnquist (closely contested) and Scalia in 1986, and Roberts (closely contested) and Alito (closely contested after the withdrawal of Harriet Miers) in 2005. With the Senate's rejection of Fortas's elevation to chief, Thornberry's nomination became moot. And while Nixon did not appoint Haynsworth until August 18, 1969, senators confirmed Burger on June 9, 1969, knowing there was another vacancy on the Court due to Fortas's resignation on May 15, 1969. On one of the other two occasions since the beginning of the twentieth century when there two vacancies—neither for chief—the Senate acted in a similar fashion, contesting the nomination of William Rehnquist but not of Lewis Powell in 1971. On the other occasion, in 1957, the Senate easily confirmed both William Brennan and Charles Whittaker. Notably, in the two occasions since the beginning of the twentieth century when presidents filled three vacancies, the Senate did not reject or contest any of the nominees. In fact, the Senate confirmed President Taft's three December 12, 1910, nominees and President Roosevelt's three June 12, 1941, nominees quickly and by voice vote. Notably, both Taft and Roosevelt selected nominees for chief who were members of the opposite party.

8. Kevin J. McMahon, *Reconsidering Roosevelt on Race: How the Presidency Paved the Road to Brown* (Chicago: University of Chicago Press, 2004); Kevin J. McMahon, *Nixon's Court: His Challenge to Judicial Liberalism and Its Political Consequences* (Chicago: University of Chicago Press, 2011).

9. McMahon, "Presidents, Political Regimes." In that article, I focused on twentieth-century Supreme Court nominations based on earlier scholarly work that distinguished that century's nominees from their earlier ones (see, for example, Richard D. Friedman, "The Transformation in the Senate Response to Supreme Court Nominations: From Reconstruction to the Taft Administration and Beyond," *Cardozo Law Review* 5 (1983); Robert Scigliano, *The Supreme Court and the Presidency* (New York: Free Press, 1971); and Jeffrey A. Segal, "Senate Confirmation of Supreme Court Justices: Partisan and Institutional Politics," *Journal of Politics* 49 (1987)). McMahon, "Presidents, Political Regimes," 921. Here, and for the same reasons, I again begin my examination of the nominees for chief justice in the twentieth century. For a study that considers all Supreme Court nominees by also employing a Skowronek-influenced historical institutional approach, see Artemus Ward, "The Nominations Presidents Make: Appointing Justices to the U.S. Su-

preme Court," *Congress and the Presidency* 28 (2001). As I discuss in the 2007 article and below, new developments in the twenty-first century—particularly the high level of party polarization—raise serious questions about the continuing usefulness of my model for understanding Supreme Court confirmations.

10. McMahon, "Presidents, Political Regimes," 920, 933.

11. The obvious exception here is Lyndon Johnson's attempted elevation of Abe Fortas, which occurred near the end of his presidency.

12. For the purposes of this chapter, I exclude the House of Representatives in defining unified or divided government.

13. Stephen Skowronek, *The Politics Presidents Make: Leadership from John Adams to George Bush* (Cambridge, MA: Harvard University Press, 1993); McMahon, "Presidents, Political Regimes." Moreover, such insights help explain how Supreme Courts—and in turn Supreme Court decision making—are constructed politically, a central argument of the regime politics scholarship. See, for example, Mark A. Graber, "Constructing Judicial Review," *American Review of Political Science* 8 (2005); and Keith Whittington, *Political Foundations of Judicial Supremacy: The Presidency, the Supreme Court, and Constitutional Leadership in U.S. History* (Princeton: Princeton University Press, 2007).

14. The contentious rates for the ten chief justice nominees under review—separated by rejection rate, closely contested rate, and overall contentiousness rate—are as follows: two nominees appointed by reconstruction presidents (0 percent, 50 percent, 50 percent); five nominees appointed by articulation presidents (20 percent, 20 percent, 40 percent); one nominee appointed by a disjunctive president (100 percent, NA, 100 percent); two nominees appointed by preemptive presidents (0 percent, 0 percent, 0 percent). Given the small sample size here, however, these figures do not advance the discussion very much.

15. As I discuss below, the rejection of Bork altered the character of the confirmation process. The presence of divided government and the low level of political authority Reagan possessed for a reconstructive president—particularly in 1987—were important factors in his rejection.

16. On the notion of appointment of a transformative thinker, see Bruce A. Ackerman, "Essays on the Supreme Court Appointment Process," *Harvard Law Review* 101 (1988); McMahon, "Presidents, Political Regimes," 934.

17. Henry J. Abraham, *Justices, Presidents, and Senators: A History of the U.S. Supreme Court Appointments from Washington to Clinton* (New York: Rowman & Littlefield, 1999), 176.

18. Quoted in Robert Harrison, "The Breakup of the Roosevelt Supreme Court: A Contribution of History and Biography," *Law and History* 2 (1984): 165.

19. Segal's scores are available at: http://www.stonybrook.edu/commcms/polisci/jsegal/QualTable.pdf (last accessed by author on May 20, 2013). Segal begins his scores with the Hugo Black nomination in 1937. See also Jeffrey A. Segal and Albert D. Cover, "Ideological Values and the Votes of U.S. Supreme Court Justices," *American Political Science Review* 83 (1989); Jeffrey Segal et al., "Ideological Values and the Votes of the U.S. Supreme Court Justices Revisited," *Journal of Politics* 5 (1995); and Jeffrey A. Segal and Harold J. Spaeth, *The Supreme Court and the Attitudinal Model Revisited* (New York: Cambridge University Press, 2002).

20. On the possibility of making distinctions between articulation presidents, see David Crockett, "The Historical Presidency: The Perils of Restoration Politics," *Presidential Studies Quarterly* 42 (2012).

21. Daniel S. McHargue, "President Taft's Appointments to the Supreme Court," *Journal of Politics* 12 (1950): 494.

22. Ibid., 502.

23. Ibid., 493, 496; and Abraham, *Justices, Presidents, and Senators*, 128.

24. Abraham, *Justices, Presidents, and Senators*, 128.

25. In the 61st Congress (1909–1911), Republicans held sixty of ninety-two Senate seats.

26. Abraham, *Justices, Presidents, and Senators*, 140. Abraham adds that Taft had significant influence over all of Harding's choices for the Court, and was focused mostly on ideology—"identity of outlook"—in finding the right men for the high bench.

27. The Republicans were William Borah of Idaho, Hiram Johnson of California, and Robert La Follette of Wisconsin. Thomas Watson of Georgia was the sole Democrat in dissent. In the 67th Congress (1921–1923), Republicans held fifty-nine of ninety-six Senate seats.

28. David A. Yalof, *Pursuit of Justices: Presidential Politics and the Selection of Supreme Court Nominees* (Chicago: University of Chicago Press, 1999), 29.

29. Abraham, *Justices, Presidents, and Senators*, 184.

30. Lewis Wood, "Vinson Expected to Bring Supreme Court Harmony," *New York Times*, June 9, 1946; according the numerous accounts, Jackson believed FDR had promised him the position once Stone's tenure ended and thought Black had maneuvered to deny him the center chair. See also Yalof, *Pursuit of Justices*, 26–33.

31. Skowronek, *Politics Presidents Make*, 43–44. "With regard to Supreme Court appointments," as I write in my 2007 article, "we should expect preemptive presidents to choose one of two strategies: (1) if they believe that an appointment might be an opportunity to broaden their base, we should expect a nominee clearly in conflict with substantial segments of the resilient regime; or, (2) if they believe that a conflictual appointment will not enhance their position and will needlessly waste political capital, we should expect a consensus nominee," 943.

32. Abraham, *Justices, Presidents, and Senators*, 200.

33. Yalof, *Pursuit of Justices*, 44–51.

34. James Reston, "Langer v. Warren," *New York Times*, Feb. 18, 1954.

35. The three opposed were James Eastland of Mississippi, Olin Johnston of South Carolina, and Harvey Kilgore of West Virginia. "Mr. Langer Votes Yes," *New York Times*, Feb. 26, 1954.

36. "Senate Confirms Warren By Voice Vote," *New York Times*, March 2, 1954.

37. See McMahon, *Nixon's Court*, for a full discussion of Nixon's appointment strategy.

38. Ibid., 88–89, 114.

39. Rowland Evans, Jr., and Robert D. Novak, *Nixon in the White House: The Frustration of Power* (New York: Random House, 1971), 159.

40. John Massaro, *Supremely Political: The Role of Ideology and Presidential Management in Unsuccessful Supreme Court Nominations* (Albany: State University of New York Press, 1990), 13, chap. 3.

41. Ibid., 14, chap. 4.

42. Fred P. Graham, "Burger and Blackmun: Opinions Similar," *New York Times*, April 15, 1970.

43. The Senate also rejected Reagan's choice of Bork (see note 15 above and discussion in text following).

44. For the specifics of these developments, see McMahon, "Presidents, Political Regimes," 939–41.

45. "The New Chief Justice," *New York Times*, Feb. 4, 1930.

46. Samuel Hendel, *Charles Evans Hughes and the Supreme Court* (New York: King's Crown Press, Columbia University, 1951), 78. By today's standards, the senators did not take that much time, confirming Hughes ten days after receiving his nomination from Hoover.

47. Paul A. Freund, "Appointment of Justices: Some Historical Perspectives," *Harvard Law Review* 101 (1988): 1153.

48. Norris quoted in Hendel, *Charles Evans Hughes*, 79.

49. Ibid., 78.

50. Earlier in his presidency, LBJ had named Fortas to his associate seat (in 1965) and Thurgood Marshall to a second associate vacancy (in 1967). At the time of their confirmations, both had Segal ratings of 1.000.

51. Segal does not provide a rating for Thornberry. His nomination became moot once the Senate rejected Fortas's elevation to chief.

52. McMahon, *Nixon's Court*, 215.

53. Yalof, *Pursuit of Justices*, 153.

54. Abraham, *Justices, Presidents, and Senators*, 292.

55. Benno C. Schmidt, Jr., "The Rehnquist Court: A Watershed," *New York Times*, June 22, 1986.

56. Quote from Wallace Johnson, a Nixon Justice Department attorney who aided with both Rehnquist confirmations; e-mail message from Johnson to author, June 8, 2013.

57. For example, Senator Kennedy's critique of Rehnquist in 1986 was strikingly similar to his famous speech on the floor of the Senate in reaction to the Bork nomination to an associate vacancy a year later.

58. "Valid Doubts About Justice Rehnquist," *New York Times*, September 11, 1986. See also Tinsley E. Yarbrough, *The Rehnquist Court and the Constitution* (New York: Oxford University Press, 2000), chap. 1.

59. Schmidt, "The Rehnquist Court: A Watershed."

60. The Ginsburg and Breyer ratings are .680 and .475, respectively. Truman's most conservative/moderate nominees were Harold Burton at .280 and Tom Clark at .500.

61. Charles Schumer, "Judging By Ideology," *New York Times*, June 26, 2001.

62. Senate minority leader Harry Reid of Nevada reportedly first proposed Miers to Bush, telling the president "If you nominate Harriet Miers, you'll start with fifty-six votes," quoted in Jan Crawford Greenburg, *Supreme Conflict: The Inside Story of the Struggle for Control of the United States Supreme Court* (New York: Penguin, 2007), 256. See also Jeffrey Toobin, *The Nine: Inside the Secret World of the Supreme Court* (New York: Doubleday, 2007), 283.

63. Lawrence Baum and Neal Devins, "Why the Supreme Court Cares About Elites, Not the American People," *Georgetown Law Journal* 98 (2010): 1518.

64. Significantly, Chafee was facing a tough—and ultimately unsuccessful—re-election fight.

65. Specifically, thirty-one senators, all Republicans, voted against Sotomayor; thirty-seven—thirty-six Republicans and Democrat Ben Nelson of the red state of Nebraska—opposed Kagan.

66. Massaro, *Supremely Political*; McMahon, "Presidents, Political Regimes"; McMahon, *Nixon's Court*.

PART III

Influence on the Bench

ARTEMUS WARD

Perhaps the most important questions surrounding the chief justice have to do with his influence on the bench. Danelski argued that chiefs can exercise both task and social leadership. But he also pointed out that associate justices can do the same. Indeed, chiefs and associates are at once both equal and different. In terms of equality, it is important to start with the premise that both chiefs and associates have many of the same powers and therefore the same chance to exert influence. For example, at the agenda-setting stage, any justice may place a case on the discuss list to be considered at conference, that justice begins the conference discussion on whether that case should be granted review, and each justice's vote is counted equally for achieving the four votes necessary to hear the case. Any justice may ask as many questions as they please during oral argument. As with accepting a case for review, each justice's vote on the merits of a case has equal weight, with five votes necessary to gain a majority. The most senior justice in the majority or minority coalition assigns opinions when the chief is not in that coalition, and any justice may write an opinion in any case. During the coalition-formation stage, justices may employ whatever strategies they deem effective to achieve their preferred outcomes. In this sense, chiefs and associates have equal power over the work of the Court.

Yet at the same time, the chief has a number of specific institutional powers that his colleagues do not possess that he can use to exert influence. At the agenda-setting stage he initiates the discuss list of cases he deems worthy of review. He begins the conference discussion for those cases, which gives him a unique opportunity to persuade his colleagues of each petition's worthiness before anyone else has a chance to weigh in.

He presides over oral argument and therefore speaks first and last at each session. On occasion, chiefs have been known to interrupt their colleagues and cut off attorneys in midsentence. At the merits stage the chief again speaks and votes first in conference, which allows him to both frame the case and suggest an outcome before his colleagues speak. By virtue of being chief, he assigns the opinion of the Court when in the majority and the principal dissent when in the minority. He can therefore choose to write these opinions himself or select a particular justice to take on the assignment. During the coalition-formation process he can press his colleagues to work quickly and threaten to withhold further opinions until outstanding assignments are completed. Thus, while chiefs and associates possess many of the same powers, the chief has a small but unique set of procedural tools he can employ to lead the Court.

Accordingly, this section contains chapters that cover the chief's task and social leadership during case selection, oral argument, opinion assignment, and case outcomes. Each chapter provides evidence of the different ways chiefs have both attempted to exercise leadership and the extent to which they have been successful in doing so. In sum, the chapters confirm Danelski's ideas about task and social leadership, demonstrate how chiefs are influential throughout the decision-making process, and show that some chiefs have been more successful than others.

In chapter 6, Timothy R. Johnson and Charles Gregory find that chiefs attempt to exercise leadership during oral argument, confirming Danelski's suppositions in his original 1960 conference paper (see chapter 1). Specifically, Johnson and Gregory examine the Burger, Rehnquist, and Roberts Courts and find that chiefs exercise task leadership by attempting to send signals to the other justices and control the debate by talking more and asking more questions. This illustrates task leadership in that a strong task leader should see little value in the individual expression of the other justices and as a result will keep the focus away from them by focusing on himself and the attorneys. In terms of social leadership, chiefs employ more emotional language when interacting with attorneys; for example, chiefs use more unpleasant language with attorneys they oppose than do the other justices. One suspects that the chief's use of emotional language pre-empts the other justices from feeling like they must do so and therefore promotes harmony and collegiality. In addition, the authors find that even though chiefs talk more, the other justices interrupt them less often than they do each other. This again suggests social leadership as interruptions annoy the interrupted justice. Fewer interruptions, therefore, promote social cohesion and collegiality. The authors conclude that these public task and social behaviors are suggestive of the chief's influence in private, where most of the Court's work is conducted.

In chapter 7, Paul J. Wahlbeck, Alyx Mark, Ryan Krog, and Phillip J. Wininger marshal the findings of prior research on opinion assignment to construct a model that predicts who opinions will be assigned to. Specifically, prior research finds that the chiefs assign the most important cases to their ideological allies while also balancing the needs of overall equitable distribution and the expertise of justices in certain areas of the law. Examining data for the Roberts Court, the authors find that these factors continue to be determinative. Thus, chiefs exercise social leadership by adhering to the objective norms of equity and expertise to minimize any hard feelings that might develop when ideological allies get assignment. One intriguing finding is that activeness during oral argument also appears to influence opinion assignment. This suggests another way that chiefs can exercise social leadership as chiefs recognize the justices who are most active and therefore most passionate about a case. The authors are then able to use their model to predict future assignments. While their results are preliminary, the authors' model successfully categorizes more majority opinion assignments than would have occurred by random chance and performs as well as the predictions made by *SCOTUSblog*.

Chapter 8 provides a nice bridge from the beginning stages of the decision-making process in the previous chapters—oral argument and opinion assignment—to the next stage of the process: decisions on the merits. Specifically, Charles M. Cameron and Tom Clark examine data from the Warren through Roberts Courts to analyze three facets of the chief's procedural power: the ability to set the agenda, assign opinions, and achieve preferred outcomes on the merits. With regard to case selection, the authors argue that the chief has considerable influence. They find that transitions from one chief to another are associated with marked transitions in the topics that make up the Court's docket. Confirming prior research, as well as the findings of the previous chapter on opinion assignment, Cameron and Clark find clear evidence that the chief uses his power to assign majority opinions in the most important cases to his ideological allies. Presumably he does this to achieve dispositions that he favors, and the authors find that case outcomes are closely associated with the chief's ideology as opposed to the median, pivotal justice as some have suggested. The authors conclude that the chief's institutional prerogatives translate into procedural power. Thus recent chiefs have exercised task leadership.

Chapter 9 asks whether new chief justices enjoy a "honeymoon effect" early in their tenures. Amy Steigerwalt, Pamela C. Corley, and Artemus

Ward suggest that the task and social leadership posited by Danelski can necessarily change from one chief to the next and therefore associate justices may seek to give a new chief the chance to establish how he best wishes to lead the Court. The authors hypothesize that associates may deliberately de-emphasize ongoing disputes and find common points of agreement to allow the chief a period of adjustment and learning. This suggests that new chiefs should exhibit high levels of social leadership as measured by fewer dissents and separate opinions in a chief's first term as opposed to later in his tenure. Accordingly, the authors examine the extent to which new chiefs are able to achieve both unanimous decisions and fully unanimous opinions without any concurrences. They find some evidence for a honeymoon effect, most notably for Chief Justice Roberts and also for Chief Justices Vinson and Burger, but none for Chief Justices Warren and Rehnquist. The authors conclude that the honeymoon effect is dependent on the extent to which new chiefs are social leaders, prioritizing consensus as a goal they wish to achieve and the extent to which the associates were predisposed to working with the new chief to achieve it. Thus, chiefs can be influential social leaders in achieving consensus.

In chapter 10, Brandon L. Bartels and Phillip J. Wininger continue the question of the chief's ability to achieve consensus by examining his role as opinion writer, the extent to which he joins majorities after initially dissenting in conference, and whether he more forcefully adheres to or cites authoritative precedent. Each of these, the authors argue, demonstrates the chief's concern for institutional legitimacy. As in the previous chapter, the authors find mixed results with Chief Justices Vinson, Warren, and Burger acting to build larger majority coalitions and exhibiting a strong propensity to change their votes in accordance with majority will—examples of social leadership. The authors suggest that the Court's increasing polarization may account for the inability of Chief Justices Rehnquist and Roberts to achieve similar results.

Ryan C. Black, Ryan J. Owens, and Justin Wedeking test Danelski's theory of social leadership in chapter 11 by examining the language used in majority opinions from the Vinson through Roberts Courts. Similar to Johnson and Gregory's analysis of language used at oral argument, Black, Owens, and Wedeking hypothesize that majority opinions written by and joined by chiefs have more agreeable language than majority opinions written by others and not joined by chiefs. While their results show a clear increase in both positive and negative emotional language in majority opinions over time, they do not find any differences between chiefs and associates in both the opinions they write and those they join. The authors suggest that asking the modern chief to be a social leader may be asking for too much, given his relatively limited powers, and that an appropriate analogy for the chief exercising social leadership would be a lot like herding scorpions. When we consider their results in tandem with Johnson and Gregory's findings, it appears that oral argument may be a fundamentally different process compared with opinion writing and coalition formation, at least in terms of the chief's ability to exercise both task and social leadership.

Douglas Rice and Christopher Zorn shed more light on this question in chapter 12. Building on the previous chapter, Rice and Zorn expand the prior analysis by considering every majority, concurring, and dissenting opinion written in the Court's history to test whether the ascension of a new chief marks a change in the degree and polarity of emotional opinion content. They suggest that task leadership can be measured by the amount of emotional language with less emotion signifying strong task leadership. At the same time, social leadership is manifested through the tone of that language, with positive language signifying strong social leadership. The authors confirm the findings of Black, Owens, and Wedeking that overall there have been more emotional opinions and the tone of those opinions has become more negative over time. But unlike the prior chapter, Rice and Zorn find large shifts in emotional language and polarity from one chief to the next. Specifically, they find that Taft was a better social leader than White, Stone failed at task leadership but was similar to Hughes in terms of his social leadership, Vinson failed at both task and social leadership, Warren succeeded on both counts, Burger failed at task leadership but was better at social leadership, and Rehnquist was more successful than his predecessor on both counts. In all, the authors confirm Danelski's argument that task and social leadership are interrelated: as task leaders lose control, demands on social leaders increase.

Finally, in chapter 13 Kirk A. Randazzo and Rebecca Reid discuss the chief's influence in statutory interpretation. Legislative statutes are interesting to examine because some are detailed while others are relatively ambiguous and therefore provide ample room for differences of opinion among the members of the Court. Using data measuring the degree of discretion afforded by legislative statutes, the authors examine how Chief Justices Warren, Burger, and Rehnquist approached statutory interpretation and whether they influenced the other members of the Court in statutory interpretation. They also take a preliminary look at the early Roberts Court. The authors find that in general, congressional statutes have the ability to either constrain or enhance the ability of the justices to vote according to their ideological preferences. In particular, Chief Justices Warren and Rehnquist, as well as their ideological allies, experienced substantial changes in their personal voting behavior as a result of statutory language, sometimes constraining, sometimes enhancing, depending on the issue area. The authors are hesitant to claim that this pattern is reflective of the chief's leadership, but it is plausible.

While these chapters are by no means the final word on the chief's ability to exercise leadership within the Court, they suggest that it is not only theoretically possible but has and is actually occurring. At the same time, the chapters point out that there are differences among the chiefs in their abilities to exercise both task and social leadership at each stage of the decision-making process. As the chapter authors suggest, these studies should be considered for what they are: initial, exploratory attempts to empirically assess the influence of the chief justice. Future research will, no doubt, build on their findings.

6 ~ The Chief Justice and Oral Arguments at the U.S. Supreme Court

TIMOTHY R. JOHNSON AND CHARLES GREGORY

Senator Strom Thurmond (R-SC) described the Chief Justice of the United States as holding "the second most powerful position in the world, second only to the Presidency of the United States."[1] Interestingly, Thurmond is not the only senator to suggest the extraordinary power chief justices wield. Senate floor speeches and confirmation hearings are replete with statements that allude to the chief's powerful position in American politics. Indeed, senators view the internal and external prerogatives attached to the chief justiceship as reservoirs of power. Internally, chiefs initiate the Court's agenda-setting process,[2] preside over conference,[3] and assign opinions when they are in the majority.[4] Externally, the chief justice chairs the Judicial Conference, the Federal Judicial Center, and the Supreme Court Historical Society.[5] In addition, chiefs supervise the Administrative Office of the U.S. Courts and are a board member of the National Gallery of Art, the Hirshhorn Museum and Sculpture Garden, and the Smithsonian Institution.[6] These prerogatives and responsibilities supposedly enable the chief justice to exercise substantial leadership over the Supreme Court, the federal judiciary, and beyond.

While senators may perceive the chief justiceship as a powerful institution, scholars and justices doubt the day-to-day power of this position. In fact, beyond the limited internal powers we explicate above, it is unclear whether the associate justices treat the chief as simply one among equals or whether they defer to the chief as the leader of the Court. The reason this distinction is unclear is that the vast majority of the Court's decision-making process is shrouded in secrecy. Data simply do not exist to make this determination. Here we employ data from the one public aspect of this process—oral arguments—to gain leverage on this intriguing question. Specifically, we compare how chief justices and associate justices act during these proceedings. We also compare how associate justices interact with (and treat) the chief in open court. To do so, we analyze data from a sample of oral arguments during the Warren E. Burger, William H. Rehnquist, and John G. Roberts Court eras.

Our analysis leads us to two broad conclusions. First, chief justices attempt to exercise leadership. Specifically, we find that chiefs talk more than associate justices during oral argument and ask more questions. We believe that by talking more, chief justices attempt to send signals to the other justices and to control the debate during oral argument. This is, as Zorn and Rice argue in a subsequent chapter, an indication of task leadership. In addition, chiefs attempt to make these signals even stronger by using more emotional language when interacting with attorneys. Again, as Zorn and Rice argue, this is akin to social leadership. Second, we find that while the chief talks more, his colleagues interrupt him less often than they do other justices. That is, associate justices do not cut off the chief in midsentence as often as they interrupt their other colleagues. This indicates they are generally willing to give chief justices at least some leeway when he speaks during these proceedings.

To flesh out these main findings, we begin by explaining why we believe the Court's oral arguments help us assess the chief's relationship with the associate justices. We then discuss the data we analyze, present an empirical assessment of these data, and discuss the implications of this analysis for understanding the relationship between associate justices and the Chief Justice of the United States.

Chiefs, Associates, and Supreme Court Oral Arguments

As the introduction to this volume (and various chapters of it) indicates, scholars recognize the potential for influence inherent in the office of the chief justice. Scholarly interest in leadership styles focuses on determining the extent to which chief justices successfully lead the nation's court of last resort. For example, Danelski suggests a chief's leadership style affects the behavior of associate justices.[7] Specifically, chiefs engage in two forms of leadership that may influence norms of behavior: task leadership and social leadership. Task leaders provide guidance on complex cases, make suggestions, and are more likely than their colleagues to frame discussions. Ultimately, task leaders present their "views with force and clarity and defend them successfully."[8] They are therefore able to secure the support and confidence of the eight associates. In contrast, social leaders soothe tension by "inviting opinions and suggestions" and by attending to the emotional needs of other justices, particularly those in losing coalitions.[9]

The primary difference between the two leadership styles is that task leaders concentrate on the Court's decisional process while social leaders focus on maintaining social cohesion and a collegial working environment. Applying this dichotomous conception to examine the William Howard Taft, Charles Evans Hughes, and Harlan Fiske Stone Courts, Danelski argues the leadership styles of Taft and Hughes maintained cohesion on the Court. In contrast, during Stone's tenure as chief justice the Court became embroiled in conflict, and its cohesiveness clearly disintegrated.

Unfortunately, styles of, and opportunities for, leadership occur primarily behind closed doors and therefore out of sight from Court watchers, scholars, and interested spectators. This makes it difficult to determine whether associate justices defer to chief justices as the latter attempt to exert influence. The Court's decision-making process does, however, have one public aspect—the oral arguments in each case granted plenary review—that may provide purchase on this phenomenon. These proceedings may, therefore, provide a rare opportunity to examine whether associate justices defer to chief justices and whether chief justices are able to exercise leadership. Indeed, oral arguments allow us to answer the following questions: Are chief justices willing to exercise leadership during oral arguments? How do associate justices respond to or interact with the chief justice during oral arguments? Are associate justices more willing to defer to a chief justice during these proceedings? To answer these questions we turn to an examination of the role oral arguments play generally in the Court's decision-making process.

As with the other aspects of the Court's decision-making process, evidence establishes that, generally, the oral arguments in cases the Court hears play an integral role in how the justices decide cases they hear.[10] Specifically, there are myriad ways in which this one-hour conversation between Court and counsel, as well as between the justices themselves, may influence case outcomes. Justices, for example, use these proceedings to gather additional information not contained in litigants' briefs.[11] Such information includes the facts of the case, the policy consequences of a decision, pertinent precedent, and how Congress or the president might respond if the Court decides in a particular way.[12]

Beyond providing information to the Court, scholars demonstrate that, during oral arguments, justices often foreshadow how they will decide the cases they hear.[13] Such signals come from the questions they ask the attorneys as well as from the emotive tenor of these questions. The key to this line of research is that when justices make these proceedings more difficult for one side (by asking that attorney more questions with less pleasant language), that side is more likely to lose.

Although the justices ostensibly speak to the attorneys during oral arguments—and while they clearly telegraph their views about the case—evidence from the academy, justices, attorneys, and keen Court watchers also suggests these questions may actually be conversations between the justices. In fact, the evidence is increasingly clear that the justices utilize these proceedings to learn about their colleagues' preferences and to make legal or policy points to one another rather than to simply ask questions of the attorneys. In so doing, they begin the coalition-building process that culminates in a majority opinion.[14] Justice Kennedy explained how this process works: "When the people come . . . to see our arguments, they often see a dialogue between the justices asking a question and the attorney answering it. And they think of the argument as a series of these dialogues. It isn't that. As [Justice] John [Paul Stevens] points out, what is happening is the court is having a conversation with itself through the intermediary of the attorney."[15]

It is these intra-bench conversations that provide the data we need to determine whether the chief acts as the leader of the Court and whether, at the same time, associate justices pay deference to the chief. To assess the former, the analysis below focuses on each justice's speech patterns during oral arguments and how the chief's penchant for asking questions and making comments compares with the associates. Additionally, we compare the degree to which the chief and the associates use language that may be classified as pleasant or unpleasant toward the attorneys arguing before them. If the chief exhibits leadership during oral arguments ***we expect him to speak more often than the associates***. At the same time ***we expect the chief to take the lead on hindering arguments that may stop the Court from reaching a particular outcome and to be more likely to help draw out arguments that may help the Court reach a desired outcome***.

In addition to understanding who controls the arguments from the bench, we are also interested in whether associate justices pay deference to the chief justice due to his position as first among equals. Our data also allow us to make this assessment because justices sometimes thwart a colleague's line of questioning during oral arguments by interrupting them with their own questions.[16] This may affect a justice in two ways. First, interruptions can keep a speaking justice from sending a signal about her intentions and preferred outcome in the case. That is, interrupting a justice stops her in her tracks and allows the interrupter to move the discussion to another topic. Second, interruptions may keep a speaker from sending signals to those with whom she hopes to coordinate when the Court reaches a final decision. The bottom line is that interrupting a justice while she is asking a question or making a comment may be an effective strategy to follow during oral arguments. But if the associate justices actually view the chief as the leader of the Court, ***we expect them to defer to him by interrupting him less often during oral arguments than they interrupt their associate colleagues***.

Data

To examine the extent to which the chief exercises leadership and how associate justices interact with the chief justice, we employ oral argument data from the Burger, Rehnquist, and Roberts Courts. Specifically, we downloaded all available oral argument transcripts for three time periods: 1970 to 1979, 1998 to 2004, and 2005 to 2009.[17] Thus, we analyze almost 1,000 cases heard by the Burger Court, more than 470 cases heard by the Rehnquist Court, and more than 350 cases heard by the Roberts Court.

Initially, we focus on the average number of times each justice speaks during these proceedings. In particular, we compare speaking patterns between associates and chiefs (the number of questions or comments made by each justice) during the first four terms of the Roberts Court and during nine terms of the Burger Court (1970–1979). As we note above, we argue this measure serves as a proxy for justices' willingness to shape policy and to move cases toward their desired outcome during oral arguments. We expect leaders—in this case the chief—to exhibit leadership by speaking more often during these proceedings.

In addition to the general speech patterns of the justices, we are also interested in the linguistic nature of the questions and comments they make, whether they are meant to help or hinder one of the arguing attorneys. Here we turn specifically to the more than 350 cases decided during the first four terms of the Roberts Court. With these data we examine how pleasant (or unpleasant) justices act toward attorneys representing the federal government, toward attorneys representing litigants other than the federal government, and toward attorneys they are predisposed to support on the merits.

Finally, we analyze how justices interact with one another during oral arguments. To do so we focus on the last six terms of the Rehnquist Court and the first three years of the Roberts Court.[18] Specifically, we examine how frequently justices interrupt one another in open court. In so doing, we seek to determine whether associate justices and chief justices behave similarly at oral argument and the extent to which associates defer to the chief during these proceedings.

Who Exhibits Leadership during Oral Arguments?

Our contention is that the Court's oral arguments are the only public opportunity for justices to shape judicial outcomes and to potentially exercise leadership in a public way. But who is most likely to attempt to shape outcomes and to exercise leadership during these proceedings? Figure 6.1 provides the data to answer this question. It compares the average number of questions asked by justices at oral argument for the first four terms of the Roberts Court (2005–2008). Specifically, we construct separate plots to compare the behavior of each associate justice with Chief Justice Roberts.[19]

The plot in the top left panel of figure 6.1 displays the average number of utterances by Chief Justice Roberts (solid bold line) compared to the average number of utterances by the associate justices collectively (dashed line).[20] The seven remaining plots depict the mean number of questions asked by Roberts (solid bold line) along with the mean number of questions asked by each associate justice (dashed line). Presented in this way, figure 6.1 provides visual data to assess our first phenomenon of interest.

Although conclusions based on visually examining plots require care, two patterns emerge from these data. First, with few exceptions, Roberts asked more questions than the associate justices. On average, he asked almost twenty-two questions per case while the average associate justice asked only about fifteen questions. This is a statistically significant difference of seven questions ($t = -8.59$, $p < .05$). More specifically, both the sign and magnitude of the t statistic indicate that Roberts asked significantly more questions than the average associate justice, a pattern that holds to varying degrees with the individual associate justices.

Certainly, some associate justices speak more often than does Roberts. For instance, during the 2005 term Justice Stephen G. Breyer asked just over twenty-four questions at oral argument, approximately three questions more than Roberts. This difference, however, is not statistically significant ($t = 1.37$, $p > .05$). In addition, during the 2005 and 2006 terms, Justice Scalia asked an average of twenty-eight and twenty-four questions respectively. That is, Scalia asked, on average, seven questions more in 2005 ($t = 3.35$, $p < .05$) and four questions more in 2006 ($t = 1.72$, $p < .1$)

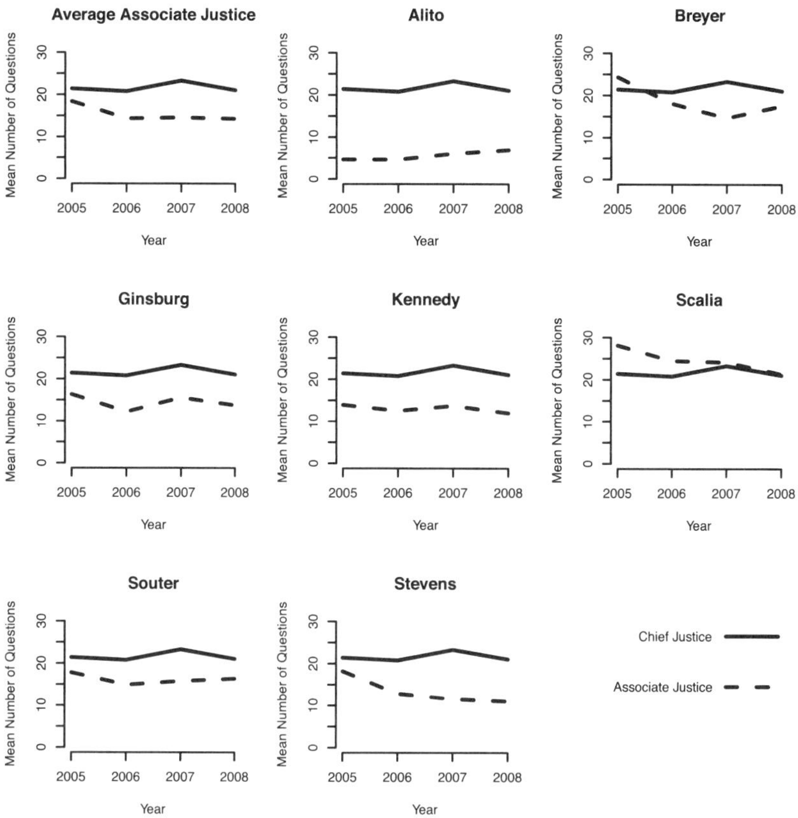

Fig. 6.1. Average number of questions asked during oral argument, 2005–2008

than Roberts asked during those two terms. On the other hand, the average number of utterances by Scalia, Breyer, and Stevens decreases during Roberts's tenure as chief. For example, both Breyer and Stevens ask almost seven fewer questions in 2008 than they did in 2005. Overall, figure 6.1 suggests that Chief Justice Roberts is willing to attempt to exercise leadership by speaking more often during oral arguments. His behavior seems to have had an effect on the behavior of the associate justices. Indeed, they have become less talkative with Roberts in the center chair.

As previous research demonstrates, chief justices differ in their willingness to exert leadership and in their ability to actually lead the Court.[21] To determine whether the Roberts Court patterns are similar to previous

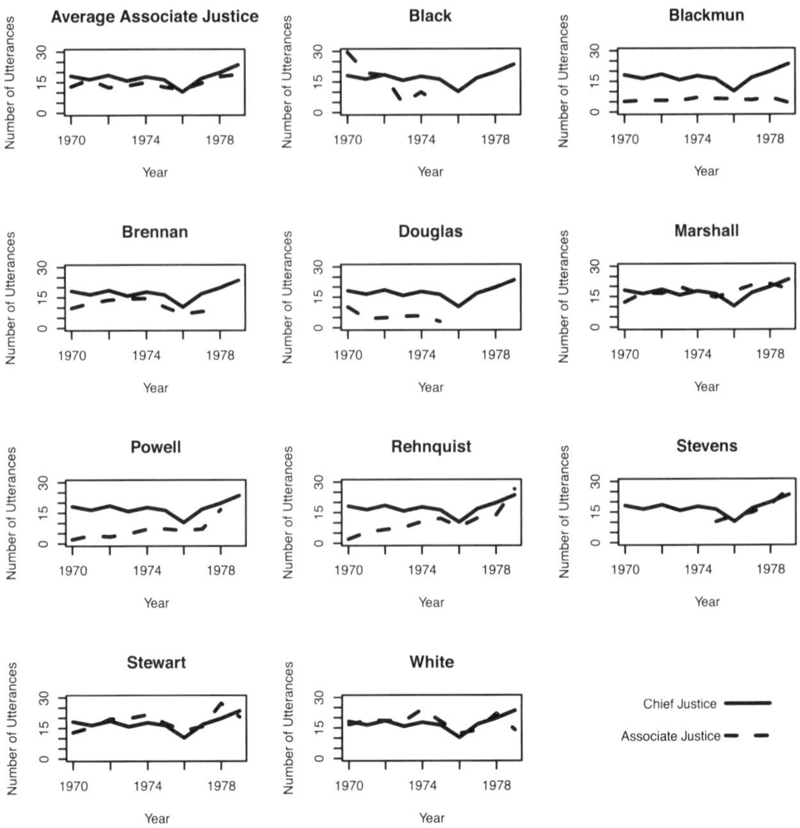

Fig. 6.2. Average number of questions asked during oral argument, 1970–1979

Courts, figure 6.2 depicts the average number of utterances made by justices during oral arguments under Chief Justice Burger. It is structured the same as figure 6.1. While variation exists in justices' utterances during the Burger Court era, it is clear that, like justices during the Roberts Court era, these justices also sought to shape policy as they sat during oral arguments.

We turn first to the chief justice. On average, Burger spoke the most often during oral arguments in our sample of cases. In fact, he spoke slightly more than sixteen times per case while the associate justices who served with him spoke slightly fewer than fourteen times. This difference suggests Burger was significantly more willing than the eight associate justices to exercise leadership and to seek to shape the policy options available to the

Court ($t = -5.93$, $p < .01$). Just as during the Roberts Court era, however, there were terms when some associates spoke more often than the chief. Indeed, for at least one term, Justices Black, Marshall, Stewart, and White spoke more often on average than did Burger.

Overall, similarities clearly exist between how justices acted during oral arguments on the Burger and Roberts Courts. That said, justices on the Burger Court demonstrated more variation in their speaking patterns. In addition, there was a relatively steady decline in utterances across justices from 1970 to 1976 and a steady increase from 1976 to 1979.[22] Despite these patterns, figures 6.1 and 6.2 generally suggest that chief justices are more willing than are associate justices to exert effort to shape policy during oral argument.

Who Takes the Lead on Probing Litigant Arguments?

Analyzing justices' utterances in different Court eras provides a first step toward examining who attempts to exercise leadership during oral arguments. Such an analysis, however, does not indicate how exactly justices attempt to do so. Therefore, we next examine how they actually treat different litigants during oral arguments. Note, initially, that the justices generally use more unpleasant language than they do pleasant language.[23] In fact, across our sample of cases, only Justice O'Connor and Chief Justice Roberts used more pleasant than unpleasant language. We speculate that the reason for this phenomenon is that, as Black and his colleagues argue, the justices often use these proceedings to knock down arguments from the side with which they disagree.[24]

Our interest lies, however, in how associate justices' behavior compares with the chief's. To make this determination we turn to figures 6.3 through 6.6, which depict the linguistic nature of the questions they posed to attorneys representing the federal government, to attorneys unaffiliated with the federal government, and to attorneys who represent the side with whom we would expect a justice to agree. Several patterns merit discussion.

First, Chief Justice Roberts uses more unpleasant and pleasant language toward attorneys representing the federal government as well as toward those unaffiliated with the federal government. Consider government attorneys first (usually the solicitor general or an assistant solicitor general). Roberts uses slightly more than twenty-four unpleasant words per case while associate justices use fewer than nineteen unpleasant words when discussing cases at oral argument with federal government attorneys. This difference is statistically significant ($t = -3.53$, $p < .05$), which indicates that the chief justice is likely to be harder on attorneys representing the federal government. Second, it is clear that that Roberts treats nonfederal attorneys similarly to their government counterparts. Indeed, he certainly probes into their arguments by hammering home points with more unpleasant language. Indeed, he uses nineteen unpleasant words on average toward nongovernment attorneys while associates use thirteen. This difference is also significant ($t = -4.14$, $p < .05$).[25]

We interpret our general finding on unpleasant language to suggest chiefs exercise leadership during oral arguments because they are more likely to be critical of arguments attorneys forward. This holds for both federal attorneys and nonfederal attorneys. At the same time, the chief is more likely than his colleagues to use pleasant language toward attorneys. This too indicates a level of leadership for Roberts because he lends a helping hand and steps up to lighten the atmosphere in tense argument sessions. Ultimately, it is not a surprise to us that Roberts uses both pleasant and unpleasant language more often than his junior colleagues.

In addition to showing that when Chief Justice Roberts interacts with attorneys during oral arguments, he is more willing than his colleagues

TABLE 6.1. Average Overall Levels of Pleasantness and Unpleasantness by Justice, 2005–2008

	Pleasant Words	Unpleasant Words
Alito	4.974	8.217
	(4.59)	(7.415)
Breyer	26.208	36.327
	(14.732)	(19.174)
Ginsburg	14.107	21.625
	(14.107)	(13.74)
Kennedy	11.416	13.884
	(8.287)	(10.891)
O'Connor	8.516	8.462
	(5.652)	(6.389)
Rehnquist	6.9	6.9
	(4.003)	(6.019)
Roberts	19.733	26.199
	(10.561)	(12.251)
Scalia	19.575	33.303
	(12.793)	(20.061)
Souter	18.902	27.219
	(12.708)	(16.894)
Stevens	9.358	12.986
	(6.94)	(10.512)
Thomas	0.017	0.026
	(0.201)	(0.361)

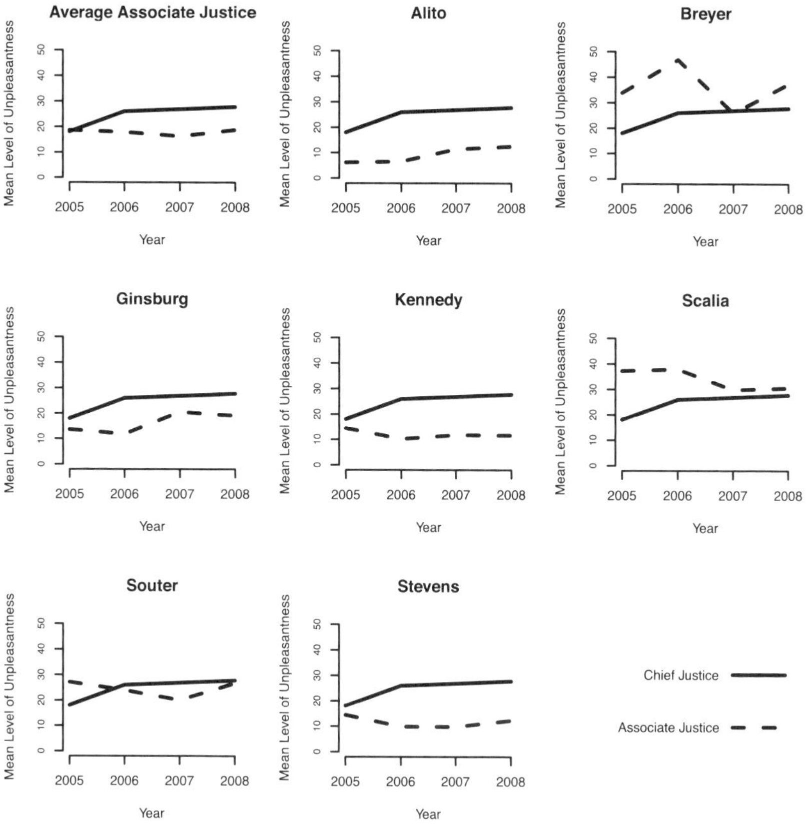

Fig. 6.3. Unpleasant questions directed at the federal government, 2005–2008

to use emotional language; the four figures indicate that Roberts's interactions with attorneys across terms has changed in his short tenure on the bench. Since his first year as chief, Roberts increased the amount of emotional language he used to interact with attorneys. The increase, however, remains more noticeable when he speaks to attorneys who do not represent the federal government. For example, in 2005 Roberts directed approximately twenty-one unpleasant words toward nongovernment attorneys. This number increased to twenty-seven during the final term in our sample.[26]

Similar patterns occur in Roberts's use of pleasant words, but the increase is not as large. This change in behavior comports with research that suggests that justices behave differently after they acclimate themselves to

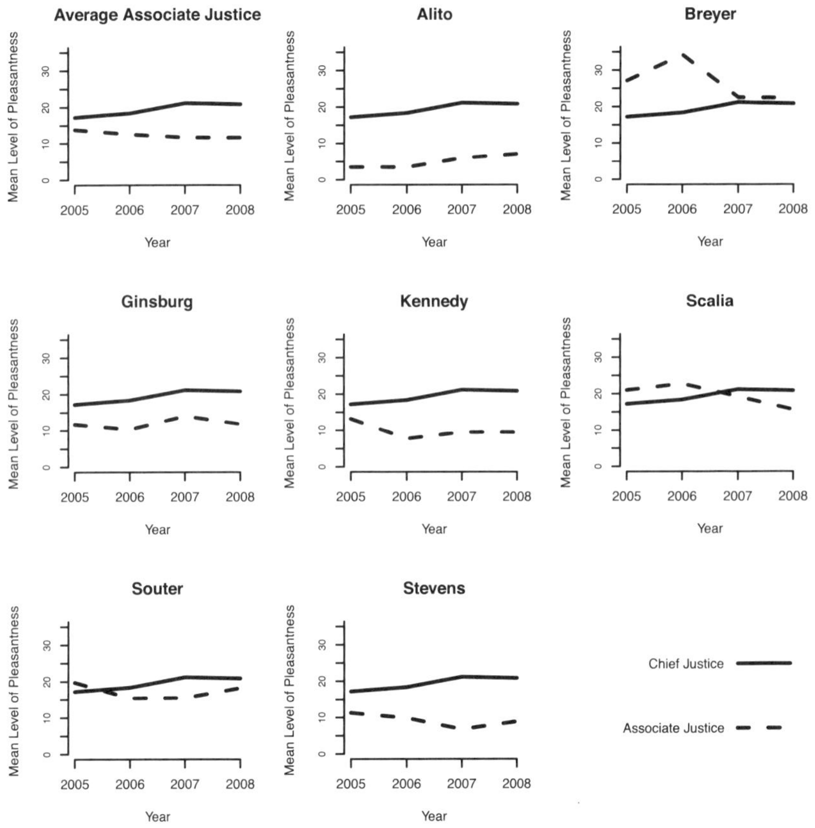

Fig. 6.4. Pleasant questions directed at the federal government, 2005–2008

their new positions.[27] As for associate justices, no single pattern accurately describes their interaction with litigants. Justices Kennedy, Scalia, and Stevens appear to use less emotional language across our sample. Justice Alito, who joined the Court at approximately the same time as Roberts, shows a similar increase, albeit a smaller one. Interestingly, Justices Ginsburg and Souter exhibit the greatest variation across terms.

Finally, because oral arguments provide justices an opportunity to shape judicial outcomes, we examine the ideological relationship between attorney's arguments and justices' use of affective language during these proceedings. In particular, as the leader of the Court, we expect chiefs to take the lead on helping attorneys who represent the side with whom they may agree and to lead the way in dissecting arguments forwarded by at-

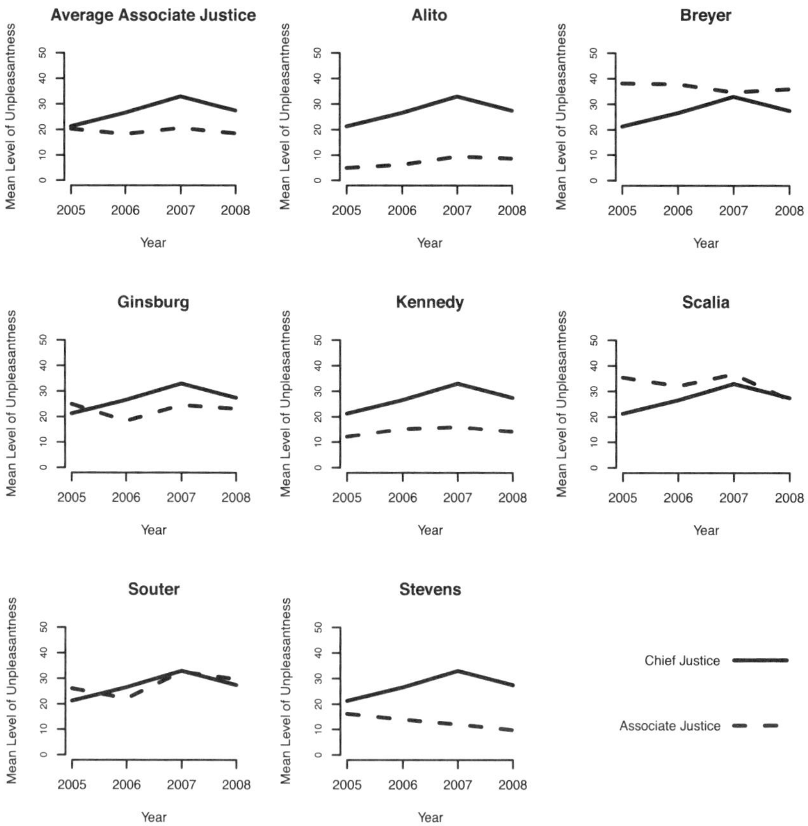

Fig. 6.5. Unpleasant questions directed at attorneys not representing the federal government, 2005–2008

torneys with whom he may disagree.[28] Again, we turn to the pleasantness of the language the chief and his associates use. We note initially that both the chief and associates are more willing to use language laced with emotional content when dealing with attorneys they oppose than with attorneys the support. On average, associate justices use approximately thirteen pleasant words when interacting with attorneys they support at the merit stage but they use approximately eighteen unpleasant words when dealing with attorneys they oppose. The chief, on average, uses approximately eighteen pleasant words while interacting with attorneys he is most likely to support at the merit stage and twenty-five unpleasant words toward attorneys he opposes at the merit stage. That is, the chief justice uses significantly more unpleasant words toward attorneys he is likely to oppose at the merit stage

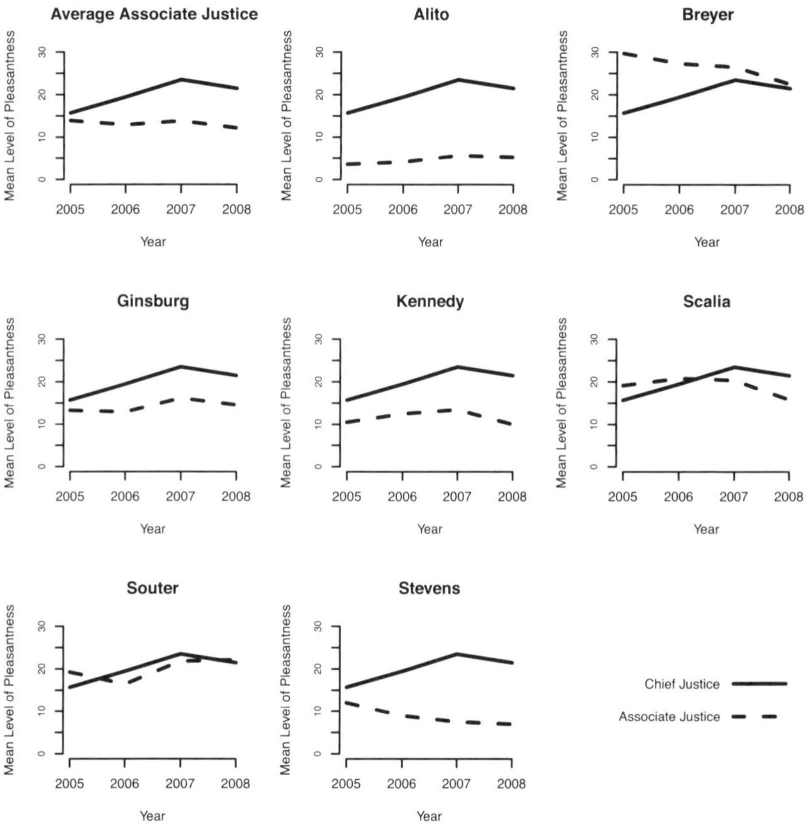

Fig. 6.6. Pleasant questions directed at attorneys not representing the federal government, 2005–2008

($t = 4.54$, $p < .05$) and significantly more pleasant words toward attorneys he is likely to support at the merit stage ($t = -6.49$, $p < .05$).

Beyond the general use of language, our interest is in the variance between the types of emotional language the chief uses versus the language associates use and at whom they direct that language. Figure 6.7 and figure 6.8 allow us to make this determination. With few exceptions, Roberts is more pleasant toward attorneys he supports than is the average associate justice. As predicted, he is also more unpleasant than are associates toward attorneys he is likely to oppose. Specifically, Roberts uses approximately eighteen pleasant words when interacting with attorneys he supports, while associate justices use approximately thirteen pleasant words

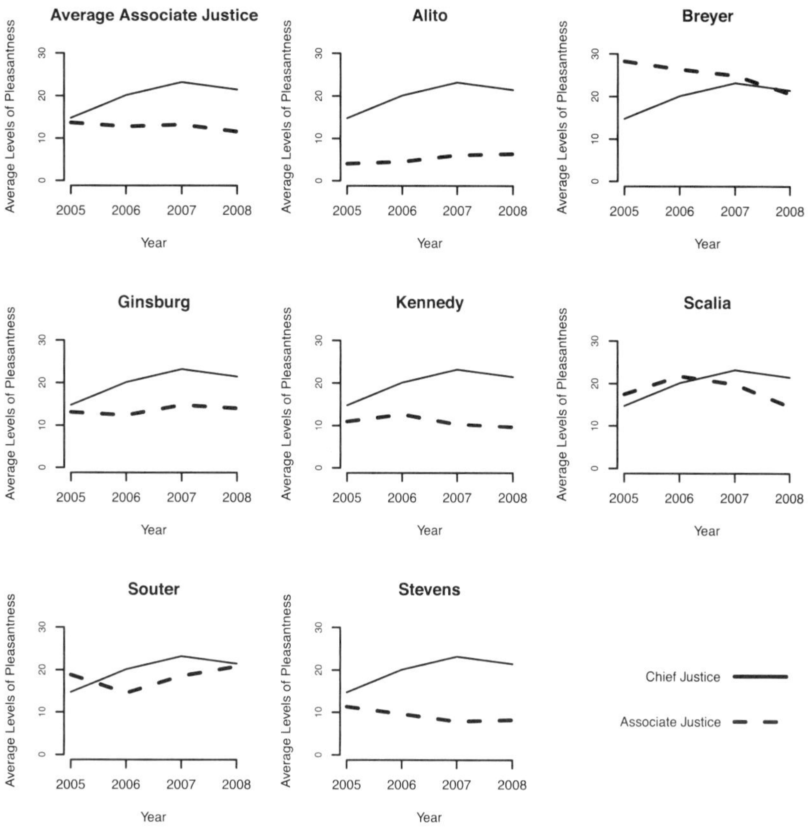

Fig. 6.7. Average number of pleasant questions directed at a side with which a justice agrees, 2005–2008

toward the side with whom they agree. At the same time he uses much more unpleasant language than the associates toward the party with whom he is predisposed to disagree. We interpret these data to indicate the chief "leads the charge" in bolstering arguments on his preferred side and in using more critical language toward the side he opposes. In short, on the affective side of justice utterances the chief clearly attempts to demonstrate leadership during oral arguments.

Roberts's leadership seems to take root early in his tenure on the bench. Figures 6.7 and 6.8 demonstrate how Roberts changes across terms and how his interactions with attorneys he supports differs from his interactions with attorneys he opposes. In his first term as chief Roberts uses ap-

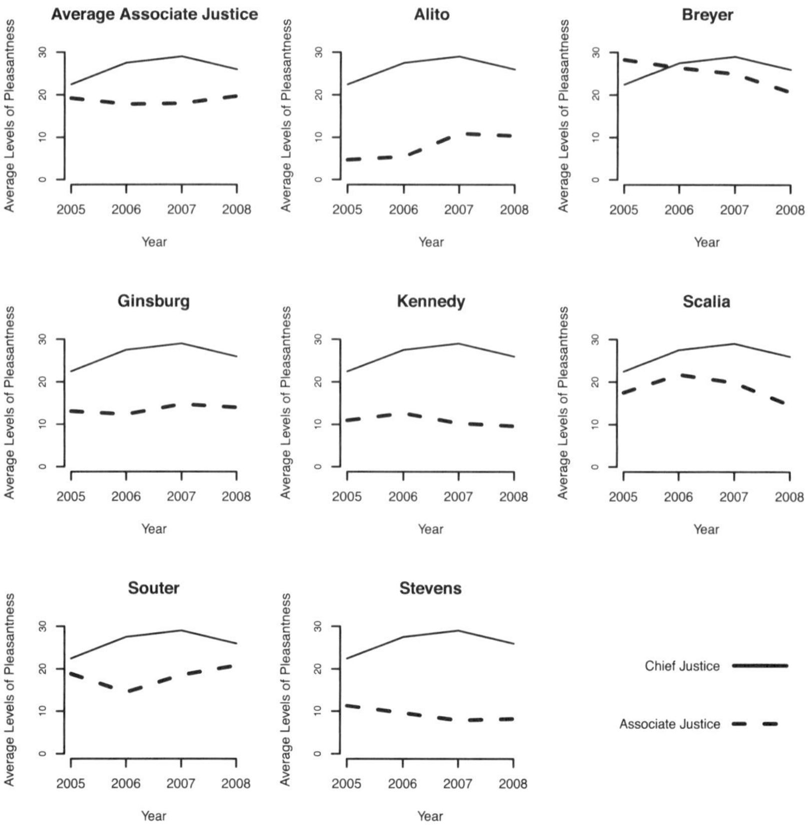

Fig. 6.8. Average number of unpleasant questions directed at a side with which a justice disagrees, 2005–2008

proximately fifteen pleasant words in his questions and comments pointed at attorneys with whom he is predisposed to agree while that average increases to twenty-one in the 2008 term. In contrast, the chief treats much more harshly attorneys with whom he disagrees. Indeed, in his first term Roberts uses approximately twenty-two unpleasant words when interacting with attorneys he opposes. This number increases, hitting a high of twenty-nine in 2007 before decreasing to twenty-five unpleasant words during the 2008 term. It remains to be seen if other chiefs act in the same manner as Roberts. These data will be available in the not-too-distant future, which will make such comparisons possible.

Overall, figures 6.3 through 6.8 offer us two insights. First, chief justices are more willing to engage actively during oral arguments in order to influence the final outcomes. Both Burger and Roberts consistently talked more during these proceedings than did their associate justices. In addition, Roberts is more willing to use unpleasant words when dealing with attorneys with whom he disagrees ideologically. This behavior indicates that he attempts to frame discussions and send signals about how he believes cases should be decided, both behaviors that indicate he tries to lead the Court.

Do Associates Demonstrate Deference to the Chief?

The previous sections indicate that chiefs (at a minimum) attempt to exercise leadership in open court by speaking more often and by attacking or defending one side of the case. Beyond the chief's own behavior, leadership may manifest itself in how the associate justices treat the chief during oral arguments. Fortunately, we have the data to test this conjecture as well. Specifically, we analyze the number of times each justice interrupts his or her colleagues. We define an interruption as when a justice is speaking (asking a question or making a comment) and another justice speaks (successfully or unsuccessfully) before an attorney can respond. This analysis is akin to the findings of Black, Johnson, and Wedeking, who find that justices use interruptions to forward their own views of the case.[29] While we agree with Black and his colleagues, we also believe interruptions can give us purchase on the degree to which associate justices defer to the chief as the Court leader.

Generally, we examine how frequently justices interrupt their colleagues during oral arguments. Figure 6.10 depicts these data for the 681 cases decided between 1998 and 2007. Two patterns are evident. First, justices rarely interrupt one another. In our sample, they take this tack, on average, less than one time per case. We posit that these data suggest a strong norm against any one justice trying to dominate the argument session. In fact, the justices clearly enforce this norm. In *U.S. v. R.L.C.* (1991), Chief Justice Rehnquist began to ask a question, and almost immediately Justice Scalia began to speak. In his oral argument observations of the case, displayed in figure 6.9, Justice Blackmun noted—on the fifth line of his notes—the chief's irritation: "CJ tells AS t[o] shut up while he is asking a q[uestion]." While Rehnquist actually used tamer language than Blackmun indicated, his point is the same given the tone of his voice; justices are sometimes annoyed by their colleagues' desire to speak over others on the bench.[30]

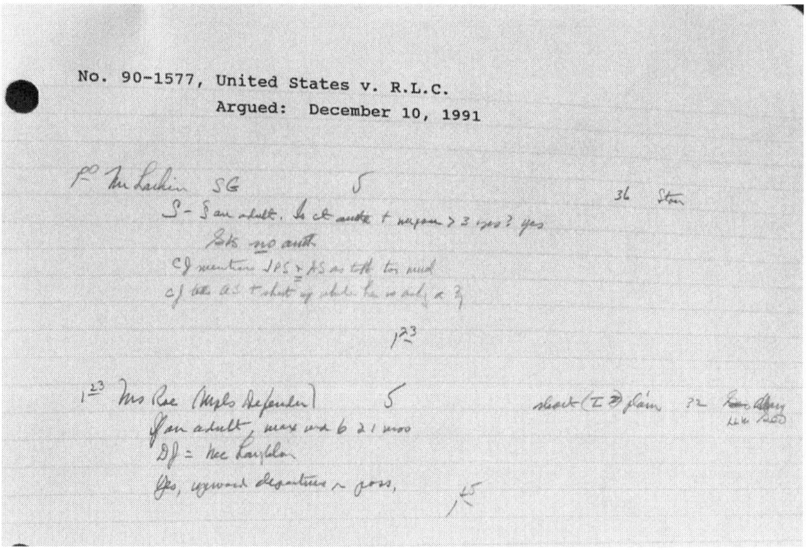

Fig. 6.9. Justice Harry Blackmun's oral argument notes in *U.S. v. R.L.C.* (1991)

Beyond the observation that justices rarely interrupt one another, figure 6.10 also makes clear that Roberts was, in general, interrupted less often than were the associate justices during this time period ($t = 8.93$, $p < .05$). This suggests that the associate justices' behavior indicates some measure of deference to the chief. In fact, the justices who speak the most often during these proceedings—Breyer and Scalia—are much more likely to interrupt their associate colleagues than they are to interrupt the chief. In addition, while variation exists, the associates all exhibit some level of deference.

Figure 6.11 provides a more nuanced picture of these data. It delineates the number of times an associate justice interrupts each justice with whom he or she sits during oral arguments. The bold black line indicates the number of times an associate justice interrupts the chief and each gray line represents interruptions of separate associate justices. For example, Justice Alito (upper left corner) interrupts Justice Scalia (gray solid line) three times in 2005, twice in 2006, and once in 2007. In comparison, Alito interrupts Roberts once in 2005, twice in 2006, and once in 2007. This suggests Alito rarely interrupts the chief or the associate justices with whom he serves. This pattern changes, however, when we turn to justices who regularly speak during oral arguments. For example, Breyer interrupts Scalia

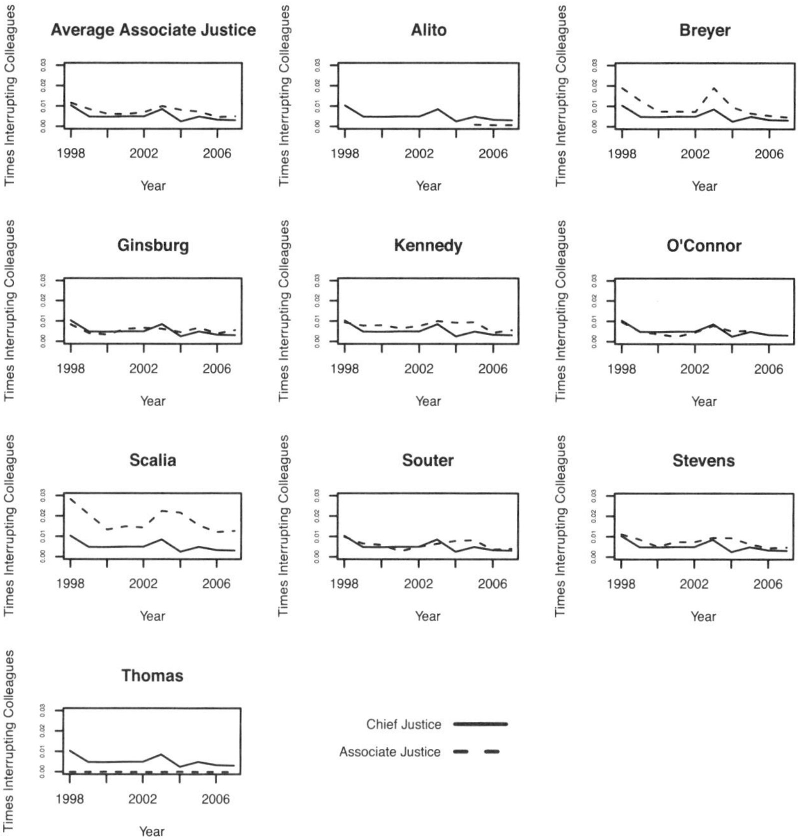

Fig. 6.10. Average number of times justices interrupt their colleagues, 1998–2007

more than sixty times in 1998 and almost fifty times in 2003. Interestingly, after both of these terms Breyer's interruptions of Scalia substantially decreased. The patterns that emerge in the Breyer plot are visible, to varying degrees, among the plots of the other seven associate justices.

Besides the overall ebb and flow of interruptions, Figure 6.11 suggests associate justices interrupt the chief justice less often than they interrupt other associate justices. In 2006 Alito interrupts the chief more than he interrupts any other associate justice. But Alito is the exception; for the most part Figure 6.11 suggests associate justices treat the chief justice as first among equals. Indeed, given that chiefs speak more during these proceedings (as we indicate in figures 6.1 and 6.2) and are interrupted at slightly

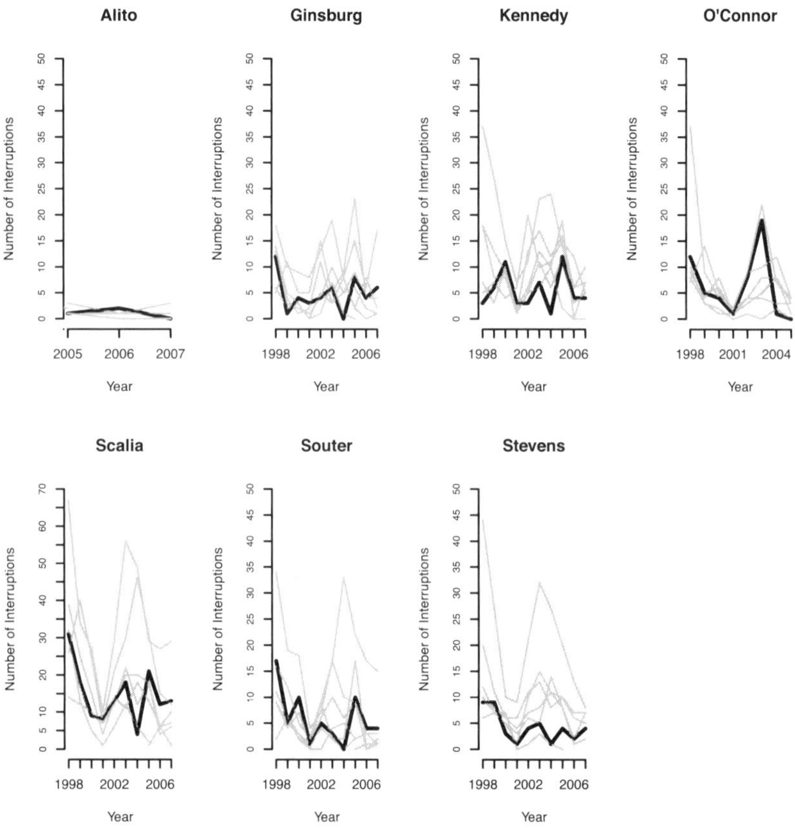

Fig. 6.11. Total number of questions that interrupt other justices by term, 1998–2007

lower rates than associates, figure 6.1 lends support to our deference argument. In fact, our analysis of figure 6.11, combined with our analysis of figure 6.1, suggests that associates interrupt the chief less often during oral arguments. This supports our conjecture that associate justices show deference to the chief.

Conclusion

Opportunities to lead or exert influence accompany the office of the Chief Justice of the United States. For example, chiefs can and do wield influence over the agenda-setting process during conference discussions[31] and when they make opinion assignments.[32] It is not always clear, however, whether chiefs are able to exercise leadership or whether associate justices treat chief justices differently. As we note from the outset, this is because justices normally interact with one another outside of the public eye. Because of this, we turned to the public part of their decision-making process.

Our analysis of the Court's oral arguments leads us to several conclusions. First, chief justices speak more during oral argument than do associate justices. With few exceptions, both Burger and Roberts asked more questions and made more statements than the other eight justices seated on the bench with them. In addition, the chief is more willing to send signals about how the case should be decided by examining how justices treat litigants during these proceedings. For example, chiefs use more unpleasant language when interacting with attorneys they oppose. Second, we find that associate justices treat chiefs as first among equals, but not all the time. Ultimately, however, chiefs do exhibit public leadership during oral arguments, and the associates often follow his lead.

NOTES

1. 115 Cong. Rec. 15,179 (June 9, 1969) (statement of Sen. Thurmond).

2. Lee Epstein and Jack Knight, *The Choices Justices Make* (Washington, DC: CQ Press, 1998); Walter F. Murphy, *Elements of Judicial Strategy* (Chicago: University of Chicago Press, 1964).

3. Epstein and Knight, *The Choices Justices Make*; David M. O'Brien, *Storm Center: The Supreme Court in American Politics* (New York: W. W. Norton, 2000); Stephen L. Wasby, *The Supreme Court in the Federal Judicial System* (New York: Holt, Rinehart, and Winston, 1984).

4. Forrest Maltzman, James F. Spriggs II, and Paul J. Wahlbeck, *Crafting Law on the Supreme Court: The Collegial Game* (New York: Cambridge University Press, 2000); Forrest Maltzman and Paul J. Wahlbeck, "A Conditional Model of Opinion Assignment on the Supreme Court," *Political Research Quarterly* 57 (2004).

5. The chief justice by federal statute oversees the Judicial Conference, the Federal Judicial Center, and the Supreme Court Historical Society (Peter G. Fish, "Judicial Administration and Organization: Chief Justice of the United States," Federal Judicial Center, www.fjc.gov/history/home.nsf/page/admin_04.html, accessed March 25, 2013.

6. Robert J. Steamer, *Chief Justice: Leadership and the Supreme Court* (Columbia: University of South Carolina Press, 1986).

7. David J. Danelski, "The Influence of the Chief Justice in the Decisional Process," in *Courts, Judges, and Politics: An Introduction to the Judicial Process*, 6th ed., ed. Walter F. Murphy et al. (New York: McGraw-Hill, 2006).

8. Ibid., 676.

9. Ibid., 676.

10. Timothy R. Johnson, *Oral Arguments and Decision Making on the United States Supreme Court* (Albany: State University of New York Press, 2004); Lawrence Wrightsman, *Oral Arguments Before the Supreme Court: An Empirical Approach* (New York: Oxford University Press, 2008).

11. Johnson, *Oral Arguments and Decision Making*; Stephen L. Wasby, Anthony A. D'Amato, and Rosemary Metrailer, *Desegregation from Brown to Alexander: An Exploration of Supreme Court Strategies* (Carbondale: Southern Illinois University Press, 1977).

12. The quality of arguments forwarded by attorneys during these proceedings also affects justices' votes (Timothy R. Johnson, Paul J. Wahlbeck, and James F. Spriggs, "The Evaluation of Oral Argumentation before the U.S. Supreme Court," *American Political Science Review* 100 (2006)). Indeed, even justices predisposed to vote for a particular side (based on their ideological predilections) tend to vote more often for the side that offers better arguments in open court.

13. Sarah Levien Shullman, "The Illusion of Devil's Advocacy: How the Justices of the Supreme Court Foreshadow Their Decisions during Oral Argument," *Journal of Appellate Practice & Process* 6 (2004); John G. Roberts, "Oral Advocacy and the Re-emergence of a Supreme Court Bar," *Journal of Supreme Court History* 30 (2005); Timothy Johnson et al., "Inquiring Minds Want to Know: Do Justices Tip Their Hands with Questions at Oral Argument in the US Supreme Court?" *Washington University Journal of Law & Policy* 29 (2009); Ryan C. Black, Timothy R. Johnson, and Justin Wedeking, *Oral Arguments and Coalition Formation on the U.S. Supreme Court* (Ann Arbor: University of Michigan Press, 2012).

14. Johnson, *Oral Arguments and Decision Making*; Timothy R. Johnson, James F Spriggs, and Paul J. Wahlbeck, "Supreme Court Oral Advocacy: Does It Affect the Justices' Decisions," *Washington University Law Review* 85 (2007); Wasby, D'Amato, and Metrailer, *Desegregation from Brown to Alexander*.

15. O'Brien, *Storm Center*.

16. Black, Johnson, and Wedeking, *Oral Arguments and Coalition Formation*.

17. Due to the current data limitations surrounding oral argument transcripts, we used three different datasets. Once all transcripts are available, we can test our conjectures more broadly.

18. We use these data, rather than the data from the previous analyses, because we draw the data from a different source: Black, Johnson, and Wedeking, *Oral Arguments and Coalition Formation*.

19. We exclude Thomas because he rarely speaks at oral argument. And when he does speak, it is national news. For example, when he spoke for the first time in almost seven years during oral argument for *Boyer v. Louisiana*, 569 U.S. ____ (2013), newspaper headlines read "Justice Clarence Thomas Breaks His Silence," "Clarence Thomas Speaks, Finally," and "Clarence Thomas speaks, but does it break his silent streak?" Ultimately, Thomas's statement was not a question or statement directed at litigants before the Court, but an offhand remark about the quality of counsel provided by Ivy League law school graduates. It was barely audible over the laughter of Thomas's colleagues. Adam Liptak, "No Argument: Thomas Keeps 5-Year Silence," *New York Times*, Feb. 12, 2011. Thomas has offered two reasons why he remains largely quiet on the bench. First, Liptak writes that Thomas has admitted to being self-conscious about the way he speaks. Second, Liptak suggests

Thomas simply wants to hear the attorneys argue if the Court has invited them to do so. As Liptak quotes from a speech Thomas gave in 2000, "If I invite you to argue your case, I should at least listen to you." Whatever the reason, Court watchers should not expect much data on Thomas's behavior in the future as he has made it clear he will not speak during oral arguments.

20. By utterance we mean any and all statements spoken during orally argument by a justice. This includes statements and questions.

21. Frank B. Cross and Stefanie Lindquist, "The Decisional Significance of the Chief Justice," *University of Pennsylvania Law Review* 154 (2006); Danelski, "The Influence of the Chief Justice."

22. While it is not clear exactly what led to this change in behavior, there seemed to be a honeymoon period for the chief in the early 1970s. By this we mean the justices spoke less often than did Burger in these early years of his tenure, but they began to speak more as Burger's era moved to its "middle years." Such a shift is also clear in the Roberts Court data. While there may be other reasons for such a change, we await future multivariate analyses to make such a determination.

23. These results are more suggestive than are the results from other sections because they are based on only one Court era. That said, there is little theoretical reason to believe the results would change once we have data from the Burger and Warren Court eras.

24. Black, Johnson, and Wedeking, *Oral Arguments and Coalition Formation.*

25. When we compare Roberts with individual associate justices, only Breyer uses more emotional language (pleasant or unpleasant words) in his interactions with attorneys across terms. Note, however, that Ginsburg, Souter, and Scalia use more affective language in a handful of terms.

26. Roberts's high water mark came in 2007 when he averaged thirty-two unpleasant words.

27. Timothy M. Hagle, "'Freshman Effects' for Supreme Court Justices," *American Journal of Political Science* 37 (1993).

28. To operationalize this concept, we used the fact that a justice voted for a particular side in the final opinion on the merits. With these data in hand, we then counted the pleasant and unpleasant verbiage used toward the side for whom the justice voted as well as toward the side against whom the justice voted. Although there are alternate ways to operationalize this concept, our blunt measure provides us with a fair glimpse of this process.

29. Black, Johnson, and Wedeking, *Oral Arguments and Coalition Formation.*

30. Interestingly, Scalia sounded equally annoyed. To hear the chief's language and Scalia's response, see http://www.press.umich.edu/resources/3_9780472118465_USvRLC.mp3.

31. Timothy R. Johnson, James F. Spriggs II, and Paul J. Wahlbeck, "Passing and Strategic Voting on the U.S. Supreme Court," *Law and Society Review* 39 (2005); Kaitlyn L. Sill, Joseph Ura, and Stacia L. Haynie, "Strategic Passing and Opinion Assignment on the Burger Court," *Justice System Journal* 31 (2010).

32. Forrest Maltzman and Paul J Wahlbeck, "May It Please the Chief? Opinion Assignments in the Rehnquist Court," *American Journal of Political Science* 40 (1996); Maltzman and Wahlbeck, "A Conditional Model"; Maltzman, Spriggs, and Wahlbeck, *Crafting Law on the Supreme Court.*

7 ~ Forecasting Opinion Assignment on the U.S. Supreme Court

PAUL J. WAHLBECK, ALYX MARK, RYAN KROG, AND PHILLIP J. WININGER

Does the chief justice possess extraordinary powers by virtue of that leadership post? One commentator, William Rehnquist, expressed skepticism, stating that the chief "presides over a conference not of eight subordinates, whom he may direct or instruct, but of eight associates who, like him, have tenure during good behavior, and who are as independent as hogs on ice."[1] Yet, as David Danelski wrote in his seminal essay on the chief justice, the chief enjoys at least one prerogative of power: the authority to assign the majority opinion.[2] Danelski outlined several ways in which the majority opinion assignment influences the policy content of the Court's decision. First, the contours of the policy articulated in the Court's opinion are dictated by the author's preferences. One justice may base the opinion on a narrow ground, while another justice may use a more broad ground. Second, the Court's legitimacy is also affected by the chief's assignment decision since some justices are more likely to write opinions that are acceptable to the public. Finally, case outcomes may be shaped by the assignment. Indeed, the chief may assign cases strategically with an eye toward maintenance or expansion of the majority coalition.

Recognizing opinion assignment as central to the Court's policymaking and case outcomes, political scientists have pursued the research agenda outlined by Danelski. An immense body of research has developed as a consequence. Employing data derived from assignment sheets found in the justices' papers, this research assesses the assignments of some previous chief justices—Vinson, Warren, Burger, and Rehnquist—and uncovers causal factors that may underlie the process.[3] As Danelski hypothesized, the chief's assignment decisions are dictated by justices' policy agreement with the chief, which is accentuated in salient cases, and efforts to maintain the majority coalition, while also balancing concerns of equitable distribution across justices and using the justices' expertise.

Our effort here is to apply these theoretically grounded explanations to forecast current opinion assignments. Legal commentators and journalists use opinion-assignment patterns as clues that allow them to predict the outcomes of the remaining cases on the Court's docket. Indeed, during the 2011 term, a whirlwind of speculation and guessing led up to the Court's highly anticipated decision regarding the constitutionality of the Patient Protection and Affordable Care Act of 2010. A week prior to the Court's announcement, for instance, various legal commentators named Chief Justice Roberts as the likely author of the opinion, since the other predicted candidate, Justice Kennedy, delivered the majority opinion in the highly salient Arizona immigration case immediately prior to the health care ruling.[4] Even as commentators and journalists toss around their predictions, political scientists have long eschewed forecasting methods. With the exception of a study by Martin and colleagues,[5] forecasting applications to the Supreme Court have been quite limited.

Our research utilizes data from the 2005 to 2009 Supreme Court terms to build an explanatory opinion-assignment model. To cross-validate the model, we then make assignment predictions with respect to cases decided during an out-of-sample 2010 term. This attempt at making a real-world application is methodologically and theoretically important. Forecasting and out-of-sample predictions provide significant analytical leverage, as testing predictions against future events is one of the most stringent checks of statistical models. To this end, Beck, King, and Zeng write, "even if we have no interest in prediction per se, the poor forecasting performance of standard models indicates that we can improve on them to provide better knowledge of real-world causal relationships."[6] Consequently, we argue that it is important to revisit (and perhaps question) our understanding of the opinion-assignment process. Testing our models of opinion assignment against future observations helps accomplish this goal. It is this challenge that we undertake as our principal responsibility in this project.

Beyond the contribution of applying our understanding of opinion assignment to the real-world scenarios, our study also allows us to investigate opinion-assignment practices during the current Roberts Court. It is important to understand Roberts's decision-making process, as he will have many opportunities to develop and change legal policy during his presumably lengthy tenure on the Court. Thus our model might provide a first glimpse into how he will lead the Court and on how law will develop under his leadership in the coming years.

In the sections that follow, we review extant research on the opinion-assignment process and use this literature to derive hypotheses about the forecasting of opinion assignment. Next we describe our data and methods and specify the series of statistical models designed to test both in-sample and out-of-sample forecasts. Along the way, we pay special attention to the challenges we face in testing our hypotheses given a lack of available data associated with several of our measures.

Opinion-Assignment Decision Making

Most reviews of opinion assignment begin with Danelski's discussion of strategies employed by chief justices.[7] Given the strategic environment within which opinion assignment operates, political scientists attempt to uncover what motivates how a chief justice executes this task.[8] An array of causal factors have been explored. But the literature has sorted these factors into two primary goals in opinion assignment: (1) the strategic pursuit of policy preferences and (2) the desire to satisfy the Court's organizational needs.[9]

Highlighting the first goal, political scientists David Rohde and Harold Spaeth aptly state, "the rational strategy for the assignor is to assign the opinion to the justice whose views are most like his own on the issue being decided."[10] This statement, of course, portrays the chief as a policy-minded justice who seeks to choose a writer who will construct a written opinion—and, thus, the content of law—that most closely reflects the chief's preferred policy. This policy-centered view of opinion assignment emanates from a large body of research demonstrating that policy motivations guide an array of judicial behavior by Supreme Court justices.[11]

There may be more to the story, however. The second goal—the pursuit of organizational needs—suggests that the chief looks beyond ideological preferences in many cases. More specifically, research indicates that formal and informal norms confer upon the chief a special job obligation: the role of an administrator and representative of the Court.[12] Internalizing this role, the chief may use opinion assignment to preserve judicial legitimacy, enhance harmony among justices, and promote the smooth operation of the Court.[13] These factors uniquely constrain the chief justice. Associate justice assignors do not weigh organizational factors.[14]

When these policy and organizational components of opinion assignment are viewed collectively, a nuanced process of opinion assignment unfolds in which the chief justice balances multiple goals.[15] To help illustrate, this review highlights a body of scholarship exploring opinion assignment as a function of both goals. And, building upon this scholarship, it iterates several empirical hypotheses relevant to a forecasting model of opinion assignment.

The Pursuit of Policy Goals

Scholars readily acknowledge that the pursuit of policy preferences underlies a variety of Supreme Court behavior, including certiorari decisions, bargaining and accommodation over opinion content, decisions to write concurring or dissenting opinions, and general voting patterns.[16] Thus it is reasonable to surmise that opinion assignment is not exempt from policy-motivated behavior. Moreover, given that opinion assignment constitutes one of the chief's primary responsibilities when voting with the majority, the chief may be able to exercise special policymaking power over the Court.[17]

In order to demonstrate how this power may operate, opinion assignment must be placed within the context of the dynamic give-and-take of opinion writing. Notably, a majority opinion generally requires five supporting votes; the opinion writer cannot institute his or her preferred policy by fiat. The opinion writer's need to collect and maintain a majority leads to a process of bargaining and accommodation whereby justices haggle over how an opinion should textually unfold.[18] An opinion writer may have to draft or alter the opinion to accommodate the views of other justices, especially when the majority appears to be small or fragile. Maltzman, Spriggs, and Wahlbeck find, for example, that writers circulate more opinion drafts—and thus engage in more bargaining—when the majority coalition is small, majority coalition members are ideologically distant from the author, or the majority coalition is ideologically heterogeneous.[19]

Given this decision-making environment, some scholars may downplay the role of the opinion writer. Several studies indicate, for example, that the median member of the majority or Court controls policy outcomes.[20] If justices' ideological preferences are arrayed along a two-dimensional scale, the median preferences arguably must be satisfied in order to reach a majority threshold. This argument suggests that median preferences may dominate the majority opinion at the expense of preferences held by the opinion writer.

A singular focus on median preferences, however, ignores the power of agenda setting. As Riker theorizes, a leader may be able to set the agenda so as to manipulate the policy alternatives available for group decision making and, consequently, alter the outcomes that ensue.[21] This logic extends to opinion writing. The writer drafts the first iteration of an opinion, which may emphasize certain policy alternatives to the exclusion of others. The collection of alternatives presented by the writer may then "set the agenda" over which the justices subsequently bargain.[22]

Research provides further evidence of the writer's agenda-setting power. As Bonneau and colleagues theorize, a majority of justices may join an opinion even if it fails to match their ideal policy preferences.[23] Arguably these justices recognize that a majority is required so that the Court can deliver binding legal precedent and maintain influence within the judicial system. The opinion writer consequently retains some leverage to move policy in his or her direction and specify the policy options. Empirically analyzing the Burger Court, Bonneau and his colleagues compared the degree to which this agenda-setting power operates or, alternatively, the preferences of the median member triumph. While finding that the median member's preferences matter, they conclude that the opinion writer's preferences also influence policy outcomes.

Similarly, Lax and Cameron utilize game-theoretic modeling to demonstrate that the opinion writer can assert special "monopoly power" over opinion content, even when other justices are able to render "counteroffers" to the opinion during the bargaining process.[24] This model shows that the opinion writer frames and shapes the majority opinion to pre-empt threats from other justices. Although the necessity of a majority moves policy toward the median, the power associated with opinion writing allows the writer to retain some control.[25]

These studies give a policy-minded chief good reason to pick wisely when choosing an opinion writer. If the writer exercises policy control over the final opinion, a policy-minded chief should choose an ideologically proximate justice to write the opinion. This method of assignment allows the chief to maximize policy outcomes in his favor by choosing the writer most reflective of his preferences.[26,27] To this end, scholars have theorized, chiefs may assign opinions to their ideological allies.[28,29] And a study of chief justice behavior between 1953 and 1990 provides some empirical support for the view that the chiefs have favored those ideologically close to them when assigning opinions.[30] A first hypothesis relevant to a forecasting model of opinion assignment, therefore, unfolds:

HYPOTHESIS 1: *Justices are more likely to be assigned an opinion when they are ideologically proximate to the opinion assignor.*

Not all cases are created equal, however. Some cases, like Social Security statutory construction cases, are deemed to be "lemons" by the justices.[31] A select group of cases, in contrast, receive more attention from the public, salient cases with broad social impact that are situated in the public spotlight. As Chief Justice Rehnquist once stated about such cases, "The office offers no greater reward than the opportunity to author an opinion on an important point of constitutional law." Moreover, research readily acknowledges that justices often display the most intense policy preferences in salient cases.[32]

Given the special role of case salience, the chief may be especially policy motivated when he assigns the writer for a high-profile decision. The behavior of Chief Justice Rehnquist offers evidence for this proposition and perhaps to extend it to future chiefs, like Roberts. Research demonstrates that although Chief Justice Rehnquist did not favor his ideological friends across all cases, he disproportionately assigned opinions to fellow conservatives when cases were salient.[33] Other studies deliver supporting conclusions or hypotheses.[34] Slotnick, for example, examines patterns of opinion assignment from Chief Justices Taft to Burger and finds that justices were less likely to equally distribute important, high-profile cases among the justices, suggesting that the chief's policy motivations may have overwhelmed concerns for equality in opinion assignment.[35,36] Collectively, this research yields an additional hypothesis for the forecasting model:

HYPOTHESIS 2: *Justices are more likely to be assigned an opinion in salient cases when they are ideologically proximate to the opinion assignor.*

While a policy-minded chief may wish to select his closest allies, the Court operates within certain constraints, namely, the need for a majority of justices to join an opinion so that it constitutes binding legal precedent. Thus the choice of an ideological ally as writer may be a poor choice in certain contexts, especially when that writer is ideologically distant from other justices who form a thin majority. Rather, a chief justice confronting a narrow majority may retreat from his policy goals in order to avoid a dismantling of the majority or to encourage original dissenters to join the opinion so as to preserve or enlarge the fragile majority coalition. This method of opinion assignment prevents policy loss that would occur if the majority were reduced to a plurality or, as a worst-case scenario, became supplanted by an alternative majority coalition that delivered policy less favorable to the chief.[37]

Empirical research supports this analysis. During the Warren Court, for example, more than 20 percent of minimum-winning coalitions broke apart, leading to a policy outcome adverse to that preferred by the original coalition.[38] On the other hand, the appointment of more moderate justices as opinion writers may prevent such outcomes. Original dissenters, for example, are more likely to switch their votes and join the majority when an ideologically moderate justice writes the opinion, thereby helping to preserve or enlarge the coalition.[39] Moreover, it has been demonstrated that Rehnquist assigned opinions to more liberal justices (rather than close ideological allies) when the victory margin was close, suggesting that Rehnquist foresaw the coalition-enhancing value of a more moderate opinion writer.[40] Thus, extant research supports a third hypothesis:

> HYPOTHESIS 3: *Less ideologically proximate justices are more likely to be assigned an opinion when the voting margin is close.*

In all, the first three hypotheses characterize the chief as a policy-minded, ideological individual who seeks to fulfill policy goals, just as a large body of political science scholarship would suggest.[41] But these hypotheses also account for strategic action by the chief within the constraints of the Court.[42] The need to maintain a shaky majority coalition may lead to alternative assignment patterns by a policy-minded chief who attempts to guard against potential policy loss.

The Pursuit of Organizational Goals

Although voluminous research demonstrates that justices are driven by ideology, the chief may pursue goals beyond policy when he assigns opinions. As Danelski expressed, the role of the chief justice carries certain formal and informal powers.[43] Along with the power of opinion assignment, the chief has a special title, speaks first at conferences where justices vote on cases, oversees judicial administration, and often represents the Court to the public. Given these special obligations and powers, the chief may internalize that he must strive to be an organizational leader. In other words, more so than associate justices, he may act in ways that demonstrate special attentiveness to judicial legitimacy, internal court harmony, and the efficient operation of the Court.[44]

The chief justices' personal statements provide some psychological insight here. Chief Justice Earl Warren stated, "I do believe that if [the assignment process] wasn't done with regard to fairness, it could well lead to a great disruption in the Court."[45] Subsequently, Chief Justice Rehnquist remarked that he strived to be "as evenhanded as possible as far as numbers of cases assigned to each justice."[46] Rehnquist even circulated a memorandum to the other justices indicating that he sought to give everyone the same number of opinions during each Supreme Court term.[47] These statements suggest that the chiefs aim for efficiency and fairness in opinion assignments so as to ensure a harmonious and smooth operation of the Court. To this end, research has hypothesized that chiefs may pursue this overriding organizational goal in several ways: evenhandedly spreading opinion assignments amongst the justices, rewarding justices with opinion assignments who have expeditiously completed previous ones, and assigning opinions to justices who exhibit relevant policy expertise.[48]

With regard to equity in assignment, research indicates that chiefs may attempt to spread out the workload. As Slotnick notes, several chiefs expressed their desire to pursue the so-called "equality" norm, whereby justices obtain an equal chance to speak for the Court.[49] He then puts these assertions to the test by examining a range of opinion assignments from Chief Justices Taft to Burger. Slotnick finds that while perfect equality in assignment was not achieved, the data revealed a clear trend toward more equal workload among the justices over time. Subsequently, Maltzman and Wahlbeck also uncover some support for the chiefs' pursuit of the equality norm by analyzing opinion-assignment data from 1953 to 1990.[50] Specifically, they find that chiefs are less likely to assign opinions to justices who have recently received assignments from a senior associate justice (when the chief is not in the majority) and, conversely, are more likely to assign opinions to justices who lack recent, pending assignments. Additionally, Maltzman and Wahlbeck have zeroed in on the equity of Rehnquist's assignment patterns.[51] This research reveals that although Rehnquist did not equitably distribute workload over the entire course of a given term, he took into account the extent to which justices had already been assigned opinions during a particular assignment cycle. Thus, it appears that equitable distribution of opinions may partially motivate assignment decisions:

> HYPOTHESIS 4: *Justices are more likely to be assigned an opinion when they have received fewer previous assignments than other justices.*

Chief justices may also be acutely aware of the so-called "June crunch," when the Court must complete its term and issue the remainder of its pending decisions. Various statements by chiefs suggest that they may reward justices who have expeditiously completed prior assignments, especially when the end of the term nears. As Rehnquist once instructed his colleagues, he would "put more weight than I have in the past" on whether justices had timely completed pending assignments.[52] And research suggests that Rehnquist may have followed his words with action: empirics show that Rehnquist punished justices who were late in finishing majority opinion drafts.[53]

As to other chiefs, Brenner and Palmer find that while Chief Justice Vinson did not appear to follow the norm of assignment equality, he disproportionately distributed assignments to justices who were expedient drafters.[54] This analysis comports with a more systematic finding by Maltzman and Wahlbeck—analyzing opinion assignments by multiple chiefs from 1953 to 1990—that justices who promptly completed assignments were more likely to receive new assignments, especially as the end of the term approached.[55] This research provides solid ground to hypothesize in a forecasting model that chiefs reward more efficient opinion drafters with new assignments:

HYPOTHESIS 5: *Justices are more likely to be assigned an opinion when they have expeditiously completed previous assignments.*

Organizational goals may also incorporate issue specialization. Scholars have recognized that specialization can be important to the Court's operation: division of labor ameliorates the troubles of a heavy workload, justices can more efficiently write in areas of law where they exhibit more knowledge, and perceptions of judicial expertise may enhance the Court's image with the public.[56] Brenner examined the relative opinion-assignment ratios of justices in different types of civil liberties cases. He uncovered evidence that certain justices appeared to become issue specialists in various areas of law, as these justices would receive a disproportionate share of cases in a particular issue area.[57] Building upon this analysis, subsequent research has examined whether a justice has been more likely to receive a new assignment in a particular issues area, dependent upon whether the justice had completed previously more opinions in that area.[58] The empirics show that, indeed, this form of policy expertise may matter to opinion assignment. Thus, the forecasting model incorporates a final hypothesis:

HYPOTHESIS 6: *Justices are more likely to be assigned an opinion in cases where they demonstrate substantive expertise.*

When one views all six hypotheses collectively, the complexity of opinion assignment becomes apparent. Chiefs, who operate as both policy-minded judges and organizational leaders, must balance multiple, competing goals. A substantial body of scholarship demonstrates that this mix of goals yields a multifaceted process of opinion assignment. In other words, rather than producing a single-minded maximizing of one goal, the political dynamics and constraints of the Court—along with the administrative and leadership obligations attached to the special job title—may force the chief to distribute assignments along several dimensions.

Data

Modeling opinion assignment in more recent terms is fraught with challenges due to data limitations. Since we do not have the benefit of the justices' personal papers for assignments made in the 2005 through 2009 terms, we draw inferences from the final vote coalition. We make the assumption that the senior justice in the majority coalition assigned the opinion to the final opinion author. Certainly that assumption introduces measurement error. Take data from the Burger Court, for example. Although Chief Justice Warren Burger assigned the opinion in about 95 percent of the cases when he signed the final majority opinion, the identity of the assigned author was a more fluid situation, with about 74 percent of first assignees authoring the final majority opinion.[59] The impact of this measurement error on our findings is unclear. At times, reassignments occur because a justice changes sides, resulting in a justice with different viewpoints writing the opinion. More commonly, however, reassignments change the author from one member of the coalition to another to maintain equity in workload. Nonetheless, we do not have an alternative when we analyze opinion assignment in more recent terms.

Using this method, there is a distribution of assignors and assigned authors in the 340 cases the Court decided by signed opinion in the 2005 through 2009 terms. Since his confirmation in 2005, Chief Justice Roberts assigned 87.2 percent of cases during the 2005 to 2009 terms, followed by Justice Stevens, who assigned 9.2 percent of the cases. In more recent terms, however, Chief Justice Roberts has been the majority assignor in more than 90 percent of the cases.

Dependent Variable

Since we have one observation for every justice who participates in a decision, the dependent variable indicates whether a particular justice wrote the majority opinion.

Independent Variables

Ideological Proximity. To measure each justice's ideological proximity to the opinion assignor, we rely on Martin-Quinn scores.[60] We take the absolute value of the difference between the justice's score and the assignor's score. The identity of the assignor, as discussed above, is inferred as the senior justice in the majority coalition. The mean difference is 2.03 with a standard deviation of 1.40.

Median Justice. We created a variable that indicates whether a justice is the median justice on the Court, using Martin-Quinn scores. The variable equals one for the median justice and zero otherwise.

Margin. The margin variable is equal to the difference of votes supporting the majority and votes in the minority.[61] The average is 3.21 with a range, as you would expect, between 1 and 9. A lower value indicates a close, e.g., 5-4, vote.

Political Salience. We measured the political salience of a case through the number of amicus briefs submitted on the merits. We obtained the amici data from the docket files made available on the Supreme Court's official website. We use a standardized measure of amicus participation. The average is –0.10 with a range of –0.94 to 5.55.

Efficiency. Past research used the average lag between the assignment date and a justice's circulation of the first draft as a measure of efficiency.[62] Without access to the justices' personal papers for these years, of course, we cannot replicate that measure. In its place, we draw on information from the average time it takes a justice to publish a majority opinion. More specifically, we calculated the time between oral argument and the opinion announcement in every case. That duration, however, can be affected by a number of considerations, such as previous experience on the bench, the justice's career stage, complexity of the case, the divisiveness of the case, the Court's docket size during that term, the justices' other workload, and time remaining in the term when the case was assigned. Consequently, we regress the time it took to publish an opinion[63] on variables associated with these considerations. Our efficiency measure is based on the residual from that regression, assuming that a justice's efficiency can be observed from the duration net these other considerations. Our measure, more precisely, is the justice's average efficiency in the previous term. The resulting measure offers some face validity: some of the renowned slow writers on the Court, like Justice Harry Blackmun, had extremely high scores, while fast writers, like Justice William Douglas, produced low scores. The average efficiency score is −0.75 with a standard deviation of 14.96.

Equity. We calculated whether a justice's running assignment total for the term deviates from the median number received by justices for the month prior to the case's oral argument. Based on the opinions written by a justice, we calculate the number of assignments received by a justice each month in which oral arguments are held.[64] For each month of oral arguments, we then calculate the median number of assignments received by the justices. A negative value, then, indicates that the justice has received fewer assignments than the median justice, while a positive value reveals that the justice has more assignments than the median. The range of values runs from −5 to +2 with an average of −0.07.

Expertise. This measure is based on the justice's propensity to write separate opinions in an issue area.[65] We calculated the separate opinion ratio for each justice in every issue area using Spaeth et al., that is, we calculated the percentage of all previous cases in an issue for which that justice wrote a concurring or a dissenting opinion.[66,67] We then took this percentage and converted it into a standardized measure for a set of justices sitting in a particular term. The average expertise is 0.05 with a range from −2.06 to +2.62.

Majority Prediction. Because justices are only eligible to author a majority opinion if they are in the majority coalition, it is necessary to control for their membership in this group. Indeed, past research excluded justices who were not members of the conference majority. Without access to the justices' personal papers, though, we do not know the composition of the conference majority. We instead created a measure of the likelihood of a justice being in the final majority. This was done by estimating a model of various case-level and justice-level factors that could be known before a decision is announced, such as the direction of the lower court decision and the number of questions a justice asks during oral argument. Using postestimation procedures, we created a score of the likelihood of a justice being in the case majority.[68] See the appendix for the details and results of this model.

Oral Argument Participation. A justice's engagement and interest in a case may act as a signal for the chief justice when it comes to opinion assignment. Research by Johnson et al. suggests that activity during oral argument may be an important predictor of the justices' decision making at later stages of the Court's processing of cases.[69] Thus, we draw upon Black et al.'s measure of the number of words each justice speaks during oral argument as a way of representing the justices' interest in a case.[70,71]

Results

Our approach begins with first specifying a model of opinion assignment using the 2005 to 2009 terms of the Court. The units of analysis are the sitting justices within a case. Because our dependent variable is dichotomous (whether a justice in the conference majority is assigned the opinion), we use a logit model, with standard errors clustered at the case level to account for the within-case correlation.[72]

Table 7.1 presents the estimated coefficients and their significance level from a logistic regression model of opinion assignments made during all cases orally argued and decided during the 2005 to 2009 terms. This model also serves as the base from which we make our out-of-sample forecasts for the 2010 term. Overall, the model provides corroborative support for many of our expectations about the opinion-assignment decisions in recent terms. Several of the variables show up as significant and in the expected direction.

Although the model's primary purpose is establishing a means for testing future decisions, a cursory review of the results provides insight into the opinion assignment under Chief Justice Roberts. It appears that many of the factors guiding his predecessors' assignment decisions also shape Chief Justice Roberts's. Consistent with earlier research, Chief Justice Roberts's opinion assignments are driven by both policy concerns and organizational needs. The likelihood of a justice winning an assignment is inversely related to his or her ideological distance from the chief.[73] As expected, however, the effect of ideology also conditions other factors associated with opinion assignment.[74] As captured in figure 7.1, which presents the effect of ideological distance conditioned on political salience, justices who are allied with the chief are more likely to win an assignment in salient cases.[75] In cases of great importance, the chief is most likely to assign the opinion to ideological friends, but in cases with fewer policy implications he is more likely to assign the opinion to justices who are ideological estranged . In addition to these factors, a justice's activeness during oral argument also appears to influence opinion assignments.

The effect of ideological distance is conditioned on the size of the majority coalition. First, when the majority is small, Chief Justice Roberts is more likely to assign the majority opinion to the median justice. The coefficient for Median Justice reflects the likelihood of the median receiving the assignment when the majority and minority possess the same number of justices. As the majority coalition grows, this likelihood drops. Outside of the effect of this one justice, we see from the significance of the interaction between margin and ideology that the effect of ideological distance varies with the size of the winning margin. This conditional relationship is presented graphically in figure 7.2. The graph demonstrates clearly that being ideologically distant from the chief justice comes with a much higher cost in cases where the majority coalition is weaker. More specifically, the

TABLE 7.1. Opinion Assignment in the Roberts Court, 2005–2009

Variable	Coefficient
Ideological Distance	–0.441*
	(0.214)
Political Salience	0.018**
	(0.006)
Margin	-0.086
	(0.061)
Median Justice	2.631**
	(0.966)
Ideological Distance * Margin	0.071**
	(0.029)
Ideological Distance * Political Salience	-0.011***
	(0.004)
Median Justice * Margin	-0.394***
	(0.145)
Equity	-0.172***
	(0.060)
Efficiency	0.001
	(0.004)
Expertise	0.048
	(0.067)
Majority Prediction	0.158
	(0.574)
Oral Argument Participation	0.179***
	(0.054)
Constant	-1.706
	(0.627)
Number of Observations	2,914
Log-likelihood	-1,002.7052
Wald Chi-square	62.61

Note: Robust standard error clustered on case in parentheses. Significance levels (one-tail): * = .05, ** = .01, *** = .001.

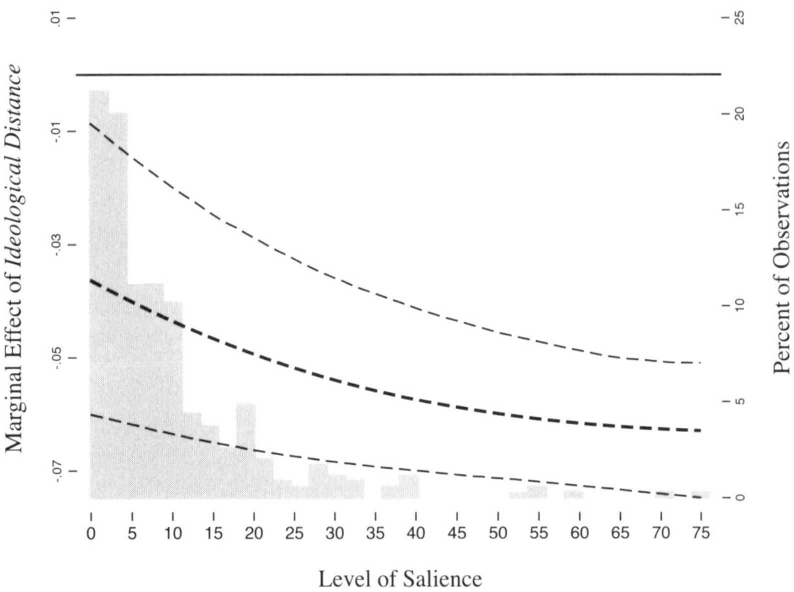

Fig. 7.1. The interaction of ideology and case salience in predicting opinion assignment

effects of ideological distance are not significant in cases with a margin of six justices.

We find support for the organizational factors in Chief Justice Roberts's assignment decisions. Equity stands out as an important factor guiding opinion-assignment decisions. Just like his predecessors, Chief Justice Roberts appears to place special emphasis on ensuring that justices have an equal workload across the span of the term. As justices receive fewer assignments than their colleagues, it is more likely that the chief will assign them the task of drafting a majority opinion. As seen in figure 7.3, justices who have received the median number of assignments to date in the term have a probability of assignment that is comparable to a one-in-nine chance. Justices who lag behind their colleagues in assignments have a greater chance of receiving the assignment. The effects of other organizational factors, however, do not manifest themselves in the same way; the variables for both expertise and efficiency are insignificant. As discussed in the previous section, there is likely measurement error associated with efficiency, and we do not condition this variable by time in the term as did

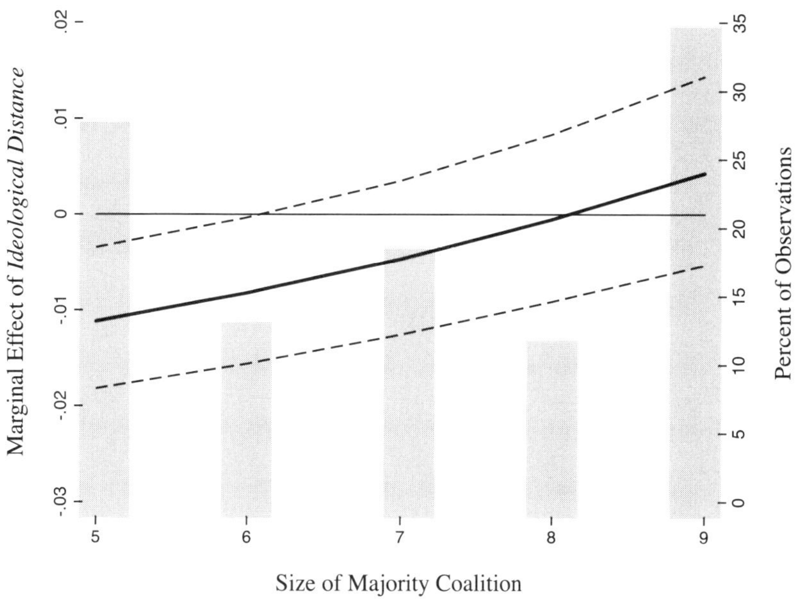

Fig. 7.2. The interaction of ideology and majority vote margin in predicting opinion assignment

past research. Similarly, expertise might be conditioned on the complexity of the case considered by the Court.[76] It is reasonable to expect that assigners will rely more heavily on experts in complex cases. Finally, another explanation for our results is that our data include all assignors, not just the chief justice. Maltzman, Spriggs, and Wahlbeck found that associate justice assignors do not weigh organizational factors.[77]

Forecasting the 2010 Term

Using the previously described 2005–2009 model, we now utilize the coefficients derived from that model to inform an out-of-sample prediction on cases in the 2010 term. Although we do, of course, know which justices were assigned particular opinions in 2010, we use the 2010 term to illustrate the usefulness of the prediction model; additionally, by using data from 2010, we can compare the predictions of our model to a popular source of assignment speculation: *SCOTUSblog*.

To compute out-of-sample predictions, we generate predicted prob-

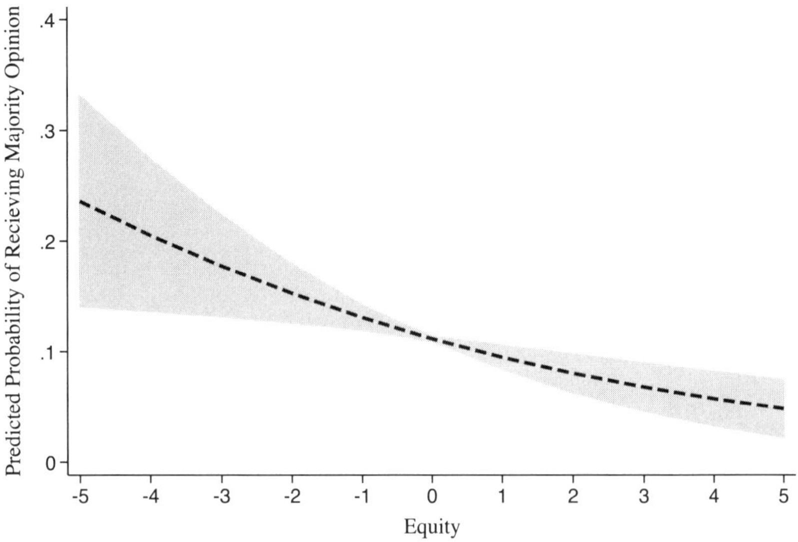

Fig. 7.3. Predicted effect of equity on opinion assignment

abilities for each round of assignments based on our presumptions of the kinds of information a forecaster would have when making a contemporaneous prediction. Thus, the model looks fairly similar to the in-sample model we have estimated. Justice-level and case-level variables, which are constant and knowable across their levels, are pieces of information we assume a forecaster would have when making a prediction. For example, an informed forecaster would have information about a justice's ideological distance from the opinion assignor and expertise in given issue areas in a given term. Additionally, the forecaster would know specifics about each case, such as the number of amicus briefs filed and the relative level of involvement of a justice in oral arguments. The model also employs an updating consideration, the number of opinions written and announced by a justice. As opinions are announced, forecasters draw inferences about likelihood that the justice will receive another assignment. We use a lagged announcement variable to best estimate the level of information a similarly situated forecaster might have when making assignment predictions.

Overall, the out-of-sample prediction model correctly predicts 16 percent of the opinion assignments in the 2010 term, or twelve of the seventy-five cases. The number of cases correctly predicted expands to twenty-four

(32 percent) of the 2010 cases for justices receiving a predicted probability that placed them in our top three most likely to receive an opinion. Although these results might not appear on their face to be particularly significant, the number of correctly predicted cases exceeds that which we would have expected from random chance (χ^2 110.07, $p < .000$). This is encouraging.

Us v. SCOTUSblog

On June 16, 2011, about two weeks before the end of the 2010 term, a prominent Supreme Court attorney and the founder of *SCOTUSblog*, Thomas Goldstein, published his prediction of the opinion authorship of the remaining fourteen cases left in the term.[78] On the whole, Goldstein did well. He accurately predicted which justice would author the opinion in five of the fourteen cases, or 35.7 percent. These predictions provide a useful marker to compare our predictions.

Figure 7.4 presents graphically our predictions of opinion assignment in each of these fourteen cases. Each point represents the predicted probability that a given justice will be assigned an opinion. An asterisk denotes *SCOTUSblog*'s prediction, while a gray diamond signifies the case's actual author.

A cursory review of the graphs suggests that the model predicts the opinion assignment with relative success. In several cases, we accurately predict which justice received the opinion, while *SCOTUSblog* was off the mark, and vice versa. For instance, *SCOTUSblog* incorrectly predicted that Chief Justice Roberts would author the opinion in *Brown v. Entertainment Merchants Association*, the much-anticipated case involving the regulation of sales of violent video games in California.[79] *SCOTUSblog* reasoned that the chief justice was the main contender through inferring the number of opinions Roberts had authored from that cycle (equity) and his past opinions (expertise): "At bottom, it seems too unlikely to me that the Chief Justice went until January before writing multiple opinions in a sitting. He is also the natural author, having written last Term's *Stevens* dog-fighting opinion." Our model, though, accurately predicted that Justice Scalia would receive the assignment.

Our model also correctly predicted that Justice Ginsburg would author the opinion in *Goodyear Dunlop Tires et al. v. Brown*.[80] In contrast, *SCOTUSblog* predicted that it would be Chief Justice Roberts authoring the opinion, citing the distribution of opinions that had been announced from that cycle (equity) and appealing to the case's importance (salience).

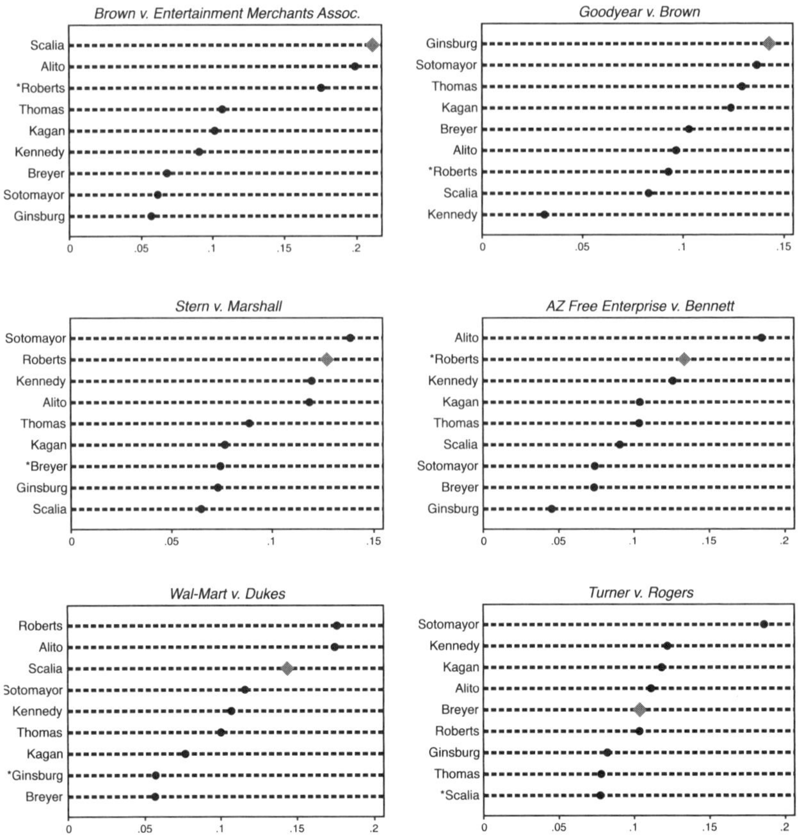

Fig. 7.4. Forecasting opinion assignment of the 2010 term. (*Note:* The gray diamonds denote the actual opinion author. An asterisk denotes the *SCOTUSblog* prediction for opinion assignment.)

The remaining graphs illustrate the model's predictions for the rest of *SCOTUSblog*'s 2010 prognostications. In the three graphs following *Brown* and *Goodyear*, the model predicts assignments for a justice with one of the three highest probabilities of receiving the assignment. For example, in *Stern v. Marshall*, *SCOTUSblog* wrongly predicted Breyer as the majority opinion writer.[81] Based on our forecasting model, we predict that the actual opinion author, Roberts, is the second most likely justice to receive the opinion, while Breyer is the fourth most likely. In a controversial case involving gender discrimination and class action lawsuits, *Wal-mart v. Dukes*, *SCOTUSblog* predicted that Ginsburg would write the majority opinion,

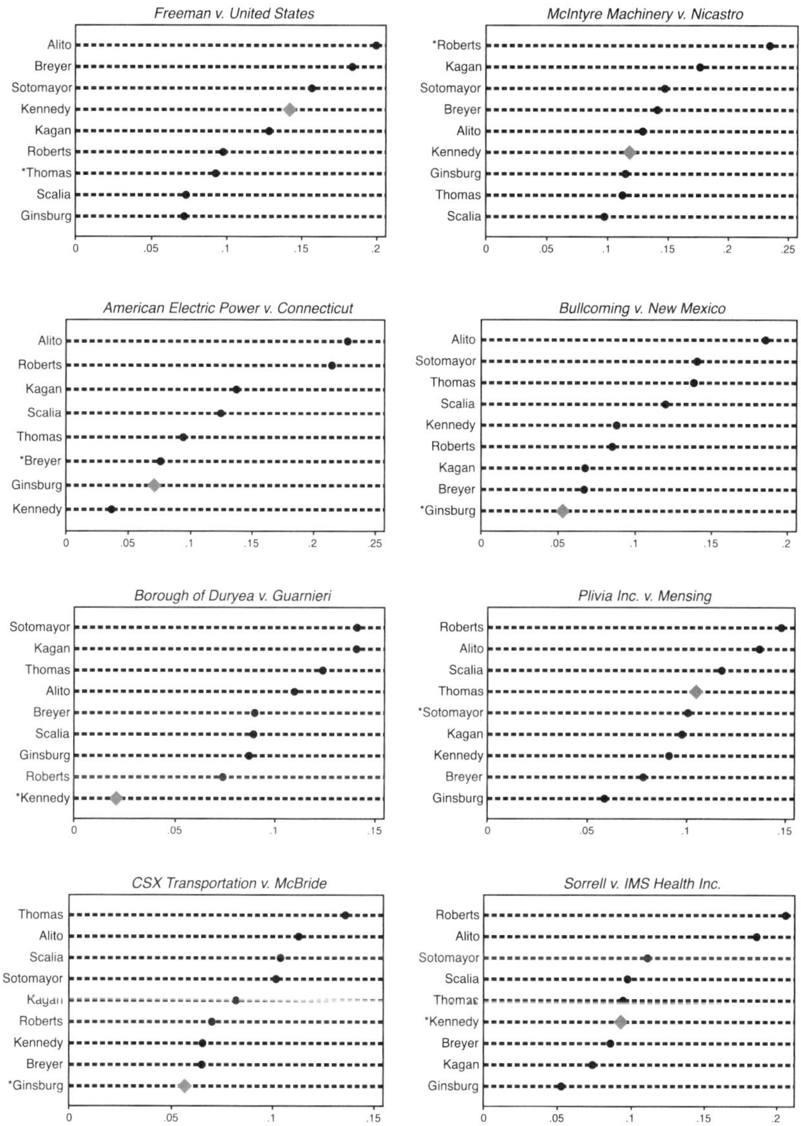

Fig. 7.4. (*continued*)

but Justice Scalia ultimately authored the opinion.[82] According to our predictions, Ginsburg was unlikely to receive this opinion, with Justice Alito being the most likely author, followed closely by Chief Justice Roberts and Justice Scalia.

Even with more idiosyncratic cases our model still holds its own. Consider, for instance, *CSX Transportation v. McBride*, an opinion authored by Justice Ginsburg.[83] Our model predicted that Justice Thomas was most likely to receive the majority opinion (quite the opposite of Ginsburg). Upon closer inspection, however, our model was not far off. The unusual case marks a complete breakdown in the traditional ideological coalitions with Justice Thomas breaking with his fellow conservatives and instead voting with the four liberal justices. Since Justice Thomas was the senior justices in the majority coalition and was responsible for assigning the opinion, he assigned the case to Justice Ginsburg.[84]

Conclusion

This chapter presents one of the first examinations of Chief Justice Roberts's opinion-assignment decisions. Consistent with findings based on Roberts's predecessors' assignments, he grounds his assignments on his colleagues' ideological positions and strategic calculations. We can expect Chief Justice Roberts to continue the practice of assigning salient cases to his ideological allies and to assign opinions to the median justice when the majority coalition is fragile. In addition, Chief Justice Roberts gives weight to organizational needs: he strives for an equitable distribution of assignments across the justices. In short, then, we conclude that the standard account of opinion assignment will explain Chief Justice Roberts's decisions.

Our second task in this chapter is to forecast opinion assignments using a theoretically grounded empirical model. We recognize that forecasting opinion assignment on the Supreme Court using theory-derived coefficients is no easy feat, and our first attempt at predictions certainly illustrates this observation. While this initial attempt was not met with the level of precision we would have liked, preliminary results indicate that the model successfully categorizes more majority opinion assignments than would have been assigned through random chance and illustrates results that are of similar strength to the predictions of *SCOTUSblog*. By using a range of variables informed by theory, we will be better situated to make reliable predictions than those not employing a dynamic information model.

APPENDIX: PREDICTING WHETHER A JUSTICE WILL BE IN THE MAJORITY

We drew upon a number of justice-level and case-level factors to predict whether a justice would be in the majority coalition. Included in these factors were ideology, the number of questions they asked each side during oral arguments, and the lower court proceedings. We also included fixed effects for individual justices and issue area. Using these relevant variables, we ran a logit model whether the justice would be in the majority, where the variable took on a value of 1 if this was the case, 0 if otherwise. After running the model, we used simple postestimation procedures in Stata to generate predicted probabilities that a particular justice would be in the majority. These scores were generated for each justice in each case of the 2010 term. Below are the estimated coefficients and the significance levels of the variables used in the model.

TABLE A7.1. Predicting the Majority Coalition

Variable	Coefficient
Ideology	–0.083
	(0.137)
Political Salience	–0.080
	(0.084)
Ideological Compatibility	–0.122***
	(0.019)
Ideological Compatibility * Political Salience	–0.010
	(0.019)
Ideology * Political Salience	–0.102
	(0.018)
Distance from Median	–0.598***
	(0.211)
Distance from Median * Political Salience	0.013
	(0.008)
Lower Court Direction	0.118
	(0.091)
Expertise	0.075
	(0.062)
Lower Court Dissent	–0.186*
	(0.091)
Oral Argument Participation	–0.163***
	(0.041)
Number of Observations	4,336
Log-likelihood	–1,973.1136
X^2	276.56

Note: Robust standard error clustered on case in parentheses. Significance levels (one-tail):* = .05, ** = .01, *** = .001.

NOTES

1. William H. Rehnquist, "Chief Justices I Never Knew," *Hastings Constitutional Law Quarterly* 3 (1975): 637.

2. David J. Danelski, "The Influence of the Chief Justice in the Decisional Process of the Supreme Court," in *Courts, Judges, and Politics*, 4th ed., ed. Walter F. Murphy and C. Herman Pritchett (New York: Random House, 1986).

3. Elliot E. Slotnick, "The Equality Principle and Majority Opinion Assignment on the United States Supreme Court," *Polity* 12 (1979); Saul Brenner and Jan Palmer, "The Time Taken to Write Opinions as a Determinant of Opinion Assignments," *Judicature* 72 (1988); Sue Davis, "Power on the Court: Chief Justice Rehnquist's Opinion Assignments," *Judicature* 74 (1990); Forrest Maltzman, James F. Spriggs II, and Paul J. Wahlbeck, *Crafting Law on the Supreme Court: The Collegial Game* (New York: Cambridge University Press, 2000).

4. Avik Roy, "On Thursday, Roberts Is Likely To Write the Supreme Court Opinion That Partially Overturns Obamacare," *Forbes.com*, June 25, 2012, http://www.forbes.com/sites/aroy/2012/06/25/on-thursday-roberts-is-likely-to-write-the-supreme-court-opinion-that-partially-overturns-obamacare, accessed Aug. 6, 2012.

5. Andrew D. Martin et al., "Competing Approaches to Predicting Supreme Court Decision Making," *Perspectives on Politics* 2 (2004).

6. Nathaniel Beck, Gary King, and Langche Zeng, "Improving Quantitative Studies of International Conflict: A Conjecture," *American Political Science Review* 94 (2000): 22.

7. Danelski, "The Influence of the Chief Justice."

8. Of course, Supreme Court norms dictate that the chief justice only assigns opinions when he is a member of the majority. When the chief joins the minority coalition, the most senior justice in the conference majority assigns the opinion. While recognizing that other justices may assign opinions, this review of literature primarily focuses on how the chief may operate in the role of assignor.

9. Paul J. Wahlbeck, "Strategy and Constraints on Supreme Court Opinion Assignment," *University of Pennsylvania Law Review* 154 (2006); Forrest Maltzman and Paul J. Wahlbeck, "Opinion Assignment on the Rehnquist Court," *Judicature* 89 (2005); Forrest Maltzman and Paul J. Wahlbeck, "A Conditional Model of Opinion Assignment on the Supreme Court," *Political Research Quarterly* 57 (2004); Forrest Maltzman and Paul J. Wahlbeck, "May It Please the Chief? Opinion Assignments in the Rehnquist Court," *American Journal of Political Science* 40 (1996).

10. David W. Rohde and Harold J. Spaeth, *Supreme Court Decision Making* (San Francisco: W. H. Freeman, 1976), 174; see also David W. Rohde, "Policy Goals, Strategic Choice and Majority Opinion Assignments in the U.S. Supreme Court," *Midwest Journal of Political Science* 16 (1972).

11. See, e.g., Jeffrey A. Segal and Harold J. Spaeth, *The Supreme Court and the Attitudinal Model Revisited* (New York: Cambridge University Press, 2002).

12. Wahlbeck, "Strategy and Constraints"; Maltzman and Wahlbeck, "A Conditional Model"; Danelski, "The Influence of the Chief Justice."

13. Wahlbeck, "Strategy and Constraints."

14. Maltzman, Spriggs, and Wahlbeck, *Crafting Law on the Supreme Court*.

15. See Maltzman and Wahlbeck, "A Conditional Model"; Maltzman and Wahlbeck, "May It Please the Chief."

16. See, e.g., Segal and Spaeth, *The Supreme Court and the Attitudinal Model Revisited*; Maltzman, Spriggs, and Wahlbeck. *Crafting Law on the Supreme Court*; Paul J. Wahlbeck, James F. Spriggs II, and Forrest Maltzman, "The Politics of Dissents and Concurrences on the U.S. Supreme Court," *American Politics Quarterly* 27 (1999); Gregory A. Caldeira and John R. Wright, "Organized Interests and Agenda Setting in the US Supreme Court," *American Political Science Review* 4 (1988); Gregory A. Caldeira, John R. Wright, and Christopher J. W. Zorn, "Sophisticated Voting and Gate-Keeping in the Supreme Court," *Journal of Law, Economics, and Organization* 15 (1999); Rohde and Spaeth, *Supreme Court Decision Making*.

17. See Danelski, "The Influence of the Chief Justice.

18. Maltzman, Spriggs, and Wahlbeck, *Crafting Law on the Supreme Court*; Walter Murphy, *Elements of Judicial Strategy* (Chicago: University of Chicago Press, 1964).

19. Maltzman, Spriggs, Wahlbeck, *Crafting Law on the Supreme Court.*

20. See Chad Westerland, "Who Owns the Majority Opinion? An Examination of Policymaking on the U.S. Supreme Court," paper presented at the annual meeting of the American Political Science Association, Philadelphia, Aug. 2003; Thomas H. Hammond, Chris W. Bonneau, and Reginald S. Sheehan, *Strategic Behavior and Policy Choice on the U.S. Supreme Court* (Stanford, CA: Stanford University Press, 2005).

21. William H. Riker, *The Art of Political Manipulation* (New Haven: Yale University Press, 1986); see also William H. Riker, *Liberalism Against Populism: A Confrontation Between the Theory of Democracy and the Theory of Social Choice* (San Francisco: Freeman, 1982).

22. Wahlbeck, "Strategy and Constraints."

23. Chris W. Bonneau et al., "Agenda Control, the Median Justice, and the Majority Opinion on the US Supreme Court," *American Journal of Political Science* 51 (2007).

24. Jeffrey R. Lax and Charles M. Cameron, "Bargaining and Opinion Assignment on the US Supreme Court," *Journal of Law, Economics, and Organization* 23 (2007).

25. See also Hammond, Bonneau, and Sheehan, *Strategic Behavior and Policy Choice*; Edward P. Schwartz, "Policy, Precedent, and Power: A Positive Theory of Supreme Court Decision-Making," *Journal of Law, Economics, & Organization* 8 (1992).

26. Alternatively, assignment to ideological allies may also prevent policy loss, when the chief's preferred position is less favored by the Court's majority. It is commonly reported, for example, that Chief Justice Burger repeatedly awaited the other justices' votes at conference and then strategically voted with the majority so that he could control opinion assignment. The method of assignment arguably allowed the chief to assign the opinion to an ally who may "do the least damage" on policy. See Lee Epstein and Olga Shvetsova, "Heresthetical Maneuvering on the US Supreme Court," *Journal of Theoretical Politics* 14 (2002).

27. See Wahlbeck, "Strategy and Constraints"; Rohde, "Policy Goals, Strategic Choice."

28. Gregory J. Rathjen, "Policy Goals, Strategic Choice, and Majority Opinion Assignments in the U.S. Supreme Court: A Replication," *American Journal of Political Science* 18 (1974). It should be noted that Rathjen performed a replication of Rohde's analysis regarding assignment to ideologically proximate justices and disputed the results.

29. See, e.g., Rohde and Spaeth, *Supreme Court Decision Making*; William P. McLauchlan, "Research Note: Ideology and Conflict in Supreme Court Opinion Assignment, 1946–1962," *Western Political Quarterly* 25 (1974); and Rohde, "Policy Goals, Strategic Choice."

30. Maltzman and Wahlbeck, "A Conditional Model."

31. Lewis F. Powell, "Note from the Chief Justice" (1986), Washington & Lee University, Justice Lewis F. Powell Papers.

32. See, e.g., Segal and Spaeth, *Attitudinal Model Revisited*; Rohde, "Policy Goals, Strategic Choice."

33. Maltzman and Wahlbeck, "Opinion Assignment on the Rehnquist Court"; Maltzman and Wahlbeck, "May It Please the Chief."

34. Slotnick, "The Equality Principle"; Rohde, "Policy Goals, Strategic Choice"; Sidney S. Ulmer, "The Use of Power on the Supreme Court: The Opinion Assignments of Earl Warren, 1953–1960," *Journal of Public Law* 30 (1970).

35. Research also shows that chiefs have been more likely to self-assign opinions in highly salient cases, arguably a policy-motivated move to control opinion content (Maltzman and Wahlbeck, "A Conditional Model"; Saul Brenner, "The Chief Justices' Self-Assignment of Majority Opinions in Salient Cases," *Social Science Journal* 30 (1993); and Rohde, "Policy Goals, Strategic Choice."

36. Elliot E. Slotnick, "Who Speaks for the Court? Majority Opinion Assignments from Taft to Burger," *American Journal of Political Science* 23 (1979).

37. See Wahlbeck, "Strategy and Constraints."

38. Saul Brenner, Timothy M. Hagle, and Harold J. Spaeth, "The Defection of the Marginal Justice on the Warren Court," *Western Political Quarterly* 42 (1989); Saul Brenner and Harold J. Spaeth, "Majority Opinion Assignments and the Maintenance of the Original Coalition on the Warren Court," *American Journal of Political Science* 32 (1988).

39. Saul Brenner, Timothy M. Hagle, and Harold J. Spaeth, "Increasing the Size of Minimum Winning Original Coalitions on the Warren Court," *Polity* 23 (1990); Brenner and Spaeth, "Majority Opinion Assignments and the Maintenance of the Original Coalition."

40. Maltzman and Wahlbeck, "Opinion Assignment on the Rehnquist Court"; Maltzman and Wahlbeck, "May It Please the Chief."

41. See Segal and Spaeth, *The Supreme Court and the Attitudinal Model Revisited.*

42. See Lee Epstein and Jack Knight, *The Choices Justices Make* (Washington, DC: CQ Press, 1998); Murphy, *Elements of Judicial Strategy*.

43. Danelski, "The Influence of the Chief Justice."

44. See Wahlbeck, "Strategy and Constraints"; Maltzman and Wahlbeck, "Opinion Assignment on the Rehnquist Court"; Maltzman and Wahlbeck, "May It Please the Chief."

45. Anthony Lewis, "A Talk with Warren on Crime, the Court, and the Country," *New York Times Magazine*, Oct. 19, 1969.

46. William Rehnquist, *The Supreme Court: How It Was, How It Is* (New York: William Morrow, 1988).

47. William Rehnquist "Memorandum to the Conference: Policy Regarding Assignments" (1989), Library of Congress, Justice Thurgood Marshall Papers.

48. Saul Brenner, "Issue Specialization as a Variable in Opinion Assignment on the U.S. Supreme Court," *Journal of Politics* 46 (1984); Brenner and Palmer, "The Time Taken"; Saul Brenner and Harold J. Spaeth, "Issue Specialization in Majority Opinion Assignment on the Burger Court," *Western Political Quarterly* 39 (1986); Maltzman and Wahlbeck, "May It Please the Chief"; Slotnick, "Who Speaks for the Court"; Harold J. Spaeth, "Distributive Justice: Majority Opinion Assignments in the Burger Court," *Judicature* 67 (1984); and Wahlbeck, "Strategy and Constraints."

49. Slotnick, "The Equality Principle."

50. Maltzman and Wahlbeck, "A Conditional Model."

51. Maltzman and Wahlbeck, "May It Please the Chief"; Maltzman and Wahlbeck, "Opinion Assignment on the Rehnquist Court."

52. Rehnquist, "Memorandum to the Conference."

53. Wahlbeck, "Strategy and Constraints."

54. Brenner and Palmer, "The Time Taken."

55. Maltzman and Wahlbeck, "A Conditional Model."

56. Maltzman and Wahlbeck, "A Conditional Model"; Brenner, "Issue Specialization as a Variable"; and Brenner and Spaeth, "Issue Specialization in Majority Opinion."

57. Brenner, "Issue Specialization as a Variable."; Brenner and Spaeth, "Issue Specialization in Majority Opinion."

58. Maltzman and Wahlbeck, "Opinion Assignment on the Rehnquist Court"; Maltzman and Wahlbeck, "A Conditional Model"; and Maltzman and Wahlbeck, "May It Please the Chief."

59. Harold J. Spaeth, "The Expanded Burger Court Database, 1969–1985 Terms," Dec. 21, 2006, http://artsandsciences.sc.edu/poli/juri/sct.htm, accessed Aug. 22, 2012. We calculated this by comparing the final majority author, identified by whether a justice authored an opinion and his or her vote, with the first assigned author in orally argued, signed opinions.

60. Andrew D. Martin and Kevin M. Quinn, "The 2010 Justice Data Files," July 25, 2011, http://mqscores.wustl.edu/measures.php, accessed Aug. 22, 2012.

61. Harold J. Spaeth et al., "Supreme Court Database," Aug. 30, 2011, http:// scdb.wustl.edu/data.php, accessed Aug. 22, 2012.

62. Maltzman and Wahlbeck, "A Conditional Model."

63. Spaeth et al., "Supreme Court Database." This is calculated as the number of days between the last argument and the date on which the opinion was announced. We determined whether a justice had prior judicial experience before appointment to the Court (Lee Epstein, Jeffrey A. Segal, Harold J. Spaeth, and Thomas G. Walker, *The Supreme Court Compendium*, 4th ed. (Washington, DC: CQ Press, 2006)). Freshman status was attributed to justices in their first two years of service on the Supreme Court. Near retirement status was attributed to justices serving their last two years on the Court. Divisiveness was calculated from the report vote recorded by Spaeth et al. The Court's docket and the number of signed opinions generated in a term were derived from two sources: the Chief Justice's Year-End

Reports on the Federal Judiciary and Epstein et al, *The Supreme Court Compendium*. The justice's workload is captured by the number of separate opinions written during a term (Spaeth et al., "Supreme Court Database"). Complexity was reflected in the number of issues presented in a case (Spaeth et al., "Supreme Court Database").

64. Spaeth et al., "Supreme Court Database."

65. Maltzman and Wahlbeck, "A Conditional Model."

66. We use the fine issue variable, which includes some 270 issues, although we combine subcategories of issues into one category. For example, Spaeth et al. have three subcategories for military issues (i.e., draftee, active duty, and veteran); we combine these three subcategories for purposes of calculating expertise.

67. Spaeth et al., "Supreme Court Database."

68. If we exclude justice observations for those individuals not in the majority, rather than include this independent variable, the results are identical.

69. Ryan C. Black, Maron W. Sorenson, and Timothy R. Johnson, "Toward an Actor-Based Measure of Supreme Court Case Salience: Information-Seeking and Engagement during Oral Arguments," *Political Research Quarterly* 66 (2013).

70. We thank Tim Johnson for graciously sharing his data on oral arguments with us.

71. Ryan C. Black, Sarah A. Truel, Timothy R. Johnson, and Jerry Goldman, "Emotions, Oral Arguments, and Supreme Court Decision Making," *Journal of Politics* 73 (2011).

72. All models, graphs, and postestimation procedures were conducted in Stata Version 12.0.

73. This does not directly test Hypothesis 1 since ideological distance is interacted with political salience and margin. With interaction terms, the coefficient for ideological distance is conditioned on the value of those two variables. Indeed, the coefficient represents the effect of ideological distance when the other variables are set at zero (i.e., average political salience and an equally divided Court). A second model with the interaction terms removed, however, produces insignificant results for ideological distance. This is not to say that Chief Justice Roberts's assignments are not influenced by his colleague's ideological views. Rather, two variables are closely related to ideology: median justice and the prediction of whether a justice would be in the Court's majority coalition. When one drops those two variables from the analysis, ideological distance nearly achieves statistical significance (p = .052).

74. Maltzman and Wahlbeck, "A Conditional Model."

75. William D. Berry, Matt Golder, and Daniel Milton, "Improving Tests of Theories Positing Interaction," *Journal of Politics* 74 (2012). The code for the visual presentation of the interactions in figures 1 and 2 was adapted from the online companion.

76. We also find that this variable might be conditioned by the justice's ideological distance from the assignor.

77. Maltzman, Spriggs, and Wahlbeck, *Crafting Law on the Supreme Court*.

78. Tom Goldstein, "Prognosticating the Remaining Opinions," *SCOTUSblog*, June 16, 2011, http://www.scotusblog.com/2011/06/prognosticating-the-remain ing-opinions.

79. *Brown v. Entertainment Merchants Association*, 131 S. Ct. 2729 (2011).

80. *Goodyear Dunlop Tire Operations, S.A. v. Brown*, 131 S. Ct. 2846 (2011).

81. *Stern v. Marshall*, 131 S. Ct. 2594 (2011).

82. *Walmart v. Dukes*, 131 S. Ct. 2541 (2011). Note, however, that Justice Ginsburg did file an opinion concurring in part and dissenting in part.

83. *CSX Transportation, INC v. McBride*, 131 S. Ct. 2630 (2011).

84. Since 2004 Justice Thomas has only been the majority opinion assigner in two cases, this being one of them.

8 ∾ The Chief Justice and Procedural Power

CHARLES M. CAMERON AND TOM CLARK

Associate justices may acquire influence on the Court through force of intellect, force of personality, political skill, or the good fortune to be ideologically pivotal. And so may the chief justice. But by virtue of the procedural rules employed on the Court, the chief justice has access to resources that the other justices do not. The chief's *procedural power* is analogous to the powers held by the Speaker of the House, the Senate majority leader, or the chairman of the Rules Committee: these officers have no right of absolute command. Rather, their power lies in the ability to manipulate the decision rules used by the members. Although some Speakers or majority leaders or committee chairs display more adroitness than others in using their procedural powers, it is in these special "vantage points" (to use Richard Neustadt's phrase) that their special influence lies. So, we argue, it is with the chief justice. Procedural power is the foundation of the chief's special impact on the Court.

This perspective on the chief is not new; indeed, it is the essence of what Danelski called the chief's "task leadership."[1] By task leadership, Danelski meant the chief's procedural steering of the Court's production of majority opinions. In his discussion of task leadership, Danelski highlighted the chief's key role in opinion assignment and suggested that the chief could exploit his special opportunities in that domain to advance his goals for the Court, for instance by minimizing the number of dissents.

In this chapter, we follow Danelski's lead in considering procedural power. Coming to the subject more than a half-century later, though, we can exploit perspectives from contemporary theories and empirical studies of Supreme Court decision making that were unavailable to the pioneers of judicial behavior.[2] Those theories formally model the decision-making procedures on the Court using noncooperative game theory, and allow a subtle analysis of the chief's incentives and ability to exploit procedural power. In some cases, the formal analysis underscores the essential validity of earlier scholars' intuitions, perhaps especially about opinion assignment. In other cases, existing theories are silent about, but nonetheless hint at, opportunities to exploit procedural power that have yet to receive much attention. In both these "new" and "old" areas, we can exploit powerful new data to gain empirical leverage. Similarly, empirical scholarship since Danelski has provided powerful insights into behavioral regularities on the Court.[3] We contribute to this line of research by bringing additional empirical data to bear on the chief justice's procedural powers.

Varieties of Procedural Power

What types of procedural power are available to the chief? Three stand out. The most obvious is *opinion assignment*. As is well-known, after oral argument the justices take a nonbinding straw vote on the proper disposition of a case. If the chief is in the dispositional majority, he has the power to assign the authorship of the majority opinion to a member of the dispositional majority in the straw vote.[4] As we discuss below, depending on one's theory of the Court this assignment power may or may not allow the chief to bend the content of majority opinions in a favorable way.

A second opportunity for procedural power arises because the chief has a special role in drawing up the "discuss list" of cases from which the Court chooses its cases. The chief creates a draft discuss list of cases he deems worthy of consideration, which he circulates. Any justice may then "nominate" additional cases to the chief's initial list. The chief has no veto power over these nominations. In forming coalitions around multiple competing cases, however, even ideologically allied justices face a coordination problem. The chief may be able to use his first draft and early knowledge of the nominated cases to organize a coalition in favor of particular cases and opposing others. Hence when the justices walk into the room to select the cases to hear, the chief may have wired the meeting, at least for particular cases. This kind of steering via *case selection* may again afford the chief some ability to affect the content of majority opinions. (We discuss how below.)

Finally, a more subtle form of procedural power may stem again from the chief's role in compiling the discuss list. The chief may be able to "seed" the discuss list with cases on topics he favors; conversely, he may hold back cases he wishes to avoid. All the other justices are free to nominate cases, so this is a weak form of agenda setting. Still, by virtue of a degree of doggedness and behind-the-scenes lobbying, the chief over time may be able to exert special influence over the topics the Court addresses. As we discuss below, this kind of *agenda setting* can have subtle yet important doctrinal consequences.

We organize the chapter as follows. First we use the lens of contemporary theories of Supreme Court decision making to view these three types of procedural power. The theories offer clues about how procedural power can work in the three venues of opinion assignment, case selection, and agenda setting. We then scour the systematic empirical record seeking the traces suggested by theory.

Theory suggests we focus our search on important cases. Accordingly, as we turn to empirical work, we identify the most important cases decided by the Court since 1946. We also derive estimates of judicial ideologies, and estimates of the location of cases selected by the Court. We then review the empirical evidence.

Broadly speaking, using new data we find clear evidence that the chief justice uses his power to assign majority opinions to his ideological allies in the most important cases. We also find that case outcomes (dispositions) are closely associated with the chief justice's own ideology and do not appear to be driven by the median, pivotal justice. This finding, we argue, is consistent with the chief justice exercising influence over case selection. In addition, transitions in the chief justice are associated with marked transitions in the topics that make up the Court's docket. Again, this suggests the chief's influence in case selection. Taken together, these findings suggest that the chief justice can use his few and seemingly paltry procedural prerogatives to strategically shape the Court's decisions. Danelski's "task leadership" appears powerful indeed.

The Foundations of Procedural Power

Many sitting justices, politicians, and legal figures have longed to hold the center chair at conference. William Howard Taft famously valued the chief justiceship over the presidency, and Associate Justice Robert Jackson's ambition for the office became an obsession that distorted his life both on and off the Court. But status aside, why is the office valuable? As Harvard law professor Noah Feldman notes, "The Chief Justice of the United States has no extra votes. His responsibilities are to handle the administrative duties of the Court, to assign opinions when he is in the majority, and to run the conferences of the justices. His influence on the other justices is not necessarily any greater than that of his peers."[5]

If the chief is no more than a housekeeper for the other justices—as

Feldman's formulation implies—then it is indeed hard to see why holding the center seat makes any difference for judicial policy. To understand why managing apparently "administrative" chores can lead to influence over judicial policy, we must take a closer look at the decision process used on the Court and at the theories developed by political scientists and judicial scholars to understand it. Then, given a clearer theoretical appreciation of how the Court operates, we can identify the leverage points the chief could use to affect decision-making, if he wanted to.

Supreme Court Decision Making

Decision making on the Court is a bargaining game played by the nine justices. The game has two distinct phases, *case selection* and *case resolution*. As we shall see, the chief has special leverage in both phases of the bargaining game.[6]

The bargaining game played by the justices is a complex one, partly because each case's resolution has two parts, not one. The two parts are a *case disposition* (the "judgment") and a *legal rule*. Literally, the case disposition either upholds or reverses a lower court's prior disposition of the case. Practically speaking, however, it resolves the dispute between the two litigants in favor of one party or the other. Thus, the case's disposition is an act of dispute resolution. In contrast, the legal rule accompanying the disposition states an abstract and general principle that leads to the Court's disposition when applied to the case in hand. In other words, it provides a "why" for the Court's resolution of the dispute. This "why" can be used by other parties to predict the Court's likely behavior in similar disputes in the future. Hence, the legal rule involves policymaking, for it creates new law or modifies old law.

To simultaneously produce the two outcomes—a case resolution and a definitive rule rationalizing the case resolution—the justices employ a distinctive process and a unique voting rule. First, a case is chosen from among those appealed to the Court (we provide some details momentarily). Then, a single justice is designated as the potential majority opinion author for the case (again, we discuss the details below). This justice pens an opinion providing both a disposition of the case and a candidate legal rule justifying the disposition. Some bickering or bargaining, in the form of memos and written suggestions, often plays a role during the author's drafting work.[7]

The justices then vote on the potential majority opinion using a strange rule. In this rule, each vote can take three values, not just two. The three values are "dissent," "concur," and "join."[8] Each of these values simultaneously indicates (first) a preference for one of the two possible dispositions of the case, and (second) an endorsement or lack of endorsement of the candidate legal rule offered in the potential majority opinion. A "dissent" vote indicates a preference for the disposition *not* offered in the potential majority opinion. Since the voting justice indicates a preference for the disposition not favored in the candidate majority opinion, a dissent automatically withholds an endorsement of the candidate rule offered in the potential majority opinion. The other two values—"concur" and "join"—both indicate a vote for the other disposition, the one favored in the potential majority opinion. The difference between the votes concerns the endorsement of the rule offered in the potential majority opinion. A join endorses that rule. It says, "I believe the case disposition offered in the opinion is correct, and the candidate legal rule is a good one." A concur withholds the endorsement of the rule. It says, "I believe the case disposition offered in the potential majority opinion is correct, but the candidate legal rule rationalizing the disposition is not a good one."[9] If five or more justices endorse the candidate legal rule, the potential majority opinion becomes the actual majority opinion of the Court (the case disposition then follows automatically) and the rule has precedential value in the lower courts. If the potential majority opinion fails to garner five or more joins, other justices can try to offer candidate rules that do so. If no justice's candidate rule gains five or more endorsements, the Court simply resolves the dispute without offering a definitive rationale for the resolution. There is no provision for a runoff or other device forcing the selection of a specific rule among those suggested, so the state of the law in this eventuality is unclear. In addition, there is no reversion to a "status quo ante" since taking the case implies a rejection of the status quo rule (which might not even exist). Rather, a judgment of the Court simply leaves the law in a confused state.

The particular votes are always presented as a bundle, but conceptually one can break them into two parts: first, a dichotomous vote on case disposition, and second, an endorsement vote held only among the dispositional majority. In other words, one can think of the Court's rule as a compound voting rule.[10] One can also distinguish the populations of eligible voters in the two distinct parts of the compound rule. That is, all nine justices vote on the case's disposition, but only members of the dispositional majority can endorse the candidate rule. In addition, the majority thresholds differ in the two parts of the compound rule. With respect to the disposition, simple majority rule applies (the winning disposition requires at least five supportive votes). But the endorsement threshold is always five joins regardless of how many justices are in the dispositional majority (assuming there are eight or more justices participating). So the effective endorsement threshold can range from simple majority rule (when all nine justices agree on the disposition, hence five constitutes a bare majority), to a unanimity rule (when only five justices are in the dispositional majority, hence five joins requires unanimity).

In short, the Supreme Court's voting rule is a *compound rule* (disposition, endorsement) with the first part using *universal franchise* (all nine justices can vote) and *pure majority rule*, and the second part using a *restricted franchise* (only members of the dispositional majority can vote) and a *variable majority threshold* which ranges from pure majority to unanimity depending on the size of the dispositional majority.[11]

The reader's head may be spinning at this point, but political scientists and legal theorists have devised a fairly simple framework for understanding what is going on. This framework, usually called "the case space approach," adapts the standard spatial theory of voting[12] to the judicial context.[13]

Figure 8.1 suggests the basic building blocks. Cases are bundles of facts, such as how fast a car was going, how much care a manufacturer exercised in producing a product, how intrusive a government search for evidence was, how entangled religious symbols were with government operations, and so on. A legal rule typically classifies cases (fact patterns) into two groups, allowable and not allowable. Thus, simple adjudication involves discovering the facts in a case and applying a legal rule to them, thereby yielding a disposition of the case. The division by a legal rule of possible facts into the two categories is shown in figure 8.1.

Justices, it is assumed, have preferences about legal rules. As shown in figure 8.2, a justice has an ideal point in a fact space, corresponding to his or her perception of the "best" legal standard or cut point separating the possible fact patterns into two classes for purposes of dispositions. (In the figures, we simplify by imagining a Supreme Court with three blocks of justices, whose memberships total nine.)

Suppose no rule yet exists for a particular class of dispute. Then the Court may take a case in order to make a rule. For instance, in the example shown in figure 8.3, the Court takes a case at location $\hat{x}$, that is, a case involving a police search with level of intrusiveness $\hat{x}$. In this example, the justices making up Block L favor one disposition of the case (e.g., "exclude the evidence"), while those in Blocks M and C favor the other ("admit the evidence"). Conversely, if the level of intrusiveness of the case had placed it to the left of Block L, all the justices would have favored the "admit" disposition; if the case had been located to the right of Block C, all would have favored the "exclude" disposition.

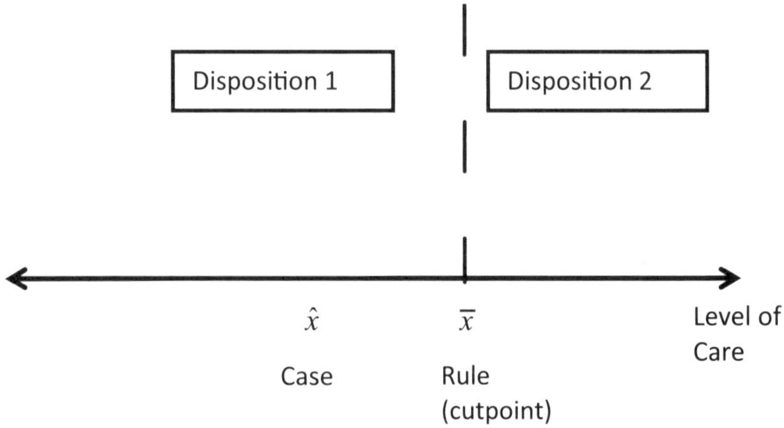

Fig. 8.1. A rule indicates how to dispose a case
A case is a bundle of facts indicating "what happened." For example, it may be the level of care exercised by the defendant. A legal rule partitions possible cases—the case-space—into equivalence classes, each class corresponding to a case disposition. For example, levels of care below a standard receive one disposition ("negligent"), while levels of care above the standard may receive the other disposition ("not negligent"). Applying the rule to a particular case yields a disposition of the case.

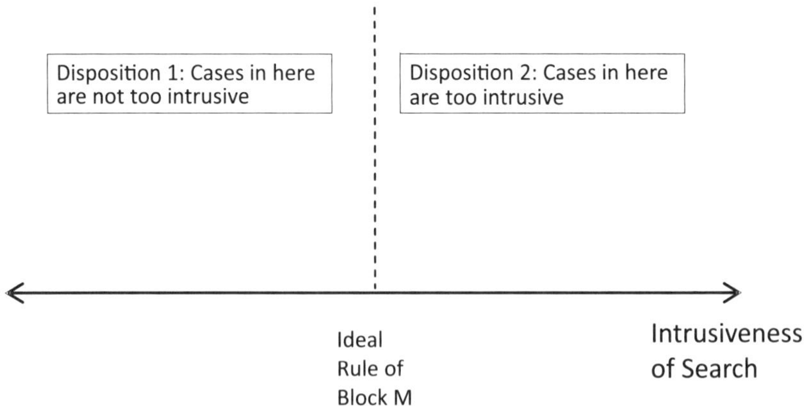

Fig. 8.2. Preferences about a search-and-seizure rule
The moderate block on the Court, Block M, prefers a moderate standard. Cases whose intrusiveness level was less than a standard yield evidence that is admissible; but cases whose intrusiveness level was too high yield inadmissible evidence.

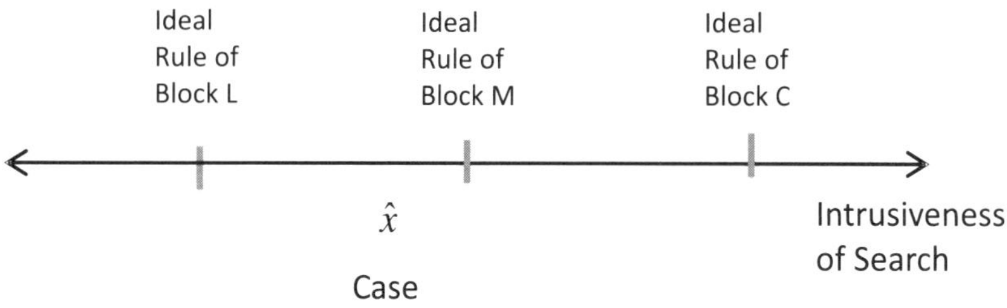

Fig. 8.3. The Court takes a case to make a rule
No rule exists that covers search-and-seizure cases of a certain type. The Court therefore takes a specific case in order to make a rule. After hearing arguments in the case, Block L favors a standard that would exclude many searches, including the one in the case at hand. Block C favors a permissive standard that would admit most searches, including the one in the instant case, though it would exclude the most intrusive. Block M favors a standard between these extremes. The moderate standard would admit the evidence in the instant case.

In turn, the case location and the winning disposition have strong implications for the possible content of rules rationalizing the disposition. For example, as shown in figure 8.4, given the case location $\hat{x}$, if the "admit" disposition prevails, then the rule must be set to the right of $\hat{x}$. But if the "exclude" disposition prevails, the rule must be set to the left of $\hat{x}$. This important feature of adjudication is sometimes called *disposition consistency*: the announced rule must yield the majority's disposition when applied to the facts in the instant case.[14] For example, if a car was going 57 mph and the Court indicates the car was speeding, a Court creating a speed limit must set it at less than 57 mph; conversely if the Court indicates the car was not speeding, the Court must set the speed limit at 57 mph or higher.

Suppose, in the search-and-seizure example, the "admit" disposition prevails (see figure 8.5). The standard must then be set to the right of $\hat{x}$ in figure 8.5. But who gets to determine the standard in the announced rule, that is, who determines the exact location of the rule from within the permissible range determined by the case location and the winning disposition? The rule is chosen by bargaining *among the justices in the winning dispositional coalition*. If Block L is committed to a dissent, it is out of the bargaining and the rule will be selected by bargaining among the justices in Blocks M and C in the figure.[15] If that bargaining is efficient, the final outcome will lie between the ideal points of these two blocks (the Pareto set). This is because both blocks can agree that points in the interval between them are better than points outside the interval. But where will the rule lie within that interval? One of the main lessons of modern bargaining

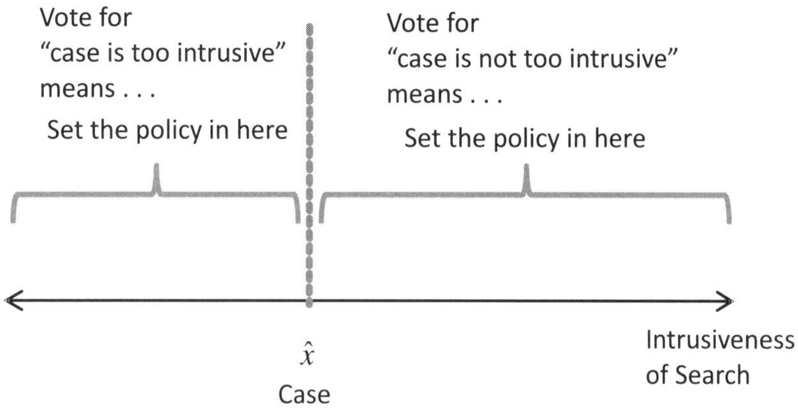

Fig. 8.4. The dispositional vote creates two distinct regions in which a new rule may be created

If the "too intrusive" disposition prevails, the new rule must be set in the left-hand region. If the "not too intrusive" disposition prevails, the new rule must be set in the right-hand region. The case location thus bifurcates the case space. Accordingly, case selection can be extremely consequential for policy making.

theory is that the exact procedures used in the bargaining determine the outcome.[16] So, given the procedures used on the Court, what is likely to happen?

Opinion Assignment: Creating and Edge in the Bargaining Game

Political scientists and judicial scholars have taken several distinct approaches to modeling the bargaining procedures used on the Supreme Court to create rules. The value of opinion assignment varies wildly across the different models, ranging from zero to very large. While there have been many empirical studies of opinion assignment, in order to derive a series of conjectures below we focus here on those that are primarily theoretical.

The oldest approach, the Median Justice Approach, simply applied a standard model from legislative and committee politics to the Court. It therefore neglected the role of the case location, case disposition, and disposition consistency in limiting the set of possible rules and determining the identity of the bargainers.[17] Instead, it assumed rules could be set at any location in the relevant space irrespective of the facts in the case and the majority disposition, and all justices could participate in bargaining over opinion content. The Median Justice Approach assumed intense competition between the justices in choosing rules. These assumptions rationalized

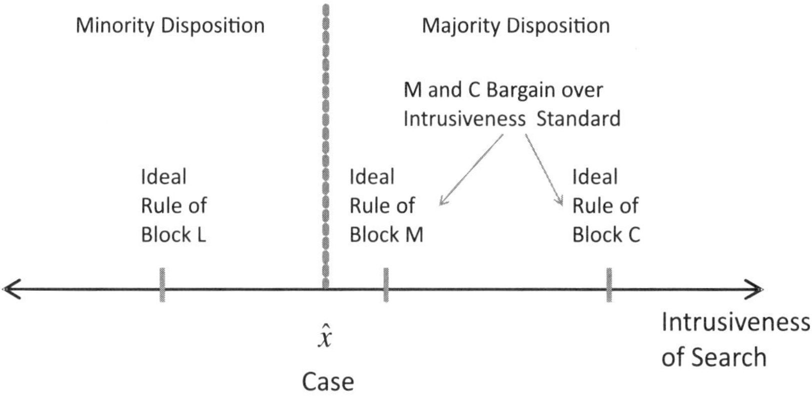

Fig. 8.5. Members of the dispositional majority bargain over the new rule
In the figure, the Moderate and Conservative blocks prevail in the dispositional vote. As a result, the new rule must be set to the right of the case location. But where? The two blocks in the dispositional majority bargain between themselves. The new rule must receive five or more endorsements ("joins") from justices in the two blocks if it is to have precedential value.

an application of the long-familiar median voter theorem.[18] The Median Justice Approach leads to the conclusion that the Court, in all cases and all circumstances, sets policy at the location of the ideal rule of the median justice on the Court. Consequently, *in the Median Justice Approach opinion assignment does not matter*; it is a resource of no value for the chief since all opinions end up in the same place irrespective of author.

Empirical tests of contemporary theories of Supreme Court decision making are in their infancy. Tests conducted using a variety of different data sets and methodologies, however, consistently and emphatically reject the Median Justice Approach when applied to the Court.[19] Perhaps this finding is not so surprising, given the poor fit of the Median Justice Approach and the actual procedures used on the Court.

No consensus has yet emerged about the best alternative to the Median Justice Approach, but two broad approaches have emerged. The first is the Majority Median Approach.[20] This approach acknowledges the importance of case location, the winning disposition, and disposition consistency in limiting the range of possible rules and the identity of the bargainers. But it retains the assumption that intense bargaining among the justices in the winning disposition drives the opinion to the ideal point of the median justice in the majority disposition. Who the median in the majority dispositional coalition will be depends heavily on the case location (the location of $\hat{x}$ in figures 8.2–8.5) and the willingness or lack of willingness of justices to vote strategically on the case disposition. But, given a specific majority dispositional coalition, opinion assignment does not matter in the Majority Median Approach, since regardless of the author the majority opinion is driven to the median of the dispositional majority. So, the Majority Median Approach holds that opinion assignment is valueless to the chief.

The third approach encompasses a set of models that for a variety of reasons depart from the median voter theorem and accordingly afford a degree of monopoly power to the opinion author. Call these models the Author Influence Approach to Supreme Court decision making. For example, the model in Cameron and Kornhauser[21] acknowledges the importance of case location and case disposition in limiting the possible rules and determining the identity of the bargainers. But in that model, the pressure of time and effort allows the assignee to pull opinion content toward his most preferred location. This ability is pronounced for cases that do not produce "tough" bargaining—for example, relatively unimportant cases—but less pronounced for ones that do. In the latter, bargaining draws opinions away from the author and toward the center of the dispositional majority coalition (if the author did not come from that center in the first place). Other Author Influence models rely on slightly different explanations for the power of the opinion author, but the basic message is the same: opinion assignment matters for the content of the opinion, and it can matter a lot.[22]

In the spirit of the Author Influence models, we suggest:

> **Conjecture 1 (Assignment Prediction):** *The chief will use his assignment power to award the majority opinion in important cases to justices who are ideologically proximate to himself.* In addition, in order to avoid overburdening his "friends" and maintaining some equity in overall opinions assigned, the chief will tend to assign unimportant cases to justices who are ideologically distant from himself.

We don't suggest that this conjecture is novel. There is considerable empirical work on opinion assignment, some of which offers an intuitive "proximity hypothesis" and some of which links proximity and "case importance." The "proximity hypothesis" suggests that the chief disproportionately assigns opinions to ideological allies.[23] The "importance hypothesis" further suggests that case importance may enhance the attractiveness of proximate justices as targets for assignment.[24] None of these studies, however, tightly links these seemingly intuitive hypotheses with Author

Influence models of bargaining or views positive evidence as smoking-gun evidence of the chief justice's procedural power through a deliberate exploitation of author influence in bargaining.

Below, we provide a new test of the proximity–case importance prediction. We make use of existing and original data on case importance in conjunction with recently developed measure of judicial preferences. We see this analysis as contributing not just to "facts," but to better knowledge about opinion assignment. In addition, the analysis speaks more broadly to how procedural power is rooted in the bargaining protocols used on the Court. In this sense, it joins other recent work that explicitly links empirics to the new theories of Supreme Court bargaining (see note 19).

Case Selection: Winning the Coordination Game

As we have seen, the location of the case used as the vehicle for making law can affect the content of the rule, for at least two reasons. First, the case location constrains the rules that can possibly be set due to disposition consistency (recall figure 8.4).[25] Second, case selection can affect or—under sincere dispositional voting—even determine the identity of the justices in the majority coalition who bargain over the content of the rule (recall figure 8.5). Hence different cases may facilitate the creation of different rules. As a result, the chief may try to influence the selection of cases to help create the most congenial law.[26]

Two questions then arise: First, what cases would the chief—or indeed any group of policy-minded justices—prefer the Court to take as the vehicle for making law? Second, what can the chief do to help his preferred group prevail in case selection?

Let's start with the second question: How can the Chief "steer" the certiorari process toward certain cases and away from others to benefit his ideological cohort on the Court? Our thinking on this question is admittedly speculative, as this question seems to have received little scholarly attention of which we are aware. H. W. Perry, though, in his authoritative study of the certiorari process, notes the widespread impression that Chief Justice Warren was a leader in the cert process, a "toreador," though—according to justices who served with Warren—generally with the acquiescence of his brethren.[27] With respect to Chief Justice Burger, Perry quotes a clerk: "It was always interesting to see which ones [cases] the chief would put on [the discuss list]; he generally lists about 70 percent of the obvious ones, then he lists some of the conservative favorites, but they are supplemented with pretty much rapid fire."[28] Perry also notes the relative infrequency with which the other justices push cases forward if the chief has not included them on the discuss list. In fact, though, Perry is skeptical of any justice's ability to shape the process: "Whether or not there is political or intellectual leadership on the Court at the opinion-writing stage, given the way the cert. process works—with most decisions made in chambers and with little discussion between chambers—there is little opportunity for leadership on cert."[29]

Before totally dismissing the idea of "leadership" during the cert process, it is important to see that cert decisions confront a group of policy-minded justices with a substantial coordination problem: there are many more cases available than the Court can possibly consider, and many of the available cases are just as good, or nearly as good, as policy vehicles. But if the policy-minded group is to rally effectively behind a few policy vehicles, it must pick and choose among the many cases, lest it split its votes ineffectually. How can it do that? One way is to effectively delegate the selection process to a like-minded chief who, after all, draws up the discuss list. In other words, the chief can create *focal points* for his fellow liberals (in the case of Warren) or fellow conservatives (in the case of Burger and the subsequent chiefs). There will be art in this, for the chief and three confederates can push forward a case, but it must be one that at least one more justice will support on the vote on the merits if not at the cert stage. Still, it seems at least possible that focal point creation can allow the chief to do some "steering." Finding direct evidence of steering—a smoking gun—will be difficult if not impossible. One should, however, be able to see its *effects*.

So let's turn to the first question. If the chief can do some steering of case selection, which cases would he and his like-minded confederates want to select? Here we turn for guidance to contemporary theories of Supreme Court decision making. The Median Justice Approach has nothing to say about strategic case selection since it ignores the roles of cases, dispositions, and disposition consistency in judicial decision making. So we put it aside. The Majority Median and Author Influence approaches offer more useful insights, which are broadly similar though not quite identical.

The key and most basic insight is that a group of policy-minded justices selecting cases want to select cases that put them in the dispositional majority. That way, a group member can receive the opinion assignment, write an ideologically attractive opinion, and garner the joins of fellow group members. Or if a group member does not receive the assignment, the group can collectively bargain with the opinion author and force her to compromise in order to receive their join votes. Conversely, cases that force the policy-minded justices into the minority disposition effectively remove them from bargaining over the content of the majority opinion. A group of policy-minded justices will wish to avoid this if at all possible.

Assume for the moment that the chief justice has some influence over which cases the Court hears. If so, he would prefer cases that result in a disposition that includes justices from his wing of the Court. Chief Justice Warren, a liberal, would want to hear cases that disproportionately result in liberal outcomes, so he would have a liberal majority, with more conservative justices more likely to be in the minority (and therefore excluded from bargaining over the majority opinion). By the same logic, Chief Justices Burger, Rehnquist, and Roberts would want to hear cases that result in a conservative majority more often, thereby excluding the liberal members of the Court from the majority more often.

> **Conjecture 2 (Disposition Prediction):** *Independent of the composition of the Court, the chief justice will use his influence over the discuss list to select cases that disproportionately result in a disposition aligned with his wing of the Court.*

To the best of our knowledge, this theoretical prediction is novel and has yet to receive any empirical study.

Agenda Setting: Shifting to More Favorable Ground

An additional way in which the chief justice may use influence over the discuss list to select the best cases for his policy agenda may manifest itself through the *topics* the Court addresses. Recent research suggests that the justices' preferences vary considerably across substantive areas of the law.[30] A consequence is that "the" Court shifts from case to case depending on the topic. Indeed, the median can well shift. Thus some areas of the law may afford the chief a more receptive or amenable Court than others. A strategic chief justice would anticipate these differences across substantive areas of the law and political cleavages and seek to direct the Court to topics in which he will have an easier time building coalitions that result in his favored doctrine. Thus if the chief justice seeks to push for cases that are good vehicles for his policy objectives, he should be most likely to push for cases in which he has a strong, homogenous block of allies.

> **Conjecture 3 (Topic Selection Prediction):** *Transitions in the chief justice's office should be correlated with shifts in the distribution of topics the Court hears.* This effect should be particularly noticeable

in increases in cases in which the chief justice has an especially strong block of allies.

Again, this is a novel prediction, which seems not to have received systematic empirical investigation in the literature on Supreme Court agenda setting.[31]

Empirical Analysis

Opinion Assignment

Conjecture 1, the assignment prediction, suggests that the chief will disproportionately assign important cases to ideologically proximate justices. We now derive new measures and evaluate the prediction.

Measuring Case Salience and Judicial Ideology

Testing the assignment prediction requires measuring case salience and judicial ideology. While there are many existing measures of each concept, we employ original measures of both, although our original measures do rely on existing data.

First, to measure case salience, we build on four different indicators often used as proxies for case salience. First, we use the measure developed by Lee Epstein and Jeffrey Segal, which is simply an indicator of whether a case decision was reported on the front page of the *New York Times* the day after it was decided.[32] Second, we use a list of the most important cases compiled by Cornell Law School's Legal Information Institute.[33] Third, we use a list of cases discussed in *The Oxford Guide to United States Supreme Court Decisions*.[34] Fourth, we use a list of landmark cases suggested by *Congressional Quarterly*.[35] To combine these lists, we specify an item-response model in which we posit a latent dimension that corresponds to a propensity to appear on each of these lists. The resulting estimates are essentially an average of the four lists, in which any given list can be more or less discriminating among salient and nonsalient cases. (We provide more detail in the appendix.)

Second, to measure judicial ideology, we employ a simple model. We again use an item-response ("IRT") model, in which justices are assumed to have unidimensional, constant ideal points, which are treated as latent variables that are predictive of dispositional voting decisions. We recognize that judicial preferences vary considerably over legal issues, and a few justices have preferences that change over time. The constant ideal point

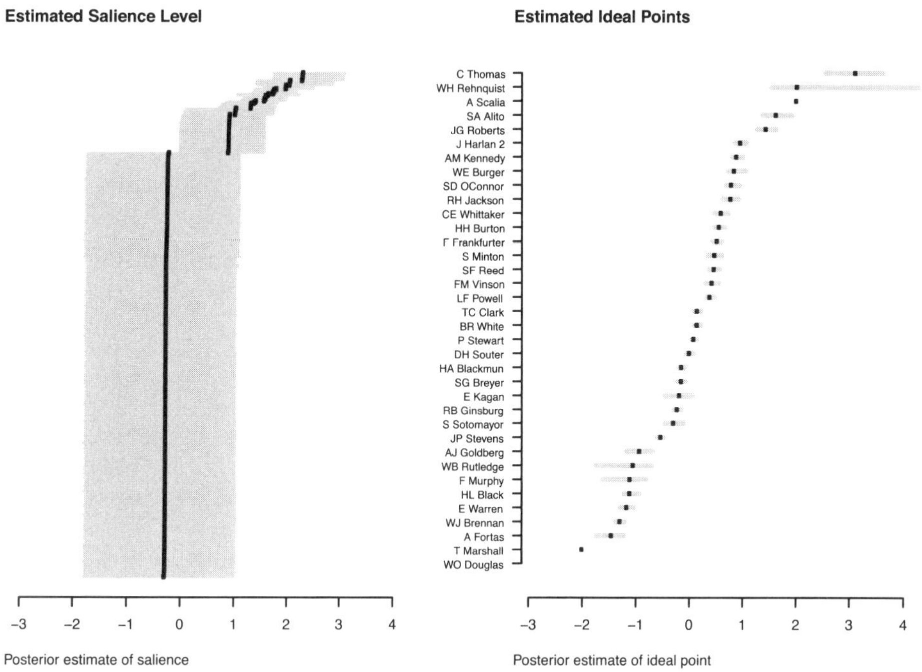

Fig. 8.6. Posterior estimates of case salience and justice ideal points
The left panel shows posterior estimates of salience; the right panel shows posterior estimates of justice ideal points. Each panel shows shows both posterior means and 95 percent high density credible intervals.

model we employ, however, is a sufficient proxy for our purposes here. Again, we provide details in the appendix.

The results of both of our measurement models are summarized in figure 8.6, which shows the distribution of our posterior estimates of case salience (using posterior means) and our posterior estimates of individual justices' ideal points (showing both posterior means and 95 percent high-density credible intervals). As the figure makes clear, both measurement models yield results that are substantively facially valid. The vast majority of cases are at the extreme low end of salience, whereas there is a long tail with a few bumps at the high end, suggesting there are a few "clumps" of extremely salient cases. Among the most salient cases are *U.S. v. Nixon* (1974) (executive power), *Thornburgh v. American College of Obstetricians and Gynecologists* (1986) (abortion), *Katz v. U.S.* (1967) (search and seizure),

U.S. v. Eichman (1990) (flag burning), and *Reynolds v. Sims* (1964) (electoral districting). These are well-known, prominent cases touching on many substantive issues (as opposed to being primarily civil liberties cases).

Assigning to Friends

With these data in hand, we can evaluate the relationship between the ideological alignment between the chief justice and the opinion assignee and the salience of the case. (We focus our analysis only on cases in which the chief justice was in the majority and therefore had the power to assign the majority opinion.)

First, consider the raw relationship, which is shown in figure 8.7. Here the gray points show cases; the *x*-axis measures the salience of the case; and the *y*-axis measures the distance from the chief justice to the majority opinion assignee. The black line is a best fit line from a linear regression model. While there is a great deal more to explaining opinion assignment than just case salience, and therefore a great deal of variation that cannot be explained by salience alone, there is indeed a negative relationship (b = –0.19, se = 0.03). In fact, the magnitude of the estimated relationship is considerable, as a two standard deviation change in salience is associated with a nearly 0.3 standard deviation change in opinion author distance. This result suggests that the chief justice assigns more salient cases to his ideological allies and less salient cases to more distant justices.

Perhaps the most important limitation on our ability to interpret this relationship is that the range of options available to the chief justice varies as the composition of the Court changes (as justices leave and are replaced by others) and even from case to case (due to disposition consistency and the identity of justices in the majority dispositional coalition). To help account for (at least) the former, we estimate a more flexible empirical model to evaluate the relationship between salience and opinion assignee distance. Specifically, we specify a random coefficients model, in which we allow the intercept and slope to vary from natural court to natural court (periods when the Court's membership is stable). This model allows for the possibility that during some natural courts there is not much variance in salience or in the ideological alignment among the justices (in which case we'd expect a flatter slope and/or a lower intercept). The model we estimate is given by:

$$\Pr(Y_{ij} = 1) = \Lambda(\alpha_{n[i]} + \beta_{n[i]}\text{Distance}_{jc[n[i]]})$$

where Y_{ij} equals 1 if justice *j* is assigned the majority opinion in case *i*; $n[i]$ identifies the natural court that decided case *i*; $c[n[i]]$ identifies the chief

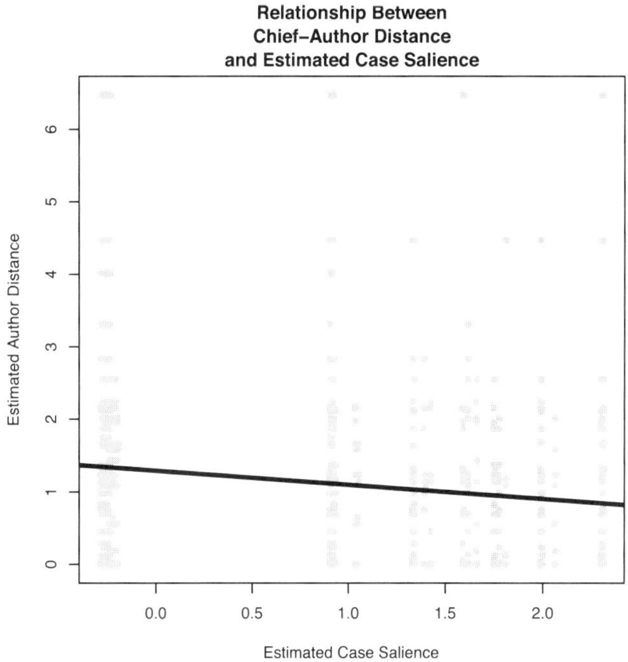

Fig. 8.7. The basic relationship between case salience and distance of assignee from the chief justice

The x-axis measures estimated case salience; the y-axis measures estimated distance from the author to the chief justice (data include only cases in which the chief justice assigned the majority opinion). The black line is a best fit line from a linear regression (OLS) model.

justice of the natural court deciding case i; and $\text{Distance}_{jc[n[i]]}$ measures the distance in our latent ideology space between the chief justice and justice j. The results of our estimation are summarized in figure 8.8.

Here each panel shows a natural court (that is, a membership-constant court). The gray points show cases, the x-axes indicate case salience, and the y-axes indicate the distance between the chief justice and the opinion assignee. The text in each panel gives the estimated intercept and slope of a linear regression fit to the data. The black line shows the natural court-specific relationship, and the gray line shows the average relationship across all natural courts.

The overall pattern is a consistent negative relationship across all natural courts. There is nevertheless some important variation. Panels with black lines that are steeper than the gray lines are natural courts where the relationship between salience and assignment is sharpest; panels where

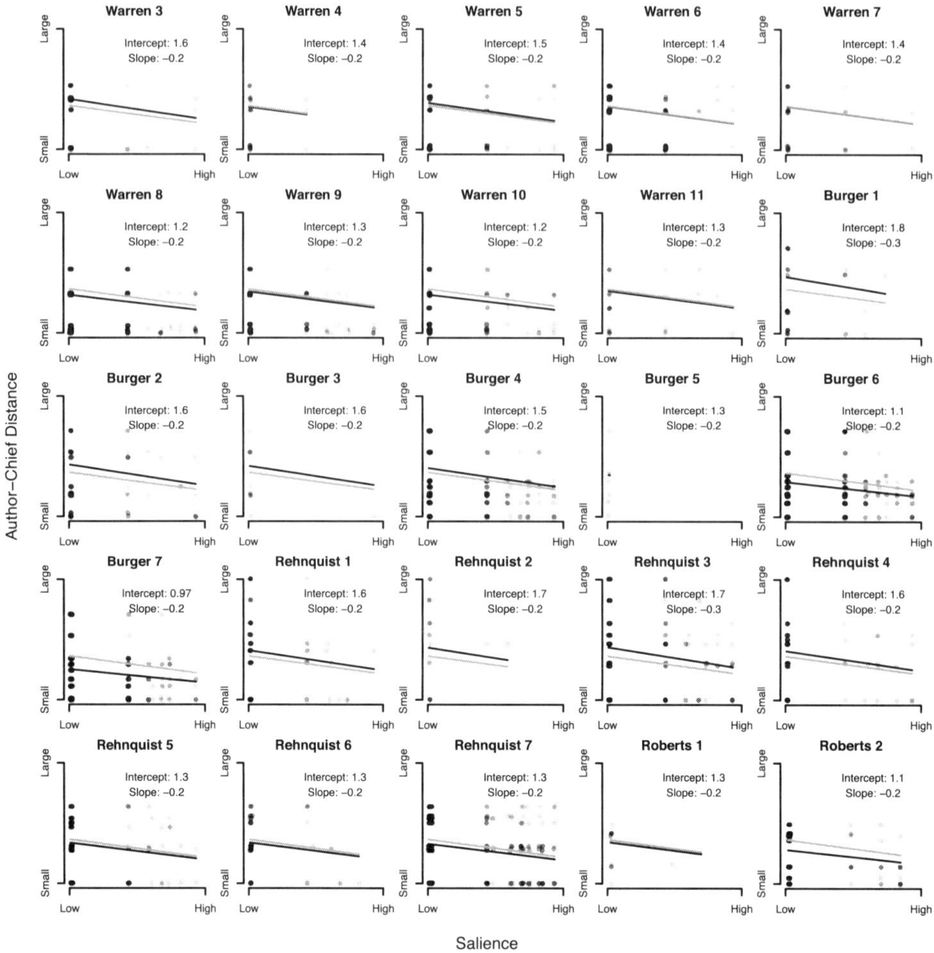

Fig. 8.8. Natural courts, case salience, and the distance of the opinion assignee from the chief justice

Each panel shows a natural court. The *x*-axes measure salience, and the *y*-axes measure author distance to the chief justice; the gray points show individual cases. The gray lines show the average relationship, and the black lines show the natural court-specific relationships.

the gray line is steeper are natural courts where salience discriminates less among opinion assignees. Among those natural courts with the sharpest relationship are the earliest Burger Courts. These natural courts are notable because Chief Justice Burger was a conservative leader of a predominantly liberal court, at least until subsequent nominations by Presidents Nixon and Reagan bolstered the right wing of the Court. And, as we see, the later Burger Courts are not characterized by such a sharp relationship. This is precisely what we would expect: When Burger was faced with an ideologically divergent Court, he had the strongest incentive to assign important cases to his ideological allies; as the Court became more homogenous and more conservative, the incentive to steer important cases to his closest allies diminished.

The correlation between salience and opinion assignment indicates the type of strategic opinion assignment we posit would characterize a chief justice who uses his institutional prerogatives to exercise influence over the Court's decisions. By selectively steering the most important cases to his ideological allies, he can shape the law by giving his allies some influence over opinion content (as the opinion author) in the cases that have the most long-run impact. We note that these results provide additional fodder for an ongoing empirical debate about how the chief justice uses his assignment power in a setting in which he is constrained by norms of equality in opinion assignments.[36]

Case Selection

Our theoretical prediction concerning case selection is that a shift in the liberalism of the chief justice should result in a shift in the Court's dispositional liberalism. We now present empirical evidence concerning this prediction.

Consider first dispositional liberalism. Figure 8.9 shows the proportion of case dispositions coded in the United States Supreme Court Judicial Database as "liberal" each term. The *y*-axis measures the proportion of liberal dispositions; the *x*-axis measures the term. The points are labeled with the initial of the presiding chief justice. As this figure makes clear, once Chief Justice Warren came to the Court in 1953, there was an immediate and sustained jump in the proportion of dispositions decided in the liberal direction. When Chief Justice Warren left and was replaced by Chief Justice Burger, there was an immediate and sustained drop in the Court's dispositional liberalism. What is particularly important is that while Chief Justice Warren's tenure is usually associated with an increasingly liberal Court—

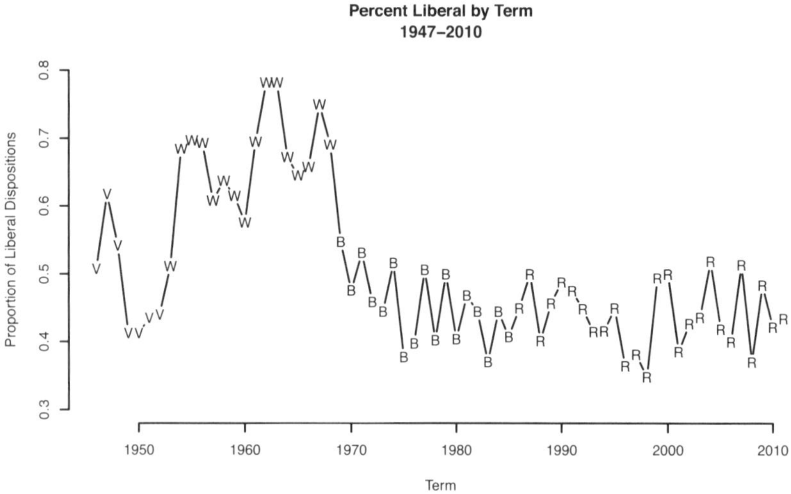

Fig. 8.9. Dispositional liberalism by term

Figure shows the proportion of case dispositions coded as "liberal" in the United States Supreme Court Judicial Database. The points are labeled with the initial of the last name of the presiding chief justice.

subsequent appointments to the Court during the 1960s are known to have been more liberal and shifted the Court's median to the left—the jump in dispositional liberalism is associated with the arrival of Warren, and subsequent appointments to the Court do not seem to have affected that pattern. What is more, the drop in liberalism is associated with the arrival of Chief Justice Burger. While Burger and Rehnquist's tenures are associated with an increasingly *conservative* Court, the dropoff in liberalism is clearly associated with the change in chief justice, whereas subsequent appointments moving the Court to the right do not have a noticeable effect on the Court's dispositional conservatism.

To make this point clearer, consider figure 8.10, which plots the proportion of liberal dispositions (same as figure 8.9) against the conservatism of the median justice (using our IRT estimates). Here the *y*-axis measures the proportion of liberal dispositions and the *x*-axis measures the conservatism of the median justice. Again, the points are labeled with the initial of the presiding chief justice. A number of findings stand out.

First, the gray line shows the fit from a linear regression of the proportion of liberal dispositions against the median justice's ideal point. As one

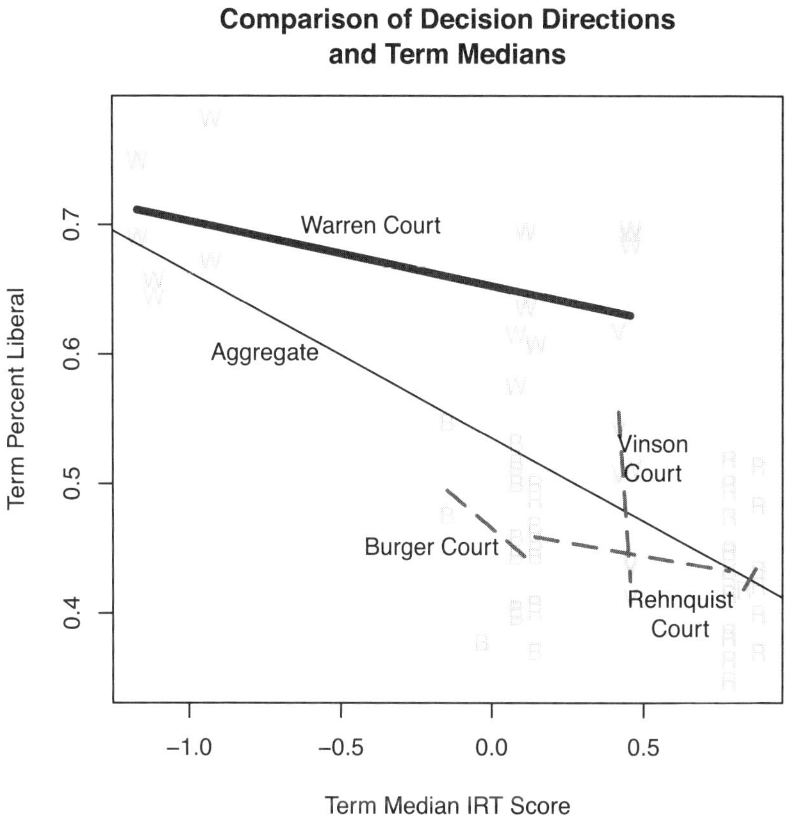

Fig. 8.10. Dispositional liberalism, median conservatism, and chief justices
Figure shows the proportion of dispositions coded as "liberal" in the United States Supreme Court Judicial Database (y-axis) against the estimated ideal point of the median justice (x-axis). Points are labeled with the last-name initial of the presiding chief justice. The thin line shows the estimated relationship among all years; the thick and dashed lines show the estimated relationships within chief justices.

can see, there is a negative correlation, suggesting that the common understanding that more conservative medians result in fewer liberal dispositions (a la Median Justice model). What is striking is that once one considers the chief justice, that relationship appears to vanish. The dashed and thick lines in the figure show the fit from a linear regression model fit to subsets of the data corresponding to each individual chief justice's tenure. What we see is that during any given chief justice's tenure, the relationship between the median's ideal point and the proportion of liberal decisions is essentially flat. Independent of the location of the median, once one knows who is the chief justice, one can effectively predict the proportion of liberal dispositions.

Indeed, if one were to estimate a linear regression model of the percent of dispositions that are coded as liberal against the conservatism of the median justice (using our measure), one would find a statistically significant relationship with an R^2 statistic of 0.40 and a residual standard error of 0.09. By contrast, estimating a linear regression of the percent of dispositions that are coded as liberal against the conservatism of the chief justice (again, using our measure), one would find a statistically significant relationship with an R^2 statistic of 0.64 and a residual standard error of 0.07. In other words, the chief justice's conservatism explains more of the variation with less error than does the median justice's conservatism. This striking pattern has not, to our knowledge, been previously documented. It appears to be one of the more dramatic pieces of evidence of the chief's impact on the Court's policymaking yet uncovered.

Before drawing this conclusion, however, we must be careful about a potential threat to this inference: perhaps the shifts in dispositional liberalism seemingly driven by changes in the identity of the chief justice were actually due to shifts in the ideological makeup of the Court coincident with those changes. For example, Warren Burger arrived on the Court in June 1969, replacing the liberal Earl Warren. Burger was soon followed by the (then) conservative Harry Blackmun in May 1970, replacing the liberal Abe Fortas. Hence the two appointments occurred fairly quickly and both moved the Court in a conservative direction. Thus the very dramatic "Burger effect" so evident in figure 8.9 may actually have been due to an ideology shift caused by the replacement of two liberals with two conservatives.

The arrival of Roberts presents the same issue but in more muted form. In particular, Roberts and Samuel Alito both arrived on the Court within a six-month period (Roberts was confirmed in September 2005 and Alito at the end of January 2006), but both replaced conservatives, not liberals (Rehnquist and O'Connor, respectively). Although most analysts scored the two new appointments as moving the median on the Court to the right—from O'Connor to Kennedy—this was hardly a dramatic ideological shift. Still, one might worry about this ideology shift. Fortunately, there is evidence that is helpful in evaluating the threat to inference. First, Warren's arrival on the Court was not a double appointment. Warren was a recess appointment who first sat on the Court in October 1953, replacing Fred Vinson. The change in the Court's ideological makeup from this shift would have been minor (in our data the ideology of the median justice is completely unaffected). No other justice joined the Court until March 1955, when the Senate confirmed the moderate conservative John Marshall Harlan II, who replaced the liberal Robert Jackson. Hence the Warren case becomes extremely interesting. In Warren's first full term, 1953, dispositional liberalism increased noticeably. But in his second, 1954, which preceded the next arrival on the Court, dispositional liberalism jumped dramatically and remained at a high level even in 1955, 1956, and 1957 (in 1957 the moderate conservative Charles Whittaker joined the Court, moving the median very slightly in a liberal direction, in our data). In short, it is difficult to tell a story in which Warren's arrival and the jump in dispositional liberalism that followed coincided with any shift in the Court's makeup in a liberal direction. We apparently have a pure Warren effect.

Additional evidence comes from close examination of figure 8.10, which arrays dispositional liberalism against the ideology of the median justice. Consider the point where the median is approximately zero. Chief Justices Warren, Burger, and Rehnquist presided over courts that had median justices in this range of the ideological dimension. Notice that all of the points from Chief Justice Warren's tenure fall above those from Chief Justices Burger and Rehnquist's tenure. That is, with an essentially identical median (in our latent ideology space), a liberal chief justice was associated with roughly 65 percent liberal dispositions, whereas a conservative chief justice is associated with roughly 45 percent liberal dispositions. Thus while it is true that the most liberal medians and most liberal dispositions occurred during Chief Justice Warren's tenure, and the most conservative medians and most conservative dispositions occurred during Chief Justice Rehnquist's tenure, the overlap of more moderate medians across liberal and conservative chief justices provides analytic leverage on the effect of the chief justice on case dispositions. This leverage points to an important influence by the chief justice.

Agenda Setting

We now turn to the final mechanism by which chief justices may influence the Court: agenda setting. To study the subjects that occupy the Supreme Court's agenda, we rely upon a topic model for text, Latent Dirichlet Allocation (LDA).[37] This model uses the different terms (words) that appear in a document to estimate a set of (fixed) topics and the probability that each document falls into that topic. In a recent paper, Lauderdale and Clark[38] employ LDA to study the voting dimensions on the Supreme Court; they conclude that approximately twenty-four different topics is sufficient for studying the cleavages on the Court. In another paper, Rice demonstrates that LDA outperforms expert coding, such as the "Issue" codes used by the United States Supreme Court Judicial Database to assign cases to discrete topics.[39]

Using LDA, we can plot over time the extent to which each topic appears on the Supreme Court's agenda. Figure 8.11, which comes from Lauderdale and Clark's study, shows the representation of each of the twenty-four topics on the Court's docket over time. The *x*-axes in each panel measure the Supreme Court term, the *y*-axes measure (essentially) the proportion of the docket represented by each topic. Above each panel are the words most closely associated with the topic (giving a sense of what the topic is about). The panels are shaded to show the different chief justices' tenures.

A striking pattern emerges. In nearly every panel, we see shifts in the topics considered by the Court that coincide with transitions in the chief justice. While the trends are smooth because we force them to be smooth, the points of transition generally stand out as sharp. Take, for example, the topic associated with the terms "speech," "ordinance," and "public." Here we see a sharp increase in that topic when Chief Justice Warren came into office, followed by a sharp drop when Chief Justice Burger took over. By contrast, there is a sharp increase in the "jury," "death," "penalty" topic during Chief Justice Burger's tenure, followed by a drop-off once Chief Justice Rehnquist was elevated to chief justice.

Another important example is the dropoff in "trial," "counsel," "testimony" cases once Chief Justice Burger arrived, followed by a subsequent rise in those cases once the Court's conservative shift (following Nixon's and Reagan's appointments) had solidified. This is precisely what our expectations regarding case selection would imply; Chief Justice Burger was interested in those cases, but upon his arrival on the Court he faced a relatively liberal group of colleagues. So he would have had an incentive to remove those cases from the docket. Once Presidents Nixon and Reagan had nominated more justices, moving the Court to the right, the Chief Justice Burger would have had an incentive to return to those cases, with a new conservative Court that could shape the law as he preferred. Notably, though, as soon as Chief Justice Rehnquist was elevated, those cases quickly dropped off of the Court's docket.

To be sure, there are myriad factors outside of the Court that affect the suite of issues that form the Court's options. Most important, external events, such as the terrorist attacks of September 11, 2001, prompt government action in certain arenas that leads to litigation. This increases the supply of cases, though it does not necessarily compel the Court to hear them. Second, organized interests often mobilize to push a subject matter on the Courts. Again, though, the availability of those cases simply means they are an option, not that they will be heard. Moreover, strategically minded interests are unlikely to pursue an issue and expend their finite resources if they anticipate a hostile Court (led by a hostile chief justice).

Of course, these patterns are only suggestive. But they are consistent with a role for the chief justice in which he exercises procedural power in a way that is consequential for the Court's policymaking. If a chief justice is able to exercise agenda-setting influence to direct the Court's attention to specific topics in the law, then he can use his other procedural powers, including case selection and opinion assignment, to shape the body of American law.

Discussion and Conclusion

Scholars have long speculated about the extent to which the chief justice has any special powers on the Supreme Court. We have identified a few of the institutional prerogatives the chief justice has—opinion assignment when he is in the majority and a potential first-mover's advantage in creating the discuss list—and contemplated the incentives created by those prerogatives. While we have not developed a full-blown theory of how those incentives work to shape the chief's behavior and the Court's decision making, we have traced a few of the implications that follow. In particular, we have argued that the power to assign the majority opinion implies that the most important cases decided by the Court should be assigned to the chief's ideological allies, while the less important cases should be reserved to those justices who are less aligned with the chief. In addition, if the chief is able to influence the discuss list by coordinating the Court on specific cases, we should see case dispositions being affected by the chief justice's preferences and shifts in the topics the Court addresses.

The empirical evidence we present corroborates those expectations. The most salient cases tend to be assigned to justices who are ideologically proximate to the chief justice. The chief justice's ideological preferences predict the distribution of case dispositions (liberal v. conservative) better than does the ideological preferences of the median justice. Indeed, for comparable median justices, liberal chief justices are associated with more liberal dispositions, whereas conservative chief justices are associated with more conservative dispositions. Finally, when there is a transition in the chief justice, we see marked shifts in the topics the Court addresses in its cases. Taken together, these findings suggest that the chief justice's institu-

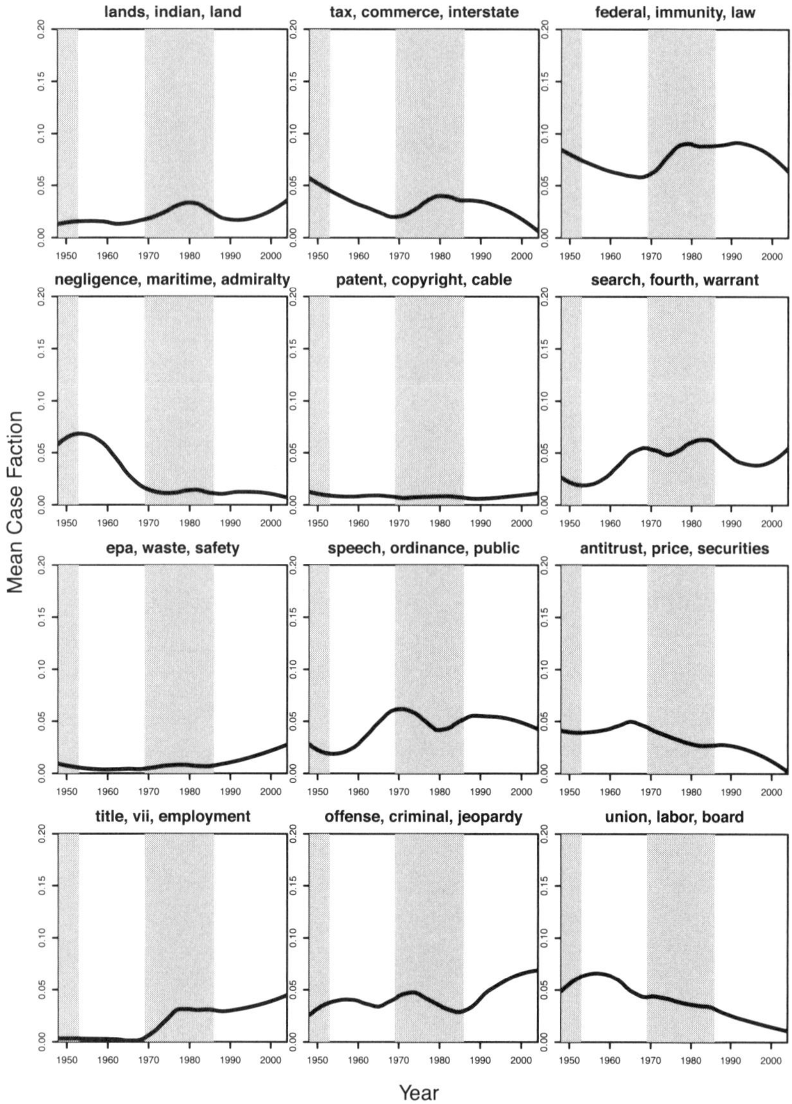

Fig. 8.11. Representation of twenty-four different topics on the Court's docket over time (data from Lauderdale and Clark, "Scaling Politically Meaningful Dimensions").

The figure shows the mean posterior assignment probability to each topic across all cases each term, using a 24-topic Latent Dirichlet Allocation model estimated via MCMC Gibbs sampling. The words above each panel show the three most topical words associated with each topic. The black lines are lowest fits.

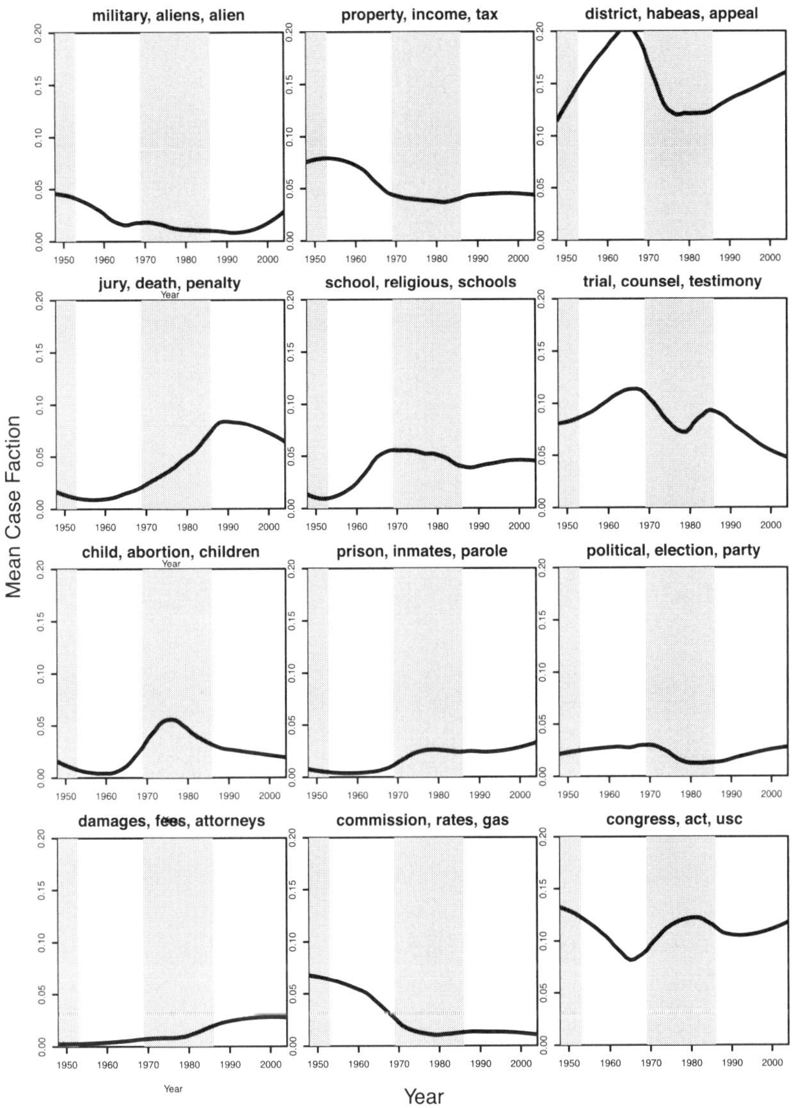

Fig. 8.11. (*continued*)

tional prerogatives translate into procedural power. Being the administrative leader of the Court comes with the benefit of being able to influence which cases the Court hears and how those cases are resolved. Of course, there remain a number of important questions that our analysis does not address, and which require deeper theorizing. For example, how does the chief justice's incentive to bring "good vehicles" to the Court affect the types of coalitions he can build or wants to build? How can the chief justice sustain an ability to coordinate the Court, without revolt by his ideological opponents? Does the Rule of Four, which allows a minority to force a case onto the Court's docket, enhance or attenuate the chief's prerogatives? These and other questions are beyond the scope of our analysis here, but we believe they are the right questions to be asking. We believe the study of the chief justice is ripe for more theoretical inquiry, and we expect this volume will lead to such work.

APPENDIX

Case Salience

As described in the chapter, to measure case salience, we reference four widely used indicators. In order to aggregate the information from those four indicators, we employ a latent variable model (essentially, an item-response theory model) to reduce the indicators into a summary of a latent propensity to appear on the four lists of important cases. Our model is given as follows:

$$\Pr(Y_{ij} = 1 \mid \alpha, \beta, \textbf{\textit{Salience}}) = \Phi(\alpha_j + \beta_j \textit{Salience}_i)$$

where j indexes the four lists of important cases, i indexes the cases, Y_{ij} equals 1 if case i appears in list j, and Φ is the Normal cumulative density function. We estimate the model via Markov Chain Monte Carlo Gibbs sampling and assign diffuse normal priors to the indicator parameters. Specifically, we assume a Normal prior for the intercept and a truncated Normal prior for the slope parameter where we put positive density only on positive values, imposing our assumption that appearing on the list of important cases is positively correlated with latent salience. We assign a standard Normal prior to the *Salience* parameters. The estimates we report in the paper are based on a 50,000-iteration simulation, with a 20,000-iteration burn-in period.

Judicial Ideology

We also use a latent variable model to develop estimates of judicial ideology. Here we employ a standard item-response theory model,[40] as follows:

$$\Pr(Y_{ij} = 1|\alpha,\beta, \boldsymbol{x}) = \Phi(\alpha_j + \beta_j x_i)$$

where Y_{ij} equals 1 if justice i is in the majority disposition coalition on case j, and 0 otherwise, and x_i is the latent ideal point for justice i. We estimate the model via Markov Chain Monte Carlo Gibbs sampling. We assign diffuse normal priors to both the intercept and slope parameters (formally $N(0,100)$ for both parameters). We assign a standard Normal prior for the latent ideal points. The estimates we report are based on a 20,000-iteration sample, discarding a 500-iteration burn-in period.

It bears noting that the IRT model we employ does not fully utilize the information provided by the Court's peculiar voting rule, as discussed early in the chapter. In particular, the model utilizes only the directional information provided by the dispositional part of the voting rule, that is, whether a justice's ideal partition of the fact space lies to the left or the right of the case location. It does not employ the additional information provided by the join/concur decision with respect to the majority opinion among the members of the Court in the dispositional majority. Indeed, it is not completely obvious how best to utilize fully the information in the Court's voting rule. Dispositional votes do, however, provide sufficient information to yield estimates of the justices' ideal points and (under the assumption of sincere dispositional voting) case locations (that is, $\hat{x}$).

NOTES

1. David J. Danelski, "The Influence of the Chief Justice in the Decisional Process of the Supreme Court," paper presented at the American Political Science Association meeting, September 8, 1960 (reprinted in chapter 1, this volume).

2. Nancy Maveety, ed., *Pioneers of Judicial Behavior* (Ann Arbor: University of Michigan Press, 2003).

3. See, for example, Forrest Maltzman and Paul J. Wahlbeck, "May It Please the Chief? Opinion Assignments in the Rehnquist Court," *American Journal of Political Science* 40 (1996); Sara C. Benesh, Reginald S. Sheehan, and Harold J. Spaeth, "Equity in Supreme Court Opinion Assignment," *Jurimetrics* 39 (1998); Forrest Maltzman, James F. Spriggs II, and Paul J. Wahlbeck, *Crafting Law on the U.S. Supreme Court: The Collegial Game* (New York: Cambridge University Press, 2000).

4. The incentive for the chief to engage in strategic dispositional voting has often been noted.

5. Noah Feldman, *Scorpions: The Battles and Triumphs of FDR's Great Supreme Court Justices* (New York: Twelve, 2010), 204.

6. Formal models of Supreme Court decision making as a bargaining game are reviewed at length in Charles Cameron and Lewis Kornhauser, "Modeling Collegial Courts III: Adjudication Equilibrium (revised)" (working paper, New York University School of Law, Public Law, New York, 2010).

7. Maltzman, Spriggs, and Wahlbeck, *Crafting Law on the Supreme Court.*

8. There is a rarely used fifth option, the "reserve" vote.

9. Sometimes a distinction is made between a "general concurrence" and a "special concurrence." Broadly, a general concurrence is a join, but offers some cavils or supplementary material. A special concurrence is a concur vote as we describe it in the text.

10. This insight was first offered in Clifford J. Carrubba, Barry Friedman, Andrew Martin, Georg Vanberg, "Does the Median Justice Control the Content of Supreme Court Opinions?" *American Journal of Political Science* 56 (2012).

11. We have slightly simplified the process, since some cases present multiple issues and voting occurs over each of the presented issues. For a discussion of some of the complexities that can then arise, see Lewis Kornhauser and Larry Sager, "Unpacking the Court," *Yale Law Journal* 96 (1986); and Christian List, "The Theory of Judgment Aggregation: An Introductory Survey," *Synthese* 187 (2012).

12. See, *inter alia*, James Enelow and Melvin Hinich, *The Spatial Theory of Voting: An Introduction* (New York: Cambridge University Press, 1984).

13. See Lewis Kornhauser, "Modeling Collegial Courts I: Path Dependence," *International Review of Law and Economics* 12 (1992); Lewis Kornhauser, "Modeling Collegial Courts II: Legal Doctrine," *Journal of Law, Economics, and Organization* 8 (1992); Cameron and Kornhauser, "Modeling Collegial Courts III"; and Jeffrey R. Lax, "The New Judicial Politics of Legal Doctrine," *Annual Review of Political Science* 14 (2011).

14. See Cameron and Kornhauser, "Modeling Collegial Courts III."

15. If Block L is willing to engage in a strategic "crossover join," it can join the other two blocks and participate in the bargaining over the content of the rule. But even so, the rule must still lie in the interval to the right of $\hat{x}$; it cannot lie to the left of $\hat{x}$ and still yield the "admit" disposition. This fact limits the attractiveness of a crossover join, which appear to be relatively rare on the U.S. Supreme Court. In contrast, they appear common on the U.S. Courts of Appeal. On the latter, see Joshua Fischman, "Interpreting Circuit Court Voting Patterns: A Social Interactions Framework," *Journal of Law, Economics, and Organization* (forthcoming).

16. David M. Kreps, *A Course in Microeconomic Theory* (Princeton: Princeton University Press, 1990).

17. The Median Justice Approach was ported directly to the study of judicial decision making in Thomas Hammond, Chris Bonneau, and Reginald Sheehan, *Strategic Behavior and Policy Choice on the U.S. Supreme Court* (Stanford, CA: Stanford University Press, 2005). The Median Justice Approach also emerges as a special case in several other models of Supreme Court decision making, for example in Lax and Cameron's Entry Blocking model when authoring costs are zero (Jeffrey R. Lax and Charles Cameron, "Bargaining and Opinion Assignment on the U.S. Supreme Court," *Journal of Law, Economics, and Organization* 23 (2007)). It also occurs in Car-

rubba et al.'s Majority Median model when the case disposition is unanimous so all justices are in the dispositional majority (Carrubba et al., "Does the Median Justice Control."). It is frequently evoked in journalistic commentary about the Court.

18. A classic reference is Duncan Black, *The Theory of Committees and Elections* (New York: Cambridge University Press, 1958).

19. At present, the key studies are Tom S. Clark and Benjamin E. Lauderdale, "Locating Supreme Court Opinions in Doctrine Space," *American Journal of Political Science* 54 (2010); Jeffrey R. Lax and Kelly T. Rader, "Bargaining Power in the Supreme Court: Evidence from Opinion Assignment and Vote Fluidity" (working paper, Columbia University, 2011); and Carrubba et al., "Does the Median Justice Control."

20. The Majority Median Approach was first proposed in an empirical paper. Chad Westerland, "Who Owns the Majority Opinion?" (paper presented at the annual meeting of the American Political Science Association, Philadelphia, Aug. 2003). The formal model in Carrubba et al., "Does the Median Justice Control," suggests that opinions should lie at the center of the join coalition; in practice this is likely to be close to the median of the dispositional majority. The game theoretic model in Charles Cameron and Lewis Kornhauser, "Bargaining on Appellate Courts" (working paper, Princeton University, 2013), indicates that opinions for very important cases will usually be located in the middle of the dispositional majority.

21. See Cameron and Kornhauser, "Bargaining on Appellate Courts."

22. Lax and Cameron, "Bargaining and Opinion Assignment"; Cameron and Kornhauser, "Modeling Collegial Courts III"; Cameron and Kornhauser "Bargaining on Appellate Courts"; See also Tonja Jacobi, "Competing Theories of Coalition Formation and Case Outcome Determination," *Journal of Legal Analysis* 1 (2009).

23. Walter F. Murphy, *Elements of Judicial Strategy* (Chicago: University of Chicago Press, 1964); David W. Rohde and Harold J. Spaeth, *Supreme Court Decision Making* (San Francisco: W. H. Freeman, 1976); Maltzman, Spriggs, and Wahlbeck, *Crafting Law on the Supreme Court*; Maltzman and Wahlbeck, "May It Please the Chief."

24. Sidney Ulmer, "The Use of Power on the Supreme Court: The Opinion Assignments of Earl Warren, 1953–1960," *Journal of Public Law* 30 (1970); Elliot Slotnick, "The Chief Justice and Self-Assignment of Majority Opinions: A Research Note," *Western Political Quarterly* 31 (1978); Saul Brenner, "The Chief Justice's Self Assignment of Majority Opinions in Salient Cases," *Social Science Journal* 30 (1993); Maltzman, Spriggs, and Wahlbeck, *Crafting Law on the Supreme Court*; Maltzman and Wahlbeck, "May It Please the Chief."

25. A great deal of legal literature suggests that learning from a case is local, and this may limit the scope of an announced legal rule.

26. Much of the scholarly literature on Supreme Court case selection focuses on its role in controlling the dispositions of lower court judges. See e.g., Charles Cameron, Jeffrey Segal, and Donald Songer, "Strategic Auditing in a Political Hierarchy: An Informational Model of the Supreme Court's Certiorari Decisions," *American Political Science Review* 94 (2000); and Jeffrey R. Lax, "Certiorari and Compliance in the Judicial Hierarchy: Discretion, Reputation, and the Rule of Four," *Journal of Theoretical Politics* 15 (2003). Some recent studies use a similar perspective but

focus on policy setting in the hierarchy, notably Tom S. Clark and Clifford Carrubba, "Rule Creation in a Political Hierarchy," *American Political Science Review* 106 (2012). A handful of studies emphasize case selection as part of social learning within the judicial hierarchy, e.g., Deborah Beim, "Finding Law: Learning in the Judicial Hierarchy" (working paper, Yale University, 2013); see also David Klein, *Making Law in the U.S. Courts of Appeals* (Cambridge: Cambridge University Press, 2002). The perspective on case selection offered in this section—emphasizing strategic selection as part of the collegial, policymaking game on the Court itself—is, so far as we know, novel.

27. H. W. Perry Jr., *Deciding to Decide: Agenda Setting in the United States Supreme Court* (Cambridge, MA: Harvard University Press, 1991), 91.

28. Ibid., 87.

29. Ibid., 91.

30. Benjamin E. Lauderdale and Tom S. Clark, "The Supreme Court's Many Median Justices," *American Political Science Review* 106 (2012); Benjamin E. Lauderdale and Tom S. Clark, "Scaling Politically Meaningful Dimensions Using Texts and Votes," *American Journal of Political Science* 58 (2014).

31. Outstanding studies on Supreme Court agenda setting are Richard L. Pacelle Jr., *The Transformation of the Supreme Court's Agenda: From the New Deal to the Reagan Administration* (Boulder: Westview Press, 1991); Vanessa A. Baird, *Answering the Call of the Court: How Justices and Litigants Set the Supreme Court's Agenda* (Charlottesville: University of Virginia Press, 2007); and Vanessa Baird and Tonja Jacobi, "Judicial Agenda Setting Through Signaling and Strategic Litigant Responses," *Journal of Law and Policy* 29 (2009).

32. Lee Epstein and Jeffrey A. Segal, "Measuring Issue Salience," *American Journal of Political Science* 44 (2000).

33. "Historic Supreme Court Decisions," Cornell University Law School, Legal Information Institute, http://straylight.law.cornell.edu/supct/cases/name.html, accessed Sep. 21, 2013.

34. K. L. Hall, *The Oxford Guide to United States Supreme Court Decisions* (New York: Oxford University Press, 1999).

35. Joan Biskupic and Elder Witt, *Guide to the U.S. Supreme Court: Congressional Quarterly's Guide to the U.S. Supreme Court*, 3rd ed. (Washington, DC: CQ Press, 1996).

36. See for example Maltzman and Wahlbeck, "May It Please the Chief"; Benjamin E. Lauderdale and Tom S. Clark, "Who Controls Opinion Content? Testing Theories of Authorship Using Case-Specific Preference Estimates for the US Supreme Court" (working paper, Emory University, 2013).

37. See David M. Blei, Andrew Ng, and Michael I. Jordan, "Latent Dirichlet Allocation," *Journal of Machine Learning Research* 3 (2003).

38. Lauderdale and Clark, "Scaling Politically Meaningful Dimensions."

39. Douglas Rice, "Measuring the Issue Content of Supreme Court Opinions Through Probabilistic Topic Models" (working paper, Pennsylvania State University, 2012).

40. Simon Jackman, "Multidimensional Analysis of Roll-Call Data via Bayesian Simulation: Identification, Estimation, Inference, and Model Checking," *Political Analysis* 9, no. 3 (2001): 227–41.

9 ~ Honeymoon on the Court?

Chief Justices and Consensus Building on the Supreme Court

AMY STEIGERWALT, PAMELA C. CORLEY, AND ARTEMUS WARD

Numerous studies highlight the impact of the chief justice on the U.S. Supreme Court. The chief justice leads the Supreme Court in setting its agenda, discussing and deciding cases, and assigning opinions when in the majority. Scholars also argue that chief justices play an enormous role in setting the tone of the Court, whether it be one of consensus, such as under Chief Justices Marshall and Warren, or one of debate, such as under Chief Justice Stone.[1] Danelski goes furthest in investigating the power and reach of the chief justice, and he argues that the most successful chief justices rely upon a combination of task and social leadership skills. In order to achieve positive results, a task leader "makes more suggestions than his colleagues, gives more opinions, and orients the discussion more frequently."[2] But because a single-minded focus on administering the business of the Court can lead to tension and discord among its members, Danelski argues a "social" leader can mitigate these potential negative effects by promoting harmony and solidarity, and being generally well-liked. Danelski argues that chief justices are uniquely positioned on the Supreme Court to exploit these leadership styles, whether they use their opinion-assignment powers to reward and punish, such as Chief Justice Taft, or use their control of the agenda to encourage discussion and debate, like Stone.[3]

Thus anecdotal and empirical evidence suggests that chief justices can substantially influence both the tone of how the Court conducts its business and the outcomes the Court achieves.[4] Furthermore, as different chiefs emphasize different traits, skills, and philosophies, exactly who the chief is and how he decides to lead the Court matters greatly as well. Important questions remain, however, as to the influence of the chief justice, and how the members of the Supreme Court interrelate. Since the Supreme Court is a majoritarian institution that relies upon collective decision making, how the justices interact to arrive at the final vote is as important as the individual views each justice holds.

Given the collegial interactions that characterize Supreme Court decision making and the power of the chief justice, along with the fact that each chief exerts a unique influence on the Court, we posit that when a new chief joins the Court, the relationships among the justices necessarily change. A new chief may adopt a different leadership style, alter the ideological orientation of the Court or the strength of the majority, or change Court processes and procedures. And, even if a new chief seems ideologically similar to his predecessor, he or she is likely to implement important changes in how the Court operates. Thus, at the beginning of a new chief's tenure, the other justices are likely to wait and see what changes and innovations the new chief brings to the Court and to give the new chief a chance to establish how he or she best wishes to lead the Court. The remaining justices may then deliberately de-emphasize ongoing disputes in order to allow the chief a period of adjustment and learning. In short, the justices are likely to give the new chief a so-called honeymoon period.

The idea of a honeymoon period stems from the literature on U.S. presidents. Following Franklin Roosevelt's inauguration, dozens of innovative and far-reaching laws were passed within the first one hundred days of his administration, many with as little as an hour of debate.[5] Scholars thus began to examine whether all presidents enjoyed such a "honeymoon" period of increased consensus and goodwill. Numerous scholars find evidence of new presidents enjoying a type of grace period whereby consensus is more likely and opposition is muted.[6] McCarty and Poole argue a "pattern of accommodation followed by later conflict" characterizes presidential-congressional relations.[7] While some studies focus on the president's first hundred days,[8] other scholars assess the president's first year in office.[9] Regardless of the time period analyzed, studies find that presidents are more likely during their honeymoon period to see their favored bills enacted,[10] less likely to encounter congressional opposition,[11] more likely to receive favorable press treatment in news stories as well as at press conferences,[12] and more likely to enjoy high public approval ratings.[13] Thus, during the presidential honeymoon period, the nation as a whole, and the specific players in the American political process, all allow the president a period of acclimation and a lessening of opposition. And a comparative study of executive leadership change and first years in office[14] finds that new executives are able to implement innovative policy changes, whether in capitalist or socialist countries; new faces are indeed able to do new things.

Scholars have also extended the idea of a honeymoon period to other ongoing relationships as well, such as marriage[15] and the creation of new businesses and business relationships.[16] In all these studies, the common thread is the idea that a new relationship or new actor should be given a period of transition and learning and that traditional or ongoing disputes will be muted during this period. These studies thus suggest that when a new actor, and especially a new leader, enters into a long-term relationship, trust and goodwill are likely to be higher and so the leader is likely to enjoy an initial "honeymoon" period of acclimation, increased attempts to find consensus, and a muting of opposition. As Fichman and Levinthal argue, "some level of commitment should be associated with the initiation of any relationship,"[17] and so the other actors should work to make the relationship run smoothly. They also find that in relationships where commitment to the relationship is higher, a honeymoon period is more likely.

We therefore posit that chief justices may enjoy a similar honeymoon period during their first term as chief. Given the consensual nature of Supreme Court decision making and that Supreme Court justices potentially serve together for decades, commitment to their ongoing relationship is necessarily high. As a new chief takes the helm, the other justices may be more likely to give the chief a period of acclimation in order to develop his leadership style and relationships with the other justices. The other justices, much like members of Congress and the press, may stanch ongoing debates or lessen opposition during this time of transition, especially as each justice determines the impact of the new chief's ideological positions and leadership decisions. As a result, the justices may be more willing to find common points of agreement and be less likely to either dissent or write separate opinions during the new chief's first term than they would later. Once the chief is settled into his role, however, the justices are unlikely to dampen their views or refrain from writing separate opinions.

Chief Justice Roberts attributed his success in achieving a high number of unanimous decisions during his first term to a type of honeymoon period, "due to the other justices' eagerness to be helpful to a newcomer, much like a fiancé meeting his future in-laws for the first time at Thanksgiving."[18] Justice John Paul Stevens also declared that Roberts was given such a honeymoon period during the 2005 term immediately following his confirmation, stating that "maybe the first few months we all leaned over backwards to try to avoid writing separately in a couple of opinions."[19] These comments suggest that the associate justices worked harder to mask dissension and to reach consensus at the beginning of Roberts's reign than they might later into his tenure.

Assessing whether chief justices experience a type of honeymoon period like that of presidents and other newly enshrined leaders broadens our understanding of elite behavior, collective decision making, and the specific factors that influence whether the Supreme Court reaches consensus in individual cases. As the Supreme Court must be concerned with seeing their decisions implemented and enforced—and thus the decisions themselves being viewed as legitimate—mechanisms to increase this legitimacy are especially important.[20] Given that many believe unanimous Supreme Court decisions carry extra legitimacy,[21] understanding what increases the likelihood of unanimity on the Supreme Court is essential to understanding both how the Court makes decisions and how the Court effectively operates as a potentially countermajoritarian institution. We specifically take up the task put forth by Epstein, Segal, and Spaeth to explore what increases the likelihood of unanimity and what role the chief justice plays in encouraging such unanimity.[22]

Data and Methods

We test the proposition that the associate justices on the Supreme Court will grant a new chief justice a type of honeymoon period whereby the justices will work harder at reaching consensus and unanimity and will therefore be more willing to vote with the majority. Additionally, we investigate whether the justices are more willing to refrain from writing separate opinions during the first year. Chief Justice Roberts made increasing unanimity a hallmark of his plan for how to lead the Court if confirmed as chief. He argued that the Court needed to return to how it operated under Chief Justice Marshall: "Marshall saw that the Court could rule authoritatively and win the public's confidence only if it functioned as a collegial body and not simply as a collection of individuals."[23] Thus unanimous and highly collegial decisions are seen by many to bolster both the legal weight of the Court's decisions as well as the level of legitimacy the decisions will enjoy. The broader question thus becomes: When are unanimity and consensus most likely to occur? And is consensus more likely in a chief justice's first term than later in his or her tenure?

We analyze all cases appealed from a lower federal court that were granted certiorari, orally argued, and decided by the United States Supreme Court between the 1946 and 2011 terms.[24] We use the data available through the U.S. Supreme Court Judicial Database.[25] Our dataset contains all cases decided under Chief Justices Vinson, Warren, Burger, Rehnquist, and Roberts. This allows us to test for the influence of five quite different chief justices and the possibility of a honeymoon period, as well as focus on chiefs who operated under similar conditions: all worked during a period when law clerks assumed much of the opinion-writing duties for their respective justices, and the Court's docket was crowded with controversial civil rights and civil liberties cases rarely present in earlier times.

The unit of analysis is the individual case, and we conduct two sets of analyses. We first examine whether the justices are more likely to reach consensus on the merits, and we utilize two separate dependent variables to reflect the degree of agreement among the justices. ***Unanimous Decisions*** reflects whether the vote in the case was unanimous and includes all instances where no justice dissented, regardless of the number of justices who participated in the case. Unanimous decisions are coded 1, and all other decisions are coded 0. ***Level of Voting Consensus*** captures the degree of consensus among the justices, and ranges from 5, highly consensual, to 1, highly divisive. Specifically, we coded unanimous decisions (9-0, 8-0, or 7-0) as 5; 8-1, 7-1, or 6-1 votes as 4; 7-2, 6-2, or 5-2 votes as 3; 6-3 or 5-3 votes as 4, and split decisions (5-4 or 4-3) as 1.

Our second set of analyses investigates whether a honeymoon manifests itself as a decrease in separate opinion writing. While a unanimous vote may reflect agreement among all the justices, it may also conceal true disagreements, particularly with regard to legal reasoning. When a justice votes with the Court on the outcome of a case but disagrees with the legal reasoning of the other justices, he or she may author a concurrence in order to express that disagreement. Separate opinions, including concurrences, thus reveal important legal disputes. Thus the third dependent variable, ***Fully Unanimous Opinions***, takes into account opinion consensus and is defined as cases in which the vote was unanimous and there were no concurrences accompanying the majority opinions. Fully unanimous opinions are coded 1, and 0 otherwise. Since ***Unanimous Decisions*** and ***Fully Unanimous Opinions*** are both dichotomous, we use logit to estimate these models and robust standard errors clustered on the case. ***Level of Voting Consensus*** is an ordinal variable, so we use ordered logit to estimate this model; we again also utilize robust standard errors clustered on the case.[26]

Our primary independent variable of interest in all three models is whether unanimity is more likely during a chief justice's first term on the Court as chief, that is, during his ***honeymoon period***. As our data includes five different chief justices, we are particularly interested in the possibility that who the chief justice is matters,[27] and thus the existence of a honeymoon period and its impact may very much depend upon the chief himself. We therefore created dummy variables for each of the five chiefs under analysis and exclude Roberts as the baseline for comparison. We then interacted each of the chief dummies with whether they were in their honeymoon year to determine whether each chief experienced a honeymoon period and the magnitude of this honeymoon effect. The results for the "Honeymoon" variable thus reflect whether Roberts experienced a honeymoon, while the interaction term results reflect whether the other four chiefs experienced a honeymoon.

We also test two competing, but not necessarily mutually exclusive, sets of hypotheses: (1) a more ideologically compatible Supreme Court is more likely to decide cases unanimously, and (2) cases with a higher degree of legal certainty are more likely to be decided unanimously. First, following the tenets of the Attitudinal Model,[28] when the Supreme Court is more ideologically compatible, unanimity should be easier to achieve. We thus control for the ***degree of ideological polarization among the associate justices***. All else being equal, the more ideologically compatible the rest of the Court, the more likely unanimity will be achieved; the more ideologically polarized the associate justices, the less likely a consensus decision can be reached.[29] This variable measures the absolute value of the distance between the median associate justice's Martin-Quinn ideology score and the most ideologically distant associate justice's Martin-Quinn ideology score.

Second, dating back to Pritchett's seminal work, we test for the possibility that certain periods see an increase in unanimous opinions not because of a honeymoon period or increased ideological compatibility,[30] but because the Court granted cert in a series of cases for which the correct legal answer was more clear and therefore "easier" to determine.[31] As Goldman explains, "In general, a consensually decided case indicates that 'objectively' the case situation (either because of clear-cut precedent, or the straight-forward applicability of the statute, or constitutional provisions to the facts of the case) offered little leeway for the judge and that institutional pressures inhibited an outcome other than that achieved."[32] Corley, Steigerwalt, and Ward find that when the level of legal certainty is high, the Court is more likely to achieve consensus.[33] The ***level of legal certainty*** is an additive index, based on the following variables: legally noncomplex cases, lack of amicus participation in the case, lack of legal conflict, lack of legal dissensus in the lower court, and statutory interpretation cases. See Corley, Steigerwalt, and Ward for a detailed discussion of the variables and index.[34]

Politically salient cases, which are of great interest to other key political actors and the nation as a whole, are also more likely to lead to division on the Supreme Court.[35] As Grossman and Wells argue, "[T]hese are the kinds of cases least likely to be decided unanimously. There is no a priori reason to expect . . . justices to be united on politically contentious issues that divide the country."[36] This variable reflects whether the case was considered politically salient at the time of the decision, and it measures whether the case was discussed on the front page of the *New York Times* immediately after the decision was handed down.[37]

Finally, certain issues may provoke more debate and controversy. Civil rights and liberties issues like abortion, criminal defendant rights, and free speech are highly divisive among American political elites and the mass public, and they divide the Supreme Court as well. Previous studies find ***cases involving civil rights and liberties issues*** are less likely to be decided unanimously,[38] and we expect to find the same result here. We included dummy variables for the issue area the case dealt with. We created dummies for civil liberties cases, economic activity cases, and governmental powers cases, and we excluded the civil liberties cases as the baseline for comparison.

For the estimation of opinion consensus (Model 3), we also examine an additional variable: time until the end of the term. Specifically, we posit that more time should lead to a decrease in opinion consensus because the justices have more time to craft separate opinions even if they agree on the merits. We calculated this number as the end date of the term in which the case was decided (July 1) minus the oral argument date.[39]

Is There a Honeymoon?

Table 9.1 presents the results of all three analyses and suggests that whether a chief justice experiences a honeymoon period, and the magnitude of this honeymoon period, depends on who the chief justice is and the willingness of the associate justices to grant him a period of adjustment. According to table 9.1, the Honeymoon variable is positive and statistically significant in all three models. Since this variable was interacted with the dummy chief justice variables and Roberts was used as the baseline category, this result shows that Chief Justice Roberts did indeed experience a honeymoon period during his first term on the Court relative to the other chiefs. Importantly, this result holds true whether we measure consensus on the merits in terms of unanimity or level of consensus. Thus, unanimity and high levels of consensus were more likely during Roberts's first term, suggesting that the Court worked together more during that first term to find common points of agreement. Furthermore, Chief Justices Warren and Rehnquist were less likely than Roberts to achieve unanimity and consensus during their first term, while Chief Rehnquist was also less likely to achieve fully unanimous opinions during his first term compared to Roberts. These results mean that even if the other chiefs did experience a honeymoon period during their first term, the magnitude of their honeymoon period was less than Roberts's.

Table 9.2 presents the predicted probability of achieving a unanimous decision or a fully unanimous decision during the first term compared with the predicted probability of achieving a unanimous decision or fully unani-

TABLE 9.1. Estimation Results for Chief Justice Honeymoon Effect

	Model 1: Unanimous Decisions		Model 2: Level of Voting Consensus		Model 3: Fully Unanimous Opinions	
Variable	Coeff.	Robust S.E.	Coeff.	Robust S.E.	Coeff.	Robust S.E.
Honeymoon	.733**	.298	.685*	.300	.771**	.329
Vinson	–.732***	.169	–.413**	.138	–.398*	.199
Warren	–.110	.141	.117	.127	.271	.166
Burger	.023	.132	.112	.124	.120	.157
Rehnquist	.263*	.124	.233*	.120	.384**	.146
Vinson*Honeymoon	–.036	.388	–.214	.365	–.016	.425
Warren*Honeymoon	–1.262**	.459	–1.084**	.378	–.784	.501
Burger*Honeymoon	–.571	.428	–.219	.368	–.573	.468
Rehnquist*Honeymoon	–.995**	.373	–1.181***	.372	–1.053**	.421
Level of Legal Certainty	.122***	.033	.136***	.029	.206***	.038
Politically salient cases	–.618***	.108	–.586***	.084	–.784***	.140
Ideological Polarization	–.092**	.033	–.090**	.029	–.055	.084
Government Power Cases	.506***	.079	.546***	.072	.676***	.088
Economic Activity Cases	.385***	.073	.408***	.064	.556***	.084
Time Left Until End of Term	—	—	—	—	–.001	.001
Constant	–.623**	.195			–1.924	.241
/cut1			–1.316*	.177		
/cut2			–.330	.174		
/cut3			.328	.174		
/cut4			.791*	.175		
N	4,642		4,642		4,584	

*** $p < .001$ ** $p < .01$ * $p < .05$, one-tailed tests.

mous decision after the first term for each chief justice.[40] These predicted probabilities allow us to determine whether each chief experienced a honeymoon period as well as the magnitude of the honeymoon period itself.

Roberts most clearly enjoyed a honeymoon period during his first term on the bench as compared to his predecessors, both in terms of voting consensus and opinion consensus. During Roberts's first term, the probability of achieving a unanimous decision was .528 compared to only .349 for his later terms, and the probability of a fully unanimous opinion was .309 during his first term as chief compared to .172 after that first term. Vinson and Burger also experienced a honeymoon effect, with the probability of achieving a unanimous decision during Burger's first term increasing by 10.73 percent compared with the rest of his tenure as chief and the probability of achieving a fully unanimous opinion increasing by 17.46 percent. During Vinson's first term, the predicted probability of a unanimous decision was .341, while after the first term it was only .205. And the predicted probability of achieving a fully unanimous opinion was .228 during Vinson's first term as chief compared to .122 after his first term. In contrast, neither Warren nor Rehnquist experienced a honeymoon period. Rather, both Warren and Rehnquist improved their ability to achieve both unanimous decisions and fully unanimous opinions after their first term. Thus it appears that Vinson, Burger, and Roberts were the only chiefs who benefited during their first terms, and Roberts obviously received a more substantial benefit during his first term. Chiefs may experience a honeymoon period, but only when the associate justices are willing to grant the new chief such a period of acclimation.

Chief Justice Roberts made the achievement of unanimity a cornerstone of his bid to be confirmed as chief justice, and unanimity was prevalent during his first term. Roberts argued that he used his leadership role

TABLE 9.2. Predicted Probabilities for Chief Justice Honeymoon Effect

	Predicted Probability of Unanimous Decision		Predicted Probability of Fully Unanimous Opinion	
Chief	First Term	After First Term	First Term	After First Term
Vinson	.341	.205	.228	.122
Warren	.221	.325	.211	.214
Burger	.392	.354	.222	.189
Rehnquist	.349	.411	.187	.233
Roberts	.528	.349	.309	.172

Note: Probabilities are computed by holding all continuous variables (such as the level of legal certainty) at their mean values, while holding all discrete values (such as civil liberties and rights issue) at their modal values.

to frame issues narrowly and to assign opinions to those who would work to breed consensus: "Say someone is committed to broad consensus, and somebody else is just dead set on 'My way or the highway . . .' Well, you assign that [case] to the [consensus-minded] person, and it gives you a much better chance, out of the box, of getting some kind of consensus."[41] But the consensus Roberts experienced during his first term did not last. According to Murphy, "[T]he chief justiceship supplies numerous opportunities to exert influence; it offers no guaranty that the incumbent can utilize these opportunities to achieve his policy goals."[42] Thus our results suggest that Roberts's first term reflected more of a honeymoon period with increased attempts at consensus, rather than a long-term break from the discord that has recently characterized the Supreme Court. Similarly, Burger was granted a small honeymoon period during his first term. While Nixon made clear that he appointed Burger as a "law and order" judge, it seems the other justices were willing to give him a chance both to find his footing as chief and to attempt to work to find points of commonality.

On the other hand, Warren and Rehnquist were not granted honeymoon periods. While the idea of a period of acclimation would seem to most apply to Warren, who lacked any previous judicial experience, it may be that the justices were unwilling to grant a honeymoon period to such an inexperienced chief. Alternatively, his inexperience may have limited any potential honeymoon effect. On the other hand, it is likely that Rehnquist's previous position as an associate justice influenced how the other justices responded to him in his new role as chief. Since Rehnquist already had established relationships with each of the associate justices (other than the newly appointed Antonin Scalia), the other justices may have had difficulty adjusting to Rehnquist in his new role as chief and/or they may not have seen the need to grant him a period of acclimation since he had already served on the Court for fourteen years before his elevation to chief justice. In sum, chief justices may indeed experience a honeymoon period much like presidents in their first term, but not all chiefs are granted such a honeymoon period and the magnitude of this honeymoon period varies as well.

In addition to the honeymoon and chief effects, we also tested two sets of alternative hypotheses concerning the likelihood of the Court reaching a unanimous decision. First, we argued that a more ideologically compatible Supreme Court is more likely to decide cases unanimously. Table 9.1 provides support for this hypothesis: as the amount of ideological polarization among the associate justices grows, the Court is less likely to issue a unanimous decision. Second, we argued that cases with a higher degree of legal certainty are more likely to be decided unanimously. Again, our results provide strong support for this theory.

Politically salient cases are less likely to result in unanimous decisions. Additionally, civil liberties and civil rights cases—those we predicted would be most divisive—are indeed less likely to be decided unanimously than governmental powers cases and economic cases. Together, these two findings illuminate the fact that divisions in American politics are present on the Supreme Court as well.

Discussion and Conclusion

Overall, we find support for each of our three main hypotheses. First, echoing the arguments put forth by Segal and Spaeth,[43] the justices are much more likely to achieve consensus when they are ideologically close than when the Court is ideologically polarized. Second, we find strong support for the notion of legal certainty. The Court can find unanimity because some cases simply lend themselves more easily to unanimous decisions. On the other hand, just like the American public and other political actors, the Supreme Court is more likely to be divided on politically salient cases and hot-button civil liberties issues. Thus, the Supreme Court reaches a unanimous decision in a sizable percentage of cases every term, and these unanimous decisions are partially guided by the Supreme Court taking on cases that lend themselves to consensus. Given the Supreme Court's need for legitimacy, and the direct tie between unanimity and legitimacy in the minds of many, these results show that unanimity can be obtained.

Third, and most important, we find some support for the proposition that chief justices may experience a type of "honeymoon period," much like U.S. presidents, during their first term on the Court. Not every Chief experiences a honeymoon, however, and not all honeymoons are equal. Vinson, Burger, and Roberts each experienced a honeymoon, but Roberts's honeymoon effect was much more substantial. On the other hand, Warren and Rehnquist did not experience a honeymoon period; unanimity and consensus were more likely *after* their first terms.

Chiefs do not operate in a vacuum and so in many ways the question is whether the other justices will *grant* the chief this period of acclimation and compromise. While our results are limited to an examination of only five chief justices, we find that not all chiefs experience a honeymoon period. These results suggest that the process of a new chief joining the Supreme Court may be qualitatively different from a new president taking office. In addition, the president's role is strikingly different than that played by the chief justice. First, the associate justices may perceive the process of a chief being confirmed much differently than the Congress views a president winning an election. While the chief must win the assent of a majority of the Senate, this vote is distinct from a president winning the general election and thus the support of the American electorate. Winning presidents usually claim a "mandate" from the people to lead the county and enact their favored proposals; the chief justice has no similar mandate to claim. As a result, the chief justice is not viewed as possessing the support of the American people to alter the Court and its decisions dramatically. For example, the *New York Times* suggested Burger might face a hard road as chief given Nixon's stated desires to overturn certain key Supreme Court precedents: "Chief Justice Burger may labor under some initial handicaps, in view of President Nixon's statements that he appointed Judge Burger as a 'law and order' proponent to attempt to turn the Court around on its criminal law decisions. The Court has been deeply split over some of these issues, and the other Justices may dig in their heels at the new Chief Justice's suggestions for change."[44] Rather than Burger possessing a mandate to push the Court toward these changes, insightful observers predicted that the associate justices would be girded for a fight on the positions they held dear.

Second, given the president's lead role in crafting the policy agenda for the nation, Congress—even during divided government—may be willing to defer to the new president at the beginning of his tenure. In the modern era, the president's role has greatly expanded to include constructing the budget for the government, taking the lead on introducing new policy initiatives, and acting as the head of his political party. As a result, in many areas Congress acts in response to the president's actions and initiatives, and the president's role is clearly one of leadership and authority.

The chief justice does not play a similar leadership role on the Supreme Court. Danelski highlighted the task leadership roles and social leadership roles chiefs can utilize to keep the Court running smoothly. However, while the chief justice may lead conference discussions and have opinion-granting powers when in the majority, the chief justice is not considered the leader of the Court in a traditional sense. Indeed, as Justice Felix Frankfurter wrote to Justice Harold Burton in 1956: "It is vitally important to remember what Holmes said about the office [of the chief justice]: 'Of course, the position of the Chief Justice differs from that of the other Justices only on the administrative side.' He is not the head of a Department; not even a quarterback."[45] Similarly, in 1958, Frankfurter wrote to Justice

William Brennan, "Any encouragement in a Chief Justice that he is the boss . . . must be rigorously resisted. . . . I, for my part, will discharge what I regard as a post of trusteeship, not least in keeping the Chief Justice in his place, as long as I am around."[46] Thus, the associate justices do not view the chief as their de facto leader in terms of crafting the Court's agenda, conceptualizing issues or determining how to vote, but rather as an administrative leader to help the Court operate efficiently. In fact, once elevated to chief justice, Rehnquist explained in his book, *The Supreme Court: How It Was, How It Is*, that the chief's role was not one of hierarchical authority: "The chief justice has some authority that the associate justices do not have, but this is relatively insignificant compared to the extraordinary independence that each justice has from every other justice." Our mixed results as to whether chief justices are granted a honeymoon period may therefore reflect the very different role the chief plays vis-à-vis the other justices in comparison to the role the president plays in relation to Congress.

In sum, given the collective nature of Supreme Court decision making, how the justices interact is crucial to their outcomes. As Danelski argued, each chief uses an idiosyncratic mix of task and social leadership traits, and how each chief pursues his job can influence these collective interactions. Danelski noted that it is uncommon to find chiefs who excel at both task and social leadership, and so the roles of task and social leadership may be played by two different justices. Our results suggest that while the justices may welcome a new task leader, they do not always view new chiefs as the Court's new social leader. The associate justices may be willing to grant a new chief a type of honeymoon period whereby disagreements are muted and consensus is favored. But not all chiefs experience such a honeymoon, and the effect, if any, differs across chiefs. We believe these results offer support for our initial proposition that who the chief justice is matters, as well as the idea that the chief justice's role on the Supreme Court is distinct from that of other leaders in the American political process. The chief justice is considered "first among equals," yet his colleagues will work to remind him that he is indeed among equals.

NOTES

1. Stacie L. Haynie, "Leadership and Consensus on the U.S. Supreme Court," *Journal of Politics* 54 (1992); Thomas G. Walker, Lee Epstein, and William J. Dixon, "On the Mysterious Demise of Consensual Norm in the United States Supreme Court," *Journal of Politics* 50 (1988); David J. Danelski, "The Influence of the Chief Justice in the Decisional Process of the Supreme Court," in *Constitutional Law and*

Judicial Policy Making, ed. Joel B. Grossman and Richard S. Wells (New York: John Wiley, 1980).

2. David J. Danelski, "The Influence of the Chief Justice in the Decisional Process," in *Courts, Judges, and Politics: An Introduction to the Judicial Process*, 6th ed., ed. Walter F. Murphy, C. Herman Pritchett, Lee Epstein, and Jack Knight (New York: McGraw-Hill, 2006), 676.

3. Walker, Epstein, and Dixon, "On the Mysterious Demise"; Haynie, "Leadership and Consensus."

4. Haynie, "Leadership and Consensus"; Walker, Epstein, and Dixon, "On the Mysterious Demise"; Danelski, "Influence of the Chief Justice" (1980); Danelski, "Influence of the Chief Justice" (2006).

5. David Kennedy, *Freedom From Fear: The American People in Depression and War* (New York: Oxford University Press, 1999), 135–53; William E. Leuchtenberg, *Franklin Roosevelt and the New Deal, 1932–1940* (New York: Harper and Row, 1963).

6. See e.g., Valerie Bunce, *Do New Leaders Make a Difference? Executive Succession and Public Policy Under Capitalism and Socialism* (Princeton: Princeton University Press, 1980); Thomas Cronin, *The State of the Presidency* (Boston: Little and Brown, 1975); Casey Byrne Knudsen Dominguez, "Is It a Honeymoon? An Empirical Investigation of the President's First Hundred Days," *Congress and the Presidency* 32 (2005); Paul Light, *The President's Agenda* (Baltimore: Johns Hopkins University Press, 1983); Nolan McCarty and Keith T. Poole, "Veto Power and Legislation: An Empirical Analysis of Executive-Legislative Bargaining from 1961–1986," *Journal of Law, Economics, and Organization* 11 (1995); James Pfiffner, *The Strategic Presidency: Hitting the Ground Running* (Chicago: Dorsey, 1987). But see John Frendreis, Raymond Tatalovich, and Jon Schaff, "Predicting Legislative Output in the First One-Hundred Days, 1897–1995," *Political Research Quarterly* 54 (2001).

7. McCarty and Poole, "Veto Power," 285.

8. Dominguez, "Is It a Honeymoon"; Frendreis, Tatalovich, and Schaff, "Predicting Legislative Output."

9. Bunce, *Do New Leaders Make a Difference?*; Cronin, *State of the Presidency*.

10. Dominguez, "Is It a Honeymoon"; Paul Light, "The Focusing Skill and Presidential Influence in Congress," in *Congressional Politics*, ed. Christopher Deering (Chicago: Dorsey, 1989).

11. Brad Lockerbie, Stephen Borrelli, and Scott Hedger, "An Integrative Approach to Modeling Presidential Success in Congress," *Political Research Quarterly* 51 (1998); McCarty and Poole, "Veto Power"; Douglas Rivers and Nancy L. Rose, "Passing the President's Program: Public Opinion and Presidential Influence in Congress," *American Journal of Political Science* 29 (1985).

12. Elmer E. Cornwell, "The President and the Press: Phases in the Relationship," *Annals of the American Academy of Political Science* 427 (1976): 53–64; Michael Baruch Grossman and Martha Joynt Kumar, *Portraying the President* (Baltimore: Johns Hopkins University Press, 1981); Jarol B. Manheim, "The Honeymoon's Over: The News Conference and the Development of Presidential Style," *Journal of Politics* 41 (1979): 55–74.

13. Richard A. Brody, *Assessing the President: The Media, Elite Opinion and Public Support* (Stanford, CA: Stanford University Press, 1991); Richard E. Neustadt,

"The Contemporary Presidency: The Presidential 'Hundred Days': An Overview," *Presidential Studies Quarterly* 31 (2001); Rivers and Rose, "President's Program."

14. Bunce, *Do New Leaders Make a Difference?*.

15. J. C. March and J. G. March, "Performance Sampling in Social Matches," *Administrative Science Quarterly* 23 (1978); William H. James, "The Honeymoon Effect on Marital Coitus," *The Journal of Sex Research* 17 (1981).

16. See e.g., Mark Fichman and Daniel A. Levinthal, "Honeymoons and the Liability of Adolescence: A New Perspective on Duration Dependence in Social and Organizational Relationships," *The Academy of Management Review* 16 (1991); James C. March and James G. March, "Almost Random Careers: The Wisconsin School Superintendency," *Administrative Science Quarterly* 22 (1977).

17. Fichman and Levinthal, "Honeymoons and the Liability of Adolescence," 445.

18. Jeffrey Rosen, "Roberts's Rules," *Atlantic Monthly* 499 (2007).

19. Ibid.

20. See e.g., Gregory A. Caldeira and James L. Gibson, "The Etiology of Public Support for the Supreme Court," *American Journal of Political Science* 36 (1992); A. Cox, *The Role of the Supreme Court in American Government* (New York: Oxford University Press, 1976); Jeffrey J. Mondak, "Policy Legitimacy and the Supreme Court: The Sources and Context of Legitimation," *Political Research Quarterly* 47 (1994); Jeffrey J. Mondak and Shannon I. Smithey, "The Dynamics of Public Support for the Supreme Court," *Journal of Politics* 59 (1997).

21. See e.g., Learned Hand, *The Bill of Rights* (Cambridge, MA: Harvard University Press, 1958); James F. Spriggs II, and Thomas G. Hansford, "Explaining the Overruling of U.S. Supreme Court Precedent," *Journal of Politics* 63 (2001).

22. Lee Epstein, Jeffrey A. Segal, and Harold J. Spaeth, "The Norm of Consensus on the U.S. Supreme Court," *American Journal of Political Science* 45 (2001): 376.

23. Bill Barnhart, "Roberts Strives for Consensus on Court," *Chicago Tribune*, February 2, 2007, http://articles.chicagotribune.com/2007-02-02/news/0702020163_1_justices-court-politics-supreme-court.

24. Because of the specific hypotheses we test, appeals cases and cases appealed from state courts were necessarily excluded from the analysis.

25. Harold J. Spaeth, *The United States Supreme Court Judicial Database, 1953–2006 Terms* (Lexington: S. Sidney Ulmer Project for Research in Law and Judicial Politics, Department of Political Science, University of Kentucky, 2007).

26. Ordered logit models assume adherence to the parallel lines assumption, or the notion that the slopes between each cut point of each variable are equal. If the parallel lines assumption is violated, alternative estimation techniques relax this assumption and estimate separate relationships for each independent variable at every cut point of the dependent variable. Using the Brant test, we found that a few of the independent variables violated the parallel lines assumption. We thus re-estimated the models using both multinomial logit and a Partial Proportional Odds model (which relaxes the parallel lines assumption only for those variables that violate it). The results from the ordered logit model presented here remained robust across the various estimation methods and so we present the ordered logit model given that the model itself is more parsimonious and the interpretation more straightforward.

27. See e.g., Danelski, "Influence of the Chief Justice" (1980); Walker, Epstein, and Dixon, "On the Mysterious Demise."

28. Jeffrey A. Segal and Harold J. Spaeth, *The Supreme Court and the Attitudinal Model* (New York: Cambridge University Press, 1993); Harold J. Spaeth and Jeffrey A. Segal, *Majority Rule or Minority Will: Adherence to Precedent on the U.S. Supreme Court* (Cambridge: Cambridge University Press, 2001).

29. Mark S. Hurwitz and Drew Lanier, "I Respectfully Dissent: Consensus, Agendas and Policymaking on the U.S. Supreme Court, 1888–1997," *Review of Policy Research* 21 (2004).

30. C. Herman Pritchett, *The Roosevelt Court: A Study in Judicial Politics and Values, 1937–1947* (New York: Macmillan, 1948).

31. See also Sheldon Goldman, "Backgrounds, Attitudes, and the Voting Behavior of Judges: A Comment on Grossman's 'Backgrounds and Judicial Decisions,'" *Journal of Politics* 31 (1969); George L. Priest and Benjamin Klein, "The Selection of Disputes for Litigation," *Journal of Legal Studies* 13 (1984); Epstein, Segal, and Spaeth "Norm of Consensus."

32. Goldman, "Backgrounds, Attitudes, and the Voting Behavior of Judges," 219.

33. Pamela C. Corley, Amy Steigerwalt, and Artemus Ward, *The Puzzle of Unanimity: Consensus on the United States Supreme Court* (Stanford, CA: Stanford University Press, 2013).

34. Ibid.

35. Lee Epstein and Jeffrey A. Segal, "Measuring Issue Salience," *American Journal of Political Science* 44 (2000).

36. Joel B. Grossman and Richard S. Wells, *Constitutional Law and Judicial Policy Making* (New York: Longman, 1989), 59.

37. Epstein and Segal, "Measuring Issue Salience."

38. Saul Brenner and Theodore S. Arrington. "Unanimous Decisions Making on the U.S. Supreme Court," *Political Behavior* 9 (1987); Thomas R. Hensley and Scott P. Johnson. "Unanimity on the Rehnquist Court," *Akron Law Review* 31 (1998); Hurwitz and Lanier, "I Respectfully Dissent."

39. If the case was reargued, we used the date the case was reargued.

40. Given the consistency of the results across model specifications, we present predicted probabilities for the two logit models as they are more easily interpretable.

41. Rosen, "Roberts's Rules."

42. Walter F. Murphy, *Elements of Judicial Strategy* (Chicago: University of Chicago Press, 1964), 89.

43. Segal and Spaeth, *The Supreme Court and the Attitudinal Model*; Spaeth and Segal, *Majority Rule*.

44. Fred P. Graham, "180 Years of Chief Justices: Some Nonentities, Some Giants," *New York Times*, June 24, 1969, 25.

45. Bernard Schwartz, *Super Chief: Earl Warren and His Supreme Court—A Judicial Biography* (New York: New York University Press, 1983).

46. Ibid.

10 ~ Genuine Leader or Merely "First Among Equals"?

Probing the Leadership Capacity of the Chief Justice

BRANDON L. BARTELS AND PHILLIP J. WININGER

During his confirmation hearings, Chief Justice John Roberts articulated one of his main objectives for the Court: "I do think the chief justice has a particular obligation to try to achieve consensus consistent with everyone's individual oath to uphold the Constitution, and that would certainly be a priority for me." Roberts's statement reflects a normative view that chief justices should use their position on the Court to pursue institutional maintenance, or act in ways that help preserve the Court's integrity, public image, and legitimacy. Such concerns recently entered the forefront during the highly salient *National Federation of Independent Business v. Sebelius*,[1] wherein Chief Justice Roberts drafted a majority opinion that upheld the controversial Affordable Care Act of 2010. Many commentators argued that he saved the statute—despite conservative views that may have led him to decide otherwise—in order for the Court to avoid the muddy waters of the intense political battle over health care.

Roberts's decision in the health care case, along with his statement, suggests a key empirical question: Do chief justices systematically behave in ways that demonstrate a special effort or ability to pursue institutional maintenance? Although generally labeled the "first among equals," chiefs do exercise certain powers that may enable them to fulfill this role. Chief justices, for example, control opinion assignment as a member of the majority coalition—a process studied by various political scientists.[2] The chief's pursuit of institutional maintenance, however, may extend beyond these more "formal" powers. While David Danelski cautioned that the role of chief justice does not guarantee special sway with the Court, he recognized that the chief can use his personal interactions with other justices to empower himself as a social leader.[3] Danelski's insights suggest that if chiefs are truly more than just "first among equals" with respect to institutional maintenance, they may demonstrate special leadership capacity or attention to these concerns even when formal norms or rules provide that they behave just like an associate justice. Thus our research seeks to explore these more "informal" contours of the chief justices' behavior and leadership capacity on the Court.

While extant research illuminates chief justice behavior in several limited contexts,[4] we shift focus to a broadly systematic study of multiple empirical implications designed to test the degree to which the chiefs may or may not use their role to pursue institutional maintenance, a study that incorporates five chief justices and data ranging from 1946 to 2010. More specifically, we contend that several empirical implications should flow from an institutionally minded chief justice, three of which we test for here: he should enhance the Court's unity by acting to build larger coalitions as the majority opinion writer, more readily join the majority following an initial conference dissent, and more forcefully adhere to or cite authoritative precedent so as to perpetuate perceptions of institutional and legal legitimacy. No formal norm mandates that the chiefs pursue these ends. But if the chiefs are in fact the caretakers of institutional maintenance, we suggest that such behavior should manifest itself in the chief to a greater extent than in the associate justices.

In order to evaluate these empirical implications, the analysis proceeds in four parts: (1) setting the context of chief justice leadership; (2) theoretical framework and associated empirical implications; (3) an overview of data and variables; and (4) a description of findings. Because this research delves into informal norms of behavior, rather than formal chief justice powers, it sets a high bar for evidence of a legitimacy-minded chief. Despite this heightened standard, some evidence emerges. The findings, even though primarily descriptive and exploratory, suggest that some of the chiefs—notably Vinson, Warren, and Burger—acted to build larger majority coalitions and exhibited a strong propensity to change votes in accordance with majority will. This research, however, does not yield conclusive evidence across all empirical implications and all chief justices explored in the study, and it suggests that factors such as increased polarization on the Court over time may impede the chief's efforts at institutional maintenance.

Probing Chief Justice Behavior

Political scientists have not shied away from studying the behavior of justices who carry the special title of chief. Much of this research centers on how chief justices use their small collection of special powers, including opinion assignment and the ability to speak or vote first at private conference, to advance policy or other goals.[5] Other studies examine how chiefs may advance goals in circumstances when chiefs and associates presumably carry equal power, such as the drafting of dissents and concurring opinions.[6] In all, this body of work lays groundwork for the research presented here, research intended to more squarely and systematically probe the chief justice's ties to institutional maintenance.

With respect to formal powers, researchers conclude that such powers have helped the chiefs advance multiple goals. Various political scientists have explored the degree to which chief justices use opinion assignment to pursue either policy goals or organizational/institutional goals.[7] Forrest Maltzman and Paul Wahlbeck, for example, analyze opinion assignments by Chief Justice Rehnquist and find that he pursued policy in close, salient cases by disproportionately assigning opinions to his ideological friends.[8] Meanwhile, he also pursued organizational goals, such as operational efficiency, by disproportionately assigning opinions to justices who timely completed prior assignments or who may have exhibited special expertise regarding the issues at hand. Scholars have extended analysis to other chief justice powers, such as the ability to speak and vote first at private conference.[9]

Collectively, this research demonstrates that chief justices may use their special powers to advance multiple goals, goals that include both policy and institutional maintenance. Execution of these formal powers gives rise to the best case scenario for chief justice leadership, as these powers directly place chiefs in a commanding role over associates. Alternatively, a more regimented test of the chief's leadership capacity should account for behavior and interactions in situations in which the chiefs and associates presumably exert equal formal power. All justices, for example, share the power to draft dissents and concurrences. To this end, multiple scholars have sought to determine whether chiefs and associates differ in the extent to which they draft dissents and concurrences. They find that chief justices write fewer of these opinions.[10] Some scholars argue that this finding may reflect the chief's special attention to institutional concerns; they may reduce the number of concurring and dissenting opinions in order to lead the way toward more consensus on the Court so as to project a positive institutional image.[11]

Although this research singularly focuses on opinion drafting, it suggests that the chiefs may exhibit special behavior and seek to lead the Court, even outside of their formal duties. As Danelski has argued, being "chief" opens the door for a justice to assert himself as a social leader on the Court, leadership that may advance beyond the mere collection of formal powers he maintains.[12] Several scholars, for example, have studied whether chief justices have been able to assert leadership to guide the Court in particular policy directions. Sue Davis explores whether Rehnquist may have been partly responsible for a rightward shift in the Court after he was promoted to chief, but she finds little support for this proposition.[13] On the other hand, Joseph Kobylka argues—based on a qualitative study of Burger's votes, assignments, and written opinions—that he was able to move the Court toward greater accommodation of religion under the Establishment Clause.[14] And Frank Cross and Stefanie Lindquist suggest that the Rehnquist Court moved in a more activist direction on certain issues such as federalism and states' rights.[15] Thus while the findings of these studies are mixed, they suggest the potential for the chief to assert broad policy leadership.

Such leadership, or lack thereof, may also advance or undermine institutional maintenance. To this end, multiple scholars have attempted to determine the causal factors behind the demise of the so-called "norm of consensus" whereby the Court historically acted in a more unified manner when voting and issuing opinions.[16] Collectively, this research suggests that multiple causal factors may underlie the demise, including ideological dispersion and polarization, the growth in "hard" cases and a discretionary docket, and the political context.[17] And, notably, much of this research also suggests another major influence: the style of chief justice leadership. Thomas Walker, Lee Epstein, and William Dixon claim that Chief Justice Stone may have caused the demise through his failure to resolve acrimonious debates on the Court.[18] Stacia Haynie shifts focus to Chief Justice Hughes and claims that patterns of dissents and concurrences increased under his watch.[19] In latter studies, scholars examine voting patterns under the Burger and Rehnquist Courts to suggest through indirect aggregate analysis that these chiefs may have been responsible for altering levels of Court cohesion as well. Marcus Hendershot, et al., suggest that Burger may have contributed to a long-term trajectory toward dissenting behavior.[20] And Frank Cross and Stefanie Lindquist compare aggregate voting patterns under the Burger and Rehnquist Courts and find that the Rehnquist

Court experienced an overall increase in cohesion.[21] While quibbling over which chief justice may be the main cause, all these studies suggest that chief justice leadership may matter in enhancing, preserving, or diminishing unity on the Court in particular contexts.

In all, an existing body of research concludes that chief justices may play a special role in either advancing, or perhaps inhibiting, policy or institutional goals. In light of this disparate collection of work that examines bits and pieces of chief justice behavior, it is important to step back for a moment and contemplate a broader, more systematic analysis of chief justice behavior, an analysis that zeroes in on institutional maintenance. In other words, while research shows that chief justice leadership may influence the Court in particular contexts or time periods, can we render any conclusions about whether chiefs systematically behave in ways different from associates with respect to institutional maintenance? And to what extent may a special attention to institutional maintenance be reflected in chief justice behavior beyond his special formal powers? These remain open questions that we intend to probe further.

Sizing Up the Chief Justice as an Institutional Legitimizer

An attempt to answer these questions starts with a theoretical account as to why the chief justice may or may not pursue institutional maintenance. On one hand, theory suggests that chiefs should be primarily policy-oriented, as predicted by the attitudinal model of Supreme Court decision making.[22] If so, chiefs may consistently favor policy goals over institutional goals so that little systematic evidence of an institutionally minded chief justice exists. Alternatively, theory also suggests that justices—notably chief justices—may care about institutional legitimacy and maintenance because the Court has no formal enforcement mechanisms and therefore relies on the goodwill of the other branches of government, the states, and the American public for implementation of and compliance with its rulings. If this is the case, certain empirical implications should follow, as set forth below.

As a starting point, many legal scholars agree with the contention that since Supreme Court justices serve life terms, sit atop the judicial hierarchy, and have discretionary jurisdiction to choose which cases they will hear, justices have significant discretion to pursue their personal policy preferences.[23] Research shows, for example, that chief justices can be policy-driven, just like any other justice, and that they may use their position as chief to this end.[24] This portrait of a policy-oriented chief justice suggests that chiefs consistently keep their eye on the ball of policy goals while downplaying attention to other worthy goals such as institutional maintenance.

Despite the predominance of the attitudinal model, however, various research demonstrates that ideology may not fully explain or predict judicial decision making. Other forces are potentially at play. Legal norms may force justices to set aside their preferred policy choice, justices may listen to public opinion or congressional preferences, or justices may be compelled to strategically accommodate others on the Court.[25] Further, as Lawrence Baum has explained, justices may seek to satisfy multiple external audiences, including the public and other political institutions.[26] Thus the portrayal of a single-minded, policy-oriented chief justice may be an oversimplification. Indeed, research recognizes that chief justices pursue multiple goals—including ideological and institutional objectives—when fulfilling their duties on the Court.[27]

Among the collection of forces that may influence judicial decision making, concerns with judicial legitimacy are particularly relevant here. It is well-recognized that the Supreme Court may constitute a weak institution in that it lacks the power of the "purse or sword." In other words, the judiciary relies upon other political and societal actors to properly enforce judicial mandates. If society loses regard for the judiciary or its rulings, judges may find themselves to be inept actors in an institution powerless to bring about societal change.[28]

While judicial legitimacy tends be resilient over time in the eyes of the public,[29] various scholars suggest that public perceptions matter to the health of the judiciary and, consequently, have deeply analyzed how these perceptions may ebb and flow depending upon various contexts and circumstances.[30] To this end, a Supreme Court that consistently projects itself as an ideologically driven, divided institution may lose esteem in the eyes of the public over time. This concern with the Court's image as a united or divided institution is widespread and readily apparent. Though scholarship has shown that the Court's legitimacy is apparently immune to even the most ideologically divided and salient decisions, like *Bush v. Gore*,[31] scholars have generated considerable research on judicial norms of consensus or dissensus.[32] And both former and current Supreme Court justices, such as Sandra Day O'Connor and John Roberts, have repeatedly expressed the importance of legitimacy, unity, and the Court's public image.

These examples illustrate that various actors, both internal and external to the Court, are mindful of and emphasize the importance of institutional maintenance, particularly with respect to unity on the Court. Thus it is logical to surmise that chief justices may feel a special pressure to pursue this form of institutional maintenance due to their unique role on the Court: they carry a special title, exercise special formal powers, oversee the Court's administration, and represent the Court to the public and other political institutions. Thus chief justices may assume the role of a social leader on the Court who must be especially attentive to institutional maintenance.[33]

While formal powers, such as opinion assignment, may be used for such institutional goals,[34] Supreme Court dynamics may also allow for special leadership by the chief outside of these formal powers. Political scientists widely acknowledge that the Court's decision making occurs within a strategic bargaining environment whereby justices may negotiate over votes and opinion content.[35] After all, no justice is a lone actor on the Court; he or she must pursue policy or other goals under the constraints of colleagues. This bargaining environment opens the door for a justice—namely, the chief justice—to assert leadership through personal interactions with others. While most research on bargaining and accommodation examines how justices pursue policy goals in this setting, it is plausible that the chief justice may leverage this environment for purposes of institutional maintenance, particularly with respect to the Court's unity.[36] The chief, for example, may use his bargaining powers to compile larger majority coalitions when he acts as the majority opinion writer. We thus expect this general empirical implication to hold:

> H1A: *Chief justices will be more likely than associate justices to build sizeable majority coalitions when acting as the majority opinion writer.*

Causal ambiguity exists with this hypothesis due to the possibility that the chief justice may assign himself opinions where large majority coalitions already exist. Alternatively, the chief may take cases where there is a close vote in order to try to persuade minority justices to join the majority. In other words, the fact that the chief will assign the majority opinion whenever he is in the majority leads to the possibility of selection effects. We can get leverage on this issue, however, by looking at "voting fluidity" between the conference vote on the merits and the final merits vote. An institutionally minded chief should be particularly intent on persuading initial dissenters to join the majority coalition and retaining large majority coalitions. Thus the following related empirical implications may unfold:

H1B: *Chief justices will be more likely than associate justices to (1) persuade initial conference dissenters to join the majority coalition, and (2) retain as many justices in the conference majority as possible.*

These first hypotheses require the chief to be particularly mindful of court unity and exert leadership to this end. In other words, the chief cannot achieve such unity absent his ability to persuade votes from other justices. But even if the chief is unable to sway the associate justices, he fully controls his own votes at all times. Voting fluidity may therefore evidence the chief's special mindfulness toward institutional maintenance and legitimacy, even when he is not the opinion writer and does not exercise power over other justices. If the chief contemplates institutional concerns more so than his colleagues, he may be more apt to rethink an initial dissent for the sake of court unity. An initial conference dissent may indicate an attitudinal predisposition against the majority, a policy position that subsequently gives way to the chief's desire to promote a unified Court. This suggests a hypothesis regarding the chief's propensity for voting fluidity:

H2: *Chief justices will be more likely than associate justices to acquiesce and join majority coalitions after dissenting in conference.*

A pursuit of institutional maintenance may extend to other areas beyond Court unity. As Lee Epstein and Jack Knight argue, institutional legitimacy demands a "norm of stare decisis," which constrains judicial behavior.[37] Research indicates that the public expects the courts to serve a legal role in consistently applying established legal doctrine over time.[38] While much of the American public recognizes that justices have discretion and do not necessarily follow a "mechanical jurisprudence" legal model, they also perceive the justices as using such discretion in a principled manner, which allows the Court to maintain ample levels of legitimacy.[39] If judges stray far from established legal rules or exercise discretion in an unprincipled manner, public or community expectations can be violated and the public's willingness to accept or comply with such decisions may diminish. Judges are socialized to defer to legal precedent in order to preserve long-term legitimacy, even though they may desire alternative outcomes in particular cases.[40] And evidence of legal norms is abundant: attorneys frame cases around legal doctrine; judges cite legal doctrine in their decisions; attorneys and judges debate legal doctrine in court hearings; and judges talk about legal doctrine in private conferences.[41]

This discussion suggests that legally principled decisions may be important to an institutionally minded chief justice. A chief justice, over and above associates, may strive to portray a norm of stare decisis by grounding his decisions in legally authoritative precedent. Thus if the chief justice constitutes the caretaker of institutional maintenance, a second hypothesis may unfold:

> H3: *Chief justices will be more likely than associate justices to forcefully adhere to or cite authoritative precedent in majority opinions.*

In our analysis, we also pay particular attention to how the chief's behavior compares to associates in highly salient cases that the public is more likely to hear about. If institutional maintenance motivations are influencing chief justices, they may be enhanced in highly salient cases in which the chief may seek to put an especially good face on the Court. We also note that these hypotheses may not exhaust all ways in which a chief justice may or may not pursue institutional maintenance. But they lay the foundation for a study of such behavior across a broad range of justices, cases, votes, and opinions. In other words, if a chief justice is more attentive systematically to institutional maintenance, some or all of these empirical implications should appear.

Data and Variables

To test Hypotheses 1a and 3, we gathered data from the Supreme Court Database[42] spanning five chief justices—Vinson, Warren, Burger, Rehnquist, and Roberts—and the years 1946–2010. Data relevant to H3 (authority of precedent) only extends to 2002. We use the Court's decision in a case as the unit of analysis, and we examine all formally decided cases that listed a majority opinion writer. We excluded formally decided per curiam decisions. This leaves us with 6,723 cases. In each case, we have a measure of which justice wrote the majority opinion.

Variables

The hypotheses call for operationalization of several variables:

- *Margin of victory* (H1a) is simply the *number of majority votes* minus the *number of minority votes*. Thus the larger the vote margin, the larger the majority coalition. This measure is preferable to the number of majority votes since not all cases contain nine votes (due to brief vacancies and recusals).

- *Unanimous outcome* (H1a): Given the traditional focus on the chief justice pushing for unanimous outcomes, we also measure whether the Court produces a unanimous outcome (=1) or not (=0).
- *Closely divided outcomes* (H1a): Essentially the opposite of the prior variable, this variables measures whether decides a case by a one-vote margin (e.g., a 5-4 outcome) (=1) or not (=0).
- *Authority of Precedent* (H3) assesses the overall authority of precedent cited within a majority opinion. To quantify precedential authority, the analysis presented here incorporates a measure developed and employed by Fowler and Jeon.[43] This measure—a "hub score"—calculates both the number of precedent citations and the authoritativeness of those citations to arrive at an overall measure, with higher values reflecting the greater extent to which a majority opinion is well-grounded in the law.
- *Case Salience* (H1a and H3): Because we are interested in whether institutional maintenance concerns among the chief justice are heightened in cases receiving greater attention from the media and public discourse, we measures salience using Epstein and Segal's measure for whether the Court's decision appeared on the front page of the *New York Times* (=1) or not (=0).[44]

Hypotheses 1b and 2. Testing these hypotheses requires an analysis of justices' conference (preliminary) votes and their final votes to investigate instances of voting fluidity and, more specifically, instances of "conforming behavior," where dissenting justices at conference subsequently join the majority opinion, and "retention behavior," where justices in the majority at conference remain in the majority for the final opinion. For this analysis, we rely on the Vinson-Warren Supreme Court Judicial Database[45] and the Expanded Burger Court Judicial Database.[46] Systematic data for analyzing voting fluidity are limited to just three chief justice eras: Vinson, Warren, and Burger. We analyze 730 cases during the Vinson Court, 1,536 during Warren, and 2,408 during Burger.

For H1b, we are interested in majority opinion authors' "conformity rates" (presiding over switches from minority to majority) and "retention rates" (presiding over instances where justices stay in the majority). To calculate conformity rates for each case, we divide the number of justices who switched from minority (in conference) to majority (final vote) by the total number of justices in the minority at conference. To calculate retention rates for each case, we divide the total number of justices who were in the majority in the final vote by the total number of justices in the majority at the conference vote. We perform this analysis at the case level and calculate these two rates for each justice when he or she wrote the majority opinion. Testing H2 requires analyzing all justice-votes and comparing justices' frequencies of switching from the minority in conference to the majority for the final vote.

Analytical Strategy and Results

Our analytical strategy for the hypotheses proceeds in two parts. For each hypothesis, we first compare the chief justice's behavior to each associate justice with whom the chief served during his tenure in order to examine whether the chief engages in each institutional-maintenance-oriented behavior to a greater degree than each of the associate justices. Second, because we posit that the chief justice might be especially attuned to institutional maintenance concerns in highly salient decisions, we provide the same analysis for salient and nonsalient decisions separately. Because just 15 percent of the decisions in our data are coded as salient decisions, a small-*n* problem arises for certain justices within certain eras. Thus, in our examinations of salient versus nonsalient decisions, we limit our analysis and comparisons to justices who were majority opinion writers in at least ten salient decisions within each chief justice's time period. We return to descriptive statistics of majority authorship in salient versus nonsalient decisions further below. In addition, because the mission of this chapter is largely exploratory, we present our results below in terms of descriptive statistics.[47] Where appropriate, we discuss results in terms of statistical significance. We discuss the voting fluidity analysis central to Hypothesis 1b following the discussion of Hypothesis 1a.

Hypothesis 1a: Majority Coalitions

We first address whether the chief as majority author presides over larger majority coalitions than his associate justice colleagues. As discussed, we use three measures to capture this concept: (1) average margin of victory (#majority votes – #minority votes), (2) proportion of unanimous outcomes, and (3) proportion of outcomes with one-vote margins (e.g., 5-4 outcomes). Figure 10.1 presents the results for each "chief justice era" separately. Within each era, we present averages of each measure among each majority author. For all three measures, justices are sorted from greatest

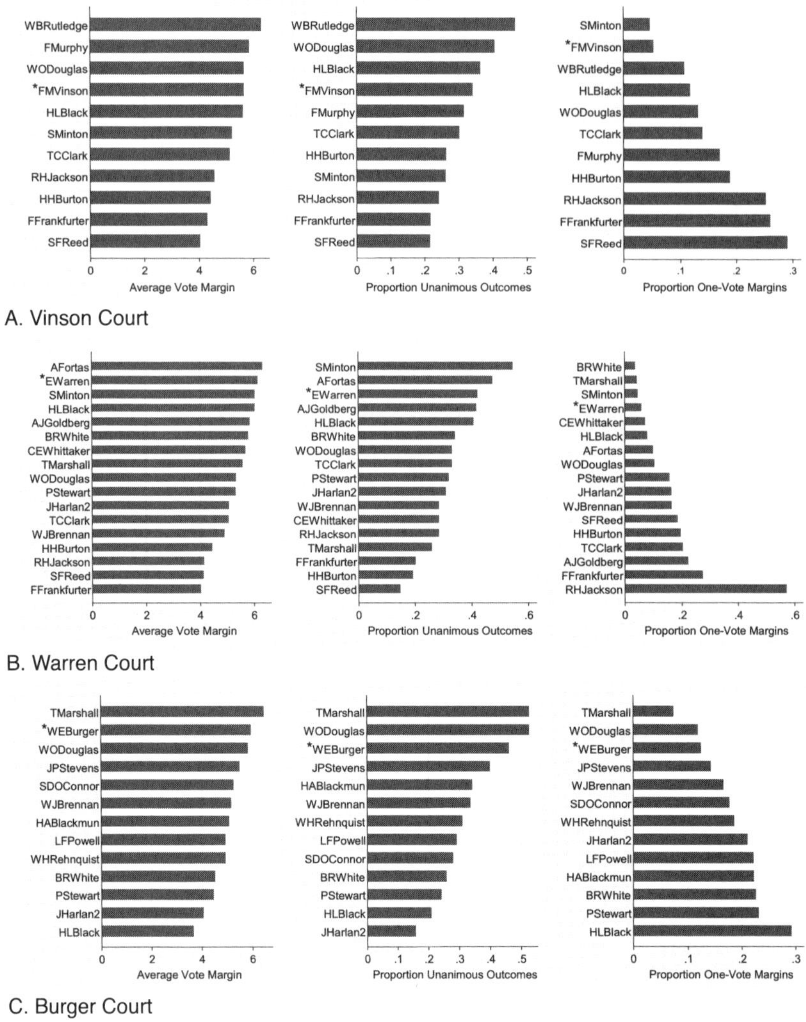

Fig. 10.1. Average vote margins, proportions of unanimous outcomes, and one-vote margins among majority opinion authors (Hypothesis 1a)

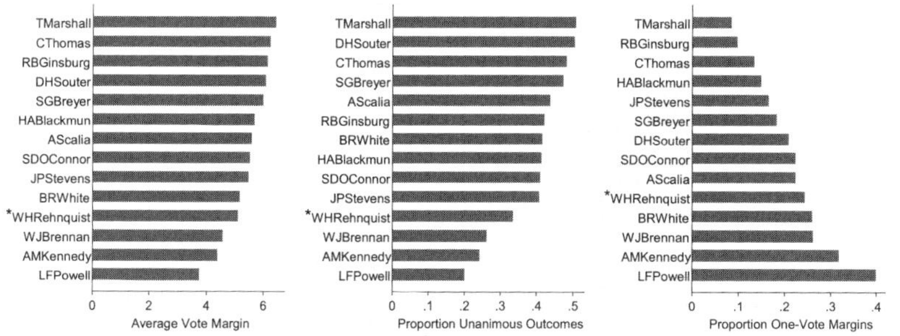

D. Rehnquist Court

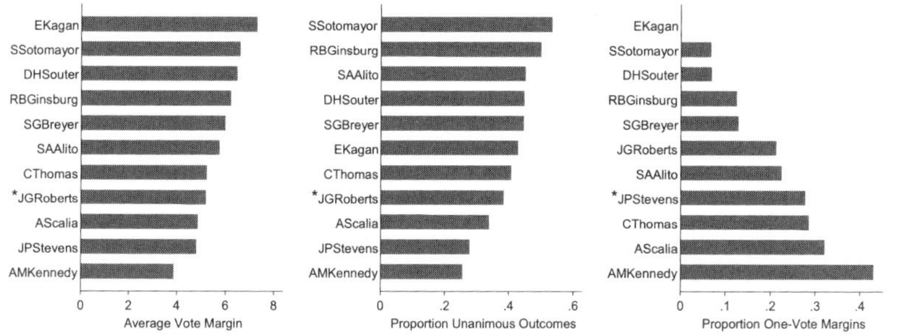

E. Roberts Court

Fig. 10.1. (continued)

"majority size" (i.e., greater margin of victory, more unanimous outcomes, and fewer 5-4 outcomes) to smallest. We have placed an asterisk next to the name of the chief justice in each set of graphs.

Figure 10.1 reveals that during the first three eras, Chief Justices Vinson, Warren, and Burger built or maintained among the largest majorities when they were majority opinion authors relative to their associate justice colleagues in their respective eras. Figure 10.1a displays how Chief Justice Vinson averaged a robust vote margin just shy of six (something between an 8-1 and 7-2 vote margin), which falls just behind Douglas, Murphy, and Rutledge (who authored just twenty-eight majority opinions in the data), though the differences between Vinson and these three justices are not statistically significant.[48] Vinson secured a substantially larger margin of victory as majority author than several of his colleagues, particularly Justices Jackson, Burton, Frankfurter, and Reed (each of these four differences is statistically significant). Vinson also secured more unanimous outcomes as majority author than his colleagues. Roughly 35 percent of the opinions he authored were signed on to by all the justices; only Black, Douglas, and Rutledge top that rate, with Douglas just topping 40 percent and Rutledge nearing 50 percent (though recall the small n for Rutledge). But Vinson did best seven of his colleagues in securing unanimous opinions, though none of those differences are statistically significant at the .05 level. Reed, Frankfurter, and Jackson are again toward the bottom of the ranking, securing unanimity at a rate between 20 and 25 percent. Finally, Vinson was among the most successful at minimizing closely divided (e.g., 5-4) outcomes, registering only about 5 percent. Only Justice Minton eclipsed that rate, though this difference is not statistically significant. In fact, Chief Justice Vinson secured a significantly lower rate of 5-4 outcomes as majority author than five (the bottom five in the graph) of his colleagues. Once again, Jackson, Reed, and Frankfurter seem to be the least likely to build unanimity during the Vinson era, which fits with past perspectives, particularly with respect to Frankfurter and Jackson and the battles they had with Justices Black and Douglas. On the whole, while Vinson was not significantly better at securing larger majorities and more unanimity than all of his colleagues, he certainly ranks among the highest in these categories.

Figure 10.1b shows that a similar story emerges for Chief Justice Warren, who topped all but one (Justice Fortas) of his fellow associate justices in average margin of victory as majority author. Like Vinson, Warren boasted an average margin victory of nearly six, and the difference between Warren and Fortas is not statistically significant. Warren's margin of victory as majority author is substantially and significantly larger than Justice Douglas and the justices that fall below him (Stewart, Harlan, etc.). As in the Vinson Court, Justices Reed, Frankfurter, and Jackson registered the lowest margin of victories as majority authors, though Jackson and Reed were not on the Warren Court for long and therefore did not author many majority opinions during this era. Warren also topped most of his colleagues in securing unanimity (over 40 percent) and minimizing closely divided voting outcomes (under 6 percent) as majority author. Minton's (who authored just twenty-two majority opinions during the Warren Court) and Fortas's unanimity rates are not significantly higher than Warren's, and Warren's rate is substantively greater than several of his colleagues and significantly higher than five of his colleagues. Results for one-vote margin outcomes is similar: Warren had among the lowest rates of closely divided vote margins, his rate is not significantly lower than the three justices above him, and he has a substantially lower rate than many of his colleagues and significantly lower than nine of his colleagues.

Figure 10.1c shows a similar pattern for Chief Justice Burger as was seen for Chief Justices Vinson and Warren. Though only Justice Marshall secured a larger vote margin (a difference that is actually statistically significant), Burger's vote margin of nearly six (similar to Vinson and Warren) is substantively higher than several of Burger's colleagues and significantly higher than nine of his colleagues (from O'Connor downward in Figure 10.1c). Burger secured unanimous outcomes in nearly 50 percent of the majorities he commanded, a figure substantively higher than Vinson and Warren, and authored closely divided (one-vote margin) opinions just 12 percent of the time. Both rates are topped by Douglas and Marshall only, though the differences between Burger and these two justices are not statistically significant for either facet. For unanimity, Burger exhibited a significantly higher rate than nine of his colleagues, and for one-vote margin outcomes he exhibited a significantly lower rate than six of his colleagues.

While Burger, Vinson, and Warren seem to show some semblance of leadership on the Court in terms of building majority coalitions as majority author and topping several, but certainly not all, of their associate colleagues, the same cannot be said for Chief Justice Rehnquist, whose average vote margin of just above five ranks toward the bottom compared to his colleagues. Moreover, Rehnquist's average is significantly lower than five of his colleagues and significantly higher than only one of his colleagues. Congruous results emerge for unanimity and closely divided votes, where Rehnquist's rate is 33 percent for the former (much lower than his predecessors) and 24 percent for the latter (much higher than his predecessors). Just as Burger, Warren, and Vinson reflected similar patterns for the 1946–1986 terms, results for Chief Justice Roberts reflect the pattern established by Rehnquist. We should note that the number of cases is not large for the Roberts Court ($n = 422$), and thus there is a small-n problem for some of the newer justices (particularly Sotomayor and Kagan). But the pattern is fairly clear: Roberts's average vote margin of just above five (similar to Rehnquist's) ranks toward the bottom compared to his colleagues. The only justice Roberts was significantly higher than was Kennedy, whose average margin is just under four. Roberts's unanimity rate is just shy of 40 percent, higher than Rehnquist's but lower than many of his colleagues. Roberts's rate for very close cases is just over 20 percent, similar to Rehnquist's and about the middle of the pack among his colleagues.

On the whole, Hypothesis 1a does not find significant support from the data, though Vinson, Warren, and Burger appear to show higher margins of victory and higher rates of unanimity as majority authors than many of the associate justices with whom they served, though they also show lower rates than some of their colleagues. The fact that Rehnquist and Roberts do not appear to be as successful as their predecessors in securing larger majorities, speaking with one voice, and reducing the occurrence of 5-4 decisions could be due to the rise of ideological polarization on the Court. Where the Warren Court was filled with several liberal justices, particularly in the 1960s, the Burger Court had more individuals on both extremes (Brennan and Marshall on the left, Rehnquist and Burger on the right), though it had a robust middle with several swing justices, including Justices Stewart, Powell, and White, and eventually Justices Blackmun and Stevens, both of whom underwent ideological drift from the right to the left during the Burger era. Of course, the middle began to shrink in the later 1980s and into the 1990s, with the retirements of these swing justices from the Burger era. By the mid-1990s, after the appointments of Ginsburg and Breyer, the Court was fairly polarized, with four quite reliable liberals (Breyer, Ginsburg, Souter, Stevens), three reliable conservatives (Scalia, Thomas, and Rehnquist) and two right-of-center justices (Kennedy and O'Connor) who were capable of casting significant liberal votes but still voted conservatively more than liberally.

From figure 10.1 and the discussion of the results, one can also see some potential "opinion-assignment effects" potentially confounding some of the patterns in the results. For instance, in the Burger, Rehnquist, and Roberts Courts, we see that many of the swing justices had among the lowest margins of victory and unanimity rates. This could be because the chief justice (or whoever the senior member of the majority coalition is) assigns cases where the preliminary merit votes are very close to a moderate, swing justice in order to preserve the majority coalition. Moreover, the chief justice could be assigning himself some of these closely divided cases in conference in order to hold together the majority. So even in closely divided cases, the chief may be exerting leadership by attempting to hold together—but not necessarily expanding—the majority coalition. In the past when the Court was not so polarized, perhaps the task of expanding the majority was simpler, especially in highly salient cases, as in the famous anecdote of Warren seeking unanimity in *Brown v. Board of Education*. But in an age with greater polarization and more rigid ideologues who resist deferring to the majority opinion when they initially vote with the minority, merely holding together a thin majority coalition may be the best a chief—or any other justice—can ask for. We return to this issue in the analysis of voting fluidity (H1b).[49]

Salience

Are chief justices even more attuned to institutional maintenance concerns in salient cases where the public, the media, and politicians are paying more attention? Might they seek to build larger majorities and produce more consensus in these cases to show that the Court is "speaking with one voice" (a la Warren in *Brown*)? Such an inquiry presents a puzzle: Prior research shows that ideological divisions are more pronounced in salient cases than in nonsalient ones.[50] Such ideological divisions in these salient cases imply smaller coalitions and lower occurrences of unanimity. At the same time, chief justices tend to be majority opinion authors in salient cases at the highest rates compared to their associate justice colleagues. This is the case in our data. Do chief justices assign themselves salient decisions in order to at least *attempt* to have the Court speak in one voice, or are these institutional maintenance/legitimacy concerns not operative and the chief instead assigns himself these cases to make a significant policy imprint? Of course, in the contemporary era marked by greater polarization, there may be a mix of these motivations, with the chief wanting control over writing an opinion for a minimum winning coalition that, for instance, avoids conflict with the other branches (which some argue Roberts did in the 2012 health care ruling). While we cannot directly answer these questions with the current data, we can get some leverage on comparing vote margins and unanimity rates between the chief and his colleagues in both salient and nonsalient cases.

Table 10.1 presents the average margin of victory and unanimity rates for all justices in each of the five chief justice time periods. But it does so separately for salient and nonsalient cases and it includes the difference between the two for each justice. Recall that we analyze only justices who were majority opinion authors in at least ten salient cases. Within each chief justice era, Table 10.1 sorts justices by average margin of victory and unanimity rates in salient cases.

First off, a clear pattern emerges in table 10.1: Nearly all majority opinion authors see their margin of victory and unanimity rates decrease in salient cases. For the most part, this difference is similar for chiefs and associates alike. Justice Fortas seems to be a clear anomaly, where his average margin of victory and unanimity rate as majority writer skyrockets in salient cases compared to nonsalient cases. In the contemporary era, Chief Justices Rehnquist and Roberts have particularly lower values of both facets in salient cases compared to their predecessors, again potentially reflecting the rise of polarization on the Court.

On the whole, the results suggest a dilemma faced by the chief justice. Chiefs may want to write the majority opinion in salient cases (they do so at a greater rate than associate justices), perhaps in an effort to attempt to get the Court to speak with one voice, but these are also the cases that elicit

TABLE 10.1. Average Margin of Victory and Proportion of Unanimous Outcomes Among Majority Opinion Authors in Salient and Nonsalient Decisions (Hypothesis 1a)

Average Margin of Victory			
Maj. Auth.	Nonsalient	Salient	Difference
Vinson Court			
Black	5.65	5.22	–0.43
Vinson	**5.84**	**5.06**	**–0.79**
Douglas	5.76	4.92	–0.84
Reed	4.13	3.22	–0.91
Warren Court			
Fortas	5.73	8.10	2.37
Warren	**6.21**	**6.04**	**–0.17**
Harlan	5.06	5.04	–0.02
Black	6.29	4.94	–1.35
Douglas	5.43	4.83	–0.60
White	5.99	4.79	–1.20
Stewart	5.50	4.68	–0.82
Clark	5.16	4.52	–0.65
Brennan	5.12	4.36	–0.76
Frankfurter	4.12	3.67	–0.45
Burger Court			
Marshall	6.48	6.40	–0.08
Burger	**6.11**	**5.27**	**–0.83**
Black	2.50	4.50	2.00
White	4.58	4.22	–0.36
Stewart	4.54	3.96	–0.58
Rehnquist	5.16	3.80	–1.36
Powell	5.26	3.55	–1.71
Blackmun	5.24	3.42	–1.82
Stevens	5.78	3.24	–2.54
Brennan	5.47	3.10	–2.37
Rehnquist Court			
Blackmun	5.69	5.55	–0.14
Stevens	5.64	4.76	–0.88
Souter	6.24	4.71	–1.53
White	5.37	4.42	–0.96
Scalia	5.79	3.74	–2.05
Rehnquist	**5.67**	**3.46**	**–2.21**
Kennedy	4.71	3.14	–1.57
O'Connor	6.04	3.03	–3.01
Brennan	5.24	2.69	–2.56
Roberts Court			
Roberts	**5.45**	**4.13**	**–1.33**
Kennedy	4.24	2.09	–2.15

Average Proportion Unanimous Outcomes			
Maj. Auth.	Nonsalient	Salient	Difference
Vinson Court			
Black	0.37	0.33	–0.03
Vinson	**0.36**	**0.28**	**–0.08**
Douglas	0.43	0.23	–0.20
Reed	0.23	0.11	–0.12
Warren Court			
Fortas	0.40	0.70	0.30
White	0.34	0.36	0.02
Black	0.42	0.34	–0.08
Warren	**0.47**	**0.32**	**–0.15**
Harlan	0.31	0.30	–0.02
Clark	0.34	0.29	–0.05
Douglas	0.35	0.23	–0.12
Frankfurter	0.20	0.22	0.03
Stewart	0.35	0.21	–0.14
Brennan	0.32	0.20	–0.12
Burger Court			
Marshall	0.54	0.40	–0.14
Burger	**0.48**	**0.36**	**–0.12**
Black	0.10	0.29	0.19
White	0.27	0.20	–0.07
Stewart	0.25	0.18	–0.07
Brennan	0.36	0.17	–0.19
Rehnquist	0.34	0.15	–0.19
Stevens	0.43	0.12	–0.32
Powell	0.33	0.11	–0.22
Blackmun	0.36	0.11	–0.26
Rehnquist Court			
White	0.44	0.33	–0.11
Souter	0.53	0.29	–0.24
Blackmun	0.43	0.27	–0.16
Scalia	0.46	0.26	–0.19
Stevens	0.45	0.24	–0.21
Rehnquist	**0.39**	**0.18**	**–0.21**
Kennedy	0.28	0.11	–0.17
O'Connor	0.47	0.11	–0.36
Brennan	0.36	0.00	–0.36
Roberts Court			
Roberts	**0.45**	**0.13**	**–0.33**
Kennedy	0.28	0.09	–0.18

the highest degree of ideological divisions because the legal and policy stakes tend to be higher. So attempting to maximize the margin of victory or the chances of unanimity may be futile. On the other hand, the chief may simply want to write for the majority in salient cases for policy reasons.

Hypothesis 1b: Voting Fluidity, Conformity, and Retention Rates

As noted, ambiguity exists over the precise mechanism driving the results surrounding H1a. We note that there is no magic bullet for ascertaining this mechanism using our current data.[51] However, examining "switching" behavior from the conference vote on the merits to the final merits vote facilitates a more in-depth look at whether the chief justice is more intent on building and maintaining larger majority coalitions than his associate justice colleagues because it examines coalition expansion and maintenance *after* the opinion has already been assigned. Figures 10.2a and 10.2b show conformity and retention rates, respectively, for each majority opinion writer during the Vinson, Warren, and Burger eras. The graphs show the proportion of the time each justice, as majority author, attracted a conference dissenter (fig. 10.2a) and retained justices in the conference majority (fig. 10.2b).[52]

Figure 10.2a shows that Chief Justice Vinson presided over a conformity rate of nearly 50 percent, which bests the colleagues with which he served by a large margin. These results work in conjunction with our prior results showing that Vinson was near the top in his attempt to forge larger majority coalitions as opinion author. These results show that after opinion assignment, Vinson sought to—and was relatively successful at—enlarging the coalition by, for instance, persuasion, bargaining, or accommodation.[53] Chief Justice Warren was not quite as successful as Vinson in this venture and, at about a 40 percent rate, falls in the middle of the pack when compared to his colleagues. It is again intriguing to see how successful Justice Fortas was at forging consensus. Chief Justice Burger possessed an even lower conformity rate than Warren, at just over 30 percent, and again falls in the middle of the pack when compared to his colleagues. It appears that both Warren and Burger were either not as successful or not as concerned with building larger coalitions after opinion assignment than their colleagues. In sum, there appears to be a chief justice effect during the Vinson Court but not for the Warren and Burger Courts.

The retention rates in figure 10.2b show little differences across justices. While Vinson was the highest among his colleagues in conformity rates, he is the lowest for retention. His retention rate is still above 90

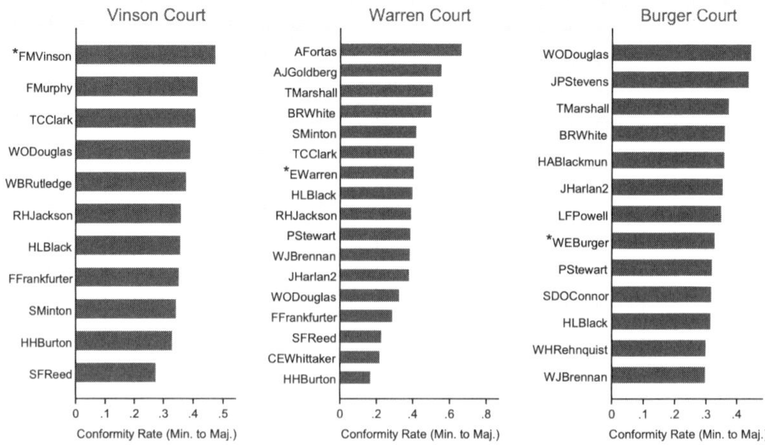

Fig. 10.2A. Majority author conformity rates (Hypothesis 1b)

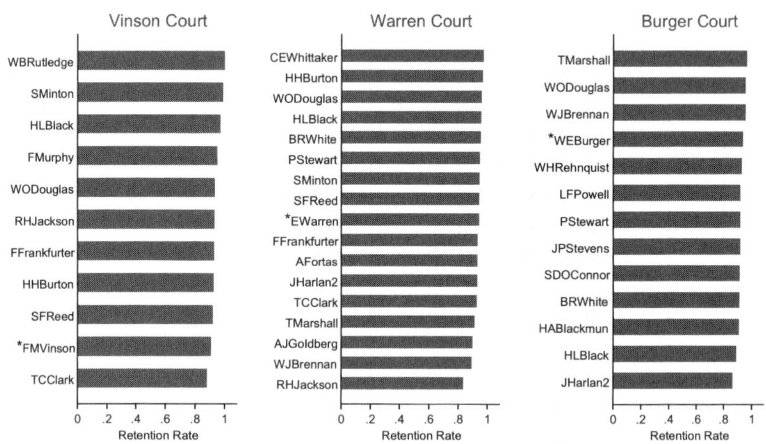

Fig. 10.2B. Majority author retention rates (Hypothesis 1b)

percent, however, which is quite high. One place to look for insight to this seeming paradox is the average size of the conference majority coalition for each justice as majority author. Vinson presided over the lowest average conference majority size—at 5.6—as majority opinion author compared to his colleagues (Rutledge presided over the highest, at 6.6). One explanation, then, is that Vinson was prone to assigning the majority opinion to himself in fairly close cases. Perhaps he bargained and accommodated the views of his dissenting colleagues to the benefit of winning them over but at the cost of losing colleagues originally in the majority. Chief Justices Warren and Burger are again toward the middle of the pack with retention rates around 95 percent. In contrast to Vinson, Warren and Burger rank near the top in average conference majority size for opinions they assigned to themselves, which means their capacity for attracting dissenters was lower than Vinson's and their capacity for retaining justices in the majority was higher. Though it is difficult to draw definitive conclusions, these results seem to suggest some semblance of "opinion-assignment effects" occurring in the analysis associated with H1a, but they do not seem to be too drastic. The results suggest that further investigation is needed to probe these dynamics.

Hypothesis 2: The Chief Justice's Rate of Switching from Minority to Majority

While voting fluidity can provide insight into the chief justice's ability to attract or retain justices as majority opinion writer, it can also help demonstrate the chief's personal voting patterns. Figure 10.3a identifies the tendency of Vinson, Warren, and Burger to subsequently join the majority after an initial conference dissent, as compared to other justices on their respective Courts. In all, the three chiefs appeared quite willing to change their initial dissenting vote. When compared to members of his Court, Vinson tops the list. In approximately 52 percent of cases in which he initially dissented, Vinson chose to subsequently switch to the majority. Notably, this rate of voting fluidity exceeds the next three highest justices—Minton, Clark, and Murphy—by several percentage points. And it far exceeds Justice Douglas, who sits at the bottom of the list with a vote change rate of just 25 percent.

Although Chief Justices Warren and Burger are not the most likely to change their votes when compared to their colleagues, they demonstrate respectable rates near the top of the lists. Warren changed his vote to majority in approximately 45 percent of cases in which he initially voted in the minority. Only four justices on his Court yield higher rates: Goldberg (53 percent), Fortas (49 percent), Minton (48 percent), and Clark (47 percent). Meanwhile, Burger switched to the majority in approximately 39 percent of cases, a rate edged out by only Powell (44 percent), White (41 percent) and Stewart (40 percent). Both chiefs were considerably more likely to change votes when compared their lowest-ranking colleagues, who conceded to the majority in less than 30 percent of cases.

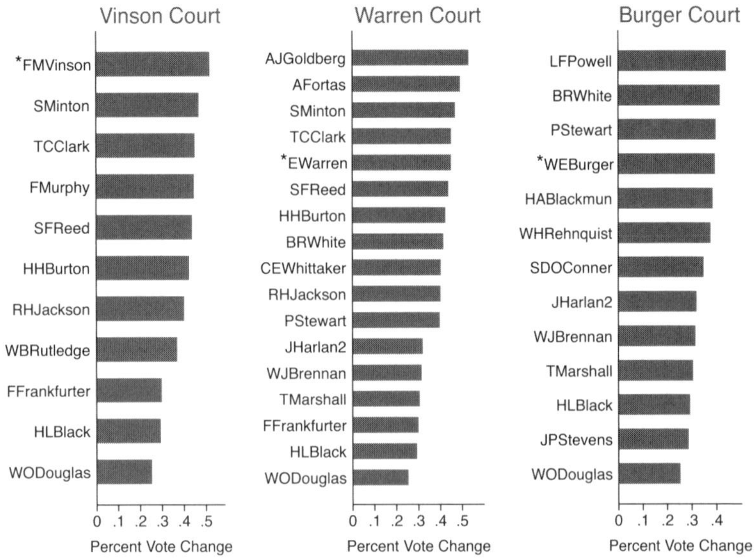

Fig. 10.3A. Justices' rates of switching from minority to majority, all cases (Hypothesis 2)

To account for the impact of case salience, Figure 10.3b ranks the justices for the three Courts based on a smaller subsample of salient decisions. Although the chiefs are slightly less willing to change votes in salient cases—perhaps due to hardened policy preferences—the results do not vary much overall. Vinson changed from the minority to the majority in 42 percent of such cases, while Warren and Burger changed votes in approximately 39 percent of such cases. Vinson moves from first to third place behind Murphy and Minton but still retains a position near the top. Warren retains his position and Burger actually moves up a notch from fourth to third place. Thus, despite the strong policy positions that often accompany salient cases, the chiefs remained willing to rethink their initial dissents, and at a rate higher than the vast majority of their colleagues.

Hypothesis 3: Citing Authoritative Precedent

As we argued, for institutional maintenance purposes the chief justice may be more attuned to citing authoritative precedent as majority author than his associate justice colleagues will. We use the "hub" score,[54] where higher

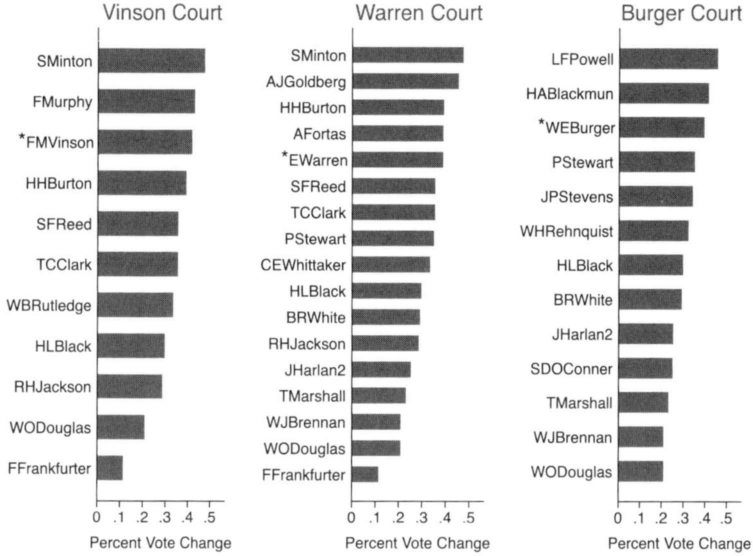

Fig. 10.3B. Justices' rates of switching from minority to majority, salient cases (Hypothesis 2)

values reflect that the majority opinion cites more "authoritative" precedent. Since this measure only goes to 2002, we exclude all years after 2002, which eliminates the Roberts Court. Since this measure is skewed and contains some extreme values toward the high end of the distribution, we report the median hub score for each majority author in each of the four chief justice time periods.

The results from figure 10.4 suggest that all the chief justices rank near the top in citing authoritative precedent when they are the majority opinion author, though they do not clearly stand out in this regard from their associate justice colleagues. Thus there is not strong support for Hypothesis 3 in this regard. Note also that while Chief Justice Rehnquist did not rank toward the top in securing a substantial margin of victory or unanimity rate, he is toward the top in terms of citing authoritative precedent, though he was also toward the top when he was associate justice during the Burger Court. Thus this may not be a "chief effect" per se for Rehnquist.

More interesting for purposes of this analysis is whether chief justices, being focused on institutional maintenance and legitimacy, are especially attuned to citing more authoritative precedent in salient cases versus non-

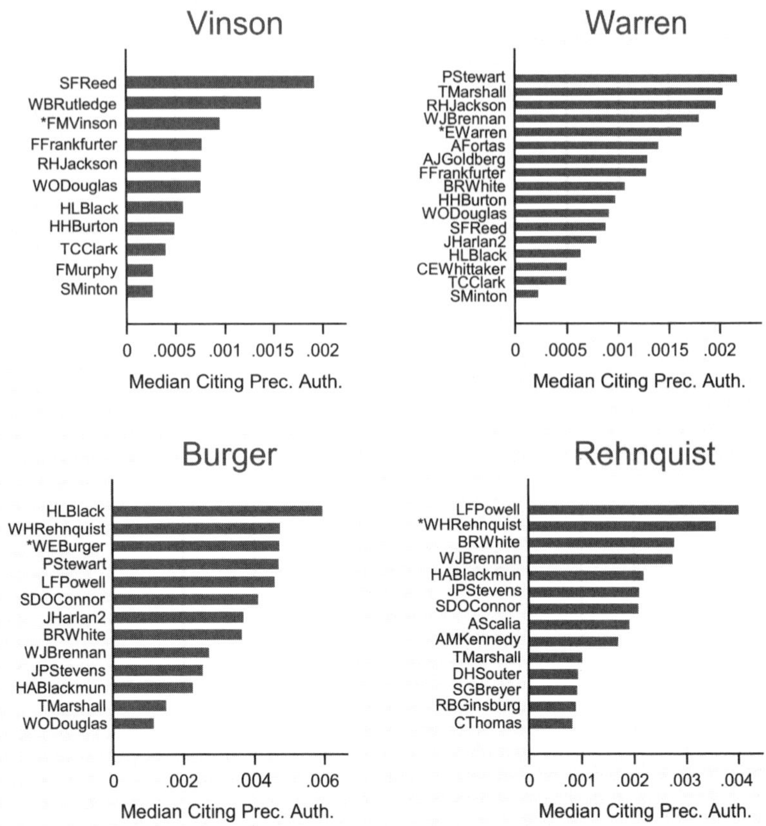

Fig. 10.4. Median citing precedent authority among majority opinion authors (Hypothesis 3)

salient cases. In salient cases, the chief justice may want to present the very strongest legal arguments in order to justify the outcome to outside audiences. Figure 10.5 presents results from this analysis. Again, median hub scores measuring authoritativeness of precedent being cited are presented for each majority opinion author, for both salient and nonsalient cases. The results are fairly clear that the four chief justices analyzed here do appear to cite more authoritative precedent in salient cases compared to nonsalient ones. But so do nearly all of the associate justices. If there is an institutional maintenance motivation underlying the chiefs' behavior, the data would

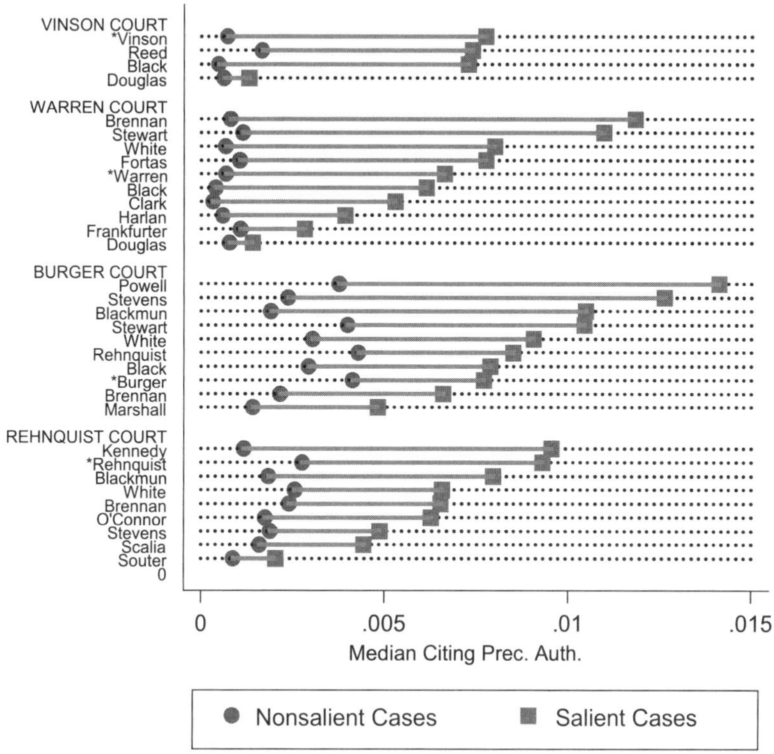

Fig. 10.5. Median citing precedent authority among majority opinion authors in salient and nonsalient decisions (Hypothesis 3)

suggest that the same motivation underlies many of the associate justices' behavior as well.

Conclusion

In theory, we may expect the chief justice to engage in behavior more reflective of institutional maintenance and legitimacy concerns to a greater extent than his colleagues. Whether the chief exhibits genuine leadership—aside from the more formal powers, like opinion assignment—or is merely "first among equals," essentially acting the same way as his associate colleagues, is a key question surrounding the leadership capacity of the chief justice. We have focused on three aspects of this issue: (1) whether the chief justice, as majority author, is more successful than his colleagues in maintaining larger vote margins and higher unanimity rates; (2) whether the chief is more likely than associates to change his vote in accordance with majority will; and (3) whether the chief justice is more attuned to maintenance and legitimacy concerns vis-à-vis the citing of more authoritative precedent. For each, we investigated whether the chief is more sensitive to institutional maintenance and legitimacy concerns in salient versus nonsalient cases.

Admittedly, the hypotheses explored in this chapter set a high bar for discovering chief justice behavior indicative of devotion to institutional maintenance and legitimacy. Our research looks beyond the chief's formal powers (e.g. opinion assignment) and assesses whether chiefs are especially mindful of institutional concerns even when they may presumably share the same power and incentives as their fellow associates. Despite this stringent test, we find some evidence of chief leadership and special sensitivity to institutional concerns, at least among certain chief justices. Vinson, Warren, and Burger were ranked toward the top with respect to margins of victory as opinion writers and their willingness to subsequently join the majority following an initial conference dissent. Vinson also ranked the highest (in relation to the colleagues with whom he served) in attracting conference dissenters to the majority.

The evidence, however, is not consistent over time. Chief Justices Rehnquist and Roberts are toward the bottom of the pack on margin of victory, though, as we discussed, this could result from the increasing polarization on the Court. The findings corroborate prior studies showing that average margin of victory and unanimity rates are lower in salient cases than in nonsalient ones. This suggests a dilemma facing the chief: While the chief likes to write opinions in salient cases (chiefs exhibit the highest, or among the highest, rates of majority opinion writing in salient cases), the chief may be unlikely to implement institutional maintenance and legitimacy goals in these decisions due to greater ideological rigidity. Thus the chief may implement institutional maintenance goals simply by trying to hold together (instead of expanding) a majority coalition, especially in the contemporary era marked by increasing ideological polarization. Evidence from the voting fluidity analysis for the Warren and Burger eras seem consistent with this argument.

With respect to citation of authoritative precedent, the results again do not suggest clear differences between chiefs and associates. Chiefs tend to cite authoritative precedent more in salient cases compared to nonsalient cases, but so do many associate justices. We are not arguing that the chief ignores institutional maintenance concerns, just that chiefs do not appear to use precedent citation to satisfy legitimacy concerns at a substantially higher rate than associate justice colleagues.

In many ways, the exploratory nature of our inquiry raises as many questions and avenues for new inquiry as it answers. Arguably, chief justices have exhibited behavior suggestive of a special mindfulness toward institutional maintenance and legitimacy, even in circumstances when they share equal formal power with associates. But this behavior has not remained consistent over time among all chiefs, perhaps due to changing dynamics on the Court that render it difficult for chiefs to influence polarized justices. To delve further into the aspects presented here, we urge scholars to probe questions of how political dynamics on the Court, including justice composition, may impact the chief justice's—and all justices for that matter—behavior and leadership with respect to institutional maintenance and legitimacy.

NOTES

1. *National Federation of Independent Business v. Sebelius*, 132 S. Ct. 2566 (2012).

2. See, e.g., Forrest Maltzman and Paul J. Wahlbeck, "May It Please the Chief? Opinion Assignments in the Rehnquist Court," *American Journal of Political Science* 40 (1996); Saul Brenner, Timothy Hagle, and Harold J. Spaeth, "Increasing the Size of the Minimum Winning Original Coalitions on the Warren Court," *Polity* 23 (1990).

3. David J. Danelski, "The Influence of the Chief Justice in the Decisional Process," in *Courts, Judges, & Politics: An Introduction to the Judicial Process*, 6th ed., ed. Walter F. Murphy, C. Herman Pritchett, Lee Epstein, and Jack Knight (New York: McGraw-Hill, 2006).

4. See, e.g, Drew Noble Lanier, "Acclimation Effects and the Chief Justice: The Influence of Tenure and Role on the Decisional Behavior of the Court's Leader, 1888–2007," *American Politics Research* 39 (2011); Saul Brenner and Timothy M. Hagle, "Opinion Writing and Acclimation Effect," *Political Behavior* 18 (1996).

5. See, e.g., Maltzman and Wahlbeck, "May It Please the Chief"; Paul J. Wahlbeck, Timothy R. Johnson, and James F. Spriggs II, "Passing and Strategic Voting on the U.S. Supreme Court," *Law and Society Review* 39 (2005).

6. Lanier, "Acclimation Effects."

7. Maltzman and Wahlbeck, "May It Please the Chief"; Forrest Maltzman, James E. Spriggs II, and Paul Wahlbeck, *Crafting Law on the Supreme Court: The Collegial Game* (New York: Cambridge University Press, 2000); Saul Brenner, Timothy Hagle, and Harold J. Spaeth, "Increasing the Size of the Minimum Winning Original Coalitions on the Warren Court," *Polity* 23 (1990); Sue Davis, "Power on the Court: Chief Justice Rehnquist's Opinion Assignments," *Judicature* 74 (1990); Elliot E. Slotnick, "Who Speaks for the Court? Majority Opinion Assignment from Taft to Burger," *American Journal of Political Science* 23 (1979); David W. Rohde,

"Policy Goals, Strategic Choice and Majority Opinion Assignments in the U.S. Supreme Court," *Midwest Journal of Political Science* 16 (1972); David W. Rohde and Harold J. Spaeth, *Supreme Court Decision Making* (San Francisco: W. H. Freeman, 1976); Sidney S. Ulmer, "The Use of Power on the Supreme Court: The Opinion Assignments of Earl Warren, 1953–1960," *Journal of Public Law* 30 (1970); Walter F. Murphy, *Elements of Judicial Strategy* (Chicago: University of Chicago Press, 1964).

8. Maltzman and Wahlbeck, "May It Please the Chief."

9. See, e.g, Wahlbeck, Johnson, and Spriggs, "Passing and Strategic Voting."

10. Lanier, "Acclimation Effects"; Frank B. Cross and Stefanie Lindquist, "The Decisional Significance of the Chief Justice," *University of Pennsylvania Law Review* 154 (2006); Saul Brenner and Eric S. Heberlig, "In My Opinion . . .": Justices' Opinion Writing in the U.S. Supreme Court, 1946–1997," *Social Science Quarterly* 83 (2002); Drew Noble Lanier and Sandra L. Wood, "Moving Up: Institutional Position, Politics, and the Chief Justice," *The American Review of Politics* 22 (2001); Saul Brenner and Timothy M. Hagle, "Opinion Writing and Acclimation Effect," *Political Behavior* 18 (1996); Sidney S. Ulmer, "Exploring the Dissent Patterns of the Chief Justices: John Marshall to Warren Burger," in *Judicial Conflict and Consensus: Behavior Studies of American Appellate Courts*, ed. Sheldon Goldman and Charles M. Lamb (Lexington: University Press of Kentucky, 1986).

11. See, e.g., Lanier, "Acclimation Effects"; Brenner and Hagle, "Opinion Writing."

12. Danelski, "The Influence of the Chief Justice."

13. Sue Davis, "The Supreme Court: Rehnquist's or Reagan's?" *Western Political Quarterly* 44 (1991).

14. Joseph Kobylka, "Leadership on the Supreme Court of the United States: Chief Justice Burger and the Establishment Clause," *Western Political Quarterly* 42 (1989).

15. Cross and Lindquist, "Decisional Significance."

16. Pamela Corley, Amy Steigerwalt, and Artemus Ward, *The Puzzle of Unanimity: Consensus on the United States Supreme Court* (Stanford, CA: Stanford University Press, 2013); Marcus E. Hendershot et al., "Dissensual Decision-Making: Revisiting the Demise of Consensual Norms within the U.S. Supreme Court" (unpublished manuscript, 2011); Lee Epstein, Jeffrey A. Segal, and Harold J. Spaeth, "The Norm of Consensus on the U.S. Supreme Court," *American Journal of Political Science* 45 (2001); Gregory A. Caldeira and Christopher J. W. Zorn, "Of Time and Consensual Norms in the Supreme Court," *American Journal of Political Science* 42 (1998); Stacie L. Haynie, "Leadership and Consensus on the U.S. Supreme Court," *Journal of Politics* 54 (1992); Thomas G. Walker, Lee Epstein, and William J. Dixon. "On the Mysterious Demise of Consensual Norms in the United States Supreme Court," *Journal of Politics* 50 (1988); Stephen C. Halpern and Kenneth N. Vines, "Institutional Disunity, the Judges' Bill and the Role of the Supreme Court," *Western Political Quarterly* 30 (1977).

17. See Hendershot et al., "Dissensual Decision-Making."

18. Walker, Epstein, and Dixon, "On the Mysterious Demise."

19. Haynie, "Leadership and Consensus."

20. Hendershot et al., "Dissensual Decision-Making."

21. Cross and Lindquist, "Decisional Significance."

22. Jeffrey A. Segal and Harold J. Spaeth, *The Supreme Court and the Attitudinal Model Revisited* (New York: Cambridge University Press, 2002).

23. Ibid.; Lee Epstein and Jack Knight, *The Choices Justice Make* (Washington, DC: CQ Press, 1998).

24. See Wahlbeck, Johnson, and Spriggs, "Passing and Strategic Voting"; Kobylka, "Leadership on the Supreme Court."

25. Brandon L. Bartels, "The Constraining Capacity of Legal Doctrine on the U.S. Supreme Court," *American Political Science Review* 103 (2009); Jack Knight and Lee Epstein, "The Norm of Stare Decisis," *American Journal of Political Science* 40 (1996); Kevin T. McGuire and James A. Stimson, "The Least Dangerous Branch Revisited: New Evidence on Supreme Court Responsiveness to Public Preferences," *Journal of Politics* 66 (2004); Maltzman, Spriggs, and Wahlbeck, *Crafting Law on the Supreme Court.*

26. Lawrence Baum, *Judges and Their Audiences: A Perspective on Judicial Behavior* (Princeton: Princeton University Press, 2006).

27. Forrest Maltzman and Paul J. Wahlbeck, "A Conditional Model of Opinion Assignment on the Supreme Court," *Political Research Quarterly* 57 (2004).

28. Gerald N. Rosenberg, *The Hollow Hope: Can Courts Bring About Social Change?* (Chicago: University of Chicago Press, 2008).

29. James L. Gibson, Gregory A. Caldeira, and Lester Kenyatta Spence, "Measuring Attitudes Toward the United States Supreme Court," *American Journal of Political Science* 47 (2003).

30. See, e.g., Brandon L. Bartels and Christopher D. Johnston, "On the Ideological Foundation of Supreme Court Legitimacy in the American Public," *American Journal of Political Science* 57 (2013); James L. Gibson, "Challenges to the Impartiality of State Supreme Courts: Legitimacy Theory and 'New Style' Judicial Campaigns," *American Political Science Review* 102 (2008); Gibson, Caldeira, and Spence, "Measuring Attitudes"; Gregory A. Caldeira and James L. Gibson, "The Etiology of Public Support for the Supreme Court," *American Journal of Political Science* 36 (1992).

31. Gibson, Caldeira, and Spence, "Measuring Attitudes"; See also *Bush v. Gore*, 531 U.S. 98 (2000).

32. See, e.g., Hendershot et al., "Dissensual Decision-Making"; Epstein, Segal, and Spaeth, "Norm of Consensus"; Caldeira and Zorn, "Of Time and Consensual Norms."

33. See, e.g., Lanier, "Acclimation Effects."

34. Maltzman and Wahlbeck, "May It Please the Chief."

35. Maltzman, Spriggs, and Wahlbeck, *Crafting Law on the Supreme Court*; Murphy, *Elements of Judicial Strategy*.

36. See David Danelski and Jeanne Danelski, "Leadership in the Warren Court," *American Court Systems* (1989).

37. Epstein and Knight, *Choices Justices Make.*

38. James L. Gibson, "The Legitimacy of the US Supreme Court in a Polarized Polity," *Journal of Empirical Legal Studies* 4 (2007).

39. Gibson and Caldeira, "Legal Realism."

40. Epstein and Knight, *The Choices Justices Make.*

41. See, e.g., ibid.

42. Harold J. Spaeth, Sara C. Benesh, Lee Epstein, Andrew D. Martin, Jeffrey A. Segal, and Theodore J. Ruger, "The Supreme Court Database, Version 2012, Release 01," http://supremecourtdatabase.org.

43. James H. Fowler and Sangick Jeon, "The Authority of Supreme Court Precedent," *Social Networks* 30 (2008).

44. Lee Epstein and Jeffrey A. Segal, "Measuring Issue Salience," *American Journal of Political Science* 44 (2000).

45. Harold J. Spaeth, *The Vinson-Warren Supreme Court Judicial Database* (Program for Law and Judicial Politics, Department of Political Science, Michigan State University, 2001).

46. Harold J. Spaeth, *Expanded Burger Court Judicial Database* (S. Sidney Ulmer Project for Research in Law and Judicial Politics, University of Kentucky, 2007).

47. We have explored various control variables and the results we have are largely robust to such controls.

48. To determine statistical significance, we regress the relevant dependent variable (here, margin of victory) on a dummied-out (nominal) operationalization of the justices in a case-level model. We include each associate justice dummy variable (e.g., Rutledge, Murphy, Douglas, etc.) and exclude the chief justice (here Vinson), which serves as the baseline of comparison. Coefficients associated with each justice dummy represent differences in margin of victory between the given justice and the chief justice (since the chief is the baseline category). Note that we do not include any control variables in these models, so these results should be considered exploratory, though still highly instructive. This is essentially akin to a simple difference of means test (*t*-test). For binary dependent variables, like unanimous outcome or one-vote margin, we use logit instead of linear regression.

49. Two other forces may be at play regarding opinion assignment. First, anecdotal evidence exists that chiefs tend to assign newer justices more consensual opinions. Thus it is possible that number of years on the bench or accounting for the "freshman phase" may exhibit some influence vis-à-vis such a phenomenon. Second, equity in opinion assignments may also complicate interpretation of these findings. Slotnick, "Who Speaks for the Court," showed that the "equality principle" did not emerge until the late Vinson era/early Warren era. Both are interesting phenomena that may have an impact on our findings, though a full examination of them is beyond the scope of the present study, which seeks to uncover broad trends in a more descriptive fashion.

50. See, e.g., Brandon L. Bartels, "Choices in Context: How Case-Level Factors Shape the Magnitude of Ideological Voting on the U.S. Supreme Court," *American Politics Research* 39 (2011); Isaac Unah and Ange Hancock, "US Supreme Court Decision Making, Case Salience, and the Attitudinal Model," *Law & Policy* 28 (2006).

51. Performing an in-depth analysis of certain justices' papers would be a promising avenue to pursue.

52. We do not account for instances where the initial dissenting opinion author becomes the majority author, which appears to occur roughly 8 percent of the time. Our results are extremely similar when excluding such instances.

53. See, e.g., Murphy, *Elements of Judicial Strategy*; Epstein and Knight, *The Choices Justices Make*.

54. Fowler and Jeon, "The Authority of Supreme Court Precedent."

11 ~ Herding Scorpions

The Chief Justice as Social Leader

RYAN C. BLACK, RYAN J. OWENS, AND JUSTIN WEDEKING

During John Roberts's testimony before the Senate Judiciary Committee to be Chief Justice of the United States, he stressed to senators that he would seek to enhance collegiality on the Court. "[I]f I am confirmed," he stated, "I think one of the things that the Chief Justice should have as a top priority is to try to bring about a greater degree of coherence and consensus in the opinions of the Court."[1] In speech after speech across the country, he declared the Court should decide cases to achieve broader agreement among the justices.[2] "[T]he rule of law," he stated, "benefits from a broader agreement."[3] His mantra seemed to be consensus and collegiality.[4]

Whether posterity will judge Roberts as a collegial consensus builder, we cannot be sure. What is clear, however, is that students of the Court often base their impressions of chiefs on their ability and eagerness to enhance collegiality on the Court and in their opinions. For example, in his seminal piece on "successful" chief justices, Danelski denoted two kinds of chiefs: those who, during the Court's conferences, are task leaders and those who are social leaders.[5] Danelski defined a task leader as one who can ensure the smooth functioning of the Court by his knowledge of precedent and past history. More important for our immediate purposes, though, was Danelski's discussion of the chief as social leader. A social leader, he argued, understands personalities, knows how to inspire others and, critically, knows how to ensure that judicial business remains collegial.[6]

To be sure, academics are not alone in imputing importance to collegiality and social leadership. Presidents also consider the chief's ability to build consensus, and they sometimes opt for nominees who carry such genes. For example, social leadership was a primary reason President Truman selected Fred Vinson to be chief justice. St. Clair and Gugin found strong evidence that Vinson was chosen because of his social skills.[7] Truman's close adviser, Clark Clifford, said of Vinson's selection, "Once the President had heard about the problems in the Court, I rather doubt he seriously considered anyone else."[8] Going further, another scholar, Richard Kirkendall, wrote that the qualities Truman admired most of Vinson were his "sociability and friendliness, his calm patient and relaxed manner, his sense of humor, his respect for the views of others, his popularity with the representatives of many factions, and his ability to conciliate conflicting views and clashing personalities, and to work out compromises."[9] In short, social leadership on the court has been recognized by academics and presidents as essential.

Despite the fairly ubiquitous belief that chiefs should be collegial and foster social harmony, little scholarship has examined whether and to what extent chiefs have been successful as social leaders. Indeed, aside from the opinion-assignment norm there is little systematic empirical scholarship focused on the chief.[10] In this chapter, we make a modest effort to highlight the chief's role as social leader. We focus not on the Court's conferences—where Danelski originally trained his sights—but rather on its majority opinions. We look to Court opinions for signs of leadership because opinions may display the levels of civility on the Court. Indeed, Justice Fortas once explained that the chief justice could use his prestige "to influence the output of the court, to a much greater degree than colleagues of equal or superior personal and professional caliber."[11] Steamer adds that a chief must "use the language with authority and with grace."[12] In sum, we believe that if chief justices are effective social leaders, we may see signs of their influence in the Court's opinions.

To that end, we analyze every majority opinion written between the Vinson Court in 1946 and the Roberts Court in 2012. Using two different textual analysis software programs, we examine "agreeable" and "disagreeable" language in the Court's majority opinions. We compare opinions written by chiefs against opinions written by other justices to analyze whether chiefs employ more or less agreeable language in their opinions than their colleagues do. We also compare the language of majority opinions joined in (but not written by) the chief against majority opinions in which the chief does not join. We do so because if the chief is able to exert a broad collegial influence over his colleagues, the opinions they write should look different when he joins them versus when he does not.

Our results suggest that modern chiefs have struggled as social leaders. Majority opinions written by chiefs tend to contain more disagreeable words and fewer agreeable words than opinions written by associate justices. We also find that the chief fails to exert a positive effect on opinions in which he is a silent member of the majority. That is, majority opinions in which the chief joins (but does not write) are just as negative (and positive) as majority opinions in which the chief does not join. Simply put, chiefs during our sample period failed systematically to apply downward pressure against negative language or to apply upward pressure and increase the amount of positive language. Finally, we observe a more emotional—and less collegial—Court in recent years, portending trouble on the horizon for the Court.

Of course, our approach is merely the starting point, and a limited one at that, in what we hope will become a long train of studies about collegiality on the Court. That is, while our approach examines the language justices use in their opinions, we do not analyze whether justices throw linguistic barbs at one another. Nor do we review how dissenters use language to attack majority opinions. Those studies would take more than a single chapter in a book. Rather, our approach is more modest. We simply examine the language of the Court's majority opinions to observe what gets "out the door" and published. In other words, while we cannot here follow the tussle among justices, we can examine the language justices use in the most public things the Court generates: its opinions.

This chapter unfolds in five parts. First, we review some of the existing literature on the chief justice's powers, with an emphasis on his informal powers as task and social leader. Second, we theorize the conditions under which we might observe more agreeable and disagreeable language in opinions and, more specifically, how social leadership on the Court might correlate with opinion language. Third, we discuss our methodology and measures. Fourth, we illustrate the agreeable and disagreeable language used by chief justices since 1946, providing a descriptive overview of opinion content across nearly seven decades. We conclude with a discussion about the behavior of modern chiefs and the consequences of their leadership.

The Chief Justice and Leadership

Despite being called the "first among equals," a title that reflects the fact that the chief's vote counts the same as an associate justice's vote, the chief has a number of significant institutional powers at his disposal, many of which he can use to influence judicial outcomes. As the other chapters in this book discuss, one of the chief's most important institutional powers (when he is in the majority) is the power to assign which justice will write the Court's majority opinion, an important prerogative because certain justices may write broad or narrow opinions.[13]

Additionally, he may be able to use informal leadership qualities to influence Court culture, votes, and opinions. The *successful* chief, at least according to many historians and political scientists, must exhibit informal leadership qualities, what Danelski calls "social leadership." A social leader knows how to inspire others and to ensure that judicial business remains collegial. When conference discussions get heated, the chief as social leader can "cool them off." The social leader is well-respected for his ability to reach consensus and keep matters from getting personally vindictive. A strong social leader on the Court can ensure harmony and minimize conflict, while a feckless social leader will oversee substantial and often personal conflict among justices. Danelski tells us that chiefs are in a good position to exercise social leadership because of their institutional powers to assign opinions, to lead discussions, to set the Court's agenda, and to recognize who may speak during conference and oral argument.[14] Thus, by extension, a successful social leader might prevent some of the Court's "dirty laundry" from being aired in public.

A few examples highlight the role of a social leader. Justice Holmes once referred to Chief Justice Fuller as "the greatest Chief Justice I have ever known,"[15] in part because of Fuller's ability to simmer down feuds before they boiled over. For example, during one conference discussion, Holmes interrupted Justice Harlan, stating that Harlan's position "just won't wash."[16] Before Harlan could respond in anger, Chief Justice Fuller smiled and made washing motions with his hand, stating, "But I just keep scrubbing away."[17] The justices responded with laughter and Fuller avoided a personal conflict.[18] In another evaluation of chief justices, Steamer noted that not all were as successful as Fuller, writing that most chiefs were:

> Extremely able personal leaders but more often than not they have been deferential to the intellects of others. Waite, Fuller, Taft, Vinson, and Warren were warm, decent human beings who possessed an ability to command, yet each could recognize and accept the intellectual leadership of men like Field, Miller, Van Devanter, Holmes, Black, or Frankfurter. White and Stone, on the other hand, while intellectually the equals of any of the brethren of their day, were incapable of running an orderly conference or orchestrating a cohesive Court. Chaos is the only word to describe the Court after Stone succeeded Hughes. The conference became a debating society with tempers out of control and tensions running high as the justices

> bickered almost endlessly, with honest intellectual differences escalating into personal antagonisms.[19]

Despite the perceived importance of collegial, social leadership, few empirical studies have examined it. Most studies of the chief look at other aspects.[20] Indeed, only a handful of studies inform our understanding of collegiality and social leadership. As we stated above, Danelski theorizes that Chief Justice Stone's poor social leadership led to a breakdown in consensus norms.[21] Haynie argues that Chief Justice Hughes oversaw a demise in consensus norms, at least as they applied to concurring opinions.[22] Cross and Lindquist find, among other things, that Chief Justice Rehnquist voted more often with the majority once he became chief, that he concurred less as chief, and that he stemmed the tide of dissent and concurrences once he took over as chief.[23] "Chief Justice Rehnquist," they found, "effectively discharged his managerial responsibility in achieving increased Court cohesion."[24] Our goal here is to build on these studies and understand which chiefs have been most successful as social leaders.

The Chief Justice, Opinion Language, and Social Leadership

It is generally assumed that small groups working to achieve a common goal (like the U.S. Supreme Court) perform better when the group operates cohesively. In a meta-analysis of more than three hundred studies on group cohesiveness and performance, Evans and Dion found a fairly strong correlation between the two ($r = 0.419$).[25] Naturally, the leader of a group plays an integral role in working toward strong cohesion, which we treat as being similar to collegiality. So what are some characteristics that enable leaders to build greater group cohesion?

In looking at leadership of small therapy groups, Antonuccio et al. found that leaders could have an impact on group cohesion.[26] Specifically, they found that leaders who have a high degree of warmth, an indirect style of leading group interaction, and an internal locus of control (a belief one can control events that affect their lives) achieved higher cohesion in their small groups. Similarly, in an examination of sports team coaches, Shields et al. found that a group's task cohesion is strengthened by leadership that is "strong in training and instruction, social support, democratic behavior, and positive feedback."[27,28]

The logic of these studies leads us to believe that cohesion and collegiality go hand-in-hand and that a chief justice can lead the Court and increase collegiality by his opinion writing. Based on the research highlighted above, opinion writers can enhance collegiality through at least four mechanisms: (1) using warm or positive language; (2) using language that does not agitate or arouse other individuals or groups; (3) using language that emphasizes inclusiveness of other group members' thoughts and opinions; and (4) using language that avoids unnecessary confrontation. All four of these mechanisms suggest that opinion language can be helpful (or harmful) for building collegiality on the Court. Since we do not have enough space in this chapter to explore all four mechanisms, however, we focus on the first two.

To begin with, perhaps the most straightforward manner a chief justice can bring about collegiality on the Court is with agreeable words in opinions. The use of warm or positive language by the chief justice should provide an example to the other justices of the kind of discourse he expects the Court to observe. Such opinion discourse is important, as many scholars have previously noted, because Court opinions shape legal policy for many years to come, and they reflect back on the Court's legitimacy. Court watchers certainly notice shifts in tone and clarity.[29] Thus it almost goes without saying that when opinions use a different tone of language, elites (and perhaps the public) notice. The connection between the use of language in opinions and its impact becomes important when we further explore the underlying meaning of these shifts in emotions. Research on the use of positive emotion (or more pleasant) words and negative emotion words has been linked to deeply felt emotions.[30] Thus the words each chief justice picks (as well as the other justices when they write) likely bears some connection to the tone he feels and that he desires the Court to take.

The second mechanism concerns use of language that may agitate or arouse others in the group. Again, if maintaining collegiality on the Court is a function of (or is otherwise correlated with) the tone of discourse in Court opinions, we should observe opinions that are consistent with the efforts of chiefs seeking to manage justices' emotions, much as Chief Justice Fuller did in the above example. If a chief wishes to lead by example and enhance collegiality through opinion writing, he will not use language that arouses negative feelings or could be personally offensive. For example, Sigelman and Whissell find that while Presidents Reagan and Clinton differed on both an emotional and "activity" dimension, partly helping to explain why some attribute rhetorical success to President Reagan (conventional history has labeled Reagan the "Great Communicator" while Clinton was labeled the "Great Talker"), Reagan's words were found to be less active than Clinton's, to be more plain-spoken, and to be closer to the average American.[31] This suggests that chief justices that are successful at enhancing collegiality will exhibit lower levels of disagreeable words (words that are less likely to arouse other justices).

If a chief is a strong social leader, we expect to observe two manifestations. First, the chief himself will author more collegial opinions. Steamer calls writing opinions "the ultimate public performance" for the chief.[32] Steamer argues that though the chief has no greater formal authority when writing opinions than any of his colleagues, "there is a subtle distinction between writing an opinion as chief and writing one as an associate justice, for in part at least the chief's ability to dominate the Court depends upon . . . [the] sort of rhetoric . . . he employ[s] to make his points."[33] In other words, the chief can write opinions in a way that showcases collegiality, that informs his colleagues how he thinks an opinion should look, and that maximizes the positive while minimizing the negative. In short, a chief who is a strong social leader will write opinions that are more collegial than the opinions of his colleagues.

Second, if the chief is a strong social leader, we might expect his presence in a majority coalition to enhance collegiality. When the chief is in the minority, his ability to influence the majority opinion is reduced considerably, making his input marginal at best.[34] Yet when the chief is in the majority, he has a more receptive audience when he comments on majority opinion drafts and other memos that are circulated among the justices. He might comment on spiteful or otherwise noncollegial language, asking the author of such language to tone it down. Alternatively, if the chief is a strong social leader, the other justices in the majority might be more inclined to shy away from disagreeable language. Put plainly, whether it comes from his comments to others to tone down disagreeable language or from the dampening effect of his mere presence, a chief who is a strong social leader will enhance an opinion's collegial appearance when he is in the majority.

Private records from the justices support our position that the chief, as well as other justices, sometimes ask others to tone down the language of their opinions. For example, after seeing Justice Stone's dissenting opinion in *Bedford Cut Stone Co. v. Journeymen Stone Cutters* (1927), Chief Justice Taft asked him to moderate and, if possible, withdraw his opinion, stating, "My dear Brother Stone, I am quite anxious, as I am sure we all are, that the continuity and weight of our opinions on important questions of law should not be broken any more that we can help."[35] Similarly, in *Mayberry v. Penna* (1971), we see Chief Justice Burger ask Justice Douglas to tone down his opinion for fear of being too harsh on lower court judges, stating, "Dear Bill: My problem is not that I disagree with your revised draft so much as that the tone of it really tends to take the Judges to task even though I don't think you intend to do so."[36]

Associate justices also will, from time to time, ask other justices to moderate their opinions for the sake of collegiality.[37] In *Hamilton v. Regents* (1934), Justice Stone made the following appeal to Justice Butler:

> I do not deny the truth of the quotations [you employ]. My only feeling about them is that they unnecessarily rub salt into the wounds of a great many very worthy people who, I am convinced, dwell on a higher spiritual plane than I do, and I am not at all sure that another generation may not conclude that their views about war are a good deal wiser than my own. The subject with which we are called on to deal is a delicate one, and I feel that we ought to avoid causing any unnecessary irritants so far as it is reasonably possible.[38]

And in *Georgia v. United States* (1973), Lewis Powell asked Byron White to modify the tone of his dissent, stating, "These suggestions [I make] obviously do not go to the substance of what you say, and simply reflect a personal feeling on my part that I would like to avoid any implication of ad hominem criticism which does not advance the legal argument which you make."[39] Simply put, these and other comments we could reference, suggest that justices recognize the important of choosing their words carefully, and that chiefs, serving as social leaders, might seek to influence their colleagues to write more collegial opinions.[40]

Data and Method: Computer Content Analysis of Court Opinions

To analyze social leadership among chiefs, we examine all majority opinions from 1946 to 2011, a period that covered five chiefs: Fred M. Vinson, Earl Warren, Warren E. Burger, William H. Rehnquist, and John G. Roberts, as well as thirty-four associate justices.[41] We analyzed approximately 6,700 majority opinions with more than 44 million words. We used two different computer content-analysis programs to examine the language of the Court's opinions. More specifically, we employed the Dictionary of Affect in Language (DAL)[42] and Linguistic Inquiry and Word Count (LIWC).[43] We discuss each of these in turn.

DAL is a dictionary-based program developed to measure the emotional meaning of words and texts. Dictionary-based programs work by identifying a set of words (or phrases) that correspond to a construct, and then observing the occurrence of the collection of words relative to overall word usage. DAL was developed by Cynthia Whissell and her colleagues[44] and has been previously used in political science[45] and, more specifically, judicial politics.[46] For this chapter, we will make use of two DAL subdictionaries: "very pleasant" words and "nasty" words.[47] Very pleasant words represent how positive the opinion tone is, while nasty words represent the amount of negativity and agitation in the tone of the opinion. Examples of pleasant words include "accomplish," "delightful," "majestic," and "serene." Examples of nasty words include "attacks," "critical," "hostile," and "rage."

As an alternative measure, we also examine two categories from LIWC. LIWC is a textual-analysis software package that examines words and operates on the same dictionary-based principles of DAL. LIWC analyzes "attentional focus, emotionality, social relationships, thinking styles" and other features of language.[48] LIWC employs a word count strategy that searches whatever text is under review for more than 2,300 words (or word stems) using specific dictionaries.[49] The analyst specifies a particular corpus of material she would like the software to examine and uploads the text, and then the software searches whether the words or word stems in its dictionary appear in the text. LIWC assigns words in a text to one of seventy predefined dimensions that have been categorized by independent examiners to measure various concepts like positive and negative emotion words, tentative words, and complex words. The program then tallies up the words used in each dimension and provides a descriptive output of their use, namely a percentage of words in the text that belong in each dimension.

We analyze two indicators from LIWC: the percentage of emotionally positive and emotionally negative words in an opinion. LIWC has specially designed dictionaries of positive and negative words that can be used to search text to determine what percentage of the material contains agreeable or disagreeable words. These special dictionaries were designed specifically for capturing tone; their validity and reliability have been extensively tested by previous scholars.[50] A sample of words for the positive emotion category, which includes more than four hundred words, is "caring," "good," "happy," "special," and "thoughtful." A sample of words for the negative emotion category, which also has more than four hundred words, includes "awful," "dread," "revenge," "sad," and "ugly."

We test whether different chief justices are more or less successful at influencing the tone of the majority opinion. To generate estimates for this test, we estimated four ordinary least squares regression models with the four measures mentioned above (percent of very pleasant, positive emotion, nasty, and negative emotion words in an opinion) each serving as a dependent variable. We then included more than twenty-five control variables to account for differences across situations and contexts. The key covariates of interest in these models were (1) dummy variables to account for the five chief justices; (2) the dummy variables for the three situations: chief writes the majority opinion, chief joins (but does not write) the majority opinion, chief not in the majority; and (3) the interactions between the chiefs and situations.[51] Although this parameterization seems initially complex, a key advantage of it is that it allows us to test for within-chief variation (e.g., whether opinions change due to Chief Justice Roberts writing the opinion versus only joining it versus being in the dissent) and also between-chief variation (e.g., whether opinions change from when Chief Justice Rehnquist wrote the majority versus when Chief Justice Roberts wrote it). Parameter estimates in hand, we then use simulations to generate point estimates and confidence intervals around how a chief justice was—or was not—able to control the tone of the majority opinion.

Results

We examine the amount of collegiality and consensus over time, looking at three dynamics. First, we look at majority opinions written by chiefs to determine whether they set collegial examples for their colleagues when they write majority opinions. Second, we compare the opinions of majorities that included the chief (but where he did not write) versus opinions of majorities that did not include the chief. If the chief is an effective social leader, we might expect that opinions of majorities that include him will contain fewer disagreeable words and more agreeable words. Third, we discuss observable trends over time.

Agreeable Language. If a chief is a good social leader, the Court's majority opinions should contain more agreeable language when he writes them than when he does not write them. Again, the chief who is a successful social leader will take his role seriously and set an example for his colleagues, authoring opinions with agreeable language. We look to the "very pleasant" language (as coded by DAL) and "positive emotion" words (as coded by LIWC) in the Court's majority opinions.

Do chiefs write more agreeable opinions than their colleagues? The answer, at least according to our analyses, is clearly not. As the first (Writes v. Joins) and second (Writes v. Dissents) rows on the right side of figure 11.1 show, not a single chief's majority opinions contained a significantly larger percent of very pleasant words than majority opinions written by associates, nor did chiefs write opinions containing a larger percent of positive emotion words. Comparing their written majority opinions versus when they join in an opinion or when they are in dissent (i.e., do not join the majority opinion) shows no significant differences in agreeable words. Simply put, when given the chance to set an example and write a majority opinion that is agreeable in nature, not a single chief since 1946 appeared to rise to the occasion. The opinions they wrote were no more agreeable than the opinions their colleagues wrote.

We also argued that if chiefs exert social leadership, majority opinions in which they join—but do not write—might also be more agreeable than majority opinions in which they do not join. If the chief can exercise social leadership and get his colleagues to write more collegial opinions, we should observe a larger percentage of agreeable language in majority opinions when he is in that coalition versus when he is not. The third (Joins v. Dissents) rows in figures 11.1(a) and 11.1(b) shoots down this notion as well. Not a single chief was able to influence majority opinion writers to craft more agreeable opinions. Majority opinions joined in by the chief were no more agreeable than majority opinions from which he dissented.

Disagreeable Language. The use of disagreeable language in majority opinions tells a similar story. Again, if a chief is a good social leader, the Court's majority opinions will contain less disagreeable language when he writes them versus when associates writes them. To determine "disagreeableness," we look to "nasty" language (as coded by the DAL) and "negative emotion" words (as coded by LIWC) in the Court's majority opinions. As the first and second rows in figures 11.2(a) and 11.2(b) show, Chief Justices Vinson and Warren's majority opinions contained just as much nasty language as associate justice majority opinions. Perhaps more importantly, however, figure 11.2(a) shows that Chief Justices Burger, Rehnquist, and Roberts all employed a *larger* percentage of nasty language in their majority opinions than did associates who wrote majority opinions. Looking at the percentage of negative emotion words (figure 11.2(b)), we find that chiefs used just as much negative emotion language in their majority opinions as associates did in theirs.

What is more, when we compare the disagreeableness of majority opinions in coalitions joined by the chief versus those in which the chief did not join, we see that *not a single chief was able to influence his majority coalition colleagues to employ less disagreeable language*. Whether the chief was in the majority did not influence the percentage of disagreeable words. Chiefs exerted no independent leadership effect of a magnitude we would expect

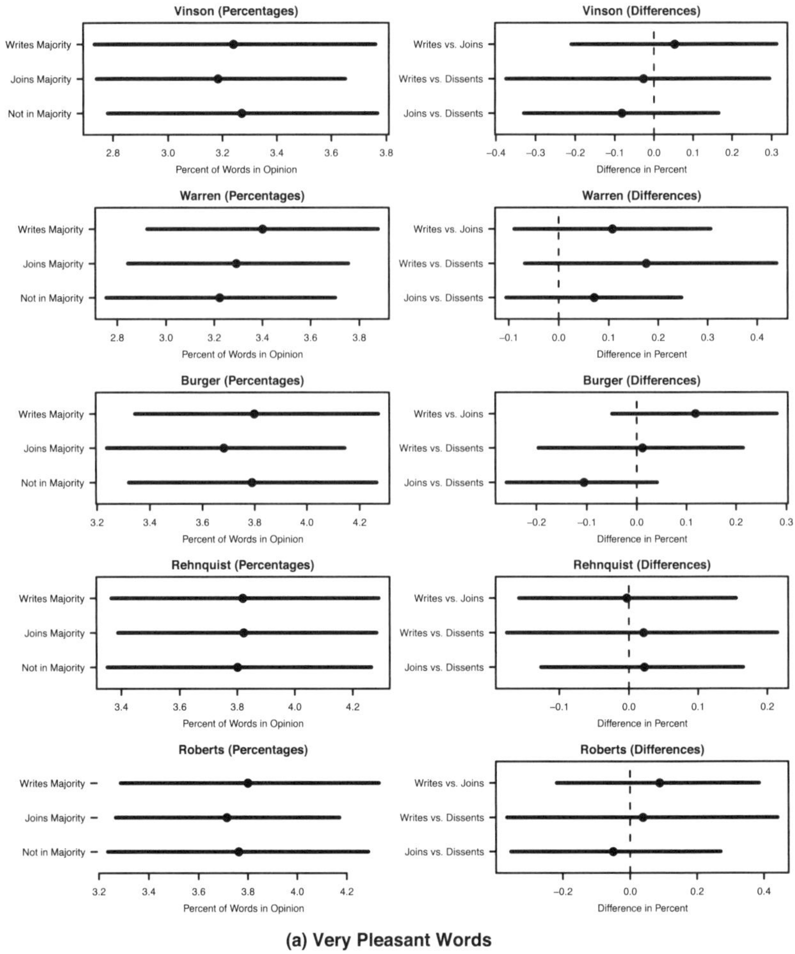

Fig. 11.1. Percent of agreeable words in majority opinions, by chief justice

if they are effective social leaders. Indeed, in many instances, they appear to behave in ways detrimental to effective social leadership. In short, the chiefs we examined tended to write more disagreeable opinions than associates *and* failed to influence their colleagues to write more collegially. Social leadership, at least as we have defined it here (to be systematic over a series of cases), seems to be sorely lacking on the modern Court.[52]

The next question, of course, is whether some chiefs are less collegial than others. Which chiefs tilted most toward disagreeable opinions and farthest from agreeable opinions? It is to this question that we now turn.

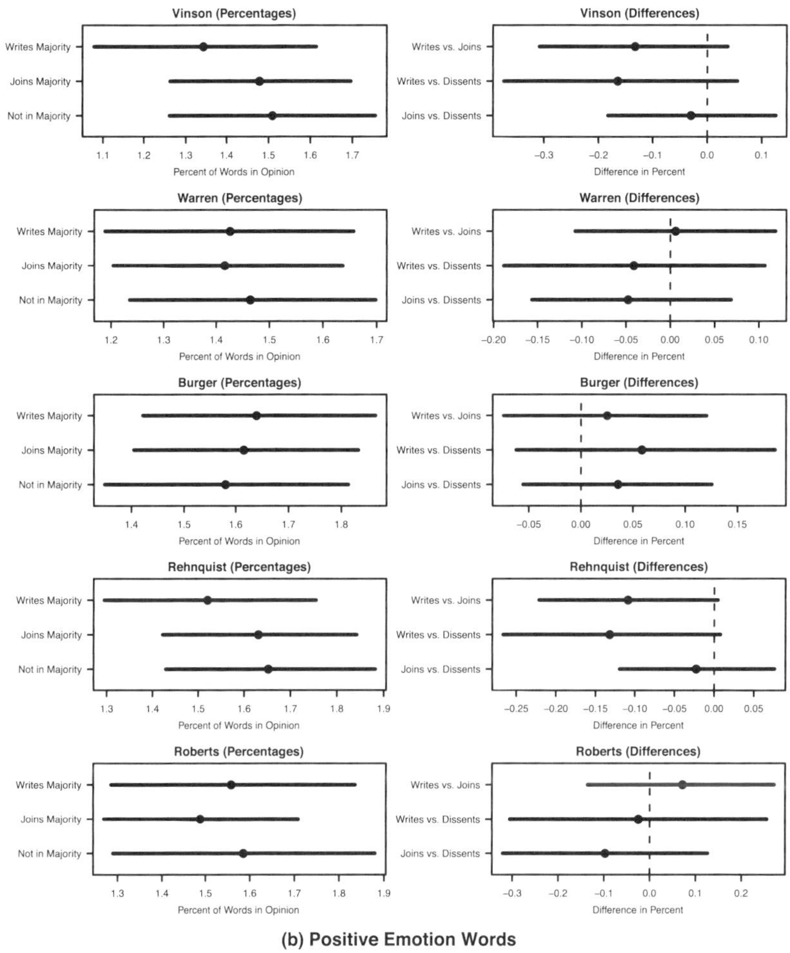

Fig. 11.1. (*continued*)

Trends Over Time. We now compare the behavior of chiefs and examine trends over time. And what we find, among other things, is that the modern Court seems to use more emotional language than Courts past. Looking first at agreeable words, what stands out is that modern chiefs appear to employ more agreeable language than their predecessors, particularly more than Chief Justices Vinson and Warren. As the top right side of figure 11.3(a) shows, all opinions written by Chief Justices Burger, Rehnquist, and Roberts contained more very pleasant words than opinions written by Chief Justices Vinson and Warren. We observe the same dynamic when

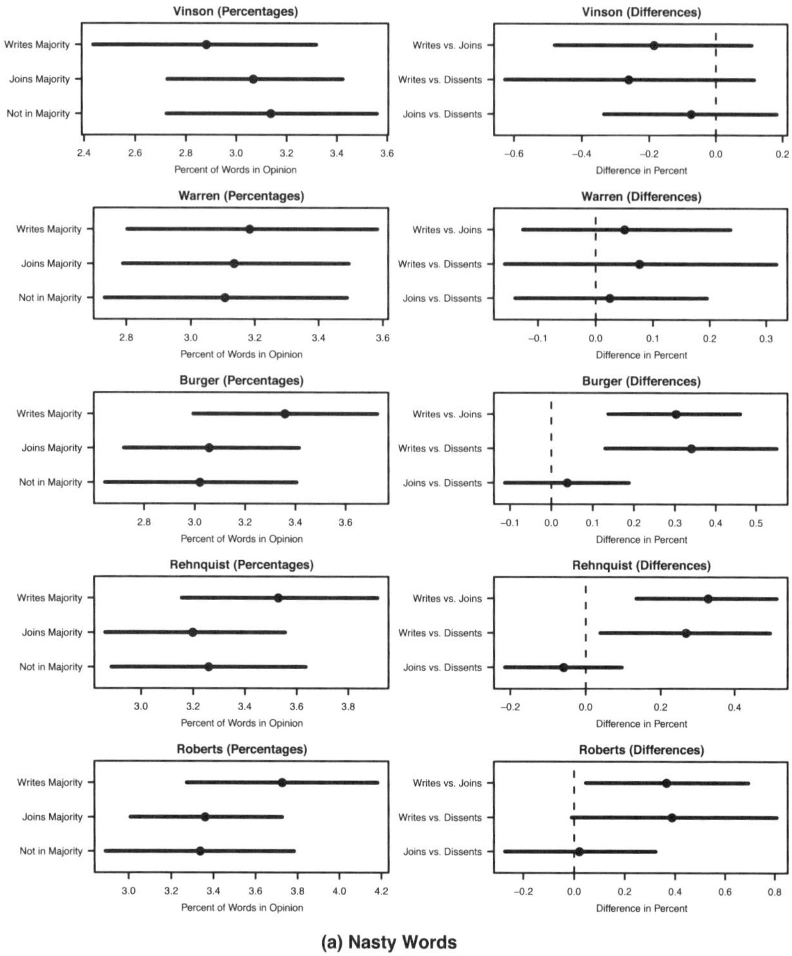

Fig. 11.2. Percent of disagreeable words in majority opinions, by chief justice

looking at majority opinions in which the chief simply joined (the second row), as well as majority opinions written when Burger, Rehnquist, and Roberts were in dissent (the third row). A similar, but less marked pattern holds when we examine the percentage of positive emotion words, as shown in figure 11.3(b).

Looking at the percentage of disagreeable words in the Court's majority opinions, however, tells a different—and less sanguine—story. Consider the percentage of nasty words in a majority opinion (fig. 11.4(a)).

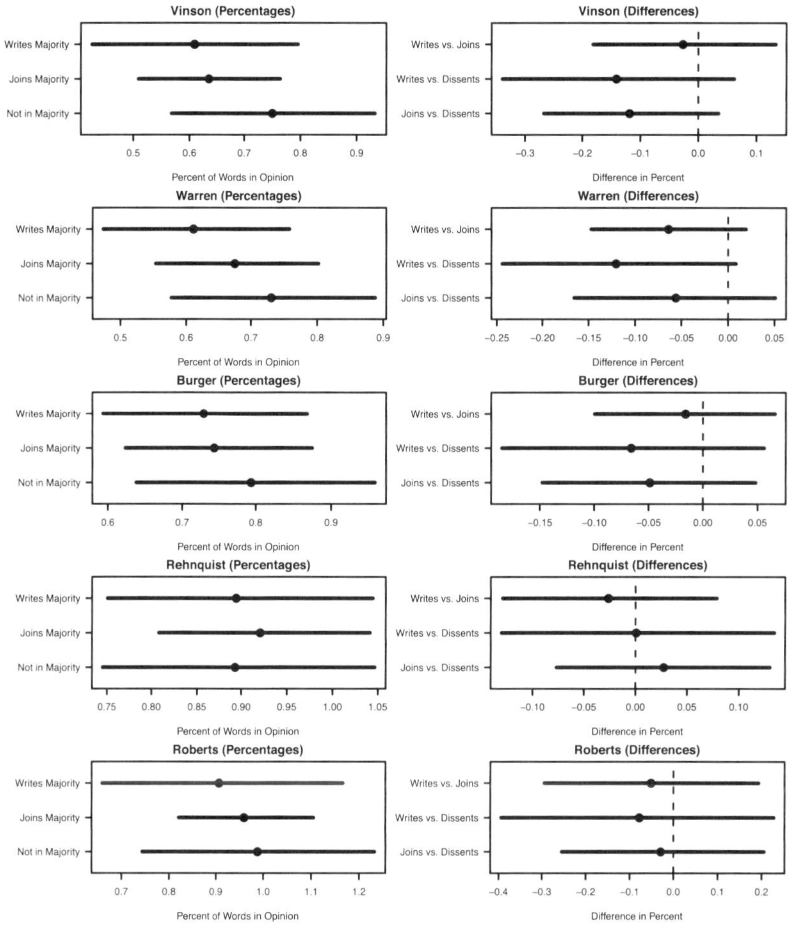

(b) Negative Emotion Words

Fig. 11.2. (*continued*)

Chief Justice Roberts employs the highest percentage of nasty words, followed by Rehnquist and Burger. The majority opinions Chief Justice Roberts writes contain a significantly larger percentage of nasty words than opinions written by Chief Justice Vinson, Warren, and Burger. Looking at majority opinions when the chief is a silent member of the majority, we see that majority opinions under the Roberts Court are the nastiest. In fact, majority opinions in the Roberts Court contain a significantly higher percentage of nasty words than those published under *any other chief*. The

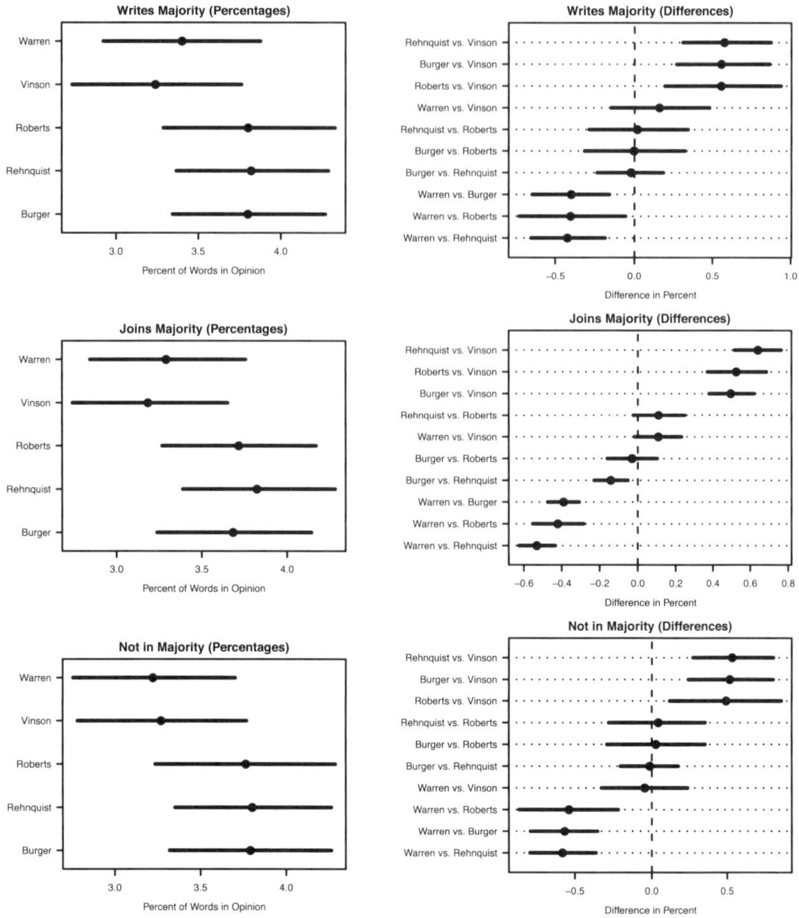

(a) Very Pleasant Words

Fig. 11.3. Percent of agreeable words in majority opinions, chief justice comparisons

LIWC approach (see figure 11.4(b)) tells nearly the same story. Roberts and Rehnquist wrote majority opinions using the largest proportion of negative emotion words, followed by Chief Justice Burger. And the majority opinions written with Roberts, Rehnquist, and Burger as silent members of the majority were among the most negative.

So, while the Rehnquist and Roberts Courts tended to employ a significant percentage of positive words, so too did they employ the most negative words. While this dynamic is perplexing, it makes one thing clear.

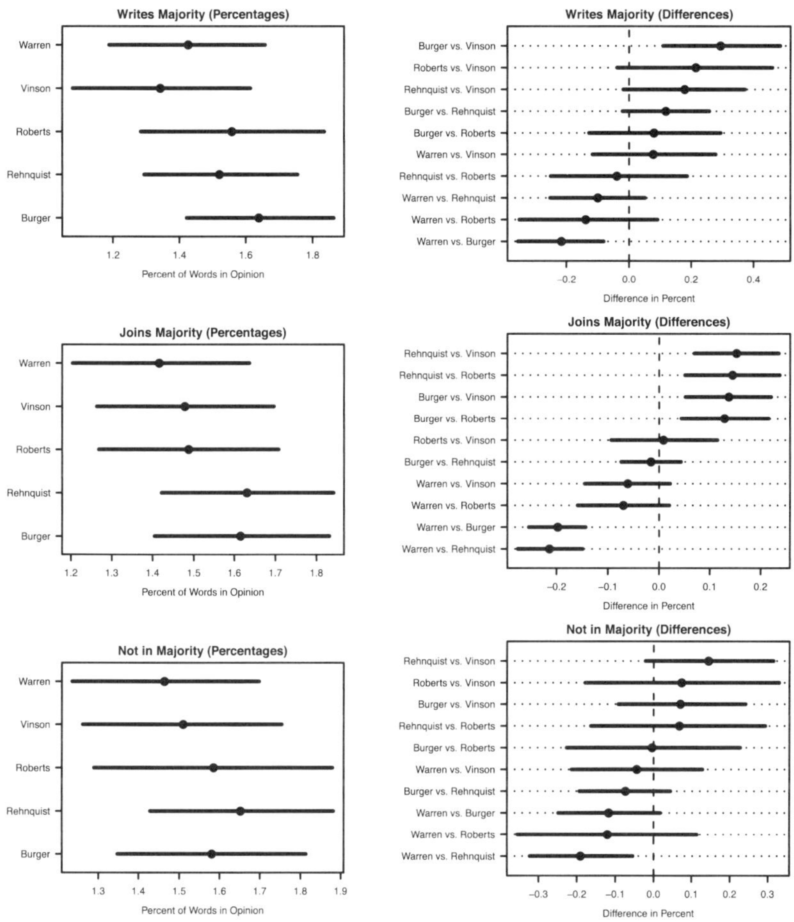

(b) Positive Emotion Words

Fig. 11.3. (*continued*)

Today's majority opinions contain a higher proportion of emotional language than past opinions.

Before we conclude, we wish to address one final concern. A skeptical reader might wonder whether the positive and negative language we examine actually taps into interpersonal relationships on the Court. That is, the positive and negative words might relate to something other than interpersonal relationships. If so, our findings would not tell us much about social leadership on the Court. To address this concern, we examined the

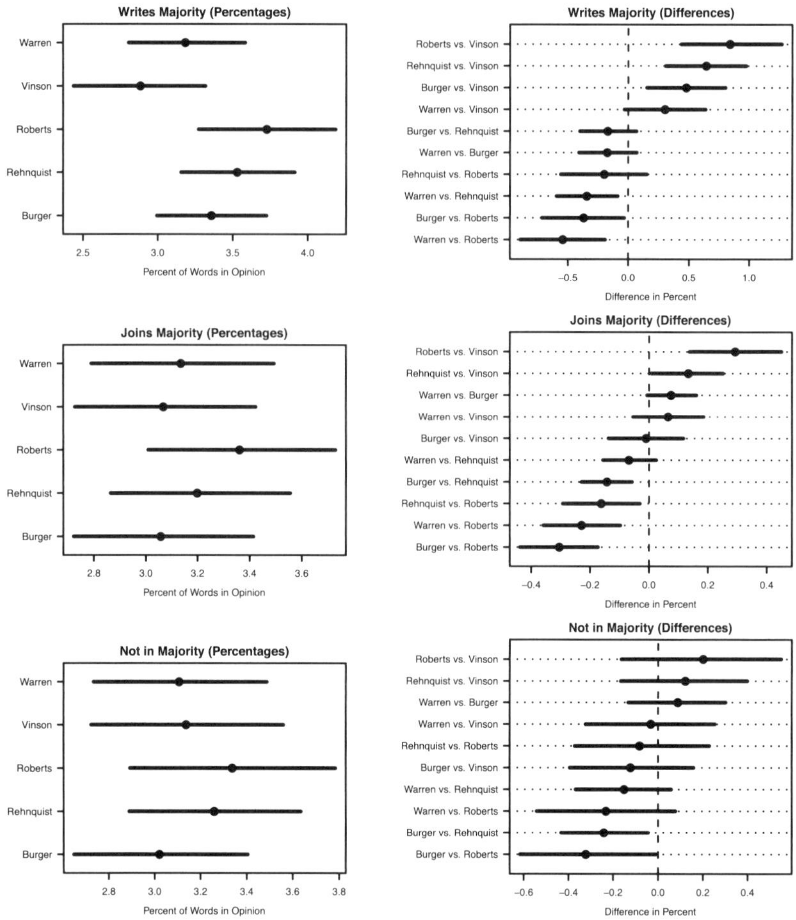

(a) Nasty Words

Fig. 11.4. Percent of disagreeable words in majority opinions, chief justice comparisons

differences between unanimous and nonunanimous opinions. If it is the case that unanimous opinions are just as "nasty," for example, as nonunanimous opinions, we might worry that our interpretation of the results is misguided. The data, however, support our inferences.

We focus on the differences in the use of negative language between unanimous and nonunanimous opinions. Looking at "nasty" language in the DAL, we discover that unanimous majority opinions have a lower nasty word score than their nonunanimous counterparts ($p < .001$). Additionally,

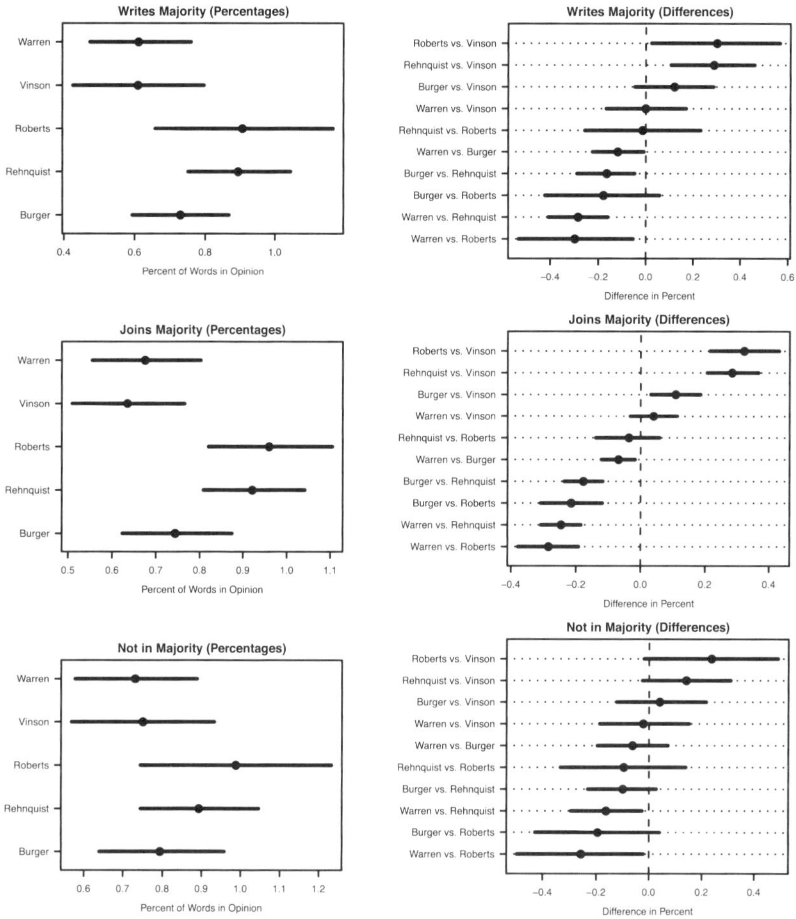

(b) Negative Emotion Words

Fig. 11.4. (*continued*)

looking at negative emotion words in LIWC tells the same story. Negative emotion words occur more in nonunanimous majority opinions than in unanimous opinions ($p < .001$).[53] We also looked at the top twenty-five nastiest opinions. Fully 92 percent of them are nonunanimous opinions. What is more, of the top twenty-five opinions with the highest values of negative emotion words in LIWC, 76 percent are nonunanimous and the top ten are *all* nonunanimous. In short, it appears that the approach we take captures the interpersonal dynamics we see to test.

Discussion

In honoring Chief Justice Warren, former justice Abe Fortas opened his essay with these two sentences: "The Chief Justice of the United States is inevitably the chairman of the judicial collegium. He is not always its leader."[54] Fortas's comments underscore the difficulties chief justices face. History judges them based on a number of things, most of which are out of their control. The chief oversees the conference of his colleagues, but he has little power over how they behave. To be sure, he can use his institutional powers to effectuate some policy change, but his ability to influence his colleagues is limited.

So, perhaps asking the chief to be a social leader is simply too much and ignores the reality of the modern office. Indeed, at least one chief justice thinks so. At his confirmation hearing for chief justice, William Rehnquist said, "I think that the Chief Justice can exercise a certain amount of leadership on the Court, but I do not think it is apt to be in a philosophical direction."[55] Perhaps he recognized that while a certain amount of leadership is possible, the lack of superior institutional rules or controls (compared to congressional leaders) means that trying to lead and shape eight other justices in a consistent direction as "first among equals" is remarkably difficult. Indeed, with a nod to Bickel's comment that justices are "nine scorpions in a bottle," keeping the justices together, focused, and united is like herding scorpions.[56] Perhaps, then, it should come as no surprise that modern chiefs would appear to have little success at influencing collegiality on the Court.

Of course, one may wonder whether the results we discover here are simply a function of the fact that law clerks in the modern era are much more involved with opinion writing than in decades past.[57] To this we have two responses. First, while it may be true that law clerks are more involved today than in years past, the clerks are supposed to act as agents for their justices. That is, they are charged with writing opinions as their justices would write them.[58] Given this, and the fact that the justices audit the opinions their clerks write, we can surmise that justices approve of the opinions written in their names. Second, if it is the case that justices have delegated opinion-writing power to their clerks, and collegiality has suffered as a result, that only supports our point that modern chiefs have failed to exercise leadership in a way that maintains collegiality. Simply put, even if clerks have become more engaged in opinion writing, our overall point about the decline of collegiality and social leadership remains.

This chapter is just the beginning of what we hope becomes a more exacting approach to examining collegiality and social leadership on the Court. We examined the content of the Court's majority opinion for the use of positive and negative language. While our results suggest that justices in recent years have used more problematic language in their opinions—and that chiefs have not stemmed that tide—we did not isolate whether the negative language was directed at other justices. Nor were we able to analyze how a justice wrote noncollegially in separate opinions. For example, in *Lawrence v. Texas* (2005), Justice Scalia's dissent exclaimed:

> At the end of its opinion—after having laid waste the foundations of our rational-basis jurisprudence—the Court says that the present case 'does not involve whether the government must give formal recognition to any relationship that homosexual persons seek to enter.' Do not believe it.

Future scholarship should look into how justices reference one another in their opinions, asking whether they go beyond mere disagreement with legal policy and question the intelligence or motives of their colleagues. Researchers also might consider examining whether, like the Court, other institutions of government show trends of negativity in language.

Still, despite the limitations with this basic analysis, the findings paint a troubling picture. Lindquist and Klein tell us that "[o]ne of the Court's most important claims to legitimacy is the proposition that its decisions are not determined solely by the justices' personal policy preferences but are influenced as well by their understandings of what 'the law' requires in a given case."[59] Most people, we suspect, would not expect the law—and legal opinions—to drip with emotional venom. So when justices attack one another's credibility, they likely damage the Court as an institution (and, ironically, their own ability to use the Court later to achieve their policy goals). Simply put, we suspect the Court loses legitimacy when justices tend toward emotion over "cold" logic; its recent trends, therefore, could spell trouble on the horizon.

NOTES

1. "Third Day of Hearings on the Nomination of Judge Roberts," *New York Times* Online, Sep. 14, 2005, http://www.nytimes.com/2005/09/14/politics/politicsspecial1/14text-roberts.html?pagewanted=all&module=Search&mabReward=relbias%3Ar&gwh=8BDD1E2A6CDCF5A878BA291200CA73B8&gwt=pay&_r=0, accessed Sep. 20, 2014.

2. Michael W. Schwartz, "Our Fractured Supreme Court," *Policy Review* 147 (2008).

3. Associated Press, "Chief Justice Says His Goal Is More Consensus on Court," *New York Times*, May 22, 2006. Of course, while some see coalition building by the chief as a virtue, others question whether an excessive concern for consensus will lead to doctrinal confusion or ideological impurities. See, e.g., Jeffrey Rosen, "Big Chief: How to Understand John Roberts," *New Republic*, Aug. 2, 2012, 13–14.

4. Once on the Court, Roberts continued to stress the importance of consensus. See Linda Greenhouse, "In Latest Term, Majority Grows to More than Five of the Justices," *New York Times*, May 23, 2008.

5. David J. Danelski, "The Influence of the Chief Justice in the Decisional Process of the Supreme Court," in *American Court Systems: Readings in Judicial Process and Behavior*, ed. Sheldon Goldman and Austin Sarat (San Francisco: W. H. Freeman, 1978).

6. Other scholars have offered similar conceptualizations. For example, Steamer used two similar terms: personal and intellectual leadership, while Stephenson offered a slight variation on Danelski's two-part leadership typology when he examined Chief Justice Waite, creating a three-part typology by splitting the "task" leadership portion into the concepts of "managerial" and "intellectual" leadership. See Robert J. Steamer, *Chief Justice: Leadership and the Supreme Court* (Columbia: University of South Carolina Press, 1986); and D. Grier Stephenson, "The Chef Justice as Leader: The Case of Morrison Remick Waite," *William & Mary Law Review* 14 (1973).

7. James E. St. Clair and Linda C. Gugin, *Chief Justice Fred M. Vinson of Kentucky* (Lexington: University Press of Kentucky, 2002).

8. Ibid., 162.

9. Ibid.

10. But see Richard L. Vining and Teena Wilhelm, "The Chief Justice as Advocate-in-Chief: Examining the Year-End Report on the Federal Judiciary," *Judicature* 95 (2012); and Frank B. Cross and Stefanie A. Lindquist, "The Decisional Significance of the Chief Justice," *University of Pennsylvania Law Review* 154 (2006).

11. Abe Fortas, "Chief Justice Warren: The Enigma of Leadership," *Yale Law Journal* 84 (1975): 405.

12. Steamer, *Leadership and the Supreme Court*, 31.

13. Ryan J. Owens and Justin P. Wedeking, "Justices and Legal Clarity: Analyzing the Complexity of Supreme Court Opinions," *Law and Society Review* 45 (2011).

14. Stacie L. Haynie, "Leadership and Consensus on the U.S. Supreme Court," *Journal of Politics* 54 (1992). Haynie points out, however, that conflict on the Court can emerge even during the watch of an effective task and social leader.

15. Willard L. King, *Melville Weston Fuller: Chief Justice of The United States, 1888–1910* (Chicago: University of Chicago Press, 1967).

16. Ibid., 290.

17. Ibid., 290; cited in Peter G. Fish, *The Office of the Chief Justice* (Charlottesville: White Burkett Miller Center of Public Affairs, University of Virginia Press, 1984), 25–26.

18. See also Charles F. Hobson, "Defining the Office: John Marshall and Chief Justice," *University of Pennsylvania Law Review* 154 (2006); Natalie Wexler, "In the

Beginning: The First Three Chief Justices," *University of Pennsylvania Law Review* 154 (2006); and G. Edward White, "The Internal Powers of the Chief Justice: The Nineteenth-Century Legacy," *University of Pennsylvania Law Review* 154 (2006).

19. Steamer, *Chief Justice: Leadership and the Supreme Court.*

20. Studies of the chief justice typically examine his opinion assignments (e.g., Cross and Lindquist, "Decisional Significance"; Paul J. Wahlbeck, "Strategy and Constraints on Supreme Court Opinion Assignment," *University of Pennsylvania Law Review* 154 (2006); White, "Internal Powers"; Timothy R. Johnson, James F. Spriggs II, and Paul J. Wahlbeck, "Passing and Strategic Voting on the U.S. Supreme Court," *Law & Society Review* 39 (2005); Forrest Maltzman and Paul J. Wahlbeck, "Opinion Assignment on the Rehnquist Court," *Judicature* 89 (2005); Forrest Maltzman and Paul J. Wahlbeck, "A Conditional Model of Opinion Assignment on the Supreme Court," *Political Research Quarterly* 57 (2004); Forrest Maltzman and Paul J. Wahlbeck, "May It Please the Chief? Opinion Assignments in the Rehnquist Court," *American Journal of Political Science* 40 (1996); Sue Davis, "Power on the Court: Chief Justice Rehnquist's Opinion Assignments," *Judicature* 74 (1990)), his influence over the agenda stage (e.g., Richard W. Garnett, "Right On," *Legal Affairs* March–April (2005), his dissenting behavior (e.g., Pamela C. Corley, Amy L. Steigerwalt, and Artemus Ward, *The Puzzle of Unanimity: Consensus on the United States Supreme Court* (Stanford, CA: Stanford University Press, 2013); Paul J. Wahlbeck, James F. Spriggs II, and Forrest Maltzman, "The Politics of Dissents and Concurrences on the U.S. Supreme Court," *American Politics Quarterly* 27 (1999)), and the size of opinion coalitions under different chiefs (Paul H. Edelman and Suzanna Sherry, "All or Nothing: Explaining the Size of Supreme Court Majorities," *North Carolina Law Review* 78 (2000); Lee Epstein, Jeffrey A. Segal, and Harold J. Spaeth, "The Norm of Consensus on the U.S. Supreme Court," *American Journal of Political Science* 45 (2001); Thomas G. Walker, Lee Epstein, and William J. Dixon, "On the Mysterious Demise of Consensual Norms in the United States Supreme Court," *Journal of Politics* 50 (1988)).

21. Danelski, "The Influence of the Chief Justice." See also Walker, Epstein, and Dixon, "On the Mysterious Demise."

22. Haynie, "Leadership and Consensus."

23. Cross and Lindquist, "Decisional Significance." See also Frank B. Cross and Stefanie A. Lindquist, *Measuring Judicial Activism* (New York: Oxford University Press, 2009).

24. Cross and Lindquist, "Decisional Significance," 1696.

25. Charles R. Evans and Kenneth L. Dion, "Group Cohesion and Performance: A Meta-Analysis," *Small Group Research* 43 (2012).

26. David O. Antonuccio et al., "Therapist Variables Related to Cohesiveness in a Group Treatment for Depression," *Small Group Research* 18 (1987).

27. David L. L. Shields et al., "The Relationship Between Leadership Behaviors and Group Cohesion in Team Sports," *Journal of Psychology* 131 (1997).

28. Philip M. Podsakoff and William D. Todor, "Relationships Between Leader Reward and Punishment Behavior and Group Processes and Productivity," *Journal of Management* 11 (1985). Podsakoff and Todor examine leadership's effect on group cohesion and find that group cohesion is related to the reward behavior of leaders. This suggests that one possible theory of why a chief justice assigns opinions

to certain colleagues could be viewed as a way to reward other group members to enhance future group cohesion.

29. Linda Greenhouse, "A Case-By-Case Ruling on Discrimination," *New York Times*, Feb. 27, 2008.

30. James W. Pennebaker, Mattias R. Mehl, and Kate G. Niederhoffer, "Psychological Aspects Of Natural Language Use: Our Words, Our Selves," *Annual Review of Psychology* 54 (2003).

31. Lee Sigelman and Cynthia Whissell, "'The Great Communicator' and 'The Great Talker' on the Radio: Projecting Presidential Personas," *Presidential Studies Quarterly* 32 (2002).

32. Steamer, *Chief Justice: Leadership and the Supreme Court.*

33. Ibid., 31.

34. See, e.g., Forrest Maltzman, James F. Spriggs II, and Paul J. Wahlbeck, *Crafting Law on the Supreme Court: The Collegial Game* (New York: Cambridge University Press, 2000).

35. Walter F. Murphy, *Elements of Judicial Strategy* (Chicago: University of Chicago Press, 1964), 47.

36. Paul J. Wahlbeck, James F. Spriggs II, and Forrest Maltzman, "The Burger Court Opinion Writing Database," http://supremecourtopinions.wustl.edu, accessed Sep. 20, 2014.

37. Indeed, the justices have even commented on how they often must tone down their own opinions, as evidenced by the following note from Justice Black to Justice Douglas in *Turner v. United States*, 396 U.S. 398 (1969): "Dear Bill: I shall circulate a dissent . . . as soon as I can tone it down to a moderate version" (available online at Wahlbeck, Spriggs, and Maltzman, "Burger Court Opinion Writing Database," http://supremecourtopinions.wustl.edu).

38. Cited in Murphy, *Elements of Judicial Strategy*, 64.

39. Wahlbeck, Spriggs, and Maltzman, "Burger Court Opinion Writing Database."

40. For a study that examines bargaining and negotiation on the federal circuit courts of appeals (including requests for stylistic changes from opinion writers), see Ryan C. Black and Ryan J. Owens, "Bargaining and Legal Development in the United States Courts of Appeals," *American Politics Research* (forthcoming).

41. We also note that the start of this time period largely coincides with the end of the time period known as *the norm of consensus*. See Epstein, Segal, and Spaeth, "Norm of Consensus."

42. Cynthia Whissell, "The Dictionary of Affect in Language," in *Theory, Research, and Experience*, ed. Robert Plutchik and Henry Kellerman (New York: Academic Press, 1989); Cynthia Whissell et al., "A Dictionary of Affect in Language: Reliability, Validity, and Applications," *Perceptual and Motor Skills* 62 (1986): 875–88.

43. James W. Pennebaker and Laura A. King, "Linguistic Styles: Language Use As an Individual Difference," *Journal of Personality and Social Psychology* 77 (1999); Yla R. Tausczik and James W. Pennebaker, "The Psychological Meaning of Words: LIWC and Computerized Text Analysis Methods," *Journal of Language and Social Psychology* 29 (2010).

44. Whissell, "Dictionary of Affect"; Whissell et al., "Dictionary of Affect."

45. Sigelman and Whissell, "The Great Communicator."

46. Ryan C. Black et al., "Emotions, Oral Arguments, and Supreme Court Decision Making," *Journal of Politics* 73 (2011).
47. DAL constructs the subdictionaries from its three main dictionaries: Pleasantness, Activation, and Imagery.
48. Tausczik and Pennebaker, "Psychological Meaning of Words," 24.
49. The internal and external validity of LIWC has been established in a series of publications (Ibid.; Pennebaker and King, "Linguistic Styles,") and has also been used in judicial politics (Owens and Wedeking, "Justices and Legal Clarity."
50. Pennebaker and King, "Linguistic Styles"; Tausczik and Pennebaker, "Psychological Meaning of Words."
51. We also control for the ideological heterogeneity of the majority coalition, the size of the majority, the number of dissenting and concurring opinions (separate measures), whether the Court was missing a justice, the length of time the natural court had served together, whether there was dissent in the lower court, and the broad issue area (civil liberties, economics, judicial power, federalism, or miscellaneous).
52. Note that this does not preclude the possibility that a chief was successful at exercising social leadership in one or two cases.
53. If we turn our attention instead to positive words, we retrieve similar results. While there is no statistically significant difference in the DAL's "nice" words between the two opinion types, we do observe differences in LIWC's positive emotion words ($p = .04$).
54. Fortas, "Chief Justice Warren."
55. *Nominations of William H. Rehnquist and Lewis F. Powell, Jr.: Hearings on Nominations of William H. Rehnquist, of Arizona, and Lewis F. Powell, Jr., of Virginia, to be Associate Justices of the Supreme Court of the United States, Before the Committee on the Judiciary, United States Senate*, 92nd Cong. 1 (1971) (Statement of William H. Rehnquist), 129.
56. Noah Feldman, *Scorpions: The Battles and Triumphs of FDR's Great Supreme Court Justices* (New York: Twelve, 2010).
57. Artemus Ward and David L. Weiden, *Sorcerers' Apprentices: 100 Years of Law Clerks at the United States Supreme Court* (New York: New York University Press, 2006).
58. Paul J. Wahlbeck, James F. Spriggs II, and Lee Sigelman, "Ghostwriters on the Court? A Stylistic Analysis of U.S. Supreme Court Draft Opinions," *American Politics Research* 30 (2002).
59. Stefanie A. Lindquist and David E. Klein, "The Influence of Jurisprudential Considerations on Supreme Court Decisionmaking: A Study of Conflict Cases," *Law & Society Review* 40 (2006).

12 ~ Troll-In-Chief? Affective Opinion Content and the Influence of the Chief Justice

DOUGLAS RICE AND CHRISTOPHER ZORN

In a 1973 article in the *William and Mary Law Review*, D. Grier Stephenson describes an exchange between Justice Stephen Field and Chief Justice Morrison Waite. Field, angered over not being chosen by Waite to author the majority opinion in an important case (*United States v. Union Pacific Railroad Co.*),[1] twice wrote to Waite complaining of the perceived slight. In his second response to Field, Waite underscores the importance for the (pro-railroad) decision's legitimacy that it not be authored by anyone perceived as too close to the railroad industry, and goes on to note that

> I knew that you were dissatisfied with the manner of the argument on the part of the government, and was afraid that this might unconsciously to you, find expression in the opinion. Once in and it would be difficult to get it out. Nothing could be more unfortunate for the court than to have it there.
>
> No one appreciates your vigorous style more than I do, and, but for these considerations I should have been glad to have had its use in this case.[2]

Stephenson's anecdote illustrates an important and underanalyzed aspect of the chief justice's role on the Court: The occasional (and sometimes more than occasional) need to consider justices' personal styles when making the decisions that shape the Court's proclamations. Such considerations, while commonly noted in historical and biographical accounts of the chief justices, have to date received little systematic analysis, at least in part because of the heretofore prohibitively massive amount of time and resources such analysis would consume. Yet matters of personal style and opinion content are at once at the core of those factors chiefs must weigh and are also likely among the things most amenable to influence by the chief himself or herself. Opinion language and content thus offers a unique window into the ways in which chief justices can shape the interpersonal dynamics of the Court.

Here we leverage recent developments in machine learning and computational linguistics to analyze the leadership of chief justices across nearly the entire history of the Supreme Court. We do so by constructing two new measures of leadership reflecting the social and task dimensions identified in Danelski's groundbreaking paper, which is printed in its entirety for the first time in this volume.[3] These measures, derived directly from patterns of word usage in the Court's opinions, provide insights into chief justice leadership across more than two hundred years of the Court's history and the tenures of sixteen chief justices. Our analysis suggests substantial shifts in the comity and productivity of the Court, as reflected in the words the justices themselves use in their opinions. Moreover, our findings generally provide substantial support both for Danelski's leadership typology and for previous biographical accounts of leadership during the tenures of individual chiefs.

We begin with a review of Danelski's leadership typology, of prior approaches to its measurement, and of the limitations of those approaches. We then introduce our method, in which we adapt and utilize tools for the analysis of sentiment in texts to measure the expressive content of Supreme Court opinions and map those measures onto Danelski's typology. In the subsequent section, building on research by Danelski and others on small groups,[4] we examine the degree to which they interrelate in the context of the Supreme Court. In the remainder of the chapter, we analyze shifts in the measures across the tenures of individual chiefs and discuss our findings and their implications for future research.

Leadership and the Chief Justice

In his seminal work on leadership in the U.S. Supreme Court, Danelski outlines two types of leaders: the *task* leader and the *social* leader. In the small group context, "the task leader is oriented primarily toward the external, task affairs of the group," while the "social-emotional leader is oriented primarily toward the internal, social-emotional affairs of the group."[5] In the Supreme Court, task leadership is focused on accomplishing the task at hand; that is, reaching an opinion of the Court for a particular case. Toward that end, the task leader "usually makes more suggestions than his colleagues, gives more opinions, and orients the discussion more frequently."[6] Often, this focus requires leaving consideration of comity on the Court by the wayside. Meanwhile, the social leader "concentrates on keeping the Court socially cohesive"; he or she "attends to the emotional needs of his associates by affirming their value as individuals and Court members."[7] For the social leader, comity on the Court is thus an important goal.

As Danelski indicates, the chief justice is uniquely positioned to assert these leadership roles. As "first among equals," the chief presides in open court and over the conference and also assigns the opinion in all cases in which he or she is in the majority, as well as undertaking various and sundry other administrative duties. Importantly, task and social leadership functions are not necessarily mutually exclusive. Instead, a chief can take on both, only one, or neither of these leadership functions. Indeed, the ability to lead and the propensity to exercise leadership has varied—sometimes dramatically—from one chief justice to the next.

In figure 12.1, we present the leadership functions asserted by the three chiefs discussed at length in Danelski's original paper. In his view, Chief Justice Charles Evans Hughes—a "great man" leader—assumed both task and social leadership functions. Chief Justice William Taft, by contrast, was particularly concerned with the amiability of the brethren, and left much of the task leadership functions to other justices, notably Justice Willis Van Devanter. Finally, Chief Justice Harlan Fiske Stone assumed neither role, leading to poor social cohesion and low productivity on the Court during his tenure. Danelski also suggests a potentially interactive effect: if task leadership duties are poorly fulfilled, then antagonisms may arise between individuals. In particular, this is hypothesized as having occurred during the tenure of Stone. Beyond reports from the Supreme Court, Burke's research on small groups suggests that greater focus and effort placed on task leadership duties could, at some point, have a deleterious effect on social cohesion as well, as they may result in greater demands being placed on the social leader.[8]

In studies of the Court, evidence for adoption of these roles primarily arises from judicial biographies, and from quantitative studies of phenomena (such as merits voting) that are not necessarily indicative of the interpersonal climate on the Court. Consider measuring task leadership. In the context of the Supreme Court, case counts—or the "rate of production"[9]—seem appropriate at first glance. The Court's actual workload, however, has varied considerably over time, with changes in various types of burdens (such as circuit riding) that would be left unaccounted for in models

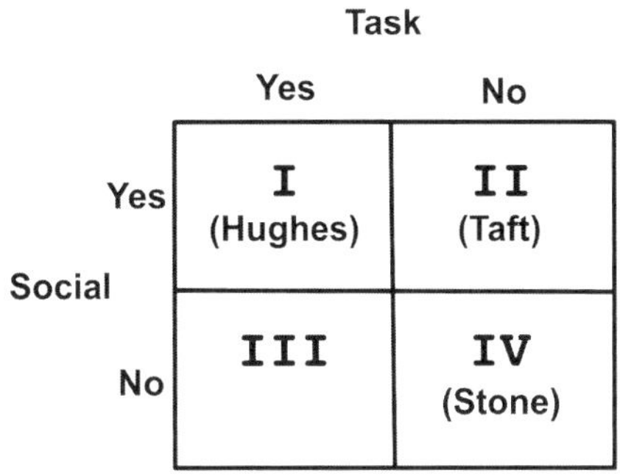

Fig. 12.1. Leadership typology

that only consider caseload. Moreover, shifts in the Court's jurisdiction, particularly through formal mechanisms like the Judiciary Acts of 1891 and 1925, mean any such measure would vary considerably independent of leadership.

Alternatively, biographical accounts have proven quite useful in understanding both the task and social leadership of individual justices. Mason's opus on Justice Harlan Fiske Stone[10] informs Danelski's original work and is the touchstone for assessing Stone's role in the development of the Court.[11] Despite their utility for the study of individual chief justices, however, such accounts are less useful for comparing the tenures of different chiefs or for assessing temporal changes in the social and task functions of the Court. Further, these studies typically rely on the reporting of conflict or cohesion as expressed in the publicly available papers of the justices or their clerks, meaning much may remain hidden from view.

Analysis of concurring and dissenting behavior is perhaps the most prevalent quantitative approach for scholars interested in studying the quality of leadership across chiefs. Concurrences and dissents are useful as they are easily observable signals; moreover, it is well-understood that "high levels of dissenting behavior are dysfunctional to the operations of the court and are specifically discouraged by the *Canons of Judicial Ethics*."[12] For this reason, scholars studying the differences in the leadership styles of Chief Justices Hughes and Stone often point to the decline in the norm of consensus during the early 1940s or to the shifts in dissenting and concurring behavior that occurred between their tenures.[13] Yet that very norm of consensus, traceable back to Chief Justice John Marshall's preference for issuing a single decision of the Court, leads to difficulties in applying the same insight to the tenures of earlier chiefs. That is, the general preference for obscuring open disagreement means dissenting and concurring opinions were relatively rare prior to the 1940s, even in times of weak leadership and strong disagreement among the Court's members.

Chief Justice Leadership and Opinion Content

We propose measuring social and task leadership by examining the language used in the justices' opinions. At the core of this approach is the (we believe, uncontroversial) idea that in writing their opinions, the justices choose their words carefully and deliberately, and that those choices will thus reflect a range of influences on their mental state at the time of that writing, including the influence of the chief. This approach also overcomes many of the limitations of prior research by providing a comparable measure of Court output across time, one that can thus be applied across the tenures of all chief justices. Moreover, by examining different opinion types separately, we build on the insight of prior research highlighting the importance of these differing types of behavior while at the same time not being constrained to recent periods of study due to the norm of consensus. More generally, we believe that by examining the linguistic content of the opinions themselves across an extended range of the Court's history, we have a consistent measure of interpersonal relations on the Court that is influenced to a far lesser degree by changes in the Court's environment.

We begin with the challenge of measuring task leadership. Recall that the task leader is said to be primarily concerned with the productivity of the court, and in particular the production of opinions. As Danelski states, the task leader is "apt to be somewhat reserved; and, in concentrating on the decision of the Court, his response to the emotional needs of his associates is apt to be secondary."[14] The task leader, concerned with the completion of the task at hand, will prioritize the effective and efficient disposition of cases. In this view, a strong task leader on the Court should see scant value in emotional interactions and extraneous emotional opinion language, particularly that which serves little purpose but to address "emotional needs." Rather, we expect that the strong task leader will act to minimize emotion on the Court insofar as the emotion is superfluous to, and perhaps counter to, the completion of the task. They will encourage the writing of more direct opinions, relatively devoid of extraneous emotional language unnecessary for the Court to reach the task leader's goal. The degree of emotional content may thus serve as an indicator of the extent of task leadership present on the Court, with less emotional language indicating superior task leadership.

With the desire to ensure the social cohesion of the Court, a strong social leader dislikes conflict and seeks to prevent it, in part through ensuring that the emotional needs of the other justices are met. To this end, the social leader will seek to decrease antagonism in conference, to cut off debate when it becomes too aggressive, and to suggest modifications to opinions in order to discourage dissents and concurrences. Moreover, even in circumstances where disagreement or dissent is inevitable, a strong social leader will work to ensure that the justices—as the saying goes—disagree without being disagreeable. Thus, while task leadership is manifested in the *amount* of emotional language, we believe social leadership may be found in the *tone* of that language. As a strong social leader works to smooth over the divisions between justices, opinions should feature language with a more positive tone. Conversely, in the absence of such strong social leadership, opinions should feature more negative language.

The question of how to assess the amount and direction of emotional content in a body of text is one that is well-understood by students of contemporary linguistics. Broadly speaking, the field of *sentiment analysis* is concerned with "the computational study of how opinions, attitudes, emotions, and perspectives are expressed in language."[15] For our purposes, we draw on two fundamental concepts in sentiment analysis. *Subjectivity* is the degree of subjective content in a document; here this refers to the fraction of the document that has either a positive or a negative emotional valence. *Polarity* is the directionality of that valence, positive or negative. Polarity is thus a measure of the tone of an opinion, while subjectivity reflects the amount of emotional language present.

Our approach addresses many of the issues present in prior research, but it also carries with it some new potential concerns. Two such concerns are whether we are actually measuring the language used by law clerks rather than the justices themselves, and whether the chief justice can actually exert any effective influence on opinion content or word usage.[16] With respect to the former, it is generally agreed that at least since the 1890s, justices have varyingly used their law clerks to draft or edit opinions. Thus clerks may shift the content of opinions and the emotional valence would thus not reflect the sentiment of the justice. At the same time, while clerks may—for some justices—play a role in shaping the content of opinions, the justices ultimately retain the final say over the opinion's content and thus will be expected to shape it as they see fit. As one-time law clerk and former Chief Justice William Rehnquist stated when discussing his clerkship under Justice Robert H. Jackson, "the end product was unquestionably the Justice's own, both in form and in substance."[17] In addition, to the extent that law clerks influence opinion content, they are also part of the Supreme Court community and thus would be expected to be susceptible to influences arising from the social environment of the Court. Finally, anecdotal accounts suggest that the justices may strategically assign opinions to clerks with the intent of expressing a certain emotional valence.[18] In all, though law clerks may influence the content of opinions, we believe the influence is not great enough to unduly influence our measurement strategy.

With respect to the chief's ability to influence language, we wish to make it clear that—except for the unusual circumstances described in the exchange between Chief Justice Waite and Justice Field at the opening of this chapter—we believe such direct micro-management of opinion language are rare. At the same time, it is important to note that such direct control is not integral to our claim about chief justice influence on opinion content. Rather, we suggest only that the interpersonal or emotional climate of the Court is likely, over time, to be reflected in the language justices employ in their written opinions. Periods of poor task and social leadership in the small group context of the Supreme Court are marked by increases in the animosity among justices. The language of opinions—both in terms of the volume of emotional content and the valence of that emotional content—will shift according to the climate of the Court.

Data and Methods

To undertake our analysis, we require data on the textual content of the opinions written by the justices. Specifically, our data comprise the full text of every opinion issued by the U.S. Supreme Court between 1793 and 2000, inclusive.[19] For each opinion, we extracted information about the type of opinion (majority, concurring, dissenting, "in part," or *per curiam*), the author of the opinion, and the date of the decision. In total, we have nearly 35,000 unique opinions spanning more than two hundred years and including the tenures of sixteen chief justices.[20]

To classify the content of opinions, we adopt a conventional dictionary-based method for automated content analysis. In dictionary methods, the researcher identifies a subset of words, the *dictionary*, that are related to some characteristic that the researcher wishes to measure. The researcher then calculates the rate at which dictionary words appear in each text, enabling classification into whatever category the dictionary is intended to capture. Because of their relative ease of use,[21] dictionaries have been employed across a host of different political science applications, including in the identification of international events from news reports[22] and media framing of racial issues.[23] The costs of constructing these dictionaries, however, can be exorbitant,[24] and costs of validation can be equally high.[25] For this reason, researchers occasionally use any of a number of publicly available dictionaries, particularly for sentiment analysis. The use of such publicly available dictionaries carries some risks as well, however, as applying any dictionary outside the realm for which it was designed can lead to potentially serious errors.[26]

A related concern that bears addressing is the issue of *semantic change*. In brief, semantic change is the idea that word usage, and the meaning(s) commonly associated with a word, may change across extended periods of time. Because we consider opinions over more than two hundred years of Supreme Court history, the valence attached to individual words may vary during the time period under study; this is particularly problematic in our case, as existing sentiment dictionaries are typically calibrated to late twentieth-century usages. To the extent that words are inaccurately labeled as "positive" or "negative," the conclusions drawn from them would be suspect.

We address this issue by deriving two alternative methods to assess word polarity directly from the texts of Supreme Court opinions themselves, and then combining the results achieved with each of these with a third set of results built upon a widely used public domain dictionary. For the latter, we use the sentiment dictionary accompanying the Linguistic Inquiry and Word Count (LIWC) software,[27] which itself has been used previously in studies of the judiciary,[28] to calculate polarity and subjectivity scores for each opinion. In addition to LIWC, we derive two specialized, context-specific dictionaries based on the texts of the opinions themselves.[29] For the first of these, we chose a seed set of nineteen positive and twenty-three negative words, then identified the five hundred words that were most likely to co-occur with our positive and negative seed sets, respectively. These thousand words were chosen by estimating the probability of other words occurring in the same opinions as the words in our seed set. More specifically, we ranked co-occurrence as a function of the log-odds ratio of a particular word co-occurring with positive or negative words in our seed set, then selected the five hundred words most likely to occur with our positive seed words, and the five hundred words most likely to occur with our negative seed words. For our third dictionary, we adapted the conjunctive approach suggested by Hatzivassiloglou and McKeown.[30] We identified a seed set of twenty-five positive and twenty-five negative seed words, then wrote a computer program to identify all words explicitly used in a conjunction with our seed words in the texts of Supreme Court opinions. We then manually removed irrelevant and inappropriate terms, yielding a "conjoined" dictionary of 520 positive and 580 negative words.

Each dictionary thus identifies a body of words classified as having either "positive" or "negative" valence. Using each of the three dictionaries, we then count the number of positive and negative words appearing in each opinion. This in turn allows us to calculate scores for each opinion for each dictionary. We calculate an opinion's *polarity* as simply the number of positive words minus the number of negative words, divided by sum of the count of positive and negative words. This score thus ranges from −1.0 (for an opinion with only negatively valenced words) to 1.0 (for one with only positively valenced words). Similarly, we calculate the *subjectivity* of an opinion as the sum of positive and negative word counts, divided by the overall number of words (both valenced and nonvalenced) used in the opinion. This score ranges (in theory) from zero to 1.0, though in practice it achieves a maximum of roughly 0.15. Finally, we average the three dictionary-specific scores for each opinion to yield an overall score.

We begin by documenting the validity of our approach. In particular, we are concerned with construct validity, or the extent to which our measure "correlates with other measures of the same construct."[31] Consider, for instance, the commonly used metric of opinion majority size. We would expect polarity to be more positive, on average, in cases with large majority coalition opinions, given the agreement of the justices on the outcome. To test this, we matched our opinion-level measures to the extensive information available from the Supreme Court Database.[32] We can then examine the relationship between our measures and other widely utilized variables to measure the interpersonal climate of the Court. To that end, in the left panel of figure 12.2, we plot the average polarity of majority opinions by the number of votes in the majority for terms 1946 through 2000. Note that, as we would expect, opinions become more positive as the Court becomes less divided on the outcome. On average, when justices agree on how to address a particular case, the opinions of the Court are more positive. This dynamic is further reflected in the right panel, where we plot the average polarity of dissenting opinions by the number of majority votes. On average, justices dissenting in highly divided cases write more negative opinions than justices facing larger majority coalitions. In both cases, we see evidence that polarity maps to the divisiveness of the Court.

Figures 12.3 and 12.4 plot three-year moving averages of subjectivity and polarity scores, respectively, for each opinion type in our data. Most of the polarity scores in figure 12.3 exhibit a slight but noticeable decline over the Court's history, suggesting that the tone of opinions has become more

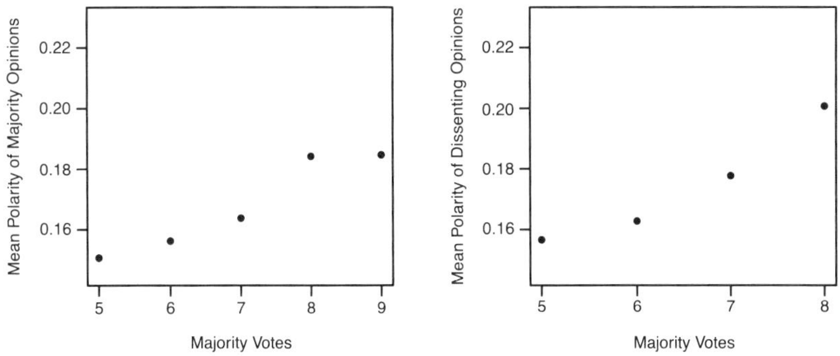

Fig. 12.2. Mean polarity of majority opinions (*left*) and dissenting opinions (*right*), by majority coalition size

Points equal the average polarity of the indicated opinion type for all cases with the indicated number of majority voters for terms 1947 through 2000. Polarity equals the sum of positive words minus the number of negative words in an opinion, divided by the sum of positive and negative words in that opinion.

negative over time. The exception is in *per curiam* opinions, where no such decrease is observed, but where average polarity scores are in general lower than for other opinion types (mean = 0.149, versus 0.181, 0.201, and 0.177 for majority, concurring, and dissenting opinions, respectively). In figure 12.4, we observe a general increase in the use of emotional language beginning in the 1930s, one that is particularly noticeable across all opinion types. Note also, however, that the rate of increase seems to be arrested, or even to be declining in the case of *per curiam* opinions, during the tenure of Chief Justice Warren.

Analysis

Our empirical analysis has two foci. First, we wish to understand whether and how social and task leadership are interrelated. Second, we wish to see how task leadership—measured as subjectivity—and social leadership—measured as polarity—have varied across chiefs. We begin by discussing how these measures relate. According to Danelski, the "constant vying for task leadership in the Stone conference led to serious conflict, ruffled tempers, severe tension, and antagonism. A social leader was badly needed."[33] This suggests that as task leadership decreases on the Court, the demands on a social leader will increase. To the extent that the social leader is not up to these demands, decreases in task leadership should correlate with decreases in social cohesion on the Court.

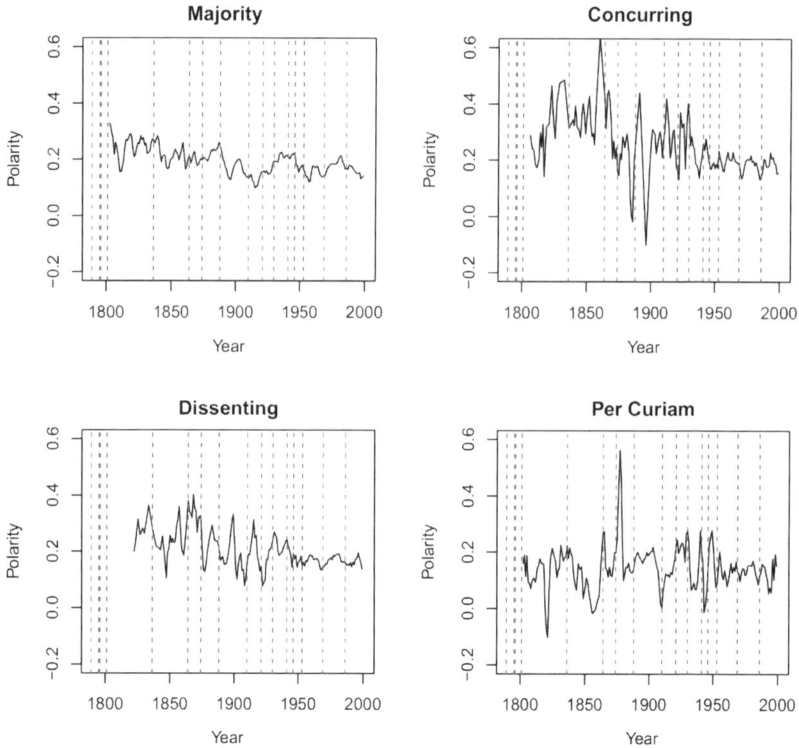

Fig. 12.3. Three-year moving average of opinion polarity, by year and opinion type

Dashed vertical gray lines represent the first year of a new chief justice's tenure. Polarity equals the sum of positive words minus the number of negative words in an opinion, divided by the sum of positive and negative words in that opinion.

To examine the relationship between polarity and subjectivity, figure 12.5 plots the annual mean of subjectivity (horizontal axis) against the annual mean of polarity (vertical axis).[34] While the relationship is not terribly strong, notice that when average annual subjectivity scores are higher than approximately 0.06, increases in subjectivity are mildly correlated with decreases in polarity. Thus, as Danelski suspects, as task leaders lose control, demands increase on social leaders.

Of course, it is also clearly evident that as we decrease mean annual subjectivity after approximately a subjectivity score of 0.06, polarity also declines. In other words, the relationship appears curvilinear across the full range of the data. The red fitted line plotted from a quadratic model of

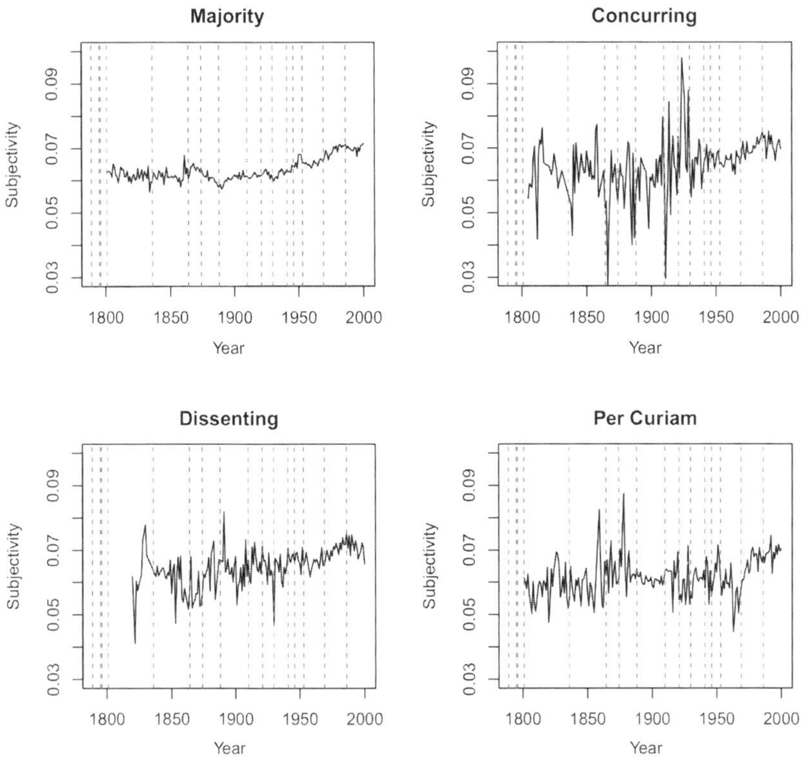

Fig. 12.4. Three-year moving average of opinion subjectivity, by year and opinion type

Dashed vertical gray lines represent the first year of a new chief justice's tenure. Subjectivity equals the sum of positive and negative words in an opinion, divided by the sum of all words in the opinion.

polarity on subjectivity offers confirmation of that relationship. While the lower levels of subjectivity the quadratic fits represent but a small number of opinions across the Court's history, they are not entirely unanticipated by research on task and social leadership of small groups. In particular, Burke discusses the demands placed on social leaders by particularly aggressive task leaders.[35]

On the more specific question of chief justices' leadership styles, our data are also informative. To assess changes in leadership style over chiefs' tenures, we examine differences in subjectivity and polarity between the tenure of each chief and that of his immediate predecessor. In figure 12.6, we plot estimates of the difference in means for each measure, along with

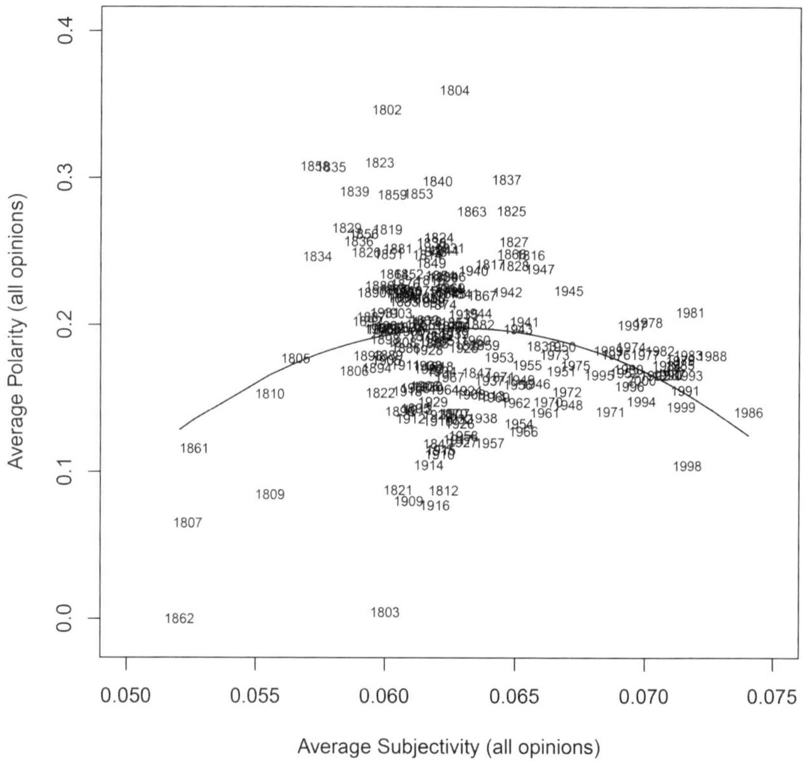

Fig. 12.5. Scatterplot of average subjectivity (annual) by average polarity (annual)
Fitted red line computed as the quadratic fit of a regression of polarity on subjectivity.

their associated 95 percent pointwise confidence intervals, using averages generated by pooling across all opinion types. Thus, each dot represents the difference in the mean polarity or subjectivity of all opinions during the tenure of each chief (for example, Rehnquist) as compared to his immediate predecessor (in that example, Burger).

A few observations from figure 12.6 bear mentioning. First, note that in the tenures of early chiefs (Jay, Rutledge, Ellsworth), there are few opinions on which to base our analyses; as a result, we can say little about the influence of these chiefs on the comity or productivity of the Court. Interestingly, when Chief Justice Marshall takes over the Court and discontinues the use of seriatim opinions, the average subjectivity of opinions decreases,

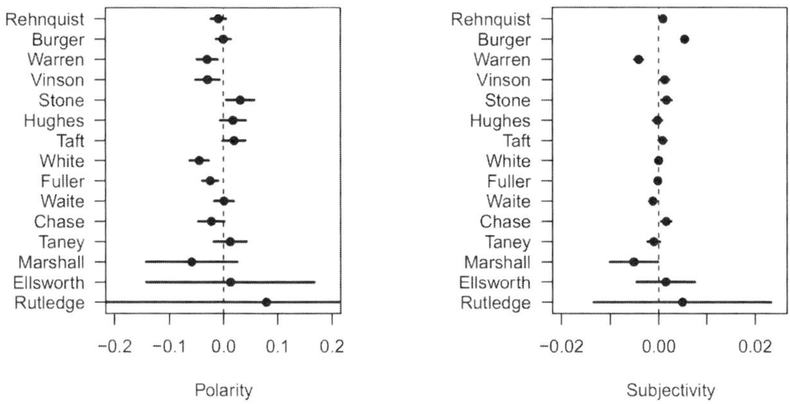

Fig. 12.6. Difference in means between a chief justice and the immediately preceding chief justice
For example, "Rutledge" indicates the change in average polarity or subjectivity from the tenure of Jay to Rutledge.

suggesting that the move to single opinions reduced the degree of personal/emotional content in the opinions themselves. Also immediately noticeable are the large shifts in subjectivity between Vinson and Warren, indicating the success of Warren as a task leader, and between Warren and Burger, suggesting the relative failure of Burger in a similar role.

Of greater import, how do Danelski's accounts of the early twentieth-century chiefs (Taft, Hughes, and Stone) stack up in comparison to expectations? In terms of task leadership (measured as subjectivity), our aggregate results offer mixed support for that narrative. Subjectivity increases slightly during Taft's leadership relative to that of Chief Justice White, though not to a statistically meaningful degree, while from Taft to Hughes there is little discernible change in subjectivity. Given that both court eras included strong task leaders, this pattern fits with Danelski's predictions. From Hughes to Stone, however, the average subjectivity of opinions increases in a manner consistent with decreased levels of task leadership. This, again, fits with expectations derived from Danelski's account of the task leadership of Hughes and Stone.

Examining polarity, however, we see an unexpected pattern: under the leadership of Chief Justice Stone, the degree of positively valenced language in the opinions actually increases from its average during Chief Justice Hughes's tenure, although the magnitude of this shift is relatively small. One possible explanation for this puzzling result lies in our initial decision to combine opinions of different types. As a substantive matter, it would be surprising if the linguistic content of majority opinions—which are necessarily the product of dialogue and compromise—were not different from that of the single-authored, discretionary statements made in concurring and dissenting opinions. And, in fact, our descriptive plots in figures 12.3 and 12.4 illustrate that the dynamics of different opinion types vary widely. In a similar vein, Caldeira and Zorn note differences in the aggregate dynamics of opinions with concurrences and dissents on the Court.[36]

To examine this in more detail, we conduct a series of similar analyses but now separated according to opinion type.[37] We begin by examining subjectivity by chief and opinion type; those results are presented in figure 12.7. In discussing these, we focus on what we believe to be the most interesting of the observed relationships. Perhaps most striking is the finding—consistent across opinion types—that opinions written during the Burger Court exhibited, on average, a higher degree of emotional content than did those written during Chief Justice Warren's tenure. For many contemporary observers of the Court, this will be unsurprising; in contrast to Warren's relatively strong task leadership, historical and journalistic accounts of the Burger Court often paint a picture of a fractured body with little in the way of internal constraints on disagreement.[38]

As for Taft, Hughes, and Stone, the shift in task leadership from Hughes to Stone is evident in the Court's concurring opinions, but relatively absent across other opinion types, yielding mild evidence of the influence of their respective task leadership. Of course, the total number of both concurring and dissenting opinions was also increasing during Stone's tenure.[39] Hughes's effort to maintain the social cohesion of the Court and the norm of consensus thus also seems to have been an effort as task leader to maintain the productivity of the Court.

We turn next to how the chiefs fared in terms of social leadership and maintaining comity on the Court; these are illustrated in figure 12.8. The shift from White to Taft was generally accompanied by a more positive Court, as would be expected given Taft's reputation as an affable chief. Changes in polarity from Taft to Hughes vary depending on opinion type; majority opinions were, on balance, more positive under Hughes, but the language in *per curiam* opinions actually grew more negative. Finally, from Hughes to Stone, we see no significant change, though on average concurrences were more positive and *per curiams* more negative under Stone than under Hughes. These results suggest that Stone was not quite a total failure as social leader; rather, during his tenure the justices do not appear to have been particularly more negative, on average, as during tenure of Chief

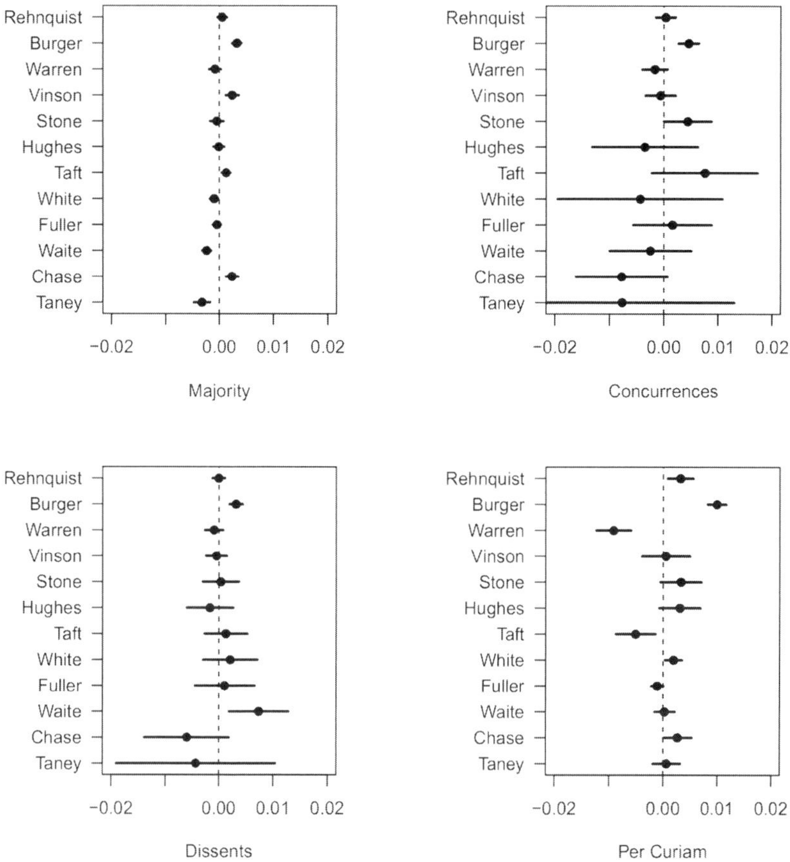

Fig. 12.7. Difference in mean subjectivity between a chief justice and the immediately preceding chief justice, by opinion type

Subjectivity reflects the amount of emotional language in an opinion and is a measure of the task leadership of a particular chief justice, with lower levels of subjectivity indicating stronger task leadership.

Justice Hughes. This is consistent with research by Haynie indicating that despite the leadership of Hughes, other justices began to act out during his tenure,[40] a finding supported by biographical accounts as well.[41]

Beyond Taft, Hughes, and Stone, other patterns emerge. Chief Justice Vinson's tenure, for example, was marked by significantly more negative majority and concurring opinions and (to a lesser degree) dissenting opinions, relative to Chief Justice Stone. This is consistent with our previous finding reported above, indicating that majority opinions became more

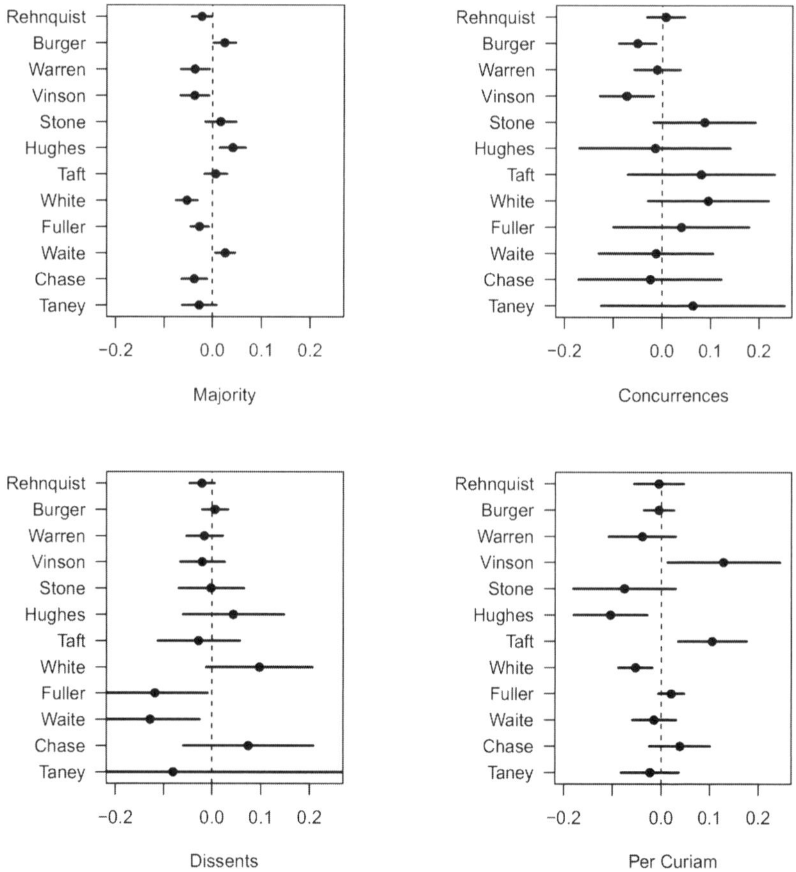

Fig. 12.8. Difference in mean polarity between a chief justice and the immediately preceding chief justice, by opinion type
Polarity reflects the relative proportion of positive language in comparison to negative language in an opinion and is a measure of the social leadership. Higher values are indicative of a more positive Court and thus better social leadership.

subjective on his watch. In totality, Vinson appears to have been both a poor social leader and a poor task leader, a characterization that is not at all at odds with historical accounts.[42]

Another interesting pattern emerges in regards to Chief Justice Burger. Recall that Burger's task leadership, as measured by average subjectivity, appeared particularly poor. In terms of social cohesion, the polarity of majority opinions under Burger is, on average, actually more positive than for majority opinions under Chief Justice Warren. This is unexpected given the earlier documentation of the relationship between task leadership and social leadership. Note also, however, that concurring opinions under Burger were, on average, substantially more negative. These dynamics may be explained by the fact that Burger was widely recognized, in biographical and journalistic accounts, as having consistently and repeatedly joined majorities not due to policy agreement but rather in order to assign the opinion to justices closer to his ideological predispositions.[43] This strategic opinion assignment is well-documented in studies of the Supreme Court[44] and warrants further exploration in subsequent studies focusing primarily on later periods, as the impact in earlier periods is likely to be minimal.[45]

To this point, we have examined only broad changes in the climate of the Court. It should be clear, though, that the broad changes presented above reflect the aggregation of changes in the sentiment of individual justices. We have argued that to the extent the chief is a successful leader, the average polarity *across justices* should be positive, while the average subjectivity *across justices* should be low. Yet these average changes certainly mask the social and task leadership of chiefs as it relates to particular justices.

To see this, we return to the Taft, Hughes, and Stone eras and examine the polarity and subjectivity of opinions authored by three long-tenured justices—Louis Brandeis, Willis Van Devanter, and Owen J. Roberts—as well as the *per curiam* opinions of the Court. In the left panel of figure 12.9, we have plotted the annual average subjectivity of all opinion types authored by the specified justice, and in the right panel we have done the same for polarity. The vertical dashed lines indicate the arrival of a new chief, and the horizontal lines indicate the average subjectivity or polarity for the specified justice during the tenure of that particular chief. For example, the plot in the first row of the subjectivity panel shows that the average subjectivity of opinions authored by Brandeis hardly shifted between the tenures of Taft and Hughes.

In general, figure 12.9 provides further evidence in support of the subjectivity results above, as the patterns again match expectations, with Brandeis and Van Devanter opinion subjectivity consistent or slightly decreasing from Taft to Hughes, and the Roberts and *per curiam* opinion subjectivity increasing from Hughes to Stone. One unexpected pattern does emerge, however, as the average subjectivity of *per curiam* opinions actually increases from Taft to Hughes. While conjectural, this shift may reflect Van Devanter's influence as task leader during the Taft years[46] and subsequent departure during the Hughes era, as well as the growing divisions on the Court during the Hughes era.

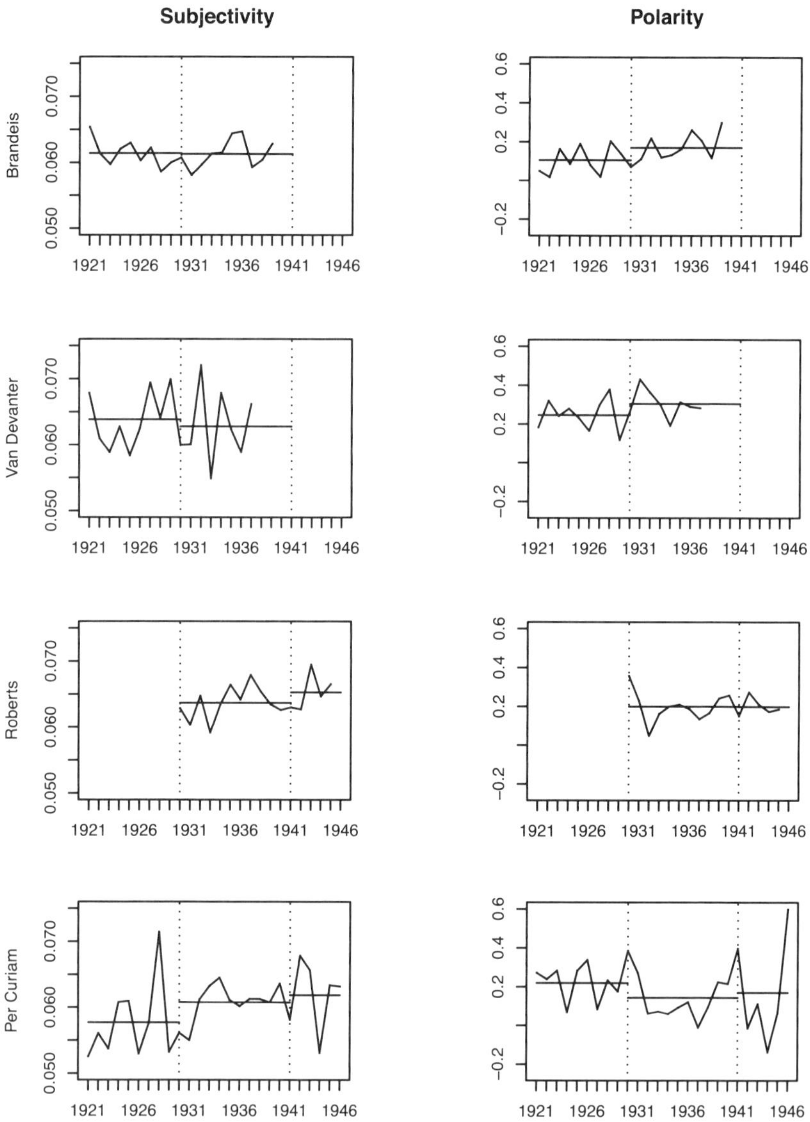

Fig. 12.9. Justice-specific shifts in annual and average polarity and subjectivity during the Taft, Hughes, and Stone eras

Vertical dashed lines indicate a change in chief justice. The horizontal bars indicate the average subjectivity (left) and polarity (right) for the justice specified at left during the tenure of the chief justice (in order, Taft, Hughes, and Stone).

Moving to polarity, Brandeis and Van Devanter both wrote slightly more positive opinions, on average, during the Hughes era than during the Taft era. In some respects, it is unsurprising that Brandeis' post-Taft opinions would reflect a more positive tone. Recall that Brandeis was deeply involved in the Taft administration's Pinchot-Ballinger scandal,[47] and that (arguably in retribution) Taft was one of seven former American Bar Association presidents to sign a 1916 letter formally opposing Brandeis' appointment to the Court. While Chief Justice Hughes was no progressive, he was significantly more open to such policies than his predecessor. With respect to Van Devanter, Pusey notes that because of Van Devanter's frequent bouts with writer's block, Hughes occasionally "reassigned the opinions in a discreet manner, taking care to avoid hurting Van Devanter's feelings."[48] Interestingly, Brandeis and Van Devanter were the two associate justices who accompanied Chief Justice Hughes in testimony against a bill (introduced by then-senator Hugo Black) that would have expanded the Court's workload;[49] they were also the only two associate justices with whom Hughes consulted prior to submitting his famous letter opposing court packing to Senator Wheeler on March 22, 1937.[50] For Roberts, in contrast, there was little shift in opinion polarity across the tenures of Hughes and Stone.

Conclusion

Danelski's theoretical framework for the study of the group dynamics of the Supreme Court set the stage for all future evaluations of leadership by the chief justice, and it has proven invaluable to subsequent generations of scholars studying the Court. Here we sought to build on Danelski's insights by developing a new approach to the study of the chief. Our approach focuses on using the written opinions of the Court to measure task and social leadership on the Court. In general, the evidence from our measures of leadership—subjectivity and polarity—suggests support for Danelski's impressions of task and social leadership under Taft, Stone, and Hughes.

With consistent measures across the history of the Court, though, our analysis expands from these three chiefs to the thirteen other chiefs as well, offering the opportunity to examine leadership across nearly the entire history of the Supreme Court. Our findings support many of the biographical and historical interpretations of the leadership of particular chiefs; for instance, in our analysis, Vinson and Burger appear to have been lacking in social and task leadership, while Warren appears to have been a good task leader, albeit one with some difficulty in maintaining a socially cohesive

Court. They also suggest more broad-based shifts in the impact of leadership on the Court, with the decline in the norm of consensus coinciding with a prolonged and sustained decrease in our measure of task leadership on the Court.

Beyond the tenures of individual chiefs, our analysis contributed additional insight into the interrelatedness of social and task leadership. The failure of the task leader invariably places additional demands on the social leader. For the Supreme Court, this has meant that years when the task leader has been particularly underwhelming, whether in terms of over- or under-controlling the Court, generally correlate with more negative opinions.

Moving forward, the analyses in this chapter have largely focused on a single explanation, the chief, for the variation in polarity and subjectivity across the history of the Court. It is important for future empirical examinations, however, to delve into alternative causes for these shifts. The issues the Court considers, the makeup of the Court during the chief's tenure, and a host of other influences, many of which are explored in this volume, could influence the comity and productivity of the Court during the tenure of a chief.

NOTES

A previous version of this chapter was presented at the Annual Meeting of the Midwest Political Science Association, April 11–14, 2013, Chicago. We appreciate comments by David Danelski, Lee Epstein, Art Ward, and the anonymous reviewers.

1. 353 U.S. 112 (1957).

2. D. Grier Stephenson, "The Chief Justice as Leader: The Case of Morrison Remick Waite," *William and Mary Law Review* 14 (1973).

3. David Danelski, "The Influence of the Chief Justice in the Decisional Process of the Supreme Court," paper presented at the Annual Meeting of the Midwest Political Science Association, Chicago, 1960.

4. E.g., Peter Burke, "Task and Social-Emotional Leadership Role Performance," *Sociometry* 34 (1971).

5. Ibid., 22.

6. Danelski, "Influence of the Chief Justice," 1.

7. Ibid.

8. Burke, "Task and Social-Emotional Leadership," 22–40.

9. Thomas Walker, "Leader Selection and Behavior in Small Political Groups," *Small Group Research* 7 (1976); Joshua C. Teitelbaum, "Age and Tenure of the Justices and Productivity of the U.S. Supreme Court: Are Term Limits Necessary?" *Florida State University Law Review* 34 (2006).

10. Alpheus T. Mason, *Harlan Fiske Stone: Pillar of the Law* (New York: Viking Press, 1956).

11. Thomas Walker, Lee Epstein, and William Dixon, "On the Mysterious Demise of Consensual Norms in the United States Supreme Court," *Journal of Politics* 50 (1988); Stacie L. Haynie, "Leadership and Consensus on the U.S. Supreme Court," *Journal of Politics* 54 (1992).

12. Walker, "Leader Selection and Behavior," 366.

13. Walter Murphy, "Courts as Small Groups," *Harvard Law Review* 79 (1965); Walker, Epstein, and Dixon, "On the Mysterious Demise," 361–89; Haynie, "Leadership and Consensus," 1158–69; Gregory Caldeira and Christopher J. W. Zorn, "Of Time and Consensual Norms in the Supreme Court," *American Journal of Political Science* 42 (1988).

14. Danelski, "Influence of the Chief Justice," 1.

15. Bing Liu, "Sentiment Analysis and Subjectivity," in *Handbook of Language Processing*, 2nd ed., ed. Nitin Indurkhya and Fred J. Damerau (Boca Raton, FL: Chapman & Hall/CRC Press, 2010), 627–66.

16. A third concern, semantic drift or semantic change, holds that the emotional valence attached to the words may shift over time. We address this concern in our description of constructing the measures.

17. William Rehnquist, "Who Writes Decisions of the Supreme Court," *U.S. News and World Report*, Dec. 9, 2008.

18. For instance, Justice Brennan reportedly assigned his most "acerbic" clerk to draft the dissenting opinion in *National League of Cities v. Usery*, 426 U.S. 833 (1976). Bob Woodward and Scott Armstrong, *The Brethren: Inside the Supreme Court* (New York: Simon & Schuster, 1979).

19. We downloaded all Supreme Court cases from 1793 through 2000 from public.resource.org, an open-source repository which maintains a compilation of various government documents. From each case file, we created opinion-specific text files, such that each file represents a written justice opinion for a particular case.

20. While our preference was to include all chiefs, including the recent tenure of Chief Justice John Roberts, our use of the public.resource.org data precludes the inclusion of the tenure of the Roberts, as the data do not reliably extend into that period. With that said, we do capture the overwhelming majority of the Court's history by using this data source, including the full tenures of all chiefs prior to Roberts.

21. Kevin Quinn et al., "How to Analyze Political Attention with Minimal Assumptions and Costs," *American Journal of Political Science* 54 (2010); Justin Grimmer and Brandon Stewart, "Text as Data: The Promise and Pitfalls of Automatic Content Analysis Methods for Political Texts," *Political Analysis* 21 (2013).

22. Philip Schrodt, Shannon G. Davis, and Judith L. Weddle, "Political Science: KEDS, A Program for the Machine Coding of Event Data," *Social Science Computer Review* 12 (1994); Philip Schrodt and Deborah Gerner, "Validity Assessment of a Machine-Coded Event Data Set for the Middle East, 1982–1992," *American Journal of Political Science* 38 (1994); Philip Schrodt, "Precedents, Progress, and Prospects in Political Event Data," *International Interactions* 38 (2012).

23. Paul Kellstedt, "Media Framing and the Dynamics of Racial Policy Preferences," *American Journal of Political Science* 44 (2000).

24. Deborah Gerner et al., "The Analysis of Political Events Using Machine Coded Data," *International Studies Quarterly* 38 (1994).

25. Grimmer and Stewart, "Text as Data."

26. Ibid.

27. James Pennebaker, Martha Francis, and Roger Booth, *Linguistic Inquiry and Word Count: LIWC2001* (Mahwah, NJ: Erlbaum Publishers, 2001); James Pennebaker et al., *The Development and Psychometric Properties of LIWC2007* (Austin, TX: LIWC.net, 2007)

28. Ryan J. Owens and Justin P. Wedeking, "Justices and Legal Clarity: Analyzing the Complexity of U.S. Supreme Court Opinions," *Law & Society Review* 45 (2011); Ryan J. Owens and Justin P. Wedeking, "Predicting Drift on Politically Insulated Institutions: A Study of Ideological Drift on the United States Supreme Court," *Journal of Politics* 74 (2012).

29. Note that for each of our specialized dictionaries, we began by addressing negations in the texts, which can invert the polarity of terms. We do so by prefacing negated terms with "not," as suggested in prior research on sentiment analysis of texts. See, e.g., Sanjiv Das and Mike Chen, "Yahoo! For Amazon: Sentiment Extraction from Small Talk on the Web," *Management Science* 53 (2007); Bo Pang, Lillian Lee, and Shivakumar Vaithyanathan, "Thumbs up? Sentiment Classification Using Machine Learning Techniques," Proceedings of the 2002 Conference on Empirical Methods in Natural Language Processing (EMNLP), 2002.

30. Valileios Hatzivassiloglou and Kathleen McKeown, "Predicting the Semantic Orientation of Adjectives," Proceedings of the 35th Annual Meeting of the Association for Computational Linguistics and Eighth Conference of the European Chapter of the Association for Computational Linguistics, 1997.

31. Quinn et al., "How to Analyze Political Attention," 221.

32. Harold Spaeth et al., "The Supreme Court Database," Aug. 30, 2011, http://scdb.wustl.edu/data.php, accessed Aug. 22, 2012.

33. Danelski, "Influence of the Chief Justice," 4.

34. For the following analyses, we remove all opinions authored by the chief justice himself. We do so to avoid conflating the polarity or subjectivity of the particular chief with the polarity or subjectivity of the Court.

35. Burke, "Task and Social-Emotional Leadership," 22–40.

36. Caldeira and Zorn, "Of Time and Consensual Norms," 891–93.

37. Note that doing so required that we remove seriatim opinions, and—as a result—chief justices Jay, Rutledge, and Ellsworth. Therefore, our analyses now begin in 1801, with the tenure of Chief Justice Marshall. In addition, the larger and more consistent number of majority opinions provides greater precision in our estimates for those opinion types, particularly for chief justices serving in the nineteenth century.

38. e.g., Bernard Schwartz, *The Ascent of Pragmatism: The Burger Court in Action* (New York: Addison-Wesley, 1990); Earl M. Maltz, *The Chief Justiceship of Warren Burger, 1969–1986* (Columbia: University of South Carolina Press, 2000).

39. Walker, Epstein, and Dixon, "On the Mysterious Demise," 361–89.

40. Haynie, "Leadership and Consensus," 1158–69.

41. Edward White, *The American Judicial Tradition* (New York: Oxford University Press, 1976).

42. Michael R. Belknap, *The Vinson Court: Justices, Rulings, and Legacy* (Santa Barbara, CA: ABC-CLIO, 2004).

43. Linda Greenhouse, "How Not to Be Chief Justice: The Apprenticeship of William H. Rehnquist," *University of Pennsylvania Law Review* 154 (2006); Sandra Wood, "In the Shadow of the Chief: The Role of the Senior Associate Justice," *Journal of Supreme Court History* 2 (1997).

44. David Rohde, "Policy Goals, Strategic Choice, and Majority Opinions Assignments in the U.S. Supreme Court," *Midwest Journal of Political Science* 16 (1972); Forrest Maltzman, James Spriggs II, and Paul Wahlbeck, *Crafting Law on the Supreme Court: The Collegial Game* (Cambridge: Cambridge University Press, 2000); Frank Cross and Stefanie Lindquist, "The Decisional Significance of the Chief Justice," *University of Pennsylvania Law Review* 154 (2006).

45. Gregory J. Rathjen, "Policy Goals, Strategic Choice, and Majority Opinion Assignments in the U.S. Supreme Court: A Replication," *American Journal of Political Science* 18 (1974).

46. Danelski, "Influence of the Chief Justice," 2. Alpheus T. Mason, "William Howard Taft: President by Chance, Chief Justice by Choice," in *The Supreme Court and Its Justices*, ed. Jesse Choper (Chicago: American Bar Association, 1987), 95–96. Mason notes that on "familiarity with technical matters of procedure and jurisdiction . . . Hughes ranks high. Taft, on the other hand, confessed inadequacy. In comparison, Justice Van Devanter's knowledge of authorities, procedure, and practice made the chief justice 'feel quite small,'" and numerous other biographers also attest to Van Devanter's skill on procedural issues (e.g., William G. Ross, *The Chief Justiceship of Charles Evans Hughes, 1930–1941* (Columbia: University of South Carolina Press, 2007), 21.

47. Philippa Strum, *Louis D. Brandeis: Justice for the People* (Cambridge, MA: Harvard University Press, 1984), 132–45.

48. Ross, *The Chief Justiceship of Charles Evans Hughes*, 228.

49. Ibid., 114.

50. Alpheus T. Mason, *Brandeis: A Free Man's Life* (New York: Viking Press, 1946), 626.

13 ~ Statutory Interpretation and the Chief Justice

Activism or Judicial Discretion?

KIRK A. RANDAZZO AND REBECCA REID

At the 1960 annual meeting of the American Political Science Association, David J. Danelski presented a paper titled "The Influence of the Chief Justice in the Decisional Process of the Supreme Court." Though the unabridged version of the paper was not published prior to its inclusion in this volume, scholars of the judiciary have regarded it as a seminal study in judicial behavior, and abridgements of the paper have been reprinted numerous times. We first encountered it in Goldman and Sarat's *American Court Systems: Readings in Judicial Process and Behavior*.[1] It is easy to understand why scholars remain impressed with Danelski's study; he collected data from the papers of William Howard Taft, Charles Evans Hughes, and Harlan Fiske Stone to determine the extent to which a chief justice leads his colleagues on the U.S. Supreme Court. Danelski recognized that "the Chief Justiceship does not guarantee leadership. It only offers its incumbent an opportunity to lead. Optimum leadership inheres in the combination of the office and an able, persuasive, and personable judge."[2]

Approximately fifty years later, the literature contains several additional studies building from Danelski's work that examine the unique role played by the chief justice, including his influence and leadership during opinion assignment and the broader decision-making process of the Supreme Court.[3] Implicit in many of these studies is the extent to which the Court engages in judicial activism by substituting its preference over policy outcomes for those of Congress or state legislatures.[4] Yet one area of inquiry that has received little attention is the degree to which chief justices shape the statutory interpretation dynamics of the courts they lead.

This question is extremely important because the justices often receive criticism for engaging in judicial activism when they strike down legislative statutes as unconstitutional. What many individuals fail to recognize, however, is that not all statutes are equal; some prescribe detailed outcomes over policy while others are vague or ambiguous, thereby providing ample discretion for interpretation. This chapter focuses on the role of the chief justice in statutory interpretation. Using a unique dataset measuring the degree of discretion afforded by legislative statutes, we empirically examine how Chief Justices Warren, Burger, and Rehnquist approached statutory interpretation during their terms. More specifically, we analyze how these chiefs personally respond to fluctuations in statutory detail and then examine how they influence the remaining justices. Additionally, we provide a qualitative assessment of Chief Justice Roberts to determine the extent to which he approaches statutory interpretation similarly to his predecessors in his initial terms.

The remaining portion of this chapter discusses how statutory language affects judicial behavior more generally and how chief justices may exercise their leadership via statutory interpretation. We then discuss the operationalization and measurement of key concepts, followed by a discussion of the empirical results pertaining to the Warren, Burger, and Rehnquist Courts. Following the discussion of our empirical insights, we offer the results of our qualitative assessment of the current Roberts Court before finally discussing our general conclusions.

The Importance of Statutory Language

During the confirmation hearing of John Roberts to replace the late William Rehnquist as chief justice, Senator Arlen Specter (chair of the Judiciary Committee) acknowledged the importance of statutory language. In his opening remarks, the senator stated, "I'm very much concerned about what I conceive to be an imbalance in the separation of powers between the Congress and the court. I am concerned about what I bluntly say is the denigration by the court of congressional authority."[5] Senator Specter then indicated that this denigration involved a lack of deference exhibited by the Court to the statutes passed by Congress. In response, John Roberts stated the following in his opening remarks: "Judges and justices are servants of the law, not the other way around. Judges are like umpires. Umpires don't make the rules; they apply them. The role of an umpire and a judge is critical. They make sure everybody plays by the rules. But it is a limited role. Nobody ever went to a ball game to see the umpire."[6] John Roberts received confirmation, in part, because these comments indicated to the U.S. Senate that he viewed a judge's role as an applier of the rules and not as a legislator in judge's robes. Stated another way, the statutes passed by Congress should receive substantial deference from judges and justices because those statutes are the law.

This example serves to illustrate the inherent tension between Congress and the courts over the law. Indeed, defining the lawmaking responsibilities of the legislative and judicial branches is "a highly dynamic process sometimes overlooked" by scholars of these institutions.[7] Fisher notes that "although it is conventional to view the judiciary—and especially the Supreme Court—as the ultimate and final arbiter of constitutional law, numerous examples over two centuries suggest a more dynamic and less hierarchical model."[8] This dynamic process is also observed by Paschal[9] when he notes that there is a "continuing colloquy" between the legislative and judicial branches over the meaning of the law. This ongoing dialogue raises important questions for scholars of the judiciary: To what extent do legal factors (such as legislative statutes) influence the behavior of justices? How does the behavior of chief justices in particular change in response to these legal influences? Providing answers to these questions will help us better understand the extent to which particular Courts engage in judicial activism and whether the law exerts a substantial constraint on judicial behavior.

One such example of the law serving as a constraint on judicial behavior is *Mansell v. Mansell*,[10] which involves an interpretation of the Uniformed Services Former Spouses' Protection Act, where the Supreme Court adjudicated a question concerning retirement pay. Though the justices preferred to rule in favor of the spouse, they were constrained from doing so by the specific language of the act. In writing for the majority, Justice Thurgood Marshall stated:

> We realize that reading the statute literally may inflict economic harm on many former spouses. But we decline to misread the statute in order to reach a sympathetic result when such a reading requires us to do violence to the plain language of the statute and to ignore much of the legislative history. Congress chose the language that requires us to decide as we do, and Congress is free to change it.[11]

While the anecdotal evidence presented above serves as a useful illustration of the tension between legislatures and the judiciary, it does not provide a systematic account of this potential dynamic. One should ask: To what extent do legal factors (such as legislative statutes) systematically influence the behavior of justices? On one side of this debate are advocates of the "attitudinal model," who argue that justices are motivated primarily by their personal ideological policy preferences,[12] while on the other side are legal advocates who contend that the law is of paramount importance.[13] While numerous analyses exist that empirically demonstrate the influence of ideology,[14] a similar pattern has not emerged for the quantitative analysis of legal influences, although more recent studies are now focusing on developing more precise ways to measure legal aspects.[15] Though qualitative research also reinforces the conventional wisdom about the influence of law, "the real question is not whether such behavior exists at all, but whether it exists at systematic and substantively meaningful levels."[16]

Our research focuses precisely on the extent to which this variation in legal factors such as congressional statutes matter as an influence on the voting behavior of chief justices and their colleagues. Unfortunately, a limited amount of research exists on this particular question. A key step in developing and testing an empirical model of legal influence involves the development of a suitable measure representing statutory influence. In a recent study of the bureaucracy, Huber and Shipan argue that "legislation is potentially the most definitive set of instructions that can be given to bureaucrats with respect to the actions they must take during policy implementation."[17] In their examination of the implementation of Medicaid laws, they discover the impact of statutes on the discretion of bureaucrats and state that "legislative statutes are blueprints for policymaking. In some cases, legislatures provide very detailed blueprints that allow little room for other actors . . . to create policy on their own. In other cases, legislatures take a different approach and write statutes that provide only the broad outlines of policy, which gives bureaucrats the opportunity to design and implement policy."[18]

Clearly, justices are not the same as bureaucrats, whose role is to administer or implement the law. Bureaucrats do not have the authority to determine which laws are constitutional, nor can they strike down specific provisions within statutes. Yet the key concept captured by Huber and Shipan is the *level of discretion* provided by congressional legislation. Randazzo, Waterman, and Fine[19] demonstrate that levels of discretion within statutes significantly affect the behavior of federal appellate judges; laws with more detailed language provide less discretion and thereby constrain appellate judges from rendering decisions according to their individual ideological preferences.

In extending this research to the Supreme Court, Randazzo and Waterman[20] discover that congressional statutes influence justices in two simultaneous ways. In some cases more detailed statutes constrain the ability of justices to vote according to their ideological preferences. These same statutes, however, also provide opportunities for other justices to enhance their ideological voting, potentially using the language of the statutes to facilitate their ideological dispositions. The logic behind this discovery is relatively straightforward: if a conservative congress passes a detailed, conservative statute one should expect the more liberal justices to be constrained from casting liberal votes, provided that the law operates as a meaningful influence. Conversely, the conservative justices can rely on this statute to provide "legal cover" for their ideological votes. While the results identified by Randazzo and Waterman are noteworthy, they examined the Court as a whole and did not examine whether individual chief justices follow similar patterns. Our analysis fills this gap by combining the theoretical expectations from Randazzo and Waterman with the discussion of chief justice influence and leadership articulated by Danelski.

What the Chief Justices Have to Say

Before turning to our quantitative results, we offer preliminary qualitative evidence from the opinions of the chief justices themselves concerning the importance of statutory language. If the chiefs are influenced by statutes then we should expect to see references of this influence written explicitly in their opinions. Of course, this does not demonstrate any systematic impact, but these references help to illustrate how the chief justices respond to statutory language.

To begin the discussion, we turn to Chief Justice Warren. Writing for the majority in the case of *Flora v. United States*,[21] he states, "In matters of statutory construction the duty of this Court is to give effect to the intent of Congress, and in doing so our first reference is of course to the literal meaning of the words employed." Warren elaborates on this initial statement in a second example, coming from the majority opinion he authored in *Hanover Bank, Executor v. Commissioner of Internal Revenue*.[22] In this case he writes, "A firmly established principle of statutory interpretation is that the words of statutes should be interpreted where possible in their ordinary, everyday senses. The statute in issue here, in plain and ordinary language, evidences a clear congressional intent [and] under such circumstances we are not at liberty to add to or alter the words employed to effect a purpose which does not appear on the face of the statute." These two cases illustrate Warren's commitment to statutory interpretation. Whenever possible his preference was to derive meaning in the law based on the actual words used in the statutes. Furthermore, Warren interprets the explicit text of the statute in plain, everyday usages and meanings in order to identify and evaluate the legislature's intent.

Chief Justice Burger followed a similar procedure when confronted with matters of statutory interpretation. In the case of *Diamond, Commissioner of Patents and Trademarks v. Chakrabarty*,[23] Burger offers an extensive account of his approach to statutory interpretation. Writing for the majority, he states:

> In cases of statutory interpretation we begin, of course, with the language of the statute. And unless otherwise defined, words will be interpreted as taking their ordinary, contemporary, common meaning. We have also cautioned that courts should not read into the law [any] limitations and conditions which the legislature has not expressed. . . . What is more important is that we are without competence to entertain these [new interpretations]—either to brush them aside as fantasies generated by fear of the unknown, or to act on them. The choice we are urged to make is a matter of high policy for resolution within the legislative process after the kind of investigation, examination, and study that legislative bodies can provide and courts cannot. That process involves the balancing of competing values and interests, which in our democratic system is the business of elected representatives. Whatever their validity, the contentions now pressed on us should be addressed to the political branches of Government, the Congress and the Executive, and not to the courts. Congress is free to amend [the statute in question] or not. But, until Congress takes such action, this Court must construe the language of [the statute in question] as it is.

It is clear from the language in *Chakrabarty* that Chief Justice Burger was extremely hesitant to read more into a legislative statute than was actually written. Similar to Warren, he argues that statutory interpretation is derived solely from the "face" of the statute, where the words are again interpreted from their plain, ordinary, everyday, and contemporary usage. Indeed, as he indicates, courts are not in a position to "legislate from the bench" and therefore should exercise careful restraint when interpreting statutes.

Finally, it is apparent from the majority opinions authored by Chief Justice Rehnquist that he follows a philosophy similar to Warren and Burger when interpreting statutes. In the case of *Bedroc Limited and Western Elite,*

Inc v. United States,[24] he states that "the preeminent canon of statutory interpretation requires us to presume that the legislature says in a statute what it means and means in a statute what it says there. Thus, our inquiry begins with the statutory text, and ends there as well if the text is unambiguous."[25] Rehnquist further reinforces this principle when he authors the majority opinion in *Louis W. Sullivan, Secretary of Health and Human Services v. Stroop et al.*[26] He indicates that "if the statute is clear and unambiguous that is the end of the matter, for the court must give effect to the unambiguously expressed intent of Congress. In ascertaining the plain meaning of the statute, the court must look to the particular statutory language at issue, as well as the language and design of the statute as a whole." Hence, again we observe the pre-eminence of the face value and explicit text of statutes as the source of interpretation (relying on plain meaning and using common, everyday usages to guide interpretation).

These examples, from Warren, Burger, and Rehnquist, reveal that the chief justices carefully examine the language of statutes. Regardless of their ideological preferences or whether additional information is used to ultimately discern meanings, it is obvious that the beginnings of all statutory inquiries focus on the language of the law. Consequently, all three chief justices strive to interpret the plain meaning of the explicit text through ordinary, everyday, and contemporary usages and warn against reading into a statute to derive implications or meanings. This qualitative evidence therefore gives greater weight to our initial question: To what extent does statutory language systematically influence the chief justices?

Research Design and Methodology

The empirical data for this study come from the three justice-centered Supreme Court databases compiled by Harold J. Spaeth.[27] Though the original datasets contain the universe of formally decided cases,[28] we limit our analyses to those cases in which the Supreme Court interprets a congressional statute. Additionally, we examine those cases involving statutes related to criminal, civil liberties, civil rights, economic regulation, and federalism issues. Consequently, we analyze approximately six thousand justice-votes from 1953 to 2000.

The dependent variable for the analysis is whether a justice voted in a sincere manner. We code the variable "1" if a liberal justice casts a liberal vote and "0" if that justice votes conservatively.[29] Similarly, the variable is coded "1" if a conservative justice votes conservatively and "0" if that justice casts a liberal vote. We should also note that in the construction of the dataset we eliminate those cases where a clear ideological decision does not exist. Thus, the six-thousand-justice-vote observations all include an identifiable ideological directionality.

Theoretically, our independent variable of primary interest is *Statutory Detail.* Following the Huber and Shipan methodology, we examine the length of congressional statutes.[30] To measure the length we rely on information in the Spaeth database to identify the statute in question,[31] and subsequently employ LexisNexis and the "word count" feature in the web browser Firefox. While this strategy provides a raw count of the number of words per statute, there is an important reason why the raw number is not particularly useful in an empirical model. From a methodological standpoint, using the raw number of words is problematic because of both the inherent noise associated with a raw count and the considerable skewness in the measure. Additionally, because we are interested in the influence brought by substantial differences among statutes, it is reasonable to take the natural log of each statute's word count as our operationalization of the variable *Statutory Detail.* Taking the natural log allows us to minimize the noise associated with raw counts and reduce the variable's skewness while preserving the expected theoretical relationship.

Because we expect that congressional statutes will affect liberal and conservative justices differently we include a dummy variable *Liberal Justice* (coded "1" if the justice is liberal) to represent the two coalitions. While this variable captures a baseline effect for liberal justices, we also include an interaction term *Statutory Detail * Liberal Justice Interaction* to measure the differential impact of statutory language on liberal justices relative to their conservative colleagues. Thus, the interaction term captures the effects of statutory language on liberal justices (i.e., when the variable *Liberal Justice* = 1).[32]

While the concept of statutory influence is related to the legal model, the attitudinal model indicates that judicial decision making is also the result of individual ideological preferences.[33] To measure the individual ideological preferences of Supreme Court justices, we rely on the ideology scores developed by Martin and Quinn.[34] We employ these measures (rather than the scores generated by Segal and Cover)[35] because they are a dynamic measure; they are calculated for each term of the Court. Using a Bayesian analysis, Martin and Quinn develop annual ideology scores for each individual justice. Rather than a static measure of general ideology, we rely on their measure that changes over time and better captures the potential dynamics of ideological influences. Because our theory argues that statutory language will limit ideological influences over judicial behavior, we "fold" the Martin and Quinn measure into a continuum from the most moderate justices to the most extreme ideologues to produce the variable *Ideological Intensity*.[36] Consequently, we hypothesize that justices with stronger ideological preferences will be more likely to vote sincerely. A positive relationship should therefore exist between our variable *Ideological Intensity* and the dependent variable.

Following the research design adopted by Randazzo and Waterman,[37] we examine the potential influence of congressional statutes across several different issue areas. First, criminal statutes tend to prescribe conservative outcomes by specifying the authority of the government over individuals and outlining the various options of punishment for transgressions. Consequently, presuming that criminal statutes affect levels of judicial discretion, it is reasonable to expect that liberal judges (who tend to rule in favor of the individual and against governmental authority, as well as impose more lenient punishments) would be most constrained. Conversely, since conservative judges generally desire a conservative outcome in criminal cases, more detailed statutes make it easier for them to reach decisions in line with their ideological preferences. Consequently, their ideological voting will be facilitated by more detailed criminal statutes.

The second area of law involves civil liberties. As with criminal law, most statutes in this area negatively impact individual rights by asserting greater state authority at the cost of individual liberty. This general trend is exemplified by many of today's most salient political issues, from abortion rights to hate crimes speech; legislatures frequently pass laws restricting individual civil liberties in the name of governmental authority. Thus, if these statutes have an impact on the level of discretion of judges, it should be liberal judges that are constrained. Conversely, the level of ideological voting of conservative judges should be facilitated by greater levels of specificity in the language of state civil liberty statutes. As most of these laws will prescribe outcomes in accordance with the ideological preferences of conservative judges, greater detail simply makes it easier for them to vote according to their predispositions.

One notable exception, however, involves civil rights statutes. In the civil rights arena legislative statutes tend to prescribe more liberal outcomes by specifying the rights of individuals that cannot be usurped by governmental authority. One needs to look no further than the Civil Rights Act of 1964 or the Voting Rights Act of 1965 for examples of these statutes. Consequently, presuming that federal civil liberties statutes affect judicial discretion, it is plausible to argue that the constraint would be felt more by conservative judges (who tend to rule in favor of state authority over individual rights). Conversely, liberal judges should be able to rely on the statutory language to facilitate their ideological voting.

Finally, with regard to economic legislation, we do not expect a significant statutory effect to exist, primarily because of the influence exerted by the bureaucracy on areas of economic policy. To examine these potential effects we examine cases related to both economic regulation and federalism. In each instance, when the Court reviews economic disputes, not only must it consider the policy prescriptions implied by the federal statutes, but the justices must also interpret subsequent rules and regulations drafted by bureaucratic agencies involved with the implementation of these statutes and any quasi-judicial rulings enacted by these agencies. Consequently, the regulatory imprint may be more pronounced during adjudication, which in turn mitigates the potential effects of any statutory language. Therefore, because bureaucratic agencies operate more visibly in the economic policy arena—instead of the criminal or civil liberties arena where the judiciary is more visible—we expect the effects of statutory language on judicial discretion to be less evident.

Empirical Results

Before turning to the more sophisticated empirical models, it is useful to examine some descriptive statistics concerning congressional statutes. Figure 13.1 displays the average statute length for the duration of the empirical analysis. What is immediately apparent is that substantial fluctuations occur over time, with peaks happening around 1963 and 1989, and valleys in 1966 and 1969. Additionally, one can detect a slightly positive trend across the duration of the time series, although this trend is not statistically significant. The overall conclusion derived from figure 13.1 is that the average length of congressional statutes remains relatively consistent across time, with notable fluctuations in specific years. While not part of the focus of this chapter, we speculate that part of this consistency is the result of the creation of the Office of the Legislative Counsel,[38] whose responsibility is to assist in the drafting of legislation. The relative consistency of statute length is important to identify in order to make certain that congressional statutes do not simply "grow longer" over time. If so, then one could expect significant differences to occur simply as a function of time rather than from an alternative theoretical perspective. Fortunately, the data depicted in figure 13.1 demonstrate that the length of congressional statutes remains relatively stable throughout the period of analysis.

To determine whether statutory language has a systematic influence on

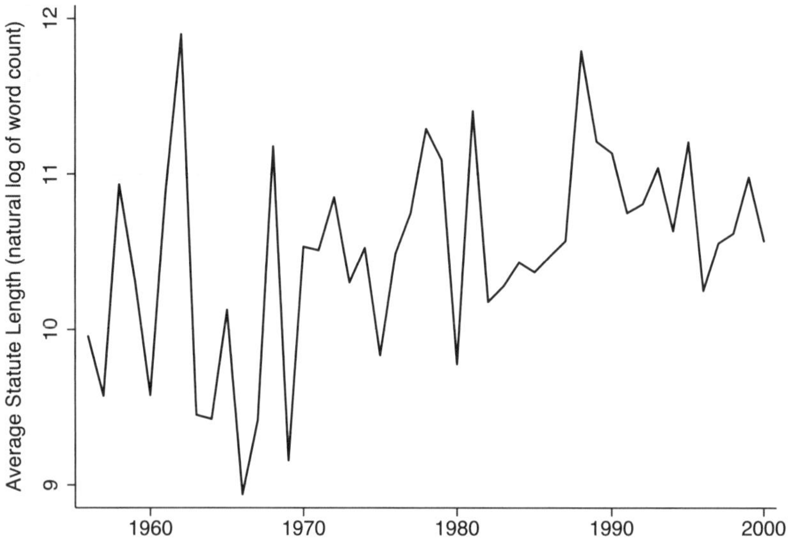

Fig. 13.1. Average statute length by year

the chief justices, we begin by initially examining the proportion of sincere votes over time. This descriptive result is portrayed in figure 13.2. Though there are substantial fluctuations over time, one can immediately observe that Chief Justice Warren cast more sincere votes than either Chief Justices Burger or Rehnquist. This is surprising, given that Chief Justice Rehnquist is credited often for leading a "conservative revolution" among his brethren. Consequently, we expected the graph to exhibit a more parabolic shape, with Warren and Rehnquist near similar levels and Burger substantially lower. Figure 13.2, however, demonstrates a decreasing trend in the proportion of sincere votes cast by the chief justices. Whether this trend is the result of legislative statutes requires a more sophisticated empirical analysis.

We now turn to a series of empirical models examining how these statutes affect the voting behavior of individual justices throughout each chief justice era. Table 13.1 provides the results for justices serving during the tenure of Chief Justice Warren (1953–1968). The first column examines criminal cases, but rather than discuss the entire table, our focus will remain on the two primary variables: *Statutory Detail* (which measures the influence of statutory language on conservative justices) and the *Statutory Detail * Liberal Justice Interaction* (which measures the influence of statu-

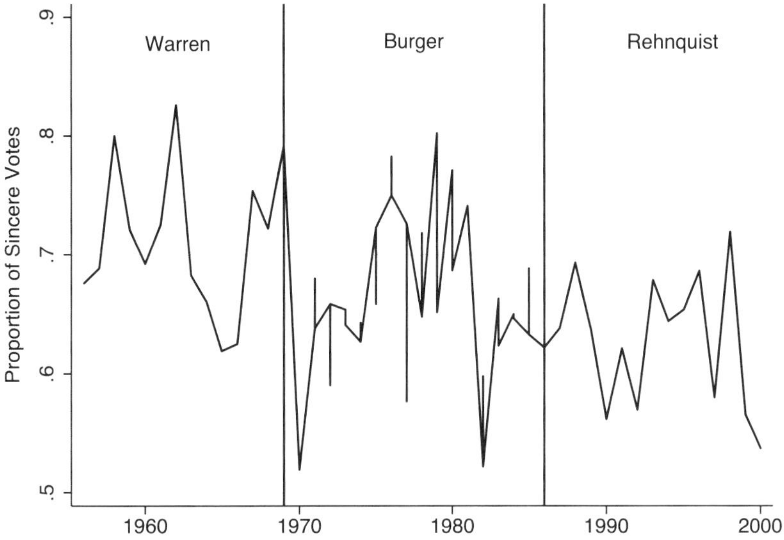

Fig. 13.2. Proportion of sincere votes over time

TABLE 13.1. Logit Analysis of the Warren Court

	Criminal Cases	Civil Liberties	Civil Rights	Economic Regulation	Federalism Issues
Statutory Detail	–.053	.012	.158	–.032	.134
	(.021)**	(.041)	(.062)**	(.023)	(.067)**
Liberal Justice	–2.269	3.463	4.592	1.745	1.817
	(.539)***	(.851)***	(.870)***	(.357)***	(.644)***
Statutory Detail * Liberal Justice Interaction	.233	–.261	–.256	.059	–.091
	(.044)***	(.093)***	(.074)***	(.040)	(.068)
Ideological Intensity	.259	.464	.221	.223	.144
	(.072)***	(.112)***	(.107)**	(.073)***	(.093)
Constant	.621	–.419	–2.141	–.724	–1.813
	(.405)	(.403)	(.698)	(.217)	(.669)
N	638	271	441	1,545	280
Log Likelihood	–410.276	–156.479	–223.145	–768.793	–181.246
LR/Wald Test	103.81	50.02	86.20	145.45	55.84
Probability > χ^2	.000	.000	.000	.000	.000
Pseudo R^2	.030	.095	.201	.244	.054

Note: Coefficients are based on a logit analysis of the likelihood of a sincere vote with standard errors clustered on individual justices.

* $p < .10$; ** $p < .05$; *** $p < .01$

tory language on liberal justices). Note that both variables are statistically significant, though the signs of each coefficient are opposite our theoretical expectation. A similar phenomenon exists for civil liberties (in the second column) and civil rights (third column) cases as well. Though the variables are statistically significant (except for *Statutory Detail* in civil liberties cases), the coefficients are opposite our theoretical expectation. Finally, the influence of congressional statutes in both of the economic issues (economic regulation in column 4 and federalism in column 5) does not seem to significantly affect voting behavior.

Examining the results listed in table 13.2 provides information concerning the voting behavior of justices serving during the tenure of Chief Justice Burger (1969–1985). In the first two columns focusing on criminal and civil liberties cases, respectively, we observe statistically significant coefficients for both the variables *Statutory Detail* and the *Statutory Detail * Liberal Justice Interaction*. Additionally, unlike the patterns observed during the Warren Court, the signs on these variables support our theoretical expectations. Liberal justices (as measured by the interaction term) are significantly constrained from casting liberal votes as congressional statutes become more detailed, while their conservative brethren are more likely to vote conservatively. Civil rights cases (the third column) possess a significant and positive coefficient for the variable *Statutory Detail* and no effect

TABLE 13.2. Logit Analysis of the Burger Court

	Criminal Cases	Civil Liberties	Civil Rights	Economic Regulation	Federalism Issues
Statutory Detail	.070	.208	.069	.095	.153
	(.040)*	(.046)***	(.017)***	(.023)***	(.050)***
Liberal Justice	1.392	2.447	.398	1.103	2.406
	(.549)**	(.455)***	(.351)	(.459)**	(.900)***
Statutory Detail * Liberal Justice Interaction	–.217	–.340	.026	–.091	–.202
	(.049)***	(.049)***	(.023)	(.046)*	(.079)**
Ideological Intensity	.261	.301	.290	.147	.295
	(.061)***	(.061)***	(.056)***	(.031)***	(.094)
Constant	–.054	-1.450	–.961	–.965	-2.003
	(.415)	(.370)	(.191)	(.236)	(.604)
N	1,249	829	2,042	2,321	475
Log Likelihood	–741.932	–488.384	–1,273.448	–1,555.182	-311.167
LR/Wald Test	177.82	156.47	212.74	86.55	30.26
Probability > χ^2	.000	.000	.000	.000	.000
Pseudo R^2	.056	.074	.057	.013	.052

Note: Coefficients are based on a logit analysis of the likelihood of a sincere vote with standard errors clustered on individual justices.

* $p < .10$; ** $p < .05$; *** $p < .01$

for the interaction term. This result runs counter to our expectations, both in terms of the sign for *Statutory Detail* and the lack of significance for the *Statutory Detail * Liberal Justice Interaction*. Finally, the economic regulations cases (fourth column) and federalism cases (fifth column) contain significant coefficients for both variables. *Statutory Detail* contains a positive coefficient while the interaction term is negative, despite our expectation that neither variable would exert an influence on voting behavior. The empirical results indicate, however, that, similar to the patterns observed in criminal cases, liberal justices are constrained from casting liberal votes as congressional statutes become more detailed, while conservatives are more likely to vote conservatively.

Table 13.3 presents the results from our analysis of voting behavior for those justices serving during the tenure of Chief Justice Rehnquist (1987–2005). The empirical evidence portrayed here resembles the patterns observed during the Burger Court. For criminal and civil liberties cases (represented in the first and second columns, respectively) the variable *Statutory Detail* is statistically significant and positive, while the *Statutory Detail * Liberal Justice Interaction* term is significant and negative. This supports our theoretical expectation and indicates that liberal justices (as measured by the interaction term) are significantly constrained from casting liberal

TABLE 13.3. Logit Analysis of the Rehnquist Court

	Criminal Cases	Civil Liberties	Civil Rights	Economic Regulation	Federalism Issues
Statutory Detail	.147	.065	–.082	.040	.152
	(.032)***	(.029)**	(.009)***	(.027)	(.033)***
Liberal Justice	1.368	.641	-2.627	1.396	2.369
	(.745)*	(.596)	(.602)***	(.442)***	(.424)***
Statutory Detail * Liberal Justice Interaction	–.153	–.082	.302	–.093	–.188
	(.062)**	(.045)*	(.040)***	(.044)**	(.039)***
Ideological Intensity	.172	.119	.332	.132	.063
	(.051)***	(.079)	(.053)***	(.031)***	(.053)
Constant	-1.208	.996	.862	–.480	-1.735
	(.400)	(.417)	(.160)	(.273)	(.311)
N	1,086	472	1,351	1,653	598
Log Likelihood	-697.409	-310.082	-804.419	-1,110.393	-405.947
LR/Wald Test	50.36	28.53	531.46	107.95	69.57
Probability > χ^2	.000	.000	.000	.000	.000
Pseudo R^2	.016	.012	.055	.012	.018

Note: Coefficients are based on a logit analysis of the likelihood of a sincere vote with standard errors clustered on individual justices.

* $p < .10$; ** $p < .05$; *** $p < .01$

votes as congressional statutes become more detailed, while their conservative colleagues are more likely to vote conservatively. The third column, capturing civil rights cases, contains a significant and negative coefficient for the variable *Statutory Detail* while the interaction term is significant and positive. Again, this supports our expectation that conservative justices will be significantly constrained from casting conservative votes, while liberal justices will be more likely to vote in a liberal direction. The final two columns (economic regulation and federalism) contain statistically significant and negative coefficients for the *Statutory Detail * Liberal Justice Interaction* term, but the variable *Statutory Detail* is only significant in federalism cases.

Substantive Impact of the Empirical Results

While the three tables above provide interesting evidence concerning the behavior of justices during each chief justice era, they do not present a complete picture. Tables of coefficients do not allow us to observe the substantive impact exerted by congressional statutes nor do they allow us to see how this influence affects individual justices. Therefore, to better understand how congressional statutes affect individual voting behavior (including the Chief Justices) we graphed the probability of a sincere vote for criminal cases. In each graph, justices are arranged according to their ideological preferences, from most conservative to most liberal.[39] Figure 13.3 captures the voting behavior of the Warren Court.

Examining figure 13.3 reveals two immediate patterns. First, as indicated by the empirical coefficients, conservative justices (with the exception of Justice White) are increasingly constrained from casting conservative votes, and congressional criminal statutes become longer and more detailed. Conversely, the liberal justices (including Chief Justice Warren) are more likely to cast liberal votes when ruling on detailed criminal statutes. A second, and potentially more interesting, pattern concerns the magnitude of this influence. For the conservative justices this magnitude is not very pronounced; the likelihood of sincere voting decreases by approximately .100, from an initial starting point of .700 to approximately .600 (in the case of Justice Clark from approximately .600 to .500). Yet the more pronounced effect appears within the liberal justices, where their likelihood of sincere voting increases by approximately .400, from a starting point of .400 to approximately .800 (in the case of Justice Douglas from approximately .600 to over .900).

If we similarly examine the substantive impact for justices on the Burger Court we observe some noticeably different patterns of behavior

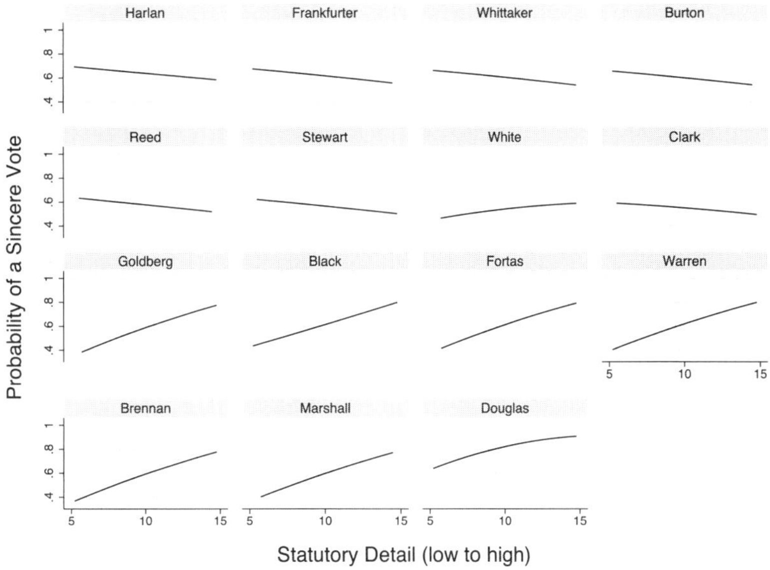

Fig. 13.3. Voting behavior in criminal cases during the Warren Court

(fig. 13.4). First, the liberal justices (with the exception of Justice Black) are now the ones constrained from voting sincerely as congressional criminal statutes become longer and more detailed. Conversely, conservative justices are more likely to cast conservative votes. Second, and consistent with the pattern exhibited during the Warren Court, the magnitude of influence is more pronounced for liberals than conservatives. Liberal justices experience approximately a .400 decrease in the likelihood of sincere voting, from an initial starting point near .800 to approximately .400 (although in the case of Justice Stevens from .600 to .300). Conservative justices, in contrast, experience only an approximate increase of .100 or .200 as criminal statutes become more detailed.

Figure 13.5 presents the substantive effects of congressional criminal statutes during the Rehnquist Court. Again we observe noticeably different patterns of behavior during this period relative to those displayed during the Warren and Burger eras. Though the coefficient on the *Statutory Detail * Liberal Justice Interaction* reported in table 13.3 was statistically significant, that does not account for the conditional nature of the interaction term.[40] When this conditional nature is included, any influence exerted by congressional statutes vanishes. This lack of substantive influence is captured

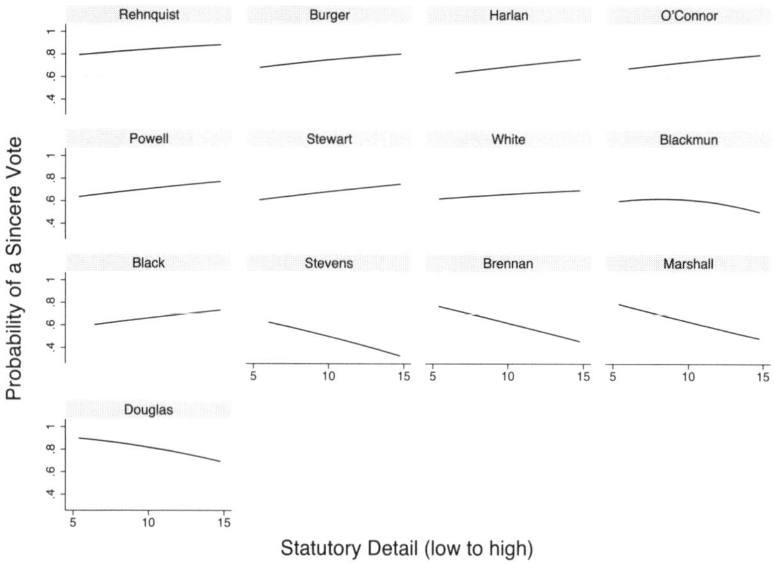

Fig. 13.4. Voting behavior in criminal cases during the Burger Court

by the relatively flat lines exhibited for the liberal justices in figure 13.5. Conversely, the conservative justices experience pronounced increases in the likelihood of their sincere voting as statutes become longer and more detailed. Unlike the relatively flat patterns displayed for conservatives during the Warren and Burger Courts, conservative justices on the Rehnquist Court experience an increase of approximately .300 (including Chief Justice Rehnquist).

What conclusions can we draw from these three figures? First, we speculate on the direction of influence exhibited by congressional statutes. Our theoretical expectation was that longer and more detailed criminal statutes would constrain liberal justices from casting sincere votes while enhancing the ideological voting of conservatives. Yet during the Warren Court we observe the exact opposite behavior. Why would this occur? We speculate that two potential explanations exist that could help understand this result. On the one hand, it is plausible that the liberal justices on the Warren Court were simply ignoring the statutory language. Certainly this explanation, if accurate, would reinforce the conventional wisdom that the Warren Court engaged in judicial activism. On the other hand, it is equally plausible that congressional criminal statutes were not focused on influencing

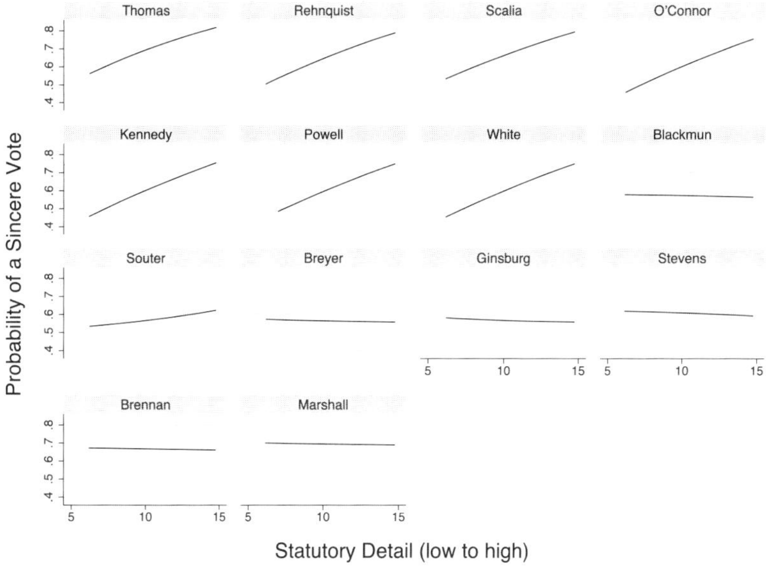

Fig. 13.5. Voting behavior in criminal cases during the Rehnquist Court

judicial behavior, but rather simply identified activities that were to be considered criminal. It is important to remember that many of the landmark decisions during the Warren Court, such as *Miranda v. Arizona*,[41] involved the interpretation of state statutes, not federal laws passed by Congress. We believe this latter alternative may better explain events because of the evidence displayed in figure 13.3 during the Burger Court, where we observe a radical change of direction for liberal justices from the steep positive trend experienced under Warren to a pronounced negative trend (especially for Justices Brennan, Marshall, and Douglas, who served during both periods). It is plausible that Congress began to draft more detailed criminal statutes in response to liberal decisions rendered by the Warren Court and that these statutes significantly constrained liberal justices.

The second conclusion involves the magnitude of influence exerted by these statutes. During both the Warren and Burger Court eras the voting behavior of liberal justices was substantially affected by longer and more detailed statutes. Regardless of whether the trend was positive or negative, the magnitude of statutory influence was pronounced. The behavior of conservative justices, however, changed only slightly over the same time period. Only when William Rehnquist became chief justice is there a pronounced impact on conservative justices. Is this change the result of particular actions taken by Rehnquist or is it the result of a change within congressional statutes themselves? We are hesitant to claim that this pattern (similar to the one exhibited during the Warren Court) is reflective of a particular leadership trait because the data do not allow us to speak to that point directly. Yet the fact that both Warren and Rehnquist demonstrate similar results concerning the magnitude of influence from statutory language is notable.

Qualitative Analysis of Chief Justice Roberts

How does Chief Justice Roberts approach the topic of statutory interpretation? While it would be interesting to examine empirical patterns, unfortunately there is not enough data at this time for a quantitative analysis. Consequently, we qualitatively examined his written opinions to determine the extent to which Roberts is influenced by legislative statutes. Based on our reading of Roberts's opinions it appears that the chief remains sensitive to the explicit language of congressional statutes, similar to his predecessors.

For example, in his dissent in *Salazar v. Ramah Navajo Chapter et al.*[42] Roberts states the following:

> It is true, as the Court notes, that each of the Tribes' contracts provides that the Act and contract "shall be liberally construed for the benefit of the Contractor". But a provision can be construed "liberally" as opposed to "strictly" only when there is some ambiguity to construe. And here there is none. Congress spoke clearly when it said that the provision of funds was "subject to the availability of appropriations". . . . The unambiguous meaning of these provisions is that when the Secretary has allocated the maximum amount of funds appropriated each fiscal year for contract support costs, there are no other appropriations "available" to pay any remaining costs.

An additional example occurs in *Dean v. United States*.[43] Writing for the majority, Chief Justice Roberts explains in detail how the Court interprets a statute related to the discharge of firearms.

> We start, as always, with the language of the statute. The text of subsection (iii) provides that a defendant shall be sentenced to a minimum of 10 years "if the firearm is discharged". It does not require that the discharge be done knowingly or intentionally, or otherwise

> contain words of limitation. . . . "We ordinarily resist reading words or elements into a statute that do not appear on its face". Congress's use of the passive voice further indicates that subsection (iii) does not require proof of intent. The passive voice focuses on an event that occurs without respect to a specific actor, and therefore without respect to any actor's intent or culpability. . . . It is whether something happened—not how or why it happened—that matters.

A final example can be found in *Knight v. Commissioner*.[44] In his opinion for the Court, Chief Justice Roberts cautions lower courts from reading too much into congressional statutes. He writes:

> In applying the statute, the Court of Appeals below asked whether the cost at issue *could* have been incurred by an individual. This approach flies in the face of the statutory language. The provision at issue asks whether the costs "would not have been incurred if the property were not held" in trust, not, as the Court of Appeals would have it, whether the costs "could not have been incurred" in such a case. The fact that an individual could not do something is one reason he would not, but not the only possible reason. If Congress had intended the Court of Appeals' reading, it easily could have replaced "would" in the statute with "could", and presumably would have. The fact that it did not adopt this readily available and apparent alternative strongly supports rejecting the Court of Appeals' reading.

These examples suggest not only that Chief Justice Roberts is conscientious of statutory language but also approaches statutory interpretation with great care and sensitivity, holding that the language of congressional statutes is extremely important and something the Court should interpret carefully. Indeed, while all three of his predecessors emphasized the explicit text of statutes, Roberts appears to go one step further by allocating a significant portion of his opinions to discussions of verb tense, diction, passive voice, and other grammatical nuances that drive his interpretations. But some notable exceptions to these conclusions are also apparent. For example, in *Citizens United v. Federal Election Commission*,[45] Roberts's concurring opinion states the following:

> Because the stakes are so high, our standard practice is to refrain from addressing constitutional questions except when necessary to rule on particular claims before us. . . . This policy underlies both

> our willingness to construe ambiguous statutes to avoid constitutional problems and our practice "never to formulate a rule of constitutional law broader than is required by the precise facts to which it is to be applied."

Yet in this case the Court arguably rendered a broad constitutional ruling when a less intrusive alternative was available.

Another exception to the general conclusion can be seen in *National Federation of Independent Business et al. v. Sebelius*,[46] involving an interpretation of the Affordable Care Act (aka the "Obamacare" statute). Though Congress justified the inclusion of an individual mandate provision as part of its authority under the Commerce Clause, the Court rejected this justification while finding the provision constitutional under Congress's Tax and Spend authority. In writing for the majority, Chief Justice Roberts states:

> The text of a statute can sometimes have more than one possible meaning. To take a familiar example, a law that reads "no vehicles in the park" might, or might not, ban bicycles in the park. And it is well established that if a statute has two possible meanings, one of which violates the Constitution, courts should adopt the meaning that does not do so. . . . Congress thought it could enact [an individual mandate] under the Commerce Clause, and the Government primarily defended the law on that basis. But, the Commerce Clause does not give Congress that power. Under our precedent, it is therefore necessary to ask whether the Government's alternative reading of the statute—that it only imposes a tax on those without [health] insurance—is a reasonable one. . . . The Affordable Care Act's requirement that certain individuals pay a financial penalty for not obtaining health insurance may reasonably be characterized as a tax. Because the Constitution permits such a tax, it is not our role to forbid it, or to pass upon its wisdom or fairness.

These examples reveal that Chief Justice Roberts maintains his sensitivity to statutory language, while simultaneously maintaining his ability to find linguistic justifications for "well-established" deferential court procedure. Hence while he exhibits delicacy and sensitivity to diction, verb tense, passive voice, and other grammatical characteristics, Chief Justice Roberts still makes exceptions in order to adhere to his ideological preferences.

Conclusions

The empirical literature focusing on the influence of statutory language demonstrates that levels of discretion prescribed in laws significantly affect the behavior of bureaucrats and federal appellate judges. This chapter examines whether a similar effect exists for chief justices and their colleagues. Do more detailed congressional statutes affect the ability of the chief justices (and their colleagues) to vote according to their individual ideological preferences?

Our empirical analyses of Chief Justices Warren, Burger, and Rehnquist demonstrate that the answer is "yes," but not in similar ways. Both the directionality of influence and the magnitude of impact fluctuate dramatically across different issue areas and the different chief justice eras. What remains consistent is the conclusion that congressional statutes have the ability to constrain some justices from voting according to their ideological preferences while simultaneously enhancing the ability of others to vote ideologically. Additionally, Chief Justices Warren and Rehnquist experience substantial changes in their personal voting behavior as a result of statutory language, and their fellow colleagues (liberals for Warren and conservatives for Rehnquist) also exhibit similar behavioral changes.

The qualitative examination of Chief Justice Roberts provides some additional clues, not only concerning the importance of statutory language, but also the manner in which he exhibits leadership and influence among his colleagues. His consistent sensitivity to statutory language, encompassing both what the statute states explicitly as well as its contextual analysis, may serve as a focal point for judicial influence. Roberts's perpetual rally of "We start, as always, with the language of the statute" may provide a sense of legitimacy concerning the importance of the law. Additionally, his careful attention to the diction and verb tense in statutes may further influence other justices to follow his lead and agree with his interpretation. But his repeated exceptions to these patterns, often to cast ideologically driven votes or reach ideologically motivated conclusions, may limit the chief's ability to consistently lead an ideologically divided Court.

NOTES

1. Sheldon Goldman and Austin Sarat, eds., *American Court Systems: Reading in Judicial Process and Behavior* (New York: Longman, 1986).

2. Quoted in Ibid., 486.

3. See, for example, Stacia L. Haynie, "Leadership and Consensus on the U.S. Supreme Court," *Journal of Politics* 54 (1992); Forrest Maltzman and Paul J. Wahlbeck, "May It Please the Chief? Opinion Assignments in the Rehnquist Court," *American Journal of Political Science* 40 (1996); and Lee Epstein and Olga Shvetsova, "Heresthetical Maneuvering on the U.S. Supreme Court," *Journal of Theoretical Politics* 14 (2002).

4. See Rorie Spill Solberg and Stefanie A. Lindquist, "Activism, Ideology, and Federalism: Judicial Behavior in Constitutional Challenges Before the Rehnquist Court, 1986–2000," *Journal of Empirical Legal Studies* 3 (2006).

5. Reported in "Transcript: Day One of the Roberts Hearings," *Washington Post*, Sep. 13, 2005.

6. Reported in "Transcript: Day One of the Roberts Hearings," *Washington Post*, Sep. 13, 2005.

7. Colton C. Campbell and John F. Stack, ed., *Congress Confronts the Court: The Struggle for Legitimacy and Authority in Lawmaking* (Lanham, MD: Rowman & Littlefield, 2001), xiii.

8. Louis Fisher, "Congressional Checks on the Judiciary," in *Congress Confronts the Court: The Struggle for Legitimacy and Authority in Lawmaking*, ed. Colton C. Campbell and John F. Stack (Lanham, MD: Rowman & Littlefield, 2001), 21.

9. Richard A. Paschal, "The Continuing Colloquy: Congress and the Finality of the Supreme Court," *Journal of Law and Politics* 8 (1992).

10. 490 U.S. 581 (1989).

11. Ibid., 594.

12. Jeffrey A. Segal and Harold J. Spaeth, *The Supreme Court and the Attitudinal Model Revisited* (New York: Cambridge University Press, 2002).

13. Richard A. Posner, *Frontiers of Legal Theory* (Cambridge, MA: Harvard University Press, 2001).

14. Since there are too many analyses to mention here, please refer to Jeffrey A. Segal and Albert D. Cover, "A Spatial Model of Roll Call Voting: Senators, Constituents, and Interest Groups in Supreme Court Confirmations," *American Journal of Political Science* 36 (1989); or Andrew D. Martin and Kevin M. Quinn, "Dynamic Ideal Point Estimation via Markov Chain Monte Carlo for the U.S. Supreme Court, 1953–1999," *Political Analysis* 10 (2002), for descriptions of ideological measurements and their effects.

15. See Howard Gillman, "Review: What's Law Got to Do With It? Judicial Behavioralists Test the 'Legal Model' of Judicial Decision Making," *Law and Social Inquiry* 26 (2001); Mark J. Richards and Herbert M. Kritzer, "Jurisprudential Regimes in Supreme Court Decision Making," *American Political Science Review* 96 (2002); Barry Friedman, "Taking Law Seriously," *Perspectives on Politics* 4 (2006); Thomas G. Hansford and James F. Spriggs II, *The Politics of Precedent on the U.S. Supreme Court* (Princeton: Princeton University Press, 2006); Stefanie A. Lindquist and David E. Klein, "The Influence of Jurisprudential Considerations on Supreme Court Decisionmaking: A Study of Conflict Cases," *Law & Society Review* 40 (2006); Ronald Kahn and Ken I. Kersch, eds., *The Supreme Court and American Political Development* (Lawrence: University Press of Kansas, 2006); Ryan C. Black and Ryan J. Owens, "Agenda Setting in the Supreme Court: The Collision of Policy and Jurispru-

dence," *Journal of Politics* 71 (2009); Michael A. Bailey and Forrest Maltzman, *The Constrained Court: Law, Politics, and the Decisions Justices Make* (Princeton: Princeton University Press, 2011); Charles Gardner Geyh, ed., *What's Law Got to Do With It? What Judges Do, Why They Do It, and What's at Stake* (Stanford, CA: Stanford University Press, 2011); Pamela A. Corley, Amy Steigerwalt, and Artemus Ward, *The Puzzle of Unanimity: Consensus on the U.S. Supreme Court* (Stanford, CA: Stanford University Press, 2013).

16. Harold J. Spaeth and Jeffrey A. Segal, *Majority Rule or Minority Will: Adherence to Precedent on the U.S. Supreme Court* (Cambridge: Cambridge University Press, 1999), 7.

17. John D. Huber and Charles R. Shipan, *Deliberate Discretion? The Institutional Foundations of Bureaucratic Autonomy* (New York: Cambridge University Press, 2002), 31.

18. Ibid., 76.

19. Kirk A. Randazzo, Richard W. Waterman, and Jeffrey A. Fine, "Checking the Federal Courts: The Impact of Congressional Statutes on Judicial Behavior," *Journal of Politics* 68 (2006).

20. Kirk A. Randazzo and Richard W. Waterman, "The U.S. Supreme Court and the Model of Contingent Discretion," *Justice System Journal* 32 (2011).

21. 357 U.S. 63 (1958).

22. 369 U.S. 672 (1962).

23. 447 U.S. 303 (1980).

24. 541 U.S. 176 (2004).

25. When the statute is ambiguous, however, Rehnquist writes that "appeals to statutory history are well taken only to resolve 'statutory ambiguity'" (*Barnhill v. Johnson*, 503 U.S. 393 (1992)).

26. 496 U.S. 478 (1990).

27. The original Supreme Court database was coded by Harold J. Spaeth. Each of the justice-centered databases (Warren Court, 1953–1969; Burger Court, 1969–1985; and Rehnquist Court, 1986–1998) was transformed by Sara C. Benesh. Links to these data are located at the University of South Carolina's Judicial Research Initiative (JuRI) website www.cas.sc.edu/poli/juri.

28. This is accomplished by setting the variable ANALU = 0 and DEC_TYPE = 1, 6, or 7.

29. We rely on the Martin and Quinn (see note 14) measure of Supreme Court ideology to determine whether a justice is considered "liberal" or "conservative" using zero as the cut point.

30. Though we use the term "statute" in reality the coding comes from the publicly available sections of the U.S. Code in which the statutes are published.

31. To identify the relevant statute, we relied on the LAW variable in the Spaeth dataset. This provides information about the sections of the U.S. Code interpreted by the Supreme Court. In some instances, Spaeth lists frequently litigated statutes by acronym (for example, NLRA refers to the National Labor Relations Act). For all cases in which an acronym occurs we recoded the specific statute in question.

32. We also note that because of the inclusion of this interactive term, the baseline variable *Statutory Detail* consequently captures the effects of constraint on conservative justices (i.e. when Liberal Justices = 0).

33. Segal and Spaeth, *The Supreme Court and the Attitudinal Model Revisited.*

34. Martin and Quinn, "Dynamic Ideal Point."

35. Segal and Cover, "A Spatial Model."

36. The folding is accomplished simply by taking the absolute value of the Martin and Quinn score for each individual justice.

37. Randazzo and Waterman, "The U.S. Supreme Court and the Model of Contingent Discretion."

38. Originally established through section 1303 of the Revenue Act of 1918 and currently authorized under title V of the Legislative Reorganization Act of 1970 (2 U.S.C. 281 et seq.).

39. These are calculated by taking the mean Martin and Quinn ideology score for each justice.

40. Thomas Brambor, William Roberts Clark, and Matt Golder, "Understanding Interaction Models: Improving Empirical Analyses," *Political Analysis* 14 (2005).

41. 384 U.S. 436 (1966).

42. 567 U.S. ___ (2012).

43. 556 U.S. 568 (2009).

44. 552 U.S. 181 (2008).

45. 558 U.S. 310 (2010).

46. 567 U.S. ___ (2012).

PART IV

Influence Off the Bench

ARTEMUS WARD

Of course, most of the work done by chief justices takes place on the Supreme Court. And chiefs may behave differently from other justices when it comes to the Court's effectiveness as a governing institution in the larger political context within which it operates. Thus chiefs may be particularly sensitive to issues of legitimacy and compliance. If lower courts, the other branches of government, and the American people perceive the Supreme Court as illegitimate, the Court's ability to gain compliance with its decisions may be jeopardized. The chief may be uniquely positioned to consider these factors as the justices go about their daily work of resolving cases and may therefore use his unique powers to promote the Court's legitimacy with outside actors.

But, as the job title—Chief Justice of the United States—suggests, chiefs have responsibilities off the bench as well. In short, chief justices are responsible not just for the Supreme Court but for the entire federal judiciary. For example, chiefs head the Judicial Conference of the United States, which brings together judges from different federal courts to frame policy guidelines for administering the federal judiciary. They issue annual year-end reports on the federal judiciary calling on Congress to enact specific reforms. In this sense, chiefs can use their unique job responsibilities to exercise influence off the bench.

In chapter 14, Richard L. Vining Jr. and Teena Wilhelm examine the chief's leadership as administrative head of the federal judiciary. They identify the chief's reform agenda by examining the content of the Year-End Report on the Federal Judiciary, which has been issued since 1975. They find that Burger, Rehnquist, and Roberts emphasized different priorities and that the more administrative experience a chief has—and each necessarily has more over time—the more items that chief will place on the reform agenda. The most senior chief justice requests nearly twice as many agenda items as an inexperienced chief, with a decade of service being the pivotal turning point for chiefs. Interestingly, they find no evidence that chiefs attempt to be strategic by taking into consideration legislative-judicial relations, divided government, economic constraints, or public opinion in crafting their reform agendas. Instead, chiefs simply ask for more over time and are more likely to ask for judicial improvements or institutional maintenance as their tenures progress.

In chapter 15, Shawn C. Fettig and Sara C. Benesh examine the extent to which the behavior of chiefs on the bench is driven by their concern for the Court's institutional legitimacy. As Danelski posited, task leadership—persuasion—and social leadership—conciliation—are connected with unanimity, which is connected with legitimacy. And Fettig and Benesh tackle legitimacy by exploring whether chiefs consider public opinion. Specifically, they examine personal correspondence and firsthand accounts of chiefs, associate justices, and clerks. They find evidence that chiefs act with more than just their own policy preferences in mind. Internal Court documents reveal that chiefs strategically use the power to assign opinions to mitigate the potential negative effects that decisions might have on the public. They show that chiefs view unanimity as a way to bolster public opinion. Chiefs manage opinion assignment, coalition formation, and opinion writing to minimize conflict and maintain the Court's prestige among the other branches of government. For example, chiefs self-assign "great cases" and choose marginal coalition members—justices who defect from their ideological blocs—in close cases. In all, the authors conclude that chiefs have been successful as the Court has consistently been among the most trusted institutions by the American people.

What each of these chapters demonstrates is that chiefs are uniquely positioned to exert their influence both on the bench and off, both for the benefit of the Supreme Court and for the federal judiciary in general. In doing so, chiefs should be viewed less in ideological or partisan terms—as they routinely are in studies of judicial decision making—and more as administrative leaders who put the institutional maintenance of both the Supreme Court and the federal judiciary above their personal attitudes about individual cases or areas of the law. In this sense, these chapters suggest that there is a very real difference between associate justices of the Supreme Court and chief justices of the United States.

14 ~ The Chief Justice as Administrative Leader

Explaining Agenda Size

RICHARD L. VINING JR. AND TEENA WILHELM

As is clear from the other chapters in this book, the bulk of scholarship on the Chief Justice of the United States analyzes his roles as task and social leader of the Supreme Court. These concepts, developed a half-century ago, dominate social scientific studies of Supreme Court leadership. Much less scholarly attention is devoted to the chief justice's role as the administrative leader of the federal judiciary. We believe this is a significant oversight given the importance of these duties. Leadership of the federal judicial branch gives the chief justice additional formal and statutory obligations.[1] The United States Code establishes more than eighty duties for the chief justice including service as chairman of the Judicial Conference of the United States and Federal Judicial Center.[2] His numerous duties and status as "first among equals" make the chief justice the most visible and consequential representative of the federal judiciary. As such, he has the ability to be the leading spokesperson for the judicial branch.

In this chapter we examine a consequential aspect of the chief justice's administrative duties, his ability to set the agenda for reforms to judicial administration and procedure. We identify the reform agenda of the chief justice by studying the content of the Year-End Report on the Federal Judiciary. The chief justice has issued this report at the end of each year since 1975. It is similar to the State of the Union Address issued by the president, including both retrospective commentary and goals for the new year, but it deals primarily with the judiciary. The Year-End Report on the Federal Judiciary receives substantial media attention and provides information to elites and the public about the reform agenda of the Third Branch. Despite its high profile and status as a rare opportunity for the courts to promote their needs, we know little about the forces that shape its content.

We examine the specific items advanced by the chief justice and their eventual success (or failure) in Congress elsewhere.[3] Here we assess determinants of the size of the agenda advanced by the chief justice each year. We focus on two alternative explanations: strategic considerations and administrative experience. Strategic considerations include political and economic conditions that can limit what is possible in American politics. The administrative experience of a chief justice is likely to foster interest in judicial reform and increase awareness of defects in the machinery of justice. We analyze the overall size of the chief justice's agenda as well as a subset of important requests with more substantial potential impacts. Our results indicate that experience in the administrative role is the more influential explanation.

The Chief Justice as Administrator, Spokesperson, and Advocate

> When an individual is asked to be instrumental on behalf of the billion-dollar agency called "The Federal Courts" (with some two thousand judges, thirty thousand in staff, and hundreds of facilities) and also to be successful jurisprudentially as a disinterested adjudicator, one role cannot help but bleed into the other. Each role amplifies the power of, distracts from, and imposes costs on the other.
>
> —Judith Resnik and Lane Dilg, "Responding to a Democratic Deficit"[4]

Mainstream political science research mostly neglects the role of the chief justice as head of the federal judiciary. His formal administrative role includes a host of statutory obligations including management, budgetary duties, and oversight. He performs these tasks while also doing the work required of him as a member of the Supreme Court of the United States.[5] Many of these responsibilities are obscure to the public and elites, but sometimes they capture their attention. For example, the role of the chief justice in selecting members of the Foreign Intelligence Surveillance Court was scrutinized in the summer of 2013 after leaks revealed the existence of government spying programs collecting data on citizens' telephone and e-mail communication. Chief Justice John G. Roberts, Jr., chose the members of this court beginning in 2005 and appointed Republicans and former executive branch employees at a far greater rate than had his predecessors

Warren E. Burger and William H. Rehnquist.[6] This prompted concerns about bias and excessive deference to the president with regard to national security and intrusive surveillance. As this single example demonstrates, the chief justice has unmatched influence on the operations of the judiciary well beyond his activities within the Supreme Court Building.

The primary source of the chief justice's administrative responsibility is his leadership of the Judicial Conference of the United States, established in 1922 after extensive lobbying by Chief Justice William H. Taft, though it was then known as the Conference of Senior Circuit Judges. The purpose of this organization was to oversee intercircuit assignments and facilitate communication among federal judges. The chief justice served as the chair of the conference and soon became its "public relations director." The Judicial Conference began making recommendations about funding, judgeships, and legislation soon after it was established. Under both Chief Justice Taft and his successor, Chief Justice Charles Evans Hughes, the reports of conference activities provided to the press and legislators tended to reflect the priorities of the chief justice. Although the conference served as a "voice" for the needs of the judiciary, Taft established that the chief justice remained the "primary national spokesperson" for the courts. These lobbying activities became routine, and Congress gradually vested the conference with additional responsibilities. Today the Judicial Conference oversees the performance of many statutory duties of the Administrative Office of the U.S. Courts as well as legislative relations, rules, and procedures for the federal judiciary. It is also obligated statutorily to provide Congress its policy recommendations for the federal judiciary, including commentary on pending legislation. As the presiding officer of the Judicial Conference, the chief justice is exposed to the operative needs of the federal judiciary.[7]

The chief justice is the primary spokesperson for the federal judiciary. While associate justices make public appearances, some of them regularly, the nature of their commentary differs from that of the chief justice. Associate justices sometimes take on the occasional speech, the visiting lectureship, or the writing of a book. These activities in the public eye typically deal with their duties and responsibilities on the Court or the nature of judging and law. The chief justice also comments on these topics but is also more likely than his colleagues to speak out publicly about administrative needs.

Because the chief justice is both the administrative leader and spokesperson for the judicial branch, he is uniquely suited to establish the agenda for the federal courts and advocate its enactment. This promotion of the judiciary's needs is necessary because the courts are dependent on the elected branches as a function of constitutional design. The Third Branch relies on Congress for both institutional maintenance and judicial improvements and must compete with other national priorities for congressional attention.

How can a chief justice advocate for the needs of the federal judiciary? One option is to use his political capital to advance the needs of the federal courts. According to Russell Wheeler, "[e]very chief justice has to decide how much political capital the office has and how to spend that capital on Congress, the bar, the press, and others."[8] He can do so in two ways. First, he may choose to use his informal influence and personal relationships to lobby elites to enact the goals of the judiciary. Chief Justice Warren E. Burger used this method early in his tenure.[9] In addition, a chief justice can advocate publicly for improvements to the judiciary. This is akin to presidential efforts to "go public,"[10] though the chief justice's audience is likely to include policymakers as well as the American people.

An overt manifestation of a chief's advocacy for the federal judiciary (and expending of political capital) occurs in his Year-End Report on the Federal Judiciary. This report is compiled every year by the chief justice and has recently become the subject of scholarly analysis.[11] These reports have been issued by Burger (1976–1985), Rehnquist (1986–2004), and Roberts (2005–present). The chief justice is at liberty to include in year-end reports the content of his choice, including, but not limited to, recommendations for judicial improvements or reforms. The issue areas to which Burger, Rehnquist, and Roberts drew attention in their year-end reports are summarized in table 14.1.[12] It is evident that chief justices emphasize

TABLE 14.1. Issue Areas of Agenda Items in Year-End Report on the Federal Judiciary, by Chief Justice

	Number of requests		
Issue area	Warren Burger (1975–85)	William Rehnquist (1986–2004)	John Roberts (2005–12)
Budget	4	14	2
Housekeeping	11	2	1
Additional Judgeships	16	19	0
Jurisdiction Change	19	6	0
Legislative Policies	10	12	0
Salary / Benefits	9	17	4
Structural Reorganization	12	3	0
Study Request	7	2	0
Vacancies	0	11	2
Total	88	86	9

Note: $N = 183$

different priorities. Burger devoted more attention to housekeeping, jurisdiction change, structural reorganization, and study requests than his successors. Rehnquist focused more on budget issues and judicial vacancies than either Burger or Roberts. Chief Justice Roberts has asked for relatively few agenda items, with the plurality of his explicit requests related to judicial salaries and benefits.

The Year-End Report on the Federal Judiciary is an opportunity for the chief justice to communicate to an audience wider than judges and lawyers or a few members of Congress. It receives coverage in national media outlets, legal trade publications, law journals, and websites and thus gives a higher profile to the proposals contained within it. For example, following the 2012 year-end report journalists affiliated with major newspapers, newswires, and news websites all reported Chief Justice Roberts's messages about the judiciary's budget appropriations and desire that vacant judgeships be filled.[13] With this visibility, the chief justice has a pulpit from which to present requests regarding the federal judiciary and therefore spend his political capital. Consequently, the reports represent his policy agenda for the judicial branch.[14] The factors that determine the size of this agenda, and the extent to which a chief justice will include important items in his report, are the subjects of this analysis.

Agenda Setting by the Chief Justice: Theory

In his 2009 Year-End Report on the Federal Judiciary, Chief Justice Roberts declined to include any reform proposals or requests for congressional action. Instead, Roberts acknowledged the public's hardship during economic recession and included only a reference to "critical needs of the judiciary" that "remain to be addressed."[15] His decision to omit requests for judicial improvements suggests two possibilities. The first is that he anticipated a slim likelihood that he would achieve them given current political and economic conditions. If so, this indicates that the chief justice is strategic and anticipatory when he creates his agenda. A second possibility is that he limited his agenda as a function of his relative inexperience as leader of the federal courts. Roberts was the chief justice for four years when the 2009 year-end report was drafted, and he had never requested more than three agenda items in a single report. If this is the case, then administrative experience carries weight as a chief justice creates his judicial agenda.

To assess the extent that strategy and experience determine a chief justice's judicial agenda, we develop a theoretical framework. This includes discussion of the chief justice's goals and strategy in building his policy agenda. Importantly, we draw from the research on agenda setting in the presidency literature to shape this framework.[16]

Goals of the Chief Justice. While the chief executive has goals that include policy enactment, re-election, and historical significance, a chief justice has more specialized motives.[17] A chief justice is motivated by policy concerns and historical significance, but not at all with re-election.[18] As administrative leader of the federal courts, his goals also relate to the health of that branch of government.

Much of his work within the Court, whether shaping the docket,[19] voting on the merits,[20] or assigning opinions,[21] reflects his policy goals. The extra-judicial activities of the chief justice, including staffing specialized courts and the Judicial Conference,[22] do so as well. In addition, the chief justice has goals related to the functions and health of the federal judiciary.[23] His administrative goals include, for example, caseload management, jurisdictional issues, and securing adequate budgetary resources for the federal courts. They may also include limiting the role of courts and promoting judicial independence. Both his policy and administrative goals are likely to be reflected in his agenda-setting activities.

Strategies of the Chief Justice. A wealth of research in the last two decades examines the strategic behavior of Supreme Court justices. This literature gives substantial scrutiny to the chief justice. We now know that chief justices are strategic with regard to setting the docket,[24] manipulating conference discussion,[25] self-assigning the majority opinion or choosing an ideological proximate,[26] and using their votes or opinion assignments to maintain majority coalitions.[27] Prior research, though limited in scope, indicates that the chief justice is also strategic when he carries out his administrative duties. Nixon found that both Warren Burger and William Rehnquist manipulated the rosters of the Executive Committee of the Judicial Conference to pursue a conservative policy agenda.[28]

If the chief justice is a strategic actor with goals related to policy and judicial administration, he is likely to consider the contemporaneous policy environment when crafting his agenda. The most important component of this environment is Congress. A rational and strategic chief executive must consider the success of potential agenda items in Congress before he gives them his support.[29] It stands to reason that a chief justice has similar concerns about the potential success of his agenda and will determine whether he is faced with support or constraint in the legislative body. Eshbaugh-Soha calls this the "rule of anticipative reactions."[30]

A strategic chief justice may also include some rational calculation about his own political capital. This capital is likely to be influenced substantially by the status of the institution he leads. If the Supreme Court is unpopular with either the public or lawmakers, we expect that the chief justice will have less clout to wield in his advocacy efforts. A chief justice whose Court is known for unpopular decisions may have less political capital to spend in support of the federal judiciary.

Experience. In addition to strategic considerations, the agenda promoted by the chief justice may also be influenced by his own administrative experience. Studies of judicial politics frequently consider whether junior justices experience a "freshman effect" or "acclimation effect" while they become acquainted with their jobs and colleagues.[31] We posit that a similar phenomenon may occur for chief justices given that their numerous administrative duties include tasks unrelated to their previous professional experience. Although many federal judges have experience as chief judges or members of administrative bodies, including the Judicial Conference, none of these positions presides over a similar range of duties or number of judicial branch employees. As a chief justice retains his position for a longer period of time, we expect he will be more aware of the vital needs of the federal judiciary and more invested in his administrative duties beyond leading the Supreme Court.

Policy Scope. Not all policy proposals requested by the chief justice are equal. Some advocate relatively minor changes, while others would change substantially the relationship between the judiciary and the American people. In general, we expect that a chief justice will approach important policies differently than minor (routine) ones. Specifically, he may choose to focus on important policy changes when the political environment is most likely to facilitate their adoption. We specify more explicitly what constitutes important and routine policies in our analysis section below.

Hypotheses

Our theoretical expectations about the effects of strategy and administrative experience on the chief justice's agenda motivate several hypotheses. His policy agenda, as expressed in the Year-End Report on the Federal Judiciary, reflects what the chief justice believes is both important and feasible in the year ahead. Our hypotheses relate to both the overall size of the agenda and the number of important agenda items requested each year.

Strategic Considerations

Congress. The expected reaction of Congress is likely to be a leading consideration when the chief justice creates his agenda. The success of his requests is a specific goal for the chief justice, and it requires the support of legislative majorities in the House and Senate. Satisfaction with the judicial branch affects how Congress responds to courts. For example, legislative overrides often follow Supreme Court rulings contrary to congressional preferences,[32] and lawmakers sometimes react to judicial activity by changing courts' jurisdiction.[33] On the other hand, satisfaction with the Supreme Court's output is correlated with budget increases.[34]

One way for the chief justice to determine the mood of Congress relative to the federal courts is to consider the quantity of court-curbing bills that Congress produced in the previous year. These bills are "legislative proposal[s] to restrict, remove, or otherwise limit judicial power" and signify hostility toward the federal courts.[35] They present a strategic tool that Congress uses to announce discontent with judicial behavior. We posit that more court-curbing bills in a given year indicates that relations between Congress and the judiciary are strained. Accordingly, if a chief justice is strategic as he creates his judicial agenda, *we expect that the chief justice will advocate fewer agenda items, as well as fewer important proposals, when the number of court-curbing bills is higher*. We use data compiled by Clark updated through 2012 to measure the quantity of court-curbing bills each year.[36]

In addition to legislative-judicial relations, a chief justice is also likely to consider the overall political climate. The presence of divided government is a strong signal that the legislative process may be more difficult to traverse. Unified or divided control of the elected branches is a key determinant of policy outputs.[37] In addition, party control of Congress affects some aspects of judicial policy, including expansion of the judiciary.[38] Thus a chief justice is likely to anticipate that his judicial policy will have a greater chance of success during periods of unified government than otherwise. If a chief justice is strategic as he creates his judicial agenda, *we expect that divided government will be associated with fewer items on the agenda of the chief justice, important or otherwise*. We measure divided government using a binary variable indicating its presence or absence.

Public Opinion. Popular perceptions of the Supreme Court are a source of prestige and political capital for the chief justice. Accordingly, we posit that the chief justice is likely to adjust the size and scope of his agenda in response to public opinion about the Third Branch. Studies of the executive branch frequently cite public approval as an important predictor of policy success.[39] Although the chief justice is a less visible political figure than the president, the general public still forms opinions about the Supreme Court and federal judiciary that reflect on him. These opinions are important to the judicial branch as perceptions about its legitimacy shape its dependence on the elected branches and subnational governments to enforce its rulings. Furthermore, Congress is likely aware of these opinions, especially in the wake of highly visible (and possibly contentious) Supreme Court opinions. Given that legislators depend on their constituents for re-election and attempt to please them,[40] Congress has little electoral incentive to shirk constituent preferences in favor of an institution out of step with the public. For these reasons, we expect that *an increase in public disapproval of the Supreme Court is associated with a reduction in both the total agenda size and total number of important items on the agenda of the chief justice.*

Economic Constraints. Economic constraints influence all outcomes in the policy process. The chief justice is likely aware that economic conditions influence how Congress may respond to his agenda items. When the economy is performing well and economic recovery is not the primary priority of lawmakers, Congress may be more amenable to legislation concerning the federal courts. Given this, if a chief justice is strategic, *we expect that greater economic growth is associated with an increase in the overall number of legislative requests made by the chief justice, whether these requests are routine or important.*

Experience. Other than strategic considerations, the size and scope of the agenda of a chief justice may alternatively be influenced by the duration of his tenure in the office. Judicial scholars have long examined whether Supreme Court justices experience a "freshman effect" or otherwise alter their behavior during the course of their careers. These shifts, when observed, are attributed to socialization, small group dynamics, or increasing comfort with the role and duties of a Supreme Court justice. We expect that similar behavior is observable in the administrative leadership of the chief justice. Individuals are nominated and confirmed for seats on the Supreme Court as a result of their judicial philosophies, professional qualifications, integrity, and temperament. Little emphasis is placed on their interest in administrative duties or ability to accomplish them. It is likely, though, that chief justices become more comfortable with these responsibilities, and more skilled at them, over time. As a result, *we expect that the overall agenda of the chief justice, as well as the number of important agenda items, will increase in size as his tenure in the center seat lengthens.*

The variables we use to test our hypotheses, as well as our data sources, are described in table 14.2. We also present the mean, range, and expected effect of each explanatory factor.

Analysis

In our analysis, we construct separate models explaining (1) the total number of items on the agenda of the chief justice and (2) the number of important items on his agenda. Because each of our dependent variables is a count, we use Poisson regression models. The models are relatively parsimonious, with four independent variables and two control variables. The independent variables indicate key aspects of the political and economic environment during the tenure of the chief justice as well as his level of administrative experience. Our controls include the calendar year in order to capture trends related to changing behavior by chief justices over time, as well as the number of agenda items requested by the Judicial Conference each year in its fall report.[41] Our data include all years in which the Year-End Report on the Federal Judiciary was issued prior to 2013 (1975 to 2012; $N = 38$).

To differentiate between important and routine agenda items in the Year-End Report on the Federal Judiciary, we develop a policy scope typology adapted from Eshbaugh-Soha's research on the president's agenda.[42] He categorized items on the president's agenda based on two dimensions defined by time and importance. In our typology, we focus on the latter dimension as analysis of Year-End Reports reveal an overwhelming focus

TABLE 14.2. Summary Statistics

Variable	Mean (s.d.)	Range	Expected Effect	Data Source
Dependent Variable(s)				
Total agenda items (Model 1)	4.66 (3.29)	0–13	n/a	Year-End Report on the Federal Judiciary
Total important items (Model 2)	2.29 (1.89)	0–6	n/a	Year-End Report on the Federal Judiciary
Independent Variables				
Chief Justice tenure	8.74 (5.22)	0.25–18.25	+	Federal Judicial Center
Court-curbing bills	7.66 (8.03)	0–32	–	Clark (2009), updated via Thomas.gov
Public disapproval of Supreme Court	14.98 (2.59)	10.3–20.9	–	General Social Survey
GDP growth	2.76 (2.09)	-3.1–7.2	+	Bureau of Economic Analysis
Control Variables				
Year	1993.5 (11.11)	1975–2012	n/a	n/a
Judicial conference agenda size	15.55 (11.27)	3.48	n/a	Report of the Judicial Conference (September/October)

Note: N = 38

on long-term goals by the chief justices. Rather than short-term political goals or contemporary national problems, chief justices tend to focus on judicial procedure, structural reorganization, systemic social problems, the creation of judgeships, and jurisdiction change.[43]

We identify important agenda items requested by the chief justices as those with the greatest impact and cost.[44] Agenda items are considered important if they would create or eliminate a judicial body, create ten or more judgeships, or alter substantially the relationship between Americans and the judicial system. We classify requests for ten or more judgeships as important because they differ in kind from requests for fewer new positions. Although we use ten judgeships as our metric for importance, an examination of requests in the year-end report reveals that requests for new judgeships tend to be either few in number, focused narrowly on specific courts with overwhelming caseloads, or number in the dozens or hundreds.[45] The latter subset includes proposals that would affect either access to justice or jury service, including, for example, the elimination of federal diversity jurisdiction and reducing the Supreme Court's mandatory jurisdiction. Although federal judges would likely disagree, we do not identify as important any requests that improve the salaries, benefits, or working conditions of individual judges. We regard these as routine matters with a limited impact on the American people. Table 14.3 illustrates the general issue areas covered by the chief justices[46] and the relative frequency of which these policies are important versus routine. Overall, 87 of 177 agenda items in our data are identified as "important."

TABLE 14.3. Routine and Important Agenda Items in Year-End Report on the Federal Judiciary, by Issue Area

Issue Area	Routine	Important
Budget	20	0
Housekeeping	5	5
Judgeships	7	28
Jurisdiction	3	22
Legislative policy	7	13
Salary and benefits	30	0
Structural reform	7	8
Study request	9	0
Vacancies	2	11

Note: N = 177 agenda items; 87 identified as important. Four housekeeping items and 2 legislative policy items excluded due to coding ambiguity. See text for details.

Results

The results of our statistical analysis are presented in table 14.4. Our findings strongly support administrative experience as a determinant for the size of the chief justice's agenda. We find no evidence that indicates strategic considerations shape the size or relative importance of the chief justice's agenda. Notably, we do not find important differences in the factors predicting the size of the agenda and the number of important items. Both are influenced primarily by chief justice experience and trends observed over time.

In terms of substantive impact, each additional year of service is associated with a rate increase of 1.05 agenda items and 1.06 important agenda items. This relationship is shown in figure 14.1. The most senior chief justice is predicted to request nearly twice as many agenda items as an inexperienced chief justice. Our data reveal that a decade of service in the position is pivotal. The mean number of requests in the first ten years is 4.0; the number increases to 6.75 per year during the remainder of his tenure. A similar trend is present for important agenda items, with an average of 1.81 per year during the first decade of service and a mean of 3.06 each year afterward. This trend is present for all three chief justices in our data, though Chief Justice Roberts has not served long enough to reach conclusions about the size of his agenda as a seasoned administrator. Notably, our

TABLE 14.4. Poisson Regression Results

	Model 1: Agenda Size		Model 2: Number of Important Agenda Items	
	Coefficient (r.s.e.)	Z	Coefficient (r.s.e.)	Z
Chief Justice Tenure	0.06 (0.02)	3.43	0.05 (0.02)	2.68
Court-Curbing bills	−0.004 (0.01)	0.67	−0.02 (0.01)	0.07
Public Disapproval of Supreme Court	−0.03 (0.03)	−0.82	−0.07 (0.05)	-1.53
GDP Growth	−0.04 (0.04)	-1.18	−0.04 (0.04)	-0.87
Control Variables				
Year	−0.04 (0.01)	−4.31	−0.06 (0.01)	-4.09
Judicial Conference Agenda Size	−0.002 (0.01)	−0.34	0.01 (0.01)	0.78

Note: $N = 38$; "r.s.e." = robust standard error.

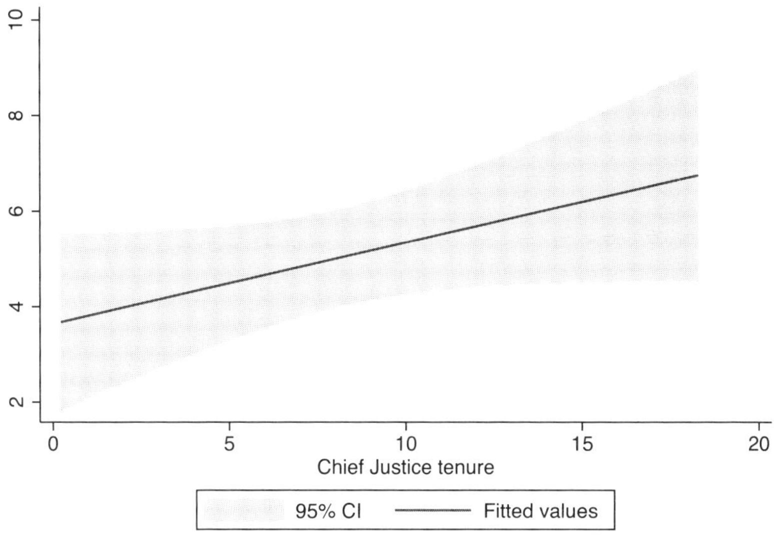

Fig. 14.1. Number of agenda items requested by chief justices

results are robust even when Roberts's years as chief justice are omitted from the analysis.

As we have already stated, none of the variables that indicate strategy on behalf of a chief justice reach statistical significance. Our lone remaining statistically significant variable is the control for the calendar year when the report was issued. We find that the size of the total agenda and the count of important items both decrease over time, all else being equal. We speculate this is due in part to the gradual, permanent removal of items from the wish list of the chief justice as problems of the mid-twentieth-century federal courts were solved. Chief Justice Burger came to office when the Third Branch was in relative disrepair, and he presented more extensive sets of proposed reforms than his successors. The mean agenda size was 7.45 items for Burger (1975–1985), 4.53 for Rehnquist, and 1.0 for Roberts.

Discussion and Conclusions

While the president is responsive to his political environment and strategic in crafting his agenda for Congress, we find no evidence that the chief justice does the same. Even though it may be logical that a chief justice would anticipate the policy environment in which he operates, including legislative-judicial relations, divided government, and economic constraints, none of these factors reached statistical significance in our models. Instead, administrative experience matters a great deal. Importantly, our results demonstrate that a chief justice who has passed the decade mark in his position will ask more of Congress than he did in his earlier tenure. Furthermore, he is also more likely to ask for judicial improvements or institutional maintenance that are of greater consequence. Overall our results show that in his relations with Congress, a chief justice is influenced more by his experience than his political leverage.

In addition, we also do not find evidence that the chief justice considers his own political capital when he determines the size of his agenda. This means that as an administrative leader, the chief justice is not susceptible to the changing mood of the American public with regard to his Court. Put another way, a chief justice will ask (or not ask) Congress for the needs of the federal judiciary without regard for public opinion. Of course, this could be a result of the relatively positive perceptions of the federal judiciary (particularly the Supreme Court) by the American public, especially when compared to the elected branches. Even after contentious decisions such as *Bush v. Gore*,[47] the Supreme Court maintains consistent levels of perceived legitimacy in public opinion polls.[48]

We believe it is important that the chief justice does not manipulate the size of his agenda in response to the political and economic environment. This is contrary to expectations expressed in studies of executive branch politics and underscores the need to devote further study to the role of the chief justice as administrative leader. Administrative experience helps determine the chief justice's ability and/or willingness to ask Congress for judicial improvements, which has important consequences for the judicial branch. This suggests that of the many hats that the chief justice wears, chief administrator of the federal courts may be one that fits better the longer it is worn.

NOTES

1. Russell R. Wheeler, "Chief Justice Rehnquist as Third Branch Leader," *Judicature* 89 (2005): 117.

2. See Judith Resnik and Lane Dilg, "Responding to a Democratic Deficit: Limiting the Powers and the Term of the Chief Justice of the United States," *Uni-*

versity of Pennsylvania Law Review 154 (2006). The administrative duties of the chief justices are sufficiently onerous that he has been provided an administrative assistant, known as a counselor to the Chief Justice, since 1972 (86 Stat. 46). The relevant statute is currently 28 U.S.C § 677.

3. See Richard L. Vining and Teena Wilhelm, "The Chief Justice as Advocate-in-Chief: Examining the Year-End Report on the Federal Judiciary," *Judicature* 95 (2012).

4. Resnik and Dilg, "Responding to a Democratic Deficit," 1575.

5. For more about the work of the chief justice, see Resnik and Dilg, "Responding to a Democratic Deficit," and Robert Post, "Judicial Management: The Achievements of Chief Justice William Howard Taft," *OAH Magazine of History* 13 (1998).

6. See Charlie Savage, "Roberts's Picks Reshaping Secret Surveillance Court," *New York Times*, July 26, 2013.

7. See Peter G. Fish, *The Politics of Federal Judicial Administration* (Princeton: Princeton University Press, 1973); and Post, "Judicial Management," for more information regarding the Judicial Conference and the chief's duties.

8. Wheeler, "Chief Justice Rehnquist as Third Branch Leader," 118.

9. See Mark W. Cannon, "Innovation in the Administration of Justice, 1969–1981: An Overview," *Policy Studies Journal* 10 (1982).

10. See Samuel Kernell, *Going Public: New Strategies of Presidential Leadership*, 3rd ed. (Washington, DC: CQ Press, 1997).

11. See Vining and Wilhelm, "The Chief Justice as Advocate-in-Chief," for a history and content analysis of these reports. See also Resnik and Dilg, "Responding to a Democratic Deficit."

12. Adapted from Vining and Wilhelm, "The Chief Justice as Advocate-in-Chief," 273.

13. E.g., Robert Barnes, "Roberts Stresses Frugality in Year-End Federal Judiciary Report," *Washington Post*, Jan. 1, 2013; Adam Liptak, "Chief Justice Prods Congress to Resolve Budget Talks and Control National Debt," *New York Times*, Jan. 1, 2013; Pete Yost, "Roberts Urges Full Financial Support for the Court," *Associated Press*, Dec. 31, 2012; and Bill Mears, "Chief Justice Laments 'Fiscal Cliff' Effects on Federal Courts," *CNN Wire*, Dec. 31, 2012.

14. While we argue that the Year-End Report on the Federal Judiciary expresses the preferences of the chief justice, we acknowledge that it is written with assistance from staff including the administrative assistant and Supreme Court fellows. The extent to which these actors influence the content of the report is beyond the scope of our inquiry.

15. Adam Liptak, "A Busy Year for Judiciary, Roberts Says," *New York Times*, Jan. 1, 2010.

16. This literature includes Jon R. Bond and Richard Fleisher, *The President in the Legislative Arena* (Chicago: University of Chicago Press, 1990). But also see Mark A. Peterson, *Legislating Together: The White House and Capitol Hill from Eisenhower to Reagan* (Cambridge, MA: Harvard University Press, 1990); Paul C. Light, *The President's Agenda: Domestic Policy Choice from Kennedy to Reagan*, 3rd ed. (Baltimore: Johns Hopkins University Press, 1999); Brandice Canes-Wrone, "The President's Legislative Influence from Public Appeals," *American Journal of Political*

Science 45 (2001); Matthew Eshbaugh-Soha, "The Politics of Presidential Agendas," *Political Research Quarterly* 58 (2005); Jeff Yates and Andrew Whitford, "Institutional Foundations of the President's Issue Agenda," *Political Research Quarterly* 58 (2005); George C. Edwards III, and B. Dan Wood, "Who Influences Whom? The President, Congress, and the Media," *American Political Science Review* 93 (1999); and Jeffrey Cummins, "State of the Union Addresses and the President's Legislative Success," *Congress and the Presidency* 37 (2010).

17. For a discussion of executive goals, see Light, *President's Agenda*.

18. Regarding the tenure of the chief justice, it is noteworthy that there have been only seventeen chiefs since the position's inception. Since the modern chief justiceship (Taft in 1921), there have been only eight chief justices compared to sixteen presidents. The average tenure for a chief justice in this time period has been 11.47 years (including Chief Justice Roberts). With fewer turnovers and an extended tenure for the chief justice compared to that of the chief executive, the pressing goal of historical significance is likely limited. A president may have only four or eight years to accomplish his goals, but a chief likely has many more. In fact, Roberts could yet have twenty years or longer to make his mark on his Court and the federal judiciary.

19. Gregory A. Caldeira and John R. Wright, "The Discuss List: Agenda Building in the Supreme Court," *Law & Society Review* 24 (1990)

20. Forrest Maltzman and Paul J. Wahlbeck, "May It Please the Chief? Opinion Assignments in the Rehnquist Court," *American Journal of Political Science* 40 (1996).

21. David J. Danelski, "The Influence of the Chief Justice in the Decisional Process of the Supreme Court," in *American Court Systems: Readings in Judicial Process and Behavior*, 2nd ed., ed. Sheldon Goldman and Austin Sarat (New York: Longman, 1989).

22. David C. Nixon, "Policy-Making by Different Means: The Chief Justice's Attempts to Shape Policy Through the Judicial Conference of the United States," *Rationality and Society* 15 (2003).

23. See Fish, *The Politics of Federal Judicial Administration*; Vining and Wilhelm, "The Chief Justice as Advocate-in-Chief."

24. Caldeira and Wright, "The Discuss List."

25. Lee Epstein and Jack Knight, *The Choices Justices Make* (Washington, DC: CQ Press, 1998).

26. Maltzman and Wahlbeck, "May It Please the Chief."

27. Danelski, "Influence of the Chief Justice."

28. Nixon, "Policy-Making."

29. See e.g. Eshbaugh-Soha, "The Politics of Presidential Agendas"; Peterson, *Legislating Together*; Douglas Rivers and Nancy L. Rose, "Passing the President's Program: Public Opinion and Presidential Influence in Congress," *American Journal of Political Science* 29 (1985).

30. Eshbaugh-Soha, "The Politics of Presidential Agendas," 258.

31. See Timothy M. Hagle, "'Freshman Effects' for Supreme Court Justices," *American Journal of Political Science* 37 (1993); Saul Brenner and Timothy M. Hagle, "Opinion Writing and Acclimation Effect," *Political Behavior* 18 (1996); Sandra L. Wood et al., "'Acclimation Effects' for Supreme Court Justices: A Cross-Validation, 1888–1940," *American Journal of Political Science* 42 (1998).

32. Jeb Barnes, *Overruled?: Legislative Overrides, Pluralism, and Contemporary Court-Congress Relations* (Stanford, CA: Stanford University Press, 2004).

33. John B. Oakley, "Recent Statutory Changes in the Law of Federal Jurisdiction and Venue: The Judicial Improvements Acts of 1988 and 1990," *University of California, Davis Law Review* 24 (1991).

34. Eugenia Toma, "A Contractual Model of the Voting Behavior of the Supreme Court: The Role of the Chief Justice," *International Review of Law and Economics* 16 (1996).

35. Tom S. Clark, "The Separation of Powers, Court Curbing, and Judicial Legitimacy," *American Journal of Political Science* 53 (2009), 978.

36. Ibid.

37. See e.g. George C. Edwards III, Andrew Barrett, and Jeffrey Peake, "The Legislative Impact of Divided Government," *American Journal of Political Science* 41 (1997); David R. Mayhew, *Divided We Govern: Party Control, Lawmaking, and Investigations, 1946–2002*, 2nd ed. (New Haven: Yale University Press, 2005).

38. John M. De Figuerido and Emerson H. Tiller, "Congressional Control of the Courts: A Theoretical and Empirical Analysis of Expansion of the Federal Judiciary," *Journal of Law and Economics* 39 (1996); John M. De Figuerido et al., "Congress and the Political Expansion of the U.S. District Courts," *American Law and Economics Review* 2 (2000).

39. See e.g. Edwards, Barrett, and Peake, "The Legislative Impact of Divided Government"; Eshbaugh-Soha, "The Politics of Presidential Agendas"; Richard E. Neustadt, *Presidential Power* (New York: Wiley, 1990).

40. E.g. Douglas R. Arnold, *The Logic of Congressional Action* (New Haven: Yale University Press, 1992); David R. Mayhew, *Congress: The Electoral Connection* (New Haven: Yale University Press, 1974).

41. This indicates whether the size of the reform agenda presented by the chief justice depends on the number of requests made by his fellow federal judges.

42. Eshbaugh-Soha, "Presidential Agendas."

43. Vining and Wilhelm, "The Chief Justice as Advocate-in-Chief."

44. See Eshbaugh-Soha, "The Politics of Presidential Agendas," 260.

45. See also Figuerido and Tiller, "Congressional Control"; and De Figuerido et al., "Congress and Political Expansion."

46. See Vining and Wilhelm, "The Chief Justice as Advocate-in-Chief."

47. 531 U.S. 98 (2000).

48. Lee Epstein and Thomas G. Walker, *Constitutional Law for a Changing America: Rights, Liberties, and Justice*, 8th ed. (Washington, DC: CQ Press, 2012).

15 Be Careful With My Court

Legitimacy, Public Opinion, and the Chief Justices

SHAWN C. FETTIG AND SARA C. BENESH

On June 28, 2012, the Supreme Court announced its decision in *National Federation of Independent Business et al. v. Sebelius, Secretary of Health and Human Services et al.*, upholding the Affordable Care Act by a vote of 5-4. Chief Justice John Roberts read his majority opinion. Almost immediately, political scientists and pundits alike began dissecting the opinion and the reason for Chief Justice Roberts's vote. Public approval of the Court, as noted by the media, was at its lowest levels ever as the Court prepared to hear the case.[1] Many argued that the Court's legitimacy weighed heavily on Roberts as he considered the case, with CBS News reporting that Roberts, as chief justice, "is keenly aware of his leadership role on the court, and he also is sensitive to how the court is perceived by the public."[2] "To be sure," wrote *New York Times* reporter Adam Liptak, "the chief justice considers himself the custodian of the Supreme Court's prestige, authority, and legitimacy, and he is often its voice in major cases."[3] He reprised the role in *King v. Burwell*, the 6-3 decision announced almost exactly one year later upholding the subsidies associated with the health care exchanges.[4] There, Jeffrey Rosen argued, the chief used the case's reason to confer legitimacy. Judicial restraint, Rosen suggests, drove the chief's decision, for "In a polarized age, it is important for the Supreme Court to maintain its institutional legitimacy by deferring to the political branches."[5]

We know that the Court is influenced by public opinion and the Court's decisions are often in line with it.[6] We also know that judicial legitimacy is fairly widespread and relatively stable,[7] and that it is drawn from diffuse support, a "reservoir of good will,"[8] that is resilient and resistant to significant fluctuation.

Perhaps chief justices believe, though, as Caldeira argues,[9] that a string of unpopular decisions could have a lasting, negative impact on the Court and its ability to render legitimate decisions. Perhaps that drove Chief Justice Roberts's vote in *Sebelius*, coming as it did after a string of unpopular decisions, and perhaps he had it in mind a year later, in *Burwell*.[10] Chief Justice Charles Evans Hughes seems to have subscribed to this belief.[11] Legitimacy is, of course, uncommonly important to the Court,[12] which is seen as undemocratic and nearly wholly reliant on its legitimacy and on the actions of other government institutions for its power.[13]

The chief justice, while endowed with no significant power over any of the other justices, is the face of the Court, assigns majority opinions when he is in the majority, and "when the Court is divided . . . is in a favorable position to seek unity."[14] Like other leaders, the chief is endowed with the opportunity to enhance and maintain the image of the Court, and some ability to affect change or direct outcomes.[15] Chiefs, like leaders more generally, vary in the extent to which they can effectively harness their administrative duties[16] and powers and channel them into influence over the Court's image and its opinion. But many of them do, via task and social leadership.[17]

The scholarship on Court legitimacy and leadership more generally, combined with conventional wisdom, suggests, then, that the chief justice may be interested in the Court's legitimacy and might take steps to ensure that the prestige of the Court is maximized and maintained. In this chapter, we explore the question of whether or not the chief justice, being the administrative head and the most recognizable justice of the Court, exhibits concern for the legitimacy of the Court and thus evidences some attention to the ways in which the Court's legitimacy might be preserved (or threatened) via various Court actions. If legitimacy matters to the Court in general and the chief justice in particular, we might expect to find two areas of evidence. First, we would find that in their private correspondence with the chief, the justices of the Supreme Court notice and discuss issues related to the approval of the Court or its decisions. We examine the personal papers of several of the justices to see whether there is any evidence in personal correspondence among the justices for attention to concerns surrounding the Court's legitimacy. We would also expect, were legitimacy a factor in his decision making, that the chief justice may sometimes vote or behave in ways seemingly at odds with his policy preferences, including in his writing, in his opinion assignments, or in his interactions with other justices, especially in particularly salient issue areas and especially when Court approval is shaky. We examine key cases, as identified by their potential to damage the Court, in an effort to determine how chiefs may have behaved to maintain institutional legitimacy and prestige. We detail several instances where this idea potentially explains the chief justice's behavior.

Working Toward Unanimity and Paying Heed to Public Opinion

The Supreme Court, as a whole, tends to respond to shifts in public opinion, such that its decisions reflect changes in it.[18] This sensitivity to public opinion is present even in the absence of any meaningful membership change on the bench. Indeed, historian Michael Klarman argues that "more constitutional law than is commonly supposed reflects this tendency to constitutionalize the consensus and suppress outliers."[19] *Brown*, he says, was decided only when the Court had at least half of the country behind it.[20] Likewise, the Court did not push hard for full-scale compliance with that decision until the civil rights movement coalesced into strong support for such action. "The justices are too much products of their time and place to launch social revolutions."[21] Indeed, Durr et al. find that support for the Court erodes when the Court deviates from aggregate public opinion on an issue, and the media's attention to cases in which the Court so deviates may help to explain the historical and recent decreases in Court favorability and confidence.[22]

Additionally, commentary suggests evidence for a concern about legitimacy demonstrated by heavy reliance on precedential case law to justify decisions that are salient to the public or that directly challenge the decision of another branch of government,[23] and an effort toward unanimous decisions when faced with outside threats.[24] Many suspect that part of the Court's legitimacy depends on the extent to which the public believes its decisions are made in accordance with the requirements of the law. Relying on precedent and speaking in legalistic language might enhance perceptions of the neutrality of the decision makers. We know from Casey that myth is a powerful force and that the Supreme Court benefits greatly from the myth of certainty in legal decision making.[25] Gibson and Caldeira rely on mythology to explain their positivity bias, noting that the couching of Supreme Court decisions in the symbols of the Court lend legitimacy to the Court's pronouncements.[26] Ulmer, as early as 1973, noted the connection among myth, symbols, and the Court's legitimacy.[27] Danelski speaks of myth when explaining why chief justices are particularly interested in unanimous decisions.[28] And unanimous decisions seemingly fit into that mythological narrative.

An astute chief may therefore take steps to enhance the Court's image and prestige and may attempt to shape decisions that will be accepted by the public. One means by which he might do so is to attempt to influence his colleagues to suppress separate opinions and instead sign on to unanimous majority opinions, especially when the public may be watching.

Danelski considered each of the chiefs and the extent to which they aimed for and achieved unanimity in furtherance of "the law's myth of certainty" necessary for Court prestige and, ultimately, power.[29] He found some variation across chiefs as to this attribute, but much evidence for its operation. Chief Justice Taft believed that unanimous decisions have greater legitimacy than divided decisions; hence he sought to "mass" his Court, urging his colleagues to "acquiesce in silence," except in cases involving fundamental principles, rather than make public their dissents.[30] Chief Justice Hughes sought unanimity (in *Schechter Poultry Corp. v. United States*[31]) when he knew that the other two branches of government would not be pleased with the Court's decision.[32] Notes in the justice's papers—where the chief justice for instance invites specific Court members to dinners or sends a note of good will to a justice who is ailing or inquires about the well-being of the justice's children—demonstrate social leadership, which may be parlayed into unanimity and hence enhanced legitimacy.

In an interview with Jeffrey Rosen in 2007, Chief Justice John Roberts acknowledged the importance of consensus on the Court as a means of signaling to the public the credibility of its decisions. Roberts, a former clerk of Rehnquist, in a moment of candor also noted that his predecessor had not been as focused on unanimity, but nonetheless did adopt a special concern for legitimacy of the institution once he donned the chief's robes. While Rehnquist did not seek consensus as a means to this legitimacy, he did take care to ensure that he signed on to an opinion as the sixth justice, though rarely as the fifth. According to Roberts, Rehnquist compromised for the "good of the Court," at least when it would not affect the outcome.[33] Two of Chief Justice Earl Warren's biographers note that in presiding over the Supreme Court's landmark decision in *Brown* (1953), Warren was keenly aware of the impact that such a decision would have on the American public and thus painstakingly sought unanimity among the Court's justices to bolster the strength of the decision, as discussed at length below.[34]

Given the research in the field, the chiefs would be right that, at least to some degree, an attempt to gain unanimity in difficult-to-implement decisions is worth the effort. Unanimous decisions over nonunanimous decisions, decisions that command at least a majority of the Court over those that are accompanied only by a plurality, and decisions accompanied only by supportive concurring opinions and not limiting or negative concurrences, are all treated better subsequently.[35] Considering Warren's famous pursuit of unanimity in *Brown* illustrates what it takes for the chief to gain this potentially important consensus.

Earl Warren

Like Hughes before him, Earl Warren believed in the power of public opinion. It makes sense, then, that he would consider it in his actions as chief. Being a skillful politician for most of his career, Warren was familiar with responding to, but also shaping, public perception. Warren's vision of American democracy and what it could accomplish comported well with his impression of the power of public perception and support. In Warren's view, democracy was not threatened by the people, but rather bolstered by it.[36]

As chief, Warren was more insulated from the politics of public opinion, and yet Warren would carry with him the belief in the importance of public opinion over the force of government. "[Warren] knew the pulsebeat of the people and the practical problems of its leaders."[37] He was, therefore, the perfect candidate to join the then-dysfunctional Supreme Court, and President Eisenhower liked his high ideals and common sense.[38] And so he appointed Warren to the seat while Congress was not in session. While at least Frankfurter was unhappy with Eisenhower's choice of a "mere politician," the public approved.[39] "He was a doer. He was an optimist. He was in the American grain. And he looked and sounded the way a chief justice should."[40]

The Court he was joining, however, was "the most severely fractured Supreme Court in history."[41] The Court had heard arguments in *Brown* in the previous term and all indications are that the Court was badly split over it. Justice Frankfurter secured a delay in asking for reargument during the next term in an attempt to achieve unanimity. Over the summer, Chief Justice Fred Vinson suddenly died, opening the vacancy eventually filled by Warren.[42] He took his seat in October of 1953, just before the reargument of *Brown*.

Warren quickly won over his brethren with his hard work, friendliness, and unpretentious manner. After reargument of the case, the new chief justice took a solid but careful stand steeped in morality that at once allayed worries of the other justices and inspired them to come his way. He argued that segregation could only be justified if one endorsed the inferiority of the African American race. "[His words] went straight to the human tissue at the core of the controversy."[43]

Warren wanted unanimity with no separate opinions, but could tell at that first conference that he would not get it. He decided, therefore, not to take the customary first vote. Warren, discussing the case later, said, "We decided not to make up our minds on that first conference day, but to talk it over, from week to week, dealing with different aspects of it—in groups, over lunches, in conference. It was too important to hurry it."[44] The Court's former clerks in looking back on it highlight that decision not to take an early vote as both unusual and likely very important.[45] These clerks recalled the guarded secrecy of the Court around the decisions and the chief's frequent discussion over lunch or during walks around the building with the other justices. At the end, Warren posed a clear question to the Court's final holdout, Justice Reed, with whom Warren had had at least twenty lunches between December and May: "Stan, you're all by yourself in this now. You've got to decide whether it's really the best thing for the country."[46] A lone dissent from Reed, a southerner, could have been catastrophic.

Indeed, unanimity was discussed frequently in the Court's internal correspondence, and the concern the justices harbored over the decision's implementation came through frequently as well, especially, of course, in consideration of the implementation decree (*Brown II*). All on the Court were paying close attention to likely public perceptions of the Court and the extent to which the opinions of the Court would be well-received. While arguments can be made about the extent to which Warren can claim credit for the Court's decision in *Brown*, he did not inherit a unanimous Court,[47] and his compatriots gave him the credit. Justice Frankfurter, arguably the most serious competition for the designation of the justice most essential to achieving unanimity, wrote to the Chief to join his opinion in *Brown*, saying,

> When—I no longer say "if"—you bring this cargo of unanimity safely to port it will be a memorable day no less in the history of the Nation than in that of the Court. You have, if I may say so, been wisely at the helm throughout this year's journey of this litigation. Finis coronat omnia.[48]

And when the decision came down, Frankfurter wrote to Chief Justice Warren again:

> This is a day that will live in glory. It's also a great day in the history of the court, and not in the least for the course of deliberation which brought about the result. I congratulate you. [49]

Justice Harold A. Burton and Justice Douglas also wrote to the Chief Justice Warren on May 17, 1954, the day *Brown* was announced, as follows:

> Burton:
>
> Today I believe has been a great day for America and the Court. Your opinions in the segregation cases were highly appropriate and were delivered in an appropriate spirit. I suspect these will be the most significant decisions made during my service on the Court. I cherish the privilege of sharing in this.
>
> To you goes the credit for the character of the opinions which produced the all-important unanimity. Congratulations.
>
> Douglas:
>
> I do not think I would change a single word in the memoranda you gave me this morning. The two draft opinions meet my idea exactly. You have done a beautiful job. [Illegible][50]

Justice Douglas, in extensive interviews with scholar Walter F. Murphy years later, attributed *Brown*'s unanimity to Chief Justice Warren. He noted the astuteness of the chief in starting the discussion of the case informally and without a solid vote. Douglas said, "the wisdom of the Chief Justice in not calling for a vote was to avoid views crystallizing too fast and too hard, trying to avoid the drawing of lines, people taking dogmatic positions. It was, I think, real statesmanship on his part."[51] He went on to discuss the "kind of a person that Earl Warren is and was at that time" to explain why the holdouts in *Brown* went along with him. "I think in other words it was the position of Earl Warren, as a very successful politician, governor, public servant before he had come to the Court, standing for this thing, standing for overruling *Plessy v. Ferguson*, rather than any intellectual arguments." The former clerks agree, giving credit to Warren and his political acumen,[52] as do scholars of the decision. Kluger likens the care taken in both the decision in *Brown* and the decree in *Brown II* to a "dexterous use of power available to him and of the circumstances in which to exploit it that had established John Marshall as a judicial statesman and political tactician of the most formidable sort."[53] Ulmer posits it as an example of the "possible value of having former political leaders on the Court."[54] Ulmer goes on: "Given the uncertainties with which some of the other justices were plagued at this time, strong leadership on the question was undoubtedly a key factor in the ultimate solution."[55] Warren, himself, would later tell of his own feelings about the decision:

> The Court was thoroughly conscious of the importance of the decision to be arrived at and the impact it would have on the nation. With this went the realization of the necessity for secrecy in our deliberations and for achieving unity, if possible.[56]

Not many expected the Court to decide the case unanimously, however, and the announcement of the opinion brought barely stifled gasps of surprise from the gallery.[57] The tale the former clerks tell of the announcement of the opinion is worth recounting. The clerks reveal that Justice Reed was working on a draft dissent and Justice Jackson a draft concurrence, but the chief's opinion ended up, happily, being something with which both could agree. They speak, like Ulmer, of the "great intake of breath" that followed the chief justice's note that the Court decided "unanimously" (which was not in the written copy from which he was reading)[58] and of then-advocate Thurgood Marshall's focus on Justice Reed, whom he had heard was drafting a dissent. "He [Thurgood Marshall] came there, said he sat there and watched Justice Reed because he heard this rumor that Justice Reed was writing a dissent. So he wanted to look him in the eye as it came down. And as it came down, he nodded to Justice Reed and Reed nodded back and gave him a big smile and he realized that he had joined it."[59] Reed's clerk later recalled a tear on Justice Reed's cheek during the announcement.[60]

Even after the decision, the justices watched for reaction. Consider, for example, Justice Brennan's circulation to Chief Justice Warren of the full text of a speech given by Erwin Griswold, then dean of Harvard Law School, to the California Bar Association. The speech was to answer critics of the Court's desegregation decisions, to defend the Court, but also to provide some thoughts about the Court's workload and propensity to make constitutional pronouncements. That Justice Brennan cared enough about the speech to pass it along to the chief justice suggests some interest of the Court in the outside perceptions of its institution.

A number of newspaper clippings made their way into the chief justice's files as well, most of them referred to him by one of the associate justices. Justice Douglas shared an article from a publication called *Peace*

News, highlighting an exchange between "a Southerner" and "Mr. Gomillion" in which the former expressed bitterness over the Court's segregation decisions (saying, "And as far as the Supreme Court is concerned, they can go to hell!") and the latter (seeming to be some sort of advice columnist) soothed him, saying, "I hope the Supreme Court will not take your suggestion to 'go to hell.' To 'go to hell' would be cowardly. There is too much work yet to be done in America."[61]

Overall, the chief was ever cognizant of the impact of the case and of its importance. His clerk recalls a draft he was given and the chief's direction to expand it into an opinion, but to keep it short and readable and nonlegalistic. "He wanted it to be something that could be understood by the layman, and he said, 'Something that even could be published on the front page of a newspaper.'"[62] He kept to his firm belief that the opinion be about education and nothing else, even though he knew it would spill over into society more generally, which was categorized by the clerks as eminently good politics.

Earl Warren may well be the poster child for considerations of public reaction to decisions as he navigated the choppy waters of racial segregation to come out with a short, unanimous decision in *Brown*. While arguments abound as to the extent to which *Brown* might be credited for desegregation of schools and other public places,[63] no one doubts the story of a chief justice determined to obtain a unanimous decision in order to avoid outright defiance from certain sections of the country, writing that opinion in easy language, and keeping it brief enough to be printed in the daily newspaper for all to read and understand.[64] Undoubtedly, all these were intrinsic to the decision's acceptance.

As mentioned above, some social science research demonstrates the disproportionate strength a unanimous decision has on the law and on the public. Our hypothesis, then, is that the chief justice will attempt to obtain unanimity whenever implementation might be difficult, again assuming that under those circumstances, the concern with the Court's power will be at its highest. One could test this notion more systematically than we have by identifying cases beyond *Brown* in which implementation might be seen as challenging and those in which implementation will likely be easier (perhaps drawing on Hall's intuition that those rulings able to be implemented directly by the lower courts are more likely to be fully implemented than those that take some outside actor to carry out[65]) and test whether the former are statistically significantly more likely to be unanimous than the latter. One might also draw on Danelski's task and social leadership conceptualization[66] to ascertain whether unanimity is more prevalent in chief justiceships characterized as stronger leaders than in others. Finally, one could approach the papers, coding all papers from all justices in all cases for discussions over unanimity to ascertain whether raising the need to decide the case unanimously has systematic characteristics, such as whether unanimity is more often discussed in important versus more routine cases, for example, or in cases able to be implemented judicially versus those that are not. What we have done was to tell a few stories where, for reasons of public reaction and implementation, the Court, pressed by the chief, took pains to decide cases unanimously. Whether chiefs do so systematically or whether chiefs vary systematically in the extent to which they pay attention to coalition size remains open to debate.

Strategic Consideration of Other Branches

Unanimity is not the only way for the Court to enhance its standing, though. The other branches have some impact on Court legitimacy as well. Several cases suggest a concern by the chief for other institutional actions, most notably when conflicts among the branches arise.

John Marshall

Chief Justice John Marshall is rightly famous for being the chief justice that created the conditions necessary for the Supreme Court to become a major force in American politics. His decision in *Marbury v. Madison*, which confirmed the power of the Supreme Court to nullify acts of Congress and the president that contravene the constitution, is considered to be the ultimate strategic play. His Court had little power, and he worried that a decision compelling the president to act would be ignored. He decided, therefore, not merely to back down to the administration, but rather to seemingly do so while grabbing much-needed power for his Court. Segal and Spaeth discuss the case, demonstrating the myriad ways in which the chief really reached to be able to hear the case.[67] Epstein and Knight agree that the decision was impressive. After all, "Marshall avoided a potentially devastating clash with President Thomas Jefferson . . . and sent a clear signal to the new president that the Court has a major role to play in American government."[68] Clearly Marshall understood the consequences of his actions and consciously avoided further angering the current administration. His care paid off as the Court gained more esteem under his tenure than it had before or since.

Charles Evan Hughes[69]

From the time Chief Justice Hughes came to the Court, he was a staunch civil libertarian, but until the spring of 1936, he was essentially an economic conservative who usually voted with the Court's conservatives. Then, in May 1936, while the Court was under attack for being too conservative, he changed his views and worked hard to gain the additional vote needed to change the Court's course, presumably in an effort to allay criticism of the Court's obstructionist rulings and end its standoff with President Roosevelt. Hughes targeted Owen Roberts because Roberts was considered the other swing vote on the Court and, of all the other justices, the one most likely to support the liberals.[70] According to a source who claimed to speak from "positive knowledge," Hughes discussed with Owen Roberts the desirability of his "taking a more liberal attitude toward legislation designed to ameliorate the social and economic ills of the country, so as to overcome the conservative bloc and relieve the Court of the pressure of increasing outside criticism."[71] This conversation probably occurred in the summer of 1936 when Hughes and his wife visited the Roberts's Pennsylvania farm.[72]

Owen Roberts eventually obliged, voting with the liberals in *Parrish* to uphold New York's minimum wage statute, the famous "switch in time that saved nine." The chief had garnered a liberal majority to avoid a further face-off with FDR and potential harm to the Court's legitimacy. Indeed, the switch seems more likely to have come from the chief's pressure than from FDR's plan, given that FDR did not announce his court-packing plan until early February, and the discussion between the chief and Roberts took place in December.

Scholars interested in empirically testing this concern with the Court's relationships with other branches have focused on congressional overrides and congressional introductions of measures to curb the Court as well as on judicial review.[73] But what we see in these two examples is the possibility that there is much concern behind the scenes over the Court's legitimacy. We also see that to test a hypothesis about the lengths various chief justices would go to ameliorate concerns about the Court would require a systematic analysis of the papers of the justices (and interviews of justices and contemporaries) to ascertain how much the chief was motivated by a concern with the other branches of government.

Care with Opinion Assignments

Chiefs may also use the opinion-assignment prerogative in ways that look toward the legitimacy of the Court, something Danelski discussed in his early work.[74] An example is Chief Justice Stone's assignment in *Smith v. Allwright*,[75] the case that declared that the Democratic Party of Texas acted as a state agency in administering primary elections and hence could not, consistent with the Fourteenth and Fifteenth Amendments, deny the right to vote in the primary election on the sole basis of race. Texas had fought for the right of the Democratic Party to discriminate. Obviously, it would not take kindly to the Court's new decision.

Originally, Stone had assigned the case to Justice Frankfurter, but Justice Jackson questioned the wisdom of Stone's choice. In a letter to Stone, Jackson explained that the assignment "overlooked some of the ugly factors in our nation's life."[76] Since *Smith* negated the "white primary," an opinion by Frankfurter, a Jewish northerner not seen as a friend to the Democratic Party, would exacerbate the sting. Jackson suggested that the decision in *Smith* would be less likely to foment opposition to the Court if it were written by a southern Democrat. Responding to Jackson's concern, Stone reassigned the case to Justice Reed, a Democrat from Kentucky.[77] While an associate justice raised the concern over the likely public reaction to a decision authored by a particular justice, the chief justice, considering potential fall-out, acceded to it.

Edwin McElwain, a former Hughes law clerk, noted that Chief Justice Hughes would often "assign 'liberal' opinions to 'conservative' judges, and vice versa," apparently to enhance public acceptance of the Court's decisions,[78] and Pusey, who interviewed Hughes, concurred.[79] This is reminiscent of psychological research that suggests that people will more often take advice if it is offered by a source acting against that source's bias.[80]

The much more recent *Citizens United*[81] case is arguably another example of strategic assignment aimed at public opinion. According to Toobin, Chief Justice Roberts first moved for reargument in the case in an attempt to avoid a particularly damaging dissent by Justice Souter, and then assigned the opinion to Kennedy rather than writing it himself. Roberts, the thinking goes, could not write this opinion given how strongly he had argued in his confirmation hearings for an umpire-like role for the justices.[82] Indeed, Justice Stevens, in his longest dissent ever, quoted the chief justice's axiom as a lower court judge: "If it is not necessary to decide more, it is necessary not to decide more."[83]

Chief justices do often assign themselves the Court's opinions in the big cases, as Chief Justice Roberts did in *Sebelius*,[84] for two reasons. First, his colleagues expect him to do so. John Hessin Clarke wrote after he left the Court, "The great cases are written, as they should be, by the chief justice."[85] Second, as Frankfurter wrote, an opinion by the chief justice has "extra weight" with the public because "of the importance of the chief justiceship as a symbol."[86] While Chief Justice Warren demurred, "Well, gee, the chief justice doesn't write all of the important decisions,"[87] he did self-assign in *Brown v. Board of Education*, *Miranda v. Arizona*, and *Reynolds v. Sims*. We examine Chief Justices Burger, Rehnquist, and Roberts to illustrate the self-assignment function. This question of self-assignment in important cases has been subjected to empirical analysis, often finding support for the hypothesis that the chief will keep the big cases. Our argument is that the reason for these findings is a concern over legitimacy (avoiding negative public opinion), which is a little harder to directly test.[88]

Warren Burger

Chief Justice Warren Burger, while much maligned as chief justice, arguably considered the Court's prestige in his self-assignment in *Miller v. California*, garnering a majority of the Court behind a definition of obscenity for the first time in many years. The Court had taken to "Redrupping"[89] obscenity cases—deciding them summarily based on the justices' viewing of the material at issue and their own idiosyncratic standards—and had failed for many years to provide any sort of guidance to the lower courts, let alone to pornographers about whether or not their conduct was constitutionally protected free speech. Burger assigned himself the task of crafting a regulation that would end the Court's involvement in this area, an end nearly everyone on the Court wished to see, though the liberals sought that end via complete First Amendment protection while the conservatives sought that end via complete deference to local communities.[90] Burger chose the latter course, removing the Court from the obscenity business, which surely was negatively affecting the Court's prestige and credibility.

William Rehnquist

Chief Justice William Rehnquist surprised many in the Court's community when he authored the Court's decision in *Dickerson v. U.S.*,[91] affirming the constitutional bases for the Court's decision in *Miranda*, with which Rehnquist clearly disagreed. Many wondered what had driven him to vote this way and to write this opinion, and many of the conjectures are consistent with our story. Bradley and Dery argue that the chief made a decision in opposition to congressional usurpation of Court power, thereby protecting his Court from override by Congress.[92] Greenhouse and Reid noted that to overrule *Miranda* would be to endure negative public opinion given how deeply entrenched the decision was in the fabric of society.[93] While there is not a unanimous view regarding Rehnquist's motivations in *Dickerson*,[94] the chief justice was potentially using strategic self-assignment to protect his Court, even though the result went against his policy preferences.

John Roberts

Finally, there is reason to believe that Chief Justice Roberts saw the health care cases as a potential turning point for the Court. The timing was precipitous. Since 2000, the Court had issued decisions in a number of cases that received negative scrutiny from both the media and the public. In *Bush v. Gore*,[95] the Court essentially ended the presidential election that had captivated the public and presented the possibility of a constitutional crisis. A *Newsweek* poll conducted in 2001 found that 65 percent of the population believed that politics and partisanship had contributed to the the Court's opinion.[96] Likewise, when the Supreme Court decided *Lawrence v. Texas*,[97] invalidating state sodomy laws and making same-sex activity legally protected, public opinion was mobilized against the Court.[98] In early 2010, the Court issued its ruling in *Citizens United v. Federal Election Commission*,[99] finding that the First Amendment protects independent political expenditures on the part of corporations and unions. A poll conducted by the *Washington Post* immediately following the Court's ruling showed that 80 percent of respondents opposed the Court's decision.

Taken together, these cases—which were decided in a relatively short period of time, were salient, and were in opposition to majority public opinion—may have contributed to a long-term loss of support for the Court. Indeed, Gallup polling shows that at the beginning of 2000, the Court enjoyed 80 percent trust and confidence from the public, but that trust had declined to 63 percent by 2012.[100] Likewise, Pew polling shows that the Court had a 68 percent public favorability rating in 2000, but by 2012 it was 52 percent.[101] In fact, a New York Times/CBS News poll conducted in June of 2012[102] showed that the Court's approval rating was at a historic low, with just 44 percent of respondents approving of the job the Supreme Court was doing.

Roberts appears to be aware of the Court's image as well as of the things the Court does that influence public opinion. When asked about the importance of unanimity of Court decisions in 2007, Roberts told interviewer Jeffrey Rosen that "If the Court in Marshall's era had issued decisions in important cases the way this Court has over the past thirty years, we would not have a Supreme Court today of the sort that we have. That suggests that what the Court's been doing over the past thirty years has been eroding, to some extent, the capital that Marshall built up. I think the Court is also ripe for a similar refocus on functioning as an institution, because if it doesn't it is going to lose its credibility and legitimacy as an institution."[103] While he did not achieve a unanimous decision in the health care cases, he did avoid overturning a major piece of legislation that was fairly popular with the public at a point where doing so may have had a detrimental impact on his Court. The media surely thought his motivation was the Court's legitimacy. CBS News suggested that a contrary decision would have cast the Court in a negative light.[104] Toobin noted that the implications of striking the Affordable Care Act in total "weighed on Roberts" and that Roberts had to sacrifice one of his dual goals (his ideological agenda) to meet his other, which was "to preserve the Court's place as a respected final arbiter of the nation's disputes."[105]

Conclusions

The Chief Justice of the United States, despite being "first among equals," is clearly a leader on the Supreme Court. He is the administrative head of the Court and the most recognizable of the justices. Since the Court relies heavily on public opinion for its legitimacy and strength, it makes sense that the justices might be concerned about its image. There are a number of ways the Court can enhance its prestige, and the chief justice is in a unique position to affect outcomes. The chief can rely on formal duties, such as opinion assignment, to influence decisions and opinions. He can also rely on personality characteristics, such as charisma, to influence how justices vote or whether or not they choose to issue a concurrence or dissent. Effective chiefs, being aware of the Court's legitimacy, have been able to manage both the formal and informal aspects of the position to maintain the Court's influence and bolster public opinion for its decisions. It is perhaps to their credit that the Court has generally been among the governmental institutions most trusted by the American people.

NOTES

The authors thank David Danelski for suggesting case studies and for reading and commenting on earlier drafts, and the University of Wisconsin–Milwaukee's Department of Political Science for financial support, which enabled travel to the Library of Congress. Finally, we thank the anonymous reviewers for excellent comments.

1. See, e.g., Pew Research Center, "Supreme Court Favorability Reaches New Low," May 1, 2012, available online at http://www.people-press.org/2012/05/01/supreme-court-favorability-reaches-new-low/.

2. CBS News Online, 7/1/2012, http://www.cbsnews.com/news/roberts-switched-views-to-uphold-health-care-law/.

3. Adam Liptak, "Roberts Shows Deft Hand as Swing Vote on Health Case," *New York Times*, June 29, 2012.

4. 576 U.S. ___, 2015, announced June 25, 2015. The chief authored the majority opinion.

5. Jeffrey Rosen, "John Roberts, the Umpire in Chief," *New York Times*, June 27, 2015.

6. Jonathan D. Casper, "The Supreme Court and National Policymaking," *American Political Science Review* 70 (1976); Thomas R. Marshall, *Public Opinion and the Supreme Court* (Boston: Unwin Hyman, 1989); William Mishler and Reginald S. Sheehan, "The Supreme Court as a Countermajoritarian Institution? The Impact of Public Opinion on Supreme Court Decisions," *American Political Science Review* 87 (1993).

7. James L. Gibson, Gregory A. Caldeira, and Vanessa A. Baird, "On the Legitimacy of National High Courts," *American Political Science Review* 92 (1998).

8. David Easton, *A Systems Analysis of Political Life* (New York: Wiley, 1965).

9. Gregory A. Caldeira, "Neither the Purse Nor the Sword: Dynamics of Public Confidence in the Supreme Court," *American Political Science Review* 80 (1986).

10. These arguably include *Bush v. Gore*, *Lawrence v. Texas*, and *Citizens United v. FEC*.

11. Charles Evan Hughes, *The Supreme Court of the United States: Its Foundations, Methods, and Achievements: An Interpretation* (New York: Columbia University Press, 1928), 52–54. The chief describes several cases as "self-inflicted wounds," including *Dred Scott* in 1857; *Knox v. Lee* in 1871; and *Pollock v. Farmers' Loan & Trust Co.* in 1895.

12. Alexander Bickel, *The Least Dangerous Branch* (Indianapolis: Bobbs-Merrill, 1962); Mishler and Sheehan, "The Supreme Court"; Barry Friedman, "The History of the Countermajoritarian Difficulty, Part One: The Road to Judicial Supremacy," *New York University Law Review* 73 (1998); Ilya Somin, "Political Ignorance and the Countermajoritarian Difficulty: A New Perspective on the Central Obsession of Constitutional Theory," *Iowa Law Review* 89 (2003).

13. A vast literature considers the legitimacy of the Court and its derivatives. The relationship between specific and diffuse support is the subject of a current debate there. The role of public opinion in decision making is similarly well-studied. See, e.g., Gerald Rosenberg, *Hollow Hope: Can Courts Bring About Social Change?*, 2nd ed. (Chicago: University of Chicago Press, 2008); David Easton, "A Re-Assessment of the Concept of Political Support," *British Journal of Political Science* 5 (1975); James L. Gibson, and Gregory A. Caldeira, "Blacks and the United States Supreme Court: Models of Diffuse Support," *Journal of Politics* 54, no. 4 (1992): 1120–45; Gregory A. Caldeira and James L. Gibson, "The Etiology of Public Support for the Supreme Court," *American Journal of Political Science* 36 (1992); Brandon L. Bartels and Christopher D. Johnston, "On the Ideological Foundations of Supreme Court Legitimacy in the American Public," *American Journal of Political Science* 57

(2013); James L. Gibson, "Understandings of Justice: Institutional Legitimacy, Procedural Justice, and Political Tolerance," *Law and Society Review* 23 (1989); Jeffrey J. Mondak, "Institutional Legitimacy, Policy Legitimacy, and the Supreme Court," *American Politics Research* 20 (1992); John R. Hibbing and Elizabeth Theiss-Morse, *Congress as Public Enemy: Public Attitudes toward American Political Institutions* (Cambridge: Cambridge University Press, 1995).

14. David J. Danelski, "The Influence of the Chief Justice in the Decisional Process," in *Court, Judges, and Politics*, ed. Walter F. Murphy and C. Herman Pritchett (New York: Random House, 1961).

15. See, e.g., Gary Yukl, "An Evaluation of Conceptual Weaknesses in Transformational and Charismatic Leadership Theories," *Leadership Quarterly* 10 (1999); J. G. Hunt, *Leadership: A New Synthesis* (Newbury Park, CA: Sage, 1991); Gary Yukl, *Leadership in Organizations*, 4th ed. (Englewood Cliffs, NJ: Prentice Hall, 1998).

16. These include constructing the calendar, managing Court staff, appointing judges to special tribunals and committees, preparing and delivering the annual Year-End Report on the Federal Judiciary, and, perhaps most importantly, assigning opinions. See Danelski, "Influence of the Chief Justice"; David J. Danelski, *A Supreme Court Justice Is Appointed* (New York: Random House, 1964); Paul J. Wahlbeck, "Strategy and Constraints on Supreme Court Opinion Assignment," *University of Pennsylvania Law Review* 154 (2006); Theodore Ruger, "The Chief Justice and the Institutional Judiciary," *University of Pennsylvania Law Review* 154 (2006); R. M. Stogdill, "Personal Factors Associated with Leadership: A Survey of the Literature," *Journal of Psychology* 25 (1948); R. M. Stogdill, *Handbook of Leadership* (New York: Free Press, 1974); F. L. Strodbeck and R. D. Mann, "Sex Role Differentiation in Jury Deliberations," *Sociometry* 19 (1956); S. Kirkpatrick and E. Locke, "Leadership: Do Traits Matter?" *Academy of Management Executive* 5 (1991); P. Hersey and K. H. Blanchard, "Life Cycle Theory of Leadership." *Training & Development Journal* 23 (1969).

17. Danelski, "Influence of the Chief Justice"; James Thompson and Hal G. Rainey, *Modernizing Human Resource Management in the Federal Government: The IRS Model* (Washington, DC: IBM Center for the Business of Government, 2003).

18. Mishler and Sheehan, "The Supreme Court."

19. Michael J. Klarman, *From Jim Crow to Civil Rights: The Supreme Court and the Struggle for Racial Equality* (New York: Oxford University Press, 2004), 453.

20. Ibid., 451. In fact, argues Klarman, the Court may have represented public opinion better than the elected branches in this regard.

21. Ibid. See also Keith Whittington, "'Interpose Your Friendly Hand': Political Supports for the Exercise of Judicial Review by the United States Supreme Court," *American Political Science Review* 99 (2005).

22. Robert H. Durr, Andrew D. Martin, and Christina Wolbrecht, "Ideological Divergence and Public Support for the Supreme Court," *American Journal of Political Science* 44 (2000).

23. Jeremy D. Horowitz, "Legitimacy, Ideology, and the Use of Precedent on the U.S. Supreme Court" (unpublished manuscript, 2012). James H. Fowler and Sangick Jeon, "The Authority of Supreme Court Precedent," *Social Networks* 30 (2008). Indeed, Fowler and Jeon make the case that *stare decisis* itself is a norm that has evolved in order to buttress the Court's legitimacy and thereby its power.

24. Stephen Wasby, Anthony A. D'Amato, and Rosemary Metrailer, *Desegregation from Brown to Alexander: An Exploration of Supreme Court Strategies* (Carbondale: Southern Illinois University Press, 1977). In making this claim, they cite David W. Rohde, "Policy Goals and Opinion Coalitions in the Supreme Court," *Midwest Journal of Political Science* 16 (1972).

25. Gregory A. Casey, "The Supreme Court and Myth: An Empirical Investigation," *Law & Society Review* 8 (1974).

26. James L. Gibson and Gregory A. Caldeira, *Citizens, Courts and Confirmations: Positivity Theory and the Judgments of the American People* (Princeton: Princeton University Press, 2009).

27. S. Sidney Ulmer, "Bricolage and Assorted Thoughts on Working in the Papers of Supreme Court Justices," *Journal of Politics* 35 (1973): 286–310.

28. David J. Danelski, "The Chief Justice and the Supreme Court," PhD diss., University of Chicago, 1961, 3.

29. Ibid., 15.

30. Danelski, "Influence of the Chief Justice," 505.

31. 295 U.S. 495 (1935).

32. This example also fits in the next section, which considers chief justice attempts to stave off threats by the other branches.

33. Jeffrey Rosen, "Roberts's Rules," *Atlantic Monthly* 499 (2007), http://www.theatlantic.com/magazine/archive/2007/01/robertss-rules/305559/, accessed July 3, 2013.

34. Leo Katcher, *Earl Warren: A Political Biography* (New York: McGraw-Hill, 1967); and John D. Weaver, *Warren: The Man, the Court, the Era* (Boston: Little, Brown, 1967).

35. John F. Davis and William L. Reynolds, "Juridical Cripples: Plurality Opinion in the Supreme Court," *Duke Law Journal* 1 (1974): 59–86; Pamela C. Corley, *Concurring Opinion Writing on the United States Supreme Court* (Albany: State University of New York Press, 2010); Thomas G. Hansford and James F. Spriggs II, *The Politics of Precedent on the U.S. Supreme Court* (Princeton: Princeton University Press, 2008); Stuart Minor Benjamin and Bruce A. Desmarais, "Standing the Test of Time: The Breadth of Majority Coalitions and the Fate of U.S. Supreme Court Precedents," *Journal of Legal Analysis* 4 (2012); Sara C. Benesh and A. Malia Reddick, "Overruled: An Event History Analysis of Lower Court Reaction to Supreme Court Alteration of Precedent," *Journal of Politics* 64 (2002); Bradley C. Canon and Charles A. Johnson, *Judicial Policies: Implementation and Impact*, 2nd ed. (Washington, DC: CQ Press, 1999); but see Jerome Frank, *Law and the Modern Mind* (New York: Bartanto's, 1930).

36. Henry M. Christman, ed., *The Public Papers of Chief Justice Earl Warren* (New York: Simon & Schuster, 1959).

37. Richard Kluger, *Simple Justice: The History of* Brown v. Board of Education *and Black America's Struggle for Equality* (New York: Vintage, 2004), 663.

38. Ibid.

39. Ibid., 664.

40. Ibid.

41. Bernard Schwartz, *Super Chief: Earl Warren and His Supreme Court—A Judicial Biography* (New York: New York University Press, 1983), 73; See also Kluger, *Simple Justice*, 584.

42. Vinson was considered a sure vote for segregation. Upon his death, Frankfurter remarked, "This is the first indication I have ever had that there is a God." Cited in Kluger, *Simple Justice*, 656.

43. Ibid., 680.

44. Ibid., 683.

45. John David Fasset et al., "Supreme Court Law Clerks' Recollections of *Brown v. Board of Education*," *St. John's Law Review* 78 (2004).

46. Ibid., 698. Reed's clerk, George Mickum, is the source for this quote. He recalls Warren as being low-key and empathetic but firm on the need for unanimity.

47. S. Sidney Ulmer, "Earl Warren and the Brown Decision," *Journal of Politics* 33 (1971): 702.

48. Library of Congress, Papers of Chief Justice Earl Warren.

49. Ibid.

50. Ibid.

51. Transcripts of conversations between Justice William O. Douglas and Professor Walter F. Murphy, Cassette No. 13, December 17, 1962. Available online at http://www.princeton.edu/~mudd/finding_aids/douglas/, accessed June 2, 2013.

52. Fasset et al., "Supreme Court Law Clerks."

53. Kluger, *Simple Justice*, 707.

54. Ulmer, "Earl Warren and the Brown Decision," 702.

55. Ibid., 689, 693.

56. Earl Warren, *The Memoirs of Earl Warren* (New York: Doubleday, 1977), 282.

57. Ibid.

58. Schwartz, *Super Chief*, 104; Kluger, *Simple Justice*, 707.

59. Fasset et al., "Supreme Court Law Clerks."

60. Kluger, *Simple Justice*, 709.

61. Library of Congress, Papers of Chief Justice Earl Warren.

62. Fasset et al., "Supreme Court Law Clerks," 549.

63. Rosenberg, *Hollow Hope*; Kluger, *Simple Justice*.

64. Fasset et al., "Supreme Court Law Clerks."

65. Matthew E. K. Hall, *The Nature of Supreme Court Power* (New York: Cambridge University Press, 2011).

66. Danelski, "Influence of the Chief Justice."

67. Jeffrey A. Segal and Harold J. Spaeth, *The Supreme Court and the Attitudinal Model Revisited* (New York: Cambridge University Press, 2002).

68. Lee Epstein and Jack Knight, "The Strategic John Marshall (and Thomas Jefferson)," in *Marbury versus Madison: Documents and Commentary*, ed. Mark A. Graber and Michael Perhac (Washington, DC: CQ Press, 2002).

69. This section is based on David J. Danelski, "Charles Evans Hughes" (unpublished manuscript).

70. See e.g., Drew Noble Lanier, *Of Time and Judicial Behavior: United States Supreme Court Agenda-setting and Decision-making* (Selinsgrove, PA: Susquehanna University Press, 2003); Glendon A. Schubert, *Quantitative Analysis of Judicial Behavior* (Glencoe, IL: Free Press, 1959).

71. Danelski, "The Chief Justice and the Supreme Court," 201, quoting Stephen T. Early, Jr., "James Clark McReynolds and the Judicial Process" (PhD diss., University of Virginia, 1954), 101. Early's source asked that he not be identified, though Danelski opines that the source was likely a Supreme Court clerk.

72. Frances Perkins, FDR's secretary of labor and a close friend of the Robertses, recounts Elizabeth Roberts's story of the Hughes visit in her oral history. Frances Perkins oral history, Columbia University Libraries Oral History Research Office: Notable New Yorkers, "Part VII, 1936–1940, Politics, the Supreme Court, the National Labor Relations Board and the Approach of War," pp. 73–74. Cf. William E. Leuchtenberg, "Charles Evans Hughes: The Center Holds," *North Carolina Law Review* 83 (2005).

73. See, e.g., Tom S. Clark, *The Limits of Judicial Independence* (New York: Oxford University Press, 2011); and Jeffrey A. Segal, Chad Westerland, and Stefanie A. Lindquist, "Congress, the Supreme Court, and Judicial Review: Testing a Constitutional Separation of Powers Model," *American Journal of Political Science* 55 (2011).

74. David J. Danelski, "Assignment of the Court's Opinion by the Chief Justice," paper presented at the annual Midwest Conference of Political Science, April 24, 1960.

75. 321 U.S. 649 (1944).

76. Quoted in Danelski, "Assignment of the Court's Opinion," 23. See also Danelski, chapter 2, this volume.

77. Danelski, "Assignment of the Court's Opinion," 23.

78. Edwin McElwain, "The Business of the Supreme Court as Conducted by Charles Evans Hughes," *Harvard Law Review* 63 (1949).

79. Merlo J. Pusey, *Charles Evans Hughes*, 2:678–79, quoted in Danelski, "An Exploratory Study of Opinion Assignment by the Chief Justice Revisited," chap. 2 in this volume.

80. See, e.g., Michael H. Birnbaum and Steven E. Stegner, "Source Credibility in Social Judgment: Bias, Expertise, and the Judge's Point of View," *Journal of Personality and Social Psychology* 37 (1979); and, for a political science application, see Charles M. Cameron, Jeffrey A. Segal, and Donald Songer, "Strategic Auditing in a Political Hierarchy: An Informational Model of the Supreme Court's Certiorari Decisions, *American Political Science Review* 94 (2000).

81. *Citizens United v. FEC*, 558 U.S. 310 (2010).

82. Jeffrey Toobin, *The Oath: The Obama White House and the Supreme Court* (New York: Doubleday, 2012).

83. Ibid., 189.

84. *National Federation of Independent Business v. Sebelius*, 567 U.S. ____ (2012).

85. Danelski, "Assignment of the Court's Opinion," 16.

86. Felix Frankfurter, "'The Administrative Side' of Chief Justice Hughes," *Harvard Law Review* 63 (1949).

87. Quoted in Ulmer, "Earl Warren and the Brown Decision," citing the *New York Times*, July 6, 1968, 42.

88. See Forest Maltzman and Paul J. Wahlbeck, "A Conditional Model of Opinion Assignment on the Supreme Court," *Political Research Quarterly* 57 (2004).

89. "Redrupping" became a popular term for summary reversals of obscenity convictions borne of the Court's 1967 decision *Redrup v. New York*, 386 U.S. 767, wherein the Court held that written material that was neither sold to minors nor forced onto an unwilling public were constitutionally protected.

90. Bob Woodward and Scott Armstrong, *The Brethren: Inside the Supreme Court* (New York: Simon & Schuster, 1979).

91. 530 U.S. 428 (2000).

92. Craig M. Bradley, "Behind the Dickerson Decision," *Trial* 36 (2000); and George M. Dery, "The Illegitimate Exercise of Raw Judicial Power: The Supreme Court's Turf Battle in Dickerson v. U.S.," *Brandeis Law Journal* 40 (2001–2002).

93. Linda Greenhouse, "The Last Days of the Rehnquist Court: The Rewards of Patience and Power," *Arizona Law Review* 45 (2003); and Mitch Reid, "Note, Dickerson v. U.S.: Uncovering Miranda's Once Hidden and Esoteric Constitutionality," *Houston Law Review* 38 (2001).

94. Daniel M. Katz, "Institutional Rules, Strategic Behavior, and the Legacy of Chief Justice William Rehnquist: Setting the Record Straight on *Dickerson v. U.S.*," *Journal of Law and Politics* 22 (2006), argues it was simply strategic.

95. 531 U.S. 98 (2000).

96. Numerous researchers sought to examine the impact of *Bush v. Gore* on the Court's support and legitimacy, some finding that the Court's reputation had been affected in some way, others finding that the Court suffered no real consequences. All agreed, however, that the Court suffered no long-term damage. See, e.g., Herbert M. Kritzer, "The Impact of Bush v. Gore on Public Perceptions and Knowledge of The Supreme Court," *Judicature* 85 (2001); Manoj Mate and Matthew Wright, "The 2000 Presidential Election Controversy," in *Public Opinion and Constitutional Controversy*, ed. Nathaniel Persily, Jack Citrin, and Patrick J. Egan (New York: Oxford University Press, 2008); James L. Gibson, Gregory A. Caldeira, and Lester Kenyatta Spence, "The Supreme Court and the U.S. Presidential Election of 2000: Wounds, Self-Inflicted or Otherwise," *British Journal of Political Science* 33 (2003); and James L. Gibson, Gregory A. Caldeira, and Lester Kenyatta Spence, "Measuring Attitudes Toward the United States Supreme Court," *American Journal of Political Science* 47 (2003). We see it as entirely reasonable, regardless of the research, for the chief to look with alarm on low levels of public support for the Court's decisions.

97. 539 U.S. 558 (2003).

98. Again, some research found that the Court suffered some short-term loss of public support, but quickly rebounded. Nathaniel Persily, Patrick Egan, and Kevin Wallsten, "Gay Marriage, Public Opinion and the Courts," Public Law Working Paper No. 06-17, University of Pennsylvania Law School, 2006.

99. 558 U.S. 310 (2010).

100. Jeffrey M. Jones. "Supreme Court Approval Rating Dips to 46%," 2011, http://www.gallup.com/poll/149906/supreme-court-approval-rating-dips.aspx, accessed July 3, 2013.

101. Pew Polling. "Supreme Court's Favorable Rating Still at Historic Low," 2013, http://www.people-press.org/files/legacy-pdf/3-25-13%20Supreme%20Court%20Release.pdf, accessed July 3, 2013.

102. New York Times/CBS News Poll, 2012, http://www.nytimes.com/interactive/2012/06/08/us/politics/08scotus-poll-documents.html?_r=0, accessed July 3, 2013.

103. Rosen, "Roberts's Rules."

104. Jan Crawford, "Roberts Switched Views to Uphold Health Care Law," CBS News, July 1, 2012, http://www.cbsnews.com/8301-3460_162-57464549/roberts-switched-views-to-uphold-health-care-law/?tag=contentMain;contentBody, accessed July 3, 2013.

105. Toobin, *The Oath*, 286.

Epilogue

DAVID J. DANELSKI AND ARTEMUS WARD

The Earliest Studies Revisited

We began this volume by revisiting and extending the earliest social science studies of the chief justice for two reasons: to provide a theoretical and empirical background for future research and to encourage such research. The 1960 study of the chief justice's influence in the decisional process (chapter 1) illustrates early theory construction using social-psychological concepts and hypotheses and preliminary theory verification using archival data. The 1960 study of opinion assignment by the chief justice (summarized in chapter 2) demonstrates that an empirical exploration using simple quantitative methods can lead to valid findings. The contemporaneous study of the relationship between personality and leadership in the Supreme Court (chapter 3) shows that revisiting a work done more than half a century ago and extending it can advance our understanding of the judicial decision making. The Jung-Myers theory used in that study suggests why Hughes, Taft, and Van Devanter were successful task and/or social leaders and why Stone was an unsuccessful chief justice but a successful associate justice. The theory also suggests that thinking introverts tend to be strategists, for they make decisions based on predictions of the logical consequences of actions. Hence, it is not surprising that Hughes and Van Devanter, both thinking introverts, were Court strategists in the 1930s.[1]

Appointment of Chief Justices

Nemacheck's study of nominations of chief justices (chapter 4) suggests that there were two approaches in choosing chief justices since 1910, one used from 1910 to 1953 and another used from 1968 to 2005. During the first period, the public stature of the nominees was so high that they were often confirmed by voice vote in the Senate. In addition, all those nominees except Stone had held major elective offices, and Stone had been dean of Columbia Law School, U.S. attorney general, and associate justice for sixteen years. During the second period, none of the nominees for the chief justiceship had the public stature of their twentieth-century predecessors, and none of them had held elective office. Further, all of them had been judges whose ideologies closely matched the ideologies of the presidents who had nominated them, which suggests that ideology was the dominant consideration in their nominations.

Illustrative of the first approach is Eisenhower's choice of Warren in 1953, which Herbert Brownell described as follows:

> [Eisenhower] believed . . . that previous experience in public affairs and administrative skill and abilities were qualities to be desired in addition to the usual requirements of judicial competence and integrity. He wanted a chief justice who would command instant public confidence—not only for integrity and professional competency but for proven success in public life. We discussed Charles Evans Hughes and William Howard Taft as examples. They had been tested in public life as well as in their professional careers before than their appointments.
>
> The president emphasized that partisan politics should have no place in the selection of a member of the Supreme Court, and he noted approvingly Governor Warren's reputation for running a nonpartisan administration in California.[2]

Illustrative of the second approach is Reagan's choice of Rehnquist in 1986, which White House Counsel Peter J. Wallison supported in a memo for Reagan. In that memo, Wallison wrote that Rehnquist was a "paradigmatic example" of a justice seeking "to reverse the excesses of the Warren Court." Wallison praised Rehnquist for his "sheer cleverness" and listed the cases in which Rehnquist had been successful and those in which he had made conservative arguments in dissent. His memo continued:

> Moreover, virtually every beneficial decision listed above grew out of a small seed of legal principle that Rehnquist had planted in a prior, seemingly innocuous case, thus further demonstrating his mastery at looking beyond the facts of an individual case to gradually achieve fundamental reform in constitutional law. . . . Further-

> more, Rehnquist possesses the leadership qualities required to make a superb chief justice. No one can question the depth of his scholarship or intellect, the clarity of his philosophical vision or his ability to build a consensus to implant that vision in the Court's decisions.[3]

The above quotation not only supports the conclusion that Rehnquist's nomination was essentially ideological; it also supports the conclusion that Rehnquist's leadership ability was an important consideration in naming him chief justice. Presidents have often taken into account a prospective nominee's leadership ability, and when they did not, the consequences in the Court were often negative, as the following analysis shows.

Taft chose White over Hughes because he thought that White would be a better social leader, but Taft was apparently unaware of White's lack of ability as a task leader.[4] When Chief Justice White encountered a difficult case in conference, he would throw up his hands and say, "Here's a baffling case. I don't know what to do with it. God help us!"[5] Rambling discussion would follow.

Harding assumed that Taft would be a great social leader. So did others. The *New York Tribune* said in an editorial that Taft's "tact," "good humor," and "spirit of fair play" would reduce the number of 5-4 decisions in Court.[6] As for task leadership, Taft relied on his friend and colleague Van Devanter to provide it.[7]

Hoover knew of Hughes's task and social leadership abilities from having served with him in the Harding and Coolidge cabinets in the 1920s; thus he expected Hughes to be a great chief justice.[8] Hughes did not disappoint him. Performing both leadership roles, Hughes ran the Court as it had never been run before.[9]

In choosing Stone as chief justice, FDR did not take into account Stone's lack of leadership ability, probably because Hughes and Frankfurter had recommended him. But Taft and others were aware that Stone lacked leadership skill. In 1929, Taft warned that it would be "a great mistake" for Hoover to choose Stone as chief justice, for "Stone is not a leader and would have a great deal of trouble *in massing the Court*."[10]

In the middle of the Black-Jackson feud in the Court in 1946, Truman chose his friend Fred Vinson as chief justice because of his reputation as conciliator and "peacemaker." But Vinson's social leadership skills were inadequate to maintain peace among colleagues who did not respect him intellectually and who competed among themselves for task leadership.[11]

Eisenhower appreciated Warren's administrative skills and abilities but chose him as chief justice primarily because of his "proven success in public life." Because Warren believed that his role as chief justice was "not to divide the Court on ideological lines, but to maintain harmony," he soon became the Court's social leader. He also exercised task leadership, which he sometimes shared with William J. Brennan, Jr., his closest friend on the Court.[12]

Johnson, wrote Laura Kalman, believed that his friend Fortas would make an outstanding chief justice. "In terms of task leadership," she added, "Fortas might have become the best chief justice in the Court's history," but social leadership "might have proven more difficult for him."[13]

Nixon chose Burger as chief justice for ideological reasons without considering any other candidate and without considering his lack of leadership ability.[14] Nixon did so because Burger had persuaded him "of his commitment to law and order and to undoing parts of the Warren Court's jurisprudence."[15] On the Court, wrote Joel K. Goldstein, Burger "forfeited his roles of task and social leader by occasional inept and obtuse conduct. Like Stone and Vinson, he failed to impose structure on the conference, to his colleagues' regret."[16] At times, added Linda Greenhouse, Burger was "irascible" and "erratic" in conference, and as result he alienated even colleagues like Rehnquist, with whom he was ideologically compatible.[17] "So, when Rehnquist became chief in 1986," wrote Jeffrey Toobin, "Burger provided him with a clear picture of how not to run a conference."[18]

As Wallison's memo suggests, Reagan took Rehnquist's leadership ability into account in naming him chief justice. As predicted by Wallison and confirmed by Nemacheck, Rehnquist became his Court's task and social leader.

One of the most important considerations in George W. Bush's selection of Roberts as chief justice was his leadership potential. Initially, Bush chose Roberts to replace O'Connor from a list of three candidates who were tied in ability and commitment to conservative principles. Inclined toward Roberts, Bush consulted a young lawyer in the White House, who told him that all three candidates would be solid justices. "The tie breaker," the lawyer added, "was which man would be the most effective leader on the Court—the most capable of convincing his colleagues through persuasion and strategic thinking." The remark was decisive for Bush. He chose Roberts, he said, because he believed that Roberts "would be a natural leader." Before the Senate held hearings on Roberts's nomination, Rehnquist died, and Bush then nominated Roberts to replace him. "John Roberts's leadership ability," Bush wrote, "made him a perfect fit for chief justice."[19]

McMahon (chapter 5) correctly identifies ideology as a major source of contentiousness concerning the nominations of Hughes (1930), Fortas (1968), Rehnquist (1986), and Roberts (2005).

Ideological opposition to Hughes's nomination had been foreshadowed in two Senate confirmations in the 1920s. In 1922, eight senators led by Senator George Norris, an insurgent Republican, voted against confirming Pierce Butler's nomination on the ground that his views were too conservative.[20] In 1925, six senators, again led by Norris, voted against Harlan Fiske Stone's nomination on the same ground.[21] Given the paucity of Senate opposition to those Supreme Court nominees, Hoover assured Hughes that there would not be a confirmation fight over his nomination, but Hoover was wrong. When Hughes's nomination came before the Senate in February 1930, the nation was in the fourth month of the Great Depression, and Norris and other Senate progressives opposed Hughes's confirmation on the ground that his business associations and conservative economic views disqualified him for the chief justiceship. In a Senate speech, Norris said of Hughes:

> The man who has never felt the pinch of hunger and who has never known what it was to be cold, who has never been associated with those who earned their bread by the sweat of their faces, but who has lived in luxury, who has never wanted for anything that money could buy, is not fit to sit in judgment in a contest between organized wealth and those who toil.[22]

Norris convinced a number of his colleagues, but the Senate nonetheless confirmed Hughes's contentious nomination by a 52-26 vote. That twenty-six senators voted to reject Hughes's nomination was remarkable, for Hughes was arguably the ablest lawyer in the country. A lesser man with his views would have been rejected. Two months later, Hoover nominated such a man—Judge John J. Parker—as an associate justice, whose nomination the Senate rejected in a 41-39 vote. He was the first nominee to the Supreme Court to have been rejected solely because of his presumed ideology.[23] Several senators later acknowledged that they had erred in voting against Parker's confirmation.[24] Parker went on to have a distinguished judicial career. His name was on Eisenhower's short list to replace Chief Justice Vinson in 1953.[25]

In 1968, a successful filibuster ended Fortas's contentious nomination. The vote was 45-43, twenty-two short of the sixty-seven votes then needed for closure. Johnson explained the nomination's defeat as follows: "The truth is that Abe Fortas was too progressive for the Republicans and Southern conservatives in the Senate, all of whom were horrified at the thought of the continuation of the philosophy of the Warren Court. The opposition was strengthened by the fact that the Republicans and the Southerners were convinced that Richard Nixon, if elected, would choose a conservative Chief Justice."[26] Fortas, one of the most liberal justices on the Warren Court, was indeed "too progressive" for the twenty conservative Democrats and twenty-three conservative Republicans who voted against cloture.[27]

In 1986, Reagan nominated Rehnquist because he was the ablest conservative on the president's short list. After a filibuster attempt by liberal senators failed, the Senate confirmed Rehnquist's contentious nomination by 65-33 vote. Only two liberal Republicans voted against confirmation, and fourteen Democrats (almost all of them conservatives) voted with fifty-one Republicans for confirmation.

In 2005, the Senate confirmed Roberts's contentious nomination by a 78-22 vote. No Republican senator voted against confirmation, and eighteen Democrats joined sixty Republicans in voting for confirmation. Both Republicans and Democrats viewed Roberts as conservative, but his ideological record was not as clear as Fortas's and Rehnquist's. Moreover, since Roberts would replace Rehnquist, a conservative, his appointment would not change the ideological balance of the Court, which was a consideration for some senators. Not all of the votes for Roberts's confirmation indicated agreement with his ideology. Some of those votes were undoubtedly strategic. So were some of the votes against confirmation, for among the senators voting against Roberts's confirmation were three candidates for the 2008 Democratic presidential nomination.

The above analysis suggests two hypotheses: (1) Ideological nominations of chief justices are likely to be contentious,[28] and (2) success or failure of contentious nominations of chief justices usually turns on the size of the majority party in Senate, its discipline, and its ideological diversity.

Leadership on the Supreme Court

Both prior research and the chapters in this volume demonstrate that once on the bench, chiefs can and have exercised leadership. They do so during each stage of the decisional process: case selection, oral argument, votes on the merits, opinion assignment, coalition formation, and opinion writing. Still, some chiefs have been more successful than others. Goldstein, in a recent study influenced by Danelski's work, concluded that Taft, Hughes, and Warren were successful chief justices and that Stone, Vinson, and Burger were not.[29]

The agenda-setting stage is perhaps the first point in the decisional process where chiefs are able to exercise influence. They do so by working with their clerks to construct a discuss list of cases they think should be formally considered by the Court and by initiating the discussion and voting in conference (see chapter 1). If four justices vote to take a case, it is granted and scheduled for oral argument. While any justice may add cases to the discuss list, by initiating the list the chief is in a unique position to set the Court's agenda. This is especially true given that the justices rely so heavily on their clerks at the agenda-setting stage. Justice John Paul Stevens explained, "We have to be honest that a lot of the cert petitions we do not actually read. I think we all use clerks to give us an awful lot of help in processing cert petitions. I tend to read the cert petition before I vote to grant, but unless one of my clerks has identified it as a potential grant, I usually will not read the original papers myself."[30]

Beyond the chief's power to initiate the discuss list is the chief's prerogative to begin the conference discussion and voting on the cases he places on the list. As discussed in chapter 1, the chief can be particularly influential at this point. Justices who might disagree with the chief's position will have to be thoroughly prepared and inclined to vocally oppose the chief in front of their colleagues. Furthermore, with limited conference time to consider the cases on the discuss list, chiefs can monopolize the discussion by speaking at length, effectively limiting if not chilling possible disagreement. As one justice explained, "When we go over them, there is not a lot of time. It is up to the chief justice how much time is spent. . . . We generally just vote. . . . Of course one may make a comment along the way saying, for example, that the case on the next page is a better one for this. It isn't a process where a vote is railroaded through, although the vote is much faster than on argued cases where there is a lot of discussion."[31]

This may account for Provine's finding that there is a significant percentage of unanimous votes to grant review, particularly in cases concerning the jurisdictional boundaries between the various layers of government and in cases brought by certain petitioners, namely the federal government. Yet this is not to suggest that chiefs, or associates, routinely base agenda-setting decisions with an eye toward votes on the merits. Provine argues that role perception—the idea that the justices take seriously their role in resolving only the most meritorious disputes—mitigates the influence of policy preferences.[32] In this sense, the chief's influence among his colleagues during case selection is likely maximized by being less ideological and more institutional.

In his interviews with justices and clerks, Perry found that most did not think that Chief Justice Burger attempted to manipulate the discuss list in any strategic sense.[33] For example, one justice said, "The chief does a good job of getting most of them on the list. He puts cases on the list even though they are ones that he would not personally vote to grant."[34] Another justice agreed: "I think the chief puts on a case automatically if he thinks it is something that others will be interested in."[35] Still, Perry reported that a minority of justices and clerks felt that Burger and his clerks were engaging in strategy. For example, one justice said, "Some that the chief justice puts on, frankly I don't know why they are on, and sometimes he doesn't know. . . . That is one of the things that makes me think his law clerks do it. . . . Or there will be cases that for everyone else is a clear deny and he will have a join three."[36] One clerk noted that "there were a little politics around the discuss list, particularly if the chief didn't put a case on."[37] Another clerk said, "It was always interesting to see which ones the chief would put on; he generally lists about 70 percent of the obvious ones, then he lists some of the conservative favorites."[38]

Cameron and Clark (chapter 8) examine case selection, and their analysis sheds further light on the relationship between institutional and ideological factors in deciding what to decide. They show that shifts in the topics considered by the Court coincide with transitions in the chief justice. For example, free speech cases increase when Warren joins the Court and sharply decrease when Burger succeeds him. Similarly, capital punishment cases increase dramatically when Burger takes office and drop when Rehnquist is elevated to chief. While these patterns are only suggestive, they are consistent with the chief exercising leadership through his agenda-setting powers, one that appears consistent with ideological influence.

Many consider oral argument to be relatively unimportant to how the justices ultimately decide cases. Justice Antonin Scalia commented that he once thought it to be little more than "a dog and pony show" but later changed his mind and recognized the value of the process. And while attorneys certainly have their chance to persuade justices during oral argument, the process is much more than that: it is a forum for the justices to discuss the case on the merits. Justice Elena Kagan explained that oral argument is more about the justices talking to each other than it is a series of individual conversations between the justices and an attorney: "Sometimes there's a conversation among the justices that's kind of happening through the lawyer but where the objective is less to ask for the lawyer's views or explanation but more to try to make a point to your colleagues."[39] Justice Kennedy said that sometimes lawyers are not prepared for this: "I think they could understand the dynamic a little bit better. They could understand that when I'm asking a question, I'm sometimes trying to convince my own colleagues, and so they could answer not just me but answer based on what they think the whole Court needs to know to decide the case."[40]

The comments of Kagan and Kennedy are instructive for understanding how chief justices can exert influence at oral argument. Specifically, they can use the process to persuade their colleagues to think about a case in a particular way and ultimately vote in conference the way the chief would like them to. Indeed, in chapter 1 Danelski notes that, as chief, Hughes was particularly adept at guiding counsel toward the arguments he wished them to make. Furthermore, he viewed oral argument as part of the decision-making process in that he would often indicate what he thought the outcome of the case would be. Stone was also an active questioner; much more so as chief than he was as an associate. These observations suggest that chiefs behave differently than associates at oral argument and attempt to exert influence during the process.

Consistent with Danelski's work, Johnson and Gregory (chapter 6) find that chiefs do indeed exercise leadership during oral argument. Specifically, they speak more than associate justices, use more emotional language (e.g., unpleasant language directed at attorneys they oppose), and are interrupted less often by their colleagues than are the other justices. This suggests both leadership on the part of chiefs and deference on the part of associates who follow his lead during oral argument.

One of the most important powers of the chief justice is assigning the Court's opinion when he votes with the majority. Chiefs can therefore choose to write majority opinions in any case they wish. John Marshall initiated the practice of delivering an institutional opinion authored by the chief justice. Prior to his tenure, the justices delivered their own opinions seriatim in each case. Marshall felt that a single opinion of the Court would promote legitimacy, and subsequent chiefs continued to follow the practice.

Often chief justices assign themselves cases for reasons of ideology and legitimacy. But some scholars suggest that judges are concerned with "audiences" and "the judgment of history" and may choose to write opinions that will raise their stature with audiences that are important to them including their colleagues, the general public, the other branches, social groups, legal professionals, policy groups, the news media, and historians.[41] Consider the landmark cases that chiefs have assigned to themselves, arguably with an eye toward building their legacies in a particular area of the law. For example, Hughes's legacy was in the area of freedom of speech, press, and association, and he chose to write the majority opinions in the symbolic speech case *Stromberg v. California*,[42] the prior restraint case *Near v. Minnesota*,[43] the assembly case *DeJonge v. Oregon*,[44] the press freedom case *Lovell v. Griffin*,[45] and the public parade case *Cox v. New Hampshire*.[46] Warren's legacy was principally in the area of equality and he wrote the majority opinions in the racial discrimination cases *Brown v. Board of Education I* and *II*,[47] *Cooper v. Aaron*,[48] *Reynolds v. Simms*,[49] *Harman v. Forssenius*,[50] *South Carolina v. Katzenbach*,[51] and *Loving v. Virginia*.[52] Similarly, Rehnquist sought to build a legacy in the area of federalism including the Commerce Clause and the Eleventh Amendment. As chief, he wrote the majority opinions in *United States v. Lopez*,[53] *Seminole Tribe v. Florida*,[54] *Florida Prepaid Postsecondary Education Expense Board v. College Savings Bank*,[55] *United States v. Morrison*,[56] *Board of Trustees of the University of Alabama v. Garrett*,[57] and *Nevada Department of Human Resources v. Hibbs*.[58]

These examples of the chief's self-assignment power do not by any means suggest that they are the only members of the Court who can appeal to audiences by choosing the area of their legacies. Yet while any justice may choose to write a separate opinion in any case they choose, majority opinions are the law of the land and are therefore likely to have the best chance of having more influence than other opinions. Thus, given his power of opinion assignment, the chief is uniquely positioned to be able to write majority opinions in order to establish a legacy.

Of course, chiefs assign majority opinions to others. When the Court's workload was particularly heavy, for efficiency reasons chiefs assigned more opinions to those who completed their assignments the fastest. But over time a norm of equity developed where chiefs sought to spread majority opinions evenly among all the justices. In chapter 2, Danelski identifies the factors that chiefs consider in opinion assignment. In addition to efficiency and equality, chiefs consider their colleagues' expertise in particular areas of the law, their ability to hold and increase majorities, their ideologies, their abilities including mental faculties and the quality of their writing, and opinion legitimacy as viewed by those outside the Court.

Subsequent research on opinion assignment, including the work done by Wahlbeck, Mark, Krog, and Wininger (chapter 7) and Cameron and Clark (chapter 8), confirms and expands on the factors identified by Danelski. For example, chiefs are especially apt to choose ideological allies to write in salient cases and to rely on the median justice when the majority coalition is fragile. Furthermore, these factors can allow for prediction of assignments in future cases, something legal commentators and journalists routinely attempt to do in order to predict the outcomes of pending decisions. Using the factors identified in the literature, Wahlbeck, Mark, Krog, and Wininger were successful in predicting opinion assignments on the

Roberts Court, suggesting that the current chief justice has been a successful task leader in assigning opinions.

The coalition-formation process is an area where chiefs can exercise leadership to promote both policy goals in the form of favorable case outcomes (e.g., dispositions consistent with their policy preferences) and institutional goals (e.g., compromise and consensus). Often chiefs attempt to exercise leadership at oral argument in order to steer their colleagues to particular outcomes; it follows that chiefs will continue that process in conference when the justices formally discuss the cases and cast their votes. Because the chief speaks and votes first, he is in a preferred position to shape the discussion and persuade his colleagues to vote his way. In addition to oral argument and conference discussion, Danelski (chapter 1) argues that because chiefs are at the center of intra-Court communication during the coalition formation process they are generally better positioned than their colleagues to reconcile differences, seek compromise, and attain unanimity. Indeed, the chief decides when opinions will be announced and can choose to delay to achieve these goals.

Have chiefs succeeded in exercising leadership during coalition formation? Cameron and Clark (chapter 8) examine the ideological influence of Warren, Burger, and Rehnquist and find that case outcomes (dispositions) are closely associated with the chief's own ideology and do not appear to be driven by the median, pivotal justice, as some have suggested. Specifically, they find that with an essentially identical median justice across each of these Courts (which accounts for changes in associates over time), a liberal chief justice was associated with roughly 65 percent liberal dispositions, whereas a conservative chief is associated with roughly 45 percent liberal dispositions. This finding is suggestive of the chief's influence on case outcomes and is consistent with the chief's exercising influence at prior stages of the decisional process.

In terms of institutional maintenance, the story of Warren's ability to achieve unanimity in *Brown v. Board of Education* (1954) is the most often cited example of this aspect of chief justice leadership during the coalition-formation process. On assuming the chief justiceship, Roberts made consensus one of his priorities, arguing that the Court needed to return to how it operated under Chief Justice Marshall:

> The Court functions most effectively as a judicial institution saying what the law is when it can deliver one clear and focused opinion of the Court. I am not talking about subordinating strongly held views

> to achieve an artificial consensus. But I am talking about deciding cases on narrow grounds, when that allows broader agreement. I remain convinced that the Court benefits most from the distinctive voices of its members when the Court meets in conference to discuss the disposition of a case and the conference takes the advantage of those views in shaping an opinion for the Court. John Marshall changed everything. He transformed the Supreme Court from a weak and ineffectual body into a powerful and independent institution of government. Marshall saw that the Court could rule authoritatively and win the public's confidence only if it functioned as a collegial body and not simply as a collection of individuals.[59]

Steigerwalt, Corley, and Ward (chapter 9) suggest that chiefs may enjoy a "honeymoon effect" whereby a new chief has some measure of political capital that his colleagues recognize and are initially deferential to. They find that Roberts exhibited the largest honeymoon effect, with both Vinson and Burger enjoying similar success initially and less success later in their tenures. Both Warren and Rehnquist, however, experienced the opposite effect: they were not successful initially but improved their ability to achieve consensus after their honeymoons. While these findings are suggestive of the chief's leadership capacity, they may also be reflective of associate justice behavior based on their perceptions of the new chief or other internal Court dynamics.

Beyond the chief's honeymoon period, Bartels and Wininger (chapter 10) show that some chiefs are able to continue to achieve consensus—in the form of building larger majority coalitions and showing a willingness to change their votes to achieve them—than others. Specifically, Vinson, Warren, and Burger were more successful than their successors on this score. The authors suggest that this is likely due to the difficulty of achieving consensus generally during eras of more polarized Courts, something confirmed by the previous chapter. Furthermore, both chapters demonstrate that consensus in general is more difficult to achieve in salient cases for both chiefs and associates (chapters 9 and 10). Thus, as Danelski posited (chapter 1), the evidence suggests that chiefs can and do exercise both policy and institutional leadership in the coalition-formation process.

Beyond case outcomes, have chiefs been able to exercise leadership by shaping the content of the Court's opinions? Both the chapters by Black, Owens, and Wedeking (chapter 11) and Rice and Zorn (chapter 12) examine this question with both complimentary and divergent findings. Both agree that emotional language—and negative language in particular—has been on the rise in majority, concurring, and dissenting opinions, particularly since the 1930s. Yet the studies diverge when it comes to whether chiefs in general, and specific chiefs in particular, have been able to shape opinion content. In short, Black, Owens, and Wedeking suggest that chiefs beginning with Vinson have failed, while Rice and Zorn argue that while Vinson may have failed, chiefs before and after him had some measure of success in shaping opinion content.

First, Black, Owens, and Wedeking find that overall, chiefs from Vinson through Roberts have not been different from associates in terms of the agreeable and disagreeable language in the majority opinions they write and join. Indeed, chiefs tended to write more disagreeable opinions than associates and failed to influence their colleagues to write more collegially. Still, they find that recent chiefs—Burger, Rehnquist, and Roberts—employed more agreeable and disagreeable language and joined more agreeable and disagreeable opinions than did Vinson and Warren. Thus, they conclude, more recent chiefs are far more emotional than their predecessors. The authors suggest that their results underscore collegiality problems for chief justices. At the same time, they realize there are limitations to their analysis in that they only examine majority opinions and that they are unable to say whether emotional language was directed at other justices or used in other contexts.

Rice and Zorn, on the other hand, examine all opinions issued under all chief justices and find that the move to a single opinion for the Court under Marshall reduced the degree of emotional content in opinions. There was little difference among the White, Taft, and Hughes years in overall emotional content, yet the Court was more positive under Taft across opinion types and again more positive under Hughes, but only with regard to majority opinions. Consistent with prior research on the Stone Court, there was an increase in emotional language. Yet, surprisingly, the proliferation of concurring opinions under Stone largely accounts for the increase in positive language. Compared to Stone, Vinson's tenure was marked by significantly more negative majority, concurring, and (to a lesser degree) dissenting opinions. Warren was successful in reducing emotional language across all opinion types, while Burger was not. Yet majority opinions under Burger were actually more positive than they were under Warren, with concurring opinions under Burger substantially more negative than they were under Warren.

Randazzo and Reid (chapter 13) examine cases where the Court interprets congressional statutes to test the chief's influence over case outcomes. They posit that relatively detailed statutes constrain judicial behavior, including the ability of chiefs to exercise leadership, while more ambiguous statutes should leave ample room for differences among the members of the Court to surface. But can chiefs stem these differences in such cases? The authors find that in general, congressional statutes have the ability to either constrain or enhance the ability of the justices to vote according to their ideological preferences. In particular, Warren and Rehnquist, as well as their ideological allies, experienced substantial changes in their personal voting behavior as a result of statutory language, sometimes constraining, sometimes enhancing, depending on the issue area. Was the chief's leadership responsible for these changes? The authors are hesitant to make this claim and thus further research will be necessary to draw more definitive conclusions.

Legitimacy, the Supreme Court, and the Federal Judiciary

Finally, we include two chapters that explore how the chief can exert leadership off the bench, both in terms of the Court's legitimacy and the needs of the federal judiciary more generally. Though associate justices can certainly exert influence over these matters, as head of the federal judiciary the chief is uniquely positioned to be the face and spokesperson both for the Court and for larger matters of concern to the judicial branch of government. One only consider that unlike the associates, chiefs have many distinctive duties such as the constitutional obligation to preside over trials in the Senate following the impeachment of the president, serving as the head of the Judicial Conference of the United States, and designating sitting federal judges to the U.S. Foreign Intelligence Surveillance Court and the Foreign Intelligence Surveillance Review Court.[60] Thus it is important to remember that the chief's powers and influence extend beyond the Supreme Court.

Can chiefs exercise leadership in the many duties they perform as head of the federal judiciary? Vining and Wilhelm (chapter 14) look to one of the chief's most visible actions outside the Court: his annual Year-End Report on the Federal Judiciary. Issued since 1975, the report gives the chief wide latitude to address whatever topic he deems appropriate. Further, he knows that the report will receive considerable press attention. For example, the report issued by Roberts at the end of 2013 prompted ABC News to declare "Chief Justice Summons Scrooge in New Year's Eve Report,"[61] while the *Washington Post* said "Chief Justice John Roberts Warns of a Not-

So-Wonderful Life for Judiciary Amid Budget Cuts"[62] and *USA Today* ran the headline "Chief Justice Warns Congress on Federal Court Cutbacks."[63]

Vining and Wilhelm study the content of these reports to identify the chief's reform agenda for judicial administration and procedure. They find that different chiefs stressed different priorities. Burger focused on housekeeping, jurisdiction change, structural reorganization, and study requests. Rehnquist was concerned with budget issues and judicial vacancies. Roberts has asked for comparatively little but has prioritized judicial salaries and benefits. The authors find that the more administrative experience chiefs have, the more items they request from Congress, particularly after chiefs have served for ten years. Perhaps this finding is not surprising given that chiefs with more experience should necessarily know more about the needs of the judiciary and generally have more confidence and gravitas over time. In addition, the authors find no evidence that strategy or political capital play a role in a chief's reform agenda. This is an intriguing finding in light of the evidence in the subsequent chapter about the chief's concern for legitimacy in shaping the work of the Court. It suggests that the chief may see his role as administrative head of the federal judiciary in different terms than his role on the Supreme Court.

Fettig and Benesh (chapter 15) examine how the chief can influence the work of the Court in order to bolster its legitimacy as a governmental institution. They begin with the recent story about how Chief Justice Roberts reportedly switched his vote in *National Federation of Independent Business v. Sebelius* (2012) to uphold the Affordable Care Act, popularly known as "Obamacare." As reported by CBS News correspondent Jan Crawford, according to two sources with specific knowledge of the deliberations, Roberts initially voted with the Court's conservatives to strike down the law 5-4 before changing his vote during the opinion-writing process to join the liberals in upholding it. Crawford reported how the switch occurred:

> As Roberts began to craft the decision striking down the mandate, the external pressure began to grow. Roberts almost certainly was aware of it. . . . Roberts pays attention to media coverage. As chief justice, he is keenly aware of his leadership role on the court, and he also is sensitive to how the court is perceived by the public. There were countless news articles in May warning of damage to the court—and to Roberts' reputation—if the court were to strike down the mandate. Leading politicians, including the president himself, had expressed confidence the mandate would be upheld. Some even

> suggested that if Roberts struck down the mandate, it would prove he had been deceitful during his confirmation hearings, when he explained a philosophy of judicial restraint. It was around this time that it also became clear to the conservative justices that Roberts was, as one put it, "wobbly," the sources said. . . . It was clear to the conservatives that Roberts wanted the court out of the red-hot dispute. . . .
>
> Roberts then engaged in his own lobbying effort—trying to persuade at least Justice Kennedy to join his decision so the Court would appear more united in the case. There was a fair amount of give-and-take with Kennedy and other justices, the sources said. One justice, a source said, described it as "arm-twisting". . . . In fact, Kennedy was the most forceful and engaged of all the conservatives in trying to persuade Roberts to stand firm to strike down the mandate. Two sources confirm that he didn't give up until the very end. But Roberts didn't focus entirely on Kennedy, the sources said. He tried to persuade the conservatives to join at least the parts of his opinion with which they agreed. . . . But despite Roberts' [efforts] . . . the conservatives would have none of it, the two sources said.[64]

This extraordinary story illustrates how the chief can exert considerable influence in protecting the Court's legitimacy, particularly in salient cases and in the face of threats from actors outside the Court. Indeed, three years later in *King v. Burwell* (2015), Roberts once again voted with the Court's liberals, assigned himself the majority opinion, and upheld a crucial portion of the Affordable Care Act.[65] As Jeffery Rosen argued in the *New York Times*, the decisions illustrate Roberts's broad vision of judicial restraint: preservation of the Court's legitimacy through deference to the political branches and generally playing a limited role in American politics.[66]

But were Roberts's decisions in the health care cases an anomaly? Fettig and Benesh demonstrate that Roberts's behavior in both health care cases—*Sebelius* and *King v. Burwell* (2015)—is no different from previous chiefs faced with similar circumstances. The authors identify key cases and situations in which the Court's image, and thus its legitimacy, has been threatened, and they provide evidence about the chief's attempts to manipulate outcomes or contain potential fallout to maintain institutional prestige. They argue that chiefs have led the Court to outcomes based on strategic consideration of other branches as with Marshall in *Marbury v. Madison* and Hughes during the New Deal. The authors show how chiefs take care with opinion assignments with examples from the Stone, Hughes,

Burger, Rehnquist, and Roberts Courts. And they highlight how chiefs promote unanimity to bolster legitimacy with examples from the Warren Court. In all, effective chiefs have managed the Court's internal processes to promote legitimacy among government actors and the public.

Future Research

The research in this volume gives rise to a number of important questions for further study, many of which are highlighted by the chapter authors. For example, because there are differences in the extent to which chiefs have been effective leaders, it makes sense that the appointment process should be different for them than it is for associate justices. Therefore studies of presidential selection, interest group activity, and the questioning and voting behavior of senators are likely to take into account a prospective appointee's personality and leadership ability.

At the agenda-setting stage, how does the chief's incentive to bring "good vehicles" to the Court affect the types of coalitions he can build or wants to build? How can the chief sustain an ability to coordinate the Court, without revolt by his ideological opponents? Does the rule of four, which allows a minority to force a case onto the Court's docket, enhance or attenuate the chief's prerogatives? Toward this end, more attention could be paid to the relationship between the chief and his clerks in reviewing cert pool memos and constructing the discuss list. Examining the substantive remarks of chiefs in the conference discussion notes of the justices will shed light on how the chief frames the issues and what happens to his framing as the other justices speak.

In terms of oral argument, conference voting, coalition formation, and opinion writing, future scholarship should examine how justices reference one another both on and off the bench in their conference discussion, internal memoranda, and draft and published opinions. Do they go beyond mere disagreement with legal policy and question the intelligence or motives of their colleagues? Does the chief attempt to promote conciliation during this process? If so, how might he go about it? Certainly evidence of overt emotional language in conference discussion or memoranda will be important, but so too could be the timing of circulations such as "preemptive" attempts by the chief or others to minimize conflict. Researchers also might consider examining whether, like the Court, other institutions of government show trends of negativity in language and whether their leaders—such as the chair of a congressional committee or the White House chief of staff—attempt to exercise leadership.

Future research on Court outcomes should look beyond chiefs to delve into alternative causes for doctrinal and policy shifts. The issues the Court considers, the makeup of the Court during the chief's tenure, and a host of other influences, many of which are explored in this volume, could influence the comity and productivity of the Court during the tenure of a chief. Indeed, as we know from the examples of Justice Van Devanter on the Taft Court and Justice Black on the Stone and Warren Courts, associate justices exercise task and social leadership. Future research will most likely explore the extent to which other associates have attempted to do the same.

The chief's influence off the bench is ripe for study. Beyond the chief's annual report, how have chiefs used the judicial conference for reforming judicial administration? Is there a strategic or attitudinal element to the chief's work with the conference? On the heels of the leaks by Edward Snowden about the surveillance undertaken by the National Security Agency, the Foreign Intelligence Surveillance Court has been controversial as of late, and popular news outlets have made it known that the chief makes appointments to this secretive tribunal. For example, a recent story about two new appointments noted that "the partisan split on the surveillance courts remains far from even."[67] Democratic senator Richard Blumenthal of Connecticut—former law clerk to Justice Harry Blackmun—has introduced legislation to change the appointment process by requiring circuit court chief judges to submit names to the chief justice, who would then seek confirmation from five associate Supreme Court justices. Democratic representative Adam Schiff of California introduced similar legislation in the House requiring presidential nomination and confirmation by the Senate.

While there is much work still to be done to understand the influence of the Chief Justice of the United States, we hope that this volume has provided some answers and has pointed the way for future inquiry. While it has been said that the chief is "first among equals," we submit that the evidence in this book suggests that he is far more than that.

NOTES

1. Irving Brant, "How Liberal Is Justice Hughes?" *New Republic* 91 (1937): 295; Irving Brant to Alpheus Thomas Mason, July 22, 1951, Library of Congress, Manuscript Division, Irving Brant Papers.

2. Herbert Brownell, *Advising Ike* (Lawrence: University Press of Kansas, 1993), 166–67.

3. Quoted in John A. Jenkins, *The Partisan: The Life of William Rehnquist* (New York: Public Affairs, 2012), 211–12.

4. Jeffrey B. Morris, "Chief Justice Edward Douglass White and President Taft's Court," *Supreme Court Historical Yearbook* 7 (1982): 36.

5. Hughes quoted in Merlo J. Pusey, "Mr. Chief Justice Hughes," in *Mr. Justice*, ed. Allison Dunham and Philip B. Kurland (Chicago: University of Chicago Press, 1956), 154.

6. Quoted in William O. Douglas, *The Court Years* (New York: Random House, 1981), 36.

7. David J. Danelski, "The Influence of the Chief Justice in the Decisional Process of the Supreme Court," chap. 1, this volume.

8. Merlo J. Pusey, *Charles Evans Hughes* (New York: Macmillan, 1951), 2:427–28, 652.

9. Danelski, "The Influence of the Chief," chap. 1, this volume.

10. Quoted in Henry F. Pringle, *The Life and Times of William Howard Taft: A Biography* (New York: Farrar & Rinehart, 1939), 2:1044.

11. James E. St. Clair and Linda Gugin, *Chief Justice Fred M. Vinson of Kentucky* (Lexington: University Press of Kentucky, 2002), 161, 171–74.

12. Leo Katcher, *Earl Warren: A Political Biography* (New York: McGraw-Hill, 1967), 350.

13. Laura Kalman, *Abe Fortas: A Biography* (New Haven: Yale University Press, 1990), 334.

14. Christine L. Nemacheck, *Strategic Selection, Presidential Nomination of Supreme Court Justice from Herbert Hoover through George W. Bush* (Charlottesville: University of Virginia Press, 2007), 108; David A. Yalof, *Pursuit of Justices: Presidential Politics and the Selection of Supreme Court Nominees* (Chicago: University of Chicago Press, 1999), 101–2; John Ehrlichman, *Witness to Power: The Nixon Years* (New York: Simon and Schuster, 1982), 114–15.

15. Joel K. Goldstein, "Choosing Justices: How Presidents Decide," *Journal of Law and Politics* 26 (2011): 462.

16. Joel K. Goldstein, "Leading the Court: Studies in Influence as Chief Justice," *Stetson Law Review* 40 (2011): 736.

17. Linda Greenhouse, *Blackmun: Harry Blackmun's Supreme Court Journey* (New York: Times Books, 2006), 160.

18. Jeffrey Toobin, *The Nine: Inside the Secret World of the Supreme Court* (New York: Doubleday, 2007), 29.

19. George W. Bush, *Decision Points* (New York: Crown, 2010), 98–99.

20. David J. Danelski, *A Supreme Court Justice Is Appointed* (New York: Random House. 1964), 190–91.

21. Ibid., 191–92.

22. Quoted in ibid., 193.

23. David J. Danelski, "Ideology as a Ground for Rejection of the Bork Nomination," *Northwestern University Law Review* 84 (1990): 912–15.

24. Ibid., 915.

25. Nemacheck, *Strategic Selection*, 149.

26. Lyndon Baines Johnson, *The Vantage Point: Perspectives of the Presidency: 1963–1969* (New York: Holt, Rinehart & Winston, 1971), 546.

27. Schubert ranked Fortas just under Murphy, Rutledge, and Douglas on his composite C (civil liberties) scale. See Glendon Schubert, *The Judicial Mind Revisited* (New York: Oxford University Press, 1974), 60.

28. Though Burger's nomination as chief justice by Nixon in 1969 was ideological, it was not contentious either because the basis of the nomination was not sufficiently known at the time or because the Senate Democrats, after being soundly beaten in their battle over the Fortas nomination only months earlier, believed they did not have the votes to defeat Burger's nomination

29. Goldstein, "Leading the Court," 721–61.

30. Bryan A. Garner, "Justice John Paul Stevens," *The Scribes Journal of Legal Writing* (2010): 41–50, 45. http://legaltimes.typepad.com/files/garner-transcripts-1.pdf.

31. H. W. Perry Jr., *Deciding to Decide: Agenda Setting in the United States Supreme Court* (Cambridge, MA: Harvard University Press, 1991), 48.

32. Doris Marie Provine, *Case Selection in the U.S. Supreme Court* (Chicago: University of Chicago Press, 1980).

33. Perry, *Deciding to Decide*, 85.

34. Ibid., 86.

35. Ibid.

36. Ibid.

37. Ibid., 87.

38. Ibid.

39. Associated Press, "Justice Kagan Describes Inner Workings of Supreme Court to University of Richmond Audience," *Washington Post*, Sep. 20, 2012. http://www.washingtonpost.com/local/justice-to-have-discussion-with-richmond-law-school-dean-before-audience-of-students-others/2012/09/20/4cedec3c-02f2-11e2-9132-f2750cd65f97_story.html.

40. Bryan A. Garner, "Justice Anthony M. Kennedy," *The Scribes Journal of Legal Writing* (2010): 89–98, 95. http://legaltimes.typepad.com/files/garner-transcripts-1.pdf.

41. See Lawrence Baum, *Judges and Their Audiences: A Perspective on Judicial Behavior* (Princeton: Princeton University Press, 2006); Frederick Schauer, "Incentives, Reputation, and the Inglorious Determinants of Judicial Behavior," *University of Cincinnati Law Review* 68 (2000): 615–36.

42. 283 U.S. 359 (1931).

43. 283 U.S. 697 (1931).

44. 299 U.S. 353 (1937).

45. 303 U.S. 444 (1938).

46. 312 U.S. 569 (1941).

47. 347 U.S. 483 (1954), 349 U.S. 294 (1955).

48. 358 U.S. 1 (1958).

49. 377 U.S. 533 (1964).

50. 380 U.S. 528 (1965).

51. 383 U.S. 301 (1966).

52. 388 U.S. 1 (1967).

53. 514 U.S. 549 (1995).

54. 517 U.S. 44 (1996).

55. 527 U.S. 652 (1999).
56. 529 U.S. 598 (2000).
57. 531 U.S. 356 (2001).
58. 538 U.S. 721 (2003).
59. Bill Barnhart, "Roberts Strives for Consensus on Court: Chief Justice Says More Unified Voice Would Strengthen Institution," *Chicago Tribune*, February 2, 2007, http://articles.chicagotribune.com/2007-02-02/news/0702020163_1_justices-court-politics-supreme-court.
60. In 1978, Congress enacted the Foreign Intelligence Surveillance Act (FISA), 50 U.S.C. 1803, which authorized the chief justice to "designate" federal judges for service on the Foreign Intelligence Surveillance Court (FISC) and the Foreign Intelligence Surveillance Review Court (FISRC). FISC members are required to be U.S. district judges and at least three of them must sit in districts within twenty miles of the District of Columbia. According to U.S. District Judge John D. Bates, who was the presiding judge of FISC from 2006 to 2009, chief justices chose judges with extensive judicial experience, particularly in Fourth Amendment cases, and the designated judges receive security checks from the FBI. "The Foreign Intelligence Surveillance Court: A Conversation with John D. Bates," Newseum Institute, February 27, 2014. FISRC members are required to be U.S. district judges or U.S. Court of Appeals judges. The vast majority of FISRC judges have been the latter. Also the vast majority of designees to both courts had been appointed to the bench by Republican presidents. The numbers of judges designated by chief justices to both courts are as follows: Burger, nineteen; Rehnquist, thirty-five; and Roberts (as of February 7, 2014), seventeen.
61. Ariane de Vogue, "Chief Justice Summons Scrooge in New Year's Eve Report," ABCNews.go.com, Dec. 31, 2013, http://abcnews.go.com/blogs/politics/2013/12/chief-justice-summons-scrooge-in-annual-report/.
62. Robert Barnes, "Chief Justice John Roberts Warns of a Not-So-Wonderful Life for Judiciary Amid Budget Cuts," *Washington Post*, Dec. 31, 2013, http://www.washingtonpost.com/politics/chief-justice-john-roberts-warns-of-a-not-so-wonderful-life-for-judiciary-amid-budget-cuts/2013/12/31/40dd7bdc-7255-11e3-8b3f-b1666705ca3b_story.html.
63. Richard Wolf, "Chief Justice Warns Congress on Federal Court Cutbacks," *USA Today*, Dec. 31, 2013, http://www.usatoday.com/story/news/politics/2013/12/31/justice-roberts-warns-congress/4266959/.
64. Jan Crawford, "Roberts Switched Views to Uphold Health Care Law," CBSNews.com, July 2, 2012, http://www.cbsnews.com/news/roberts-switched-views-to-uphold-health-care-law/.
65. 576 U.S. ___ (2015).
66. Jeffrey Rosen, "John Roberts, the Umpire in Chief," *New York Times*, June 27, 2015, http://www.nytimes.com/2015/06/28/opinion/john-roberts-the-umpire-in-chief.html.
67. Tal Kopan, "Roberts Names 2 New FISA Court Judges," Politico.com, Feb. 7, 2014, http://www.politico.com/blogs/under-the-radar/2014/02/roberts-names-new-fisa-court-judges-182921.html.

Selected Bibliography

Abraham, Henry J. *Justices, Presidents, and Senators: A History of U.S. Supreme Court Appointments from Washington to Bush II.* 5th ed. Lanham, MD: Rowman & Littlefield, 2008.

Bailey, Michael A., and Forrest Maltzman. *The Constrained Court: Law, Politics, and the Decisions Justices Make*. Princeton: Princeton University Press, 2011.

Bales, Robert F. *Interaction Process Analysis: A Method for the Study of Small Groups*. Chicago: University of Chicago Press, 1950.

Bales, Robert F. "Task Roles and Social Roles in Problem-Solving Groups." In *Readings in Social Psychology*, edited by Eleanor E. Maccoby, Theodore M. Newcomb, and Eugene L. Harley, 437–47. New York: Holt, 1958.

Bales, Robert F. "Task Status and Likeability as a Function of Talking and Listening in Decision-Making Groups." In *The State of the Social Sciences*, edited by Leonard D. White, 148–61. Chicago: University of Chicago Press, 1956.

Baum, Lawrence. *Judges and Their Audiences: A Perspective on Judicial Behavior*. Princeton: Princeton University Press, 2006.

Belknap, Michael R. *The Vinson Court: Justices, Rulings, and Legacy*. Santa Barbara, CA: ABC-CLIO, 2004.

Benesh, Sara C., Reginald S. Sheehan, and Harold J. Spaeth. "Equity in Supreme Court Opinion Assignment." *Jurimetrics* 39 (1998): 377–89.

Berkowitz, Leonard. "Sharing Leadership in Small, Decision-Making Groups." *Journal of Abnormal and Social Psychology* 48 (1953): 231–38.

Berkowitz, Leonard. "Some Effects of Leadership Sharing in Small, Decision-Making Conference Groups," Unpublished PhD dissertation, University of Michigan, 1951.

Beveridge, Albert J. *The Life of John Marshall*. 4 vols. Boston: Houghton Mifflin, 1916–1919.

Bickel, Alexander. *The Least Dangerous Branch*. Indianapolis: Bobbs-Merrill, 1962.

Black, Ryan C, Timothy R. Johnson, and Justin Wedeking. *Oral Arguments and Coalition Formation on the U.S. Supreme Court: A Deliberate Dialogue*. Ann Arbor: University of Michigan Press, 2012.

Black, Ryan C., and Ryan J. Owens. "Agenda Setting in the Supreme Court: The Collision of Policy and Jurisprudence." *Journal of Politics* 71 (2009): 1062–75.

Blue, Frederick J. *Salmon P. Chase: A Life in Politics*. Kent, OH: Kent State University Press, 1987.

Bonneau, Chris W., Thomas H. Hammond, Forrest Maltzman, and Paul J. Wahlbeck. "Agenda Control, the Median Justice, and the Majority Opinion on the US Supreme Court." *American Journal of Political Science* 51 (2007): 890–905.

Borgatta, Edgar F., Robert F. Bales, and Arthur S. Couch. "Some Findings Relevant to the Great Man Theory of Leadership." *American Sociological Review* 19 (1954): 755–59.

Boskey, Bennett. "Mr. Chief Justice Stone." *Harvard Law Review* 59 (1946): 1200–1202.

Brant, Irving. "How Liberal Is Justice Hughes?" *The New Republic* 91 (1937): 296–330.

Brenner, Saul. "The Chief Justices' Self-Assignment of Majority Opinions in Salient Cases." *Social Science Journal* 30 (1993): 143–50.

Brenner, Saul. "Issue Specialization as a Variable in Opinion Assignment on the U.S. Supreme Court." *Journal of Politics* 46 (1984): 1217–25.

Brenner, Saul. "Strategic Choice and Opinion Assignment on the U.S. Supreme Court: A Reexamination." *Western Political Quarterly* 35 (1982): 204–11.

Brenner, Saul, and Timothy M. Hagle. "Opinion Writing and Acclimation Effect." *Political Behavior* 18 (1996): 235–61.

Brenner, Saul, and Jan Palmer. "The Time Taken to Write Majority Opinions as a Determinant of Opinion Assignment on the Vinson Court." *Judicature* 72 (1988): 179–84.

Brenner, Saul, and Harold J. Spaeth. "Issue Specialization in Majority Opinion Assignment on the Burger Court." *Western Political Quarterly* 39 (1986): 520–25.

Brenner, Saul, and Harold J. Spaeth. "Majority Opinion Assignments and the Maintenance of the Original Coalition on the Warren Court." *American Journal of Political Science* 32 (1988): 72–81.

Brown, William G. *The Life of Oliver Ellsworth*. New York: Macmillan, 1905.

Caldeira, Gregory A. "Neither the Purse Nor the Sword: Dynamics of Public Confidence in the Supreme Court." *American Political Science Review* 80 (1986): 1209–26.

Caldeira, Gregory A., and James L. Gibson. "The Etiology of Public Support for the Supreme Court." *American Journal of Political Science* 36 (1992): 635–64.

Caldeira, Gregory A., and John R. Wright. "The Discuss List: Agenda Building in the Supreme Court." *Law & Society Review* 24 (1990): 807–36.

Caldeira, Gregory A., and Christopher J. W. Zorn. "Of Time and Consensual Norms in the Supreme Court." *American Journal of Political Science* 42 (1998): 874–902.

Casper, Jonathan D. "The Supreme Court and National Policymaking." *American Political Science Review* 70 (1976): 50–63.

Casto, William R. *The Supreme Court in the Early Republic: The Chief Justiceships of John Jay and Oliver Ellsworth*. Columbia: University of South Carolina Press, 2012.

Chemerinsky, Erwin. "Assessing Chief Justice William Rehnquist." *University of Pennsylvania Law Review* 154 (2006): 1331–64.

Christman, Henry M., ed. *The Public Papers of Chief Justice Earl Warren*. New York: Simon & Schuster, 1959.

Cook, Beverly Blair. "Testing a Model of Opinion Assignment: The Burger Court."

Paper presented at the annual meeting for the American Political Science Association, 1992. Tulane University, Newcomb Archives, Beverly Blair Cook Papers.

Corley, Pamela C., Amy Steigerwalt, and Artemus Ward. *The Puzzle of Unanimity: Consensus on the United States Supreme Court*. Stanford, CA: Stanford University Press, 2013.

Corwin, Edward S. *John Marshall and the Constitution*. New Haven: Yale University Press, 1919.

Coyle, Marcia. *The Roberts Court: The Struggle for the Constitution*. New York: Simon & Schuster, 2014.

Cross, Frank B. and Stefanie Lindquist. "The Decisional Significance of the Chief Justice." *University of Pennsylvania Law Review* 154 (2006): 1665–1707.

Danelski, David J. "The Assignment of the Court's Opinion by the Chief Justice." Paper presented at the Midwest Conference of Political Scientists, April 28, 1960.

Danelski, David J. "The Chief Justice and the Supreme Court." PhD dissertation, University of Chicago, 1961.

Danelski, David J. "The Influence of the Chief Justice in the Decisional Process of the Supreme Court." Paper presented at the American Political Science Association Meeting, September 8, 1960.

Danelski, David J. *A Supreme Court Justice Is Appointed*. New York: Random House, 1964.

Danelski, David J. "A Supreme Court Justice Steps Down." *Yale Review* 54 (1965): 411–25.

Danelski, David J., and Jeanne Danelski. "Leadership in the Warren Court." *American Court Systems* (1989): 500–510.

Danelski, David J., and Joseph S. Tulchin, eds. *The Autobiographical Notes of Charles Evans Hughes*. Cambridge, MA: Harvard University Press, 1973.

Davies, Ross. "William Cushing: Chief Justice of the United States." *University of Toledo Law Review* 37 (2006): 101–62.

Davis, Sue. "Power on the Court: Chief Justice Rehnquist's Assignments." *Judicature* 74 (1990): 66–72.

Davis, Sue. "The Supreme Court: Rehnquist's or Reagan's?" *Western Political Quarterly* 44 (1991): 87–99.

Douglas, William O. "Chief Justice Stone." *Columbia Law Review* 46 (1946): 693–95.

Ducat, Craig R., and Victor E. Flango. *Leadership in State Supreme Courts: Roles of the Chief Justice*. Beverly Hills, CA: Sage Publications, 1976.

Edelman, Paul H., and Suzanna Sherry. "All or Nothing: Explaining the Size of Supreme Court Majorities." *North Carolina Law Review* 78 (2000): 1225–52.

Ely, James W. *The Chief Justiceship of Melville W. Fuller, 1888–1910*. Columbia: University of South Carolina Press, 1995.

Epstein, Lee, and Jack Knight. "The Strategic John Marshall (and Thomas Jefferson)." In *Marbury versus Madison: Documents and Commentary*, edited by Mark A. Graber and Michael Perhac. Washington, DC: CQ Press, 2002.

Epstein, Lee, and Jack Knight. *The Choices Justices Make*. Washington, DC: CQ Press, 1998.

Epstein, Lee, Jeffrey A. Segal, and Harold J. Spaeth. "The Norm of Consensus on the U.S. Supreme Court." *American Journal of Political Science* 45 (2001): 362–77.

Epstein, Lee, and Olga Shvetsova. "Heresthetical Maneuvering on the U.S. Supreme Court." *Journal of Theoretical Politics* 14 (2002): 93–122.

Fahy, Charles. "Mr. Chief Justice Stone." *Harvard Law Review* 59 (1946): 1196–99.

Fish, Peter G. *The Office of Chief Justice*. Charlottesville: White Burkett Miller Center of Public Affairs, University of Virginia Press, 1984.

Flanders. Henry. *The Lives and Times of the Chief Justices of the United States Supreme Court*. Philadelphia: J. B. Lippincott, 1874.

Fortas, Abe. "Chief Justice Warren: The Enigma of Leadership." *Yale Law Journal* 84 (1975): 405–12.

Frank, John P. "Harlan Fiske Stone: An Estimate." *Stanford Law Review* 9 (1957): 621–35.

Frankfurter, Felix. "'Administrative Side' of Chief Justice Hughes." *Harvard Law Review* 63 (1949): 1–4. In *Of Law and Men: Papers and Addresses of Felix Frankfurter*, edited by Philip Elman, 133–44. New York: Harcourt, Brace, 1956.

Frankfurter, Felix. "Chief Justices I Have Known." *Virginia Law Review* 39 (1953): 883–905. In *Of Law and Men: Papers and Addresses of Felix Frankfurter, 1939–1956*, edited by Philip Elman, 129–38. New York: Harcourt, Brace, 1956.

Frankfurter, Felix. "The Impact of Charles Evans Hughes." *New York Times*, November 18, 1951, 1 In *Of Law and Men: Papers and Addresses of Felix Frankfurter, 1939–1956*, edited by Philip Elman, 162. New York: Harcourt, Brace, 1956.

Freund, Paul. "Charles Evans Hughes as Chief Justice." *Harvard Law Review* 81 (1967): 4–43.

Gibson, James L., and Gregory A. Caldeira. *Citizens, Courts and Confirmations: Positivity Theory and the Judgments of the American People*. Princeton: Princeton University Press, 2009.

Gibson, James L., Gregory A. Caldeira, and Vanessa A. Baird. "On the Legitimacy of National High Courts." *American Political Science Review* 92 (1998): 343–58.

Glad, Betty. *Charles Evans Hughes and the Illusions of Innocence*. Urbana: University of Illinois Press, 1966.

Goldstein, Joel K. "Leading the Court: Studies in Influence as Chief Justice." *Stetson Law Review* 40 (2011): 717–59.

Greenhouse, Linda. "Chief Justice Roberts in His Own Voice." *Judicature* 97 (2013): 90–97.

Greenhouse, Linda. "How Not to be Chief Justice: The Apprenticeship of William H. Rehnquist." *University of Pennsylvania Law Review* 154 (2006): 1365–72.

Greenhouse, Linda. "The Last Days of the Rehnquist Court: The Rewards of Patience and Power." *Arizona Law Review* 45 (2003): 251–67.

Gross, Neal, Ward S. Mason, and Alexander McEachern. *Explorations in Role Analysis*. New York: Wiley, 1958.

Hagle, Timothy M. "'Freshman Effects' for Supreme Court Justices." *American Journal of Political Science* 37 (1993): 1142–57.

Hammond, Thomas H., Chris W. Bonneau, and Reginald S. Sheehan. *Strategic Behavior and Policy Choice on the U.S. Supreme Court*. Stanford, CA: Stanford University Press, 2005.

Hansford, Thomas G., and James F. Spriggs II. *The Politics of Precedent on the U.S. Supreme Court*. Princeton: Princeton University Press, 2006.

Haw, James. *John and Edward Rutledge of South Carolina*. Athens: University of Georgia Press, 1997.

Haynes, Dennis. "Rolling Back the Top on Chief Justice Burger's Desk." *University of Pittsburgh Law Review* 39 (1977): 631–95.

Haynie, Stacie L. "Leadership and Consensus on the U.S. Supreme Court." *Journal of Politics* 54 (1992): 1158–69.

Hendel, Samuel. *Charles Evans Hughes and the Supreme Court*. New York: King's Crown Press, Columbia University, 1951.

Hettinger, Virginia, Stefanie A. Lindquist, and Wendy L. Martinek. "The Role and Impact of Chief Judges on the United States Court of Appeals." *Justice Systems Journal* 24 (2003): 91–117.

Highshaw, Robert B. *Edward Douglass White: Defender of the Conservative Faith*. Baton Rouge: Louisiana State University Press, 1981.

Hobson, Charles F. "Defining the Office: John Marshall and Chief Justice." *University of Pennsylvania Law Review* 154 (2006): 1421–61.

Homans, George C. *The Human Group*. New York: Harcourt, Brace, 1950.

Hughes, Charles Evans. *The Supreme Court of the United States, Its Foundations, Methods and Achievements: An Interpretation*. New York: Columbia University Press, 1928.

Jenkins, John A. *The Partisan: The Life of William Rehnquist*. New York: Public Affairs Press, 2012.

John, Oliver P., Laura P. Naumann, and Christopher J. Soto. "Paradigm Shift to the Integrative Five Trait Taxonomy." In *Handbook of Personality: Theory and Research*, edited by Oliver P. John, Richard W. Robins, and Lawrence A. Pervin, 115–58. New York: Guilford Press, 2008.

Johnson, Herbert A. *The Chief Justiceship of John Marshall*. Columbia: University of South Carolina Press, 1997.

Johnson, Timothy R. *Oral Arguments and Decision Making on the United States Supreme Court*. Albany: State University of New York Press, 2004.

Johnson, Timothy R., James F. Spriggs II, and Paul J. Wahlbeck. "Passing and Strategic Voting on the U.S. Supreme Court." *Law and Society Review* 39 (2005): 349–77.

Jung, C. G. *Psychological Types*. In *Collected Works of C.G. Jung*, translated by R. F. C. Hull, vol. 6, *1970–1979*. Princeton: Princeton University Press, 1979.

Katcher, Leo. *Earl Warren: A Political Biography*. New York: McGraw-Hill, 1967.

Katz, Daniel M. "Institutional Rules, Strategic Behavior, and the Legacy of Chief Justice William Rehnquist: Setting the Record Straight on *Dickerson v. U.S.*" *Journal of Law and Politics* 22 (2006): 303–39.

King, Willard L. *Melville Weston Fuller: Chief Justice of the United States 1888–1910*. New York: Macmillan, 1950; Chicago: University of Chicago Press, 1967.

Klarman, Michael J. *From Jim Crow to Civil Rights: The Supreme Court and the Struggle for Racial Equality*. New York: Oxford University Press, 2004.

Kluger, Richard. *Simple Justice*. New York: Vintage Books, 1975.

Kobylka, Joseph F. "Leadership on the Supreme Court of the United States: Chief

Justice Burger and the Establishment Clause." *Western Political Quarterly* 42 (1989): 545–68.
Konefsky, Samuel J. *Chief Justice Stone and the Supreme Court*. New York: Macmillan, 1945.
Lanier, Drew Noble. "Acclimation Effects and the Chief Justice: The Influence of Tenure and Role on Decisional Behavior of the Court's Leader, 1888–2007." *American Political Research Quarterly* 39 (2011): 682–723.
Lanier, Drew Noble, and Sandra L. Wood. "Moving Up: Institutional Position, Politics, and the Chief Justice." *American Review of Politics* 22 (2001): 93–127.
Lax, Jeffrey R., and Charles M. Cameron. "Bargaining and Opinion Assignment on the US Supreme Court." *Journal of Law, Economics, and Organization* 23 (2007): 276–302.
Lazarus, Richard J. "The Opinion Assignment Power, Justice Scalia's Un-Becoming, and UARG's Unanticipated Cloud Over the Clean Air Act." *Harvard Environmental Law Review* 39 (2015): 37–39.
Leuchtenberg, William E. "Charles Evans Hughes: The Center Holds." *North Carolina Law Review* 83 (2005): 1187–99.
Lindquist, Stefanie A., and David E. Klein. "The Influence of Jurisprudential Considerations on Supreme Court Decisionmaking: A Study of Conflict Cases." *Law & Society Review* 40 (2006): 135–62.
Magrath, C. Peter. *Morrison R. Waite: The Triumph of Character*. New York: Macmillan, 1963.
Maltz, Earl M. *The Chief Justiceship of Warren Burger, 1969–1986*. Columbia: University of South Carolina Press, 2000.
Maltzman, Forrest, James F. Spriggs II, and Paul J. Wahlbeck, *Crafting Law on the Supreme Court: The Collegial Game*. New York: Cambridge University Press, 2000.
Maltzman, Forrest, and Paul J. Wahlbeck. "A Conditional Model of Opinion Assignment on the Supreme Court." *Political Research Quarterly* 57 (2004): 551–63.
Maltzman, Forrest, and Paul J. Wahlbeck. "May It Please the Chief: Opinion Assignments in the Rehnquist Court," *American Journal of Political Science* 40 (1996): 421–43.
Maltzman, Forrest, and Paul J. Wahlbeck. "Opinion Assignment on the Rehnquist Court." *Judicature* 89 (2005): 121–26, 181.
Marshall, Thomas R. *Public Opinion and the Supreme Court*. Boston: Unwin Hyman, 1989.
Martin, Andrew D., and Kevin M. Quinn. "Dynamic Ideal Point Estimation via Markov Chain Monte Carlo for the US Supreme Court, 1953–1999." *Political Analysis* 10 (2002): 134–53.
Mason, Alpheus T. *Harlan Fiske Stone: Pillar of the Law*. New York: Viking Press, 1956.
Mason, Alpheus T. *William Howard Taft, Chief Justice*. New York: Simon & Schuster, 1965.
McElwain, Edwin. "The Business of the Supreme Court as Conducted by Charles Evans Hughes." *Harvard Law Review* 63 (1949): 5–26.

McLauchlan, William P. "Research Note: Ideology and Conflict in Supreme Court Opinion Assignment, 1946–1962." *Western Political Quarterly* 25 (1974): 16–27.

Mishler, William, and Reginald S. Sheehan. "The Supreme Court as a Countermajoritarian Institution? The Impact of Public Opinion on Supreme Court Decisions." *American Political Science Review* 87 (1993): 87–101.

Mondak, Jeffrey J. "Institutional Legitimacy, Policy Legitimacy, and the Supreme Court." *American Politics Research* 20 (1992): 457–77.

Morris, Jeffrey B. "Chief Justice Edward Douglass White and President Taft's Court." *Supreme Court Historical Yearbook* (1982): 27–45.

Morris, Jeffrey B. "What Heaven Must Be Like: William Howard Taft as Chief Justice, 1921–30." *Supreme Court Historical Yearbook* 8 (1983): 80–101.

Morris, Richard B. *John Jay, the Nation, and the Court*. Boston: Boston University Press, 1967.

Murphy, Walter F. "Courts as Small Groups." *Harvard Law Review* 79 (1965): 1565–72.

Murphy, Walter F. *The Elements of Judicial Strategy*. Chicago: University of Chicago Press, 1964.

Myers, Isabel Briggs. *Gifts Differing*. Palo Alto, CA: Consulting Psychologists Press, 1980.

Myers, Isabel Briggs, and Mary H. McCaulley. *Manual: A Guide to Development and Use of the Myers-Briggs Type Indicator*. Palo Alto, CA: Consulting Psychologists Press, 1989.

Nemacheck, Christine L. *Strategic Selection: Presidential Nomination of Supreme Court Justices from Herbert Hoover through George W. Bush*. Charlottesville: University of Virginia Press, 2007.

Niven, John. *Salmon P. Chase*. New York: Oxford University Press, 1995.

Nixon, David C. "Policy-Making by Different Means: The Chief Justice's Attempts to Shape Policy Through the Judicial Conference of the United States." *Rationality and Society* 15 (2003): 345–60.

O'Brien, David M. *Storm Center: The Supreme Court in American Politics*. New York: W. W. Norton, 2000.

O'Connor, Sandra Day. "William Howard Taft and the Importance of Unanimity." *Journal of Supreme Court History* 28 (2003): 157–64.

Oppenheim, Felix E. "An Analysis of Political Controls: Actual and Potential." *Journal of Politics* 20 (1958): 516–34.

Pellew, George. *John Jay*. Boston: Houghton Mifflin, 1890.

Perry, H. W., Jr. *Deciding to Decide: Agenda Setting in the United States Supreme Court*. Cambridge, MA: Harvard University Press, 1991.

Pettys, Todd E. "Choosing a Chief Justice; Presidential Prerogative or a Job for the Court?" *Journal of Law and Politics* 22 (2006): 231–81.

Post, Robert. "Judicial Management: The Achievements of Chief Justice William Howard Taft." *OAH Magazine of History* 13 (1998): 24–29.

Post, Robert C. "Mr. Taft Becomes Chief Justice." *University of Cincinnati Law Review* 76 (2007–2008): 761–92.

Pratt, Walter F., Jr. *The Supreme Court under Edward Douglass White*. Columbia: University of South Carolina Press, 1999.

Pringle, Henry F. *The Life and Times of William Howard Taft: A Biography*. 2 vols. New York: Farrar & Rinehart, 1939.

Pritchett, C. Herman. *The Roosevelt Court: A Study in Judicial Politics and Values, 1937–1947*. New York: Macmillan, 1948.

Provine, Doris Marie. *Case Selection in the United States Supreme Court*. Chicago: University of Chicago Press, 1980.

Pusey, Merlo J. *Charles Evans Hughes*. 2 vols. New York: Macmillan, 1951.

Pusey, Merlo J. "Mr. Chief Justice Hughes." In *Mr. Justice*, edited by Allison Dunham and Philip B. Kurland. Chicago: University of Chicago Press, 1956.

Pusey, Merlo J. *Mr. Chief Justice Hughes*. Chicago: University of Chicago Press, 1956.

Rathjen, Gregory J. "Policy Goals, Strategic Choice, and Majority Opinion Assignments in the Supreme Court: A Replication." *American Journal of Political Science* 18 (1974): 713–24.

Rehnquist, William H. "Chief Justices I Never Knew." *Hastings Constitutional Law Quarterly* 3 (1976): 637–55.

Rehnquist, William H. *The Supreme Court: How It Was, How It Is*. New York: William Morrow, 1988.

Resnik, Judith, and Lane Dilg. "Responding to a Democratic Deficit: Limiting the Powers and the Term of the Chief Justice of the United States." *University of Pennsylvania Law Review* 154 (2006): 1575–1664.

Rohde, David W. "Policy Goals, Strategic Choice and Majority Opinion Assignments in the U.S. Supreme Court." *Midwest Journal of Political Science* 16 (1972): 652–82.

Rohde, David W. "Strategy and Ideology: The Assignment of Majority Opinions in the United States Supreme Court." PhD dissertation, University of Rochester, 1971.

Rohde, David W., and Harold J. Spaeth. *Supreme Court Decision Making*. San Francisco: W. H. Freeman, 1976.

Rosen, Jeffrey. "Big Chief: How to Understand John Roberts." *New Republic*, August 2, 2012.

Rosen, Jeffrey. "Roberts's Rules." *Atlantic Monthly* 499 (2007): 104–13.

Ross, William G. *The Chief Justiceship of Charles Evans Hughes, 1930–1941*. Columbia: University of South Carolina Press, 2007.

Ruger, Theodore W. "The Chief Justice and the Institutional Judiciary." *University of Pennsylvania Law Review* 154 (2006): 1323–30.

Ruger, Theodore W. "The Chief Justice's Special Authority and the Norms of Judicial Power." *University of Pennsylvania Law Review* 154 (2006): 1551–74.

Ruger, Theodore W. "The Judicial Appointment Power of the Chief Justice." *University of Pennsylvania Journal of Constitutional Law* 7 (2004): 341–402.

Savage, Charlie. "Roberts's Picks Reshaping Secret Surveillance Court." *New York Times*, July 26, 2013.

Schwartz, Bernard. *The Ascent of Pragmatism: The Burger Court in Action*. New York: Addison-Wesley, 1990.

Schwartz, Bernard. *Super Chief: Earl Warren and His Supreme Court—A Judicial Biography*. New York: New York University Press, 1983.

Seddig, Robert G. "John Marshall and the Origins of Supreme Court Leadership." *University of Pittsburgh Law Review* 36 (1974–75): 785–833.

Segal, Jeffrey A., and Harold J. Spaeth. *The Supreme Court and the Attitudinal Model Revisited*. New York: Cambridge University Press, 2002.

Sharp, Daryl. *Personality Types: Jung's Model of Typology*. Toronto: Inner City Books, 1987.
Sill, Kaitlyn L., Joseph Ura, and Stacia L. Haynie. "Strategic Passing and Opinion Assignment on the Burger Court." *Justice System Journal* 31 (2010): 164–79.
Slater, Philip E. "Role Differentiation in Small Groups." *American Sociological Review* 20 (1955): 300–310.
Slotnick, Elliot E. "The Chief Justice and Self-Assignment of Majority Opinions: A Research Note." *Western Political Quarterly* 31 (1978): 219–25.
Slotnick, Elliot E. "The Equality Principle and Majority Opinion Assignment on the United States Supreme Court." *Polity* 12 (1979): 318–32.
Slotnick, Elliot E. "Who Speaks for the Court: The Chief Justice and the Assignment of Majority Opinions." PhD dissertation, University of Minnesota, 1976.
Slotnick, Elliot. "Who Speaks for the Court? Majority Opinion Assignment from Taft to Burger." *American Journal of Political Science* 23 (1979): 60–77.
Smith, Christopher E., Christina DeJong, and Michael A. McCall, eds. *The Rehnquist Court and Criminal Justice*. Lanham, MD: Lexington Books, 2011.
Smyth, Russell, and Paresh Kumar Narayan. "Hail to the Chief! Leadership and Change in the Level of Consensus in the High Court of Australia." *Journal of Empirical Legal Studies* 1 (2004): 399–421.
Spaeth, Harold. "Distributive Justice: Majority Opinions in the Burger Court." *Judicature* 67 (1984): 299–304.
St. Clair, James E., and Linda C. Gugin. *Chief Justice Fred M. Vinson of Kentucky*. Lexington: University Press of Kentucky, 2002.
Steamer, Robert J. *Chief Justice: Leadership and the Supreme Court*. Columbia: University of South Carolina Press, 1986.
Stephenson, D. Grier. "The Chief Justice as Leader: The Case of Morrison Remick Waite." *William and Mary Law Review* 14 (1973): 899–927.
Stevens, John Paul. *Five Chiefs: A Supreme Court Memoir*. New York: Little, Brown, 2011.
Stone, Harlan F. "Fifty Years' Work of the United States Supreme Court." *American Bar Association Journal* 14 (1928): 428–36.
Stone, Irving. *Earl Warren*. New York: Prentice-Hall, 1948.
Swaine, Edward T. "Hail, No: Changing the Chief Justice." *University of Pennsylvania Law Review* 154 (2006): 1709–28.
Swisher, Carl B. *Mr. Chief Justice Taney*. Chicago: University of Chicago Press, 1956.
Swisher, Carl B. *Roger B. Taney*. New York: Macmillan, 1935.
Toobin, Jeffrey. *The Oath: The Obama White House and the Supreme Court*. New York: Doubleday, 2012.
Toma, Eugenia. "A Contractual Model of the Voting Behavior of the Supreme Court: The Role of the Chief Justice." *International Review of Law and Economics* 16 (1996): 433–47.
Tribe, Laurence, and Joshua Matz. *Uncertain Justice: The Roberts Court and the Constitution*. New York: Henry Holt, 2014.
Tushnet, Mark. "The First (and Last?) Term of the Roberts Court." *Tulsa Law Review* 42 (2006–2007): 495–503.
Ulmer, S. Sidney. "Earl Warren and the Brown Decision." *Journal of Politics* 33 (1971): 689–702.
Ulmer, S. Sidney. "Exploring the Dissent Patterns of the Chief Justices: John Mar-

shall to Warren Burger." In *Judicial Conflict and Consensus: Behavior Studies of American Appellate Courts*, edited by Sheldon Goldman and Charles M. Lamb. Lexington: University Press of Kentucky, 1986.

Ulmer, S. Sidney. "The Use of Power in the Supreme Court: The Opinions Assignments of Earl Warren, 1953–1960." *Journal of Public Law* 30 (1970): 49–67.

Umbreit, Kenneth B. *Our Eleven Chief Justices*. New York: Harper & Bros., 1938.

Vining, Richard L., and Teena Wilhelm. "The Chief Justice as Advocate-in-Chief: Examining the Year-End Report on the Federal Judiciary." *Judicature* 95 (2012): 267–74.

Wahlbeck, Paul. "Strategy and Constraints on Supreme Court Opinion Assignment." *University of Pennsylvania Law Review* 154 (2006): 1729–55.

Wahlbeck, Paul J., Timothy R. Johnson, and James F. Spriggs II. "Passing and Strategic Voting on the U.S. Supreme Court." *Law and Society Review* 39 (2005): 349–77.

Wahlbeck, Paul J., James F. Spriggs II, and Forrest Maltzman. "Marshalling the Court: Bargaining and Accommodation on the United States Supreme Court." *American Journal of Political Science* 42 (1998): 294–315.

Walker, Thomas G. "David J. Danelski: Social Psychology and Group Choice." In *The Pioneers of Judicial Behavior*, edited by Nancy Maveety. Ann Arbor: University of Michigan Press, 2003.

Walker, Thomas G., Lee Epstein, and William J. Dixon. "On the Mysterious Demise of Consensual Norms in the United States Supreme Court." *Journal of Politics* 50 (1988): 361–89.

Warren, Earl. *The Memoirs of Earl Warren*. New York: Doubleday, 1977.

Weaver, John D. *Warren: The Man, the Court, the Era*. Boston: Little, Brown, 1967.

Wetstein, Matthew E., and C. L. Ostberg. "Strategic Leadership and Political Change on the Canadian Supreme Court: Analyzing the Transition to Chief Justice." *Canadian Journal of Political Science* 38 (2005): 653–72.

Wexler, Natalie. "In the Beginning: The First Three Chief Justices." *University of Pennsylvania Law Review* 154 (2006): 1373–1419.

Wheeler, Russell R. "Chief Justice Rehnquist as Third Branch Leader." *Judicature* 89 (2005): 116–20.

White, G. Edward. "The Internal Powers of the Chief Justice: The Nineteenth-Century Legacy." *University of Pennsylvania Law Review* 154 (2006): 1463–1510.

Whittington, Keith. *Political Foundations of Judicial Supremacy: The Presidency, the Supreme Court, and Constitutional Leadership in U.S. History*. Princeton: Princeton University Press, 2007.

Wood, Sandra L. "In the Shadow of the Chief: The Role of the Senior Associate Justice." *Journal of Supreme Court History* 2 (1997): 25–35.

Wood, Sandra L., Linda Camp Keith, Drew Noble Lanier, and Ayo Ogundele. "'Acclimation Effects' for Supreme Court Justices: A Cross-Validation, 1888–1940." *American Journal of Political Science* 42 (1998): 690–97.

Wood, Sandra L., Linda Camp Keith, Drew Noble Lanier, and Ayo Ogundele. "Opinion Assignment and the Chief Justice, 1888–1940." *Social Science Quarterly* 81 (2000): 798–809.

Woodward, Bob, and Scott Armstrong. *The Brethren: Inside the Supreme Court*. New York: Simon & Schuster, 1979.

Yalof, David A. *Pursuit of Justices: Presidential Politics and the Selection of Supreme Court Nominees*. Chicago: University of Chicago Press, 1999.

Contributors

Brandon L. Bartels is Associate Professor of Political Science at George Washington University. His research and teaching interests center on American politics, judicial decision making, the U.S. Supreme Court, and public perceptions of law and courts. His work has appeared in the *American Political Science Review*, *American Journal of Political Science*, *Journal of Politics*, *Public Opinion Quarterly*, and other outlets. His current work focuses on legal change and the constraining capacity of law on the Supreme Court and the consequences of Supreme Court policymaking for public perceptions of judicial legitimacy and democracy.

Sara C. Benesh is Associate Professor of Political Science at the University of Wisconsin, Milwaukee, where she teaches courses on civil liberties, Supreme Court decision making, research methods, and American government. She received her PhD in 1999 from Michigan State University and her BA in 1995 from St. Norbert College. Her research focuses primarily on confidence in the U.S. courts, though she has also published work on Supreme Court decision making, decision making on the U.S. Courts of Appeals, the impact of the Supreme Court, and state court behavior. She is coauthor of *The Supreme Court in the American Legal System*, with Harold J. Spaeth and Jeffrey A. Segal (Cambridge) and author of *The U.S. Courts of Appeals and the Law of Confessions* (LFB Scholarly). Her work has appeared in the *American Journal of Political Science*, *Journal of Politics*, *American Politics Research*, and *Justice System Journal*, among others. She is a contributor to the Supreme Court Database and her work has been supported by the National Science Foundation.

Ryan C. Black is Associate Professor of Political Science at Michigan State University. His research focuses on U.S. Supreme Court decision making. He is a coauthor of two books on the Supreme Court: *Oral Arguments* *and Coalition Formation on the U.S. Supreme Court* (University of Michigan Press, 2012) and *The Solicitor General and the United States Supreme Court* (Cambridge University Press, 2012). His work has also been published in a variety of journals, including the *American Journal of Political Science*, the *Journal of Politics*, *Political Research Quarterly*, and the *Journal of Law, Economics, and Organization*. He received his PhD from Washington University in St. Louis in 2009.

Charles Cameron is Professor of Politics and Public Affairs at Princeton University. He specializes in the analysis of political institutions, particularly courts and law, the American presidency, and legislatures. The author of numerous articles in leading journals of political science, he is also the author of *Veto Bargaining: Presidents and the Politics of Negative Power* (Cambridge University Press, 2000), which won the American Political Science Association's Fenno Prize for best book in legislative studies, and the William Riker Award as best book in political economy. A recipient of multiple grants from the National Science Foundation, he has been a Research Fellow at the Brookings Institution, a National Fellow at the Hoover Institution, a Visiting Scholar at Princeton's Center for the Study of Democratic Politics, has a recurrent visiting affiliation as professor at New York University School of Law, and is a member of the American Academy of Arts and Sciences (class of 2014). He taught for fifteen years at Columbia University. He holds an MPA and PhD (Public Affairs) from Princeton University.

Tom Clark is Asa Griggs Candler Professor of Political Science at Emory University. His research focuses on legal institutions and has examined conflict between Congress and the Supreme Court, the influence of public opinion on elected judges, learning and rule-making in the judicial hierarchy, and the statistical measurement of judicial preferences.His book *The Limits of Judicial Independence* (Cambridge University Press, 2011) received the William Riker Award for the best book in political economy, and his articles have appeared in top disciplinary journals, including the *American Political Science Review*, the *American Journal of Political Science*, *Journal of Politics*, and *Political Analysis*, among others. The recipient of multiple grants from the National Science Foundation, he has been a Visiting Scholar at Princeton's Center for the Study of Democratic Politics and the Institute for Advanced Study in Toulouse. Clark received his BA from Rutgers University and his MA and PhD from Princeton University.

Pamela C. Corley is Associate Professor in the Political Science Department and Director of the Law & Legal Reasoning Minor at Southern Methodist University. She received her JD and PhD from Georgia State University. She specializes in judicial politics and American political institutions. Her work focuses on three questions regarding judicial decision making. The first evaluates the content of court opinions, the second examines how consensus is formed on the United States Supreme Court, and the third analyzes how courts are constrained by Congress. Professor Corley is the author of *Concurring Opinion Writing on the U.S. Supreme Court* (State University of New York Press, 2010), which is the first systematic examination of the content of Supreme Court concurrences. She is also the coauthor of *The Puzzle of Unanimity: Consensus on the United States Supreme Court* (Stanford University Press, 2013), which provides the first comprehensive account of how the Court reaches consensus.

David J. Danelski (volume editor) is the Mary Lou and George Boone Centennial Professor Emeritus at Stanford University. He previously taught at Illinois (Champaign-Urbana), Washington (Seattle), Yale, Tokyo, Cornell, and Occidental (where he was also dean of the faculty and academic vice president). After his retirement from Stanford, he taught at Whitman, Johns Hopkins, and Maryland, while he continued to do research and writing on the Supreme Court. He has a law degree from DePaul and a PhD from Chicago. He has published or edited seven books or special issues of journals and has published more than fifty articles and reviews. His most recent book is *Constitutional Law: Civil Liberty and Individual Rights* (with William Cohen and David Yalof, Foundation Press, 2007), and he contributed to Melvin Urofsky's *Biographical Encyclopedia of the Supreme Court: The Lives and Legal Philosophies of the Justices* (CQ Press, 2006). An inactive member of the bars of the Supreme Courts of Illinois, Washington, and the United States, he is a former Navy JAG officer and a former trial and appellate lawyer. He has been a Guggenheim Fellow, a Japan Foundation Fellow, a National Endowment for the Humanities Fellow, a Center for Advanced Study in the Behavioral Sciences Fellow, a Woodrow Wilson Center Fellow, and a Fulbright Lecturer in Japan. Among his awards are the E. Harris Harbison Prize for Gifted Teaching from the Danforth Foundation (which he received when he was at Yale), the Humanities and Science Dean's Award for Distinguished Teaching from Stanford, the Hughes-Gossett Award for Historical Excellence from the Supreme Court Historical Society, and a Lifetime Achievement Award from the Law & Courts Section of the American Political Science Association.

Shawn Fettig is a Visiting Teaching Assistant Professor at the University of Denver. He holds a PhD from the University of Wisconsin–Madison. His dissertation examines the question of why people might prefer one institution of government (courts, legislatures, executives) over another to handle certain issues. Employing a large, national survey, Shawn examines what factors might influence an individual's preference(s) for a particular policymaking entity to handle certain issues or issue typologies. He is currently working on a book project that highlights the story behind the issuing of the first same-sex marriage licenses in the United States, out of Boulder, CO, in 1975.

Sheldon Goldman is Distinguished Professor of Political Science at the University of Massachusetts–Amherst. Over the course of nearly fifty years, Goldman has become one of the nation's leading judicial politics experts. In the 1960s, his research effectively shifted the focus of federal court scholarship from a singular examination of the Supreme Court to a broader and more inclusive study of law and the courts. In the late 1970s, Goldman began a series of articles in *Judicature* on federal judicial selection. In total, he has published more than fifty articles in professional journals, two constitutional law casebooks, several other books including (with Thomas P. Jahnige) *The Federal Courts as a Political System.* Goldman is also the author of *Picking Federal Judges: Lower Court Selection from Roosevelt Through Reagan*, published by Yale University Press (1997, 1999) which won several awards. In 2006 he received the Lifetime Achievement Award from the American Political Science Association's Law and Courts Section. Over nearly five decades he has appeared on or been interviewed by NBC Nightly News, Bill Moyer's Journal, CBS, Voice of America, CNN, *Rolling Stone*, *Ms.* magazine, the *Wall Street Journal*, and the *New York Times*, among many other regional and national media outlets.

Charles Gregory is Assistant Professor at Stephen F. Austin State University. He received his PhD in Political Science from the University of Minnesota in 2014. His teaching and research interests concentrate primarily on American political institutions, judicial decision making on the Supreme Court, and the judicial appointment process.

Timothy R. Johnson is Morse Alumni Distinguished Teaching Professor of Political Science and Law at the University of Minnesota. He received his PhD from Washington University in St. Louis. Johnson's research and teaching interests include American politics, judicial politics, Supreme Court decision making, Supreme Court oral arguments, executive-judiciary relations, and the evolution of the norm of respecting precedent. He has published articles in a wide variety of political science journals and law reviews and is the coauthor of *Oral Arguments and Coalition Formation on the U.S. Supreme Court: A Deliberate Dialogue* (University of Michigan Press, 2012, with Ryan C. Black and Justin Wedeking), coeditor of *A Good Quarrel* (University of Michigan Press, 2009, with Jerry Goldman), and the author of *Oral Arguments and Decision Making on the U.S. Supreme Court* (State University of New York Press, 2004).

Ryan Krog is a PhD candidate in the Political Science Department at George Washington University. His research centers on American politics, judicial politics, and political methodology. He is currently working on projects examining judicial decision making, legal argumentation, and agenda setting in the U.S. Supreme Court.

Alyx Mark is Assistant Professor of Political Science at North Central College in Naperville, IL, where she teaches courses on public law and American politics. She received her PhD and MA in political science from George Washington University in 2015 and her BA from Southern Illinois University–Edwardsville. Her research focuses on the American civil legal system, the ways in which individuals interact with legal institutions, and the relationship between the federal courts and Congress. Her current research, which examines the civic and political effects of interacting with legal services offices, has received the support of the National Science Foundation and the Economic Club of Washington, D.C. Her work appears in, or is forthcoming at the *Denver University Law Review*, *Hastings Law Review*, *Law and Society Review*, and the *Journal of Law and Courts*.

Kevin J. McMahon is the John R. Reitemeyer Professor of Political Science at Trinity College in Hartford, Connecticut. His research mainly focuses on the examination of the presidency and the political origins and consequences of Supreme Court decisions. In 2014, the Supreme Court Historical Society award his book, *Nixon's Court: His Challenge to Judicial Liberalism and Its Political Consequences* (University of Chicago Press, 2011), its Erwin N. Griswold Book Prize. *Nixon's Court* was also selected as a 2012 CHOICE Outstanding Academic Title. Professor McMahon's first book, *Reconsidering Roosevelt on Race: How the Presidency Paved the Road to Brown* (University of Chicago Press, 2004), won the American Political Science

Association's Richard E. Neustadt Award for the best book published that year on the American presidency in 2004. He is also the coauthor/coeditor of three books on the presidency and presidential elections and author of numerous book chapters and journal articles.

Christine L. Nemacheck is the Wilson & Martha Claiborne Stephens Associate Professor of Government and a Fellow with the Center for the Liberal Arts at The College of William & Mary. She received her BA from the University of Michigan and her PhD from George Washington University. Her research focuses on judicial selection and the role of the courts in a separation-of-powers system. Her book *Strategic Selection: Presidential Selection of Supreme Court Justices from Herbert Hoover through George Bush* was published in 2007. Along with her two coauthors, David Magleby and Paul Light, Nemacheck wrote *Government by the People*, an introductory American politics textbook. Her work has also appeared in political science and law review journals and several book chapters. Her research, which is primarily archival, has been funded by numerous foundation grants and awards. Nemacheck has received a number of awards for her teaching and research activity, including the Alumni Fellowship Award for excellence in teaching at the College of William & Mary, the Coco Faculty Fellowship, the 2010 Dean's Distinguished Lecturer award, and from 2010 to 2013 she held the Alumni Memorial Term Distinguished Professorship.

Ryan Owens is Professor of Political Science at the University of Wisconsin–Madison. He also enjoys an affiliate status with the law school and is an Honorary Fellow in the Institute for Legal Studies. Owens studies judicial politics and American political institutions. His work analyzes, among other things, agenda setting on the United States Supreme Court, strategic behavior on the United States Courts of Appeals, and unilateral executive behavior. Dr. Owens's work has appeared in the *American Journal of Political Science*, *Journal of Politics*, *Political Research Quarterly*, the *Georgetown Law Journal*, the *William & Mary Law Review*, the *University of Illinois Law Review*, *Law & Society Review*, and the *Journal of Law and Courts*.

Kirk A. Randazzo is Professor of Political Science and Director of the Carolina Leadership Initiative at the University of South Carolina. He has published three books, including *Checking the Courts: Law, Ideology, and Contingent Discretion* (State University of New York Press), *Judicialization of Politics: The Interplay of Institutional Structure, Legal Doctrine, and Politics on the High Court of Australia* (Carolina Academic Press), and *Defenders of Lib-*

erty or Champions of Security? Federal Courts, the Hierarchy of Justice, and U.S. Foreign Policy (State University of New York Press). Additionally he has published numerous articles on issues related to law and judicial politics in leading journals such as the *American Journal of Political Science*, *Journal of Politics*, *Journal of Law & Courts*, and the *Justice System Journal.*

Rebecca Reid is Assistant Professor of Political Science at the University of Texas at El Paso focusing on judicial politics and research methodology. Her main research interests include the establishment and maintenance of the rule of law, the tensions and interactions between international and domestic law, and the role of courts in democratizing and consolidating countries. She has research either published or forthcoming in the *Justice System Journal* and *Judicature*.

Douglas Rice is Assistant Professor in the Department of Political Science at the University of Mississippi. He earned a PhD in political science from Pennsylvania State University (2013), an MA in political science from Villanova University (2008), and a BA in political science from Elizabethtown University (2005). His research examines judicial behavior, agenda setting, American political institutions, and computational methods for the analysis of legal texts.

Amy Steigerwalt is Associate Professor of Political Science at Georgia State University. Her research focuses on the federal judicial selection process, as well as the role of courts as institutions and the differing influences on court operations and decision making. She has published three books to date, including *Battle Over the Bench: Senators, Interest Groups and the Politics of Courts of Appeals Confirmations* (University of Virginia Press, 2010), as well as articles in journals such as *Journal of Politics*, *Political Research Quarterly*, and *Justice System Journal*. Her most recent book is *The Puzzle of Unanimity: Consensus on the U.S. Supreme Court*, coauthored with Pamela Corley and Artemus Ward (Stanford University Press, 2013). Dr. Steigerwalt, along with Drs. Corley and Ward, was recently awarded the 2013 Hughes-Gossett Award for the best article published that year in the *Journal of Supreme Court History*.

Richard L. Vining Jr., PhD, is Associate Professor in the Department of Political Science at the University of Georgia. Dr. Vining joined the faculty at the University of Georgia in 2007 after completing his graduate studies at Emory University. His research focuses on judicial selection, judicial departures, judicial decision making, and the interaction of courts with exogenous institutions. He frequently participates in professional conferences and provides expert commentary to the press and legal groups regarding judicial selection and tenure. He has published articles in a number of peer-reviewed outlets including the *Journal of Politics*, *Political Research Quarterly*, *American Politics Research*, *Social Science Quarterly*, *Political Communication*, *Judicature*, and *Justice System Journal*.

Paul J. Wahlbeck is Professor of Political Science at George Washington University. His research focuses on legal change, oral argument before the Supreme Court, strategic interaction among justices, and institutional development. Wahlbeck is coauthor of *Crafting Law on the Supreme Court: The Collegial Game* (Cambridge University Press, 2000). His work has appeared in many journals, including the *American Political Science Review*, *American Journal of Political Science*, *Journal of Politics*, and *Law & Society Review*.

Artemus Ward (volume editor) is Professor of Political Science at Northern Illinois University. He received his PhD from the Maxwell School of Citizenship at Syracuse University and served as a Congressional Fellow on the House Judiciary Committee in Washington, DC. His books include *Deciding to Leave: The Politics of Retirement from the United States Supreme Court* (State University of New York Press, 2003), *Sorcerers' Apprentices: 100 Years of Law Clerks at the United States Supreme Court* (with David L. Weiden, New York University Press, 2006), *In Chambers: Stories of Law Clerks and Their Justices* (edited with Todd C. Peppers, University of Virginia Press, 2012), and *The Puzzle of Unanimity: Consensus on the United States Supreme Court* (with Pamela C. Corley and Amy Steigerwalt, Stanford University Press, 2013). His articles have appeared in such journals as *Political Analysis*, *Congress & the Presidency*, *White House Studies*, *Justice System Journal*, and the *Journal of Supreme Court History*. He is a two-time winner of the Hughes-Gossett Award for Historical Excellence from the Supreme Court Historical Society.

Justin Wedeking is Associate Professor of Political Science at the University of Kentucky. His research examines judicial behavior and decision making, oral arguments, Supreme Court confirmation hearings, and the role of courts in American society. He has two coauthored books—*Supreme Court Confirmation Hearings in the U.S. Senate: Reconsidering the Charade* and *Oral Arguments and Coalition Formation on the U.S. Supreme Court: A Delib-*

erate Dialogue—that were recently published by the University of Michigan Press. In addition, his work has been published in the *American Journal of Political Science*, *Journal of Politics*, *Law & Society Review*, *Journal of Law and Courts*, *American Politics Research*, *Justice System Journal*, *Judicature*, *Hofstra Law Review*, and *Loyola Law Review*, and has been discussed in the *New York Times*, McClatchy Newspapers, PBS, and NPR.

Teena Wilhelm is Associate Professor in the Department of Political Science at the University of Georgia. Her authored or coauthored research has appeared in major political science and legal studies journals and has been honored by the Southern Political Science Association. Her research has also garnered a grant from the National Science Foundation. Her teaching and research specialties are judicial politics, state politics, and constitutional law.

Phillip J. Wininger is a PhD candidate in political science at George Washington University. His research centers upon the institutional design of state and federal courts, judicial independence, and judge decision making. Prior to pursuing his PhD, he worked for several years as an attorney, where he litigated cases across state, federal, and administrative courts. He holds a BA in political science and economics from Western Kentucky University, an MA in political science from the University of Kentucky, and a JD from the University of Kentucky College of Law.

Christopher Zorn is the Liberal Arts Research Professor of Political Science, Professor of Sociology and Crime, Law, and Justice (by courtesy), and Affiliate Professor of Law at Pennsylvania State University. He holds a PhD in political science from Ohio State University (1997) and a BA in political science and philosophy from Truman State University (1991). Prior to coming to Penn State, he was professor of political science at the University of South Carolina (2005–2007), a Visiting Scientist and Program Director for the Law and Social Science Program at the National Science Foundation (2003–2005), and Winship Distinguished Research Professor of Political Science at Emory University, where he taught from 1996 to 2003. His research focuses on judicial politics and on statistics for the social and behavioral sciences. He is the author of two forthcoming books and three dozen refereed articles that have been published in the *American Political Science Review*, the *American Journal of Political Science*, the *Journal of Politics*, *Political Analysis*, and other journals. Professor Zorn is also the recipient of six grants from the National Science Foundation and numerous other fellowships and awards. In addition, he currently serves as vice president of the Midwest Political Science Association (2013–2016) and on the editorial board of the *American Political Science Review* and the executive boards of the American Judicature Society and the Empirical Legal Studies weblog.

Index